Medicine
and
Health
1985

GROLIER INCORPORATED, DANBURY, CONNECTICUT

Jean Paradise, *Group Editorial Director*
Robert Famighetti, *Executive Editor*
Zelda Haber, *Design Director*

EDITORIAL STAFF

John P. Elliott, *Senior Editor*
Richard Hantula, *Senior Editor*
William A. McGeveran, Jr., *Senior Editor*

Michael E. Agnes, *Editor*
Jacqueline Laks Gorman, *Editor*

Robert Sorenson, *Associate Editor*
Martha G. Wiseman, *Associate Editor*
Rosalie Fadem, *Assistant Editor*
Marjorie Holt, *Assistant Editor*
Patricia R. Howe, *Assistant Editor*

Charlotte Fahn, *Adjunct Editor*
Vitrude DeSpain, *Indexer*

ART/PRODUCTION STAFF

Joan Gampert, *Design Manager*
Gerald Vogt, *Production Supervisor*
Trudy Veit, *Senior Designer*
Marvin Friedman, *Senior Designer*
Emil Chendea, *Designer*
Joyce Deyo, *Photo Editor*
Margaret McRae, *Photo Editor*
Marsha Rackow, *Photo Editor*
Mynette Green, *Production Assistant*
Patricia Brady, *Editorial Assistant*

Medicine and Health 1985 is not intended as a substitute for the medical advice of physicians. Readers should regularly consult a physician in matters relating to their health and particularly regarding symptoms that may require diagnosis or medical attention.

PUBLISHED BY GROLIER INCORPORATED 1985.
This annual is also published as *Health & Medical Horizons 1985.*

ISBN 0-7172-8149-3

Library of Congress Catalog Card Number 82-645223

Grolier Incorporated offers a varied selection of both adult and children's book racks. For details on ordering, please write:
Grolier Incorporated, Sherman Turnpike, Danbury, CT 06816, Attn: Premium Department.

Manufactured in the United States of America

For Good Health

The latest developments in medical science can help us stay healthy and help doctors treat us when we are sick. This book explains recent trends and breakthroughs in health care—in clearly written, easily understood articles prepared by experts.

Page 4

Page 38

Page 62

FEATURE ARTICLES

Contents Continues

SPOTLIGHT ON HEALTH

A series of concise reports on practical health topics.

Health and Medical News

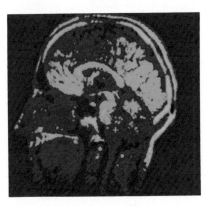

THE COMMON COLD

Diane J. Rosenthal

ILLUSTRATION BY WALLY NEIBART

Among diseases, the common cold is our most frequent and universal tormentor. Each year the cold exacts a staggering economic toll: close to 50 million workdays are lost annually in the United States alone, which translates into a cost of billions of dollars. On the more philosophical side, colds guarantee family physicians a steady stream of customers from late fall to early spring, help keep afloat the manufacturers of innumerable cough syrups and nasal sprays, and provide millions of workers with a good excuse for a day off.

The common cold has probably been with us ever since human beings came in from the wild and gathered in caves or huts in numbers large enough to support a contagious disease. Given all that time and all those colds, it seems to be a major failing of medical science that a cure has not yet been found. To be fair, however, it must be said that common cold researchers didn't really have much to work with until the 1950's, when cold-causing viruses were first isolated in the laboratory. Today, as the study of infectious disease continues, it appears that the ordinary cold is a problem much more complex than previous generations of researchers could have suspected.

The commonness of the common cold is reflected in the broad vocabulary used to describe it: We speak of head colds, chest colds,

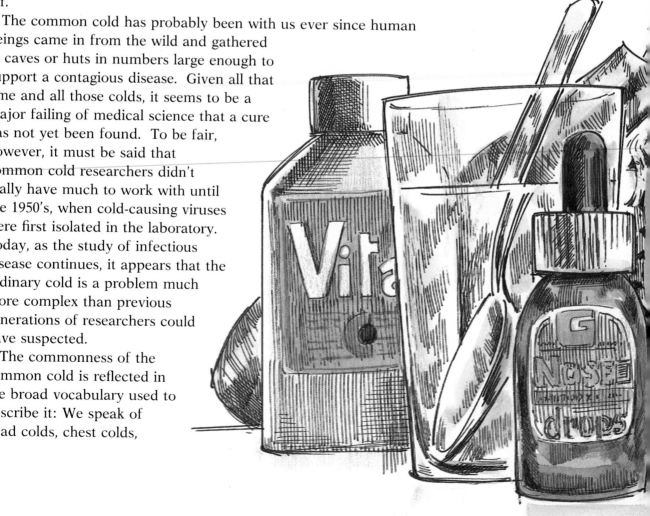

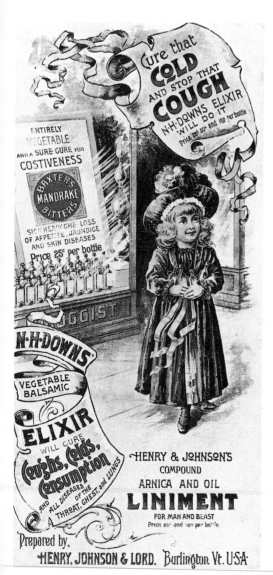

A sure cure for coughs and colds was advertised by a turn-of-the-century poster. Effective or not, such elixirs and potions presumably sold as well as today's ubiquitous over-the-counter remedies.

sinus colds, and lingering summer colds, as well as the grippe, the blahs, a touch of the flu, and feeling run-down. The medical definition of the common cold is an infection of the upper respiratory tract (the airways of the nose and throat). Sometimes, doctors will describe a cold according to the specific part of the tract that is most affected. Pharyngitis, therefore, is an infection in the pharynx, or upper portion of the throat, and laryngitis is a problem in the larynx, which is lower down in the throat.

To the cold sufferer, however, it usually comes down to this: a few days of stuffed and runny nose, sore throat, coughing and sneezing, and mild but general misery.

Causes and Effects

The common cold is caused by a virus—an entity so small that it can be viewed only through a powerful electron microscope and so primitive that its status as a living organism is a subject of scientific debate. Rhinoviruses, the most common cold-causing agents, consist of little more than a strand of genetic material called RNA, protected by a protein coat. Viruses have no ability to carry on basic life functions by themselves. About all they can do is replicate, and even for that they need a host cell to, in effect, do the reproductive work for them.

Rhinoviruses seem to be specifically designed to attack the epithelial cells of the mucous membrane lining the upper respiratory tract. Their protein coats serve as a kind of identification badge that allows them entrance at certain chemical receptor points on the epithelial cell walls. Once inside, the virus sheds its protein coat, and its RNA invades the cell nucleus, where the host cell's own replicative machinery is housed. The virus RNA commandeers the genetic control room, forcing the host cell to expend all its energy in making more virus RNA and more protein coats. Within two or three days, the host cell collapses from this overtime effort, releasing a thousand or more new viruses, which move out into the epithelial tissue seeking new host cells to attack. Before the host cell collapses, however, it sends out a warning message in the form of a protein called interferon. Interferon seems to alert neighboring cells of the presence of infection and helps to trigger preventive action. But viruses are fast workers, and an infection with a good head start can often outrun or overwhelm the protective effects of naturally produced interferon.

Up to this point, the human cold sufferer has probably felt nothing unusual, even though armies of viruses are amassing inside the nose and/or throat. As the infection spreads, however, the body reacts with a range of defensive maneuvers—and these protective actions, rather than the virus itself, bring on the discomforting symptoms of a cold. One of the first defensive measures is inflammation, whereby blood supply to the infected area increases and the area swells, reddens, and becomes warmer and more sensitive to the touch. The swollen cells leak some of their excess fluid, which combines with stepped-up production of mucus to create a nasal drip, or runny nose. Swelling of the nasal lining tissues also causes congestion—the familiar stuffed nose—which may block off the

---

Diane J. Rosenthal is a free-lance medical writer and editor.

normal air flow to the sinus cavities, producing headache. All this heavy traffic in the nose triggers sneezing, which is a dramatic attempt to clear the area and expel some of the viruses. If the activity extends to the throat, the cough center in the brain will set off its own minor explosions to prevent virus-laden secretions from reaching the lungs.

A rise in body temperature may also occur. Fevers of 103°F and above are not uncommon in young children with colds. In adults, fever is less frequent and less severe, rarely exceeding 101°F.

By now, the infected person is well aware of being sick, though he or she may not realize that the body is actually on its way to healing itself. The decisive battle of the cold war is conducted by the various white blood cells of the body's immune system, which have congregated and multiplied at the infection site. One group of large white cells, known as macrophages, goes about gobbling up every virus particle within reach; other defenders, called killer T cells, destroy infected cells on contact. Toward the end of the fray, neutralizing antibodies appear. These agents are programmed to attach themselves to a particular virus and prevent it from entering host cells. It takes some time for the body to manufacture these specialized antibodies, and as a result they don't play a major role in fighting off the initial invasion. Their value lies in the fact that once produced, they remain active and alert long after the infection has run its course. The next time that particular virus appears, the antibodies are ready and waiting to thwart the infection.

Unfortunately, there are over 100 different strains of cold-causing rhinoviruses, and the antibodies that protect against one strain may not do the job against any of the others. Furthermore, rhinoviruses account for only about 30 to 40 percent of colds. Coronaviruses, another family of cold-causing agents, account for an additional 15 to 20 percent. There are also adenoviruses, parainfluenza viruses, respiratory syncytial viruses, Coxsackieviruses, and echoviruses, which together are responsible for 10 to 15 percent. In all, some 200 different strains of cold-causing viruses have been identified, leaving room for a substantial number of colds of unknown, but presumably viral, origin. Our bloodstreams, therefore, can be stocked with all kinds of cold-stopping antibodies, and we will still be vulnerable to slightly different strains of virus. As we age, however, we do tend to have fewer colds—they are relatively rare in people over 65—probably because we have built up immunities to the most common cold-causing viruses over the years.

How Colds Spread

How do we catch colds? From someone else, to begin with—usually a member of the immediate family, often a school-age child. Young children are the most vulnerable population group because they have had the least exposure to cold viruses and thus the least opportunity to develop protective antibodies. It is true that babies are born with some natural immunities acquired from the mother, but these wear off after a few months. At that point, an infant's life often becomes a cold-ridden affair, with as many as a dozen infections during the first year.

Colds seem to spread best in the home and at school. In fact, in the grade-school classroom—where there is constant daily contact among

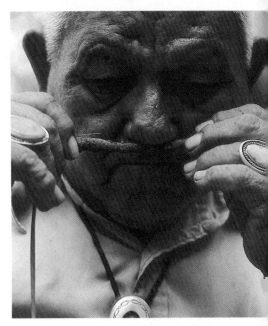

A Navajo medicine man sniffs a piece of osha root, a variety of parsley used as a folk remedy for colds. Cold sufferers chew the root or drink a tea made from its leafy top.

7

dozens of susceptible youngsters—cold viruses have a relative field day. The children bring their germs home with them, infecting their parents and siblings. This is why adults in their 20's and 30's—the typical child-rearing years—tend to have frequent colds (four to six annually) and why women, who usually spend more time with young children, have a higher infection rate than men.

Contrary to popular belief, we do not catch cold by simply *being* cold. Researchers at the Common Cold Unit in Salisbury, England, proved this years ago by marching lightly-clad volunteers through the hillsides in chilly weather, or by letting them shiver in wet bathing suits in unheated rooms. Despite their ordeals, the volunteers were no more likely to catch cold than a control group not subjected to these uncomfortable experiences. (Research suggests, though, that there may be one exception: In some studies, women in the middle third of their menstrual cycle did seem to catch cold more readily after being chilled.) People often feel a chill just before the onset of a cold, but this is most likely a preliminary symptom, not the cause, of an infection that is already under way. The prevalence of colds in cold or rainy seasons is probably attributable to the natural tendency to stay indoors in bad weather, thereby making it easier for cold viruses to spread. It has also been suggested that the warm dry air generated by central heating systems may have an inhibitory effect on certain cells of the nasal mucous membrane that help to filter out foreign particles entering the respiratory tract.

Scientists are quite certain that colds are passed from one person to the next, but the mechanism of transmission is not fully understood. Laboratory studies conducted by Dr. Jack M. Gwaltney, Jr., of the University of Virginia School of Medicine indicate that so-called hand-to-hand self-inoculation is the most effective means identified so far. What happens is that an infected person often has quantities of cold virus on the hands (the viruses probably got there when the person rubbed the nose or covered nose and mouth when coughing or sneezing). The viruses then travel to new hosts through hand contact, and the unsuspecting recipients complete the job by touching their faces, thereby introducing the viruses to the moist linings of the nose and eyelids, where they thrive.

Viruses also can survive for hours on common household surfaces—coffee cups, water faucets, tile floors and walls—where members of a family can easily encounter them. In addition, colds can be spread by tiny virus-bearing droplets expelled during coughing or sneezing, but laboratory tests have shown that this airborne transmission of viruses is not nearly as effective as the hand-to-hand or surface-to-hand routes. It should also be noted that kissing—even prolonged kissing—does *not* seem to be an efficient means of transmitting cold viruses.

Such simple measures as frequent hand-washing and spraying disinfectant on common household surfaces may cut down the circulation of cold viruses. Researchers are also looking into the possibility of nontoxic disinfectants that could be applied directly to the hands, perhaps in lotion form. Another approach may be disposable tissues treated with an antiviral agent, which cold sufferers could use to blow the nose. Dr. Elliot C. Dick of the University of Wisconsin has been experimenting with "killer Kleenex," different types of tissues laced with iodine or various chemicals, which seem to limit the spread of cold viruses.

Close to 50 million workdays are lost each year in the United States alone as a result of colds.

A number of studies have shown that there is a correlation between emotional stress brought on by abrupt changes in normal life patterns and either the frequency or the severity of cold symptoms. It is thought that stress can weaken the body's immune defenses and make people more susceptible to disease. This weakening of the immune system has been proposed as a partial explanation for seasonal variations in cold incidence. Colds proliferate in inclement weather because people tend to stay indoors; it is also possible that the associated changes in life patterns produce enough stress to cause certain vulnerable individuals to catch cold more easily. The seasonal-stress hypothesis goes hand-in-hand with another controversial—and unproven—theory: that cold-causing viruses may lie dormant for long periods of time in a human host and that sudden stress may tip the delicate immunological balance in favor of the infectious agents.

A classroom full of youngsters can be a cold-ridden place. Young children, who have had little exposure to cold viruses, are highly susceptible—and hence, often sick.

When a Cold Is More Than a Cold

The common cold is a "self-limiting" disease; that is, it usually goes away (with the help of the immune system) within a week to ten days of the initial infection. Noticeable cold symptoms—congestion, sore throat, sneezing, and so on—rarely last more than the two or three days in which the body's battle with the virus is at its peak. The apparent lingering of cold symptoms may actually be the result of allergies, which can often produce similar effects. Hay fever, caused by an allergic reaction to ragweed pollen in the air, is most prevalent during the fall months and can bring on sneezing and other nasal symptoms. Itchy and watery eyes often accompany hay fever, however, and these symptoms are not associated with the common cold.

By themselves, colds are never a serious health threat and usually do not require medical attention. But especially in the very young and the very old, and in those whose immune systems are weakened by chronic disease or certain medical treatments, colds can sometimes open the door to more serious bacterial infections. Young children weakened by cold viruses seem to be particularly susceptible to bacterial infections of the middle ear, while older people who catch cold are at greater risk of developing potentially life-threatening pneumonia. There is a slim possibility that a viral upper respiratory tract infection can spread to the air passages, or bronchi, in the lungs; more often, colds precede bacterial bronchitis. When a cold does seem to spread to the chest area, with coughing that brings up large amounts of phlegm, it is best to consult a

Research volunteers at England's Common Cold Unit play long-distance chess by calling their moves across a 30-foot gap. Participants in the unit's experiments on cold viruses must keep away from everyone but their roommates to stave off possible contact with stray viruses.

physician. Severe sore throat and difficulty swallowing should also be brought to a doctor's attention; they may be signs of strep throat, an infection caused by the bacterium streptococcus.

Secondary bacterial infections can be readily treated with antibiotics. However, antibiotics are useless against viral infections and should never be given to treat a simple cold unless the patient is at risk of bacterial complications. Cold sufferers nevertheless frequently demand that their doctors give them "a shot" to make them feel better, and doctors occasionally comply, apparently figuring that it will improve the patient's state of mind. Yet antibiotics are powerful drugs, and it is possible that an unnecessary dose might make bacteria harbored in the body more resistant to future treatment, when it may be truly needed. Also, antibiotics may suppress the normal bacteria contained within the body, allowing more dangerous organisms to grow and cause infection.

In people with a history of asthma, colds can sometimes bring on episodes of wheezing and breathlessness. Again, a physician should be notified when a person with asthmatic tendencies catches cold. Wheezing attacks can often be treated or prevented with drugs such as theophylline.

Nobel Prize–winning chemist Linus Pauling relaxes in his California home, well stocked with oranges. Pauling believes that vitamin C helps prevent the common cold—a still unproven theory.

Occasionally, a case of laryngitis in very young children turns into croup. This condition can be frightening to parents and child because it may involve blockage of airways and cause its victim to gasp and struggle for breath. It often comes on at night and is characterized by a high-pitched, barking cough. Disturbing as these symptoms can be, croup is rarely a serious problem. Treatment often consists of calming the child and placing the child in an enclosed environment fed by humid air, which may ease the blockage; a humidifier or vaporizer is often helpful, as is turning on a hot shower and then sitting with the child in the steamy bathroom. Parents should exercise caution, however—if they are in doubt about how serious the problem is, a doctor should be called; occasionally, the child may need to be hospitalized.

"A cold" and "the flu" are terms used interchangeably by many people, but the common cold and influenza are two very different—sometimes fatally different—diseases. Like cold-causing agents, influenza viruses usually enter through the nose and attack the upper respiratory tract. Mild cases of the flu are practically indistinguishable from ordinary colds. But influenza infections can also be quite severe, putting ordinarily healthy people on their backs for a week or more and posing a serious threat to the elderly and those with heart or lung conditions. Furthermore, influenza viruses sometimes invade the lower respiratory tract, where they can cause potentially deadly fluid buildup in the lungs.

The risk of secondary infection, such as pneumonia, is also greater with influenza than with the common cold.

Although influenza and the common cold share many of the same symptoms, the general rule is that the flu comes on stronger and more suddenly. A bad sore throat, painful to the external touch, is more typical of the flu than of colds. So are generalized symptoms, such as high fever, weakness, achiness, and pain in the joints and muscles. Short of laboratory analysis, however, there is no surefire way to tell a flu infection from a bad cold, although doctors can usually make accurate diagnoses based on similarity of symptoms to those caused by a known flu virus circulating in a given region.

It is unlikely that scientists will develop a vaccine against all 200 or so cold viruses.

A Cure for Colds?

The possibility of a vaccine that protects against the common cold has been bandied about in scientific circles for several years. Vaccines against specific types of cold viruses have been developed, but an inoculation, or even a series of inoculations, that protects against all 200 or so cold viruses is not a likely prospect. Even if such a vaccine were feasible, health officials would have to decide whether the cost of developing it and administering it to the general population could be justified in view of the minimal health risk that colds present.

In the absence of a vaccine or any medical cure, many people have been willing to believe that vitamin C is the answer to the common cold. The vitamin C fanfare began in 1970 with the publication of the book *Vitamin C and the Common Cold* by Linus Pauling, the Nobel Prize–winning chemist. Pauling argues that vitamin C helps build the network of connective tissue that holds the cells together. Without enough vitamin C, he claims, this connective tissue is weakened and is more easily penetrated by viruses. Unlike those animals that produce vitamin C in their bodies, human beings must obtain their vitamin C from dietary sources. However, Pauling believes that the modern Western diet simply does not include enough fresh fruits and vegetables to supply sufficient quantities of vitamin C. According to the Food and Nutrition Board of the U.S. National Academy of Sciences, the Recommended Daily Dietary Allowance (RDA) for adults is 60 milligrams of vitamin C; most people, Pauling says, actually need between 1,000 and 2,000 milligrams a day to stay healthy. When one does catch cold, this dose should be increased, he maintains—up to 10,000 milligrams a day, if necessary.

Since the publication of Pauling's book, hundreds of scientific studies have attempted to determine the effectiveness of vitamin C against the common cold. Here and there, some findings have supported Pauling's claims, but the conclusion reached by an overwhelming majority of medical researchers is that vitamin C in any quantity neither prevents colds nor reduces the severity of cold symptoms. There is a chance that vitamin C may shorten the duration of cold symptoms by a few hours, but this effect does not seem to depend on particularly large dosages. Furthermore, the long-term effects of taking massive amounts of vitamin C are not known.

Despite this scientific skepticism, many people continue to swear by the curative powers of vitamin C. There is always the possibility that a small subgroup of the population may actually benefit from vitamin C megadoses. More likely, however, is what researchers call the placebo effect: if people believe that something will make them better, that conviction alone may speed recovery.

Probably the brightest prospect on the cold-cure horizon is interferon, the chemical substance released by damaged cells to warn their neighbors and help them fend off impending attack. Researchers believe that by boosting the body's supply of interferon, endangered cells will become more resistant to disease. Manufactured by the body in minute quantities, interferon until recently has been very difficult and exceedingly expensive to harvest. Through contemporary gene-splicing techniques, though, it is now possible to "grow" large quantities of interferon outside the body.

Interferon does seem to be effective in preventing common cold infections, and it may also be able to stop infections if administered shortly after exposure to the virus. (It cannot reduce cold symptoms once the infection is well under way.) It works best when introduced directly into the nasal passages in spray form. The drawback is that the interferon spray must be administered regularly, several times a day, before and after exposure to the virus, and these repeated dosages have caused nasal irritation in volunteers. Until another effective application method is developed, we won't be seeing interferon on the local pharmacist's shelves.

During a card game among staff members at the University of Wisconsin (below), cold sufferers use iodine-laced "killer Kleenex" to test their effect on cold viruses. At right, Dr. Jack Gwaltney of the University of Virginia washes the nose of a student volunteer who was given a cold virus.

Self-Care

Neither vitamin C nor medical technology can cure the common cold, but there are several measures cold sufferers can take to make themselves more comfortable. For starters, the standard advice about resting in bed and drinking plenty of fluids makes good sense. It may not be necessary to skip work and stay in bed all day, but taking it easy on the job, cutting back on social activities, and going to bed early for a few days can help the body conserve its strength while battling the virus. If you feel truly rotten, it probably is best to stay home. It's hard to accomplish much with a bad cold, and exhaustion increases the risk of secondary infection.

Fluids, especially warm fluids, help by loosening the mucus in the nose and throat, thus easing congestion. Traditionalists will be pleased to hear that chicken soup really does work: Investigators at Mount Sinai Medical Center in Miami Beach demonstrated that hot chicken soup clears mucus at a slightly faster rate than plain hot water. But another age-old remedy—alcohol—may do more harm than good by increasing nasal irritation and worsening headaches. More important, alcohol's interaction with certain cold medications can be downright dangerous.

The old saw "feed a cold and starve a fever" has its drawbacks as well. It's difficult to enjoy food when the nose is stuffed and taste buds

Annoying as they are, colds by themselves are not a serious health threat.

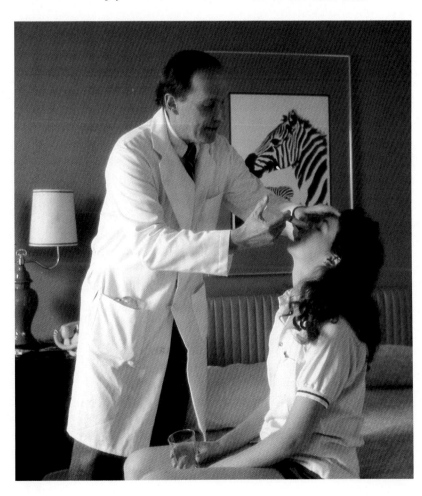

15

Chicken soup—an age-old remedy—really does help, by clearing the mucus in the nose and throat.

deadened by a cold. Furthermore, a heavy meal, combined with a reduction in normal activity, can make one feel even more lethargic and uncomfortable. On the other hand, a cold victim's craving for spicy food may be quite reasonable, since the sharp flavoring can cut through the general deadening of taste sensations.

As for self-medication, *The Essential Guide to Nonprescription Drugs* states that over 50,000 different products are available over-the-counter for treating the common cold. It is important to remember that even the best of these drugs do nothing to reduce the duration or severity of the infection; they can only ease symptoms. And some don't even do that. A massive review of cold remedies done in the 1970's by a U.S. Food and Drug Administration advisory panel found a number of products to be unsafe, ineffective, or both. The panel itself had no enforcement power, but the FDA, which does have such power, is still reviewing its findings. Ingredients found to be unsafe generally have already been removed from the market by the manufacturers themselves—perhaps to forestall FDA action—although ineffective (but not harmful) substances often have not been. A brief rundown on the six basic categories of nonprescription cold medications follows. Consumers should check ingredient lists and instructions for use on the package before taking any drug. Even though they are sold without prescription, over-the-counter drugs can cause side effects. Their use should be reported to a doctor if patients are also taking other medications on a regular basis.

Analgesics are pain-killing drugs that help to reduce the achiness and fever that often accompany a cold. For years, aspirin and acetaminophen (the active ingredient in Tylenol and other products) were the only nonprescription analgesics available in the United States. In 1984, ibuprofen—formerly sold only as the prescription drugs Motrin and Rufen—was also approved for sale, in lower dosages, on a nonprescription basis, under the brand names Nuprin and Advil. (As of early 1985, ibuprofen was still sold only as a prescription drug in Canada.) Acetaminophen is the analgesic usually recommended for children.

Anticholinergics usually contain small quantities of atropine or belladonna alkaloids, which dry out the nasal passages. The FDA advisory panel on cold remedies found that no nonprescription anticholinergic agents could be recommended as "safe and effective." Nevertheless, many combination products still contain anticholinergics along with other active ingredients.

Antihistamines can ease the sneezing, runny nose, and watery eyes produced by colds and allergies. They tend to cause drowsiness and should not be used if one intends to drive or operate heavy machinery. They also should not be used with alcohol, tranquilizers, or sleeping pills. Antihistamines deemed safe and effective by the FDA advisory panel are those that contain these active ingredients:

> brompheniramine maleate
> chlorpheniramine maleate
> doxylamine succinate
> phenindamine tartrate
> pheniramine maleate
> pyrilamine maleate
> thonzylamine hydrochloride

Antitussives, or cough suppressants, may be used to reduce dry, "nonproductive" coughing—the kind that irritates the throat but doesn't bring up mucus or clear air passages. The most effective cough suppressants contain codeine preparations. Codeine is a narcotic drug, and although the amount contained in over-the-counter cough remedies is small, it can be dangerous if taken before driving or with alcohol. In some states, purchasers of codeine products must sign a special register in the pharmacy; in others, codeine is available only on a prescription basis. Other safe and effective antitussive agents are dextromethorphan, dextromethorphan hydrobromide, and diphenhydramine hydrochloride.

Decongestants act by constricting the swollen blood vessels in the lining of the nose and sinuses. They are sold in three forms: topical (nose drops and nasal sprays), inhalant (usually a steam vapor), and oral (liquid or tablets). Nasal spray decongestants should be applied only as often as the label advises; if they are used too frequently, they can cause what is called rebound congestion, in which the blood vessels become even more swollen than they were before. A nasal spray dispenser can transmit infection if used by more than one person. Safe and effective nasal decongestants may contain the following active ingredients:

> ephedrine preparations (topical)
> naphazoline hydrochloride (topical)
> oxymetazoline hydrochloride (topical)
> phenylephrine hydrochloride (topical or oral)
> phenylpropanolamine preparations (oral)
> propylhexedrine (inhaled)
> pseudoephedrine preparations (oral)
> xylometazoline hydrochloride (topical)

Expectorants are claimed to soothe sore throats and to thin nasal secretions and promote the passage of mucus (thereby increasing the productiveness of a cough). The FDA advisory panel decided that none of the over-the-counter expectorants on the market could be recommended as safe and effective.

In recent years, drug manufacturers have been placing greater promotional emphasis on combination cold products, those that contain active ingredients from two or more of the above categories. The FDA advisory panel frowned on this "shotgun" approach and recommended that consumers stick to cold products with one or at most two active ingredients. ☐

Over-the-counter drugs do not reduce the severity of a cold—they can only ease symptoms.

SUGGESTIONS FOR FURTHER READING

ANDREWES, CHRISTOPHER. *The Common Cold.* New York, Norton, 1965.

MURPHY, WENDY. *Coping With the Common Cold.* Alexandria, Va., Time-Life Books, 1981.

WILLIAMS, RICHARD L. "For the All-Too-Common Cold, We Are Perfect, If Unwilling, Hosts." *Smithsonian*, December 1983, pp. 47–55.

ZIMMERMAN, DAVID R. *The Essential Guide to Nonprescription Drugs.* New York, Harper & Row, 1983.

Milk

Good for Everyone?

Susan Walton

In the late 1970's the Federal Trade Commission filed suit against the California Milk Producers Advisory Board. Among other things, it claimed the board's advertising slogan—"Everybody needs milk"—was wrong. A number of people, the FTC noted, lack a key enzyme—lactase—needed to digest milk, and they experience such symptoms as nausea, cramps, excessive gas, and diarrhea when they drink it. Other people are allergic to milk protein. Therefore, the agency reasoned, not everybody needs milk. However, the judge ruled that the slogan was close enough to the truth so that it could not be regarded as misleading advertising; whatever health risk milk presented for some was more than outweighed by its benefits for most people.

The fact is that milk is an extraordinarily rich source of many nutrients, most notably calcium. An 8-ounce glass of whole milk provides more than a third of the 800 milligrams of calcium that most adults should take in each day, according to the Recommended Daily Dietary Allowances (RDA's) established by the Food and Nutrition Board of the U.S. National Academy of Sciences. That same glass of milk also contains 150 calories, 8 grams of protein (roughly 20 percent of the RDA), 8 grams of fat, and 11 grams of carbohydrate. From a glass of milk, an adult gets 25 percent of the RDA for riboflavin (vitamin B_2), 15 percent of the recommended vitamin B_{12}, 20 percent of the phosphorus, 8 percent of the magnesium, and various amounts of other nutrients. In addition, U.S. and Canadian producers add vitamin D to milk to help prevent rickets, a childhood disease resulting in softened and, sometimes, deformed bones.

With all these health benefits, the case for milk is an easy one to make. Of course, those few who have an allergic reaction, such as breaking out in hives when they drink milk, may have to avoid it or at least severely

Milk from dairy animals has been a source of food for thousands of years.

Cows, sheep, and goats—the most popular dairy animals—are depicted in a medieval farmyard in this old Belgian print.

limit their consumption. But for most people milk, in one form or another, can play a valuable role in the diet. Lactase-deficient individuals often can digest milk to which the enzyme has been specially added. And using milk with a reduced fat content helps to eliminate potential problems caused by the fact that whole milk is high in fat and cholesterol, which have been linked with some kinds of cancer (fat) and with heart disease (both).

Sales figures, however, suggest that the general public doesn't take seriously the vital role that dairy products play in health. In the United States, sales of whole milk, whose fat content is about 3.4 percent, dropped sharply between 1960 and 1983, the latest year for which statistics are available, falling from 250.87 pounds per person to 130.46. Although the figures for low-fat milk (generally either 1 or 2 percent fat) climbed significantly—from 2.27 pounds per person to 77.75—the increase did not offset the decline for whole milk. Sales of skim milk, which is less than 0.5 percent fat, were 10.68 pounds per person in 1960 and 10.88 in 1983. Milk sales in Canada have shown a similar trend in recent years. Studies by the U.S. National Center for Health Statistics show that many people consume

Susan Walton is a free-lance writer who specializes in health topics.

less than half of the recommended 800 milligrams of calcium each day. Surveys do not reveal why the drop in milk sales has occurred, but both history and recent medical research do show why it matters.

How Dairying Began

Humans probably started domesticating dairy animals, such as cows, sheep, and goats, before recorded history, and by 3000 B.C. people were using the animals as sources of milk. The practice of milking began in Northwest Africa and Southwest Asia, and spread across Europe and Asia and into sub-Saharan Africa. Milk use was common in biblical times; there are more than 50 references to cows and milk in the Old Testament.

Why people began milking their animals remains unknown. The 19th-century American physician Robert M. Hartley speculated that early humans saw milking as a trade-off. Since they hesitated to simply "appropriate this unlabored gift of nature for their own use," they gave the animals food and shelter "that would tend to augment their numbers and increase their enjoyments."

Not all cultures that kept herds of animals used them for milking. Early European explorers who encountered such peoples were offered various explanations for the failure to use the animals' milk. Some said they did not milk the animals because they viewed it as an "unnatural manipulation of the animals' udders." In parts of Asia, religious beliefs proscribed milking because it would deprive the animals' young of their rightful food.

Others told the explorers that they did not use the milk because it produced such unpleasant effects as stomach cramps, nausea, and diarrhea. These tales are among the earliest known reports of a condition that actually occurs among most of the world's adults, particularly those who are not of northern European ancestry—lactase insufficiency.

Trouble Digesting Milk

The body cannot digest lactose (also known as milk sugar), the major carbohydrate in milk, if lactase is not present in the small intestine. This enzyme is produced by all young mammals, including humans. But as the young grow up, there is a significant drop in lactase production. Researchers once believed that the fall in lactase levels was a response to dietary changes after weaning. More recently, however, they have found that lactase production slows in people of most ethnic groups regardless of how much milk is in the diet. Adults not suffering from a lactase deficiency tend to be of "northern" European origin, such as Danes, Germans, French, Dutch, Poles, Czechs, and northern Italians. (A few isolated ethnic groups in Africa and India have also been found to have a high percentage of adults without lactase deficiency.)

Just why it is that some people do remain "lactose tolerant" is something of an enigma. Scientists generally think (although there is not universal agreement on the matter) that the ability to tolerate lactose developed in "dairying" cultures. This capacity, they note, would offer an advantage in terms of survival, since those who could digest lactose could continue to benefit from the nutritional value of milk into adulthood. In

The Effects of Lactose Intolerance

What happens when people who cannot tolerate lactose drink milk? Not digested in the small intestine, because not enough of the enzyme lactase is present, the milk's lactose passes into the large intestine. There bacteria act on it, with unpleasant results. Symptoms, which occur to different degrees in different individuals, may include gas, rumbling sounds, abdominal bloating, cramps, loose bowel movements, diarrhea, and nausea. Children who cannot digest lactose may not gain weight as they should. Similar symptoms may also be produced, of course, by other conditions. A lactose-tolerance test will readily determine whether bowel problems are due to lactase deficiency.

Many people who can't digest milk may be able to eat yogurt.

the book *Lactose Digestion* the nutritionist Dr. Norman Kretchmer suggests that such an evolutionary advantage, arising with the beginning of dairying, would be important "in an environment characterized by the consumption of large amounts of milk and milk products in lactose-rich forms. In such a dairying culture, lactose absorbers would enjoy greater health and vigor, multiply better, and fare more successfully in general."

Physicians have broken the problem of low lactase production into several subcategories. If a person has a lactase deficiency, then he or she probably suffers from a condition called lactose malabsorption, in which the body does not use the lactose consumed. If this person shows symptoms—like those reported to the European explorers—after being given a test dose of lactose, undiluted or mixed with water, he or she is said to be lactose intolerant. And if the person drinks milk and then suffers problems, the condition is called milk intolerance.

Overcoming the Problem

Recent studies suggest that the last distinction is an important one, because many lactose-intolerant people can tolerate at least a little milk. A number of individuals who react badly to the test dose of lactose—the same amount found in a quart of milk—can nevertheless drink a glass of milk without experiencing the side effects. Hence, someone who has been tested and found lactose intolerant may actually be able to continue to drink milk in small quantities.

In addition, such people may be able to consume certain other dairy products, notably yogurt. A study reported in 1984 found that yogurt—commonly eaten in many parts of the world where adults tend to be lactase deficient—can often be digested by people who cannot tolerate milk. A research team headed by Dr. Joseph C. Kolars of the University of Minnesota compared the amount of hydrogen in the breath—a measure of lactose absorption by the body—in ten lactase-deficient individuals who consumed equivalent (with respect to lactose content) amounts of milk, a lactose-and-water mixture, and yogurt. Eating the yogurt resulted in only one-third as much hydrogen as drinking the milk or the lactose-and-water mixture, which indicated that far more lactose was absorbed when the yogurt was consumed. Moreover, eight of the ten people complained of diarrhea or gas after drinking the milk, but only two after eating the yogurt. The researchers noted that lactase from bacteria in the yogurt seems to substitute for that missing in a lactase-deficient person's intestines. Another point in yogurt's favor, by the way, is that a cup of it contains less lactose to begin with than does a cup of milk.

Some lactase-deficient people may also be able to consume other dairy products—such as buttermilk, hard cheese, and sour cream—that have less lactose than milk. Another alternative is to use milk (or milk products) pretreated with lactase, which is available in some areas in stores; lactase itself may be bought from pharmacies and added to milk. In addition, a tablet form of lactase, to be taken before eating, was recently introduced. Acidophilus milk, which contains bacteria thought to digest lactose, has sometimes been suggested for use by lactase-deficient individuals, but studies by researchers have not generally found it to be effective.

In any case, a problem with lactose digestion need prevent only those individuals who are most sensitive to milk sugar from drinking milk or eating milk products.

What About the Fat in Milk?

Because whole milk is high in cholesterol and in the type of fat called saturated fat (which tends to increase cholesterol levels in the blood), many physicians and nutritionists advise that adults drink low-fat or skim milk. One reason for this is, of course, that any high-fat food may promote obesity, which is considered a risk factor in heart disease and other ailments. Another is that high levels of cholesterol in the blood have been linked to heart disease. Studies indicate that the risk of heart disease can be reduced by lowering the blood cholesterol level. And there is evidence that eating a diet low in cholesterol and saturated fat can lower the level of cholesterol in the blood. Scientists have not yet been able to definitely prove that decreasing people's blood cholesterol levels by dietary means will reduce the incidence of heart disease. Nonetheless, many physicians argue that prudence dictates a diet low in cholesterol and saturated fat, at least for adults.

The American Academy of Pediatrics has warned against routinely giving low-fat or skim milk to children up to three years of age. Since milk is usually a major part of a growing child's diet, using low-fat or skim milk may deny the child sufficient calories and a proper balance of nutrients; it should be kept in mind that some components of milk fat are necessary for proper growth.

A connection has also been made between a high-fat diet and certain

The lineup of milk containers on school lunch trays is recognition of the importance of milk throughout the growing years.

types of cancer. In a 1982 report the U.S. National Research Council's Committee on Diet, Nutrition, and Cancer reviewed studies involving various dietary components and concluded that "the combined epidemiological and experimental evidence is most suggestive for a causal relationship between fat intake and the occurrence of cancer." Cancers of the breast, large intestine, and prostate, in particular, were linked to a high-fat diet. Conversely, those who eat less fat were found to have lower rates of these cancers. The mechanism behind the fat-cancer connection is not clear, but the committee speculated that high fat consumption may change the body's metabolism in ways that promote tumor formation and growth. As an aid in preventing cancer, the committee recommended that people decrease their fat intake, including that from whole milk. Some scientists and representatives of the meat and dairy industries, however, objected that the committee's dietary recommendations were based on too little evidence.

Wholesomeness Guaranteed

Lowering milk's fat content and adding lactase and vitamin D to milk are not the only ways that people have improved on nature. Modern ways of processing milk also ensure that, barring exceptional circumstances, it is free of contamination. In the 19th century, as more and more people moved from farms to cities, where they had to buy their milk, physicians became increasingly aware of significant health problems resulting from milk contamination. Some milk came from diseased cows, and some was processed under unsanitary conditions. Eventually, strict controls were established, with general standards in the United States set by the Public Health Service. Dairy farms must now meet strict sanitation rules, and cows must be certified as free of disease. To kill harmful bacteria, milk undergoes pasteurization, named for its inventor, the French chemist Louis Pasteur.

A far cry from the old red barn is this sanitary tile-floored milking parlor.

As soon as it is taken from the cow, milk is cooled to prevent the growth of undesirable microorganisms. (The nutritional qualities that make milk an excellent food for people also make it an ideal medium for the growth of bacteria.) Pasteurization takes place at the processing plant and involves heating the milk to prescribed temperatures, followed by rapid cooling. As a result, disease-producing bacteria present are killed (along with many of the microorganisms that can cause spoilage). Pasteurization affects the nutritional quality of milk only slightly. A significant fraction of its vitamin C may be lost, but milk is not considered a major source of that vitamin.

Another pasteurization method, called ultrahigh temperature treatment (UHT), makes it even less likely that milk will contain dangerous germs. In this process, milk is heated to temperatures higher than in regular pasteurization, then reheated to even higher levels either before or during packaging. The effect is to kill virtually all microorganisms and greatly extend the shelf life of the product. UHT milk has another great advantage: it may be stored in the cupboard for up to three months and need not be refrigerated until after it is opened. Used in Europe for many years, the UHT process was only relatively recently approved for milk in Canada and the United States, where it has not been widely adopted, largely because of a reluctance by consumers to buy unrefrigerated milk.

Despite the obvious benefits of the pasteurization process, some people argue that unpasteurized, raw milk is better. They say it has a richer flavor and, when processed under proper conditions, is more healthful. There is no guarantee, however, that even raw milk produced under ideal conditions will be free of harmful microorganisms, and there have been calls in both the United States and Canada for a ban on its sale, which is now allowed in some areas.

Milk is commonly sold in a homogenized state. In homogenization, the fat globules are broken up and evenly distributed, preventing a layer of cream from forming at the top of the container.

In regular pasteurization, milk is heated to a high temperature and then cooled; in the UHT process, it is twice heated to much higher temperatures.

The Need for Calcium

Milk is celebrated for its calcium. Although other foods contain the mineral, very few offer as rich a supply in as concentrated a form.

For people of all ages, calcium is essential for maintaining strong bones; in fact, 99 percent of the calcium in the body is found in the bones and teeth. Calcium also circulates in the blood, where it plays an important role in regulating many functions, including heartbeat, transmission of nerve impulses, and muscle contraction; it is also needed to regulate hormone levels and to activate certain enzymes. The blood calcium level is regulated by hormonal mechanisms, with the mineral being withdrawn from bones as needed.

When the body is growing, its need for calcium is particularly great. The RDA for children up to age ten is 800 milligrams, the same as for adults. For adolescents—ages 11 to 18—even more is recommended: 1,200 milligrams daily. (The RDA for pregnant and breast-feeding women is also 1,200 milligrams.) Even after the period of peak bone growth, the bones continue to change. In a process called remodeling, old bone is reabsorbed by the body and replaced by new bone.

Generally between the ages of 30 and 35, the rate of bone reabsorption begins to exceed the rate of replacement; this net bone loss continues throughout the rest of life. It is important for people to have built up their bones to the maximum mass possible by the time they enter the period of bone loss. Once this period has begun, maintaining an adequate intake of calcium is believed to help keep bone loss to a minimum.

In general, taking in enough calcium is a good way to help prevent calcium-deficiency problems, although there is no straightforward relationship between the amount of calcium a person ingests and the amount the body uses. Researchers have found that in adults, on the average, only about 30 percent of the calcium consumed in food is actually absorbed; the remaining 70 percent is excreted. Exactly how much calcium is absorbed depends on a number of dietary and other factors. Several substances that increase absorption are found in milk: lactose, certain amino acids, and vitamin D (in fortified milk). Substances found in some other foods decrease absorption, including oxalates (in cocoa, beet greens, spinach, and chard) and phytates (in bran or whole grains). The absorption of calcium may also be diminished by psychological stress, aging, the ingestion of alkali (in antacids), and the immobilization of the body (as when a person is confined to bed for a prolonged period).

A recent study has suggested that large amounts of fiber in the diet may reduce calcium absorption. This finding, if confirmed by further research, is a good example of the complex effects and countereffects that people must consider when they try to modify their diets to improve their health. Low-fat, high-fiber diets are said to lower the risk of atherosclerosis (clogging of arteries with fatty deposits), coronary heart disease, and certain types of cancer; however, people who lower their calcium intake may place themselves at greater risk for such health problems as osteoporosis and, perhaps, high blood pressure.

Calcium and Osteoporosis

Osteoporosis is the development of excessively weak, fragile bones; many people who suffer from it break bones in accidents that would leave a healthy person undamaged. The condition is a serious public health problem. According to the U.S. National Institutes of Health, 15–20 million Americans may suffer from osteoporosis in some degree. Each year, about 1.3 million Americans over the age of 45 experience fractures that probably occur because their bones have been weakened by the disease. Among those who live to be 90 years old, 32 percent of women and 17 percent of men will suffer a hip fracture that can usually be blamed on osteoporosis.

Scientists now know that many things can play a role in the development of osteoporosis. At an NIH conference on the disease in spring 1984, it was noted that complex hormonal and other physiological factors may underlie the occurrence of osteoporosis. One "probable cause" is a deficiency of calcium in the body; adequate intake of the mineral (and normal levels of vitamin D), along with moderate exercise, may help to ward off the disease. There is some evidence that for the elderly the current calcium RDA of 800 milligrams may be too low; for

The old as well as the young need milk in their diets.

women past the age of menopause, who are at much higher risk for osteoporosis, it was suggested that increasing the intake of calcium to 1,000–1,500 milligrams daily may reduce the chances of getting osteoporosis.

The NIH conference cautioned, however, that those who have a tendency to develop urinary-tract stones may raise their risk of doing so if they begin taking unusually large amounts of calcium. Although drinking a lot of water—about 2½ quarts daily—may prevent the stones from forming, susceptible people should add extra calcium to their diets only under the guidance of their physicians.

Calcium and Blood Pressure

Since calcium is a major component of bones and teeth, it is almost a matter of common sense to consume calcium to keep them strong. Less obvious, however, are the links between calcium and various body functions.

One of the most intriguing ideas that researchers have proposed is a possible link between calcium and blood pressure levels. The mineral may act as a protective force in the prevention of high blood pressure (or hypertension), and there is some evidence suggesting that it may be useful in treatment as well. One study, for example, found that a group of people with hypertension who received daily calcium supplements for eight weeks showed significant drops in blood pressure compared with a group of hypertensive individuals who were not given extra calcium.

Wide publicity was accorded a study published in mid-1984 that found evidence that diets low in calcium (and also potassium and sodium) are associated with hypertension. The study, carried out by a team of scientists headed by Dr. David McCarron of the Oregon Health Sciences University, was based on data from a survey in which people were asked to recall all the foods and beverages they had consumed in the preceding 24-hour period. Many scientists, however, voiced caution about accepting the McCarron team's findings without further study. One problem is that the methods used were not capable of accurately establishing people's usual dietary intake of nutrients, including calcium, potassium, and sodium. An additional complication is that blood calcium levels are not greatly influenced by diet. Dr. McCarron himself stressed that his study did not prove that hypertension is actually caused by a diet low in the three nutrients; that remains to be established by future laboratory and other studies. His claim that "the greater an individual's consumption of dairy products, the less likely it was that he or she was hypertensive" also, of course, needs to be corroborated by further studies. But regardless of whether milk is ultimately proved to help prevent hypertension, the fact remains that the calcium it contains in abundance is vitally needed by the body.

What should people do who want to cut back on their fat intake while ensuring themselves of getting enough calcium? The obvious answer is to drink skim or low-fat milk, a glass of which actually contains more of the mineral than does a glass of whole milk. A good source of many other nutrients as well—riboflavin, for example, and potassium—milk is low in only a few, notably iron and vitamin C. It is easy to see why you never outgrow your need for milk. ☐

Some Good Sources of Calcium

FOOD	MILLIGRAMS OF CALCIUM
Low-fat yogurt, plain (1 cup)	415
Sardines, canned (3 oz.)	372
Collard greens (1 cup)	357
Low-fat yogurt, fruit-flavored (1 cup)	343
Almonds, chopped (1 cup)	304
Skim milk* (1 cup)	302
2% low-fat milk* (1 cup)	297
Whole milk (1 cup)	291
Buttermilk (1 cup)	285
Whole-milk yogurt (1 cup)	274
Swiss cheese (1 oz.)	272
Kale (1 cup)	206
Cheddar cheese (1 oz.)	204

* No milk solids added

Source: U.S. Department of Agriculture

CHOOSING A HEALTH CLUB

Barbara Scherr Trenk

Physical fitness has become something of a North American pre-occupation. In the United States, more than 90 million adults engage in some form of exercise on a regular basis. A 1981 Canadian survey found that participation in sports by the 55–64 age group had doubled during the previous five years—and tripled for those aged 65 and over. While some of these people choose to run, bike, swim, play racket sports, or do calisthenics on their own, many others are flocking to health clubs, also known as health spas.

Choose a health club to fit your needs.

For many men and women, membership in a health club is more than a matter of physical fitness. Some people join largely for the social benefits. Singles often find the health club a more comfortable place to meet members of the opposite sex than bars or discos, and mothers can enroll in clubs that offer baby-sitting along with exercise. While executives still like to make contacts and entertain clients on the golf course or at the country club, more than one business connection has been made at a downtown fitness center.

There is as much diversity in health clubs as in the reasons people join them. Some clubs specialize in helping individuals at high risk, such as cardiac patients, become more active. Others emphasize appearance and weight loss. A health club may occupy thousands of square feet on several levels and include an indoor jogging track and Olympic-size pool or it may be simply a large room with a smooth floor where exercise classes are conducted. Some health clubs offer restaurants and cocktail lounges for post-exercise relaxation and socializing; others have a juice bar to provide a nutritious "one for the road." Some sell vitamins and diet formulas, some provide nutrition consultation and smoking-withdrawal clinics, and others offer nothing more than the opportunity to twist and bend yourself into shape.

The cost of joining a health club can vary even more dramatically than the kinds of services available. You are likely to pay more if you have one-on-one instruction rather than little or no trainer supervision. Clubs with the most extensive facilities are often the most expensive, but a posh neighborhood location may boost the fees as well. A well-equipped Y may be more reasonably priced than a private club, but it could lack a fresh paint job and other aesthetic amenities. The annual price of a club membership may range from under $200 to $2,000 or more. Sometimes a reduced rate is available if you want only limited services (for instance, calisthenics or aerobic dancing without use of the strength-building equipment).

The American Heart Association suggests that if you choose an exercise program that emphasizes an activity you really enjoy, you'll work at it more consistently and so get the health and fitness benefits more quickly. This should be a guideline for choosing a health club as well. If you like to swim or play tennis or racquetball, you'll want to find a club that offers these activities, perhaps with exercise classes and various kinds of equipment that will provide variety and new experiences.

Convenience is another factor in regular use of a health club and its facilities. Think about whether you'd rather join a club near home, where you can go on evenings and weekends, or one close to your job so you can enjoy the benefits of an early morning or lunch-hour workout. Some clubs have more than one location and let members use all of the sites, enabling you to visit a business-center club during the week and one near your home on weekends. Prospective members will want to be sure that the club's hours fit their own schedules: a nurse or police officer who works rotating shifts, for instance, may want to be sure that favorite

---

Barbara Scherr Trenk is a free-lance writer who specializes in health; her articles have appeared in USAir, Amtrak Express, *and* Long Island Life.

activities are available during a wide range of hours. The salesperson who is frequently on the road may want to find a club that has a reciprocal arrangement with another club in a city frequently visited. The several hundred clubs that belong to the Association of Physical Fitness Centers (5272 River Road, Bethesda, Md. 20816) have such an arrangement.

Shopping Around

Health clubs are becoming so popular that there are several choices in virtually every community. Some are part of large chains or are franchise operations; some are run by the YMCA-YWCA or YMHA-YWHA. Certain colleges and universities have fitness centers that are open to the public on a membership basis; others make their gymnasium facilities, swimming pools, and tennis courts available to alumni or community residents during selected hours. There are also high schools and community recreation departments that offer at least some of the activities that might be found at a health club—often at far more modest cost.

Prospective members should visit one or more clubs before actually joining. Often the best way to do this is to ask a friend who is a member to obtain a guest pass. The other alternative is a tour of the club with a staff member (who may well have been trained as a sales representative rather than an exercise specialist). If this tour is your introduction to the club, it's a good idea to also try an exercise class, some of the exercise machines, or the pool before you join. (However, some facilities will not allow prospective members to work out because the clubs do not wish to be liable in case an individual is injured.) By participating in an activity, you'll learn whether the club you're visiting is one where you'll feel comfortable, and you will have more opportunity to speak with members and learn their opinions about the benefits and disadvantages of membership. It's important as well to tour the facilities during the hours you expect to use them; peak hours can be very crowded, and you may be forced to wait to use the pool or a particular machine.

When visiting the club, you will want to learn all you can about the activities available, the hours, and the fee structure. You should also observe the quality of the housekeeping. If there is a shower room (a must if you plan to go straight to work or social engagements after a sweaty workout), is the floor reasonably well drained? Is the floor of the exercise area clean? Are the pool and whirlpool properly cared for? Ask to use the bathroom during the tour, and be sure it meets your personal standards of cleanliness.

See whether the equipment is in good repair. One health club administrator, Daniel J. Lynch of the Executive Fitness Center in New York City's Vista International Hotel, suggests that maintenance of equipment is the most critical sign a consumer should look for when visiting a facility. "If there are many pieces of equipment that are not in working order," he says, "that should indicate to the individual user that there is no professional expertise on site."

Think about the amenities you'll want. If you will be using the club during your lunch hour, it would be helpful if towels are supplied so you can avoid having to keep a wet towel in your desk drawer all afternoon. Are hair-driers provided, or do you have to bring your own? Are lockers

NEW YORK HEALTH & RACQUET CLUB

Some exercise clubs have restaurants or snack bars for nutrition and relaxation.

31

NO FRILLS vs. FIRST CLASS

Facilities at good clubs can range from no-nonsense spartan to the sybaritic. Some patrons look for few, if any, extras; above, the pared-down pool area of a McLean, Va., sports club. Others prefer posh, luxurious surroundings (right).

available that really lock (or are designed so that you can bring your own padlock), so that your wallet, jewelry, and street clothes will be safe? If you will be driving to the club, be sure the parking lot is convenient and well lit at night. If snow is heavy in your area, ask a member whether the lot is cleared during winter months.

Notice the way people dress when you visit a health club. Even leotards and exercise shorts come in high-fashion (and high-priced) styles; if you've always wanted a designer gym suit, the opportunity to wear it might be an incentive to exercise. But if you are more comfortable in less stylish surroundings, you might want to consider looking at other clubs.

Meeting Your Specific Needs

At some health clubs the swimming pool is a place to relax after a game of racquetball or a workout on the weight machines. It can also be a pleasant place for informal conversation. There's nothing wrong with this, except that if your favorite exercise is an invigorating 30 minutes of swimming laps, such a pool will probably be both too small and too crowded for your needs. If you plan to swim laps, you will want a pool at

least 60 feet long. Be sure to find out whether lap swimming is restricted to certain hours, and visit the pool at least once during the time you'd be most likely to use it, to see how crowded it gets.

Exerting yourself in summer heat and humidity is uncomfortable and can be unhealthy; an air-conditioned club can be as important in summer as a warm one in winter. If you're especially heat-sensitive, you'll want to be sure the club is not too frugal with the air-conditioning. Don't be unreasonable—everyone's equipment breaks down occasionally—but if the cooling system is not working properly for several weeks during the summer, you should be given an extension on your membership period to compensate.

If tennis or racquetball is your primary reason for joining a club, ask if there are extra charges for court time. Also find out whether the staff will arrange partners and competition with people of similar skills, if this is what you want. Conversely, if you have friends you wish to play with, will mutually convenient court times be available by reservation?

Vigorous exercise should be preceded by a five-minute warm-up period, to stretch the muscles and tendons and to prepare for more vigorous activity by increasing body temperature and heart and respiration rates.

After exercising, you should allow five minutes for cooling down, to let the body readjust gradually. It's not a good idea to stand still or sit down right after vigorous exercise, experts warn. When you visit a club before joining, you'll want to see whether members are encouraged to follow this widely accepted procedure.

Supervision and Instruction

According to Dr. Willibald Nagler, head of New York Hospital–Cornell Medical Center's Department of Rehabilitative Medicine, ideally a physical therapist should supervise a health club's exercise activities, aided by instructors who have studied anatomy and physiology. At some exercise centers, activities are supervised by physicians trained in sports medicine or another exercise-related specialty. However, in many cases instructors have only minimal training, if any at all. The American College of Sports Medicine has developed a Fitness Instructor Certification program to train these exercise instructors in the rudiments of working with basically healthy individuals. The ACSM feared that many instructors were unable to recognize possible health problems in their students and so might actually encourage them to do exercises that could cause injury. Since the ACSM program is so new, most instructors today are not certified. Because many of them may not be well trained, it's important for you to know your own exercise limits.

One Los Angeles grandmother may have saved herself from serious injury by being cautious. The woman joined an exercise class at a local health club because she was bored with doing stretching exercises on her own. When she found that some of the movements she was encouraged to do at the club were too strenuous for her, she used good judgment and substituted her own exercises instead. It would have been better, of course, if a trained instructor had recommended to her variations in the standard program, based on her age and medical history.

Know Your Limitations

Anyone with a chronic disease that might be aggravated by an inappropriate exercise program—including a heart condition, hypertension, diabetes, hyperthyroidism, or asthma—will want specific advice from a personal physician about an appropriate level of physical activity. Medical advice is also a good idea for anyone who has arthritis or a history of back, neck, knee, or foot problems.

Experts seem to agree that anyone who is 45 or older or who has not been exercising regularly should have a complete physical examination before beginning an exercise program; some say that anyone over 35 should do so. Special precautions, including an exercise stress test to check the body's response to physical exertion and temporary restrictions on strenuous activities, may be suggested for those who are obese, smoke, or have a high cholesterol level. If your physician recommends limits on your activities, be sure the health club staff understands this and is willing to help you develop an appropriate program.

Be wary of instructors who encourage participants to move in ways that seem to cause pain or strain, and avoid those trainers who make exercisers

Everyone can benefit from exercise, but people—especially the elderly or those with medical problems—should be aware of their limitations and should avoid activities that seem painful or too strenuous.

feel they must live up to an athlete's standards of fitness instead of gradually improving their own abilities. Don't be afraid to ask an instructor why a particular exercise is being done. After all, you're the customer, and certain exercises do have the potential to cause injury. Some specialists, for instance, suggest that sit-ups be done with the knees bent instead of straight out, to avoid back strain. If you find an exercise painful, consult your instructor or physician before continuing with it, and don't allow a coach to shame or browbeat you into doing it. On the other hand, some discomfort is to be expected while you're getting into shape—sore muscles may occur after the first few sessions.

Signing on the Dotted Line

While visiting a health club you'll undoubtedly be given a sales pitch, sometimes a very hard sell. So your first step toward fitness should be to exercise restraint. Before signing anything or making even a small down payment, get solid information—in writing—about the club's services and activities, what your membership fee covers, and what rights are guaranteed to members.

Many health clubs are reputable businesses, providing high-quality services in exchange for a membership fee. But perhaps because there are so many people who are concerned with improving their health and appearance, abuses have occurred. Some customers have been talked into paying for clubs that failed to provide the services that had been promised, and other people have been sold multiyear contracts or even lifetime memberships when they would have been better off with a three-month trial, or a full year at the most.

Careful supervision by trained instructors can go a long way toward helping you exercise most effectively.

A health club can provide bonuses in addition to physical fitness—such as the opportunity to meet people in a more comfortable place than a bar or a disco.

The U.S. Federal Trade Commission, which has had many complaints about health clubs, suggests not signing a contract unless it includes in writing everything the salesperson promised. The FTC also recommends that such contracts include a cooling-off period, giving you some time to change your mind after you've signed. In New York State, for example, a three-day period is required by law, and the Association of Physical Fitness Centers endorses this policy in its code of ethics. Of course, you should be allowed to use the club during these days to be sure it meets your expectations.

The contract should also list the services provided by the club—pool, exercise classes, exercise equipment, sauna, indoor track, and so on—and the hours during which these services will be available during the contract period. This prevents a club from simply saying "sorry" when, for instance, the exercise teacher leaves for another job.

Another FTC suggestion is to contact your local consumer affairs office, state attorney general, or Better Business Bureau to learn whether complaints have been lodged against a particular health club or spa. If you feel you do not get what you were promised when you joined, register a complaint with one of these agencies. Not only will you be helping to warn other consumers, but you may be able to encourage legal action against a club that does not honor its contracts.

Some clubs sell memberships before they even open their doors, a practice criticized by consumer agencies. More than once, large sums of money have been collected from prospective members, and the club either never opened for business or opened for only a short time. In order to discourage fly-by-night operations, the state of Maryland now requires health clubs to register with the Consumer Protection Division of the attorney general's office and to post a bond with a private bonding agency or deposit $50,000 with the state.

Should You Join a Health Club?

There is good reason to be careful when choosing a health club, and medical advice should sometimes supplement common sense as you decide on an exercise program. But many people do benefit from a structured program of exercise, which may include membership in a health club. Some people find that investing in a club membership is an incentive to exercise regularly: they want to get their money's worth. Others find that they are more likely to twist and bend into shape if they are in a class with other people, rather than at home exercising in front of a televised instructor or on their own. (If you do prefer to exercise independently, you should know that various aerobic activities—riding a bike regularly, taking a long, brisk walk, jogging, or swimming laps—are equally effective wherever they are done. Just be sure to do some warm-up stretches and to cool down gradually at the end so that your session will be a healthy one.)

Investing in a club membership can be a big incentive to exercise regularly.

The manager of one club that is especially watchful of its members' state of health says he sometimes recommends that previously inactive people spend a few weeks just walking before they begin a more strenuous program at his facility so that they'll be ready for vigorous activity once they've spent their money. Anyone who is self-conscious about being out of shape might be comfortable taking this advice; when walking a mile or two is no longer tiring, membership in a health club could be an appropriate reward.

If you decide that a health club is the best place to improve your level of physical fitness, and you find one that is convenient and priced within your budget, why not start getting fit right away, while your enthusiasm is high? Build up your program gradually—there's no rush. Chances are you'll soon begin to feel and look better than you have in years. □

SUGGESTIONS FOR FURTHER READING

About Your Heart and Exercise (1984). American Heart Association, 7320 Greenville Avenue, Dallas, Texas 75231; or contact your local chapter.

"E" is for Exercise (1983). American Heart Association.

Exercising Your Right to Know: A Consumer Guide to Choosing and Using Exercise Training and Stress Testing Facilities (1981). New York Heart Association, 205 East 42nd Street, New York, N.Y. 10017.

Health Spas: Exercise Your Rights (1982). Federal Trade Commission, Bureau of Consumer Protection, Office of Consumer and Business Education, Washington, D.C. 20580.

How Pets Aid Health

Aaron Honori Katcher, M.D.

At the Green Chimneys School in Brewster, N.Y., black and Hispanic children from New York City who are emotionally disturbed and cannot attend public schools are exposed to life on a working farm. The children attend classes, but they also learn how to raise and care for farm animals, tend crops, and ride horses. Tough street kids who never saw a cow before win 4-H prizes for calves they have tenderly reared.

In a nursery school in France, an autistic child who has played only with blocks and toys and paid no attention to other people suddenly notices the flight of a dove brought into the classroom. She smiles for the first time. As days pass, she focuses attention first on the bird, then on other classroom pets, then on other children and the teacher. Finally, she makes the first stumbling efforts to speak.

In a mental hospital in Ohio, an active wirehaired fox terrier was brought to the bed of a passive, uncommunicative adolescent who was not responding to doctors, nurses, or drug therapy. First the dog started to play with the boy; then the boy began to play with the dog. Soon the boy volunteered his first question and left his bed—a very significant step—when the dog jumped to the floor.

The Impact of Animals

In all of the cases just described, there is a common thread: the immediate and transforming impact of ordinary animals. The general public has always put great faith in the value of pets, especially for children. But until quite recently, most scientists paid little attention to the notion that contact with animals has healing power. Now, though, there is increasing scientific interest in the possibility that animals provide effective therapy for a wide variety of physical and emotional problems. Pioneers like psychologists Boris Levinson, Samuel Corson, and Elizabeth O'Leary Corson and veterinarians Ange Condoret in France and Leo Bustad in the United States have documented cases in which the human-pet bond has radically and positively altered courses of psychiatric and physical therapy. Research in this area is going on at the University of Pennsylvania's Center for the Interaction of Animals and Society, under Dr. Alan Beck of the university's School of Veterinary Medicine.

Evidence that animals can have tremendous impact also has come from the many humane society volunteers who for years have been bringing animals to homes for the aged and have found their efforts well rewarded. The volunteers have seen elderly residents who had been sitting in glum and apathetic silence reach out for a puppy that has been brought in. They hold the animal close, bending their heads down to meet its inquiring nose. Suddenly, they smile. Still holding the animal, they begin to talk, reminisce, and ask questions about the animal and the people who brought it. With the pet, they are able to reach out to others, and soon patients, staff, and volunteers are all talking animatedly.

A researcher examines a woman's blood pressure readings as she talks to and pets a dog. Studies have shown that such contact with an animal has a calming effect.

Case histories in which contact with animals has played a pivotal role have been documented on film, on videotape, and in photographs. The pictures have convincing force; in them, you can actually see people's behavior dramatically change because of the presence of pets. The transformation is particularly apparent in the emotionally disturbed and others who are often placed in institutions. The patients' facial expressions are so changed and so animated by contact with animals that one sees them no longer as patients, but simply as fellow humans. The character of the smile, the tender care expressed in the face and in the protective cuddling of the animal, and the sense of contentment and peace bridge the gap between viewer and subject.

The transformation may be brief. The next day, without the animal present, institutionalized patients again may be withdrawn. But however fleeting, the alteration in manner and behavior reminds both staff and visitors of the human potential in everyone, no matter how ill. The field of pet therapy is relatively new, and we do not yet know just how therapeutic pets are or the degree to which they can make lasting changes in patients. Nevertheless, the happiness the pets bring and the renewal of human contact they inspire certainly justifies the current trend toward making institutions more humane through the introduction of animals as companions.

Aaron Honori Katcher is associate professor of psychiatry at the University of Pennsylvania Schools of Medicine and Dental Medicine and is the coauthor, with Alan Beck, of Between Pets and People *(1983).*

A visit from a warm, loving animal is something to look forward to for elderly nursing-home residents, who find the pets a source of enjoyment and affection.

Pets and Health: Initial Clues

Why do pets have these transforming, revitalizing effects on people? I first looked into the question and came upon some initial clues when a chance research finding suggested that pet ownership could make a real contribution to the health of patients with severe physical illness. I was involved in a cooperative study between the universities of Pennsylvania and Maryland in which we were testing the hypothesis that *human* companionship could significantly increase the survival rates of patients with severe coronary artery disease. We conducted long, detailed interviews to determine if living with a family, having friends to see and talk to, attending church or other social gatherings, or living in friendly neighborhoods would help these patients survive. Among all of the questions we posed to patients was one about the presence of pets.

After one year, we examined the data and found, unexpectedly, that those heart disease patients who had a pet had better survival rates than patients without pets. Only three out of 53 patients with pets (under 6 percent) died, whereas 11 out of 39 patients without pets (or over 28 percent) died. These results suggested that pet ownership could make a real contribution to the survival and recovery of severely ill patients, and

Aquarium fish can provide a sense of peace and tranquility.

the findings opened up a whole new area of investigation. How could these results be explained? How could a dog or a cat, a horse or an iguana, affect the outcome of a life-threatening disease?

What Pets Do for Us

To begin to answer questions like these, we must first understand what pets do for their millions of essentially healthy owners. Over half the families in the United States own pets. How do these people benefit?

For people who might otherwise find themselves at loose ends, such as retired men and women whose days are no longer structured by work, pets can provide a focus of activity. The necessity of feeding and exercising an animal can form the basis of a daily routine and help instill a sense of purpose. Pets can also improve people's social lives. An activity like walking a dog can combat isolation simply by getting the owner out of the house, and several studies have shown that owning a dog increases opportunities for meeting and talking to people and for making friends. A series of experiments done in England demonstrated that people are more approachable for conversation in public places and have longer conversations if they are accompanied by a dog. Pets seem to make both their owners and others feel psychologically safer—more able to deal with the unfamiliar—and to lend increased social acceptability. Another study showed that people photographed with pets are perceived as more socially attractive than those in pictures without pets. (Politicians have long recognized this and almost always pose with a pet at some time during a campaign.)

Because pets must be cared for, they make their owners feel wanted and needed. Feeling needed is an important psychological antidote to depression and the overwhelming sense of helplessness that often accompanies it, both of which are believed to increase a person's susceptibility to illness. Pets also engage people in play and sometimes are the only source of lightheartedness and humor in their owner's lives. Such play and laughter can be another factor in preventing depression.

Pets offer valuable, loyal companionship, which has been shown to have a positive influence on health. For some people, their pets are their only friends or their closest companions, and the animals are treated like members of the family. Pets, after all, do not judge but give and return love unconditionally. In addition, pets may be an important source of physical contact and affection in their owners' lives. Affectionate physical contact keeps us very literally in touch with our ability to love and be loved. Holding or stroking a pet is reassuring, reduces anxiety, and strengthens self-esteem. In times of loss and mourning, many a pet has provided true comfort and solace.

The play and laughter that pets bring their owners can be important in preventing depression.

Attending to details of the outside world and putting aside personal worries is an effective way of reducing tension. Pets effectively draw our attention from our problems. Just watching a cat stretch elegantly can exert a calming influence; a dog's frolicking can entertain and amuse. To drain away the residual tensions of the workday, most pet owners intuitively turn to their pets. Being greeted by your dog or cat when you get home in the evening can make it all seem worthwhile; a few minutes spent caressing or playing with an animal can be as effective in combating stress at the end of a long day as a drink or a jog around the block. Pets may also help to reduce anxiety because they increase their owners' sense of physical safety. Some dogs provide real protection, but the presence of any pet can calm fears and make people feel more secure, especially people who live alone. As has been documented, another way to lessen tension and anxiety is exercise, and pets can be of help here, too. Some pets, like dogs and horses, provide both a stimulus and a reward for taking exercise.

Lower Blood Pressure and Calmer Souls

The calming effects pets have on their owners have been well documented by researchers. Pets can actually calm people enough in some cases to significantly lower blood pressure.

Chirping birds often help to dispel loneliness.

Experiments have shown that being with a pet can actually reduce blood pressure.

A set of experiments conducted with dog owners and their canine companions at the clinic of the University of Pennsylvania School of Veterinary Medicine contrasted the effects on blood pressure of talking to a person and talking to and petting a dog. When one person talked to another, blood pressure almost always rose. But when people talked to and caressed their dogs, a number of striking effects on both blood pressure and behavior were observed. Their faces became more relaxed, with a general decrease in muscle tension around the eyes and the brow. Smiles, usually present during interaction with pets, were more relaxed than during conversations with people—there was less tension at the corners of the mouth. Voices became much softer and higher in pitch, and the overall speech pattern was slower and was broken into small series of words, frequently phrased as questions and concluding with a rising intonation. These questions were followed by silences during which eye contact and answering gestures were solicited from the animal. All of these distinct behavioral changes were associated with definite alterations in blood pressure. When people were talking to their dogs, blood pressure was significantly lower than when they were talking to another person and sometimes even fell below the level measured when at rest. Other experiments have shown that when people speak more slowly, blood pressure tends to decrease. Some patients with borderline hypertension can in fact be treated by training them to speak more slowly and softly and with more pauses for breath—just the way people speak naturally to their pets.

People don't have to talk to or touch animals to benefit from them—gains can be achieved simply by gazing at fish in an aquarium. Everyone has experienced the almost hypnotic calm induced by the sight of waves breaking on a beach, an open fire blazing on the hearth, the patterns of cloud and sunlight seen through the leaves of a tree. Perhaps because they provide some of that same peace, aquarium fish are among the most popular pets in American homes. And aquarium fish can do more than produce a relaxing state of calm—it has even been demonstrated that an ordinary aquarium can have beneficial effects on blood pressure and the ability to tolerate stress.

In one set of experiments, people with high blood pressure and normal blood pressure were asked to watch a tank stocked with a variety of common, relatively inexpensive tropical fish. Just before watching the fish, the subjects had been sitting quietly in a chair for 20 minutes to stabilize their blood pressure levels. As they watched, the blood pressure of both the hypertensive and normal subjects fell to even lower levels. Contemplating the aquarium was found to be as effective for lowering blood pressure as meditation and biofeedback (a technique for developing conscious control over certain body processes).

In other research, either aquarium contemplation or hypnosis was used to calm anxious subjects who were about to have one or more teeth pulled under local anesthesia. The investigators found that a period of restful watching of an aquarium before the tooth extraction enabled patients to get through the procedure with relatively little discomfort and anxiety and was as effective as hypnosis in inducing calm. Watching the fish distracted anxious patients. When their attention was directed outward, they were less likely to ruminate about their private concerns or dwell on the impending dental procedure. This study confirmed the wisdom of the many dentists and physicians who place aquariums in their waiting rooms. Moreover, it suggested that many environments in which people are anxious or under pressure could be made more comfortable if there were pleasant living displays there to watch.

The aquarium experiments raise another important point. Undisturbed animals and plants are traditional symbols of safety, just as sudden agitation is a sign of danger—symbols probably based on our evolutionary history. Animals in the wild use the flight and agitation of other animals as signals of imminent danger. We know, for example, that apes depend upon the flight of animals with more acute senses as warnings; the sudden agitation of grazing antelopes when they catch a leopard's scent would alert apes to the danger as well. By the same token, the sight of antelopes grazing peacefully would be a signal of relative safety. Such symbols pervade Western culture. The flight of animals and trees whipped into motion by storm winds are classic visual signals of danger, while the sight of cows grazing in a meadow or deer in the forest gives us a sense of bucolic serenity. That the sight of nature undisturbed should be relaxing—such as calmly swimming fish and gently swaying plants—is not at all surprising.

Pets and Prisoners

To those who have been isolated from the rest of society and confined to prisons and hospitals, animals can have special meaning. This has been

Prison inmates participate in dog-training classes (below). The women learn new skills and also make new friends (above).

shown by a pet-therapy program at the Lima State Hospital for the Criminally Insane in Ohio, instituted by prison social worker David Lee. The program has given some convicts a better grip on reality, softened some of the harshness of their existence, enlivened their environment, and improved the relations between inmates and staff. In one maximum security ward, inmates were permitted to have caged birds, small animals (rabbits, guinea pigs, and gerbils), and tropical fish. The prisoners became dedicated to nurturing their animals; they built cages for them, grew some of the pets' food, and began to raise money so that other inmates could have pets as well. Larger animals are also kept on the hospital grounds, including ducks, geese, goats, deer, and chickens.

A visiting turtle can teach students valuable lessons about nurturance and gentleness, as well as biology.

The Lima program has been documented on film. Seeing these rough, dangerous men tenderly stroke their animals and hearing them say that these animals are the only living things they could love and nurture offer

perhaps the most convincing evidence of the program's success. David Lee has also reported that the frequency of suicide attempts and episodes of violence have decreased strikingly among the inmates on the wards with pets.

Inspired by the Lima pet-therapy project, Dr. Earle Strimple, a Washington, D.C., veterinarian, introduced a similar program at Lorton Reformatory in Lorton, Va. Studies of human-animal interaction were conducted there by the University of Pennsylvania veterinary school. Prisoners' blood pressure and heart rate were measured, and their facial expressions were recorded while they talked to the researchers and played with their pets. The presence of the pets modified the behavior of aggressive prisoners in the same way they affected the pet owners studied at the veterinary school clinic. The prisoners talked more softly and slowly to the animals, and their blood pressure was lower than when they talked to researchers. The mere presence of a pet in the same room tended to lower the prisoners' blood pressure and permitted them to deal with researchers with less tension. The prisoners talked of the importance of the animals in their lives, not as hobbies, but as other beings who could be loved and nurtured and who gave love in return. Prison records showed no change in the frequency of episodes requiring disciplinary measures or infirmary visits for prisoners with pets. But direct observation of the prisoners with their pets clearly demonstrated the potential of such programs to humanize the prison environment.

Animals can have special meaning for the institutionalized, who are isolated from the rest of society.

Pets Should Go to School

Birds, gerbils, rabbits, and goldfish are frequently residents of nursery and elementary school classrooms. There is evidence that they are more than playthings and provide more than basic lessons in biology. In another series of experiments by the University of Pennsylvania Center for the Interaction of Animals and Society, children were brought individually into a room that contained either a female researcher and a pet dog or the woman alone. After a period for stabilization, each child's blood pressure was measured while the child was quiet and while the child read aloud. It was discovered that when the dog was in the room, the children had significantly lower blood pressure, whether they were silent or whether they were reading aloud.

These findings have important implications for nursery and elementary schools in particular. Animal residents introduce an element of calm, helping to reduce the stress of learning and performance. The classroom pets may also teach children about nurturance and gentleness in dealing with others—both humans and animals.

The Therapeutic Potential of Pets

Animals have proved a great boon for many handicapped people, serving as companions, as eyes and ears for the blind and deaf, and even as physical therapists. We are all familiar with the usefulness of Seeing Eye dogs; Hearing Ear dogs for the deaf also exist. One of the most remarkable and successful examples of pets' therapeutic value is the use of horses and horseback riding in the treatment of the physically disabled.

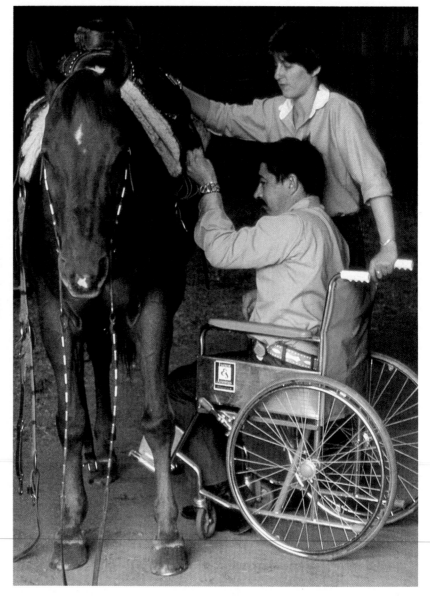

A wheelchair-bound patient prepares to take a rehabilitative horseback ride (right), while a retarded boy shares a close, quiet moment with a pet rabbit (above).

At riding centers around the world, children who cannot walk are taught to ride horses, in seemingly miraculous programs of physical therapy. In one case, a handicapped boy moves his wheelchair up a ramp to the horse's side, discards his braces, and mounts. That child who could not walk now rides above the world, and his face reflects the joy of that conquest. In his own eyes and those of the people around him, he has gained stature, sharing in the power and beauty of the horse he controls. In addition to learning to ride, he learns how to exercise, to compete in games, and even to take his mount over hurdles. The warmth of the horse's body and the motion of the gait loosen the spasms in his muscles, improving his coordination and permitting him to do the exercises that will further increase his muscle tone and coordination.

Another kind of therapeutic potential is evident in the immediate effects that pets have on one's emotional state and responsiveness to other people. In a study with chronically ill mental patients at the Haverford State Hospital outside Philadelphia, the presence of a cage of four finches increased the amount of talking by patients in group therapy. The presence of the birds also decreased the amount of hostility and aggression the patients displayed.

Animals can be trusted even by those who have been too emotionally damaged to trust people. An animal does not argue, criticize, talk back, or threaten rejection, making it much less painful for withdrawn patients to approach and talk to an animal than to another person. The ability to touch and establish communication with the animal is reassuring to the patient, who may never have expected to respond to or care about anything. A therapist is perceived as more trustworthy and less threatening because of the animal's presence, and the animal provides a safe and stimulating topic for discussion. Once contact and trust are established, therapy can move forward.

Unfortunately, it has not been documented whether a pet's positive influence persists when the pet is no longer present. But the results of studies emphasize that a major benefit of pet therapy, particularly for institutionalized patients, is improved communication with other human beings. The pet can be thought of in such instances, not as a substitute for a person, but as a bridge to other people.

Carefully designed investigations are identifying the specific kinds of people likely to be helped by animal contact. One interesting finding is that rural women are among the least likely to be helped by pets. Women living and working on farms frequently treat cats and dogs more like farm animals than like members of the family. For these people, pets may actually be associated with decreased health and morale and may seem, in times of stress, to be just another burden. On the other hand, pets may be most helpful to urban men, since city dwellers tend to treat a pet like a person and since men often have more difficulty expressing affection than women. For many men, a pet may be their only outlet for the expression of affection, tenderness, and nurturance.

Other research efforts are focusing not just on the long-term effectiveness of pet therapy for the ill and handicapped but also on the importance of natural settings and companion animals to the health and emotional balance of those without diseases or handicaps. □

There is now convincing evidence that animals provide effective therapy for many physical and emotional problems.

SUGGESTIONS FOR FURTHER READING

ANDERSON, ROBERT K., BENJAMIN HART, AND LYNETTE HART, eds. *The Pet Connection.* Minneapolis, Center to Study Human-Animal Relationships and Environments, 1984.

BECK, ALAN, and AARON KATCHER. *Between Pets and People.* New York, Putnam, 1983.

FOGLE, BRUCE. *Pets and Their People.* London, Collins Harvill, 1983.

FOGLE, BRUCE, ed. *Interrelations Between People and Pets.* Springfield, Ill., Charles C. Thomas, 1981.

KATCHER, AARON, and ALAN BECK, eds. *New Perspectives on Our Lives With Companion Animals.* Philadelphia, University of Pennsylvania Press, 1983.

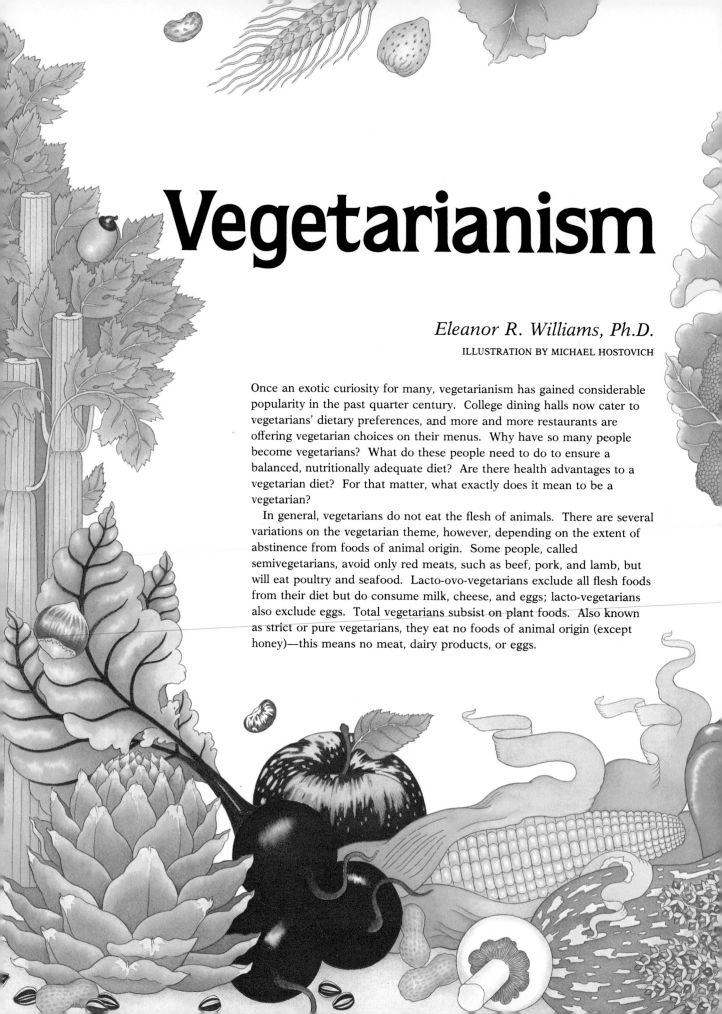

Vegetarianism

Eleanor R. Williams, Ph.D.

ILLUSTRATION BY MICHAEL HOSTOVICH

Once an exotic curiosity for many, vegetarianism has gained considerable popularity in the past quarter century. College dining halls now cater to vegetarians' dietary preferences, and more and more restaurants are offering vegetarian choices on their menus. Why have so many people become vegetarians? What do these people need to do to ensure a balanced, nutritionally adequate diet? Are there health advantages to a vegetarian diet? For that matter, what exactly does it mean to be a vegetarian?

In general, vegetarians do not eat the flesh of animals. There are several variations on the vegetarian theme, however, depending on the extent of abstinence from foods of animal origin. Some people, called semivegetarians, avoid only red meats, such as beef, pork, and lamb, but will eat poultry and seafood. Lacto-ovo-vegetarians exclude all flesh foods from their diet but do consume milk, cheese, and eggs; lacto-vegetarians also exclude eggs. Total vegetarians subsist on plant foods. Also known as strict or pure vegetarians, they eat no foods of animal origin (except honey)—this means no meat, dairy products, or eggs.

Vegans are a special group of total vegetarians who abstain not only from eating but from using animal products. They do not eat honey or wear wool, silk, leather, furs, or pearls, nor do they use any household items containing animal derivatives. Their life-style is based on their belief that animals should not be exploited or caused to suffer. Fruitarians go a step further, claiming that plants should not be killed for food. The diet of a fruitarian is made up of grains, fruits, nuts, and seeds—those plant products that can be obtained without destroying the plant.

The macrobiotic diet followed by adherents of the Zen sect of Buddhism is often considered vegetarian. The goal of the diet, as strictly practiced by Zen Buddhists, is in fact a fairly restricted vegetarianism, toward which it moves in stages. Both seafood and poultry are included in early stages but not in later ones. This gradual exclusion of foods is not typical of vegetarian diets generally. Many non-Buddhists follow diets referred to as macrobiotic that they believe promote health and longevity. These diets may be more or less restrictive, with their content depending on individual needs and preferences.

Just as there is not a single set of eating habits, there is not a life-style that is typical of all vegetarians. Some avoid alcohol and tobacco, while others do not; some consume only unrefined or organically grown foods, and others devour large quantities of junk foods.

Why Vegetarianism?

Doing without meat is not always a matter of choice. In the less developed countries of the world, many people are vegetarians simply because they are too poor to obtain any flesh foods. Throughout history, however, there have been men and women who have chosen to practice vegetarianism—for religious, philosophical, ethical, or health reasons.

The ancient Eastern religions of Buddhism, Jainism, and Hinduism prohibit the killing of animals, a prohibition stemming from the belief that animals, like people, are capable of feeling and should therefore not be harmed. Animals also enjoy a protected status because many followers of these religions believe that after a person dies, the soul may pass into the body of an animal.

In the Roman Catholic Church, Trappist monks take vows of simple living that traditionally require them to avoid meat, which is considered a luxury. Although the Catholic ecumenical council Vatican II (1962–1965) freed Trappists from mandatory abstinence from meat, a majority are still vegetarian.

Seventh-Day Adventists view the body as the temple of God. They consider it their religious duty to avoid eating meat and using substances deemed injurious to health, such as tobacco, caffeine, and alcohol. Most Seventh-Day Adventists are lacto-ovo-vegetarians.

Since the 1960's flesh-free diets have had a widening appeal among young people in the United States and Canada with no family history of vegetarianism. Many have turned to vegetarianism for the same reasons

The personification of vegetables was a fanciful tool of late 19th-century agricultural advertising. Here a man made of cucumbers urges farmers to plant Rice's Seeds.

Eleanor R. Williams is an associate professor in the Department of Food, Nutrition and Institution Administration at the University of Maryland.

A Bombay, India, vendor displays his wares—an enticing array of the vegetables that constitute staples of the Hindu diet.

people did earlier. Some, for example, find it repugnant to kill animals for food. Some have become vegetarians out of a belief that meat eating is ecologically and economically wasteful; they point out that raising animals for meat production requires larger amounts of land, water, and other valuable resources than growing plant foods directly for human consumption. There are vegetarians who regard their diets as more healthful than diets containing meat, and there are some who claim that meat is inherently toxic to the human body. The 1960's saw an increased interest in the ancient Eastern religions and practices, which also influenced many to follow vegetarian diets.

Of Poets and Politicians

Vegetarianism dates back to ancient times in the West as well as in the East. The Greek mathematician and philosopher Pythagoras, who lived in the sixth century B.C., was a vegetarian; because of his fame, vegetarians were in the past sometimes called Pythagoreans. Around the first century B.C. the poets Horace, Vergil, and Ovid espoused vegetarianism in reaction to the dietary excesses of their fellow Romans. The asceticism and temperance advocated by many early Christian leaders often included a vegetarian diet. St. Francis of Assisi, who loved animals, abstained from meat, as did the Renaissance artist and inventor Leonardo da Vinci.

In England, John Wesley, the founder of Methodism, and the poets Alexander Pope and Percy Bysshe Shelley were among proponents of vegetarianism in the 18th and 19th centuries. The critic and playwright George Bernard Shaw was probably England's best-known vegetarian in the first half of the 20th century.

Benjamin Franklin, an advocate of simple living, was perhaps the most famous 18th-century American vegetarian. Sylvester Graham, for whom

Famous Vegetarians

An unlikely trio is formed by Percy Bysshe Shelley (left), Benjamin Franklin (center), and St. Francis of Assisi, who were all vegetarians.

the graham cracker was named, Dr. John Harvey Kellogg, inventor of ready-to-eat breakfast cereals, and Ellen White, a Seventh-Day Adventist leader, were prominent vegetarians and dietary reformers in the 19th and early 20th centuries. Upton Sinclair, whose 1906 novel *The Jungle* described life in the Chicago stockyards and the conditions under which animals were slaughtered for meat, also adopted a vegetarian diet.

Perhaps the most influential vegetarian in the world in the 20th century was Mohandas Gandhi, who led India's struggle for independence from Great Britain. Gandhi's practice of vegetarianism was closely allied with his doctrine of nonviolence. At a time when large numbers of Hindus were beginning to view their traditional diet as out-of-date and meaningless, Gandhi's example inspired many of his followers to return to vegetarianism.

Adolf Hitler was also a vegetarian. The fact that such different men as Gandhi and Hitler both abstained from flesh foods drives home the point that vegetarianism cannot be associated with any one set of beliefs or way of life. People choose nonflesh diets for various, often highly personal reasons.

Well-known modern American vegetarians include the historian Will Durant; Scott and Helen Nearing, advocates of self-sufficiency and living off the land, which they celebrated in *Living the Good Life* (1954); the Nobel Prize–winning writer Isaac Bashevis Singer; and the comedian and political activist Dick Gregory.

Health Pluses

Is there any truth to the belief of many vegetarians that their diets are more healthful? Or is an omnivorous diet—one that includes both animal and plant foods—best? Scientists have found that both health benefits and health risks can be associated with a flesh-free diet. Whether the risks or advantages are foremost depends upon the specific content of the diet. There is some evidence, however, that in general vegetarians may be less at risk than omnivores for such conditions as obesity, constipation, heart disease, diabetes, and diverticular disease.

Take body weight, for example. It is closely associated with health. People who are extremely underweight or overweight generally run a much greater risk of developing various health problems than those who are near their optimum weight. Studies done in the United States show that vegetarians, particularly total vegetarians, are, on the average, closer to their desirable weight than nonvegetarians. The most likely explanation for this is that vegetarian diets tend to be lower in fat and higher in fiber, or roughage. Less fat, of course, means fewer calories. Meals with large amounts of fiber—from whole grains, legumes (peas, beans, and lentils), other vegetables, seeds, and fruits—result in a feeling of fullness, allowing a sense of satisfaction from a lower-calorie diet.

A high intake of dietary fiber also accounts for vegetarians being less bothered with constipation than nonvegetarians. The fiber increases fecal bulk, stimulating nerve endings in the colon and rectum to move the fecal mass without strain.

Vegetarians, some studies suggest, may have lower death rates from heart disease than omnivores. One possible reason for this has to do with cholesterol. In the blood, cholesterol is carried by substances known as lipoproteins, most notably by so-called high-density and low-density

Reflecting the new health consciousness, many restaurants now offer simple, fresh foods that fit well into a vegetarian diet.

lipoproteins. High blood levels of cholesterol and of low-density lipoproteins, which transport cholesterol to body cells, increase one's chances of developing heart disease; high levels of high-density lipoproteins, believed to carry cholesterol away from body cells for excretion, diminish the risk of heart disease.

Generally, vegetarians have lower blood levels of cholesterol and low-density lipoproteins and higher levels of high-density lipoproteins. This may be because, in comparison to omnivores, vegetarians are relatively lean and consume less total fat, less saturated fats (which are obtained primarily from meat and dairy products), and more polyunsaturated fats (which are generally obtained from plant sources). Saturated fats in the diet tend to increase blood cholesterol and low-density lipoprotein levels, whereas polyunsaturated fats tend to lower them.

High blood pressure also increases the risk of heart disease. Here, too, vegetarians may be at an advantage: they tend to have lower blood pressure than omnivores. The evidence is not conclusive, but vegetarians' lower blood pressure may be due to the lower amounts of fat as well as the type of fats they consume—a high ratio of unsaturated to saturated fats; or it may be a result of the relatively high levels of the mineral potassium in their diets. Potassium is found in fruits, vegetables, and dairy products; some studies have indicated that it may help lower blood pressure. Moreover, vegetarian diets are often low in sodium (found in salt and, therefore, in salty foods), and there is evidence suggesting that too much sodium may be associated with high blood pressure.

Vegetarians also seem to be less prone than nonvegetarians to develop non-insulin-dependent diabetes, the most common form of the disease. In diabetes, the body's needs for the hormone insulin are not met. Either the pancreas simply does not secrete enough, or the body is unable to utilize effectively the insulin it produces. The disorder affects the body's ability to use carbohydrates (such as sugar) and fats. Eventually, such complications as diseases of the arteries and kidneys may develop. Individuals who produce little or no insulin must receive injections of the hormone and are said to be insulin-dependent. Treatment for those who simply cannot make use of their insulin includes a carefully controlled diet and, sometimes, orally administered drugs (but not insulin). Obesity increases the risk of developing non-insulin-dependent diabetes. The fact that obesity is relatively rare among vegetarians may account for their being less likely to develop the disease.

Following a vegetarian diet makes it easier to control both non-insulin-dependent and insulin-dependent diabetes. To explain this, many researchers point to vegetarians' high intake of "complex" carbohydrates—as in high-fiber starchy foods, including legumes and whole-grain cereals and breads. They believe that consuming such carbohydrates, as opposed to simple carbohydrates like sugar, results in a smaller and more gradual increase in blood sugar after meals, possibly because complex carbohydrates are digested and absorbed more slowly than simple ones.

Diverticular disease is another condition that appears to occur less frequently among vegetarians. In this disorder, small distended pouches, or sacs (called diverticula), form along the outside of the colon. They are believed to be produced by increased pressure inside the colon, which causes the colon wall to balloon out at points of weakness. If fecal matter

Vegetarians may be less likely to develop heart disease, high blood pressure, or diabetes than meat eaters.

56

becomes trapped in the pouches, infection can develop; sometimes ruptures occur, requiring surgical repair. Many scientists think that by increasing the bulk of the fecal mass and moving it through the colon more quickly, the large amount of fiber in the vegetarian diet keeps pressure from building up within the colon and thus helps to prevent diverticular disease.

Evidence as to the effect of a vegetarian diet on the incidence of cancer is conflicting. Some reports have noted fewer deaths from cancer among Seventh-Day Adventist lacto-ovo-vegetarians than among nonvegetarians. There is also debate about whether vegetarianism can help ward off osteoporosis, a disorder affecting mainly the elderly, in which bone mass is lost, making fractures more likely to occur. Recent studies have found increased bone loss in nonvegetarian females (but not in males) over age 60 in comparison with Seventh-Day Adventist lacto-ovo-vegetarians. It is not clear, however, to what extent these observations are actually diet-related. They could have been due to genetic, hormonal, or metabolic differences between the omnivores and vegetarians studied. In the case of osteoporosis, differences in amounts and types of physical exercise could have been an important factor, and in the case of cancer the fact that most Seventh-Day Adventists abstain from smoking and drinking must be taken into account. Further research is needed to determine whether or not vegetarianism can indeed help prevent these diseases.

The Danger of Malnutrition

The major danger of vegetarianism is that malnutrition or particular deficiency diseases may develop in those who limit their food choices or who suffer from illnesses that affect their vitamin and mineral requirements. At particular risk are those vegetarians who reject orthodox medicine and rely instead on lay healers or homeopathic remedies. (Homeopathy is a 200-year-old system that treats a disease with very small doses of substances that are capable of producing symptoms like those of the disease.)

Since they abstain from fewer types of food, lacto-ovo-vegetarians or semivegetarians are more apt to have adequate diets than total vegetarians. The chances of malnutrition are especially great for total vegetarians with very restrictive diets, such as fruitarians and devotees of raw plant foods to the exclusion of all else.

To avoid nutritional deficiencies, vegetarians should keep certain problem areas in mind when putting together their diets. Although plant foods tend to be good sources of most vitamins and minerals required by the human body, they cannot provide them all. Neither vitamin B_{12} nor vitamin D is found in plant foods. Total vegetarians must also make special plans to meet their bodies' needs for calcium and for riboflavin (vitamin B_2).

Some vegetarians use fermented soy products and seaweeds in the mistaken belief that the process of fermentation produces adequate B_{12}, which is required for normal functioning of the nervous system and for the formation of red blood cells. These fermented products are not reliable sources. To be assured of obtaining sufficient vitamin B_{12}, total vegetarians should take vitamin B_{12} pills or use nutritional yeast rich in

A corn woman and a turnip and carrot couple ingratiatingly invite us to partake of vegetables in these 19th-century advertisements.

vitamin B_{12}, soybean milk fortified with B_{12}, or B_{12}-fortified meat analogues (food made from soybeans and wheat gluten to resemble meat, poultry, or fish). Although full-blown vitamin B_{12} deficiency is relatively uncommon among total vegetarians, they cannot afford to ignore this vitamin's importance. Lacto-ovo-vegetarians generally obtain sufficient vitamin B_{12} from eggs and milk products.

Vitamin D regulates the body's absorption and utilization of calcium and thus is required for healthy teeth and for normal growth and calcification—hardening—of bones. Deficiency of this vitamin results in rickets (softening of the bones) in children and a similar condition, osteomalacia, in adults. Adequate vitamin D may also be necessary for prevention of osteoporosis; the vitamin is often used in treating this disease. Milk is often fortified with vitamin D, but total vegetarians must obtain the vitamin from D-fortified soybean milk, vitamin D supplements, or sufficient exposure of the skin to the sun, whose ultraviolet rays convert a substance in the skin to vitamin D. Sun exposure may not provide sufficient amounts for children, who need more vitamin D than adults do.

Since total vegetarians do not drink cow's milk, the most important source of calcium and riboflavin in the U.S. diet, they must make special efforts to obtain enough of these nutrients. Among the best plant sources of calcium are legumes, almonds, unhulled sesame seeds, calcium-fortified soybean milk, and dark green vegetables such as broccoli, kale, and collard greens, mustard greens, and turnip greens. Although spinach, chard, and beet greens have considerable calcium, they are poor dietary sources of it because they also contain oxalic acid, which inhibits the absorption of calcium. Dark-green leafy vegetables, legumes, and whole grains can provide all the riboflavin needed.

Because the iron in food is not absorbed easily by the body, both omnivores and vegetarians may suffer from iron deficiency, particularly women of reproductive age and children. Iron from plant foods is actually less readily absorbed than iron from red meats. Well-chosen vegetarian diets are relatively high in iron, but it is apt to be poorly absorbed unless a source of vitamin C is consumed at the same time, or unless the iron source is also a source of vitamin C, as in dark-green leafy vegetables. (Vitamin C appears to bond with iron chemically, making it more readily absorbable.) All vegetarians should include a source of vitamin C with each meal or snack to aid in iron absorption.

Some questions have been raised about the extent to which zinc is absorbed from vegetarian diets based on minimally refined and unrefined foods. Studies of long-term lacto-ovo-vegetarians have indicated no zinc deficiencies. Further research is needed to determine whether obtaining adequate zinc, which is necessary for cell division and replacement, is a problem for other types of vegetarians.

What About Protein?

"How will you ever get enough protein?" ask many parents when they learn their teenager has become a vegetarian. But the notion that only flesh foods can provide adequate protein is very far from true.

The body needs to receive from food not specific proteins but specific amino acids, the building blocks of all proteins. Dietary proteins are

Protein-packed vegetarian burgers, made from soybeans and wheat products, are prepared at a factory for sale in health food stores and restaurants.

FOOD GUIDE FOR ADULT VEGETARIANS

FOOD GROUP AND SERVING SIZE	SERVINGS PER DAY		NUTRIENTS SUPPLIED
	Lacto-Ovo-Vegetarians	Total Vegetarians	
1. Legumes, meat analogues, soybean curd (tofu), soybean cake (tempeh) 1 cup cooked legumes, 2–3 oz. meat analogue, 4 oz. tofu or tempeh	1	1 1/4	Protein, thiamine, riboflavin, niacin, iron, calcium, phosphorus, vitamin B_6, folic acid, magnesium, zinc, vitamin E, pantothenic acid, fiber
2. Nuts and seeds, nut and seed butters 1/4 cup	1	1	Thiamine, riboflavin, niacin, phosphorus, vitamins E and B_6, pantothenic acid
3. Bread, grains, pasta (preferably whole-grain products) 1 slice bread, 1/2–3/4 cup rice, 1 cup dry breakfast cereal, 1/2–3/4 cup pasta	4–6	7–12	*Whole-grain:* Thiamine, riboflavin, niacin, iron, phosphorus, zinc, magnesium, vitamin B_6, pantothenic acid, folic acid, vitamin E, protein, fiber *White enriched:* Thiamine, riboflavin, niacin, iron, protein
4. Dark-green leafy vegetables 1 cup raw or 3/4 cup cooked broccoli, spinach, dark green lettuce, or turnip, mustard, or collard greens	1	3	Vitamins A, C, E, and B_6, folic acid, riboflavin, iron, magnesium, calcium, fiber
5. Other vegetables, fruits 1 cup raw or 3/4 cup cooked vegetables, 4–6 oz. fruit juice, 2/3 cup raw or cooked fruit, 1 piece whole fruit	3 or more	2 or more	Vitamins C and A, as well as varying amounts of vitamin E, B vitamins, magnesium, zinc, phosphorus, fiber
6. Milk, cheese 1 cup milk, 1 cup yogurt, 1 1/2 oz. cheddar cheese, 1 1/3 cups cottage cheese	2*		Protein, calcium, phosphorus, vitamins D, A, E, B_6, and B_{12}, zinc, magnesium
7. Soybean milk (fortified with 10 micrograms vitamin D, 3 micrograms vitamin B_{12}, and 800 milligrams calcium per quart) 1 cup		0–2**	Protein, calcium, vitamins D and A, B vitamins, including B_{12}
8. Eggs 1 egg	3–4 per week		Protein, vitamins A and B_{12}, pantothenic acid
9. Fats, oils 1 tbsp. margarine, oil, mayonnaise, or salad dressing	2	2	Vitamin E, linoleic acid (an essential fatty acid)

* 3–4 for children and adolescents, 4 for pregnant women, 5 for lactating women.
** Adults who do not consume fortified soybean milk should take a vitamin B_{12} supplement. For children and adolescents, 3–4 servings per day; for pregnant and lactating women, 4 servings per day.

broken down in the digestive system into their component amino acids, which are then used in the tissues to create the appropriate proteins for the body's needs. The body can synthesize certain amino acids but not others. Those it cannot synthesize are called the essential amino acids; they must be obtained from food.

It is true that the essential amino acids are more concentrated in animal foods than in plants. Animal proteins conform more closely in the proportions of essential amino acids to the human body's needs than do plant proteins and are thus considered more complete proteins. But by combining different types of plant foods (grains, seeds, nuts, legumes, and certain other vegetables) or by combining plant foods with nonflesh animal foods, the necessary amino acids can be obtained. Those amino acids that are low in one food can be supplied by another. This is called supplementing, or complementing, proteins.

Vegetarians should consume complementary sources of proteins at each meal. This is actually not at all difficult to do. A peanut butter sandwich with a glass of milk is a complementary combination. Other complementary combinations include grains (wheat, oats, corn, rice, and barley) with seeds (sesame or sunflower seeds); legumes (soybeans, lentils, peas, and garbanzo, black, navy, pinto, and kidney beans) with seeds or grains; and milk products or eggs with grains, legumes, or seeds.

A Cardinal Rule and Basic Guidelines

A cardinal rule for all vegetarians is to eat a wide variety of foods, especially unrefined or minimally refined foods, in sufficient quantities to promote normal growth in children and to maintain normal weight in adults. The greater the variety of foods, the higher the chances of obtaining all the nutrients needed. Eating enough of the right foods ensures an adequate supply of calories. A diet too low in calories is, moreover, less likely to provide all the nutrients required, including protein. In fact, when too few calories are taken in, the body is forced to use part of the dietary protein to supply energy, thereby diminishing the dietary protein that can be used to manufacture body proteins.

The Food Guide on page 59 can be a valuable aid in planning a nutritious vegetarian diet. Apply the cardinal rule, and choose a wide variety of foods within each of the first five groups. Vegetarians should use relatively small amounts of sugar, honey, and syrups; these furnish calories but few nutrients and are therefore not included in the Food Guide. Complementary protein combinations and a source of vitamin C should be consumed as part of each meal. Total vegetarians should choose those dark-green leafy vegetables that are free of oxalic acid for their sources of calcium.

Pregnant and breast-feeding women will do well on vegetarian diets if they follow the Food Guide. A woman of normal weight at the start of pregnancy should gain 2 to 4 pounds during the first three months and about ¾ to 1 pound each week thereafter; her total weight gain should be 24 to 28 pounds. Iron supplements may be needed depending on the amount of iron the woman has stored in her body when pregnancy begins. Total vegetarians must make sure they get sufficient calcium and vitamins B_{12} and D, all most easily obtained from properly fortified soybean milk.

The appeal of fresh fruits and vegetables is the selling point in this condiment ad from the late 1800's.

Sufficient vitamin B_{12} is of particularly vital importance to breast-feeding women. There are documented cases of vitamin B_{12} deficiency among nursing infants of total vegetarian mothers who had no known source of this vitamin in their diets while nursing. This deficiency can cause serious damage to the infant's nervous system.

Infants and children do well on sensibly planned lacto-ovo-vegetarian diets. The Food Guide, however, is basically geared for adults. If it is used for children, be sure to make serving sizes smaller, according to the child's age. The child's growth rate should be monitored to be certain that it remains within normal limits.

Total vegetarian diets require a little more careful planning in order to meet the needs of infants and children. Many cases of malnutrition and abnormal growth have been reported among children of total vegetarians. Often these problems arise simply because parents are not aware that children's dietary needs are different from those of adults. Again, it is important to remember that the total vegetarian diet outlined in the Food Guide is a bulky diet, designed principally for adults. Young children cannot easily consume this volume of food. In order to satisfy their calorie and nutrient needs, they should be fed smaller amounts at each meal and eat more than three meals a day. Ideally, small children should receive most of their calories from soybean milk and from groups 1, 2, and 3 in the Food Guide. To reduce bulk further, dark-green leafy vegetables can be cut down to one small serving daily.

Properly fortified soybean milk should be used so that sufficient calcium, vitamin D, and vitamin B_{12} can be obtained and the child's growth will not be compromised. Many vegetarians prefer the flavor of fortified soybean milk made at home. A good recipe is in *Laurel's Kitchen: A Handbook for Vegetarian Cookery and Nutrition* (see Suggestions for Further Reading).

Most people have their own beliefs and priorities about the food they eat; vegetarians are perhaps more conscious of their food views and values and more deliberate about their choices. It is unfortunate that in some cases vegetarians who are skeptical of orthodox medical systems have been driven away from good health-care facilities or services by dictatorial or unsympathetic health professionals. Many vegetarians simply need advice and information sensitively presented in order to be motivated to follow a diet that promotes health and reduces the risk of diet-related illnesses. With proper planning, all vegetarian diets can be nutritionally adequate and satisfying. □

SUGGESTIONS FOR FURTHER READING

LAPPÉ, FRANCES MOORE. *Diet for a Small Planet*, 10th anniversary edition. New York, Ballantine, 1982.

ROBERTSON, LAUREL, CAROL FLINDERS, and BRONWEN GODFREY. *Laurel's Kitchen: A Handbook for Vegetarian Cookery and Nutrition*. Berkeley, Calif., Nilgiri Press, 1976. Paperback edition: New York, Bantam, 1978.

SUSSMAN, VIC S. *The Vegetarian Alternative: A Guide to a Healthful and Humane Diet*. Emmaus, Pa., Rodale Press, 1978.

Running and Walking for Fitness

Allan J. Ryan, M.D.

Hordes of people are pounding highways, byways, and tracks today, running or walking for fitness or simply for the fun of it. A recent estimate put the number of runners in the United States at over 35 million. If you're not already one of this myriad of exercisers, you may be wondering if you too should join in.

Both running and walking—if done regularly and for a sustained period—can increase your physical fitness and sense of well-being. They are both good aerobic exercises. This means they improve your body's ability to use oxygen to produce energy, thereby increasing the efficiency of your lungs and cardiovascular system and improving your endurance. Another plus of regular, vigorous walking or running is that it can make you leaner by reducing excess fat stored in your body. This decreased weight means increased overall efficiency and stamina.

To Walk or to Run?

If you are a potential walker or runner, you have to first decide which type of exercise is best for you. People who are reasonably healthy and without a serious physical handicap may feel fairly confident of their ability to walk a good distance or for an extended time. But the idea of running (or jogging, which is essentially just a slower form of running) for, say, 20 minutes straight may seem intimidating. Running, however, like walking, is actually relatively easy if you follow a sensible program and build up your time gradually. As with any sport, there is risk of injury, but that can be minimized by learning proper techniques and not pushing yourself beyond your capacity.

Your choice of running or walking may be affected by where you will be able to do your exercise—city dwellers with easy access to a running track, for example, might find jogging on it more pleasant, and safer, than walking through the streets, while a person living in a country area might prefer walking because of the greater chance of injury when running on uneven roads or ground. If you want companions—some people find it boring to run or walk alone—you will have to take into account your friends' desires. Consider as well which exercise you are most likely to grow to like. Experience shows that no matter how well you do something or how much you get from it, if you don't enjoy it, you probably won't keep at it for very long. A major advantage of running and walking, after all, is that if you remain in generally good health, you will be physically able to continue with either of them for as long as you live.

There are some basic differences between the two activities. Running will enable you to reach a higher level of fitness, depending on how long, hard, frequently, and efficiently you do it. And runners appear to derive a greater exhilaration from their exercise. Some scientists have proposed that what is known as runners' high may have a physiological basis, being triggered by morphine-like chemicals called endorphins whose production in the body is stimulated by strenuous exercise. An additional advantage of running, for people interested in competitive exercise, is that it offers far more opportunities for competition.

Walking, even if done vigorously, puts less physical strain on the body. Since the pace is slower, you are less likely to fall victim to some of the hazards faced by runners—including heat stress, leg injuries, and fast-moving cars. On the other hand, the slower pace means you will have to spend more time walking to get the same aerobic benefit you would from running.

Whichever exercise you choose, before you begin your fitness program it is a good idea, especially if you have not been physically active, to see your doctor for a checkup. People who are over 35 or who have a personal or family history of heart disease are often advised to undergo a stress test to check their heart function.

Gearing Up

Whether your walking or running is recreational or competitive, you will want your gear to be as comfortable, safe, and lightweight as possible. If you are exercising outdoors, your selection of clothing should take into

Running can be more exhilarating, but walking puts less strain on the body.

account the temperature, humidity, and wind velocity, which will all, of course, vary during the year. Your choice of shoes will depend on the surface on which you walk or run and whether it is affected by precipitation and temperature. Indoors, what you wear may vary according to the ventilation and heating of the facility you use.

Your clothing should be close-fitting enough to stay in place but loose enough not to restrict your movements. Clothes designed specifically for walkers or runners are certainly not essential, but they can make your exercising a lot more comfortable and efficient. Because of the surge of interest in walking and running in recent years, a wide range of suitable garments is now available.

The basic outfit for both walking and running is a sleeveless, collarless top (often called a tank or singlet) and shorts, although the all-purpose T-shirt may suit you better than the tank. Most T-shirts are cotton; so are many tanks, though the most popular are combinations of cotton and some synthetic—such as nylon tricot—with wide mesh areas for ventilation. Arm holes should allow freedom of movement, and the T-shirt or tank should be long enough to keep it from riding up, whether you wear it inside or outside of your shorts. Cotton shirts, worn under a jacket or another shirt, are more comfortable in cold weather.

Shorts are available in cotton and in nylon tricot and other synthetic fabrics. The better ones have a built-in athletic supporter for men and a cotton panel for women. Wide openings for the legs are desirable to avoid binding; some openings are cut diagonally for this purpose. Side slits with or without a covering flap are popular and convenient.

For warming up and cooling down after walking or running, a warm-up suit is desirable. These suits may be made of cotton-polyester blends, nylon tricot, flannel, or wool and should be cut generously across the shoulders and around the arms. Suits made of synthetics should have mesh panels across the shoulders for ventilation. One-piece warm-ups are available, with a zipper or snap front. Two-piece outfits tend to be more popular and more versatile. Separate trousers often have an elastic waistband and a zipper along the side of each leg.

Windproof and water-resistant outerwear is available for cold and wet weather and may be worn directly over shirt and shorts or over the warm-up suit. Some types have hoods, attached or detachable. Again, mesh panels across the shoulders provide ventilation.

Visored caps are popular for outdoor wear both as sunshades and as a means of holding hair in place. Cold weather calls for wool hats; earmuffs or overall face masks may be necessary for very cold and windy conditions. Many runners and walkers with long hair wear headbands of some absorbent material both indoors and outdoors to keep hair and sweat out of their eyes.

Socks made of a light cotton or a cotton-synthetic blend are comfortable in mild weather for most people. Socks should fit well, so that they don't slide into the shoe and wrinkle under the foot, which would cause blisters. In cold weather, socks made of wool or a wool-synthetic blend are best for warmth, and some people prefer them year-round.

Walkers in the city, on their way to work or school, don don *running shoes and pound the pavements for health.*

Allan J. Ryan is editor in chief of The Physician and Sportsmedicine.

Off and Running

Left, a city skyline provides the back-drop for avid runners on a rooftop track. Above, employees jogging on company grounds prove that work and exercise are compatible. Many corporations now support some kind of fitness program.

The Right Shoes

Proper shoes are a must—both for comfort and for safety. Such a variety
of shoes is available today that it is not difficult to find a pair suitable to
your needs and pocketbook. For most people, including walkers, these
will be running shoes. Recreational walkers and those engaged in low-
level long-distance walking competition should use a sturdy runner's
training shoe rather than a light racing shoe.

Ideally, look first for shoes whose upper parts are made entirely of
leather (although many runners and walkers use shoes with uppers made
of some combination of leather and another material, such as canvas).
Not only does leather adapt itself best to the foot's exact shape, but it is
less likely to cause excessive foot perspiration.

When you try on a running shoe, you should be able to press the broad
side of your thumb down on the outside of the toe box to the insole
without pressing on your big toe. At an inch from the tip of the shoe, the
box should be an inch high. Look for a shoe that fits your foot width as
exactly as possible. Although some brands of running shoes are made in
only one width for each length, others offer several widths. You should
avoid shoes with lacing that comes down to the toe, since this may cause
uncomfortable constriction of the toes.

The sole of the shoe needs to be moderately flexible to allow the foot to
bend slightly during its contact with the ground. But the sole should be

stiff enough through the shank (the narrow part beneath the instep) to prevent too much flattening or rolling inward of the foot (overpronation). The insole should be cushioned for shock absorption. To improve traction, you may want to use shoes that have a special tread or are studded with short cleats.

The back of the shoe, the heel counter, has to be stiff, to hold the heel perpendicular to the running surface. There should be cushioning for the heel and some padding where the Achilles tendon attaches to the heel base. Also desirable is a padded cuff around the top that extends to 3 inches above the heel cup. Most running shoes today have some built-in correction to hold the foot in the proper relation to the running surface. If you need special corrective adjustments in your shoes, you should see a podiatrist or orthopedic surgeon for custom-made corrective shoe inserts (orthotic devices) rather than relying on off-the-shelf inserts.

Even the best running shoes wear out under heavy and repeated use. Don't be surprised if they have to be replaced in three months or less. When the heels are excessively worn or the supporting elements in the shoe are broken down, it is better to replace the shoes than to risk developing foot or leg problems that could require expensive and lengthy treatment.

Walking and Running Correctly

People tend to think of walking and running as instinctive, but these actions are in fact learned. Your manner of walking or running, or gait, changes with age and growth and may also be affected by any number of

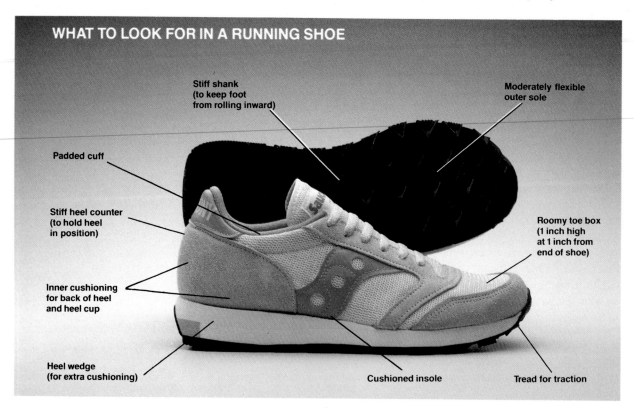

WHAT TO LOOK FOR IN A RUNNING SHOE

Stiff shank
(to keep foot
from rolling inward)

Moderately flexible
outer sole

Padded cuff

Stiff heel counter
(to hold heel
in position)

Roomy toe box
(1 inch high
at 1 inch from
end of shoe)

Inner cushioning
for back of heel
and heel cup

Heel wedge
(for extra cushioning)

Cushioned insole

Tread for traction

internal and external factors; once your gait has been established, however, it becomes to a large degree automatic—second nature to you.

Gaits vary widely from person to person. Even people of the same age, size, and build who are not suffering from any marked physical handicaps may walk or run quite differently. Some gaits are more efficient than others, but barring anatomical problems or defects, inefficient ones can be corrected.

Such correction is particularly important if walking or running is your principal means of regular exercise, since an efficient gait reduces the risk of injury. If you have questions about your gait, an orthopedist can analyze it and determine the optimal gait for you.

Getting Started Walking

According to the U.S. President's Council on Physical Fitness and Sports, rates of walking may be described as slow (3 miles per hour), moderate (4 mph), or fast (4½ mph). You are the best judge of your own pace. If you have not had experience in long walks, a good way to get started is to follow the 12-Week Walking Program at right. For the first four weeks, it is best to stay on fairly level ground. After 12 weeks, you should be able to develop your own walking program according to your interests and needs. You may wish to enter a walking competition if it is offered on a level appropriate for you—that is, if the distances and surfaces covered and the paces expected are comfortable for you.

It is not necessary to walk every day in order to derive benefit and pleasure from the exercise. But you should walk at least three days a week (preferably not on consecutive days). Otherwise, you are not as likely to develop strength and stamina or to derive the potential benefits to your cardiovascular system.

Getting Started Running

If you have never run before, or are not used to running regularly, a very slow beginning is safest. A lot has been written about the pain and injuries sometimes associated with running. But it does not have to be an uncomfortable or painful experience if you go about it the right way: it can and should be enjoyable.

As a beginner, you will make the most progress if you run every day, or at least every other day. Following the Ten-Week Program on page 71 will get you off to a good start. Do not force yourself to exercise if you are too stiff, sore, and tired; it is better to wait an extra day or two. Once your body gets accustomed to the routine, you will find that you can maintain your state of conditioning and even make progress by running three times a week, about every other day.

When the ten weeks are up, you can tailor your program to your individual needs. If you are interested principally in general conditioning, running at a steady pace for about 30 minutes three times a week should be sufficient. Some people like to run every day, but that is a matter of personal preference. A possible drawback to running every day is that it may make you more vulnerable to overuse injuries—injuries resulting, basically, from pushing your body too hard. Those who are in training for

Following the Ten-Week Program on page 71

A 12-WEEK WALKING PROGRAM FOR BEGINNERS

Week 1
Pace: slow
Distance: 1 mile a day at first, gradually increasing to 2

Week 2
Pace: slow
Distance: 2½ miles at first, gradually increasing to 4

Week 3
Pace: slow
Distance: 4½ miles at first, gradually increasing to 6

Week 4
Pace: moderate
Distance: 3 miles at first, gradually increasing to 4½

Week 5
Pace: moderate
Distance: 3½ miles at first, gradually increasing to 5
Include some hills in each of this week's and every subsequent week's walks.

Week 6
Pace: moderate
Distance: 5 miles at first, gradually increasing to 6

Week 7
Pace: moderate
Distance: 6 miles at first, gradually increasing to 7
On alternate days do 3 miles at a fast pace.

Week 8
Pace: moderate
Distance: 7 miles at first, gradually increasing to 8
On alternate days do 3½ miles at a fast pace.

Weeks 9–10
Pace: moderate
Distance: 8 miles at first, gradually increasing to 10
Include half-mile bursts at a fast pace.

Weeks 11–12
Pace: moderate
Distance: 10–15 miles two or three times a week and, if you desire, shorter distances on other days

Easy does it: Suited up warmly, a jogger does stretching exercises before setting out.

racing must run more often and usually for longer distances than those running for fitness.

Special training is something you may wish to consider if you want to get involved in competitive running. Among the techniques used are speed play, interval training, and pace training. Speed play alternates slow running with short bursts of fast running over distances of several miles. In interval training you run a set distance in a time somewhat slower than your fastest possible time, take a short rest, repeat the distance in the same amount of time, rest, run again, and so on. The number of repetitions may be five to ten or more, and the rest intervals may be shortened progressively over a period of days. Pace training gradually increases your speed, requiring you to run distances at approximately the pace you would use in competition, with longer rest periods than in interval training. The pace is gradually increased over days or weeks.

70

Warming Up and Cooling Down

You have probably noticed that when you are cold, your muscles feel harder and stiffer than usual. When you take a hot shower or bath, they feel relaxed, softer, and more pliable. Changes in temperature affect the ways in which muscles contract in responding to a stimulus. They respond more rapidly and effectively when they are warm than when they are cold and are thus much less apt to be injured by a forceful contraction.

Walking and running, like all physical activity, can raise your body temperature as much as several degrees, depending on how hard you are working. But you may have to go some distance before your temperature rises and you have worked up a sweat. Up to that point, your muscles will be less efficient and at a greater danger of injury. That is why it is important to warm up before you start to walk or run: this is one of the principal means of preventing injury.

Light calisthenics, including very gentle stretching of your arms and legs, are good for warming up. (Intensive stretching should be avoided at this time, since it is likely to injure muscles; it is best saved for immediately after exercise when the muscles are thoroughly warmed up.) Your warm-up may involve simply jumping up and down in place or easy jogging in a small circle, arm swings, and light stretching of leg muscles. Lifting very light weights, such as 1-pound or 2-pound dumbbells, is another method.

When you finish your walk or run, you will feel a natural desire to sit or lie down. You will be better off cooling down by walking or jogging slowly for five to ten minutes. This helps the body to reduce concentrations of lactic acid, a substance that builds up in the muscles during vigorous exercise and contributes to the feeling of fatigue. A brief cooling down period may also lessen any stiffness or soreness you might experience the next day.

Some Possible Injuries

The injuries suffered by walkers and runners generally involve the feet, legs, hips, or lower back. Some are the result of accidents, but many more are overuse injuries, occurring gradually as a result of repeated stress on muscles, bones, joints, and connective tissue. The kinds of possible injuries are many. Joints may be sprained, with ligaments—the fibers that connect bones to one another—being stretched or torn. Tendons, connecting muscles to bones, may become inflamed—a condition called tendinitis. Muscles may be strained. Bursitis may develop; this condition is an inflammation of a protective fluid-filled sac (bursa), such as the one covering the knee. Bones may be dislocated or fractured; in a complete fracture, a bone is broken through entirely, while a stress fracture involves a hairline crack that results from repeated pulling by muscles or too much weight bearing by the bone.

Some of these and other injuries may occur no matter what you do. But many—probably most, particularly overuse injuries—can be avoided if you follow proper running or walking techniques and do not ignore aches and pains, which are your body's warning signals. When an injury does

A 10-WEEK RUNNING PROGRAM FOR BEGINNERS

Week 1
Alternate 100 yards of moderately fast walking with 100 yards of running until you have covered half a mile.

Week 2
Alternate 100 yards of walking with 150–200 yards of running until you have covered a mile.

Week 3
Run a mile slowly and then walk a quarter mile.

Week 4
Run 1¼ miles.

Week 5
Run 1½ miles.

Week 6
Run 1¾ miles.

Week 7
Run 2 miles.

Week 8
Run 2½ miles.

Week 9
Run 3 miles.

Week 10
Run 3½ miles.

occur, prompt diagnosis and treatment will help to minimize any potentially disabling effects.

Here are a few examples of injuries a runner or walker might experience:

Foot. The Achilles tendon may become inflamed just above the place where it attaches to the base of the heel. Resulting from overuse or from abnormal foot structure, this condition is best treated with rest and anti-inflammatory drugs. If the tendon is not rested, it can weaken and eventually tear, necessitating surgical repair.

The sheet of fibrous support tissue (or fascia) called the plantar fascia, one of the basic structures of the sole and arch of the foot, can become painfully inflamed. This injury, known as plantar fasciitis, may result from excessive inward rotation (overpronation) or too much outward rotation of the foot or from poor shoe support. Treatment usually includes taping the foot to support the arch; an orthotic device may need to be inserted in the shoe, and exercises are often prescribed to stretch the fascia.

Toes can be sprained, dislocated, or fractured, usually as a result of being stubbed or stepped on. Injured small toes can generally be treated by taping them to adjacent toes after correcting any dislocations or sprains. Big-toe injuries are disabling, since the big toe is the push-off point of the foot. Sprains of the big toe require the use of a splint; dislocations should be X-rayed for possible fractures and splinted. For big-toe fractures, the bone must first be returned to its proper position. Then the foot must be placed in a non-weight-bearing cast for three weeks and in a walking cast for another three.

A common foot injury that is painful but not serious is hemorrhage under the toenail (especially the nail of the big toe), with the nail becoming discolored and tender. This problem is usually due to shoes fitting too tightly or too loosely, causing the toe to jam against the toe box. The doctor will probably drill a hole in the nail to release the blood.

Sprains involving the ligaments in the metatarsal (instep) area of the foot may develop because of lack of proper shoe support or because the foot lands off balance. The foot should be taped up for support and rested for two to four weeks. Using poor or worn-out running shoes, stepping in a hole, or running or walking too much can cause fractures of the metatarsals themselves, the five bones that extend from the top of the arch to the base of the toes. If a fracture is not displaced—that is, if the bone has not changed position—it may be treated with rest and the use of an orthotic device. However, a displaced fracture may have to be repositioned and held with metallic fixation (plates, pins, rods), then placed in a cast for eight to ten weeks.

Poorly fitting shoes can also cause corns, which are horny outgrowths on the toes; bunions, or bony protrusions from the joint at the base of the big toe; and hammertoes, in which a toe (usually the second) curls and lifts into a shape similar to a piano hammer. A genetic predisposition, however, may contribute to the development of hammertoes and bunions. Treatment includes correcting the shoe fit. Corns resulting from two toes rubbing together can often be relieved by inserting lamb's wool between the toes and wearing cotton socks to keep moisture from building up. Hammertoes are sometimes aided by use of splints. Serious cases of all three conditions call for surgery.

Many injuries can be avoided if you use correct running or walking technique and do not ignore any aches or pains.

Heels may be bruised by walking or running in improper or thin-soled shoes on hard or rocky surfaces. Spurs of calcium sometimes form on the bottom of the heel bone near the ankle, where the plantar fascia attaches. Rest, correctly fitted shoes, and some padding in the heel will usually correct these problems.

Ankle, knee, and leg. Ankle sprains may occur when the ankle is turned over by a misstep or fall. Sprains of both the inner and outer ankle ligaments must be treated with complete rest for 24 to 48 hours; the ankle will then be taped or supported with an Air-Cast, an inflatable plastic cast. The injured ankle can begin to bear weight but should not bear its normal load until all swelling and pain are gone.

Everyone has heard of "runner's knee." This is often used as a catchall term for any pain in the knee, but it can also refer specifically to a softening of the cartilage behind the kneecap (chondromalacia). The kneecap's tendency to slide sideways from its normal position may also cause pain, particularly if the foot rotates inward too much and hits the ground too flatly. In addition, knee pain may be due to inflammation of the tendon attaching the kneecap to the shinbone, of the cartilage behind the kneecap, or of the bursa covering the kneecap. All of these conditions are treated primarily with rest, medication, and exercises that involve a limited range of motion and strengthen the thigh muscles.

Painful strained muscles in either the front or the back of the lower leg, or both, commonly called shinsplints, usually result from attempting to do too much too soon. Shinsplints can also be caused by overstriding or by running or walking on concrete. Rest and stretching exercises are generally prescribed to help the muscles heal. A more serious problem is compartment syndrome, in which a very tight fascia shuts off the circulation in the calf muscles as they swell with exercise. This condition may be so painful that it becomes impossible to run or walk for any length of time. An operation may be necessary to split the fascia.

Stress fractures of the lower leg bones—the shinbone and fibula—and the thighbone must be treated with reduced activity. Healing may be slow. A leg bone that suffers a complete fracture needs to be repositioned and held in place with metal plates, rods, or pins. The leg must then be placed in a cast for eight to ten weeks.

Hip and back. Adolescent runners may suffer painful injuries in which one or more points of the pelvic bones where ligaments attach are pulled off. Rest and support generally suffice to deal with the problem, but sometimes surgical repositioning and fixation are necessary. Runners with poor technique and improper alignment of the spine may fall victim to strained muscles, sprained ligaments, and even stress fractures in the lower back. Treatment for these injuries includes rest, lower-back supports, exercises for strengthening the abdominal and buttocks muscles in order to control the position of the pelvis properly, and correction of running technique.

If one leg is shorter than the other, tilting of the pelvis or curvature of the spine to one side (scoliosis) may result. In both cases, walking or running for any length of time is likely to cause pain, which can be eased with a heel lift for the shorter leg.

See also the Spotlight on Health article FRACTURES, SPRAINS, AND STRAINS. □

President Harry S. Truman was a famous advocate of brisk morning walks.

STRESS

in the Workplace

Jere E. Yates, Ph.D.

A growing body of evidence indicates that for many people, work and work-related problems contribute a great deal to the stress in their lives. A certain amount of stress both on and off the job is unavoidable and not a cause for concern. But for some people, prolonged high levels of job stress can have a serious effect on their health.

Many people assume that stress is always bad. In fact, it is normal for the body to be under almost constant stress from both external and internal sources, called stressors. External stressors can include family, friends, and government, as well as one's work. Internal stressors may be ambition, creativity, and perfectionism—in short, the individual values that make a person unique. To ask people whether they are under stress is like asking them whether they have temperatures. Where there is life, there is temperature—and stress.

Stress is the body's reaction to any demand. Whether the stressor is physical danger, a family crisis, or a new and demanding assignment at the office, the same complex physiological reaction occurs. Epinephrine (adrenaline) pours into the system from the adrenal glands, located on top of the kidneys. This hormone causes blood pressure to rise, breathing and heart rates to quicken, and blood to rush to the lungs, heart, and muscles throughout the body, so that we will be able to operate at peak capacity. Brain wave activity increases, additional sugar is released into the bloodstream for quick energy, muscles tense in preparation for action, and senses are heightened. When the demand on the body is removed or the crisis is overcome, the body slows down, sometimes dropping below normal resting, or baseline, levels.

Short-term stress is not worrisome, since the body's response is useful—providing energy to deal with emergencies, deadlines, and even the pleasures of life—and since the body soon returns to a resting state. Long-term stress, however, can be dangerous because it causes the body to continue running at high speed, never fully returning to baseline levels. Research on people who find their jobs continually stressful has discovered that their resting heart rates may go from 70 beats per minute to 75 or 80 within a single year. This kind of prolonged stress may lead to

Portions of this article are based on the author's book, *Managing Stress: A Businessperson's Guide,* © 1979 by AMACOM, a division of American Management Associations, New York. All rights reserved.

the development or aggravation of various disorders, such as heart disease, emotional problems, ulcers, diabetes, migraines, allergies, or arthritis. It is readily apparent, then, why companies and workers—and their health and life insurance providers—are becoming increasingly concerned about long-term stress.

Individual Stress Reactions

Different people react differently to the same stressors. Some people actually thrive on deadlines, busy schedules, and work-related problems, but for others, the stress resulting from these pressures takes a toll on their physical and emotional well-being. Some of us may be able to stand more job pressure because we inherently react less strongly or because we have been conditioned to cope with certain kinds of stressors. Some people may simply be "made of tougher material."

As long as the amount of stress we experience is within our personal limits, it is good for us, keeping us motivated and free from boredom. (Pioneering stress researcher Hans Selye coined the term eustress, or "good stress," for the type that is productive and not a threat to health.) But if we are pressed beyond our natural limits for an extended period, then job demands can lead to what Selye called distress, and the risk of health problems increases unless we improve the situation.

In other words, the job itself is not necessarily what determines whether distress occurs. Rather, individual personality characteristics are intrinsically involved in stress and productivity levels. Over the past 20 years, two cardiologists, Dr. Meyer Friedman and Dr. Ray Rosenman, have made the relationship between stress and personality clearer by identifying what they call Type A and Type B personalities. Type A personalities have a chronic struggle with time and are always trying to do as much as they can as quickly as possible. They are competitive and aggressive, and they often have feelings of hostility below the surface (see the box at left for a more detailed list of Type A traits). Type B people may have some of these same qualities, but they are far more likely to take their time, postpone decisions, and take a relaxed view of deadlines and other pressures—though this does not necessarily mean they get less done than Type A's. It is believed that roughly half of the American population consists of Type A personalities. Most doctors are convinced that these people experience more stress in their lives, and are more likely to suffer from stress-related disease, than people with Type B personalities.

Some words of caution are in order here. First, although people with a pure Type A personality may be statistically more prone to certain illnesses, this does not mean that every Type A individual will have a heart attack or other stress-related problems. Statistics tell us only of probabilities in groups and nothing definite about any one person. It should be emphasized that some of us may be better equipped than others

---

Jere E. Yates is a professor of organizational behavior and management and is chairman of the Business Administration Division at Seaver College, Pepperdine University in Malibu, Calif. He specializes in stress management and has served as a consultant for business and government.

to handle the stress resulting from Type A behavior. Moreover, just as a race horse that is not allowed to run and stretch its limbs will deteriorate quickly, a Type A person might well suffer if forced to follow a pure Type B behavior pattern. Nevertheless, Drs. Friedman and Rosenman recommend that Type A personalities attempt to modify their behavior to make it more like the pattern of Type B people, in order to reduce the risk of heart disease or other stress-related illness.

These personality types play an important role in determining the amount of stress in people's lives. However, other factors, such as a person's levels of emotionality and anxiety, are also significant. Some of us are more prone than others to anxiety—a feeling of apprehension or dread about something we expect or fear in the future. Often there are legitimate reasons for feeling anxious. Job-related stressors, such as changes in management, lack of feedback about one's work, job insecurity, and intense competition, may contribute to anxiety. Although moderate anxiety can be productive, habitual anxiety can cause distress.

Emotionality refers to individual differences in emotional make-up. A highly emotional person is likely to have frequent mood fluctuations; tendencies toward guilt, worry, and low self-esteem; sensitivity to environmental sources of stress, such as noise or crowds; or excessive concern about physical health. As with anxiety, not all emotionality is detrimental. Moderate emotional arousal is necessary to focus one's energy so that problems can be solved. It is when the arousal is severe or prolonged that it becomes undesirable.

The extent to which people get anxious or emotional about their work will depend upon both the job itself and the person's own makeup. For those prone to anxiety or emotionality, a well-structured job with clear-cut tasks is most desirable. Someone less anxiety-prone or emotional could probably better cope with a job which has less structure.

Some people thrive under stress that would exact a heavy toll on others: this bond trader appears composed in the high-pressure atmosphere of Wall Street.

Sources of Stress in the Workplace

Although every job is different, certain sources of stress common to many types of work can be identified. The following is a sampling of some of these stress-producing factors.

Lack of participation in decisions. When asked to name major job stressors, people often rank at the top of the list unresponsiveness of management. Employees who are allowed to participate in the decision-making process frequently experience eustress; however, when workers are barred from helping to make decisions which directly affect their jobs, distress can easily be the result. Interestingly, people often find even a negative response to their suggestions less stress-producing than no response at all.

Time pressures and deadlines. The urgency of deadlines is real; the word itself evokes an image of a line beyond which death lies. Medical research confirms that heavy deadline pressures year after year can take a toll on overall health.

Role conflict. The role one plays within an organization can be another primary source of stress. Role conflict can arise in a number of situations: (1) a job which is not clearly defined, as in the case of the person who is asked to complete a task but doesn't know whether he or she has the

The Many Sources of Stress

The difficulties of commuting (left), the monotony of assembly-line work (above), and the frenetic activity of some workplaces, like the New York Mercantile Exchange (above right), are just a few of the environments that can contribute to an overload of stress.

authority to carry out the details; (2) unrealistic demands made by a superior, such as a deadline which cannot be met because of factors beyond the employee's control; (3) the failure of colleagues to communicate their expectations, as when someone works hard to complete a report, only to be told that another department has already taken over the project; (4) a job which is in basic conflict with the person's values, as in the case of an executive who is expected to travel a great deal but who wants to spend time at home with the family. People who suffer from role conflict report lower job satisfaction and higher job-related tension than those without such problems.

Boredom. Boredom can be an important factor in work stress. Many assembly-line workers, for example, report that anxiety, depression, irritation, and fatigue result from the day-in, day-out performance of the same task, which often bears little apparent relation to the finished product. For professionals, boredom may be called burnout, but whatever the label, it is a serious stressor (and a drain on productivity in the workplace).

Responsibility for people. Research shows a definite link between stress and the amount of responsibility one has for others. Executives who have influence over their subordinates' careers, professional development, and job security generally experience more stress than executives primarily responsible for budgets, projects, equipment, or property.

Ambition and success. Some people suffer stress when their careers do not progress as they had hoped. If people find themselves several positions lower than they expected to be at a particular time, disappointment may lead to distress. Even successful people may experience distress as they push themselves to surpass previous achievements. In recent years, a great deal has been written about midlife crisis, which usually occurs between the ages of 35 and 45. For many, this is a time of value clarification in every area of life—including occupation; it is a time when they reflect on their careers to date and, perhaps, make a basic decision either to push ahead for advancement or to slow down and enjoy life more. Whether midlife crisis is a source of distress or eustress will vary with the individual. Some people emerge from this stage of life cynical and bitter; others derive both growth and fulfillment.

Relationships at work. Some associates at work can be a "pain in the neck." Poor working relationships may be a result of lack of trust or lack of interest in mutual problems. Whatever the causes, difficult working relationships can bring on distress. Workers seem to experience more distress when their relationships are poor with peers or supervisors than when they cannot work well with subordinates.

Commuting. Perhaps no stressor connected with urban life is as devastating as long commuting to and from work. Researchers have found that, in many cases, commuting causes more stress than work-related deadlines. For example, a pulse monitor attached to the wrist of a newspaper editor who traveled from his suburban home to his downtown office by automobile showed that his peak pulse rate occurred not during an unexpected crisis at work—such as the presses breaking down—but during his trips to and from work.

Many other sources of job-related stress could be discussed, including working conditions, job design, job insecurity, and financial difficulties. People who find their jobs excessively stressful need to reflect seriously on their own personal stressors, since identification of the specific problem is an essential first step in solving it.

An increase in smoking may be a sign that stress is building past the limits of tolerance.

Red Flags: Symptoms of Stress

When our bodies endure long-term stress, certain predictable reactions occur. Some of these, such as a rise in blood pressure or in the electrical conductivity of the skin, are not readily observable. There are other signs we can observe, however. Our bodies tend to signal stress with red flags, or danger signs—some physical, some psychological. The particular symptom (or symptoms) any individual experiences depends on that person's vulnerabilities. Whatever the way excessive stress manifests itself, the problem should not be ignored.

One possible sign of stress is decreased productivity at work. An inability to concentrate, frequent absenteeism, and attention to busywork while avoiding important but unpleasant tasks can all result from excess stress. Stress can also lead to a general irritability and emotional instability that can make relations with people on—and off—the job more difficult.

Excessive stress can bring on physical aches and pains.

Another common sign of excess stress is depression (although depression is certainly not always caused by stress). Depression is characterized by sadness, lethargy, anxiety, and difficulty in sustaining concentration. Obviously, some sadness is inevitable in life, as when one must cope with the death of a loved one. Depression, however, either has no apparent cause or is of greater magnitude and duration than is appropriate to its cause. Insomnia, fatigue, and changes in eating habits may accompany depression—and can also be warning signs of stress even when depression is not present.

Increased consumption of tobacco, alcohol, or coffee may also signal excessive stress; unfortunately, none of these substances is particularly effective as a stress reducer. People who smoke more when under stress are making matters worse; nicotine at first acts as a stimulant in the body, which then "comes down" again, and such artificially induced highs and lows actually add to stress. The caffeine in coffee can also be an unneeded stimulant for people under stress. The amount of caffeine in as little as two or three cups of coffee has been linked to nervousness, insomnia, and headaches, and excessive caffeine can even cause people to exhibit symptoms usually associated with severe anxiety. The problem with alcohol as a stress reliever is that it may work too well, allowing people to forget the source of their stress and focus instead on a temporary feeling of elation or tranquillity. Some people are tempted to "solve" their problems by neglecting them with the help of alcohol, and this strategy for dealing with stress can easily lead to alcoholism.

Stress can also bring about physical aches and pains. Upset stomachs, migraine headaches, neck pain, or backaches may all be signals that the body is overloaded with stress. Another warning sign is grinding the teeth.

If people do not heed such warning signs and do not take measures to deal with the sources of their excessive load of stress, the ultimate result may be serious illness. There is a risk of heart disease or of a serious mental disorder. Other afflictions possibly linked with stress include peptic ulcers, ulcerative colitis, bronchial asthma, hay fever, arthritis, hyperthyroidism, and impotence or other sexual dysfunctions. Research has found that people who heed the warning signals of stress early are better able to prevent disease or to minimize its impact and duration.

Reducing Stress

If we determine that job-related stress is threatening our health, we have a number of options besides resigning and going to the countryside to live on a farm. We can build up our resistance to stress, adjust our attitude toward stressors so that they affect us less, or work at eliminating the stressors in our lives. A number of strategies for reducing stress are outlined below.

Exercise. One of the most effective means of reducing stress and combating the effects of stress on the body is exercise. The benefits of vigorous exercise are twofold. First, it develops cardiovascular fitness, thereby reducing the risk of heart disease. (If people with well-conditioned hearts do have heart attacks, they are two or three times more likely to survive.) Regular exercise—15 to 20 minutes of continuous activity (such as running, swimming, or biking) three or four times a week—strengthens the heart muscle, improving its ability to pump blood to the body. Someone who exercises regularly may have a resting heart rate of only 60 beats per minute, compared with a rate of, say, 80 beats per minute for a person with a deconditioned heart. The first person's heart will beat 86,400 times in 24 hours, whereas the second person's heart will beat 115,200 times—almost 30,000 extra beats per day. It is not hard to see that in the long run the heart actually works harder and less efficiently when we "take it easy" than when we make reasonable exercise demands.

Besides building cardiovascular fitness, a sound exercise program will help the body directly reduce stress. Since vigorous activity makes it

Reduction of stress can be accomplished in many ways: here, a moment of meditation in the midst of a trying day, a satisfying social life outside the office, and the sense of stability provided by a tightly knit family.

likely that we will rest afterward, exercise can provide a form of forced relaxation as the body insists upon recovery time. Vigorous activity also provides a good way of getting rid of frustrations and pent-up feelings.

The relaxation response. Aside from the kind of relaxation that follows exercise or goes with lying on the beach, there is a deeper form of relaxation that can be even more valuable in breaking up stress. Dr. Herbert Benson, who has studied the links between stress, high blood pressure, and heart disease, uses the term relaxation response for a state in which the body actually runs at very low speed, consuming less oxygen and using less energy than in its usual resting state. This kind of relaxation can be induced by meditative techniques similar to those practiced for centuries in certain religions. The relaxation response can also be brought about by biofeedback, in which subjects receive information about their bodily processes through monitoring devices and then attempt to control these processes. Research has shown that regular practice of such techniques—including Benson's own basic method of meditation—can help most people lower their blood pressure and increase their resistance to stress. Of course, a relaxation technique is not a panacea and cannot eliminate stress by itself, but someone who has a positive attitude toward such a technique and practices it regularly will probably be better able to resist stress.

Stability zones. Another stress-reduction strategy is to establish "stability zones." Everyone needs some part of life in which there is little or no change taking place, or in which change occurs at a comparatively slow pace. For some people, religion provides a source of stability, since it offers a framework of enduring values that help to put problems in

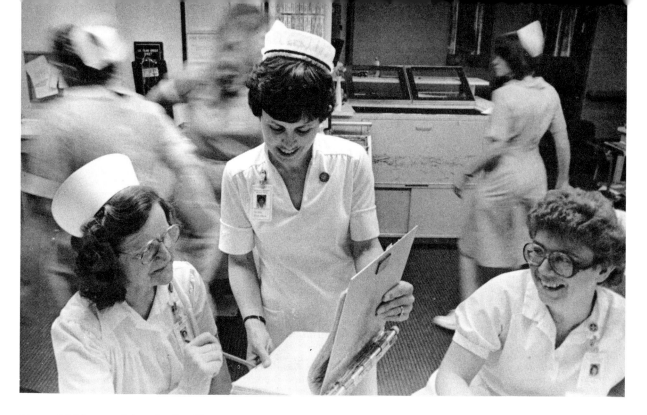

Even a highly stressful profession like nursing can provide considerable satisfaction; the pressures of meaningful and important work can be stimulating rather than distressing.

perspective. A close-knit family may also serve as a stability zone, helping to provide a sense of security. Engaging in the same line of work, or perhaps even working for the same company, for many years can also be a source of stability, as can living in the same house or neighborhood, keeping the same close friends, following the same routine, or even owning certain material possessions for a long time. If people have several sources of stability, they should hang onto them tenaciously. If they have few stability zones, they should consider how they can add more of them to their lives.

Maintaining a confidant. Having someone to confide in can help keep the stressors you experience in perspective. The person can be your spouse or anyone else with whom you can share your feelings. Talking about what bothers you can play a vital role in combating stress.

Interacting with people besides co-workers. It is not particularly healthy to socialize exclusively with people you work with, because many of us have a tendency to talk shop with co-workers and a person's social life should provide an opportunity to get away from job problems. Certainly, a network of social relationships is necessary at work, but people who associate only with co-workers may spend too much time being reminded of job stresses.

Doing meaningful work. If you have a job you thoroughly enjoy, you should be very reluctant to give it up, even if a new job comes your way that would mean more money or status. People who have jobs they enjoy will still have stressors associated with their work, but they will tend to perceive them differently than people who have jobs they don't enjoy very much. Rather than being harmful, the stressors in a job you enjoy may be stimulating, offering you a more fruitful life.

Thinking rationally about your problems. Use your analytical skills to help you deal with stressful problems at work. Suppose your immediate response to having a new task assigned to you or a deadline moved up is "I can't cope with this." Instead of growing panicky, examine that response a word at a time. Look at the word "I." Are you the only one who can do the work, or can someone else help? Next, look at the word "can't." Are you sure you can't cope, or is it that you don't want to deal with the problem? Could you substitute "can try to" for "can't"? Look at the word "cope." Do you have to cope perfectly? What are some ways you could try to cope? Finally, what exactly is "this?" Getting a clear definition of the exact problem may put it in a new light.

Another aspect of thinking rationally about a problem is to recognize that the stress will not last forever. This will help you keep your head during the stress, rather than "freaking out." Action based on "freaked out" thinking is rarely effective or appropriate.

Use coping self-statements. These are statements you have decided ahead of time to say to yourself as you deal with stressful situations. There are four times during a crisis when you would do well to utilize such statements. (1) In planning your course of action, you might say, "I've handled harder situations than this one before." (2) When acting to solve the problem, you might say, "I'm in control. I'll take one step at a time." (3) If you feel overwhelming anxiety in the midst of stress, you might say, "It will be over soon. Keep calm." (4) In rewarding yourself after the stress has passed, you might say, "Hey, that wasn't so bad. I really was able to do well." People need to develop their own statements of this kind, since we each know best what we will respond to and what will calm us.

Vacations. Taking vacations is another way to control stress, as long as you don't try to crowd so much into the vacation that you are more stressed and exhausted when you return than when you left. Even an afternoon or morning off can be successful at breaking up a harmful buildup of stress.

Clarifying values. Take the time to analyze what your basic values are and whether your job responsibilities are in harmony with them. Behavior that is at cross-purposes with a person's ideals is bound to increase that individual's stress level. If your job requires behavior that conflicts with important values, or takes so much time that it interferes with things that are more meaningful to you, you should consider finding a new position or even a new career. □

You can cope with problems better by thinking about them rationally rather than reacting emotionally.

SUGGESTIONS FOR FURTHER READING

BENSON, HERBERT, and MIRIAM KLIPPER. *The Relaxation Response.* New York, Avon, 1976.

FRIEDMAN, MEYER, and RAY H. ROSENMAN. *Type A Behavior and Your Heart.* New York, Knopf, 1974.

HOUSE, JAMES S. *Work Stress and Social Support.* Menlo Park, Calif., Addison-Wesley, 1981.

MOSS, LEONARD. *Management Stress.* Menlo Park, Calif., Addison-Wesley, 1981.

SELYE, HANS. *Stress Without Distress.* New York, New American Library, 1975.

YATES, JERE E. *Managing Stress: A Businessperson's Guide.* New York, AMACOM, 1979.

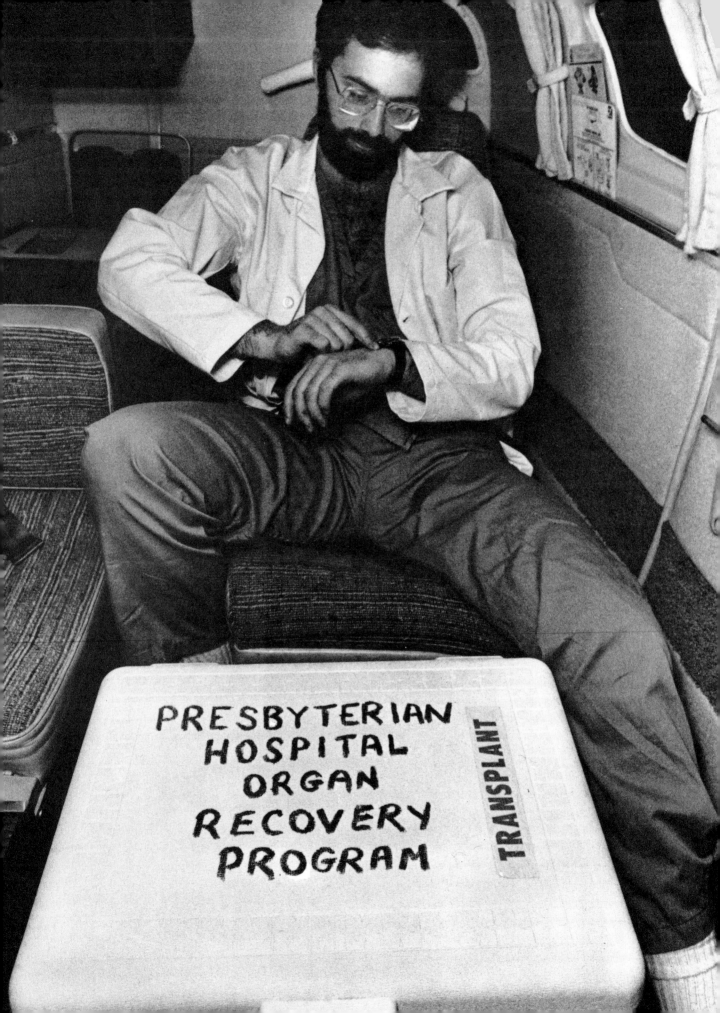

New Successes in Transplants

Sharon Begley

Transplant surgery has been undergoing a renaissance. The revival, after the grim early days of such procedures when few patients survived even a month, is being sparked by medical breakthroughs like improved surgical techniques and the use of a drug that helps prevent rejection of the transplanted organ, as well as by technological advances like computer networks that track and match prospective donors and recipients. In the United States, the recent decisions of some major insurance companies, the federal government, and some state medicaid programs to cover certain types of transplants reflects the judgment that the procedures are no longer experimental. Instead, they must increasingly be considered standard medical practice. Many physicians and health care experts believe this decision to be a watershed event in transplant history.

But all of these developments have proved a mixed blessing. As transplants enter the medical mainstream, various problems arise. With more top hospitals performing transplants, health care officials face the prospect that other, less glamorous hospital services will suffer. This is hardly an idle worry: some transplant operations require 20 hours or more, 35 to 50 medical people, and 100 units of blood. Lack of full insurance coverage also raises troubling questions. The cost of transplants is astronomical, often topping $100,000, and is not likely to come down. Yet another problem is the lack of donors and the difficulties of procuring what organs are available. The system for

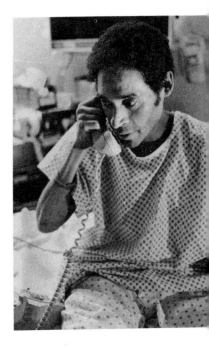

Speed is essential in transporting a donated heart, packed in ice. At left, a transplant courier checks traveling time; right, the patient who will receive the heart waits anxiously for its arrival.

organ procurement, although improving, is far from comprehensive or completely efficient.

Early History

A transplant is the removal of living tissue or a complete organ from its natural site to a new place in the same individual or in another person. Tissue transplants were recorded as early as 600 B.C., when surgeons in India reportedly used grafted skin from patients' foreheads to reconstruct their noses. A Bolognese professor of anatomy, Gasparo Tagliacozzi, introduced the technique to Western medicine in the 16th century, using tissue taken from the arm. It was also Tagliacozzi who recognized the effect of the immune system, the great barrier to organ transplants from one person to another. "For such is the force and the power of individuality," he wrote, "that if anyone should believe that he could . . . achieve even the least part of the operation, we consider him . . . badly grounded in the physical sciences."

Individuality—today known as the immune system—would indeed prove to be the greatest barrier to successful organ transplants. Only recently have medical developments begun to overcome this obstacle. Early success was achieved in transplanting the cornea—the tough, transparent tissue covering the front of the eyeball—only because the cornea does not receive any direct blood supply and is thus segregated from the rest of the body. It can be transplanted with success in 90 percent of cases.

The first cornea transplant was performed early in the 20th century, and the operation has been an accepted medical procedure since the 1940's. But transplantation of major body organs initially fared less well. In the early 1950's, Chicago surgeon Richard Lawler was one of a number of physicians who attempted to perform a kidney transplant. When Lawler saw that during the eight months following the transplant, the new kidney, taken from a cadaver, seemed to be failing, he operated again—and found that the implant had shrunk to a mere shadow of its original size. The patient's immune system had attacked and destroyed the foreign organ.

The first successful kidney transplant took place at the Peter Bent Brigham Hospital in Boston in 1954, when a patient received a kidney from his identical twin; their genetic similarity forestalled rejection complications, and the patient lived into the early 1960's. The first liver transplants were performed in the spring and early summer of 1963 at the University of Colorado Medical Center; none of the first four patients lived more than 22 days. The first lung transplants, done at the University of Mississippi Medical Center in June 1963 and at the University of Pittsburgh School of Medicine a month later, were no more successful. Dr. Christiaan Barnard of Cape Town, South Africa, won the race to perform the first heart transplant in December 1967; the patient lived 18 days.

The basic reason most transplant recipients in the 1960's lived only a short time was tissue rejection, part of the response of the body's immune system. The body's white blood cells, which play a key role in the immune system, treat a donated, foreign organ much as they do a bacterium, virus, or any other invader. The so-called T lymphocytes, a type of white blood cell, detect the presence of foreign tissue and trigger other white cells to attack the invader directly or to produce the substances called antibodies, which fight to repel the invader. In the early years of kidney transplants, physicians showered their patients with near-fatal doses of whole-body radiation in an attempt to kill the white blood cells and thus prevent rejection by the immune system. But the organ recipients died anyway, often because their weakened immune systems were helpless against disease.

Next, doctors tried drugs which suppressed the actions of the patient's immune system. These drugs boosted the success rate for kidney transplants: 70 percent of patients with organs donated by relatives (whose tissues were similar to the patient's own) survived after one year; patients with cadaver-donated kidneys had a survival rate of 50 percent. But the drug regimen frequently produced side effects ranging from brittle bones to diabetes. And rejections of organs other than kidneys occurred all too often—so often, in fact, that most heart transplant surgeons had withdrawn from the field by 1970.

Into the Medical Mainstream

What helped get transplants back on track was the discovery, in 1970, of the immunosuppressive drug cyclosporine, which suppresses the immune response associated with organ rejection but does so without killing white blood cells.

Exactly how the drug works remains unclear. Broadly speaking, cyclosporine inhibits T-cell function.

Sharon Begley is science editor of Newsweek.

Kidney transplants are more likely to succeed if the donor is a close relative. The woman above received a kidney from her brother; the woman in front at left received an organ donated by her identical twin.

It seems to prevent these cells from proliferating but apparently leaves other cells of the immune system active. As a result, the risk of infection is lower than with other immunosuppressive drugs.

Cyclosporine has dramatically improved survival rates for transplant recipients. In addition, the reduced incidence of rejection and the lowered risk of infection mean that patients at Stanford University Medical Center, the leading heart transplant center in the United States, can now leave the hospital after a heart transplant in 42 days, as compared to 72 days without cyclosporine. That cuts costs considerably. Also, cyclosporine does not stunt growth, as immunosuppressive steroid drugs do, and it is thus the drug chosen for very young transplant patients. One of the drawbacks is the long-term cost of the drug: a patient must take cyclosporine for life to prevent infections and tissue rejection, at an annual cost, at present, of at least $5,000. Heart transplant patients, who must take higher doses of the drug, can face a bill of $18,000 a year.

Transplant centers began using the drug experimentally in the late 1970's; the U.S. Food and Drug Administration approved it for general use in late 1983. There is no doubt that the higher patient survival rates seen with cyclosporine, along with new surgical techniques, encouraged more and more young surgeons to join transplant teams.

Partly because of cyclosporine, some 70 percent of patients receiving liver transplants now survive the crucial first year; in contrast, only 30 to 35 percent survived one year on conventional immunosuppressive drug therapy. The one-year survival rate for heart transplant patients is up, thanks in part to the drug, from 40 percent a decade ago to 80 percent today.

As would be true with any new drug, cyclosporine and its effects are currently being reassessed. It is now known that the drug can cause damage to the kidneys as well as to other organs. Use of cyclosporine has also been reported to produce lymphomas (tumors of the lymph glands) in a small percentage of transplant cases. One of the basic problems is the drug's narrow effectiveness range: the toxic dose and the dose required for immunosuppression are very close, and optimal dosages have not yet been established. Doctors must monitor their transplant patients very carefully for signs of any adverse effects of cyclosporine as well for signs of rejection of the transplanted organ. But because cyclosporine inhibits the rejection process, the drug may also make early detection of a rejection episode more difficult—some of the classic symptoms of rejection may be absent.

Better surgical and monitoring techniques also deserve much of the credit for the resurgence of transplants. For example, at Stanford University,

Saving Children's Lives

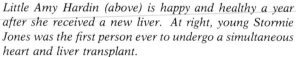
Little Amy Hardin (above) is happy and healthy a year after she received a new liver. At right, young Stormie Jones was the first person ever to undergo a simultaneous heart and liver transplant.

surgeons developed a procedure called heart, or cardiac, biopsy, in which a tiny piece of the transplanted heart muscle is snipped off, with a scissors at the end of a catheter, and examined for early signs of rejection.

Matching Donor and Recipient

In their efforts to understand and to circumvent the rejection response in transplant patients, immunologists continue to develop new techniques to get the best possible match between donor and recipient.

The surfaces of body cells are studded with protein molecules called antigens. It is by these molecules that the immune system recognizes alien agents in the body. Through a process called tissue typing, doctors attempt to identify the antigens of both donor and recipient and thus to assess the compatibility of their tissues. Identical twins have identical antigens; siblings have a 25 percent chance of having the same antigens. But unrelated individuals have only a one in 1,000 chance of matching up antigenically, and doctors turn to tissue typing in order to increase the odds of choosing the best match.

In the basic tissue-typing test, researchers take a

blood sample from a potential recipient and combine it with serums containing antibodies against different tissue antigens. (Antibodies and antigens are specific: a particular antibody is produced to act only against a distinct antigen.) If the lymphocytes being tested have the particular antigen that matches the antibodies in the serum, the lymphocytes will be killed. By running the same test with samples from a transplant donor, and comparing the results, researchers can determine how many antigens the donor and potential recipient have in common.

Tissue typing is not perfect, because scientists have not yet identified all of the genes that determine lymphocyte antigens—which is why immunosuppressive drugs still matter. But the great benefit of tissue typing is that it makes the decision about who shall receive an available organ a medical one and not an ethical one: almost always, there is only one best immunological match for a given organ.

The State of the Art

Cost, eligibility requirements, postoperative treatment, surgical procedures, the rate of success, and the degree to which a transplant is or is not accepted as standard medical practice—each of these factors varies according to the organ involved. Some organs can now be transplanted with relative ease; others continue to pose enormous difficulties for the medical profession.

Kidneys. Of all the major organs, kidneys have the best transplant record. A kidney is the only major internal organ that can be donated by a living person; we each have two, and kidney function is not permanently affected by the loss of one of the pair. The top hospitals report that with the use of cyclosporine, 80 percent of transplanted cadaver kidneys still work after a year, and 90 percent or more of those from living relatives are functioning at the end of this first critical period.

Although an individual can live only a few days after total kidney failure, those who need a new kidney also have the longest grace period of all patients awaiting organs. Even after a kidney begins to fail, a few months of kidney dialysis treatment can reverse the buildup of waste products and the inflammation of the covering of the heart and the lining of the stomach that may occur. (Dialysis is also used as a backup when a transplanted kidney fails.) Periodic dialysis on a long-term basis is both debilitating and expensive, however. Of the

approximately 70,000 Americans now on dialysis, about 10,000 are ill enough to be considered candidates for a transplant. But only 5,000 or so kidney transplants are done each year (some 1,600 of these use a kidney from a living relative).

The operation costs between $25,000 and $35,000, depending on postoperative complications; dialysis costs about $25,000 a year. The procedure is fairly simple. After the donor kidney is removed, a needle is inserted into it to draw out blood and any residual waste. Then, surgeons connect the internal iliac vein in the pelvis of the recipient to the main vein in the donated kidney, and make a comparable artery attachment. (The new organ is often placed in the pelvis instead of its natural place in the back to bring it nearer the bladder.) Finally, the ureter, the duct that transports urine to the bladder, is attached to the new kidney. Transplant patients usually stay on dialysis until physicians are sure that the new organ is functioning.

Liver. Only about 160 liver transplants were performed in the United States in 1983 (up from 30 in 1981). But some 27,000 Americans die each year from diseases of this largest internal organ. Diseases that can lead to liver failure include cancer; cirrhosis, in which normal liver cells are destroyed and fibrous tissue is formed; and biliary atresia, a congenital disease, probably due to viral infection during fetal development, in which nonfunctioning bile ducts cause a buildup of bile in the liver.

Transplant eligibility criteria vary from center to center, but because of the acute organ shortage, most people are not considered eligible until doctors give them only a short time to live. Generally, the recipient's liver disease must not be alcohol-related. (Doctors fear that an alcoholic might continue to drink and thus endanger the new organ.) In addition, the patient must have a viable portal vein—the vein that transports blood from the digestive system to the liver—to establish blood flow to the new organ. The age requirements are flexible, with transplants going to infants (most of them afflicted with biliary atresia) as well as to 50-year-olds.

A liver transplant is one of the most expensive transplant procedures, ranging from $55,000 to $250,000, and surgically, this is the most challenging transplant operation. Simply removing the donor liver can take four hours; the tiniest slip can cause enough damage to blood vessels and bile ducts to make the new organ useless. The transplant itself requires five separate surgical attachments, compared with only three in a kidney transplant. And unlike kidneys, livers must work as soon as they are inserted. There is no equivalent of dialysis to back the new liver up.

Lungs. A lung transplant requires a donor organ free of infection and of exactly the right size to meet the specific respiratory needs of the recipient. Even with cyclosporine, rejection is a constant threat, for even a mild reaction can severely impair the ability of the organ. Transplanting a single lung poses the risk that the remaining original lung will interfere with the transplant by robbing it of air and routing too much blood into it. In addition, heart damage tends to accompany lung disease. For these reasons, surgeons prefer to transplant both lungs and the heart at the same time. The heart-lung transplant operation remains in its infancy, with only 13 such procedures having been performed in 1983.

Bone Marrow. Bone marrow is the easiest tissue to transplant, from the surgeon's point of view, but it is the riskiest transplant for the patient. Unlike other transplants, in which the recipient's immune system threatens to attack the transplant, in this case the transplant can attack the body. Patients with leukemia, aplastic anemia (in which the tissue of the bone marrow, where blood cells are formed, is depleted), and other life-threatening diseases can be saved by a marrow transplant, in which marrow is removed from the donor's pelvic bone and injected into the recipient's arm. However, the marrow contains the progenitors not only of red blood cells but also of the white blood cells that cause rejection. Unless the marrow of the donor is very closely matched to that of the recipient, these so-called stem cells might manufacture lymphocytes that attack the transplant patient, in the potentially fatal condition known as graft-versus-host disease.

Now, however, researchers have developed a procedure to treat the donated marrow so that it will not attack the recipient. The marrow is first processed and cleaned in a blood bank. Then, it is combined with monoclonal antibodies (special antibodies created through genetic-engineering techniques). These antibodies are specific for mature T cells in the bone marrow, which the antibodies seek out and destroy. That leaves only the young stem cells, the T cells' precursors. Twelve to 14 hours later, the treated marrow containing these stem cells is injected into the transplant recipient in a procedure that takes just ten minutes. The T cells produced by these stem cells do not recognize the recipient's tissue as foreign and therefore do not attack their host; the reasons for this are not yet clear. By and large, the technique is proving successful.

Heart. Heart transplants have become the stars of the transplant field. Cardiovascular disease is the number one killer in the United States. Although many people with heart disease would not be helped by a transplant, the American Heart Association estimates that there are perhaps 75,000 potential heart transplant recipients in the United States each year. The cost of the surgery and a year of postoperative treatment can surpass $100,000, compared with the $80,000 a year it costs to care for someone in the final phases of cardiac disease.

A heart transplant is one of the easier cardiac operations, simpler than open-heart surgery. Frequently, only the ventricles (the lower chambers of the heart and the primary pumping mechanisms), the major valves, and parts of the atria (the upper chambers) are removed from the recipient. (A heart-lung machine circulates the patient's blood throughout the body until the new heart is in place.)

The procedure has been called the new surgery of the 1980's because after years of being bested by the immune system, heart surgeons are again entering a field once regarded as vaguely raffish. But even today the numbers of donor hearts available and of experienced surgeons and adequately equipped hospitals are sufficient to treat only a small percentage of potential transplant recipients. In 1983, 172 hearts were transplanted at 11 U.S. medical centers; that was a sharp increase over the figure for 1982. The number of operations should keep rising with the number of heart transplant centers, which had reached 17 by mid-1984.

Most candidates for heart transplants have a form of cardiomyopathy, which gradually destroys the heart muscle. Eligibility varies from center to center, but usually candidates must be younger than 50 and have no circulatory disease or diabetes. Recently, surgeons have begun accepting younger and younger children, including infants, as heart transplant patients.

It is possible that permanent artificial hearts may someday be able to fill the gap between potential transplant recipients and donors. By early 1985, three permanent artificial heart implants had been done: on Barney Clark, who lived 112 days with the device implanted in late 1982, on William Schroeder, who received an artificial heart in November 1984, and on Murray Haydon, who received one in February 1985. But the implantation of mechanical hearts remains highly experimental.

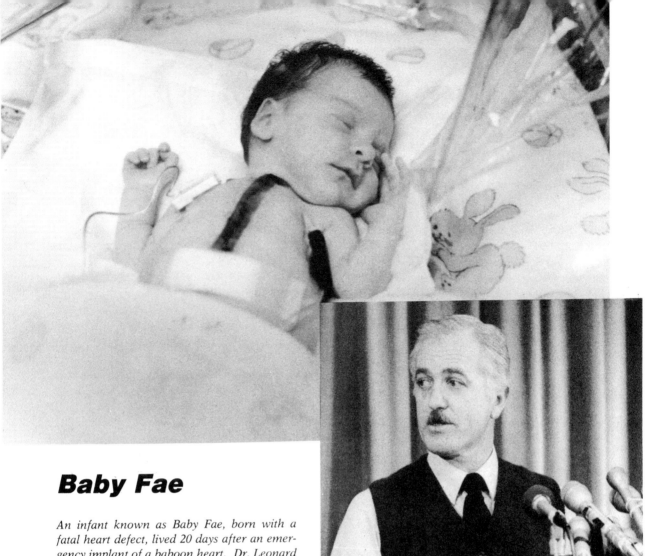

Baby Fae

An infant known as Baby Fae, born with a fatal heart defect, lived 20 days after an emergency implant of a baboon heart. Dr. Leonard Bailey (right) has defended the controversial operation he performed.

Another possible solution to the shortage of donor hearts is the use of animal organs. This was dramatized in late October 1984 when a surgical team at Loma Linda University Medical Center in California implanted the walnut-sized heart of a female baboon in an infant about two weeks old, known as Baby Fae. Baby Fae was born with a usually fatal condition, hypoplastic left heart syndrome, in which the left side of the heart is much smaller than the right, rendering the heart useless as a pump. The child reportedly did remarkably well immediately after the operation. However, despite the use of cyclosporine and other immunosuppressive drugs, Baby Fae's body began to reject the baboon heart, and she died 20 days after the transplant. Baby Fae survived longer than any other human recipient of an animal heart.

Some regarded the highly experimental procedure as a major advance in transplantation, maintaining

that animal organ transplants could be an increasingly important solution to the severe donor shortage problem, particularly for very young children. (Some researchers believe that immediate rejection of an animal organ is less likely in an infant, whose immune system is not fully developed.) But the Loma Linda transplant team also faced much criticism for undertaking the experiment, including the charge that it had failed to make a diligent search for a suitable human heart.

Split-Second Timing

Transplant operations still garner banner headlines in the press—as the case of Baby Fae illustrated—and perhaps they will never achieve the ho-hum status of, say, appendectomies. Transplants carry more than a tinge of drama, partly because of the split-second

93

timing and coordination necessary for surgical teams in different cities to extract an organ from a cadaver and prepare a patient to receive it.

Organs cannot remain viable for very long either inside or outside a cadaver: after the heart stops, surgeons have only half an hour or so to remove the kidneys, for example, before they begin to deteriorate. Once an organ is removed, the race against time places geographic constraints on transplants; how far doctors can travel to retrieve a heart is influenced by the fact that the organ can survive for only four to six hours outside the body. Livers can be sustained for eight to 12 hours after all circulation ceases, but surgeons prefer to start the transplant operation within eight hours. Lungs deteriorate so rapidly that they cannot even be transported—the recipient must be at the same hospital as the donor. Kidneys have the longest life outside the body: with the use of a portable machine that pumps oxygenated plasma and a salt solution through the organ and with the temperature maintained at 50°F, a kidney can be sustained for three days after removal.

The short life of organs means not only that establishing an organ bank is extremely difficult—though there are research efforts currently directed toward this end—but also that the logistics of a transplant easily rivals the actual medical procedure. A typical prelude to an operation might begin with an early morning phone call from a transplant coordinator at a hospital in Dayton, Ohio, to his counterpart at the University of Pittsburgh School of Medicine—one of the leading U.S. centers for liver transplants. Ten days earlier, a five-year-old Ohio boy was hit by a car. He never regained consciousness and is now brain dead, kept alive by a mechanical respirator. Since the Dayton hospital does not perform liver transplants, doctors there are offering the boy's liver to Pittsburgh. The Pittsburgh organ procurement director calls the university's liver transplant specialist, Thomas Starzl, to get the go-ahead. Starzl, consulting with pediatric physicians, decides that a five-year-old Texas boy with biliary atresia who is near death is the proper recipient. The child's parents are phoned, and they arrange to get the boy to Pittsburgh by that evening.

Meanwhile, the Dayton director has received permission from the parents of the brain-dead boy to donate their son's liver. Then Starzl, accompanied by Pittsburgh's organ procurement director and a surgical assistant, flies to Dayton on a chartered jet. At the hospital there, the surgeons remove the dead child's liver in a two-hour operation and chill it in a salt solution. Back in Pittsburgh, another surgical team is alerted that the Dayton surgery has begun. After the little boy from Texas has arrived, they begin their own operation, so that the recipient's own liver is removed when the new one arrives with Starzl. Upon his return to Pittsburgh, he and another surgeon install the new liver in a four-hour operation.

Systems for Obtaining Organs

Many patients awaiting transplants die for want of an organ donor. There is no lack of potential donors: an estimated 20,000 Americans a year die from head injuries, brain tumors, and other conditions that leave the major internal organs intact. But in only about 2,500 of these cases are the organs donated. People may agree in advance to donate their organs and carry donor cards indicating their wishes; however, too few in the United States have done so to meet the organ need. In Canada, there is a comparable problem procuring enough organs for transplants. Although several provinces have organ-donor cards for drivers to carry, the family legally can override the deceased's request that his or her organs be donated.

The lack of donors is partly attributable as well to the reluctance of many physicians to approach a grief-stricken family about donating the organs of a loved one they have just lost. In addition, many families have trouble understanding the concept of brain death, in which there is no neurological function but respiration and blood pressure can be maintained mechanically; indeed, it is often difficult to accept that someone whose chest is moving in and out, whose kidneys are making urine, and whose heart is beating is in fact dead.

About 110 organ procurement agencies around the United States serve as matchmakers, alerting hospitals with potential donors as to what organs are needed. Most of these agencies, which until recently have been largely voluntary and regional, deal only with kidneys. The more than 150 hospitals and medical centers nationwide that perform kidney transplants can hook up with the computer listings of the agencies to see if donors are available for their patients.

For transplants other than kidneys, the North American Transplant Coordinators Organization (NATCO), which among other things serves as an information and education clearinghouse, operates two 24-hour computerized hot lines that tell physicians and officials which centers need hearts, livers, and lungs, what the recipient's blood type and weight requirements are in each case, and how far hospital staff members can travel to retrieve an organ. The NATCO system, health experts agree, has worked well.

Recently, U.S. lawmakers took action to streamline the organ procurement process. The National Organ Transplant Act, which was signed by President Ronald Reagan in October 1984, sets up a federal office of transplantation within the Health and Human Services Department. The legislation requires that office to establish a computerized registry for matching transplant donors and recipients and to administer a grant program that would strengthen and consolidate existing organ procurement agencies.

Efforts are under way as well to improve the transplant situation in Canada, where under the national health insurance program, citizens are covered for all costs relating to a transplant once it has been deemed medically necessary. A government task force is currently studying how to provide such services cost effectively, including improving the organ procurement system and perhaps establishing regional transplant centers. Relatively few transplants currently are performed in Canada, but the government foresees a growing demand.

High Costs

Even a perfect organ procurement system leaves the problem of the cost of transplants, which is not likely to come down anytime soon. Hospitals can be squeezed financially by these costs, which if not covered by insurance—as is many times the case in the United States—often cannot be met by transplant recipients, so that institutions still willing to perform the surgery must make up the difference elsewhere. Many hospitals demand substantial deposits in advance—perhaps $100,000. In some cases where state medical insurance programs would not pay for transplants, a call to an influential politician has put pressure on the governor to make an exception.

Clearly, the funding dilemma is one of the biggest problems in the transplant field. As insurance companies begin to cover the costly operations, eligibility criteria have to be set—and that forces some hard social decisions. Should a reformed alcoholic suffering from cirrhosis of the liver be accepted as a transplant patient? What about cases in which a transplant might improve the quality of life for a year but would not stave off death from other diseases for much longer than that?

Health-cost experts expect insurers to place restrictions on which drugs and other maintenance therapies will be paid for, but such limits will leave a big gap in coverage, since postoperation costs are so high. In general, the health benefits of transplants will have to be weighed against the high medical bills and insurance premiums. Some experts predict that society is severely underestimating the demand for transplants and the attendant strain on the health care budget. They point to the current U.S. situation with kidney dialysis, which the federal government funds at an annual cost of some $2 billion—much higher than had been anticipated.

A natural cap on the transplant boom is the number of donors. Ideally, of course, that number would meet a reasonable demand set by conscious social decisions and not act as the limiting factor itself. Several European countries meet their demand for organs (which is much lower than in the United States) with what is known as a presumed consent law: potential donors, such as accident victims, are presumed to have consented to organ donation unless they have specifically indicated otherwise, with the added stipulation that families have the right to rescind the presumed permission.

Almost everyone agrees that such a law would never be accepted in the United States, and bioethicists have suggested an alternative—required request. This policy would require physicians to ask permission of the family to remove the organs of a brain-dead patient. By making the question routine instead of leaving it to a doctor's discretion, required request could dramatically increase the number of available organs. How society chooses to deal with these vexing issues of cost and procurement will, even more than medical advances, determine the future of transplants. □

SUGGESTIONS FOR FURTHER READING

"A Breakthrough Transplant?" *Newsweek*, November 12, 1984, pp. 114–116, 118.

KALSON, SALLY. "A Link to Life." *New York Times Magazine*, June 19, 1983, pp. 20, 22, 24, 60, 62, 69.

"The New Era of Transplants." *Newsweek*, August 29, 1983, pp. 38–44.

"Transplants—Progress Along With Agony." *U.S. News & World Report*, November 26, 1984, pp. 78–79.

Children of Divorce

Judith S. Wallerstein, Ph.D.

O utward appearances provide no clues that anything is amiss in four-year-old Linda's life. When she is asked what is happening at home, the pretty, well-groomed child becomes perhaps a little subdued. She replies that her father now lives in the city because he doesn't like Mommy anymore, but Mommy still likes Daddy and is sad.

When Linda plays with a dollhouse, however, the scene that unfolds belies her composure. At the beginning, a mother and father are sleeping in the same bed. A baby is also asleep, and the other children are playing contentedly in an adjoining room. The mother gets up and prepares a delicious breakfast, and a little boy brings a bowl of cereal to another child.

But soon the aura of togetherness disappears. Linda puts the entire family on the roof, where they start teetering precariously back and forth. Suddenly she knocks over the furniture and the dolls. She picks up animal puppets and has them attack each other viciously. A whale bites a crocodile; the crocodile bites a giraffe. Finally, Linda herself bites the crocodile ferociously, pummeling it out of shape.

Linda's view of the world is clear. What once seemed a tranquil place has been transformed into a jungle in which aggression runs wild.

Linda is one of 131 youngsters studied as part of the Children of Divorce Project, now associated with the Center for the Family in Transition in Corte Madera,

Calif. The center was established in 1980. The project, which began in 1971, is the longest-running and largest effort in the United States to evaluate the impact of divorce on children and their parents. The project studies normal youngsters ranging in age from 2½ to 18 at the time of the divorce.

Linda's dilemma is much more common than it once was. The number of divorces in the United States each year is far greater than it was just 25 years ago. It is estimated that 45 percent of the children born in 1983 will experience their parents' divorce, 35 percent will experience a remarriage, and 20 percent will experience a second divorce.

For most children, including adolescents, divorce and its immediate aftermath constitute the most stressful period in their lives up to then. The fact that many of their friends and neighbors are going through the same thing does not seem to lessen their pain. For only 10 percent of the children, the Children of Divorce Project found, did divorce turn out to be a welcome relief. Most youngsters feared the breakup and opposed it vigorously, even though half of them had seen physical violence in their homes. Five years after the divorce, over one-third of the children were still moderately to severely depressed.

Most children oppose their parents' breakup even when there has been fighting or violence in the home.

Many factors influence how a child weathers divorce. Two crucial elements are the child's psychological attributes—behavioral patterns, needs, fears, and level of intellectual and emotional development, which is closely linked to age—and the degree to which the mother and father can maintain their parenting roles during and after the divorce.

Do Boys and Girls React Differently?

There has been a lot of speculation as to whether boys and girls respond differently to marital breakdown. Findings of the Children of Divorce Project indicate that at the time the rupture occurs, the behavior of children younger than adolescents is more likely to be governed by their age than by their sex. It does appear, however, that girls regain their equilibrium significantly faster than boys. A year after the separation, the girls studied seemed to have recovered better; the boys, especially those below the age of seven, were by comparison more depressed and still preoccupied with the divorce.

Until very recently, most courts gave custody to the mother in divorce settlements. Thus, most of the children of divorce studied by researchers have lived with their mother. It is not known whether this is a crucial factor—that is, whether boys and girls appear to adjust at different rates because they react differently to living with their mother or because little boys may be more vulnerable to stress than little girls. A study in Texas has shown that boys of school age do better when they live with their father than with their mother. Since only a few boys were studied, however, this finding needs to be confirmed.

Judith S. Wallerstein, coauthor of Surviving the Breakup: How Children and Parents Cope With Divorce, *is executive director of the Center for the Family in Transition in Corte Madera, Calif., and senior lecturer at the University of California at Berkeley.*

A Question of Age

Although youngsters react to divorce in very different ways, certain patterns of behavior are typical for specific age groups. Age-related problems are normal reactions to the acute stress caused by the trauma of divorce. They are often severe and can be quite troublesome to parents and teachers, although many of them may lessen or even disappear within the first year or two after the parents' separation. Some children, of course, show little or no change of feelings at the time of the separation, or even in the succeeding year or two; it must be kept in mind that such youngsters may actually be just as troubled as those openly distressed.

Preschoolers. Preschool children are very likely to show some behavioral or mood change after the departure of a parent from the family. Regression to earlier behavior is common, with newly learned skills, such as toilet training or self-feeding, the most likely to be temporarily lost. Children may return to thumb-sucking or a security blanket, and masturbation may increase.

Personal relationships may be affected. Any separation from the remaining parent is likely to become threatening. The child may not want to let that parent out of his or her sight, for fear of being abandoned once more. This fear also accounts for sleep disturbances, which are frequent at this time: a child may be terrified by the possibility of awakening to an empty house, with both parents gone. Preschoolers may also regress in their ability to control hostile impulses. They are likely to become irritable and cranky; they may hit the baby or behave more aggressively with other children.

Children of divorce must cope with bewilderingly intense feelings of loss and rejection.

A visiting father greets his daughter. Such visits can be emotionally charged for parent and child alike: parents are brought back into painful contact, and the child often feels caught in the middle.

Preschoolers may see the separation as punishment for being "bad" and blame their own misbehavior for the parent's departure: "Daddy left because I played too noisy."

Ages six to eight. Children who are six to eight years old at the time of divorce are most likely to show their grief. They frequently appear downcast and tearful; sometimes they sob openly. Their central and underlying concern is with their feelings of loss and rejection.

Youngsters in this age group often long for the departed parent—usually the father. They fear they will be completely abandoned by him and are especially worried about being replaced in his affections: "Will Daddy get a new dog? . . . a new Mommy? . . . a new little boy?" Little girls, refusing to believe that their father's absence is permanent, weave elaborate fantasies about his eventual return to them. This longing for an absent father does not appear to depend on whether the child had a good relationship with the father before the divorce: poor fathers are evidently missed just as intensely as caring and attentive ones.

Six-year-old Wanda told a psychologist who interviewed her that she saw her father all the time. "He lives with me," she explained. "You mean," said the interviewer, "you wish he still lived at your house." Wanda replied, "Yes, I mean that, but some day he really, really will. He promised me that he would."

A few days later, the interviewer told Wanda that he had seen her father and had conveyed to him her wish that he visit more often. "Don't say that. It makes me sad, because I really don't get to see him very much," she confessed sadly. Wanda's father was hardly visiting her at all during this period.

Fantasies of somehow rescuing the broken marriage are also common in youngsters in this age group. The way children studied at the Corte Madera center play with dollhouses often shows undisguised wishes for an intact family. They create a peaceful, well-ordered family life in which mother doll and father doll sleep side by side in one bed, while the children help themselves liberally to the fantasy contents of the well-stocked toy refrigerator.

The Children of Divorce Project has noted a precipitous decline in school performance in half of the youngsters of this age. Anxious about their parents and preoccupied with their own sense of rejection, these children have difficulty concentrating at school.

Ages nine to 12. Intense anger—either at both parents or at the parent blamed for seeking the divorce—marks the responses of children aged nine to 12. These youngsters also typically suffer grief, anxiety, acute loneliness, and a sense of powerlessness.

> *Ten-year-old Gwen was in despair. She was extremely angry at her father for leaving and she said she never wanted him to return. She had lost interest in school, her friends, and her piano lessons. She kept thinking all day that her father was with his girlfriend, and she could not stand that. She also kept thinking of her mother with her boyfriend and shuddered at the idea that her mother might fall in love again. "I don't want anyone that she would marry. How can I concentrate at school, thinking about Mom and Dad kissing and making love with other people?"*

Youngsters in this age group are likely to be caught up in one parent's desire to humiliate or harass the other. As battle lines are drawn, a child may identify with the angry, revengeful parent and become a faithful ally. Such a strong alignment was formed by over one-fifth of all the youngsters in the Children of Divorce Project, many aged nine to 12.

An unhappy parent may also find a son or daughter of this age to be very helpful and comforting, since such youngsters are generally quite capable of responding with loyalty and love to the parent's new needs for companionship and solace. But sometimes these new demands overtax the child's still limited capacities.

Children at this age may complain of physical problems, usually stomachaches and headaches. Chronic illnesses such as asthma are likely to get worse. Some of these youngsters engage in petty stealing or similar types of delinquency; others learn to lie, wheedle, and otherwise manipulate children and adults in order to get something they want. In roughly half the youngsters in this age group who were studied in the project, both school performance and relationships with friends deteriorated.

Adolescents. The effects of a divorce on adolescent children are not always immediately apparent but can be quite serious. About a third of those studied in the project appeared more troubled one year after the divorce than when their parent's marriage broke up.

The new vulnerability of their parents may cause adolescents acute anxiety. The adolescents also tend to feel more apprehensive and uneasy about their entry into young adulthood; they fret about their own future marriage, fearing that, like their parents, they too will fail. Moreover, they may be disturbed by their parents' suddenly more visible sexual needs.

"I can yell too!" In the midst of escalated fighting between parents, children may turn their own hostile impulses against siblings and friends.

Preoccupied with their own burgeoning sexuality, most adolescents prefer to think of their parents as old and beyond sex.

After the divorce, adolescents are likely to spend more time away from home than they might otherwise and may, in anger at their parents, begin acting out their aggressions and frustrations in various ways. Increased or premature sexual activity is not uncommon, particularly as parental controls loosen or fade completely and as parents' sexuality is more evident.

Hard Times for All

Youngsters' reactions to divorce are closely tied to the feedback they get from their parents. It is important therefore to understand what parents are going through at this disruptive time.

Divorce in a family with children is usually initiated by one spouse. The other partner often feels helpless, angry, jealous, and depressed. The home can become a battleground. A flood of hatred and anger may pour out, as well as revelations and taunts about sexual behavior. Physical fighting between the adults at this time is much more common than many people would like to believe.

The period of instability in the home may be long; it may take several months to several years for a sense of order to be restored. The Children of Divorce Project found that the average amount of time required for adults to restabilize their lives was 2½ to 3½ years.

During this turbulent period, the husband and wife understandably become so preoccupied with their own problems and worries that their capacity to be good parents is considerably diminished. Women who suddenly become single parents are likely to find the clashing demands of home, work, and children too much to cope with. Moreover, parents who are newly separated or on the verge of separation have a great need for affection and adult companionship at the very time that their children also need increased attention and care.

It is unfortunate that when separation and divorce require parents to make important, long-range decisions about their children—about custodial, financial, and educational arrangements, for example—their judgment may be colored and impaired by their own conflicts and needs. Because of the stress they are under, the same parents who would normally spend hours preparing their children for other upsetting or potentially frightening experiences, such as going to the hospital for minor surgery, may fail to tell them about the impending divorce. Eighty percent of the preschoolers in the project were not told about their parents' divorce beforehand. These youngsters essentially awoke one morning to find that one parent was gone.

The parent who remains in the home after a divorce frequently withdraws emotionally from the children, showing less concern and sensitivity—or none at all. It is no wonder, then, that at the same time that youngsters are most insecure about themselves and their future, they also often feel they are losing both parents.

Instead of getting increased support for their needs, youngsters may be left, to varying degrees, on their own while the parents attempt to cope with their new circumstances. The children are often forced to take new

Young children routinely take on many household tasks to help out their divorced or separated parents. Sometimes youngsters are saddled with more responsibility than they can realistically handle.

and extraordinary responsibility for themselves. It is not unusual to see children as young as six putting themselves to bed, taking themselves to school, getting their own lunch—or going without lunch when they don't remember to fix it. This is in most cases simply more than such a young child can handle.

The consequences and repercussions of parental self-absorption, burdensome demands, fighting, and tension can be serious and long-lasting.

In a letter received by the Center for the Family in Transition, a 30-year-old woman whose parents had divorced when she was a child wrote: "Psychotherapy helped me realize that I felt that my parents did not care that they had hurt me. I know this probably isn't true, but the child is more or less overrun by the parents' choices.

"I am firmly committed to never having children, as I am determined not to repeat the bitterness and irreparable harm that results to people who hate. However, I am experiencing a great deal of difficulty in interpersonal relationships, and despite my desire to date and to be in love with a man, I have yet to develop a romantic relationship that lasted more than eight months."

A divorced father and his daughter seek help in working through the difficulties that beset them at this stressful time in their lives.

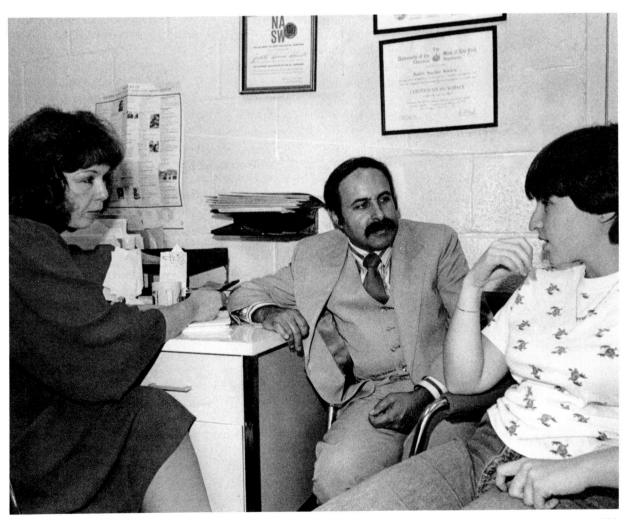

Absorbing the Shock

The center has found, however, that divorce does not have to lead to such a disastrous outcome. In fact, the most valuable finding of the center's work is that the happiness of children depends much more on the quality of their life in the postdivorce family than on the stressful events of the breakup itself. This means that some of the potentially destructive aftereffects of divorce can be reduced or even prevented. Parents who are able to understand and anticipate their children's preoccupations, fears, and behavioral problems are in an excellent position to help ease the emotional trauma of divorce and find ways of resolving some of the problems that children face in their new life.

Explaining the Divorce. First of all, youngsters need to be told about the divorce in advance so that they can prepare for the changes that lie ahead. This should ordinarily not be done in a single announcement. Ideally, both parents should meet with all the children to discuss the pending divorce shortly before it takes place. The children should be made to feel that parents expect and encourage their questions.

The reasons for the divorce must be made as clear as possible to children. They need assurance that their parents are rational people who have thought carefully, who have tried and exhausted every resource, before making such a weighty decision that will so powerfully affect everyone in the family.

Explanations of the divorce must be appropriate to each child's age and level of understanding. Young children can be told that the parents have been unhappy and in conflict and that the purpose of the divorce is to bring an end to the fighting and unhappiness. Older children can be given more specifics—the various attempts the parents have made to resolve their conflicts, and their disappointment and sorrow over the marital failure. Details of sexual infidelity are not helpful to youngsters. If a child is already aware of an extramarital relationship, however, there is no point in denying such a relationship; instead, it should be described as symptomatic of the unhappiness within the marriage.

Children must understand as clearly as possible that they have not caused the divorce and that no effort of theirs can mend the broken marriage. The divorce needs to be accepted as simply a decision the parents have taken to rectify the discord between them.

It is important to explain what the divorce will mean for the children— what will alter, what will remain the same. They need to understand what the family structure will be like in the immediate future and what immediate changes they can expect in their daily lives. Since they are likely to fear getting lost in the shuffle, they must be assured and reassured that they will continue to be cared for and that their needs will be considered and their wishes given some priority in the new, postdivorce family.

Contact With the Absent Parent. It is essential that the youngsters believe their relationships with each parent will survive and continue, despite the altered circumstances: neither parent, in other words, will abandon them. Indeed, studies show that children's continued self-esteem is linked with their ability to maintain ongoing, meaningful relationships with both parents. After the separation, children must be made to

A parent's assurance of continued love and support is tremendously important.

Pulling together: A single father and his daughters attack the job of running their household.

understand that the absent parent has not disappeared and has a place to live, food to eat, and people to care for him or her. It is helpful for children to see where the absent parent is living.

Visiting patterns must be based on the child's needs and the prior relationship with the absent parent, not on the amount of tension between the mother and father. In general, the younger the child, the more regular and more frequent the visits should be. Because their sense of time is not fully developed, young children have difficulty keeping track of when the absent father or mother will appear. Although there can be no absolute rule, children below the age of nine probably should see the absent parent at least once a week and more frequently if possible.

The visits should include overnight and weekend stays, so that neither child nor parent feels rushed or pressured. Generally, children are frustrated by hurried, fleeting contacts. (Adolescents, however, do sometimes prefer a dinner meeting or a brief contact at irregular intervals.) It helps a great deal if children are ready to be picked up and parents are on time.

Both ordinary activities and special treats are important when planning visits. Children need a parent, not an entertainer or a sugar daddy. A child who seems to be pulling away before the visit ends is probably preparing for the separation, not rejecting the parent; the parent must understand this. Also, visits will go more smoothly if parents do not introduce complications into the situation by bringing up their own disagreements.

If the parent without custody is psychologically unstable, visits should be discouraged, but not totally discontinued, as long as the child is not in jeopardy. Children who are forbidden to see a parent are more likely to idealize and romanticize the unseen mother or father. Physical separation does not necessarily lead to psychological disengagement and sometimes may even have the opposite effect.

Assurance that they are not expected by either parent to take sides against the other is of tremendous importance to youngsters. They need permission to love both parents.

The Postdivorce Family.   Freedom to give vent to feelings of sadness, anger, and disappointment is yet another need of children attempting to cope with separation and divorce. But they also must be made to understand that violent or destructive expression of anger will not be tolerated. Such restraints will help them to see that the family structure has not been and will not be utterly destroyed, though it has been dramatically altered, and that order and routine will eventually replace the instability and difficulty of the immediate future.

Many divorced men and women will eventually remarry and form a stepfamily, like the one shown here, with its own attendant conflicts and joys.

A single parent can expect to have problems as the only disciplinarian. Many single mothers relied on their husbands to enforce discipline before the divorce and find themselves at a loss when they must take over this role. In addition, newly separated or divorced custodial parents are often more vulnerable to children's criticism and anger: fear of rejection by their children may make parents loath to set limits and rules, or to say "no" at all. Inevitably, roles in the household will change as a result of the divorce. But order in the home will make it easier for children to adjust; they will benefit from clear-cut rules and consistent expectations. The parent must temper this firmness with greater emotional support, which children desperately need at this time.

Perhaps most important to regaining some sense of equilibrium and stability, the postdivorce family must find ways of having fun, times when problems can be temporarily put aside. An activity as simple as baking cookies or flying a kite can provide a welcome respite from day-to-day pressures and anxieties and can help solidify the family. Also, even a small amount of time spent alone with each child will become special to both parent and child.

If parents can put their conflict behind them, their children stand a good chance of ultimately faring well.

The Opportunity for a New Life

Parents need to understand that divorce, in itself, is not always harmful to children in the long run. The Children of Divorce Project found that ten years after the parents' separation, half of the children who had been preschoolers when the rupture occurred had no memories of the frequently violent and stormy breakup period. This was the age group that generally had been the most distressed and frightened at the time of the separation. Ten years later, there appeared to be something of a reversal: the younger children tended to be much more optimistic and less fearful about their future than their older brothers and sisters, who were still tormented by memories of the divorce.

However, when the divorce itself "fails"—when parents continue to fight bitterly every time they see each other, when their pain is not at least eventually eased—then children of all ages remain bewildered and angry, unable to make sense of the persisting stresses and conflicts. It is not unusual for them to fall into a chronic depression that may later require prolonged psychiatric treatment.

If on the other hand the parents are able to put their conflict behind them and make use of the new opportunities provided by the divorce, the children too can learn to understand and accept the breakup; they then stand a good chance of ultimately faring well. "Divorce is not as bad as you think, not near as bad as it looks in movies or on television," thoughtfully explains 11-year-old Harold. "Mom is not as sad as she was, and she's getting much stronger. Dad was unhappy during the marriage, and he's much happier now."

For Harold, who is speaking five years after his parents split up, the divorce has acquired a finality, a permanence. He has realized that putting the shattered marriage back together again is as impossible as repairing a broken glass. The divorce makes sense to him now because both his parents are happier. He has come to terms with their separation and can move ahead with his own life. □

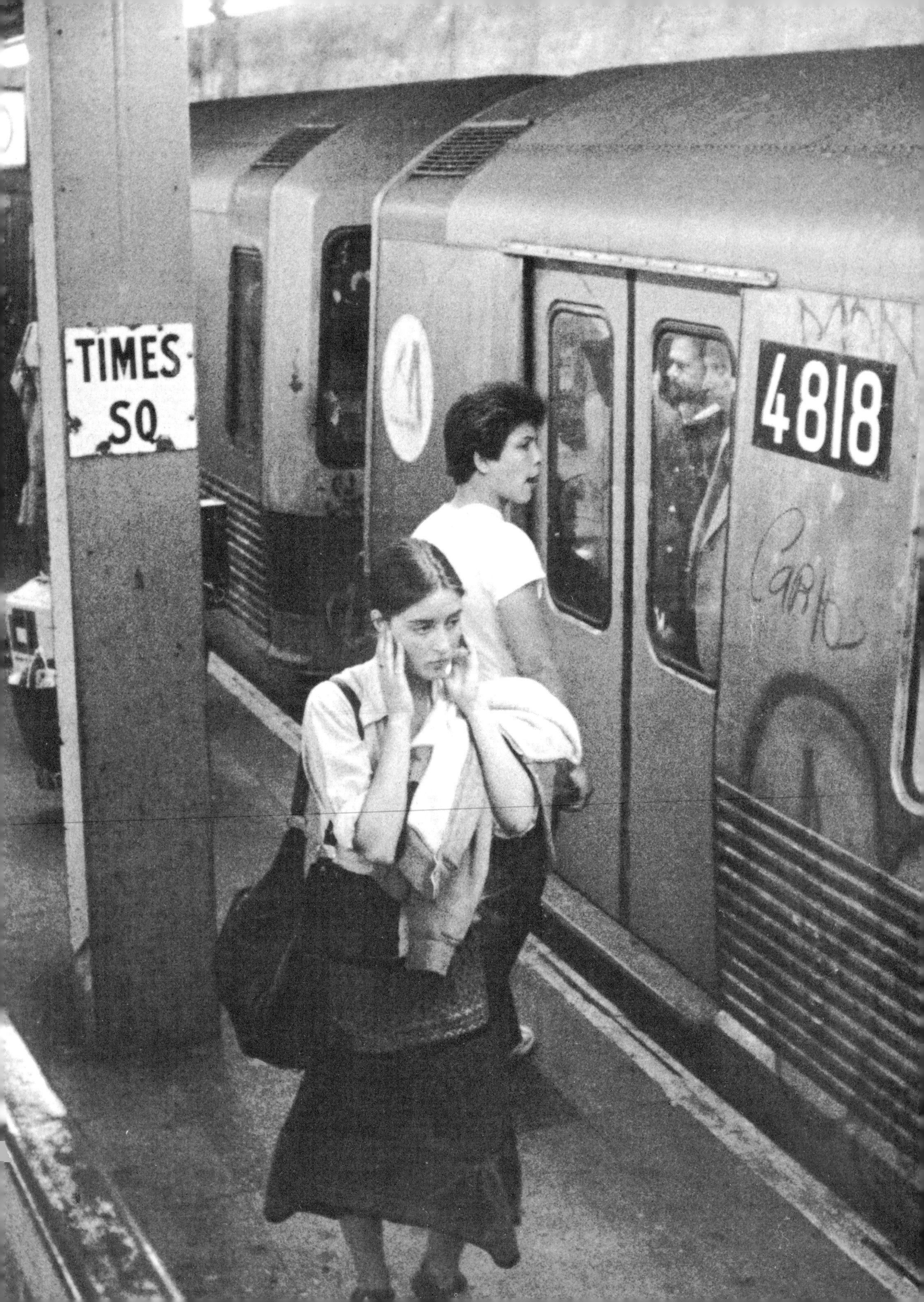
TIMES
SQ
4818

Hearing Impairment

Richard J. H. Smith, M.D.

Our world is filled with sounds. Some, like the quiet ticking of a watch, are almost inaudible. Others, like the noise of a jet engine, are intensely painful. We take for granted this constant exposure to noise; often, only in the wake of deafness is the full importance of hearing appreciated.

Hearing loss, whether its onset is sudden or slow, is a subtly cruel handicap. The affliction is not instantly apparent to others, and for a hearing-impaired person, misunderstandings and frustrations become a part of everyday social interaction. Failure to respond is interpreted as dullness or stupidity, and incorrect responses elicit ridicule or mirth. Self-confidence is lost, tension mounts, social isolation occurs, and in some instances, extreme demoralization results. Obviously, then, measures to prevent or limit hearing loss are immensely important. A number of such measures will be discussed in this article.

The study of sound, known as acoustics, began in the late 17th century when Robert Boyle demonstrated that sound cannot travel in a vacuum. Sound waves require a medium to carry them from one point to another. The medium can be a gas, liquid, or solid, and the characteristics of the sound produced will vary accordingly. In air, for example, sound travels relatively slowly—only 1,120 feet per second (the speed of light is 186,300 *miles* per second). This is why, during a thunderstorm, we see bolts of lightning before we hear the peals of thunder. In freshwater, sound travels roughly four times faster than it does in air, and in steel, it travels faster still, moving at 16 times its velocity in air.

The intensity of sound waves—what the listener perceives as loudness—is measured in units known as decibels. The decibel (dB) is one-tenth of a bel, named in honor of Alexander Graham Bell. On the decibel scale, an increase of 20 decibels represents a hundredfold increase in intensity. Such a scale is convenient for dealing with the amazing sensitivity range of the ear. The highest sound intensity that can be tolerated (120 dB) is a million times that of the quietest audible sound (0 dB).

The Ear and Its Structure

Our ears function very efficiently as sound receivers. Each ear is subdivided into three sections: the outer, the middle, and the inner ear. All of us are familiar with the flaplike appendage on the side of the head, technically known as the pinna, but deep within the skull are several intricate structures far more essential for hearing.

The pinna is part of the outer ear. It helps to collect sound waves, to increase the ear's ability to hear sound in the upper frequencies (sound that has a higher pitch), and to determine the direction of the source of sound. It is built on a framework of gristlelike tissue called cartilage, and although the pinna has some muscle tissue, in humans this is minimal. Extending inward from the pinna is another part of the outer ear, the ear canal. The canal extends rather deep into the side of the skull and ends abruptly at the eardrum. The ear canal is formed from both cartilage and bone. The skin overlying the cartilage portion contains glands which secrete earwax. The wax acts as an important barrier to infection by preventing moisture within the ear canal from softening and breaking down the skin. The acidity of earwax also inhibits the growth of bacteria and fungi.

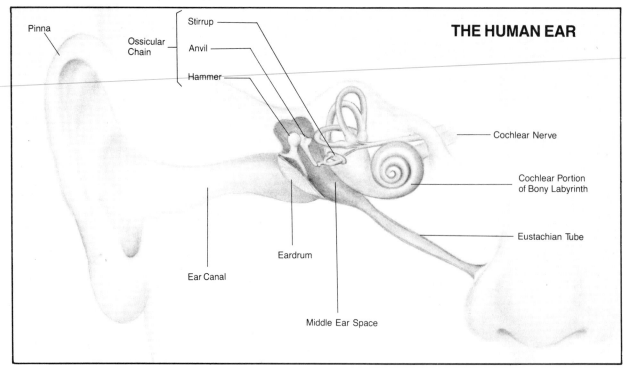

THE HUMAN EAR

Pinna

Ossicular Chain

Stirrup

Anvil

Hammer

Cochlear Nerve

Cochlear Portion of Bony Labyrinth

Eustachian Tube

Eardrum

Ear Canal

Middle Ear Space

The eardrum separates the outer ear from the middle ear. The middle ear is an irregularly shaped cavity that houses a series of three connected bones known collectively as the ossicular chain. Although their scientific names are the malleus, incus, and stapes, they are probably better known (because of their shapes) as the hammer, anvil, and stirrup. Sound waves traveling down the ear canal cause the eardrum to vibrate, and these vibrations are transmitted to the ossicular chain. Proper functioning of the ossicular chain depends upon the eustachian tube—the tube connecting the middle ear cavity to the back portion of the nose. Ideally, the eustachian tube drains away the natural fluids secreted by the walls of the middle ear. This ensures that the middle ear cavity contains air, thus providing optimal conditions for the transmission of vibrations through the ossicular chain. It is possible for the middle ear cavity to become filled with fluid, as when an infection causes the eustachian tube to swell and become blocked. This prevents the eardrum and the three bones from functioning properly. The vibrations of both are lessened by the fluid, and the result is a mild to moderate hearing loss.

The stirrup abuts a series of interconnecting tubes in the portion of the skull known as the inner ear. These tubes form the sensory organ for both hearing and balance. Collectively, they are referred to as the bony labyrinth, because of the mazelike, intricate quality of the structure. Within the bony labyrinth is a second labyrinth, similar in appearance but formed from membrane. This membranous labyrinth is suspended in fluid and is subdivided into specific areas essential for normal hearing and balance. The hearing portion is called the cochlear duct. Within this duct is a fine network of hair cells that converts into electrical energy (nerve impulses) the vibrations the ossicular chain transmits to the fluid within the bony labyrinth. The nerve impulses then travel down the cochlear nerve to the brain.

Types of Hearing Loss

Hearing impairment is a very frequent occurrence. It is estimated that one out of every 1,000 to 2,000 children in the United States is born with a hearing problem or suffers a severe hearing loss before speech and language development occurs. Among adults, approximately 20 percent have some type of hearing impairment. This is largely due to the condition called presbycusis, the slow, progressive decline in hearing sensitivity that tends to occur with age. This hearing loss is usually greater in the higher frequencies, and numerous factors play a part in its development, including diet, metabolism, cholesterol levels, blood pressure, exercise, smoking, stress, and heredity.

Two basic types of hearing impairment can occur: conductive and sensorineural. With conductive hearing impairment, sound is not effectively transmitted to the inner ear. A foreign object lodged in the ear

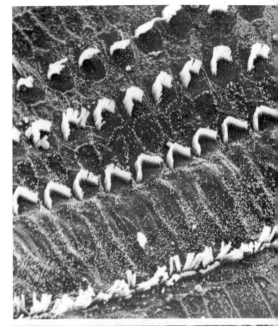
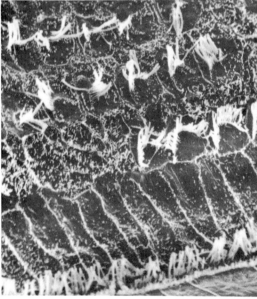

How noise can injure the ear: the top picture shows normal hair cells (in rows) in the inner ear of a guinea pig; the bottom picture, damaged hair cells after 24 hours of exposure to extremely loud noise.

Richard J. H. Smith is a board-certified otolaryngologist (ear, nose, and throat specialist) and an assistant professor in the Department of Otorhinolaryngology and Communicative Sciences at the Baylor College of Medicine in Houston.

Even very young children can be given hearing tests to detect possible problems.

canal can produce a temporary conductive hearing loss. More permanent types of conductive hearing loss can occur if the ear canal or the eardrum does not develop normally in the fetus before birth. For example, if the eardrum forms as a bony plate instead of a very thin layer of skin, sound waves cannot be efficiently transmitted to the ossicular chain.

Middle ear abnormalities can also cause conductive hearing impairment. The example of fluid in the middle ear cavity has already been given. This typically results when the eustachian tube does not effectively drain fluid from the middle ear. Another example would be an abnormality involving the ossicular chain. If the hammer, anvil, and stirrup are either firmly fixed (so that they cannot vibrate) or completely separated from each other (so that they cannot transmit vibrations), sound vibrations will not reach the inner ear.

With sensorineural, or perceptive, hearing loss, the inner ear mechanism designed to convert the energy of fluid movement into nerve impulses is defective. The most common cause of sensorineural impairment is an abnormality within the cochlear duct, such as damage to or degeneration of the hair cells. Extremely loud noises, certain drugs, certain genetic disorders, and the normal aging process all can cause hair cell destruction.

Detection and Correction

It is often possible to determine whether hearing loss is conductive or sensorineural by means of a series of hearing tests. Such testing is usually simple, but it is also extremely important, as most types of conductive hearing loss can be treated, either with medication or with surgery.

Medications are useful in cases where the hearing loss is caused by an infection of the outer or middle ear.

In some cases surgery is needed for both diagnosis and treatment. While the patient is under anesthesia, the surgeon can lift up the eardrum and inspect the middle ear, using a special viewing instrument; the surgeon may then be able to identify and correct the problem responsible for the conductive hearing loss. The corrective surgery may be either a relatively simple or an extremely complex undertaking.

It should be understood that very few types of sensorineural hearing loss can be corrected by current medical or surgical techniques. Some people have a mixed hearing loss; that is, there are both conductive and sensorineural problems. Knowing the degree of each makes it possible for a physician to recommend therapy and predict the results of treatment.

If neither medical nor surgical treatment is likely to eliminate the problem, a hearing aid may be beneficial. Simply stated, a hearing aid is any device which brings sound more effectively to the listener's ear. (The simplest aid is the hand cupped behind the ear. By deflecting more sound waves into the ear canal, the hand provides a small amount of amplification.) The best available hearing aids can help even severely hearing-impaired patients. No hearing aid, however, can compensate for every component of a hearing loss. Hence, it is important to discuss the use of amplification with a doctor, and if possible, to wear an aid on a trial basis to see whether added amplification helps.

The familiar gesture of cupping a hand behind the ear actually creates a primitive hearing aid.

Inherited Problems

The causes of both conductive and sensorineural hearing impairment can be broadly divided into two categories: inherited and environmental. Often, the difference between inherited and acquired hearing loss is not entirely clear-cut. It is possible, for example, to have normal hearing but to be more susceptible, because of hereditary influences, to damaging agents such as loud noises or certain drugs. In many cases, the cause of hearing impairment cannot be attributed with certainty to either inherited or environmental factors and remains unknown.

Inherited traits are transmitted to us from our parents through distinct units called genes. In some cases the gene from one parent for a certain trait takes precedence over its counterpart from the other parent. In the case of eye color, for example, if you inherit a gene for blue eyes from one parent and a gene for brown eyes from the other, you will have brown eyes. The gene for brown is said to be dominant, and the gene for blue is said to be recessive. The recessive genes can be passed on to future generations, however. Some offspring of blue-eyed ancestors, even several generations back, may thus receive two recessive genes for blue eyes. With no dominant gene present, these people will have blue eyes.

Virl Osmond, seen here (center) in a game with his wife and children, is one of two brothers of Donny and Marie Osmond born with a severe hereditary hearing impairment. All of his children hear normally.

The genetics of hearing problems is far more complex. There are well-documented cases of deaf parents having only deaf children. In other instances, deaf parents can have children with normal hearing. This does not mean that hearing impairment in those parents was not hereditary; rather, it could mean that the problems of the parents were due to different genetic causes and that each parent contributed a dominant gene to the children to correct the defective recessive gene transmitted by the

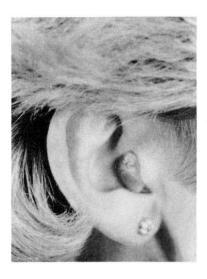

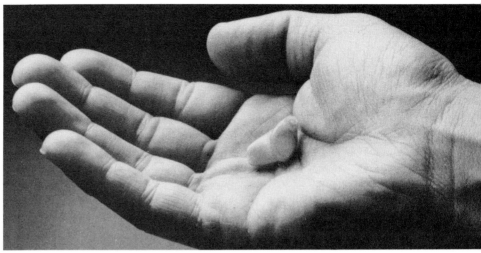

other parent. These genes for defective hearing do not disappear. They remain hidden, like the gene for blue eyes, and may reappear generations later to produce hearing problems.

Although the specific genes responsible for hearing have not been identified, it has been determined that recessive genes cause hearing impairment more frequently than dominant genes. Nearly 90 percent of all cases of hereditary hearing impairment are thought to result from recessive genes. Two of the more common forms of recessive hereditary impairment are Pendred's syndrome and Usher's syndrome. These result in a severe sensorineural hearing loss that tends to be more severe in the high frequencies.

Dominant genes account for only about 10 percent of cases of hereditary hearing impairments. Usually, the problem is less severe than one produced by recessive genes. The trait may even appear to skip a generation because the degree of deafness produced may vary from individual to individual. Examples of hearing impairment inherited through dominant genes include Waardenburg's syndrome (a disorder that affects the function of the hair cells in the cochlear duct) and Treacher Collins syndrome (an abnormality in the development of the jaw bones and the ossicular chain). Both syndromes can cause a mixed type of hearing impairment (conductive and sensorineural).

Eradicating hereditary types of hearing impairment is probably impossible, in part because parents may not realize they carry an abnormal gene and because spontaneous mutations of genes constantly occur. Genetic counseling can be invaluable for parents of a child born with a hearing impairment. Through counseling, it may be possible to predict the likelihood that other children will be similarly affected. Counseling may also guide hearing-impaired individuals when they wish to start a family.

Another type of hearing problem that tends to run in families is known as otosclerosis. In this condition, abnormal bone formation results in impaired mobility of the stirrup, and transmission of sound through the ossicular chain is therefore impeded. This conductive hearing loss can usually be surgically corrected by removing the stirrup and replacing it with a tiny artificial rod.

SOME COMMON SOUNDS:

HOW LOUD? HOW DANGEROUS?

	Decibel level	Sound
	0	Softest sound audible
	10	Normal breathing
	20	Rustling leaves
	30	Whisper
	40	Quiet residential community, freezer or refrigerator
	50	Rain, electric toothbrush
	60	Average speaking voice, air conditioner at 20 feet, sewing machine
	70	Vacuum cleaner, food mixer, noisy restaurant
Critical level: continual exposure can affect hearing	80	Lawn mower, hedge clippers, heavy city traffic, factory noise
	90	Truck traffic, shop tools
	100	Chain saw, pneumatic hammer
Immediate danger: exposure can injure the ear	120	Thunderclap, rock concert (in front of the speakers)
	130	Jet at takeoff
	140	Gunshot blast

Portions of this table are taken from *Noise, Ears and Hearing,* published by the American Academy of Otolaryngology — Head and Neck Surgery, Washington, D.C.

Special ear protection is a must for those who work in noisy environments, such as this welding shop.

There may be a direct genetic influence on the susceptibility of certain people to drugs known to cause hearing impairment (either permanent or reversible) as a side effect. Such drugs include aspirin, quinine, some diuretics, and some antibiotics, for example, neomycin and streptomycin. It is difficult to identify susceptible people prior to their exposure to these "ototoxic" drugs, and often the only clue comes from other family members who have suffered a hearing loss after taking medication. When a family history of drug-induced hearing loss exists, potentially damaging drugs should be avoided. It is also wise for anyone with a hearing problem to avoid such drugs unless their use is absolutely necessary.

Noise and Hearing

In many cases, hearing loss occurs as a result of trauma to the ear. Although direct trauma, such as a blow to the side of the head, may cause hearing impairment, the commonest type of trauma that results in hearing loss is long-term exposure to excessive noise. Indeed, noise exposure is the most important determinant of hearing ability once the effect of age has been accounted for.

The damaging effect of noise on hearing was first measured in blacksmiths in England in 1830. Since that time, it has been well documented that continual noise exposure on the job (or elsewhere) causes permanent hearing impairment if the intensity of the noise is high enough and the exposure to the noise is long enough. Initially, hearing loss is temporary, but with repeated exposure it may become permanent. The rate at which permanent damage occurs decreases as the time of exposure increases. The greatest loss occurs within the first five to seven years. The process then slows down, and after about 15 years have elapsed, unless exposure time and noise level are changed, very little

118

further noise-induced hearing impairment occurs. Generally, both ears are equally damaged; initial hearing loss occurs in the high frequencies, and later the low frequencies are affected.

If you work in a noisy environment, you should wear ear protectors and have an annual hearing test. Generally, noise is loud enough to damage your hearing if you have to raise your voice over background noise to make yourself heard. A slight hearing loss, ear pain, or ringing in your ears after noise exposure also indicates that irreversible damage may occur if special precautions are not taken. Earplugs or special earmuff-like "ear defenders" provide from 15 to 25 decibels of protection. Ordinary cotton is too porous to make a good earplug and is not recommended. Since the initial hearing loss is in the high-frequency range, early symptoms include difficulty in understanding the higher-pitched voices of women and children. Because the damage occurs gradually, it is easy to remain unaware of the developing problem.

With loud pulsed sounds, such as explosions, gunfire, or riveting, the situation is more complicated. As in the case of exposure to constant noise, the hearing impairment that pulsed noises cause may be restricted to the high frequencies. However, it is also possible to have both a high-frequency and a low-frequency loss or, sometimes, a predominantly low-frequency loss. The ultimate effect may not be predictable for several months after the period of acoustic trauma has occurred. Again, earplugs, ear defenders, or both should be used to minimize damage.

Background noise is loud enough to damage your hearing if you have to raise your voice to make yourself heard.

Hearing Loss in Children

Several types of infections that can cause hearing impairment are especially common in children. Some of these infections can be acquired prenatally (before the child is born). The prenatal infection that is most likely to cause hearing impairment is rubella (commonly known as German measles). Over 50 percent of infants infected with rubella before birth have some form of hearing problem. If women are immunized against rubella before they become pregnant, such birth defects can be prevented. Appropriate rubella immunization programs could eventually eliminate the disease as a cause of hearing impairment.

Prenatal infection with the virus known as cytomegalovirus, or CMV, can also cause hearing impairment. However, only a small percentage of unborn babies become infected if their mother does. Some of these babies are left with impaired hearing, and often, other handicaps are present as well. Unfortunately, preventing CMV infections in pregnant women is very complicated. One vaccine available uses live CMV virus and is effective, but the virus may persist in the body and cause an infection at a later time. Using a killed virus for the vaccine circumvents this problem, but the current killed-virus vaccines provide the mother with only a low level of protection from CMV infections.

Postnatal infections that cause hearing impairment include meningitis, measles, mumps, and various forms of the condition called otitis media. Meningitis (inflammation of the membranes around the brain and spinal cord) is a major cause of hearing impairment in young children, especially the type of meningitis caused by bacteria. Early diagnosis and treatment, however, can reduce the likelihood of any hearing loss.

Measles may cause a sensorineural hearing impairment if the infection spreads to the brain. This type of hearing loss can best be prevented by immunizing all children against measles. Similarly, mumps may cause sensorineural hearing impairment, usually in only one ear. Although hearing loss occurs in 5 to 25 percent of mumps cases, partial recovery occurs in 50 to 90 percent of the affected children. Again, vaccination against mumps can eliminate this risk.

One of the commonest types of conductive hearing impairment in children results from a collection of fluid in the middle ear because of ineffective functioning of the eustachian tube. If the fluid becomes infected, the condition is known as otitis media. It is often very painful, and occasionally the eardrum may even burst. Fortunately, the resulting hole usually heals spontaneously. If it does not, a new eardrum must be made surgically, using the outer membrane of nearby muscle tissue.

One-fifth of four-year-olds entering preschool programs have a mild hearing loss from recurrent ear infections.

It has been estimated that in the United States approximately one-fifth of children entering preschool programs at age 4 to 4½ have a mild conductive hearing loss because of recurrent episodes of otitis media. This hearing problem may affect their development of language skills. However, otitis media can usually be treated with antibiotics or, in certain cases, by making a tiny incision in the eardrum and inserting a small tube. This tiny tube allows air to ventilate the middle ear cavity until reduced swelling permits normal functioning of the eustachian tube to return.

For many other hearing-impaired children—and adults—the cause of hearing loss cannot be determined. Nevertheless, everyone with a hearing problem should be monitored on a regular basis by a doctor and an audiologist. The doctor can identify any anatomical abnormalities of the ear, and the audiologist can evaluate hearing limits. Appropriate recommendations can then be made.

Symptoms and Effects

The insidious nature of hearing impairment often makes early detection difficult. Initially, an individual may not recognize that a hearing problem exists. In the case of a hearing-impaired child, it is the parents who must watch for signs of hearing difficulty. Both normal and hearing-impaired infants pass through the same early stages of language development. Both will coo and babble, and then, at about seven months of age, the amount of babbling will decrease. Normal infants will then begin to mimic sounds, and more sophisticated language skills will start to develop. Severely hearing-impaired children, on the other hand, will fall behind in speech and language acquisition and may even resort to a system of gestures to express themselves. They may not respond to loud voices or sounds and may appear to be oblivious to those around them. Behavioral problems may arise, and unless care is taken, such children may be erroneously labeled "hyperactive."

Children with only a mild or moderate hearing loss (especially if it is in the high frequencies) may hide the handicap for a much longer time because they appear to respond well to the noises they do hear. It is only when parents recognize that there are problems with speech and vocabulary development that the hearing problem is detected. This is unfortunate, because children with this type of problem can probably benefit more than children with a severe loss if hearing aids are fitted at an early age.

Good hearing in the high frequencies is very important because high-frequency sounds play a major role in speech intelligibility. The most informative parts of speech, consonants such as *s, f,* and *th,* are high-frequency sounds. Vowels, in comparison, impart less information and are of lower frequency. The intensity (or loudness) of the high-frequency consonants, however, is less than that of the low-frequency vowels. To compare the plight of someone with a high-frequency hearing loss to someone with a low-frequency hearing loss, first read aloud the sentence "The red fox jumped over the white fence," omitting the consonants. The sentence becomes unintelligible. Now repeat it again with the consonants and only one vowel sound, such as *ah.* The sentence, though strange, is understandable.

The first case, illustrating a high-frequency hearing loss, shows how difficult it is for a child with this problem to learn speech and to acquire expressive language without help. If the loss is less severe but still in the high-frequency range, the child may acquire expressive language, but this will be largely unintelligible to others. With an even milder high-frequency loss, the only clue that a problem exists may be sound substitutions. "Dish" is pronounced as "ditch," "seat" as "heat," and "sea" as "tree," because that is how the child hears the words. Such a child may be judged inattentive or "slow," when in fact the problem is a hearing impairment.

Hearing damage in adults usually develops over several years. The high frequencies are generally affected first, and this causes frequent misunderstandings and makes everyday social interaction frustrating. Other signs of a possible problem include intermittent or continuous ringing in the ears (caused by damage to hair cells in the cochlear duct) and difficulty in understanding conversation in a noisy environment.

If you suspect that you, or someone around you, may have a hearing problem, it is important to have this checked by a doctor. Anyone can be tested, even a baby. Hearing can be checked by computer (this method is used for babies and those incapable of cooperating), or conventional testing can be done in a soundproof booth. The importance of these tests cannot be overstated. If a hearing problem is found, it can be evaluated and treated, but the patient must take the first step. Additional information on hearing impairment is available from the American Academy of Otolaryngology—Head and Neck Surgery, 1101 Vermont Avenue, NW, Washington, D.C. 20005. □

If you suspect you have a hearing problem, you should be checked by a doctor.

SUGGESTIONS FOR FURTHER READING

BURNS, WILLIAM. *Noise and Man.* Philadelphia, Lippincott, 1973.

CANFIELD, NORTON. *Hearing: A Handbook for Laymen.* Garden City, N.Y., Doubleday, 1959.

NORTHERN, JERRY L., and MARION P. DOWNS. *Hearing in Children.* Baltimore, Williams & Wilkins, 1978.

YOST, WILLIAM A., and DONALD W. NIELSEN. *Fundamentals of Hearing: An Introduction.* New York, Holt, Rinehart & Winston, 1977.

CONTROLLING PAIN

C. Richard Chapman, Ph.D.

ILLUSTRATION BY ROBERT SHORE

Pain is a common but unpleasant experience that becomes increasingly familiar as we age. Although we think of it as a physical sensation and associate it with bodily injury, it involves emotional upset and mental anguish as well. Pain can help protect us from injury and disease by providing a valuable warning signal when we hurt ourselves or become ill, but it can also cause prolonged suffering that serves no useful purpose. Despite the great strides made by modern medical science, many accident victims, burn patients, and people with arthritis, cancer, and other diseases still suffer significantly, as do many women undergoing childbirth, patients recovering from surgery, and others whose pains cannot be safely or satisfactorily brought under control by drugs and other treatment. The conquest of pain remains one of the major challenges faced by medicine today.

The physical conditions that give rise to pain are many and varied; however, researchers find it useful to speak of two general types of pain: acute and chronic. The causes, nature, medical diagnosis, and treatment of the two types are very different. Acute pain is associated with a new or recent injury or disease, and it persists only until healing is complete; the pain accompanying most sports injuries and the pain that follows surgery or tooth extraction are typical examples. Chronic pain, on the other hand, is pain that continues beyond the healing of the injury or disease, sometimes indefinitely. Back pain is perhaps the most common example. Some diseases, such as arthritis, last over long periods of time, and the pain they produce is also considered chronic.

When pain is chronic, patients often become discouraged, irritable, and unable to function normally. Many people afflicted with chronic pain suffer fatigue and progressive physical deterioration as a result of poor sleep and disturbed appetite, lack of activity, and prolonged or excessive use of drugs. When the pain interferes with gainful employment, financial hardships often follow, and family life and friendships deteriorate as the patient becomes more and more preoccupied with pain and with ways of relieving it.

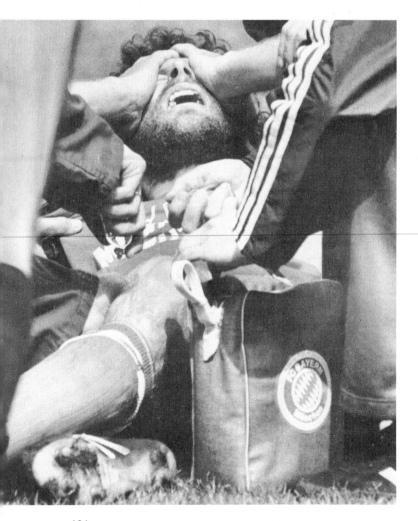

Acute pain, such as that suffered by the injured soccer player at left, will subside once healing has occurred. But the pain of the arthritis patient pictured below is chronic, interfering with the woman's daily life.

How Does Pain Occur?

Pain is the brain's response to special signals from the nervous system warning us that injury has occurred or is occurring. These signals come from two types of nerve fibers, called nociceptors, that are located in the skin, teeth, muscles, and deep tissues of the body. They are smaller than most other sensory nerves and comparatively slow in transmitting signals to the brain.

The faster of the two types of nociceptors sends warning signals that enable the brain to realize rather quickly that injury is occurring and to identify the injury's precise location. These signals, which are of very short duration, also trigger muscle reflexes, enabling us to withdraw our arms and legs from a source of injury even before the brain can receive and react to the warning signal. Thus, when you touch a hot stove, you instantly pull your hand back. Almost as quickly, you feel a flash of sharp pain. The second type of nociceptor sends signals that arrive more slowly but persist longer, often beyond the duration of the injury itself. This type of pain appears to serve a reminding rather than a warning function. It generally involves a more diffuse burning or aching sensation that comes perhaps a second later than the initial flash of pain.

Nociceptors are excited into activity when you experience a direct injury—for example, when your skin is pricked by a needle, when you bang your shin against a hard object, or when you tear a muscle or ligament during exercise. Diseases sometimes cause pain in a similar way. For example, a growing tumor may stretch a hollow organ in the abdomen or press tissues against a bony structure. A tumor can also create conditions in which nerve endings are deprived of the oxygen they normally get from circulating blood; this circumstance can cause nociceptors to send alarm signals.

More often, however, the mechanism involved is chemical. The inflammation associated with an infection, such as a sore throat, or with an injury in the process of healing releases chemicals that affect the nerve endings in the area. One type of chemical acts by sensitizing the nociceptors so that they can be excited by minor pressures or stresses they ordinarily would not pick up. Another type of chemical excites the nociceptors directly upon contact. These chemical substances, which also produce redness and swelling, cause us to feel pain in response to simple stimulation. They serve a useful function by compelling us to shun activity and rest our bodies when we are sick.

Natural Defenses Against Pain

Fortunately, human beings are not helpless victims of injury and disease, with no inner resources to control pain. Science has recently begun to understand how we can limit, or even eliminate, feelings of pain under certain circumstances.

Not all pain is bad—it can help protect us from injury and warn us when we are hurt or ill.

C. Richard Chapman, a psychologist, is a professor at the University of Washington School of Medicine in Seattle, where he also serves as associate director for research at the Pain Center.

Oddly enough, when injury occurs in the midst of extreme activity or stress, the injured person may not feel any pain at all. Soldiers wounded in battle have sometimes said that they noticed the warmth and wetness of blood before they actually realized they had been wounded. Similarly, accident victims sometimes deny they have been injured immediately after an automobile crash, only to find out later that they have suffered a broken bone, torn ligaments, or worse. Athletes occasionally sustain a significant injury during play but realize only later that they have been hurt. And in some ceremonies performed by primitive peoples and others, celebrants endure serious injuries while denying or minimizing any pain involved. In one American Indian tribe, dancers traditionally submitted to the insertion of hooks into the muscles of the chest; these hooks were attached to a pole that the dancer was required to circle in the ritual ceremony. Some African tribes still engage in mutilating rituals in which the skin is cut to form scar patterns that are considered beautiful; this seeming ordeal is endured with perfect composure and without evident suffering. Such examples make it clear that, at least in certain circumstances, human beings have within them some power to control pain.

Patients suffering chronic pain may be discouraged and irritable and unable to function normally.

Several systems in the human body may play a role in controlling pain, but our knowledge of most of the mechanisms involved is quite limited. The best known mechanism for pain control is a set of nerve pathways that run from the base of the brain (the brain stem) down along the spinal cord. Signals traveling downward along these paths, from a small area in the brain stem, block injury signals ascending to the brain from nociceptors. In effect, the signals from the brain shut a "gate" located between two structures in the nervous system: the peripheral nerve receiving the injury signal and the central transmission nerve in the spinal cord that carries the injury signal to the brain. When this happens, injury signals do not progress farther, and the brain does not receive information that gives rise to pain.

Certain types of painkilling drugs and certain natural pain-blocking chemical products manufactured by the brain work by binding themselves to special receptors in different parts of the brain—in particular to receptors in the brain stem, where they can turn on the pain-blocking system. The natural chemical products released by the brain are called endorphins; they are constantly at work, helping to reduce our sensitivity to minor injuries and muscular stresses and strains. When our endorphin production is too low, we may feel more aches and pains than usual, and some scientists think differences in pain sensitivity among different people depend partly on their endorphin levels. Of course, willingness to complain of pain is another matter; two people experiencing the same degree of pain may differ greatly in how they describe it and in how much they complain.

Can we learn to block pain at will? Although the brain can act to limit or prevent pain, this power is not usually under our conscious control. The one brain area we know of that influences susceptibility to pain is located at the base of the brain—not in the part where we do our thinking or imagining. Some scientists have speculated that the prevention of pain through hypnosis involves the control of this part of the brain stem through conscious effort, although there is no scientific evidence to support such a theory. A more likely explanation is that other pain control systems that exist in higher brain structures come into play.

How Painkillers Work

Because pain is a complex event, there are many ways to control it. One of the best-known ways is with painkilling drugs such as aspirin. Aspirin works in the tissues surrounding the nociceptors by affecting the chemicals produced during inflammation. It attacks those chemical substances that sensitize the nerve endings located at the site of an injury or disease; as a result, the nerves are less readily stimulated to signal an injury. In this way, aspirin can make a sore throat, a sunburn, or an injured thumb less painful.

Other drugs that work in the same way include acetaminophen (the aspirin substitute found in a variety of nonprescription drugs, such as Tylenol and Datril) and ibuprofen. Ibuprofen, previously available only by prescription, is now marketed in smaller doses as an over-the-counter drug in the United States (but not, as of early 1985, in Canada) under the brand names Nuprin and Advil. Still other painkilling drugs that work by desensitizing nerve endings are available only by prescription because they can cause severe side effects.

It is also possible to prevent pain by stopping nerves from conducting injury signals. This is often done by injecting a local anesthetic drug onto the nerve; the dentist's nerve block injection is a common example. Anesthesiologists also use such injections for the control of pain in surgery, for the treatment of painful conditions, and sometimes to aid in diagnosing cases of chronic pain. In some instances, they apply a local anesthetic to the spinal cord pathways rather than to the nerves directly involved at the site of the injury. Local anesthesia is highly effective and safe, but it cannot be used for long-term pain control because the drugs employed could then be harmful.

Relief Without Drugs

Electrical stimulation can also be used for pain control. Small, battery-operated stimulation units can be prescribed by doctors for patients to operate themselves. These units, which are smaller than a deck of playing cards, can produce electric currents that the patient can control by adjusting current strength and pulse rate. Electrodes are taped to the patient's skin, usually in the area of the pain. When the pain is chronic, many patients clip the stimulator unit to their belt so that they can use the electrical stimulation as often as needed.

It is not yet known for certain how this process (technically known as transcutaneous electric nerve stimulation, or TENS) acts to relieve pain. However, most scientists think it works by exciting the large nerves that carry touch and movement signals to the brain. A massive barrage of such signals at the dorsal horn of the spinal cord tends to close a gate against the signals from smaller nerves carrying injury messages. Some scientists think that electrical stimulation also helps release endorphins at higher centers in the brain, but others disagree with this theory. What is certain is that if endorphins are released at all by electrical treatments, it

People have some power to control or withstand pain. Without apparent suffering, this African girl took part in a ritual in which her skin was cut to form a decorative scar pattern.

127

happens only when certain combinations of pulse rate and current strength are used.

Electrical stimulation has proved useful for the control of certain types of postsurgical pain. Special sterile electrodes made of conductive tape can be attached by the surgeon alongside the surgical incision just before the bandage is applied. Electric currents can be started even before the patient awakens from the anesthetic, to help control pain during the first hours or days of recovery. Electrical stimulation can also be used for painful sports injuries and other muscular or skeletal pains and can serve as a supporting therapy for patients with many different types of chronic pain.

In recent years, physicians and others have increasingly made use of acupuncture to control pain, although there has thus far been little systematic scientific research to define exactly what conditions it can treat effectively. The procedure, which involves inserting steel needles into the skin and underlying muscles, originated in the ancient folk medicine of China. In Chinese folk medicine, physical disorders were believed to come from imbalances in the flow of "life energy" through certain paths that run through the body. Most scientists regard these folk beliefs themselves as of historical interest only, but the technique of acupuncture has frequently been found effective in relieving pain.

There are several scientific explanations as to how acupuncture may work. First, when acupuncture is combined with electrical stimulation methods, it differs little from the electrical treatments described above and probably involves the same mechanisms of therapy. Second, when used alone, acupuncture closely resembles the trigger-point therapy practiced by some Western physicians.

Trigger-point therapy involves identifying specific points in tight, sore muscles that, when pressed, cause a radiating pain related to the patient's complaint. These pain points are injected with local anesthetic or saline, and over a series of treatments, patterns of aching and stiffness, such as back or shoulder pain, may disappear. The acupuncturist uses a similar procedure when sticking the pain point with a needle over repeated treatments. What probably happens is that reflex patterns are activated and blood circulation altered in sore muscles, causing them to relax and heal.

Opiates and Opioids

Drugs derived from opium are among the oldest medicines for pain control. Opium, which is obtained from a species of poppy, has been given for thousands of years to control pain and to treat diarrhea and other problems. Morphine, a drug derived from opium, is still considered the most effective drug of its kind by most doctors, but new synthetic drugs, called opioids, are now available as well. They have been designed to provide pain control over varying lengths of time and to have certain special effects. Thus, opioids can be applied in many different settings, depending on the need of the patient. Like endorphins, these substances bind to many parts of the brain and to special receptors in the brain stem, where they turn on the pain-blocking system that shuts off incoming injury signals.

The latest methods of administering drugs may help doctors avoid some serious problems in the use of strong painkillers.

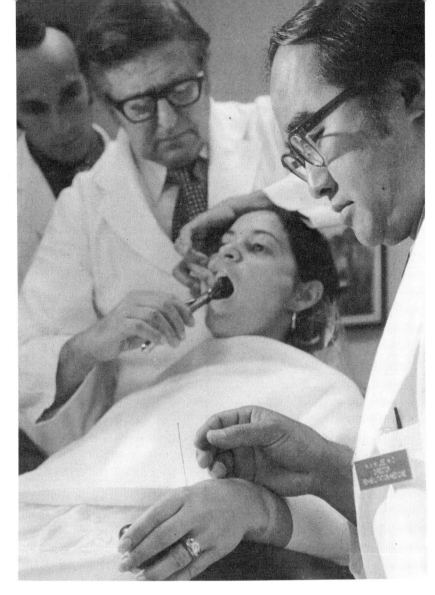

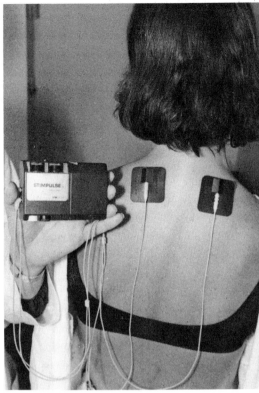

Inserting an acupuncture needle into a patient's hand (left) enables her to tolerate painful dental work without discomfort. The so-called TENS device (above) produces electric currents that act to relieve pain.

Because of their similarity to brain chemicals, the natural opiates and synthetic opioids are perhaps the most reliable way to control pain. However, they are suitable for only short-term use for several reasons. For one, these drugs bind to many different parts of the brain and body and cause extreme side effects, most of which are undesirable or even dangerous. Patients who take morphine, for example, experience confusion and mental clouding. Although some may experience euphoria, others feel restless and disoriented. Most experience varying amounts of sedation, depending on the amount of drug given.

The most serious problem associated with morphine is that the drug can reach a sufficiently high concentration in the blood to shut down brain mechanisms that control breathing. When this happens, the patient will die unless breathing is supported by medical equipment or unless a drug that blocks the effect of morphine is given at once. Another problem is that the body adapts itself to the presence of morphine over time. If patients use the drug for several weeks, they will require greater and greater doses to reach the same level of pain relief. As time progresses, they are thus increasingly likely to come close to the danger point where breathing may be affected. The prolonged use of opiates and opioids, say for a month or more, can also cause addiction. Doctors and nurses try to avoid this possibility, except when treating patients who do not have long to live.

New Technology

There are several new developments in the use of opiates and opioids to control pain. One development combines use of a computer in the administration of a drug to achieve better control of drug levels in the bloodstream. Ordinarily, when a single injection of a drug is given, the level in the blood is at first very high, causing undesirable side effects; the drug gradually becomes less concentrated, so that pain typically returns before the next injection can safely be given. In the new technique, a small computer is used with a drug infusion pump. The pump can inject a drug slowly and with precise control into the bloodstream, and the computer can control the rate of delivery so that it just matches the rate at which the patient's body clears the drug from the bloodstream.

There is a variation of this method, known as patient-controlled analgesia. With this system, the computer-controlled pump is operated by the patient, who pushes a button to get small amounts of the drug

In a system called patient-controlled analgesia, individuals can press a button to release a painkiller into the bloodstream. A computer is programmed to make sure that only safe doses are given.

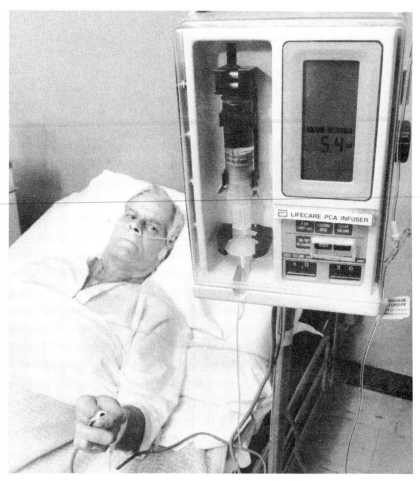

injected into the bloodstream. The computer's program sets a safe upper limit for drug levels in the blood, registers the passage of time, and remembers past doses so that the patient cannot receive an overdose. If the patient requests an unsafe level of the drug, the computer will refuse to deliver it. The computer can also be used to print out a detailed record of the patient's drug use for study by the physician or nurse. This technology is still new, but some scientists predict that patients using it will take smaller amounts of a drug and be less anxious about pain relief. Initial research on patient-controlled analgesia shows that the method can be successful in controlling pain after surgery.

Another new way for doctors to administer opiates and opioids is to inject the drugs into spaces in the spinal cord instead of into the bloodstream. The brain and spinal cord have canals and reservoirs of fluid that are connected with one another and with the brain stem center that blocks injury signals. Injections of small amounts of a drug directly into the fluid can provide excellent, long-lasting pain relief. Because the drug is not in the blood, it does not bind itself to other parts of the brain, and the patient does not feel sedated, confused, or emotionally abnormal. This method solves many of the problems involved with treating patients who have pain for long periods of time, such as cancer patients, since it allows doctors to treat them without problems of increasing drug tolerance, mental clouding, or sedation. However, because there is a small risk patients will stop breathing, in the United States and Canada this treatment is limited to intensive care situations or other settings where there is constant supervision of patients.

Multidisciplinary pain clinics may help relieve the problems of the chronic pain patient.

Mind Over Pain

Psychological methods are also used to control pain. Among the most effective techniques for dealing with acute pain are relaxation therapy, biofeedback, and hypnosis.

Relaxation therapy involves teaching the patient to relax the muscles fully. When a person has a large wound after surgery or a major injury, the muscles in the affected area become tense and hard. This makes them painful, and the places where the muscles attach to bone also become sore. Muscle pain and sometimes muscle spasm commonly accompany pain after an operation. Pain can also arise from muscle as a result of emotional stress; a common example is tension headache. Patients who are taught muscle relaxation may be able to reduce their pain to a manageable level, or even eliminate it entirely.

Biofeedback is a technique that helps patients learn relaxation and other skills useful in pain control. In biofeedback, the body is attached by electrodes to electrical devices that can sense and measure muscle tension and other physiological states. These instruments provide constant feedback by means of tones or lights, so that patients attempting to relax can see from moment to moment how well they are doing. This approach has proved valuable for a variety of acute and chronic pain problems.

Hypnosis can be used to prevent the pain associated with many different conditions such as childbirth, dental work, or even surgery. It involves an interaction between the hypnotherapist and the patient, which usually requires practice over several sessions and full cooperation from

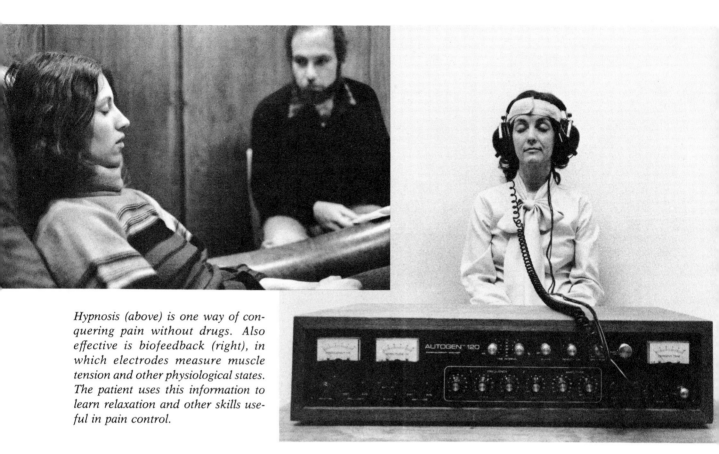

Hypnosis (above) is one way of conquering pain without drugs. Also effective is biofeedback (right), in which electrodes measure muscle tension and other physiological states. The patient uses this information to learn relaxation and other skills useful in pain control.

the patient. Just how hypnosis works to control pain is not yet known. It seems likely that hypnotic pain control uses higher-level brain functions rather than the brain stem mechanism that involves endorphins. Some research suggests that consciousness is partitioned during hypnosis so that patients deny experiencing pain at certain levels of awareness, while at other levels they can report it accurately. One explanation is that hypnosis involves such a strong control of attention that pain is excluded from the patient's explicit awareness, even though injury messages are received at deeper levels of the brain.

Chronic Pain

Pain serves no useful function when it persists beyond the healing of an injury or a disease, and its continuing presence can constitute overwhelming stress for a patient. In such cases, the nature of the pain's sensations typically change with time, and the patient becomes increasingly more helpless, discouraged, and hypochondriacal. It is still not known why pain becomes chronic for one person after an injury but not for another. Even more puzzling is the question of why some patients develop chronic pain without any preceding injury or disease whatever.

Psychological research has provided some important clues. Chronic pain patients often have a history of serious stressful events that occurred prior to acute injury or disease or to the onset of unexplained pain. Also, depression is often associated with chronic pain. Sometimes it precedes the pain; in other cases patients who develop persistent pain eventually become depressed. Chronic pain patients often sleep poorly, just as depressed patients do.

There are many forms of chronic pain. Back pain is perhaps the most familiar problem. In most cases, well-defined back injuries can be corrected by surgery, but many of the patients seen by doctors for back pain appear to have no physical problem that can be pinpointed and diagnosed. Some researchers attribute such pains to unobserved abnormal conditions in the muscles of the back. Others believe the explanation is at least partly psychological.

Although severe mental illness is rarely implicated, some patients can develop a habit of exaggerating their pains, complaining about them frequently, visiting doctors, and taking medications. Behavior of this kind brings them attention, sympathy, and, in some cases, financial gain through compensation or litigation. Over months or years such habits can become entrenched, and the patient may become addicted to prescription drugs or even injured or debilitated by repeated surgery. When this happens, the patient may need both psychological and medical therapy.

The treatment of chronic pain disorders has been a major problem over the years. Patients suffering from chronic pain usually should not be given treatments suitable for acute pain, such as opiate or opioid drugs or surgery; such measures will rarely succeed and often make the patient worse. Treatments that help relieve chronic pain are often therapies developed for other purposes, such as antidepression medications and relaxation therapy. When the pain has gone on for many years, a comprehensive rehabilitation therapy is often needed. Pain patients need to rebuild their energy, stamina, and activity levels. They may need assistance in the restructuring of family habits, so that they can be treated as normal people rather than as invalids.

Multidisciplinary pain clinics have now been established in many medical centers in the United States and other countries. In these clinics patients are seen by specialists in several different areas of medicine, as well as by clinical psychologists and social workers. The various health care professionals confer among themselves to consider the problems of each patient from all perspectives and to develop a long-range treatment plan. In this way, the complex problem of chronic pain can be addressed strategically and comprehensively for the individual patient. □

The conquest of pain remains one of the major challenges faced by medicine today.

SUGGESTIONS FOR FURTHER READING

LIPTON, SAMPSON. *Conquering Pain.* New York, Arco, 1984.

MELZACK, RONALD, and PATRICK D. WALL. *The Challenge of Pain.* New York, Basic Books, 1982.

PRUDDEN, BONNIE. *Pain Erasure: The Bonnie Prudden Way.* New York, Ballantine Books, 1982.

SAPER, JOEL R., and KENNETH R. MAGEE. *Freedom From Headaches.* New York, Fireside Books/Simon & Schuster, 1981.

WHITE, AUGUSTUS A. *Your Aching Back: A Doctor's Guide to Relief.* New York, Bantam Books, 1983.

Identifying Mental Problems

Bruce Shapiro, M.D.

Today, there is more help available for the mentally ill than ever before. Psychiatrists and other mental health professionals have made significant advances in accurately identifying the various types of mental disorders. Researchers have developed effective treatments for many of them. But treatment for a mental problem can be of help only if it is used. And it can be used only if the existence of the problem is recognized.

As is the case with physical illness, the earlier a mental problem is recognized and treatment begun, the greater the chances for quick and sustained recovery. Of course, determining exactly what is wrong with a seriously troubled individual is a job for a specialist. Knowing when and how to help an emotionally disturbed or confused friend or loved one to seek treatment, however, is a problem that potentially concerns everybody.

Bruce Shapiro is clinical director of the Department of Psychiatry of the Psychiatric Institute at the Westchester County Medical Center in Valhalla, N.Y., and associate professor of clinical psychiatry at New York Medical College in Valhalla.

Recognizing the Need for Help

Probably 15 to 20 percent of the U.S. population suffers from some form of mental illness. Many of these individuals have physical disorders as well as mental difficulties; studies reveal that a significant proportion of those admitted to hospitals with mental disorders also have physical illnesses that had not previously been detected. The majority of visits to family physicians are actually due to unrecognized emotional disorders; often, for example, headaches, abdominal pains, or stomach problems reflect underlying anxiety or depression. On a practical level, early recognition and treatment of mental disorders may be life-saving: a person with severe depression runs a significant risk of suicide.

When someone has a mental illness, that person's spouse, parents, children, other loved ones, and employer are almost always affected. Estimates of the loss to the U.S. economy each year from mental disorders run in the billions of dollars.

Many people, however, will suffer from the pain of mental illness for years before consulting a psychiatrist or psychologist. Some may never do so. At least part of the reason for this is the continued prevalence of age-old myths and misunderstandings about what mental illness is and how it should be treated. People often do not want to recognize it in family or friends because of the stigma it unfortunately carries in the minds of many. Some still believe the notion that those suffering from anxiety or depression just do not have "enough willpower." The fact is that a person cannot stop being depressed simply by wanting to stop. There is no reason for the parents of a child suffering from some form of psychosis (that is, seriously out of touch with reality) to feel responsible for the problem, yet such guilt feelings are still commonly found.

The plain truth is that mental disorders are real illnesses and that effective treatments are often available. Scientists' knowledge of mental illnesses has come a long way since the Middle Ages, when they were often attributed to demonic possession or witchcraft.

Many people feel nervous about seeking help from a psychiatrist. But psychiatrists are simply skilled professionals who have been trained to evaluate, diagnose, and treat mental disorders. The initial consultation is usually enough to calm most nervousness, and people often report they are glad that they finally got their concerns off their chest.

Mental illness, of course, is a broad concept that encompasses a number of different problems having different symptoms. In reading the following descriptions, with early warning signs, of some of the more common mental disorders, it should be kept in mind that such factors as a person's age can affect how the illnesses first reveal themselves. A child who is depressed will most likely exhibit some change in behavior or complain of a physical problem (such as a stomachache); the child's face may express unhappiness, but otherwise there generally will not be any explicit signs of sadness or lowering of mood. In contrast, a depressed adult will often display a "blue mood" that is clearly identifiable as depression. Among the elderly, however, depression may be manifested more in a loss of memory or concentration, sometimes leading to a misdiagnosis of senility. Socioeconomic differences can influence how readily symptoms are recognized. A wealthy suburban housewife with severe depression or agoraphobia (fear of being alone or in public places from which escape might be difficult) might not attract notice for years, while a young male laborer's job performance and manner of relating to others might be immediately impaired.

Recognizing Schizophrenia

Schizophrenia is a major mental disorder, or psychosis, in which an individual loses touch with reality and shows a deterioration in ability to function. Early signs of it usually become apparent in late adolescence or the early 20's. As time passes, the person becomes increasingly isolated or withdrawn from others and exhibits odd behavior. Delusions may develop that cannot be overcome by logic or reasoning. People suffering from schizophrenia may look or act as if they hear voices or see things that are not there. Many tend to have a rather dull expression except when they are upset.

These changes in behavior sometimes begin abruptly, but more often their onset occurs over a period of months. An abrupt personality change

may signal a drug-induced psychosis, a manic-depressive psychosis, or some other psychosis that may or may not eventually turn out to be a schizophrenic illness. Moreover, the sullen rebelliousness and inner turmoil sometimes seen in teenagers can be difficult to differentiate from the onset of schizophrenia; distinguishing between them may require the services of a specialist who has experience in dealing with adolescent patients.

People falling victim to schizophrenic disorders may not understand that they are becoming ill or may attribute what is happening to them to external factors—a typical comment is "Someone is planting these thoughts in my mind." Thus, it is often the family that must first bring the problem to medical attention. On the other hand, those suffering from schizophrenia who begin to experience severe anxiety or depression may ask for help directly. When schizophrenics do not realize that they are ill and refuse to seek assistance, a family member would be well advised to consult with a psychiatrist or other mental health professional on how to bring the person to treatment. The local mental health association or a hospital psychiatric outpatient department may be of help to the family.

It is always useful, and sometimes necessary, for the family to seek professional guidance and to educate itself on the problem before the sick individual comes for treatment. The first consultation with the psychiatrist may have to take place without the patient's being present. To deal with cases where the schizophrenic person refuses any consultation or treatment, some communities have mobile crisis-intervention centers based in hospitals that will come to the home in an attempt to get treatment started.

Acute psychotic attacks are possible, in which people seem to be capable of harming themselves or appear threatening to others. If such a person refuses help, the local police may have to be called to bring the individual to a psychiatric or general emergency room for psychiatric evaluation. Many hospitals have either a psychiatrist or a psychiatric resident on duty or on call; others can usually transfer the uncooperative patient to a hospital where there is a psychiatrist on duty. Hospitalization is sometimes needed; at other times it is possible to stabilize the person with intensive daily outpatient treatment, but this decision must be made with the help of a qualified psychiatrist.

Recognizing Mania

Attacks of mania may be encountered, along with periods of depression, in manic-depressive illness. In the manic state people experience an elated or irritable, overactive "high" in which they lose touch with reality. In the depressed state, by contrast, they may feel "blue" or "down in the dumps," they may no longer take an interest in or enjoy their usual pursuits, and they may become less active. Today, specialists tend to use the term "bipolar disorder" for manic-depressive illness, in reference to the fact that those who suffer from it swing between the elated (high) pole and the depressed (low) pole.

If the first attack in a biopolar disorder is a manic one, it is likely to occur between the late teenage years and the 30's. As in schizophrenia, family and friends notice a personality change. The change is characterized by—in addition to elation and sometimes irritability—rapid, "pressured" speech; increased, occasionally ceaseless activity; high self-esteem (which can develop into delusions of grandeur); and a decreased need for sleep. The individual may begin to act recklessly—spending a lot of money, engaging in indiscreet sexual behavior, making foolish business decisions, or driving carelessly.

As is common with schizophrenia, a person experiencing a manic attack may not recognize that he or she is ill, may deny that there is anything wrong, and may fight the notion of seeking assistance. In general, the manic individual feels "terrific" and sees no need for help for what feels like an excited, enjoyable state. Family or friends may be the first to sense the presence of mental illness and the need to do something about it.

People with an acute manic psychosis tend to be preoccupied with grand, unrealistic ideas or plans. They may have religious or paranoid delusions, such as imagining they are great religious leaders or believing they are being persecuted because of their great importance. Such situations often need to be handled in the same way as acute schizophrenic psychosis—that is, family or friends should get help from a professional, a mental health association, a hospital emergency room, a crisis-intervention team, or the police.

Symptoms of a manic attack include elation, overactivity, rapid speech, and sometimes delusions of grandeur.

Although the early signs of schizophrenia and manic psychosis may appear similar, the treatments used and the long-range outcome can be quite different. In fact, one of the basic rules of thumb in psychiatry is that people with schizophrenia often deteriorate in their level of functioning between acute phases; they may become more isolated, relate poorly to others, and show a decline in their ability to work. People with manic-depressive illness, on the other hand, often continue to function as well as ever when they are between attacks.

Treatments available for these major psychiatric illnesses include drugs, individual and family psychotherapy, and electroconvulsive therapy (also called, misleadingly, electroshock therapy). They can often restore afflicted individuals to excellent mental health. This fact alone should encourage anyone who is hesitant about seeking help.

Recognizing Depression

There are actually several types of depressive illnesses. One is the bipolar, involving both major depressions and manic states. If a person suffers from major depression without manic periods, the illness is said to be unipolar. Another type is the minor, or neurotic, depression, technically known as dysthymic disorder. A single individual may have more than one type of depressive illness. For example, someone may suffer from a neurotic depression for years while also experiencing two or three attacks of major depression.

Major Depression

With the onset of major depression, a person begins to lose interest or pleasure in activities usually found enjoyable. There may be a decrease in appetite and/or a loss of weight, difficulty in sleeping, irritability, episodes of easily provoked or spontaneous crying, slowed speech, or slowed body movements. Such individuals may sometimes show agitation, wring their hands, be easily fatigued, or experience feelings of worthlessness or of hopelessness about the future. Other possible symptoms include slowness in thinking or concentrating and verbal remarks that hint at suicide, such as "Oh, life just isn't worth living anymore" or "You would be better off if I weren't around." The signs of depression may appear quickly or over a period of weeks.

The majority of people who commit suicide show some signs of depression beforehand.

In contrast to a schizophrenic illness or manic attack, a major depression is usually first recognized by the person suffering from it. Victims of depression also are more likely to ask for help than those suffering from schizophrenia or a manic attack. Since depressed people most often realize that they are suffering from some form of mental or emotional disturbance and wish to be helped, it is generally not very difficult for their family and friends to bring them in for treatment.

Neurotic Depression

Neurotic depression involves a more or less constant sense of chronic unhappiness or inability to take pleasure in usual activities. It may occur in children, adolescents, or adults and usually is treated by psychotherapy, which helps those suffering from the disorder to face, and deal with, the reasons why they are unhappy. Failure to receive treatment often results in a substantially reduced enjoyment in living.

Suicide Prevention

Early recognition and treatment of depression can be major steps toward the prevention of suicide. Although it is true that some people who attempt suicide give little indication beforehand that something is wrong, the majority do show some signs of depression. It is important to keep in mind that suicidal thoughts are often part of the pain of a depressive illness and that such illnesses are some of the most easily treatable disorders known to modern psychiatry. In this sense it is appropriate to regard suicidal thinking as a treatable problem.

Recognizing Anxiety Disorders

People who begin to experience an anxiety disorder are themselves always acutely aware that something is wrong; the problem may also be obvious to others in their family, at work, or elsewhere. Phobias are familiar forms of anxiety disorders. Individuals with a phobia have a persistent irrational fear of an object or situation, which they try to avoid. By contrast, generalized anxiety disorders involve a more pervasive anxiety not occasioned by a specific object or situation. In what are known as panic disorders, an individual is beset by severe, unpredictable attacks of anxiety that extend to intense panic or terrified states. Sometimes anxiety disorders follow a traumatic event, in which case they are called posttraumatic stress disorders.

An anxiety attack typically couples a sudden onset of unexplainable fear with such physical symptoms as a rapid pulse and heartbeat, difficulty in breathing, a feeling of dizziness, sweating, hot and cold flashes, trembling or shaking, or feelings of lightheadedness and faintness. Sometimes, especially in initial panic attacks, people believe that they may be dying or losing their mind or that they may do something uncontrollable during the attack. It is not difficult to persuade those who have had anxiety attacks to seek help because they are often severely frightened and realize that they need assistance to feel better. Identifying the exact reason for the anxiety attack should be the job of a psychiatrist skilled in making such a determination, who will be able to recommend the most beneficial treatment.

Various forms of treatment are used for anxiety disorders, including medications, psychotherapy, and behavior therapy. It is most important that family and friends try to direct a person suffering from an anxiety disorder to a mental health professional who can provide reassurance that there is no danger of "going crazy" or of going "out of control." Although anxiety or panic may sometimes be part of a psychosis, the anxiety or panic state most often is not a sign of major mental illness.

Recognizing Alcoholism

A case of alcohol abuse or the more serious condition of alcohol dependence (alcoholism in the strict sense) can be difficult for the problem drinker to recognize. Beginning alcoholics often deny that there is a problem and fight with those who tell them otherwise. In fact, denial is frequently the major initial roadblock to their recognizing their alcohol problem and seeking treatment for it.

Signs of alcohol abuse include a need to drink daily in order to function adequately and an inability to reduce consumption. Alcohol abusers typically make repeated unsuccessful attempts to stop drinking and will continue drinking even if they have a serious medical condition that is made worse by it. They may go on binges where they stay drunk for at least two straight days. Blackouts may occur, in which activities while drinking are totally forgotten. Abusers drink to such an extent that they impair their job performance or social relationships.

If the drinking problem continues unchecked, alcohol dependence may follow. Tolerance of a given level of alcohol consumption and the need for more alcohol develop, so that withdrawal symptoms occur if alcohol intake is decreased. Alcohol withdrawal symptoms can range from morning shakes, nausea and vomiting, sweating, anxiety, and high blood pressure to becoming psychotic or delirious or having seizures and running the risk of coma or death. Prolonged use of alcohol can cause severe medical conditions affecting the liver, the heart, and the brain. The personal dangers in remaining alcoholic and not receiving treatment are obvious and devastating. No less devastating, however, are the effects of alcoholism on others. Alcoholics make poor spouses and parents and are often deadly drivers.

Alcohol is the most commonly abused drug, and people's reasons for abusing it are various. Sometimes abuse is actually a result of another disorder, such as anxiety or depression. It is not uncommon to see people begin drinking in an attempt to "treat themselves" for their anxiety, tension, or feelings of depression or to try to lessen an emerging psychosis.

Some alcoholics themselves seek treatment, but many refuse it, denying that they have a problem in controlling their alcohol intake. In such cases, the local chapters of Alcoholics Anonymous or Al-Anon (an organization for families and friends of alcoholics), local mental health associations, or psychiatrists can provide extremely valuable assistance. Other alcoholics unwilling to get help for their drinking may seek it for "family problems" or other reasons. If all else fails, this may provide a way of drawing them into treatment.

Anyone suffering from alcohol abuse should see a medical doctor to determine what physical effects, if any, the alcohol has had. Alcoholism rarely goes away by itself. Facing the problem squarely can save much suffering, and perhaps a life.

Recognizing Eating Disorders

Eating disorders have received much attention in the media lately, particularly the two known as anorexia nervosa (the "self-starving illness") and bulimia (uncontrolled binge eating).

Anorexia

The major symptoms of anorexia nervosa—which occurs almost exclusively in females (up to 95 percent of all cases) and generally appears in the adolescent years or the 20's—revolve around an intense fear of becoming overweight. Anorexics feel "fat" even though they clearly are not. They refuse to eat enough to keep their weight up to a normal level. They may exercise, use laxatives, or induce vomiting to lose weight, and the amount lost is extreme—over 25 percent of the original body weight. Some authorities put the death rate for cases that are not treated at over 15 percent.

Anorexics often fail to recognize that they have an illness. It is relatively easy for the family to see that there is a problem, but it can be enormously difficult to get the anorexic to accept treatment. Psychiatrists with experience in treating anorexic patients are a good source of help. Another, relatively new source are the clinics for eating disorders that in recent years have been established at some hospitals and medical school departments of psychiatry.

Treatment for anorexia nervosa may include individual psychotherapy, medication, and family psychotherapy. Of course, any medical problems the anorexic may have developed need to be attended to. Often anorexics can be treated on an outpatient basis, but in cases of serious weight loss, hospitalization may be required.

Bulimia

Bulimia usually makes its initial appearance in adolescence. It is characterized by repeated binges in which large amounts of food are rapidly consumed. The foods eaten are often sweet or high in calories. The binges may end with the person developing abdominal pain or inducing vomiting and are frequently followed by a feeling of depression. Bulimics, like anorexics, often try to diet, but they do not experience severe weight loss. Unlike anorexics, they are aware that their eating pattern is abnormal, but it is very difficult for them to stop the binge eating without outside help. As with anorexia, it is advisable to turn to an experienced psychiatrist or a clinic specializing in eating disorders for treatment.

Recognizing Hyperactivity

Children (most often boys) with the disorder commonly known as hyperactivity have a very short attention span for their age and are often quite impulsive. They are easily distracted and frequently do not seem to listen. (Because of the prominent role played in the disorder by problems with attention, specialists now call it attention deficit disorder.) At times these children can be highly overactive in a haphazard, poorly organized, and undirected way. When the overactivity is severe, they can be constantly "on the go," as if their "motor never stops running," and it can be hard to quiet them down. They often have great difficulties in school.

Children who have such problems should be seen and evaluated by a child psychiatrist or at a specialized clinic. They can often be helped to achieve relatively normal behavior through treatment aimed at reducing their overactivity and attention difficulties. It is important to understand that these children are not "bad kids" or children who "don't want to listen." They are suffering from a clearly defined and treatable psychiatric disorder. □

SOURCES OF FURTHER INFORMATION

The following organizations can provide assistance and referrals, primarily through regional and local groups and chapters:

Al-Anon World Service Headquarters, 1 Park Avenue, New York, N.Y. 10016.

Alcoholics Anonymous, P.O. Box 459, Grand Central Station, New York, N.Y. 10163.

American Psychiatric Association, 1400 K Street, N.W., Washington, D.C. 20005.

Canadian Mental Health Association, 2160 Yonge Street, Toronto, Ontario M4S 2Z3.

National Mental Health Association, 1021 Prince Street, Alexandria, Va. 22314.

DIABETES
Advances in Treatment

Ethan A. H. Sims, M.D., and Dorothea F. Sims

The numbers tell how serious the problem is. About 6 million people in the United States alone are known to have diabetes. An estimated 6 million more have the disease but don't realize it. Together with its complications, diabetes is now the third leading cause of death among Americans. The annual cost of the disease, including medical care and time off from work, comes to over $10 billion. The past few years, however, have seen impressive advances in doctors' understanding of diabetes, and there has been a veritable revolution in techniques for controlling the disease, particularly in the area of self-care. Diabetes is actually not a single disease but a group of disorders, all involving a defect in the body's ability to make use of glucose—a simple form of sugar that is the main end product of carbohydrate digestion and is one of the body's principal sources of energy. Underlying this defect is a lack of, or an inability to effectively utilize, the hormone insulin. In normal people, insulin is continuously produced by so-called beta cells, located in tiny areas of the pancreas known as the islets of Langerhans. The insulin moves through the bloodstream and attaches to the surfaces of cells in the body, enabling them to take in glucose for energy and the amino acids that are the building blocks for growth and repair of tissues. Insulin also promotes the storage, for later use, of extra calories—in the form of glycogen, a starch, in the liver and muscles and in the form of fat in fat cells. In addition to the continuous, steady secretion of insulin they provide, the beta cells respond to a meal—and the resulting rise of glucose in the blood—by promptly secreting more insulin as needed. By promoting the use or storage of glucose by body cells, insulin keeps the glucose level in the blood within a normal range. Other hormones in the body counterbalance the action

---

People with diabetes are now able to monitor their own blood sugar levels with portable kits.

of insulin. An example is glucagon, which is secreted by "alpha cells" in the islets of Langerhans, particularly when blood sugar levels are low; it stimulates the release of glucose from glycogen stored in the liver, and its production from protein.

In diabetes, glucose tends to accumulate in the blood. At a certain point this excess sugar is passed into the urine, carrying water with it. The body's attempt to rid itself of the sugar through increased urination can lead to dehydration—and the extreme thirst that, along with fatigue, is often an early symptom of diabetes. Since food energy in the form of glucose is being flushed away unused, the person with diabetes may begin to consume more food as well as water, causing blood sugar levels to go higher still. The body's use of fats for food energy is also affected, and this can lead to a variety of potentially dangerous complications.

Complications

There is no cure for diabetes. Even with conscientious use of the accepted techniques for "managing" the condition, debilitating or life-threatening complications may develop after a number of years.

People who have diabetes, for example, are vulnerable to a unique kind of damage to the smallest blood vessels, the capillaries. Glucose combines chemically with proteins in the capillary walls, which thicken, impeding the flow of blood; at the same time the walls tend to leak proteins from the blood into the surrounding tissues. In the retina of the eye, such leakage can cause scarring and the formation of new blood vessels, which can lead to blindness. Similarly, damage to the capillaries of the filtering units of the kidneys can result in kidney failure. In cases of diabetes that are poorly controlled, glucose may be converted into other sugars that accumulate in nerve tissue, causing damage that can keep nerves from working properly. In the lens of the eye such a build-up may produce cataracts.

In recent years more and more doctors have come to believe that maintaining blood sugar at very close to normal levels, rather than just keeping it from

Ethan A. H. Sims is professor emeritus of medicine at the University of Vermont and a specialist on diabetes. Dorothea F. Sims is a member of the National Diabetes Advisory Board.

causing immediate problems, may minimize or postpone complications. There is strong evidence for this from animal experiments, but evidence from studies with humans is less decisive. In addition, it appears that some people are simply genetically more susceptible to various complications than are others. Still, as one researcher puts it, "No one has shown that normal blood glucose is harmful." Those who succeed in keeping blood glucose within narrow limits are motivated to persist by the fact that they feel well most of the time.

The Two Major Types of Diabetes

There are at least two main types of diabetes. Type I is characterized by loss of the ability to produce insulin. It is often called insulin-dependent diabetes, since the regular injection of insulin is essential for survival. (Insulin cannot be taken orally, because it would be broken down during digestion.) This type has long been the form of diabetes most familiar to the general public. It used to be known as juvenile-onset diabetes because it usually—though not always—develops in young people.

About eight times more common in the United States is Type II, or non-insulin-dependent diabetes. It was formerly called adult-onset diabetes, but it may develop in youth. Type II diabetes differs from Type I in that the main problem is not an absolute lack of insulin; people with Type II do produce insulin, but they have developed resistance to its action. Ultimately the pancreas may fail to make enough insulin, so that the situation becomes similar to Type I diabetes. Unless and until that happens, however, the administration of insulin is not necessary for survival, except perhaps temporarily during acute illness. Today, many adults with Type II diabetes are successfully managing their blood glucose by eating properly, getting enough exercise, and monitoring their condition with home blood tests. Quite a few people with Type II who are taking insulin could get along without it, particularly if they restricted their calorie intake and increased their physical activity. Such persons should be called insulin receiving, not insulin dependent.

When Type I diabetes is out of control, resistance to insulin similar to that in Type II develops within body cells. Conversely, when Type II diabetes is out of control, it becomes similar to Type I, in that the secretion of insulin is impaired. Thus, measures that improve one type may also improve the other.

One of the differences between the two types is that Type I diabetes is more likely to damage small blood vessels in the long run, especially affecting the eyes and the kidneys. In contrast, Type II diabetes is more strongly associated with disease of the heart and large blood vessels; among the possible consequences are heart attack and stroke, as well as gangrene, which can require amputation.

People with Type I diabetes are at daily hazard from wide fluctuations in blood glucose if their diabetes is not well monitored and managed. When a person who has Type I diabetes is deprived of insulin, the blood sugar level rises rapidly, yet body cells are unable to use the sugar for nourishment. Then, to overcome the lack of nourishment, the body turns to fats for food energy, and they increase in the blood. The breakdown of the fats produces small fragments called ketone bodies, some of them acidic, which drastically disturb the metabolism as they accumulate. Much sugar, along with vital salts and water, is lost in the urine, and the blood becomes increasingly acidic. Before long a condition called diabetic acidosis develops, which can result in coma and death if not promptly treated. The opposite extreme—too much insulin—may lead to low blood glucose with symptoms ranging from mental confusion to loss of consciousness. These two extremes do not occur frequently with the use of modern techniques of self-care.

An overweight person with poorly controlled Type II diabetes (most people who have Type II are overweight) will develop high blood glucose levels but stop short of acidosis, thanks to the action of the body's own insulin, unless there is an infection or a severe injury. Occasionally the glucose in the blood may reach a level high enough to cause severe dehydration of the body's cells, leading to a condition called hyperosmolar coma.

Coping With Type I Diabetes

The chances of a person's developing insulin-dependent diabetes are higher if there is a family history of this type of diabetes or if a number of close relatives have had babies with large birth weights. An important warning sign in lean women is the development during pregnancy of an apparently temporary diabetic condition known as gestational diabetes. About 40 percent of women who are not overweight and experience gestational diabetes develop persistent Type I diabetes within 15 years.

Onset. The onset of Type I diabetes is often rapid, with abrupt development of thirst, frequent and excessive urination, weight loss, and fatigue. It is often associated with viral infections during the winter months. While Type I diabetes typically appears in the teens or 20's, it may develop at any age.

Scientists are just beginning to understand why some people lose their ability to secrete insulin. Studies of identical twins suggest that long before diabetes becomes apparent, the body may develop an allergic reaction to the beta cells. A tendency for such a reaction to arise may run in families. There is some evidence that a viral infection, such as mumps or German measles, may first damage the islet cells. Then the body's immune system develops antibodies against the islet cells, attacking them as if they were foreign tissue and gradually destroying them.

Monitoring blood glucose. People with Type I diabetes have to assume the major responsibility for their own daily care. The greatest recent advance in self-care for diabetes has been the development of test strips that change color when exposed to a blood sample, the exact shade depending on the amount of

Type I diabetes, which requires the lifelong injection of insulin, often develops early in life.

glucose in the blood; these strips make it possible, at any time and place, to ascertain the blood glucose level simply and virtually painlessly—a drop of blood obtained by pricking the finger is enough. In addition, there is a new laboratory test for checking on blood glucose control over a period of several months, which provides more valuable information than the traditional blood sugar test done during a visit to the doctor. The new test makes use of the fact that some glucose in the bloodstream combines with hemoglobin, the compound in red blood cells that carries oxygen through the body. Since red blood cells last about 100 days in the bloodstream, measuring this glucose-hemoglobin combination—called glycosylated hemoglobin—can indicate what average blood glucose levels have been over several months.

Diet and exercise. Recent years have seen a marked liberalization of dietary recommendations for people with insulin-dependent diabetes. Formerly the recommended diet was relatively low in carbohydrates and high in fats. This tended to promote heart disease by providing considerable amounts of cholesterol and saturated fats. Doctors have learned that a more generous allowance of carbohydrates may actually improve the ability of the body to use glucose. Moreover, the form in which the carbohydrates are eaten makes a difference. Carbohydrates consumed in the form of large molecules of starch, rather than simple molecules of sugar, are generally absorbed more slowly and can be better handled by the body. There are some exceptions: the complex starches of potatoes have been shown to raise blood glucose levels quickly, at least when consumed alone, while fructose, the simple sugar found in fruits, raises glucose levels much more slowly than other simple sugars. Also, a recent study suggests that a small amount of sucrose, or table sugar, has no adverse effect on glucose levels as long as it is taken as part of a mixed meal. In general, however, people living with diabetes—as well as everyone else—should consume their carbohydrates in the form of complex starches. Another dietary element that helps slow the absorption of carbohydrates is fiber, or roughage.

Foods that are rich in complex starches and fiber include whole grain breads and cereals and dried beans, peas, and lentils. Preparing vegetable dishes at home from fresh produce and eating raw fruits and vegetables are good ways to make sure a diet has enough fiber, since processed fruits and vegetables tend to have much of the fiber removed.

Today, the diet recommended for a person with diabetes does not differ from the ideal diet for anyone else. Its usual nutrient composition is about 15 percent protein, 30 percent fat, and 55 percent carbohydrates, with a substantial proportion of starches, and it should include a reasonable amount of fiber. It is important that calorie intake be suitable to a person's stage of life. Obviously, a growing adolescent or active adult needs more food than a sedentary person over 70. The amount and timing of meals need not be rigidly controlled, especially when small doses of insulin are taken more than once a day, before eating.

Exercise produces an increase in sensitivity to insulin both during the actual activity and for some time afterward; making allowances for this helps the person taking insulin come closer to the goal of mimicking the insulin output of the normal pancreas and permits flexibility in daily life. Home blood glucose monitoring is invaluable in making decisions about insulin dosage, meals, and activity.

Insulin. The insulin used in diabetes has traditionally been drawn from the pancreases of

Learning to Live With Diabetes

Children who develop diabetes are encouraged to do as much as possible to care for themselves. The boy attending a diabetes summer camp (left) weighs his food to help him keep track of his calorie intake; the children at right use a doll, aptly named Sugar Babe, to practice the difficult task of injecting themselves with insulin.

animals, usually cows or pigs. Since it is not identical to human insulin, it may produce allergic reactions in some people. In addition, the body's immune system may react to the "foreign" insulin, diminishing its effectiveness. There are many new and purer forms of insulin now available that minimize such reactions. These vary in the duration and intensity of their effects and can be mixed in various proportions to provide a schedule of injections suitable for each individual. (In recent years many people have turned to multiple injections daily, in an effort to achieve better blood glucose control.) The latest development is the use of genetic engineering techniques to obtain human insulin from genetically altered bacteria. This "biosynthetic" insulin minimizes the chance of an allergic reaction and so is especially advantageous in cases where the hormone is used only temporarily, as in gestational diabetes. Moreover, a young person who starts out taking such insulin may be less apt to develop an adverse immune system response over the years.

There has been a wave of enthusiasm for the insulin pump, a device that delivers insulin continuously. The pump thus can mimic the constant secretion of "background" insulin in the normal body. The wearer can either program the pump to inject higher dosages before meals or inject the insulin manually, varying the quantity as necessary. With the aid of home monitoring, fluctuations of blood sugar can be kept close to normal limits. Such stability has been shown by some studies to retard the deterioration of nerve function associated with diabetes, as well as some of the retinal changes in the eye that can lead to blindness. Still, the degree to which complications can be reduced in the long run remains unclear. (A long-term study sponsored by the U.S. government is currently investigating how tight glucose control should be to minimize complications.)

There are, however, limitations and disadvantages in using a pump. Keeping a needle continuously under the skin of the abdomen may cause local infection and may be inconvenient for those leading very active lives or engaging in sports. Also, some technical difficulties remain; the incidence of diabetic acidosis, for example, appears so far to be higher than with other methods of strict control.

151

Perhaps the greatest advantage of the pumps in their present state of development is that people using them learn what it is like to feel well through close monitoring and better control. Comparable results, without some of the pump's disadvantages, can be achieved by multiple injections of regular insulin—with long-acting insulin also being used, to provide continuous background insulin. Many who have tried the pump are choosing this option instead.

New Horizons for Type I Diabetes

Much is being learned by scientists about the immune system response that seems to cause destruction of the beta cells and about possible means of blocking it. Cyclosporine, a drug ordinarily used in organ transplants to prevent rejection of the transplanted organ by the body, partially reverses the loss of insulin secretion in people who have had diabetes for less than six months. There is, however, a prompt relapse when the drug is discontinued, and cyclosporine's potential toxic side effects may make this "cure" worse than the disease. Development of drugs that could block just the body's immune system reaction against the beta cells, without the more widespread effects of cyclosporine, would be preferable.

It is already possible to determine whether relatives of those with Type I diabetes are at risk of developing the disorder. If antibodies targeted against the islet cells are identified in the bloodstream, diabetes will probably develop, although they may be present for up to ten years before the onset of the disease. When such antibodies are found, the lack of a prompt release of insulin in response to a test injection of glucose usually means that frank (that is, clearly recognizable) diabetes can be expected within a year or so. Tests allowing early identification of those susceptible to the disease will become more important when scientists develop a reliable and safe means of prevention.

Medical research also holds the hope of future advances in diabetes management. Development of a practical implantable sensor for glucose would be one such advance. Used alone, it could help a person with diabetes to "think for the pancreas." Linked to an insulin pump, it could lead to a true artificial

A regular exercise program, along with a healthful diet, is an important factor in managing diabetes.

pancreas. A glucose sensor that is apparently well tolerated in the body is now being tested in large animals.

Doctors have long looked to pancreas transplants as a possible cure for diabetes, and several hundred such transplants have been tried, although only a relatively small number have succeeded. Moreover, transplanting only the islets of Langerhans, rather than the whole pancreas, is becoming a real possibility. Scientists have learned that white blood cells accompanying such transplants help trigger rejection by the immune system, and destroying these cells by any one of a number of methods has greatly increased the chances for success. There has also been progress in growing pancreatic cells in the laboratory, so that adequate numbers will be available. Experimentation with transplanting such cells into humans has just begun, however.

Type II Diabetes and the Problem of Fat

The tendency to develop Type II diabetes is more strongly controlled by heredity than is Type I. If one identical twin develops Type II, the other is almost certain to do so eventually.

On the other hand, Type II diabetes is potentially the more preventable or reversible, since it is often brought on gradually by obesity and lack of exercise. It is most prevalent in affluent countries, where food is abundant and diets are high in fat and sugar. It is rare in less affluent regions of the world, but where urban living, soft drinks, and fast food have penetrated, Type II has increased rapidly.

Among people with Type II diabetes, 80–90 percent are clearly overweight or have too much fat in relation to their muscle mass. Some of their bodies' resistance to the action of insulin may be a result of having gained weight. When normal individuals in one research study deliberately put on weight, they developed insulin resistance, and consequently the amount of insulin produced by their bodies increased. People with Type II diabetes, however, have inherited a reduced ability to produce insulin promptly in amounts sufficient to overcome such resistance—even though the level of insulin in their blood may actually be higher than normal.

The fat cells of the body are not as resistant to insulin as the muscle and liver cells, and so the increased insulin continues to promote fat storage in them. Meanwhile, the liver keeps putting excess amounts of glucose into the bloodstream. If weight

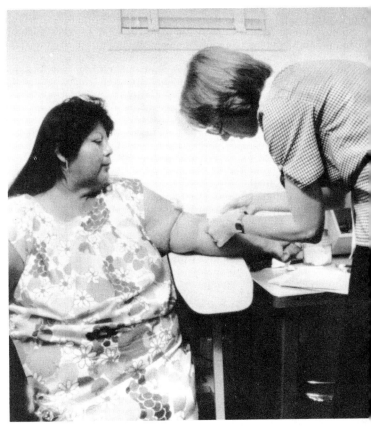

An overweight woman has her blood sugar checked. Obesity increases susceptibility to Type II diabetes.

increases further, so does resistance to insulin, and a vicious cycle occurs, with weight gains leading to worsening diabetes.

Coping With Type II Diabetes

Since Type II diabetes is strongly dependent on heredity, people with a history of it in their family should be alert for early signs of the disease. A pregnant overweight woman who develops gestational diabetes has a 60–70 percent chance of developing diabetes (often Type II) within 15 years.

Onset. Type II diabetes develops gradually, becoming apparent, or overt, only after considerable time has elapsed. Preventive measures should be instituted early and continued. A gain in weight in late adolescence or in the adult years is a warning sign. The accumulation of fat in the central areas of the body, rather than on the arms and legs, is particularly associated with later diabetes and hypertension. Fatigue, apathy, excessive urination, and change of vision herald the overt stage.

153

Successful actress Mary Tyler Moore, who has had diabetes for nearly 20 years, is active in the Juvenile Diabetes Foundation.

Diet and exercise. Since most people with Type II diabetes are still making plenty of insulin on their own, the key to managing the condition is to reduce the body's resistance to the action of the insulin. Toward this end, there is no substitute for a lifelong program of balanced diet and exercise.

For the overwhelming majority of people with Type II diabetes—those overweight—the critical element in diet is reducing one's intake of calories to ensure gradual loss of at least some of the excess weight. This is much easier said than done; there are powerful mechanisms within the body that resist weight reduction. These include a lowering of the rate at which food energy is used when food intake is restricted. And there is recent evidence that overweight people may lack some of the mechanisms that tend to protect others against gaining weight when excess calories are consumed.

In some instances the diabetic state may be reversed by a period of sharp restriction to a diet supplying just enough protein and carbohydrates to prevent malnourishment. In the long run, however, a balanced, low-calorie diet will be needed. As in Type I

diabetes, it is useful to include a high proportion of carbohydrates in the form of complex starches and a generous amount of fiber to slow the rate of absorption of glucose.

Restricting food intake on a daily basis means continual self-denial and is hard to sustain. Modifying a sedentary life-style to include some vigorous exercise, as well as an increase in the daily level of physical activity, can be very rewarding and a real help in maintaining weight loss. The net effect of a good exercise program is usually a reduction in appetite and in caloric intake, although this takes patience and persistence to achieve.

Various approaches can be used to improve one's physical condition. Household and other chores can be done in ways that include more stretching and moving. There is no need, for example, to use a riding power mower for a tiny suburban lawn. An elevator is not necessary in order to go up two flights of stairs. Sports enjoyed in one's teens and 20's may gradually be taken up again. Aerobic exercise is another good approach. It reduces insulin resistance and tends to normalize the body's processing, or metabolizing, of sugar, even though little weight may be lost. These aerobic benefits can be achieved by doing exercise that raises the heart rate significantly for 30 minutes, three times a week. Swimming, jogging, or vigorous walking are good aerobic activities. Individuals who are badly out of shape, however, should not start such a program without consulting a physician. It is important that any increase in activity be gradual, and when exercising, time should always be taken for warming up and cooling down.

Oral drugs and insulin. If an intensive program of diet and exercise does not bring blood glucose to within a narrow range, either oral drugs or insulin injections may be called for, as part of a combined approach involving both diet and exercise. The principles governing insulin use are essentially the same as for Type I diabetes.

Approximately a third of those who do not respond adequately to a conscientious program of diet and exercise will be helped by sulfonylureas, drugs commonly known as oral agents. They stimulate the pancreas to produce more insulin and act on the cells of the body to reduce resistance to the hormone. Much controversy and confusion has been associated with their use since a large study sponsored by the U.S. government showed about 20 years ago that, under certain circumstances, they may be linked to an increase in deaths from heart disease. Although the methods of that study have been criticized, the U.S. Food and Drug Administration has cautioned that the drugs may present possible cardiovascular hazards and has stressed that they should be used only along with treatment by diet and exercise.

A danger associated with using oral drugs and insulin is that they may come to be regarded as a substitute for carrying out essential changes in diet and level of physical activity. Both the oral medications and insulin promote weight gain, and a vicious cycle of increasing weight and increasing insulin resistance may develop. Blood fats may increase, adding further risks of complications. A person taking insulin or oral drugs must be constantly monitored to check for continued effectiveness and possible adverse reactions. Home blood glucose monitoring is as essential here as in Type I diabetes, and laboratory tests of glycosylated hemoglobin should be performed to check on overall control.

Type II Diabetes and the Future

The greatest hope for the future regarding "the other diabetes"—Type II—lies in the fact that it is beginning to receive the attention it deserves as a major health problem. Scientists do not yet fully understand what is cause and what is effect in Type II diabetes. The precise relationship between genetic effects and the effects of environment and personal habits must still be determined. Emphasis is now being placed on characterizing the different subtypes of the disease and on studying just how they come about, whether the genes that predispose a person to diabetes can be detected, and what measures of management are most appropriate. New education programs for people with diabetes are helping to motivate individuals who have to live with the difficult challenge of overcoming the dangers of overweight and inactivity. For cases where the body's energy production mechanisms do not function properly, current research on appropriate drugs for specific defects may prove useful. However, no single approach can be expected to solve a problem that is so complex.

Easing the Psychological Burden

The psychological burden of living with diabetes can be severe. For one thing, the disease interferes with people's flexibility in choosing their daily activities. Smoking, for example, is particularly hazardous for those who have diabetes, and they have to be more careful than most about their eating habits. In addition, no matter how hard they try to do what is right for their condition, there is likely to be a recurrent sense of failure, because the lack of a cure means that complete success can never be attained. People who have diabetes have to think for the pancreas for the rest of their lives. Growing recognition by doctors of these psychological stresses has led to a new emphasis on partnership with the patient. The fact that blood glucose monitoring can now be done at home gives people with diabetes more control over their condition. This permits doctor and patient to work out a treatment plan together. A sharing of knowledge and responsibility can lighten the burden of frustration and contribute to effective management of the condition. Today, those with diabetes who eat sensibly, keep physically active, and avail themselves of the latest advances in care may be in better shape over the years than many people who believe they have no health problems. □

SOURCES OF FURTHER INFORMATION

American Diabetes Association, 2 Park Avenue, New York, N.Y. 10016.
Canadian Diabetes Association, 78 Bond Street, Toronto, Ontario M5B 2J8.
Juvenile Diabetes Foundation, Parktown Place, South Building, Philadelphia, Pa. 19130.
National Diabetes Information Clearing House, P.O. Box NDIC, Bethesda, Md. 20205.

SUGGESTIONS FOR FURTHER READING

BIERMAN, J., and B. TOOHEY *The Diabetic's Total Health Book.* Los Angeles, Calif., J. P. Tarcher Inc., 1980.
Diabetes Forecast. Bimonthly publication of the American Diabetes Association.
LODEWICK, PETER A. *A Diabetic Doctor Looks at Diabetes: His and Yours.* Cambridge, Mass., RMI Corporation, 1982.
Progress and Promise in Diabetes Research: Report of the Second National Diabetes Research Conference, September 1983. Washington, D.C., National Institutes of Health, 1984.
SIMS, DOROTHEA F., ed. *Diabetes: Reach for Health and Freedom.* St. Louis, Mo., C. V. Mosby Company, 1984.
SIMS, ETHAN A. H., and DOROTHEA F. SIMS, eds. *The "Other" Diabetes.* New York, American Diabetes Association, 1983.

Hair

Up-to-date knowledge about hair can help us keep it healthy—and perhaps prevent its loss.

Lynne Lamberg and Stanford Lamberg, M.D.

During World War II a soldier suffered a hand wound that was repaired with the help of a skin graft taken from the side of his head. Some hair-bearing scalp was inadvertently included, and for many years the man found it necessary to clip hairs that consequently grew on his thumb. As he aged, however, the part of his scalp that was the source of the graft became bald, and the hairs on his thumb disappeared.

It was as if the skin of the scalp had a built-in timer that determined when hair would stop being produced. Scientists still cannot explain fully how hair grows and why it sometimes falls out, nor why it sometimes grows excessively where it is not wanted. But these questions are currently the focus of vigorous study. Such research, if successful, promises better treatment for the problems of too little, or too much, hair—problems that, because they affect appearance, often exact a heavy emotional toll.

Hair has just a few practical advantages. For example, it acts both as a permanent headgear, protecting the wearer from the sun, and as an insulator, helping to retain body heat. But hair is less effective than a hat—as much as 10 percent of body heat may be lost through the scalp on a cold day. The fact that large numbers of bald men lead a healthy existence suggests that a full head of hair is not necessary for survival.

In other parts of the body, eyebrows and eyelashes serve to deflect the sun's rays and keep out dust particles. The hairs in the nostrils also filter out dust. Hair in body folds cuts down friction from arm and leg movements, minimizing potential iritation. All over the body, hair aids in sensation. Hairy parts of the underarm and groin are the sites of specialized sweat glands—known as apocrine glands—that contribute to body odor and play a role in social and sexual recognition in animals, and perhaps a minor role in humans as well.

Fashion and religious beliefs play a major role in determining whether hair is allowed to grow or is removed, or whether it is adorned, braided, colored, or concealed. Only a quarter of a century ago, most men in the United States were clean-shaven; today, beards are commonplace. Popular male hair styles in recent years have ranged from crew cuts to shoulder-length locks. American women are more likely to remove their underarm and leg hair than are Western European women. Monks in some orders shave their heads, while in some Orthodox Jewish sects it is the women who shave their heads and wear wigs and the men who allow their hair to grow.

How Hair Grows

Hair is not alive; that is why cutting it is painless. Each hair grows in the lining of a pocket-like indentation in the skin called a follicle. Follicles begin to form in a fetus's third month, and their number is complete at birth. Every hair consists of tightly packed cells that contain large quantities of a fibrous protein, keratin.

At puberty, body hair becomes longer, coarser, and darker and begins developing in the underarm and pubic areas, as well as on the face in males. Scalp hair does not change significantly at puberty, although it may become slightly darker and coarser. There are three main types of hair, all present by adulthood: the soft, light body hair called vellus hair; the coarser and darker hair of the scalp, pubic and underarm areas, eyelashes, and eyebrows, known as terminal hair; and the short, bristly hair of the lining of the nose, called vibrissae.

In some animals, such as Merino sheep, hair grows continuously. In others, such as rabbits and deer, cycles of growth are synchronized; that is, hairs grow at the same time, and fall out at the same time. This molting process produces a lighter-colored coat in winter and a darker one in summer, so the animals blend into their surroundings for protection.

Lynne Lamberg is a medical journalist and the author of The American Medical Association Guide to Better Sleep. *Stanford Lamberg is associate professor of dermatology at the Johns Hopkins University School of Medicine and chief of dermatology at the Francis Scott Key Medical Center in Baltimore.*

HAIR ANALYSIS

The claims by some commercial laboratories that chemical analysis of hair can detect vitamin and mineral deficiencies are simply not valid. Analysis of hair does, however, have an established role in the detection of lead, mercury, and other poisons. In fact, the discovery of arsenic in a sample of Napoleon's hair has led to conjecture that he died from arsenic poisoning. Hair analysis can provide comparative data on the eating habits or the exposure to toxic substances of different population groups; it has been found that rural populations, for example, have lower levels of lead in their hair than city dwellers. And hair analysis can help in criminal investigation; hair found at the scene of a crime can be matched to a small group, thus narrowing down suspects.

In humans, by contrast, while some hairs are growing, others are resting. Each hair grows for a variable amount of time, then stops. When the process restarts, the old hair is pushed up and out by a new hair, which takes its place. The period of active growth is known as anagen and the resting phase as telogen, while the transition from the growth to the resting phase is called catagen.

At any given time, about 80 to 90 percent of the hairs on the scalp are growing, and 10 to 20 percent are resting. The scalp contains approximately 100,000 hairs, and 25 to 100 of them normally fall out each day. Because the follicles of growing hairs are intermingled with those of resting hairs, this shedding is generally inconspicuous. When a scalp hair is in its growth phase, the cell multiplication rate in the follicle is one of the highest in the body, with cells reproducing themselves approximately once a day and adding about half an inch to the length of the hair each month. Hence, a shoulder-length hair is two to three years old. Scalp hairs grow for about two to four years and rest for two to four months.

Sex and race account for certain obvious tendencies in the distribution of hair among different people. For example, men are usually hairier than women, and whites are usually hairier than blacks. Among whites, Mediterranean and Semitic peoples are hairier than Nordics or Anglo-Saxons. Asians and American Indians are the least hairy races.

Hair color is genetically determined. Whether your hair is red, blond, brown, or black depends on the amount, distribution, and types of pigment the hair contains, as well as on the way light is reflected by the hair surface. Nobody knows exactly why hair turns gray as the years pass. In most people, however, pigment production begins to slow in middle age. Heredity plays a role here, too; members of some families become gray earlier or later than average.

The appearance of hair is affected by the shape of the individual strands, which is also genetically determined. Round hairs grow out straight, while hairs that are alternately oval and round form waves. Hairs shaped like twisted ribbons are curly; the greater the twist, the tighter the curl. Extremely twisted stands have a wiry appearance. Chemicals are available that can make hair temporarily straighter or curlier by rearranging the bonds between molecules in the strands.

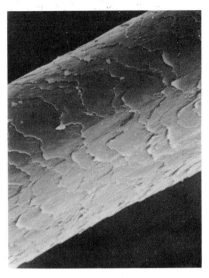

As revealed by an electron microscope, the outer layer of a hair is made of tiny overlapping scales.

How Hair Is Lost

A person may lose a substantial amount of hair, perhaps as much as 30 percent, without a change in appearance if the individual hairs fall out uniformly throughout the scalp. People whose hair is thinning in this way usually notice the problem before it becomes obvious to others; telltale signs include excessive quantities of hair on a comb or brush, or in the drain after shampooing. Sometimes, however, hair loss occurs in patches or at the margins of the scalp.

Particularly in Men. In both sexes, hair grows more slowly and becomes sparser with age. Thinning, however, is usually more extensive in men than in women and starts earlier, since female hormones have a protective effect. Male pattern baldness, as the common type of baldness in men is known, generally begins with a receding hairline. The first signs of this may appear as early as the late teens, and it affects four out of five

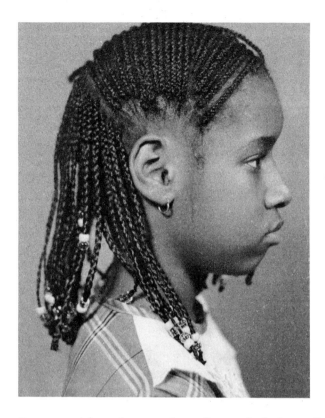

Cornrows, tight curlers, or other styling methods that pull on hair for prolonged periods can lead to thinning at the edges of the scalp; the hair usually grows back if the practice is stopped.

men by age 50. As balding proceeds, the hairline comes to form an **M**. The thinning of the hair on the crown of the head causes the point of the **M** to gradually recede, eventually producing the characteristic horseshoe of hair surrounding the thinned or bald pate. (Actually, the bald scalp is not truly hairless, since invisible short, fine hairs are present.)

The genetic factors that cause balding are complex and are thought to involve both parents, although the thatch on the son so often mismatches that on the father that some authorities believe inheritance from the mother's side is more critical. Balding is also racial: Caucasians are more likely to become bald than Asians or American Indians.

Even though, according to the biblical tale, Delilah robbed Sampson of his strength by cutting his hair, baldness does not signal loss of virility. In fact, baldness doesn't occur in eunuchs (males castrated before puberty), who lack the male hormone testosterone, which is thought to trigger hair loss as people age.

Particularly in Women. Pregnancy, as well as the use of certain oral contraceptives, may trigger sudden and profuse loss of hair. Both alter the body's hormone balance, often with the result that more hairs than usual continue growing, instead of shifting at the appropriate time into the resting phase. When the hormone stimulus stops—after the child is born or the pill is discontinued—the growing hairs simultaneously enter the resting phase. Typically about three months later, growth restarts, with resting hairs being shed en masse.

Thinning from hormonal causes generally occurs diffusely over the head, but in some women it is particularly marked at the crown. After childbirth or the use of birth control pills, hair usually returns to its previous thickness, but in some women the thinning is permanent. In most other women such thinning is delayed until after menopause, when the female hormone levels fall and the male hormones that are normally present in small amounts in women have a more noticeable effect. This female pattern baldness is not reversible.

An often temporary problem generally seen only in women is thinning at the edges of the scalp. This may be a result of the scalp's being damaged by a continuous tugging force, or traction. Women who curl their hair tightly, sleep with curlers, and use "hot combs" are most likely to develop this problem, and it can also occur in children who wear their hair in cornrows, tight pony tails, or braids or use tight barrettes. Hair usually regrows normally after the practice is stopped unless the hair follicles have been permanently damaged.

Perhaps less of a problem are the strong chemicals contained in hair bleaches, dyes, and curling and straightening agents. While some of these chemicals could potentially damage hair, most products available today generally are not damaging if used as directed. But leaving a bleach on too long, for example, could pose a problem.

Shocking Events, Drugs, and Disease. In both men and women, hair loss that occurs within a period of weeks is usually the result of a physical, chemical, or emotional "event" that occurred approximately three months before the hair began to fall out. Such events alter the normal hair cycle by shocking many growing hairs and causing them to enter a resting phase prematurely. These hairs are then shed after growth restarts.

Events known to alter hair growth include a high fever, generally 102° Fahrenheit or more; a severe illness; surgery, especially with a general anesthetic; and treatment with radiation and some medications. Hair loss may also be triggered by severe fright, such as from an automobile accident, by acute mental illness, by crash dieting, or by an injury that causes blood loss.

Sudden shedding of hair after a frightening event accounts for the false belief that hair can turn white overnight. Actually, once they are formed, hairs will lose their color only if they undergo bleaching by chemicals or strong sunlight. If, however, someone with both dark and white hairs loses a large quantity of hair rapidly, the white hairs that remain may appear more conspicuous. While it is unlikely that only dark hairs would fall out, it is possible that extreme stress could have a selective effect on pigmented hairs, and there have been stories told of persons losing only their dark hairs. If pigment production suddenly shuts down, as sometimes occurs after a stressful event, hair that grows in afterward will, of course, be white.

Medications associated with hair loss include anticancer drugs and certain epilepsy, gout, thyroid, and blood-thinning drugs. Large doses of vitamin A may also lead to hair shedding, as may the related drug isotretinoin (trade name, Accutane), sometimes prescribed for severe acne.

Anticancer drugs can cause hair loss because they have their most destructive effect on rapidly growing cells. This means that hair follicles in the growing phase, with their rapid cellular turnover, are particularly

KEEPING HAIR HEALTHY

- Eat a nutritionally sound diet. Vitamin supplements are not necessary if your diet is adequate.

- Brush or comb only as needed for styling; overly vigorous brushing may damage hair. Avoid back combing and teasing the hair.

- Wash gently, and comb wet hair carefully. Tangles should be eased, rather than pulled, out.

- Avoid brisk toweling, and don't overdry your hair with an electric dryer. Curling irons should be used as quickly and infrequently as possible.

- Trim ends regularly to minimize splitting.

- When dyeing, bleaching, waving, or straightening hair, follow package directions scrupulously.

- Don't sleep with rollers or clips in your hair. Avoid styles that pull hair, such as tight ponytails and buns.

- Wear a hat on the beach or at the pool—the sun can damage hair as well as skin. After swimming in a pool, shampoo to remove chlorine.

- Keep in mind that massage won't help hair growth and that wearing a hard hat or similar head covering for safety on the job won't harm it.

- If hair falls out suddenly or grows where it is not wanted, see your doctor.

A hairpiece is a relatively inexpensive "treatment" for baldness, while potions that claim to restore lost hair are generally worthless. However, a drug used to treat high blood pressure called minoxidil (being applied above) has shown some value against hair loss in preliminary tests.

susceptible to damage. Hairs produced at the time these drugs are taken typically have a thin segment that breaks easily; because 80 to 90 percent of scalp hairs are in the growing phase at any one time, sudden and nearly complete hair loss may occur shortly after treatment is started. Fortunately, hair almost always regrows normally after drug treatment ends; sometimes the hair is even more profuse and darker than before.

Many diseases can cause hair to fall out. When loss of hair on the scalp occurs in patches that develop within days or weeks and are accompanied by inflammation, the culprit is often an infection. One of the most common is the fungal disorder tinea capitis; it often affects young children and, as it is highly contagious, may occur in minor epidemics.

Sharply defined round or oval patches of hair loss without inflammation are typical of alopecia areata. This baffling disorder, which may develop anywhere on the body, strikes people of all ages. It is thought to result from an autoimmune reaction to the hair follicle—that is, the body's immune system attacks the follicle as if it were a foreign substance. While hair lost as a result of this disorder tends to regrow, about one-quarter of the time it falls out again at the same spot or elsewhere. With each attack, the likelihood increases that the hair lost will not return. Certain drugs may help alleviate the condition, but permanent and even total hair loss sometimes occurs.

Such diseases as seborrhea and psoriasis may cause severe itching of the scalp, which can lead to intense scratching and, sometimes, overzealous shampooing. These may in turn produce mild temporary thinning and may make hairs more likely to break.

Thyroid disorders and iron-deficiency anemia can interfere with hair growth; indeed, hair loss may be the problem that first brings a person suffering from such a condition to the doctor's office.

Some people, of course, simply have congenitally weak hair shafts. The resulting tendency of their hair to break easily may be apparent throughout life or may not show up until adulthood. Another possible cause of brittle and easily broken hair is crash dieting, which can rob the body of essential nutrients.

Diagnosing Hair Loss

Often a family doctor, internist, or pediatrician can readily identify the reason for hair loss after talking with the patient and examining the scalp. If not, or if the problem is severe, the doctor may advise seeing a dermatologist, a specialist in disorders of hair and skin. Dermatologists may use one or more of the following procedures in making a diagnosis:

Hair Pluck. The dermatologist removes a clump of ten to 20 hairs from the scalp and examines them, particularly their roots, under magnification. Resting hairs have a bulbous end, while growing hairs have a sheath of living cells. These hair roots will be counted to see if a normal 80 to 90 percent are growing and 10 to 20 percent resting. The hairs will also be

In some cases, an ice pack can help prevent baldness caused by chemotherapy for cancer. By slowing blood circulation to the scalp, it minimizes the effects of certain drugs on hair follicles.

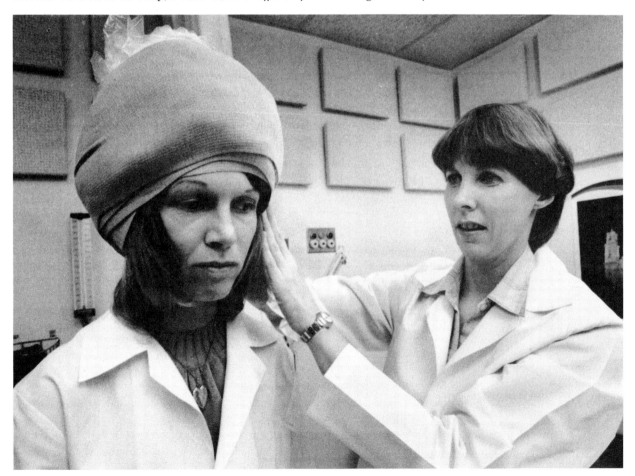

In alopecia areata, the body's immune system attacks hair follicles as if they were foreign tissue.

Severe cases of alopecia areata can cause total, permanent hair loss, which can be socially and psychologically devastating. The support group shown here helps its members adjust to the condition.

examined all along their length, to see if weakened segments, constrictions, or frayed or split ends are present. If the patient has an underlying medical illness such as thyroid disease, the hair may appear dry and lusterless, and the hair shaft may be thinned or shaggy.

KOH Exam. This test utilizes the chemical potassium hydroxide (KOH) to dissolve hair proteins, making fungi, if present, more easily seen.

Wood's Light Exam. Certain infections of the scalp appear greenish yellow when viewed under this ultraviolet light.

Biopsy. Here, a plug of skin the size of a pencil eraser is removed. In many skin disorders, skin cells viewed with a microscope have characteristic patterns. These include skin cancers, which may cause hair loss either by taking the place of normal hair-bearing skin cells or by damaging hair follicles.

Treatment for Hair Loss

No treatment is necessary for the shedding of hair in the aftermath of an illness, pregnancy, or stressful event; time brings a cure. Medication relieves some diseases of the scalp that cause hair loss. There is no way, however, to reverse the baldness that accompanies aging.

Although balding is controlled by hormones in the body, taking hormones internally can have unwanted side effects such as breast development and loss of sex drive in men and menstrual irregularities in women. Experiments with external use of hormones, on the scalp, have not been successful in producing hair. The hope of restoring hair to bald heads has fostered the development of hundreds of potions and lotions, all, so far, to no avail. In early 1985, in fact, the U.S. Food and Drug Administration announced that since all these nonprescription remedies for baldness were ineffective, it would seek to introduce a regulation barring them from the marketplace. Such baldness cures, an FDA spokesman said, were being produced and sold by "a lot of shady figures on the fringes of the medical profession," and although not actually harmful, they failed to meet the requirement that medications be effective. Researchers, meanwhile, have focused attention on drugs used to treat a variety of illnesses that have as a side effect the growth of hair in places where it is not wanted.

The most common effective treatment for male pattern baldness is the hair transplant.

One of these is the drug minoxidil (trade name, Loniten). When given by mouth to reduce high blood pressure, it often triggers the growth of hair on the forehead, across the bridge of the nose or elsewhere on the body. To investigate its possible benefits for baldness, the drug's manufacturer, the Upjohn Company, undertook a one-year study that enlisted 2,200 patients at about 20 medical centers across the United States. The treatment phase of the study was concluded in late 1984, and results are expected to be made available in 1985. The participants were carefully monitored for possible adverse side effects. (In its oral form, the drug sometimes causes fluid and salt retention and congestive heart failure.) Even if the drug is shown to work, and to be safe, Upjohn says it most likely would not be on the market before 1987.

Minoxidil may also prove useful in the treatment of alopecia areata, the disorder in which hair falls out in patches. According to a report published in April 1984, 48 people with severe, long-standing alopecia areata were treated at an Illinois medical center with twice daily applications of minoxidil solution to the scalp. In 25 of the 48 some hair growth resulted, and almost half of these developed enough hair so that they no longer felt the need to wear a wig or cap.. Additional studies, also sponsored by Upjohn, are under way at about a dozen U.S. medical centers, using stronger concentrations of the drug. Since the normal growing phase of scalp hairs lasts several years, it is too early to tell if the drug can truly restore normal growth and prevent recurrent hair loss.

The most common medical treatment for male pattern baldness involves transplanting "plugs"—tiny cylinders of tissue containing active hair follicles—from a still-hirsute area of the scalp to the bald area. The rationale is that the plugs will follow the growth pattern of the area they came from rather than that of the area into which they are placed. In most cases, plugs are taken from the sides or back of the head—areas

How Electrolysis Works

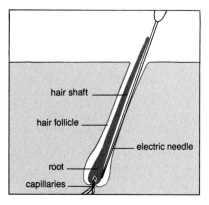

A very fine needle is used to apply a mild electric current to the base of a hair follicle, destroying the hair root and sealing off the capillaries that nourished it.

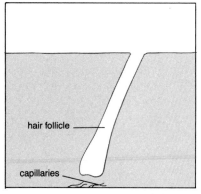

With the blood supply cut off, generally the hair will not regrow.

where hair growth tends to persist throughout life—and transferred to the front or top. In order that nourishment may reach their center, the plugs must be no larger in diameter than a pencil; they typically contain just five to ten hairs. Because it takes several hundred plugs to give significant coverage, the transplantation process is time-consuming and costly.

Sometimes a different procedure is used, with a surgeon moving a flap of hair-bearing scalp, approximately 1 inch wide, from the side of the head up over the top, leaving it attached at the bottom end to assure a continuous blood supply. In a third technique, the surgeon removes portions of the bald area and pulls up the sides and back of the scalp, bringing hair-bearing areas closer together.

The implantation of synthetic fibers into the scalp is often advertised as a permanent means of hair attachment, but it is not a medically approved treatment for baldness. Indeed, it invariably leads to infection and permanent scarring, since the body rejects the foreign material. The FDA has repeatedly issued warnings about these dangers.

What About Too Much Hair?

Some people's hair is naturally more profuse than others'. For example, it is normal for women of certain ethnic backgrounds, such as those of Mediterranean descent, to have some facial hair. The best way to tell whether a particular woman has excessive facial hair is if she has markedly more than close female relatives. Such an abnormal abundance of hair may be caused by a surplus of androgen-related (masculine) hormones. More rarely, a tumor of the ovaries or adrenal glands may be the cause; in such cases, the excess hair is usually accompanied by the appearance of masculine characteristics. Although the reason for the excess hormone production cannot always be found, countering the androgen-related hormones with other hormones, such as estrogens or corticosteroids, can sometimes be a successful means of inhibiting the growth of the unwanted hair.

Hair can also grow excessively as a reaction to friction (such as might occur under a cast) or as a side effect from a wide variety of drugs. But such increased growth can usually be stemmed by removing the cause.

Unfortunately, once they are stimulated, follicles sometimes continue to produce hair even after the instigator of the excessive growth is removed. No drugs are currently available to turn off excessive growth in people who are otherwise healthy. For this reason, such unwanted hair can only be removed or concealed.

The only safe, permanent method of hair removal is electrolysis, which destroys individual hair follicles with an electric current. Shaving is the most popular temporary method of hair removal. Depilatories, chemical agents that break down hair structure so that the hairs can be washed away from the skin, are often preferred for the face, since they leave the skin smoother than does shaving. Another method of removing unwanted hair is waxing, in which either a melted wax that quickly hardens or prepared strips are applied to the skin; when these are pulled off, hairs are drawn out of their follicles. Scattered hairs can be plucked out with tweezers. A different approach is to make unwanted hair less obvious by bleaching it. □

SPOTLIGHT
ON HEALTH

CHECKUPS
What to Expect

Richard E. Allen

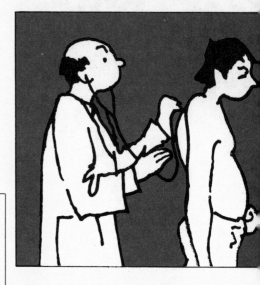

Should you ever see a doctor even if you don't feel sick? Most physicians would say "yes" (although there is less agreement about how often or exactly what your examination should consist of). A routine periodic checkup may pick up at an early stage—before symptoms develop—such potentially treatable conditions as diabetes, weight problems, vision problems, certain kinds of cancer, and high blood pressure. It may also tell if you have a heart murmur, which does not always require treatment but may mean you should receive antibiotics in the event you have to undergo, say, dental treatment or bowel surgery. Beyond that, the checkup fosters a trusting doctor-patient relationship and gives you a chance to receive from your doctor useful advice on good health practices.

Basic Procedures

What kind of checkup should a healthy person with no serious symptoms expect to have? Certain procedures, of course, are appropriate only for some types of patients—women, for example, or the elderly. Factors placing a patient at higher than average risk for some health problem will influence what the doctor looks for in the examination, factors like occupation, life-style, and family history.

Still, there are a few basic procedures common to most checkups, beginning with the taking of a medical history.

Especially if you're a new patient, the doctor will ask you for standard biographical data, as well as information about the health and longevity of your parents and other family members, your past medical problems, and any current symptoms or recent changes in, say, sleep patterns, appetite, or weight. (You should, of course, volunteer such information if the doctor neglects to ask for it.)

The actual physical exam will likely begin with a physician's assistant or nurse measuring your height, weight, and vital signs—blood pressure, pulse rate, temperature, and respiratory rate. This information, like the history, can help focus the doctor's attention on possible problems.

Problem areas can be identified.

The doctor will usually examine you visually for such things as deformities, bruises, or other skin abnormalities and then feel certain areas with the fingers and hands. This procedure, known as palpation, can yield clues of some respiratory and circulatory disorders, as well as reveal abnormally warm or tender regions and, sometimes, growths beneath the skin. In another technique, called percussion, the doctor will put an outspread hand on, say, your chest and tap one of the fingers with a finger of

the other hand, repeating the procedure in several areas. The sounds produced may help the doctor detect fluid in a body cavity, an abnormal mass such as a tumor, or the enlargement of such organs as the heart, liver, or spleen. Using a stethoscope, the doctor will listen to the sounds made by your heart, lungs, and other organs. You will be asked to inhale, exhale, take a deep breath, hold your breath, and so on as the doctor assesses certain lung functions. An unusual odor in the exhaled air may be a sign of a bacterial infection in the lungs or of diabetes.

The doctor ordinarily will note your posture and gait. A slouch or one shoulder held higher than the other might reflect an abnormal curvature of the spine. A person's walk may indicate the presence of a muscle or bone disorder or a problem involving the nervous system (which controls the muscles). The doctor may want to check the working of your nervous system in other ways as well. For example, a simple method of assessing whether you can utilize your muscles with reasonable strength is to have you do various movements with your head, trunk, arms, or legs against resistance supplied by the doctor.

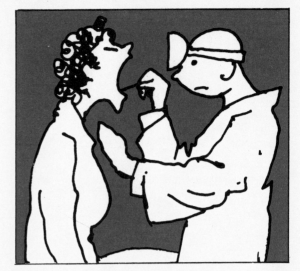

Checking your reflexes can be another way the doctor assesses the functioning of your nervous system. This is why the doctor may tap the tendon just below the kneecap with a rubber-headed mallet.

With the aid of special viewing instruments, the doctor may examine your eyes, ears, nose, and throat. (The reason you have to say "ah" is that this raises the uvula, a small fleshy projection hanging from the upper throat above the back of the tongue, giving the doctor a better view.) This part of the exam can be quite revealing. Telltale signs in the blood vessels of the retina of the eye, for example, may give early warning of diabetes, hypertension, or heart disease.

Some Special Tests

A checkup may include more elaborate procedures involving special equipment or laboratory analysis. Among the more familiar of these are blood tests, urinalysis, X rays, and electrocardiograms.

Laboratory blood tests can reveal many things. For example, a complete blood count yields information about the number, size, and shape of red blood cells; the number of white blood cells; and the proportions of the different kinds of white blood cells. A shortage of red blood cells could be a sign of anemia, perhaps caused by an underlying disease or by an iron or vitamin deficiency. An abnormal white blood cell count may be a sign of infection, leukemia, or some other disorder. Blood can be analyzed for a great many other substances, such as excess sugar (a possible sign of diabetes) or cholesterol and triglycerides (fatty substances that play a role in some types of heart disease). The blood to be tested, seldom more than one or two teaspoonfuls, is usually drawn from a vein in the arm. You may be asked to fast overnight for these blood tests.

Analysis of the urine can reveal information about a number of body systems. Signs of kidney and bladder problems or of diabetes, for example, may be found. The urine sample may be taken in the doctor's office, or you may be asked to bring one in. The doctor's instructions concerning the time of day to take the sample and whether or not to eat or drink beforehand should be followed faithfully, since the daily round of eating, drinking, and sleeping affects the composition of the urine.

Chest X rays can yield valuable information about the heart and lungs. They have not generally been able to help in the early detection of lung cancer, however, and many authorities have argued that their routine use is probably not worthwhile. Less controversial, though, are chest X rays for people with symptoms of heart or lung problems, patients who show evidence of such problems in a physical examination, and individuals in certain high-risk groups, such as smokers, asbestos workers, and coal miners.

Also part of some checkups is an electrocardiogram. In an ECG (or EKG), sensors attached to your chest, arms, and legs pick up the small electric current produced by your heartbeat; this is then translated into a series of tracings on a moving roll of paper. By interpreting the tracings, the doctor can sometimes detect a heart abnormality. The ECG is more sensitive in detecting disease if it is done when you're exercising on a treadmill or stationary bicycle (stress ECG) than when you're lying down (resting ECG). Even the stress ECG, however, will sometimes not detect existing heart disease. In fact, some experts have argued against the routine use of the test for people without heart disease symptoms. Nonetheless, many doctors advise at least having a "baseline" ECG done in mid-life, to be used for comparison if an ECG is called for later because of a possible heart problem. A stress ECG is also often recommended as part of the complete physical that is generally advised for people planning to begin an exercise program, especially those over 35.

For Women Only

It is a good idea for women to undergo at regular intervals a Pap test and a breast X ray. Both help detect cancer at an early stage, improving the chances of recovery. The Pap test is a simple procedure. The doctor collects a few cells from the cervix (the neck of the uterus) and endometrium (the uterus's lining), which are then studied under a microscope. Many doctors recommend that their women patients have a Pap smear once a year.

Breast X rays, or mammograms, are an excellent tool for detecting cancer of the breast, the leading cause of cancer deaths among women in the United States. Mammograms can find cancers that are too small to be felt by even the experienced examiner. The American Cancer Society advises women to have a baseline mammogram done between the ages of 35 and 40, a mammogram performed once every year or two between the ages of 40 and 49, and annual breast X rays from age 50 on. The society also recommends a physical examination of the breasts at three-year intervals for women between the ages of 20 and 40, and once a year thereafter, and it urges all women to do a self-examination once a month.

How Often

The question of how often general checkups should be done, like the question of what a checkup should consist of, has no precise answer. Quite frequent checkups (or at least specific tests) are often recommended for people in special situations or at high risk of certain health problems: pregnant women, for example; people with a family history of high blood pressure, high cholesterol, or diabetes; and coal miners (susceptible to black lung disease).

Such special considerations aside, the traditional recommendation used to be that all adults have an annual physical. That recommendation has come under fire in recent years, however. Many doctors now say that a thorough checkup every year is often not sufficiently worthwhile to justify the time and expense—although that certainly does not mean that the basic idea of monitoring people's health by periodic exams is bad.

High-risk people should have frequent checkups.

In a 1983 report, the American Medical Association, taking account of the recommendations of various authorities, advised that, in general, young adults should have a medical evaluation every five years until they are 40. After that age, a checkup at intervals of one to three years was recommended, the exact length of the interval depending on the person's type of work, health, medical history, age, and other personal factors.

For children, the association supported the recommendations of the American Academy of Pediatrics. Children who are developing satisfactorily and who have no major health problems should be seen by a doctor two to four weeks after birth, four or five more times in their first year, and then every year or two until they are 21.

For pregnant women, the recommendation of the American College of Obstetricians and Gynecologists were cited; these included visits to the doctor every four weeks in the first 28 weeks of pregnancy, every two to three weeks in the next eight weeks, and then weekly until delivery.

The AMA cautioned that all these recommendations are only "informed guidelines," subject to modification in accordance with new research findings and the individual characteristics of each patient.

Some experts have proposed more radical reform of the existing system of preventive medicine, including the checkup. For instance, particularly detailed recommendations have been made by the Canadian Task Force on the Periodic Health Examination, a group of doctors and scientists that began its work in 1976 and published a comprehensive study three years later. The group suggested, in place of the traditional general checkup, a series of 18 different "health protection packages," to be performed at 35 specified times from the prenatal period to old age. Each package of procedures and tests was aimed at spotting the emergence of particular disorders most likely to occur at the time of life when the package is performed. The task force was reestablished in 1982 to reassess the study and make any necessary revisions and updates.

Between Checkups

When a person comes through a checkup with flying colors, that does not mean, of course, that a serious health problem cannot develop before it's time for the next physical. See your doctor immediately whenever disturbing symptoms of any kind are noticed. It is definitely a bad idea to wait for the next scheduled checkup—even if it is just a few months away. □

The Importance of Fiber

Jacqueline Laks Gorman

We've all heard a great deal lately about fiber. Like honey, granola, and herbal tea, it has taken its place on health food shelves, and some claim that fiber—which is found in whole grains, fresh fruits, and vegetables—is the answer to such diverse conditions as cancer and constipation, hemorrhoids and heart disease. As if that weren't enough, others say that eating such foods as whole-wheat bread, bran cereal, and crunchy raw carrots will also help people lose weight, control diabetes, and prevent a range of common but troublesome digestive disorders.

How much solid medical evidence is there for all these claims? There is one thing we do know. The degree of certainty about fiber's role varies with each affliction. It is firmly established that fiber combats constipation and the intestinal disorder diverticulosis. Its role in easing or preventing other digestive problems, however, is not well documented, and whether fiber can prevent cancer or cardiovascular disease remains a matter of promising evidence and theory rather than proven scientific fact. But even if not all the claims are borne out, it is clear that fiber should be an important part of a balanced, healthful diet.

Five Kinds of Fiber

Dietary fiber—which is sometimes called roughage—is a material of complex composition that is found in the walls of plant cells. There are actually five kinds of fiber—called cellulose, hemicellulose, pectin, gum (or mucilage), and lignin. Each type has distinctive properties in the body and is found most abundantly in different foods. Cellulose, which has a strong laxative effect, is found in bran, unpeeled apples, and such

Americans used to eat more fiber.

vegetables as cabbage, beans, and broccoli. Whole-grain products, brussels sprouts, and beets are good sources of hemicellulose, which also prevents constipation. Pectin and gum both may affect the way cholesterol and sugar are treated in the body. Apples, citrus fruits, cabbage, and cauliflower are good sources of pectin (which also prevents

constipation), while oatmeal and dried beans supply gum. Lignin, found in such foods as pears, strawberries, and eggplant, may play a role in preventing cancer of the colon (large intestine).

In the early 19th century, North Americans and Europeans consumed much more fiber than they do today, as their diet was high in vegetables and bread made of whole-grain flour. Whole grains contain all the parts of the grain kernel, including the bran, or outer coating, which is an excellent source of fiber (and also B vitamins). When new milling processes were developed in the 1840's, less nutritious white flour, from which the bran has been removed, became widely available. Ironically, the various digestive disorders that became common in the early 20th century were often blamed on fiber, even though little of it was consumed by that time. Fiber did not come into favor with the medical profession and with consumers until about a decade ago.

An Indigestible Substance

Although fiber plays an important role in the digestive system, it is itself indigestible. The enzymes, or digestive juices, that break down the sugars, starches, fats, and proteins in food into nutrients that can be absorbed

171

into the bloodstream have virtually no effect on fiber. Most of the absorption of nutrients takes place in the small intestine; the waste products that remain pass (in liquid form) into the large intestine, where fiber plays its major role.

An important property of most types of fiber is the ability to hold water. When fiber is present in the undigested matter in the colon, it soaks up the water in these wastes. The soft, bulky stool that results can pass through the intestine and be eliminated more easily.

Keeping Things "Regular"

If you suffer from constipation, a few spoons of bran or a daily bowl of whole-grain cereal may be enough to solve your problem. Moderate amounts of fiber can also be used to treat diarrhea, because bulking agents like fiber-rich foods help avoid stools that are too liquid as well as too hard.

Fiber-rich foods are filling, low in calories, and taste good too.

Diverticulosis can be treated—and perhaps even avoided—with a high-fiber diet. In this disorder, which affects a third of middle-aged and older Americans, small pouches called diverticula form at weak spots in the wall of the large intestine. People with diverticulosis may have no symptoms and may be unaware of the condition, but some experience cramping, gas, and bouts of diarrhea alternating with constipation. If one or more of the diverticula become inflamed, the condition is called diverticulitis, which can cause severe abdominal pain, tenderness, and fever. Recurrent

attacks can result in a narrowing of the colon, sometimes leading to an obstruction (or blockage), as well as to inflammation of nearby organs. If the diverticula burst, the lining of the abdominal cavity may become inflamed—a painful and dangerous condition called peritonitis.

There has been a sharp increase in the incidence of diverticular disease in industrialized countries in the 20th century, coinciding with the decreased consumption of fiber-rich foods. Scientists have discovered that increasing the amount of fiber in the diet will reduce the pressure within the large intestine that helps cause diverticula to form. Eating a high-fiber diet may thus reduce the risk of diverticulosis. Once a person has the condition, fiber is often prescribed to ease mild symptoms, as well as to perhaps prevent hard fecal matter from settling in the pouches and causing inflammation.

There is relatively little scientific evidence that fiber is useful in treating or in lowering the risk of developing other digestive system disorders, but some advocates of high-fiber diets contend that it can help those who suffer from various conditions, including hemorrhoids and irritable bowel syndrome. Hemorrhoids are veins in the rectum that have swollen as a result of pressure within them; such pressure may occur when there is persistent straining during bowel movement. Since eating fiber will produce softer stools and so ease straining, it is argued that many cases of hemorrhoids can be prevented or controlled by a high-fiber diet.

Irritable bowel syndrome, or IBS, is a very common, uncomfortable, and emotionally upsetting gastrointestinal problem in Western societies. IBS is actually a catchall diagnosis for certain symptoms—periodic bouts of diarrhea or constipation,

nausea, gas, and abdominal pain—that have no known cause. Following a high-fiber diet sometimes seems to help IBS sufferers control their symptoms (as may taking an antispasmodic drug, undergoing counseling, and avoiding possibly irritating

The optimal amount of fiber that is comfortable varies with individuals.

"triggers," like coffee and fried foods). However, the exact role of fiber—if any—in easing IBS is not known.

A Cure-all for Many Ills?

The doctor who is perhaps the current chief advocate of fiber is British physician Denis Burkitt. Burkitt worked for 20 years in tropical Africa, where the diet is very high in fiber, and he noticed that many illnesses common in present-day Britain and North America—including heart disease, gallstones, diabetes, colon cancer, and a wide range of digestive problems—were virtually unknown there. He linked these conditions to the low-fiber diet that became prevalent in industrialized countries in the 20th century.

Numerous scientists remain skeptical about Burkitt's claims, stating that they are based on speculation and circumstantial evidence rather than proof. However, recent reports indicate that fiber may be beneficial in certain medical conditions. For instance, evidence suggests that pectin and gum may lower the level of cholesterol in the blood, which could help lower the risk of heart disease. In addition, the same kinds of fiber may help diabetics. Eating any meal causes an increase in blood sugar, but when the meal is high in pectin and gum, the rise is much more modest. This finding suggests that fiber can help diabetics stabilize their blood sugar levels and possibly reduce their dependence on insulin or other medication. Many diabetics are now advised by their doctors to follow a high-fiber diet.

The Cancer Connection

A controversial claim made about fiber is that it lowers the risk of cancer of the colon, which is one of the most common cancers in North America but is quite rare in Africa and other regions where a high-fiber diet is followed. Critics charge that this is only circumstantial evidence and that other factors may be involved. For one thing, in many parts of Africa people tend to eat much less beef and less of other high-fat foods than do Westerners, and fat definitely has been linked with increased risk of cancer of the colon.

According to the fiber hypothesis, roughage helps to reduce the risk of cancer in part by absorbing bile acids. These acids are produced by the body to aid in the digestion of fat, but in the colon, certain bacteria may convert them into carcinogens (cancer-causing agents). Moreover, the fact that fiber makes wastes move faster through the colon may mean that carcinogens are in contact with body tissues for a significantly shorter time.

In 1982, the National Research Council, an arm of the U.S. National Academy of Sciences, issued a report on diet and cancer. The panel found that there was "no conclusive evidence" to indicate that fiber had a protective effect. However, in February 1984, when the American Cancer Society issued a set of dietary guidelines, high-fiber foods were recommended. While acknowledging that "agreement on fiber's role in cancer prevention is not

universal," the ACS concluded that people should eat more fiber anyway. Even if fiber itself should prove not to directly protect against cancer, the ACS said, fiber-rich foods would be a healthful, nutritious substitute for fatty foods, which are widely believed to be dangerous in excessive amounts.

A similar argument could be made about fiber and heart disease, and since fiber-rich foods are filling and generally low in calories, they may even help people keep slim and avoid the health risks of obesity. Add to this the known benefits of fiber, and it is easy to see why most health experts believe it should be an important part of the diet.

Following a High-Fiber Diet

How much fiber is enough? There are no official rec-ommendations. The average American adult currently consumes about 20 grams (less than three-quarters of an ounce) of fiber each day, only about a third as much as many people in Africa take in; some doctors say that adult Americans should increase their daily fiber intake to perhaps 40 grams. However, the amount that's comfortable for different individuals varies, and in general, too much fiber added to the diet too quickly can cause bloating, gas, and diarrhea. These problems are often temporary, but a certain amount of trial and error may be necessary, if you're trying to increase fiber intake, before the best diet is found.

To increase the amount of fiber in the daily diet, whole-grain products such as bran cereal, whole-wheat bread, and pasta should be substituted for foods made from refined flour (white bread, for example). Several servings of fiber-rich vegetables (those already mentioned, as well as various legumes, squash, and potatoes, including the skin) should be eaten, as well as lots of fiber-rich fruits (bananas, berries with seeds). Bran is the most concentrated form of roughage, and it can be sprinkled on fruit, yogurt, and cereal or added to dishes like meat loaf. Nuts and seeds are also good sources of fiber. □

THE FIBER IN FOODS

(grams of total dietary fiber)

Breads and Cereals		Legumes	
Rolled oats, 1/4 cup dry	2.2	Kidney beans, 1/2 cup cooked	9.5
Rye bread, 1 slice	1.9	Peanuts, roasted, 1 oz.	2.2
Shredded wheat, 1 oz.	3.5	White beans, 1/2 cup cooked	7.4
Wheat bran, 1 oz.	11.2		
Wheat bran cereal, 1 oz.	7.6	**Vegetables**	
White bread, 1 slice	0.8	Broccoli, 6-oz. stalk, raw	6.1
Whole wheat bread, 1 slice	3.2	Brussels sprouts, 1 cup	5.6
Whole wheat flour, 1 cup	17.9	Cabbage, boiled, 1/2 cup	2.1
		Cabbage, raw, 1 cup	1.9
Fruits		Carrot, raw, 1 medium	1.4
Apple, 1 medium	2.7	Cauliflower, cooked, 1/2 cup	1.1
Avocado, 1 cup pureed	4.6	Corn, 1/2 cup	3.9
Banana, 1 medium	4.1	Green peas, 1/2 cup	4.2
Nectarine, 1 medium	2.5	Potato, 1 medium	3.6
Orange, 1 medium	3.6	Potato chips, 1 oz.	3.4
Peach, 1 medium	2.6	Radishes, 4 small	0.9
Pear, 1 large	5.0	Spinach, raw, 1 cup	0.6
Prunes, dried, 2 oz.	5.4	Sweet potato, 4 oz.	2.7
Strawberries, 1 cup	3.1	Tomato, 1 medium	2.5

Based on U.S. Department of Agriculture figures. Actual values may vary.

Contact Lenses

Carmen A. Puliafito, M.D.

At least 11 million people in the United States wear contact lenses to correct refractive errors, or the failure of their eyes to focus properly. Like eyeglasses, contact lenses can be used to compensate for nearsightedness, farsightedness, and astigmatism, which produces distortion or blurring of images at any distance. Certain types·of contacts can also be used to treat eye diseases, serving as a "bandage" lens to protect the cornea, the transparent membrane at the front of the eye. Impressive advances in contact lens technology in the past decade have increased the range of their usefulness as well as their comfort. The number of wearers is increasing each year.

Hard Lenses

Contact lenses are made of a variety of plastics. Standard hard lenses, manufactured from a hard plastic, have been in use for many years and are suitable for many people. They are easily cared for and are sturdier than soft contact lenses; thus they are more economical in the long run. Moreover, they correct astigmatism better than soft

lenses do. However, they are more difficult to adjust to and must be "broken in" by increasing the wearing time gradually over a period of days. If they are not worn for several days, this adjustment process must be repeated.

A newer type of hard lens is the gas-permeable lens, whose primary advantage over a conventional hard lens is that it transmits more oxygen from the air through the lens to the cornea, making for greater comfort and longer wearing times. Gas-permeable lenses are more flexible than standard hard lenses as well, which also helps make them more comfortable. Like standard hard lenses, they are more durable and easier to care for than soft lenses.

Soft Lenses

Soft contact lenses are made from plastics with the remarkable ability to absorb water molecules. When on the eye, they have a water content ranging from 30 to 70 percent. They have a number of advantages over hard lenses, including the fact that they can be worn for longer periods without damaging the cornea.

Like gas-permeable hard lenses, soft lenses allow significant amounts of oxygen to get through to the cornea. This quality may be increased by making them thinner or by increasing their water content.

Soft lenses tend to be more comfortable than hard ones because they fit under the eyelids and flex as the eyes blink. Patients generally adapt rapidly to them, and an adjustment period is not usually necessary. Moreover, soft lenses can be worn intermittently, unlike hard lenses. They are also better for use in active sports because they are less likely to pop out of the eye as a result of sudden movements or to cause injury to the eye as the result of a blow.

Soft lenses do have some disadvantages, however. They require more care than hard lenses, including daily cleaning and disinfecting, either by boiling the lenses or by using a chemical disinfectant. They are also less durable than hard lenses and may be spoiled by the formation of deposits on the lens surface. Such deposits interfere with the visual effectiveness of the lens and may irritate the eye. The deposits, which may consist of calcium, protein, or other organic materials, must be removed, usually on a weekly basis, by soaking the lenses in a special enzyme solution. Soft lenses are also subject to chipping, tearing, and loss of flexibility.

More important, soft lenses are not as effective as hard lenses for correcting astigmatism. Soft lenses that correct for astigmatism are available, but they are more difficult to fit than conventional soft lenses. In addition, some soft-lens wearers develop inflammation of the eyelids or conjunctivitis (inflammation of the delicate membranes that line the eyelids and cover the whites of the eyes). Inflammation is especially likely if lenses are not cleaned properly or if saliva is used to moisten them before insertion into the eye. It can also come about because of reactions to chemicals in contact lens solutions; some people, for example, are allergic to a chemical often used as a preservative in such solutions.

Extended-Wear Lenses

The development of thin, soft lenses with an especially high water content has made it possible for many people to wear contacts 24 hours a day for weeks without removing them from the eyes. (Neither hard nor standard soft lenses should be left in overnight.) Besides being convenient, extended-wear contact lenses may be useful for treatment in several situations. In cataract surgery, for example, the lens of the eye (the part of its focusing mechanism behind the cornea) is removed because it has become cloudy, interfering with vision. After the surgery, the focusing power of the eye can be restored in one of three ways: with eyeglasses, by implantation of a tiny plastic lens into the eye, or with contact lenses. The thick eyeglasses traditionally used after such surgery magnify images and reduce peripheral vision; although lens implants are increasingly successful, contact lenses provide an alternative without many of the disadvantages of cataract glasses.

Extended-wear lenses may be worn for periods of up to three months between cleanings, but they are not for everyone. They are generally not suitable for people who have had recurrent eye infections or inflammation, or for those whose eyes do not produce enough tears to keep the lenses sufficiently moist to allow the cornea to breathe. Moreover, patients with extended-wear lenses can develop bacterial infections of the cornea, sometimes from careless lens maintenance; proper lens care and hygiene are important. The care of an ophthalmologist to ensure a continuing good fit and the overall health of the eyes is also important. Patients should consult the ophthalmologist at the first sign of redness or discomfort.

HARD LENSES OR SOFT?

Both hard and soft contact lenses have particular advantages and disadvantages that people considering contacts should be aware of.

HARD LENSES

- More durable and thus more economical in the long run.
- Easier to care for.
- More effective for correcting some vision problems—particularly astigmatism.
- Can be difficult to adjust to and must be worn according to a regular daily schedule.

SOFT LENSES

- Much easier to adjust to because they conform to the shape of the eye.
- Can be worn for longer periods and are less likely to irritate the eyes.
- Preferable for wear during active sports.
- More difficult to care for, since they must generally be cleaned and disinfected daily and also soaked weekly in a special solution.

Adapting to Contacts

Today, with both hard and soft lenses available, many people can wear contacts comfortably all day long. However, there are a number of people, especially those who are farsighted or who have a large degree of astigmatism, whose tolerance of contact lenses is limited by the shape of their eyes. Many such people can wear contacts successfully as long as their daily wearing time is restricted to six to 12 hours. The lenses may start to become uncomfortable toward the end of the wearing period.

Unfortunately, there is no generally reliable way of predicting how comfortable contact lenses will be until the lenses are actually worn. It is sometimes possible to identify beforehand patients whose eyes are unsuitable for contact lenses, but in most cases, tolerance for both hard and soft lenses can be evaluated accurately only after they have been worn for some time. Therefore, the decision to begin wearing contact lenses should be made only after weighing the reasons—cosmetic and otherwise—for wearing the lenses against their inconvenience and the possibility that they will never become entirely comfortable.

New Technology

Bifocal contact lenses have been introduced recently, permitting the same lenses to be used both for distance vision and for reading. (At present, bifocal lenses are available only in a soft version.) Another option for nearsighted patients who are also in need of reading correction is to fit one eye for distance vision and the other for near vision. Patients do well with this approach as long as the disparity in vision between their eyes is not too great. A third recent development is the tinted soft contact lens without any corrective optical power; such lenses are expected to be used widely for cosmetic purposes in the future.

Future developments in contact lens technology will probably include improved bifocal lenses. In the future, more people will probably be able to use extended-wear lenses because of improved materials and greater medical experience in preventing the possible complications. Efforts at developing a disposable contact lens are also under way; such a lens would have to be of high quality and yet inexpensive enough to be replaced frequently. ☐

Are VDT's Dangerous?

Michael E. Agnes

The video display terminal (VDT) was introduced into the workplace only in the 1960's, but it is fast becoming as familiar to office workers as the electric typewriter. As the use of VDT's has increased, many workers have become concerned that the new technology poses a health threat—that VDT's may cause headaches, eye problems, muscle and back pain, and even miscarriages and birth defects. A considerable amount of recent research has focused on VDT's and the safety of their operation.

The VDT consists of a screen much like an ordinary television screen and, usually, a keyboard. It is also known under a variety of other names, including video or visual display unit (VDU) and cathode-ray tube (CRT). The unit functions as a computer terminal, with the operator feeding in data using the keyboard and with information displayed on the screen. In 1984 more than 12 million VDT's were in operation in U.S. businesses alone, used by airline reservation clerks, telephone operators, secretaries, newspaper reporters, and operators of word processors. It

has been estimated that the number of workers using VDT's may reach 40–50 million by 1990. In addition, millions of people operate personal computers, whose screens and keyboards use essentially the same technology as do VDT's.

Radiation Studies

Like television sets, VDT's can produce two types of radiation: powerful, high-frequency radiation (called ionizing), such as X rays, and less powerful, lower-frequency radiation (called nonionizing); examples of nonionizing radiation are visible and infrared light and microwaves.

Questions about the safety of VDT radiation emissions first surfaced in the mid-1970's, when two young newspaper employees developed cataracts after VDT's were installed in their newsroom. Some feared that VDT radiation emissions were responsible. Several investigations of radiation from VDT's followed, including rigorous studies by U.S., Canadian, and British government agencies and independent groups. Researchers have been

unanimous in their findings: no significant radiation hazards of any type have been detected. In fact, the levels of various kinds of radiation from VDT's are virtually undetectable or well within existing exposure standards and recommendations. X-ray emissions, in particular, are often too low to be detectable above natural background levels, and most studies have failed to detect any microwave emissions. Other common sources of radiation, such as fluorescent lights and space heaters, produce more radiation of some specific types than VDT's do, with no apparent harmful effects.

In 1983 a report of the National Research Council of the U.S. National Academy of Sciences concluded that "present knowledge indicates that the levels of radiation emitted by VDT's are highly unlikely to be hazardous to health." This echoed a 1982 statement by the American Academy of Ophthalmology that VDT's are "safe for normal use and present no hazard to vision." No study has uncovered any direct link between VDT use and eye disease, including cataracts.

Complaints and Symptoms

Despite the reassurance of such findings, it is impossible to ignore the rising tide of complaints from VDT operators, many of whom spend eight hours a day, five days a week, in front of VDT screens. Symptoms most commonly reported include muscle aches and pains, general job stress, and, in particular, vision problems, such as itchy and irritated eyes and eyestrain, which can lead to eye fatigue, blurred vision, eye pain, and headaches. The symptoms are similar to those reported by workers who do not operate VDT's but whose jobs require that they use their eyes for long periods of time at relatively close distances.

Several studies have found that equipment design and VDT use in offices often disregard factors known to affect the way workers interact with their environment—for example, how comfortably operators can reach the keyboard and how well they can read the screen. Furthermore, some VDT jobs involve repetitive, boring tasks and are associated with low worker satisfaction. Such problems are clearly not inherent in the technology of VDT's, and solutions are available. Careful selection, installation, and use of VDT equipment and associated office furniture will help alleviate many of the symptoms experienced by VDT operators. Improved job design can help to reduce stress and raise levels of job satisfaction. As might be expected, good vision—properly corrected by glasses or contact lenses if necessary—is a must for any worker whose job involves constant and concentrated use of the eyes. (See the accompanying table for recommendations.)

VDT's and Pregnancy

By far the most disturbing health question has been whether VDT use is dangerous during pregnancy. There have been alarming accounts of "clusters" of cases of miscarriages, premature births, and birth defects among women who work with VDT's. Such clusters have been reported at as many as two dozen sites in the United States and Canada since 1979. Scientific investigations have failed to detect any connection between VDT use (and specifically, VDT radiation emissions) and the problem pregnancies, and researchers point out that the clusters may be simply the result of statistically normal coincidence. However, some critics object that the research to date is inconclusive. The U.S. National Institute for Occupational Safety and Health is planning a study of pregnancies among 4,000 women, half of whom work with VDT's and half of whom do not. Results of the study are expected to be released in 1987.

In any event, the fears of VDT operators can be very real. A few groups of operators have taken a "better-safe-than-sorry" stance and have sought flexibility concessions from employers. For

---

TIPS ON USING VDT'S

1. Adjust the VDT screen and keyboard, as well as office furniture, to the positions most comfortable for you.

2. Adjust room lighting, window blinds or curtains, and screen contrast to get the sharpest screen image and minimize glare.

3. Try to switch to different tasks or activities periodically during the day.

4. Make use of work breaks to rest your eyes.

5. Have your eyes examined regularly, and if you need eyeglasses or contact lenses, be sure to wear them.

---

example, some workers now ask for and are granted extra unpaid leave or temporary transfers to other jobs during pregnancy. Others limit their daily exposure time.

Design Standards

Although VDT's must meet federal safety requirements for radiation emissions, there are as yet no mandatory standards in the United States governing the various factors of VDT design that affect worker comfort and operating conditions. Equipment manufacturers and trade organizations resist any such regulations, on the ground that medical research has not proved that there is a need. They cite the 1983 National Research Council report, which termed the establishment of mandatory design standards "premature" and called instead for more research in this area.

Still, the governments of such countries as Sweden and West Germany have issued design standards, and Canada has debated similar standards and legislation. Connecticut, Maine, Rhode Island, and New Jersey have passed bills that call for the study of VDT operation and possible hazards. Other states are expected in 1985 to consider legislation regulating VDT use, including measures giving pregnant VDT operators the right to be transferred to other positions if they wish.

Common Sense

Some critics claim that there is cause for further investigation of the possible effects of prolonged use of VDT's. For instance, some would like to see new studies of the effects of radiation in the very low-frequency (VLF) band, despite the fact that the preponderance of medical opinion holds that exposure to such radiation in the amounts emitted by VDT's presents no danger whatsoever.

Clearly, however, it is impossible to ignore the considerable body of knowledge already collected attesting to the safety of VDT operation. The great majority of physicians and researchers see no link between VDT's and cataracts or miscarriages, and they see no reason for concern about risk from radiation produced by VDT's. The health problems that have been associated with the use of VDT's, such as eyestrain and back pain, can often be dealt with effectively by means of intelligent equipment design, proper structuring of tasks, and common-sense attention to good posture and eye care. □

Straightening Teeth

Joel P. Douglas, D.M.D.

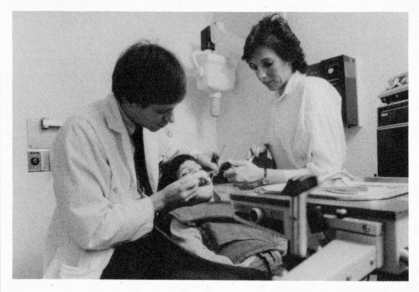

Who doesn't want to make a good first impression when meeting people? Who doesn't like an attractive smile? Few things can do more to spoil the effect of a smile than seriously crooked or protruding teeth. Besides being unsightly in themselves, they can undermine the appearance of the entire face. Straightening badly aligned teeth is the job of the dental specialty called orthodontics. In both children and adults, orthodontic treatment, using braces or other "appliances" to move teeth into their proper position, can bring tangible and sometimes dramatic changes in facial appearance with a minimal amount of discomfort. By improving people's self-image, treatment can enhance their self-confidence and sense of well-being, and make social interaction more pleasant.

But orthodontics is not just a matter of appearance. Correcting a "bad bite" promotes effective chewing of food and helps stiffen resistance to periodontal disease, which can gradually destroy the tissues supporting the teeth. (Although it is primarily caused by the buildup of bacteria-containing plaque and tartar between the gums and teeth, periodontal disease can be aggravated by a bad bite.) In addition, properly aligned teeth make it easier for tongue, lip, and cheek muscles to function normally in speech, eating, and breathing. Finally, orthodontic treatment can often help prevent or alleviate problems involving the joint of the lower jaw.

What Makes a Bad Bite?

First and foremost, orthodontics is concerned with the bite, or occlusion, which is the way the teeth come together when the jaws are closed. A bad, or abnormal, bite is called a malocclusion. Not every case of bad bite is serious enough to need treatment. According to one study, however, about half of all U.S. children between the ages of 12 and 17 have mal-

Straightening teeth is important for many reasons.

occlusions that are sufficiently severe for orthodontic treatment to be considered desirable or even mandatory.

The size and shape of the teeth, of the dental arches (the curves formed by the upper and lower rows of teeth), and of the jawbones are all primarily determined by heredity. A disharmony in the relationships between any of these structures can lead to a malocclusion. The best example is when the size of the teeth is greater than that of the dental arch. There is not enough space in the jawbone to fit all the teeth, and they become crowded and overlapped.

One common example of a malocclusion is buckteeth—protrusion of the upper front teeth. This is often due to an inherited protruding upper jaw or a short receding lower jaw, but it may also be caused by thumb-sucking, the pressure of the thumb against the roof of the mouth causing the front teeth to protrude.

Inheritance of a lower jaw that is larger and longer than the upper jaw can lead to a different problem—"crossbite" of the front teeth, with the lower front teeth outside the upper teeth when the person bites down. Similarly, a lower dental arch that is broader than the upper arch can give rise to crossbite of the back teeth, with one or more of the lower back teeth biting outside the upper back teeth.

Besides genes, there are other factors that can cause or contribute to orthodontic problems. A bad bite, for example, may result when baby teeth are extracted before they should be, owing to unfilled cavities. An important role in the growth and development of the dental arches is played by the forces exerted on the teeth by the muscles in the tongue, lips, and cheeks. If these muscles apply an abnormal or unbalanced pressure—as a result, say, of lip biting or persistent breathing through the mouth—a malocclusion may develop.

The situation where the top and bottom front teeth fail to meet when back teeth are in contact is known as an open bite. It is sometimes a result of thumb-sucking or tongue thrusting—the constant thrusting of the tongue between the front teeth, particularly when swallowing. The opposite of an open bite is the deep overbite, wherein the lower front teeth actually strike the gum tissue on the roof of the mouth behind the upper front teeth when biting. When both top and bottom front teeth lean forward (a double protrusion) so that the lips must strain to close properly over the teeth, one result may be mouth breathing, which in turn makes the orthodontic problem worse.

Muscles at Work

The case of mouth breathing provides a good example of how teeth can be moved out of their proper positions when muscles do not work in a harmonious way. Normally people breathe through the nose; the lips are closed, and the tongue is up near the roof of the mouth. The tongue exerts a gentle outward pressure on the upper side teeth, which is balanced by an inward pressure from the muscles in the cheeks and lips. In a child with, say, chronic nasal congestion from an allergy or enlarged adenoids, who must constantly breathe through the mouth, the lips are always kept open, and the tongue is held low, in the floor of the mouth, so that air can pass over it. This abnormal tongue posture forces teeth in the lower jaw outward, while the upper back teeth move inward because of the unopposed force exerted by the cheek muscles. Thus, children who breathe through the mouth often have narrow upper dental arches, resulting in crossbite of the back teeth, crowding of teeth, and possibly an open bite. Orthodontic treatment of malocclusions associated with persistent mouth breathing may not produce a stable result if the habit is continued. Breaking the habit may involve the removal of the adenoids and tonsils which is declining in popularity.

Orthodontic treatment can dramatically improve appearance.

Jaw Problems

The various consequences of an abnormal bite can be far-reaching. For example, problems involving the joint connecting the lower jaw to the skull—the temporomandibular joint, or TMJ—may be associated with failure of the back teeth to fit together properly when the jaws close. A person with faultily positioned back teeth—where the tooth cusps do not mesh as they should—may habitually and unconsciously deflect the lower jaw away from its proper path when closing it. This may lead to grinding of the teeth (bruxism), spasms of the facial muscles, and headache-like pain radiating up the side of the head and neck.

In a few cases the problem may be eased by shaving the cusps down to allow the jaw to close properly in its intended position. If this is unfeasible, moving the offending teeth into the proper bite by orthodontic treatment may be called for. Most cases of chronic TMJ discomfort, however, have multiple causes and very diverse symptoms. Diagnosing and treating them can be an extremely complex matter and may require the services of a person specially trained to deal with such cases.

Braces

The treatment of a malocclusion is based on the principle that light, steady pressure applied to a tooth will cause it—slowly but surely—to move to a new position. Braces are a common means of achieving this: typically, metal brackets are bonded onto the teeth to serve as anchors for wires, springs, and elastic bands that are used to apply forces against the teeth in the appropriate direction. As the teeth move, they become slightly tender to bite on, and a little loose, until new bone fills in around them.

Recent years have seen the development of alternative

devices that, in some cases, are as effective as conventional metal braces but are less visible. These include tooth-colored ceramic braces, clear plastic braces, and so-called invisible, or lingual, braces. Metal brackets are used in invisible braces, but they are bonded to the teeth on the inside (the lingual side). All of these newer braces have disadvantages of their own. The plastic and ceramic types are brittle and tend to break more often; in addition, they may become discolored. Invisible braces are more expensive, are more difficult for the orthodontist to work with, and do not provide the precise control of tooth movement afforded by conventional braces.

Other Applicances

A wide variety of removable appliances—inserted and removed by the patient—may be used prior to or along with fixed braces. Among them are the so-called functional appliances, which are rather bulky, although not uncomfortable, acrylic devices containing heavy wires and expansion screws.

One type of functional appliance is designed to allow the force of the tongue (the strongest muscle in the body) to widen and expand the dental arches outward, thereby making space for slightly crowded teeth. This is accomplished by actually shielding the teeth from the inward counterforces exerted by the lips and cheeks. The underlying assumption—still open to question—is that the original tooth crowding is due to constriction and narrowing of the dental arches caused by excess pressure from the outside lip and cheek muscles.

The purpose of another type of functional appliance is to aid in the treatment of buckteeth, particularly in cases where such upper protrusions are partly or wholly due to underdeveloped chins. The appliance forces the

Adults as well as children can benefit from orthodontics; more and more older patients are taking advantage of new techniques and appliances. Most orthodontic work for children starts around age 12.

patient to hold the lower jaw forward when closing the mouth, the aim being to induce the jaw to grow more than heredity intended. It is, however, very difficult to prove that this kind of functional appliance really accomplishes its purpose, since it must be used during puberty, when the jaws are actively growing in any case.

Functional appliances have been gaining in popularity in the United States since they were introduced about a decade ago from Europe (where their popularity is now waning). But it still remains to be established whether they yield results that are stable and that stand up over the long term.

Less controversial is the use of removable acrylic "retainers" at the conclusion of treatment to hold the teeth in their new positions. Retainers are ordinarily worn for about six to 12 months. They may not even be needed if the orthodontist finds when the

braces are removed that the teeth are meshing well and are in balance with the muscle forces around them.

Another major type of orthodontic appliance is the headgear, or night brace. Typically anchored by elastic straps around the back of the neck and over the head, it provides the strong force that is often required to correct protrusions of the front teeth and to move upper back teeth to the rear.

When Should Treatment Start?

The best time to begin orthodontic treatment depends on the specific type of problem and the patient's stage of dental development. Certain problems that may be keeping the jaws from growing, or functioning, as they should—such as crossbites of the front or back teeth—are generally best treated as soon as they are detected, regardless of the patient's age. The American

Association of Orthodontists recommends that children be initially examined by an orthodontist at the age of seven, since by then most problems can be detected and a few even prevented.

Orthodontic treatment cannot be completed until the last permanent teeth have come in and are aligned—that is, around ages 12 to 14 in most children. (Girls usually get their teeth earlier than boys.) Generally, treatment for crowded or protruding teeth can be done in about two to two and a half years if it is begun at age 11 or 12, when the child's last baby teeth are being shed and patient motivation and the growth spurt of puberty, the two biggest allies of the orthodontist, are at their peak.

The patient's cooperation is crucial not only in keeping regular appointments but also in wearing headgear, elastics, and removable appliances. Also vital throughout treatment is a commitment by the patient to keep both braces and teeth scrupulously clean. The end result of the treatment can be compromised if the patient loses motivation and falls victim to "cooperation burnout."

Orthodontic treatment for a malocclusion does not have to be done only in childhood or adolescence. Over the past decade, in fact, more and more adults have been seeking help from orthodontists. Some have been drawn by the growing availability of alternatives to conventional metal braces for certain problems. Most have always been unhappy about the appearance of their smile but for one reason or another never decided to undergo orthodontic treatment. Once they realize the importance of a good bite and a pleasing smile, they become slightly reluctant but highly motivated candidates for braces.

Overall duration of treatment for adults is comparable to that for children. Although adults' teeth move slightly more slowly than children's, adults generally cooperate better in wearing the removable parts of their braces, particularly elastics.

Adults are also good candidates for a combined surgical-orthodontic approach to the treatment of certain severe problems in which movement of teeth alone is not enough to correct the situation. The upper jaw, the lower jaw, and even entire segments of teeth and bone within the jaws can be moved backward or forward by an oral surgeon, in conjuction with orthodontic treatment.

Pulling Healthy Teeth

Few dental procedures cause as much anxiety in patients and parents as the extraction of

---

Sometimes healthy teeth must be pulled to provide space for other teeth.

---

sound, healthy permanent teeth. Yet in about 40 percent of all orthodontic patients the extraction of either two or four first bicuspid teeth is a necessary part of treatment. (The first bicuspids are directly behind the pointed eyeteeth.)

Whether these permanent teeth should be extracted depends largely on how crowded the bottom front teeth are. In most instances crowded lower front teeth cannot be permanently straightened just by moving them forward or outward to obtain the necessary space for their alignment. If moved forward, they are likely to relapse back inward after treatment and again become crowded. In such cases, most specialists believe, the required space should be obtained by extracting the lower

first bicuspid teeth. If these teeth are extracted, the corresponding upper teeth must also be removed to maintain a normal bite. For protruded or crowded upper front teeth, on the other hand, upper first bicuspids are sometimes extracted without removal of any lower teeth, provided the latter are straight.

Mindful of past criticism that the treatment could produce a "dished-in" look, today's orthodontist places significant emphasis on maintaining a pleasing lip profile. This means exercising extreme care in bicuspid extraction cases to fully close all the spaces without pushing the front teeth too far in.

A Cautionary Note

It's always a good idea, of course, to get a second, or even third, opinion before anyone decides to embark on a course of orthodontic treatment. Since every patient is unique, and since orthodontic diagnosis and treatment planning are extremely complex, experts may sometimes differ in their recommendations for a particular case. Whatever treatment plan is ultimately decided upon, the patient, or the patient's parents, should make every effort to choose a well-qualified and experienced practitioner to carry it out. In the United States this usually means turning to a trained orthodontic specialist who is a member of the American Association of Orthodontists. (Any licensed dentist can legally perform orthodontics, but only the specialist has the advantage of having completed two to three years of postgraduate courses after finishing dental school.)

Orthodontic treatment is a long-term investment. It cannot be redone readily, and it should therefore be performed correctly in the first place, with an end result that is not only functional and aesthetically pleasing, but also capable of lasting a lifetime. □

How to Preserve NUTRIENTS IN FOOD

Eleanor R. Williams, Ph.D.

The best way to get all the nutrients you need for good health is to consume a wide variety of foods. But some methods of handling, cooking, and storing can lead to the loss or destruction of essential vitamins and minerals. To get the full value of a well-balanced diet, it is important to know how to preserve the nutrients in foods.

What Nutrients Can Be Lost

Vitamins and minerals are the nutrients most likely to be lost or destroyed by improper handling, cooking, or storage. Minerals can dissolve into the water in which foods are soaked or cooked; they go down the drain if that water is discarded. The same thing happens to water-soluble vitamins (all vitamins except A, D, E, and K). Some vitamins are also destroyed by heat or by exposure to alkaline liquids, light, or air. Enzymes that occur naturally in vegetables can destroy vitamins if the vegetables are bruised or otherwise damaged. Methods of protecting foods against nutrient losses are designed to avoid or minimize exposure to such destructive conditions.

Vegetables

Vegetables are among our best dietary sources of vitamins A and C, as well as many other vitamins and minerals. If you have a home garden, you should harvest vegetables immediately before you cook, freeze, or can them. If you cannot use them right away, put them in the refrigerator in plastic bags or covered containers to prevent wilting, which leads to the release of the enzymes that can destroy vitamins. In any case, use the vegetables within a few days. Vitamin C in particular is lost with the passage of time after harvest even under the best of conditions.

Commercially grown vegetables, even those that are transported across great distances, retain a high proportion of their nutritive value if shipped and stored under proper conditions of temperature and humidity. They will also retain their original color, shape, firmness, and texture. Thus, if vegetables appear to be fresh when you buy them, their nutritive value will still be high. You should get

> To get the full value of a healthful diet, it is important to handle and cook your food without wasting nutrients.

them home from the store as quickly as possible and refrigerate them in plastic bags or covered containers. Potatoes, sweet potatoes, and other roots or tubers need not be refrigerated, but they should be kept cool and moist enough to prevent any shriveling.

Use a sharp knife for trimming, cutting, or shredding vegetables, and a sharp vegetable peeler for removing skins, to avoid bruising the tissues. Exposing cut or peeled vegetables to air for any length of time causes loss of vitamins A and C, since they react with the oxygen in the air. (Although you may have heard that nutrients are concentrated in and immediately under the skin, they are actually found throughout the vegetable.)

A general rule to follow in cooking vegetables is to use a small amount of water for as short a time as possible. You should not add bicarbonate of soda to the water (to brighten the color of green vegetables); it creates alkaline conditions that can destroy some vitamins. To minimize water evaporation, use a pan with a tight-fitting lid. An alternative method, in which sliced or shredded vegetables are cooked quickly in a small amount of oil or fat with no added water (stir-frying or braising), also helps retain nutrients. Learn to like cooked vegetables that are still somewhat crisp; longer cooking time results in greater destruction of vitamins. Root vegetables, such as carrots, potatoes, and beets, retain more nutrients if they are cooked in their skins.

Steaming vegetables is a good cooking method only if the cooking time is kept brief. Steaming in a pressure cooker is a very fast way to cook many vegetables—so fast that just a few minutes too long will overcook them. Keeping vegetables warm or reheating them results in large losses of vitamin C and some of the B vitamins. It is generally best to cook only as many vegetables as will be eaten at one meal.

Fruits

Many fruits, especially citrus fruits and strawberries, are excellent sources of vitamin C. Yellow fruits, such as cantaloupes and peaches, are good sources of vitamin A. Under proper temperature and humidity conditions, fruits can retain their nutritive value for ten weeks or so in commercial storage. Most whole fruits keep well in the refrigerator for two or three weeks if covered. Berries are highly perishable, however, and lose vitamin C readily, so plan to use them within a day or so after you buy or pick them.

Citrus juices are lower in nutritive value than the whole fruit simply because edible parts of the fruit are left behind when the juice is extracted. They are still a good source of vitamin C, which they retain for several days in the refrigerator because their acidity helps preserve it. Usually the flavor deteriorates along with the level of vitamin C.

Meats, Poultry, and Fish

Meats, poultry, and fish supply protein, B vitamins, and minerals, especially iron, zinc, and phosphorus. Vitamins and minerals are lost from these foods chiefly through drippings from thawing frozen products or from cooking or slicing. Use meat drippings, after skimming off the fat, in soups or gravies. Thiamine (vitamin B_1) and vitamin B_6 also may be partly destroyed by heat, especially if meat is cooked until well-done.

Milk

Milk is our best source of calcium and vitamin D (which is added in processing); it also supplies

Cooking Vegetables to Keep in the Vitamins

1. Use a sharp knife or peeler for cutting and paring.

2. Cook vegetables as briefly as possible.

3. Use a small amount of water for cooking, or toss vegetables quickly in a small amount of hot oil.

4. Don't add bicarbonate of soda to brighten the color of green vegetables.

5. Serve the cooked vegetables right away—keeping them hot or reheating them destroys vitamins.

protein, riboflavin (vitamin B_2), and vitamin A. All of these nutrients are stable except for riboflavin, which is destroyed by light; light-proof containers help preserve it. Pasteurization of milk does not destroy any of these nutrients—but does destroy organisms that can cause disease.

Cereals

Cereals and grains—especially whole-grain products—are important in the diet for their contributions of B vitamins and minerals (including iron, phosphorus, magnesium, and zinc). Cereals, rice, and other grain products that require cooking should be prepared in just the amount of water that will be absorbed when the food is done. Do not wash packaged rice before cooking it, for this washes away some of the vitamins and minerals. Brown rice purchased in bulk, however, may require washing.

Frozen Foods

Fruits lose little of their nutritive value when properly frozen. Vegetables lose some water-soluble vitamins and minerals when blanched before freezing to inactivate enzymes that might otherwise damage the flavor, texture, or nutritive value of the

vegetable. Frozen meats, poultry, and fish keep their nutrients well. Proper packaging of frozen foods keeps out air; this is essential for retaining flavor and nutrients.

Frozen foods should be stored at temperatures of 0° Fahrenheit or lower. Even at 0°F some nutrients are lost with time; the longer foods are stored, the greater the losses. Thawing and refreezing will harm flavor and nutritive value; the food may also spoil.

Cook frozen vegetables without first thawing them. Since the blanching that is done before freezing partially cooks the vegetable, the cooking time should be very short.

Canned Foods

Canned vegetables lose some vitamin C and B vitamins and canned meats lose some thiamine because of exposure to heat during processing. Modern commercial food processing techniques have reduced losses significantly, however. Canned foods retain their nutrients best when stored at 65°F or less. The liquid from canned vegetables and fruits contains nutrients, so try to consume the liquid with the food or use it in soups, gravies, or sauces. ☐

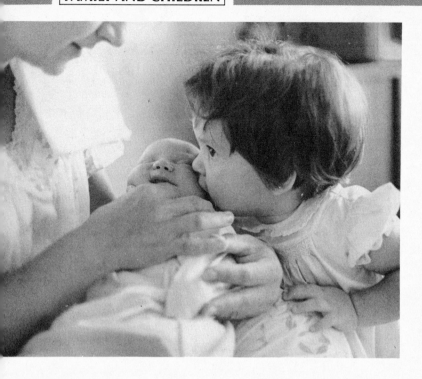

Having a SECOND CHILD

Carole E. Calladine

Three-year-old Becky peeked into the bassinet where a friend's newborn son lay waving his fists in the air. "Our baby won't be so little," Becky said.

"Why won't our baby be so little?" asked Becky's mother, who was two weeks away from her second child's due date.

"Our baby will be big like baby Jennifer at Aunt Susan's house. I'll be able to play with our baby."

Becky's mother had been hesitant to take her daughter to visit her friend's new baby, not sure what Becky's reaction would be. But having read about the importance of preparing a child for a new baby, she had decided to arrange the get-together. It would give her and Becky an opportunity to talk about somebody else's baby.

Becky's reaction surprised her mother until she realized that her daughter had never seen a newborn before. It made sense that Becky thought the baby would be like nine-month-old Jennifer. After all, wasn't Jennifer always called the baby by everyone? The visit to the newborn turned out to be extremely helpful. Becky watched with great interest as the baby was nursed and changed. "Babies can't do anything, can they?" she observed.

Talking About the Baby

Preparing a first child for a baby sister or brother is important. Such preparation sets the tone for a newborn's arrival and helps minimize the inevitable jealousy children feel toward a new sibling. Silence about a coming baby, on the other hand, hinders the family's psychological readiness for this big event.

Talking about the coming baby is natural in light of the changes already starting to occur in the daily interaction between the mother and her first child. Research has shown that mothers spend less time with their toddlers during pregnancy than they did before. The change, a physical and psychological reaction to pregnancy, is important because it prepares the child to be a little less dependent on the mother. This increasing independence is helpful in making the child feel capable and a little more grown-up—which all children like to feel.

Talking about the new baby also helps the first child to understand what's coming and to feel a part of the process, rather than an outsider. Pointing out the helplessness of the newborn can aid the first child in developing a feeling of responsibility and helpfulness toward the newcomer that will work against feelings of jealousy and rivalry. The older child might be given a T-shirt to wear that reads "I'm a Big Brother" or "I'm a Big Sister."

Telling the child about the newcomer should take into account the older sibling's need to feel secure in parental love. The hardest thing for any child to share is a parent. It is not helpful for parents to tell a child that they are having a baby to provide a brother or sister to play with. Such a message is almost as if a spouse were told that a lover was being added to the family to help out in the household and be good company. Children are likely to reject such a trumped-up explanation and feel hurt. Besides, they will not really be able to play with the new child for at least several months after birth.

It is better for parents to emphasize that they want a second child because they like children and want their family to grow. The message should be, "You are special and important to us. We like our family. We want to add another special person to the family, and we have enough love for everyone."

Explaining where a baby grows helps prepare a child for a new sibling.

As the pregnancy progresses, any of the child's questions or worries should be discussed. The child may well have some practical questions. ("Where will the new baby sleep? Will I have to share my toys with him? Who will look after me and play with me?") In addition, most psychologists and educators believe it's a good idea for a mother to explain to her child that the new baby is growing inside her and to let the child feel it move. Some children even accompany their mother on a visit to the obstetrician's office, where they can hear the baby's heartbeat through the stethoscope.

Anticipating Changes

Many changes are going to come about in the first child's life because of the new baby. Some can be anticipated and planned for ahead of time. It is not a good idea to have the older child start nursery school near the time of the baby's birth to ease the mother's workload. If she does need assistance in caring for two children, a mother's helper might be hired; this solution gives both children the attention they will be needing.

If the older child is to move to a new bedroom, the change should be made at least six weeks before the delivery date. This gives the child time to settle comfortably in the new room and gives everyone time to get the baby's room ready. The older child might even want to place something he or she has outgrown in the baby's room to welcome the new sibling.

Anticipating changes and problems, and finding preventive solutions to them well ahead of the baby's arrival will help keep the first child from feeling displaced by the newcomer. Instead, the older child can actively participate in implementing the changes— which helps promote the child's new "helper" role in the family.

The jealousy felt by an older child can be minimized by talking about a new arrival in the family beforehand.

Age-Related Problems

Children of different ages respond differently to the birth of a baby, depending on their needs and personalities. One-year-olds will pay more attention to their parents than to a new baby. Since their needs are so similar, the one-year-old and the new baby can almost become like twins—two children in diapers who need to be fed, bathed, and cuddled.

Two-year-olds are becoming more independent from their parents and are developing a separate identity. Often, they can feed themselves and use the toilet, and they have minds of their own. The arrival of a baby can affect them in various ways. Some two-year-olds are comfortable with the role of big brother or sister, but others may feel ambivalent about giving up their own "baby" status. They may regress temporarily by having accidents after having been successfully toilet trained, or by refusing to drink from a cup and demanding a bottle instead.

Calm parenting is essential. Saying "you're not a baby" won't help the child feel more secure. But giving such children responsibilities, like helping to clean up after themselves, will help them feel capable and will reinforce the more mature aspects of their behavior. Their regressive behavior should be gently discouraged rather than punished; two-year-olds need assurance that they are still loved, even when their behavior is less than desirable.

185

Three-year-olds are beyond the stage of just acquiring words and are developing the rudiments of abstract thinking. They can understand that when mother goes to the hospital to have the baby, she will come back in a few days. Having them use a hand-drawn calendar to mark off the days until mother and the new baby come home can help get three-year-olds involved in the birth of a new sibling. They can also draw pictures to put over the baby's crib. Because of their understanding of co-operative behavior, many three-year-olds take a new baby in stride—as long as parents are sensitive to their need for continued attention.

Four-year-olds, on the other hand, can be difficult with new babies. They often are bossy, test the rules laid down by parents, become silly, and have many new fears. They may ignore the new baby or even try to hurt the intruder, since all boundaries are subject to question at this stage of childhood. Or they may want to take over completely and be the parent of the baby, telling mother what to do. Parents can guide such impulses into helpful channels by giving a four-year-old simple chores to do, but parents must remain in control.

Five-year-olds and older children are often jealous of the fussing over the new baby, but they frequently feel guilty over their jealousy. Because older children are usually finding a place for themselves outside the home—among their playmates or at school—their jealous feelings may be more easily diluted than those of younger children.

Settling Conflicts

Parents must think through the effects a new baby may have on their family and work at ways of promoting healthy relations between brothers and sisters. When the baby arrives, a well-prepared child is usually able to handle the inevitable jealousy. True rivalry often doesn't develop until a few months later, when the baby sleeps less, becomes more mobile, and is perhaps more demanding. The parent is then faced with the question of how to settle conflicts.

What should a mother do, for instance, if the baby cries while she is in the middle of reading a favorite storybook to the older child? A solution for that problem may be to get the baby and hold it while finishing the story. But other daily decisions may be more difficult. For this reason, parents must learn to act as mediators rather than as judges or referees. By involving the children in finding the solutions, they won't feel that a parent is taking sides with one or the other. Instead, everyone's needs and feelings will be recognized.

If, for example, a crawling baby bulldozes her way through her brother's blocks, involve him in finding a solution as you pick up and hold the baby. Where could he play in peace? Would he like to play in another room with the door shut? Would he like to put away his blocks and play peeka-boo with the baby? The right answer is the one the child likes and feels good about.

This approach, which doesn't judge the children and put the blame on one of them, is helpful in teaching children how to solve problems and get along with others. What better place to learn this than in the safe and caring atmosphere of the family.

When having a second child, parents must make sure that the firstborn still feels special and important as a son or daughter—and begins to like the idea of becoming a big brother or sister. When this occurs, the special bond the child shares with the parents continues, and a close, new relationship to the sibling begins. The result is a family where caring and love are shared. □

Try to get the older child to help solve the problem.

Conquering Childhood Diseases

Lois A. Pounds, M.D.

Mr. and Mrs. Cooper were a middle-class couple living in Philadelphia at the turn of the century. They had eight children. The oldest child, a boy, was healthy and normal as an infant and toddler. He had the usual childhood diseases of the era—whooping cough, measles, and chicken pox—by the time he was two. When he was seven, he started school; after a few months he became ill with scarlet fever and died within a week.

The next two Cooper children, both girls, were healthy as newborns but died of diarrhea in their first summer. The next baby was a girl who enjoyed good health until she developed an abscess (a collection of pus, caused by an infection) in her right ear at the age of two. For the next several years she suffered from a chronic ear infection, which eventually left her deaf in the right ear.

The Coopers' fifth child, a boy, had mild cases of diphtheria and measles during citywide epidemics, and he also had a bout of chicken pox. Despite missing about two months of school each year because of various illnesses,

he remained in general good health. The next child was a girl, born prematurely; she survived despite the fact that it took nearly six months for her to begin to grow properly. She had many infections as an infant and preschooler, but none was life-threatening. The seventh child, a boy, was not so lucky. He had meningitis as an infant, which left him severely mentally and physically handicapped. He subsequently died of pneumonia when he was four years old. The youngest Cooper child, also a boy, was ill much of his infancy with ear infections, whooping cough, and diarrhea, but he survived and became a productive young man.

The Coopers' family medical history was not unusual in the first part of this century, and Mr. and Mrs. Cooper counted themselves lucky to have had four children survive and reach adulthood. The situation today is radically different. Medical advances—vaccines and antibiotics, for example—have played a major role in this change. In addition, children today are better nourished, have safer water and food, and live in

cleaner environments, and their parents are better educated about health and disease.

All of the children of Mr. and Mrs. Brown, a present-day Philadelphia couple, can be expected to survive infancy and childhood to become healthy adults. The Browns expect their children to have colds and flu and perhaps an ear infection or pneumonia, and to miss ten or 12 days of school a year. They know their children might get appendicitis or break an arm. But Mr. and Mrs. Brown do not fear many of the communicable diseases that were so devastating in the past.

Disease Prevention Today

The development, since the 1930's, of various vaccines—and comprehensive immunization programs—have brought about a dramatic decline in the United States in the great epidemic diseases of childhood (see the accompanying table). Infants and toddlers can now be protected from diphtheria, pertussis (whooping cough), tetanus, polio, measles, rubella (German measles), and mumps. The vaccines are remarkably safe and effective, and children now contract these diseases only if the vaccines are not given or are given too late.

The development of medications, such as sulfa drugs and antibiotics, have made it possible to treat children for other infectious diseases that once caused major chronic conditions or disabilities. For instance, in the past, osteomyelitis (a bone infection) and mastoiditis (inflammation of part of the skull behind the ear) were often lifelong problems; now, with early antibiotic treatment,

Research proceeds on new vaccines.

they can be quickly brought under control and cured. Before the advent of antibiotics, meningitis (inflammation of the membranes surrounding the brain and spinal cord) was fatal in half of all cases and caused severe disability in those who survived. Now the disease can be promptly diagnosed and treated, and both death and disability have been markedly reduced.

The infectious diseases to which children are most vulnerable vary with age and development. The special problems of each age group—and the state of the art in protecting children today—will be reviewed.

Protecting the Fetus

In the 1960's, an Australian ophthalmologist established the link between mothers who contract rubella during the first three months of pregnancy and infants born with such eye defects as cataracts. The potential dangers of rubella were shown dramatically in 1964, when the United States had a major epidemic and thousands of infants were born to mothers who had the disease while they were pregnant. Rubella is a mild

disease in adults, and the women were only briefly ill. But their babies were severely affected— suffering eye defects, deafness, heart disease, and varying degrees of mental and physical retardation.

The birth of these handicapped infants pushed the research community to speed up development of an effective rubella vaccine, which became available in 1966; vaccination is now required by law throughout the United States and in some Canadian provinces. The vaccine is given to children at 15 months, in an attempt to eradicate the disease so that pregnant women will not be in danger of exposure. Adult women who plan to become pregnant and who do not have immunity—from having had rubella previously or from vaccination—can be immunized as a preventive measure.

Fetuses can be harmed by other infections as well. There is a whole category of fetal infections called Storch, which is an acronym for *s*yphilis, *t*oxoplasmosis, *r*ubella, *c*ytomegalovirus infection, and *h*erpes. Syphilis is caused by a type of bacterium called a spirochete. This bacterium, if present in the mother, can invade the fetus to cause liver, bone, and brain disease. Toxoplasmosis is caused by a protozoan parasite widely found in animals and birds. The main source in urban areas of the United States and Canada is believed to be house-

hold cats. The parasite can be acquired by both children and adults, causing a rather mild disease. However, if the parasites are in the mother's body during pregnancy, they can cause extensive injury to the developing fetus.

Cytomegalovirus is a widespread virus that causes upper respiratory infections and flu-like illnesses in adults and children. In the developing fetus, it can cause inflammation of the liver, bone marrow injury, and brain, ear, and lung disease. Some of the effects of the cytomegalovirus may not be apparent until years after birth. Infants may appear healthy and behave normally, but they are suffering from a "silent" infection now known to be related to learning problems and poor school performance in later years.

The last of the Storch infections is herpes. Herpes simplex viruses are responsible for, among other things, the painful, recurrent condition known as genital herpes. Once a person has been infected, the virus remains in the body for life, although it may be dormant most of the time. Herpesviruses can be acquired by the infant during birth, but they can also be passed from the mother to the fetus during pregnancy and can invade the membranes surrounding the fetus. If the mother has been infected, some hospitals today

automatically perform a cesarean section to lessen the danger to the baby of exposure during birth. Others do so only if the mother exhibits the skin blisters characteristic of a flare-up of genital herpes. Several current research efforts are looking at this whole problem for a better solution. It is not yet entirely clear if performing a cesarean is the best approach, if successful treatment of the infant with new antiviral drugs is possible, or if treatment of the mother with drugs just before delivery can be effective.

Dangers for Newborns

A newborn infant arrives from a special world, where protection from many infections (other than Storch) is provided by the membranes and fluid that surround the fetus. Prior to birth, the fetus receives some of the mother's immunity to certain diseases because her antibodies (disease-fighting agents) enter the fetus's bloodstream via the placenta. However, the mother's antibodies gradually disappear in the infant; by three months of age, the baby is no longer protected.

Even before then, the protection a baby derives from the mother's immunity does not prevent all infections. In part because not all elements of the immune system are fully developed at the time of birth, the newborn will actually be more susceptible to certain infections— and these infections can be particularly severe. For example, the herpes simplex type II virus, the most common cause of genital herpes, produces a potentially deadly infection in newborns. Intestinal organisms such as the bacteria *Escherichia coli*, klebsiella, and Group B streptococcus also can invade babies, causing bloodstream infections that can spread to the lungs, liver, brain, and kidneys.

Newborns cannot respond to these infections in the usual ways that alert parents and doctors to

Childhood Diseases

(number of cases
in the United States)

	1955	1983
Diphtheria	1,984	5
Measles	555,156	1,497
Whooping cough	62,786	2,463
Polio	28,985	15
Rubella	56,552	970

the presence of illness. They may not run a fever, for instance, nor can they complain of not feeling well. If undetected, the infections quickly spread and can be fatal within hours.

Treating Newborns

Over the years studies have shown that many infections in infants can be recognized and treated promptly. There are several clues to infections in newborns. The first is a fluctuating temperature, going from high, as in fever, to below normal. The second is that sick babies refuse to eat. Other clues include jaundice (yellow coloring of the skin), either lethargy or irritability, and mottled skin.

Any combination of these signs in a newborn calls for swift medical action. Samples of the baby's blood and urine are taken for bacterial culture. The doctor performs a spinal tap to look for bacteria and white blood cells (which combat infection) in the spinal fluid. Even before test results are received, antibiotics are prescribed to treat the most likely causes of the infection.

The infant is watched very carefully for 48 to 72 hours—the time it takes for the culture tests to identify any bacteria causing the symptoms. Often the cultures do not reveal anything,

and the baby who only recently was restless and had an abnormal temperature now seems to be doing well; this shows that the episode was not caused by a bacterial infection. Even when culture tests show a bacterium was present, the infant already may be well on the way to recovery because of the prompt antibiotic treatment. The swift response to warning signs is now common in hospital nurseries and has had a major impact on the success of newborn care.

Infants and Toddlers

Since the immunization of infants and toddlers ensures that children will be protected from diphtheria, pertussis, tetanus, polio, measles, rubella, and mumps, attention is being directed to other infections. With increasing numbers of mothers entering the work force, many thousands of infants and toddlers are now in day-care programs. As a result, they receive greater exposure to infectious diseases than if they remained at home and came in contact with fewer people. This does not mean that children in day-care programs are doomed to multiple infections. It does mean, however, that the people running and working in such programs need to be alert to prevent infections within the group. They should, for example, be conscientious about washing their hands after changing diapers, avoid overcrowding, and exclude children with obvious signs of active infection.

One prevalent ailment is the common cold—many very young children today will have more colds simply because they are exposed to more people. But they will also develop antibodies to the various cold viruses to which they are exposed, and they can thus be expected to have fewer colds in future years when they enter school.

Colds do present a special problem for infants and toddlers, however, since a frequent complication of colds in very young children is a middle ear infection. The infection, known as otitis media, is treatable with antibiotics, and a great deal of research is being done on the problem of recurrent otitis media.

Young children have always been susceptible to infections with the bacterium *Hemophilus influenzae*. One strain of this bacterium, Type B, causes joint infections, meningitis, and epiglottitis (swelling of the tissue flap in the throat that covers the opening to the air passages). This organism has been under intensive study for many years in an effort to develop a vaccine to protect youngsters.

Infectious diarrhea also can be a major illness during a child's early years. Infants and toddlers cannot tolerate too much fluid loss from diarrhea; they quickly become dehydrated. Diarrhea was a leading cause of death in the past, when children often were infected by contaminated milk and water. Today, the prime source of these infections is person-to-person contact. The disorder can thus be expected to occur within families and among children in day care. Some types of infectious diarrhea call for treatment with specific drugs. Most others are managed simply by keeping the infant hydrated with fluids (either by mouth or intravenously) and allowing the infection to run its course, since medication can actually complicate the problem.

Older Children

Preschool and school-age children are in general a healthy group; with immunizations against the epidemic diseases, these youngsters generally are affected only by various apparently unavoidable sporadic infections. Good nutrition, good hygiene, and a healthful environment by and large enable these children to handle these unavoidable infections.

Some infectious diseases become a problem when the child already has another disease. Children who have a chronic illness, such as leukemia or another type of cancer, kidney failure, cystic fibrosis (which affects the pancreas and lungs), or liver disease, are susceptible to infections that do not occur in healthy children. Children who have undergone kidney or liver transplants or have any immune system deficiency are similarly susceptible. These conditions and/or their treatment alter the body's defense mechanisms against organisms that a normally functioning immune system easily defeats or brings under control.

> **The devastating diseases of the past no longer pose a threat to young children.**

The yeast organism *Candida albicans,* for example, commonly causes thrush (an infection of the mouth) in newborns and vaginal irritation in adult women; in a child with acute leukemia, however, it can cause a life-threatening infection. Children with cystic fibrosis can be affected by a common bacterium called pseudomonas, an organism that is resistant to many antibiotics.

Another organism, called *Pneumocystis carinii,* is a major problem in children with leukemia and those whose immune systems have been suppressed to prevent rejection of a transplanted organ. It causes a form of pneumonia that is difficult to diagnose but can be treated with a combination of antibiotics, and susceptible children can often be protected with small daily doses of

antibiotics to prevent the organism from establishing itself in the lungs.

New Frontiers

As medicine approaches the 21st century, new areas of research will further reduce the impact of infectious diseases on children. Studies are now under way to improve methods of detecting viruses and to understand how the body's cells can defend themselves. Researchers are also working on new vaccines to protect children against viruses, including the one that causes chicken pox. In 1984, a team of researchers reported success in a test of a chicken pox vaccine. Much more testing remains to be done, however, and a vaccine is not expected to be generally available for a number of years.

Work continues on finding safer means of preventing diseases for which there are already vaccines. Concerns have been raised about the side effects of the vaccine currently used to prevent whooping cough. The vaccine is highly effective and the risks are quite low, but children do have reactions to the pertussis vaccine more often than to other inoculations, and in rare cases, children have died. The rising costs of lawsuits and liability insurance caused two of the three American firms manufacturing the vaccine to announce in 1984 that they would stop producing it. The announcements led to fears of a vaccine shortage, despite a subsequent promise by one of the withdrawing manufacturers to continue production in 1985. All this has generated major efforts to find a purer, less potentially dangerous new vaccine.

Infectious diseases are an important enemy of normal health and development in children. The progress in combating them has been very impressive, and new knowledge should make more and more diseases obsolete. ☐

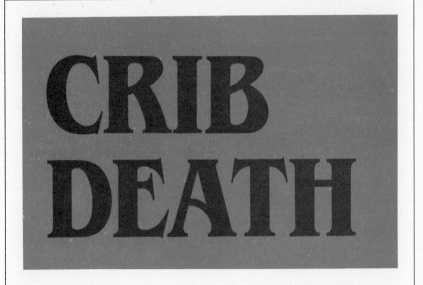

CRIB DEATH

Frederick Mandell, M.D.

Crib death is the sudden, unexpected, and unexplainable death of an infant. It is a tragedy that arouses deep and troubling emotions, shattering the joys of new parenthood. Feelings of shock, despair, guilt, helplessness, and anger are common. While parents grieve, often blaming themselves for the mysterious death, their other children are bewildered, unable to understand the meaning of their baby brother or sister's disappearance or its impact on the family.

A Sudden, Silent Killer

Crib death, technically known as sudden infant death syndrome, or SIDS, is the leading cause of death in infants between the ages of one week and one year in both the United States and Canada; most SIDS deaths occur between the ages of two months and four months. About 8,000 babies will die of the syndrome in the United States this year.

SIDS deaths are silent, and most occur during sleep. Typically, a well-cared-for and apparently healthy infant is placed in a crib at night—and found dead the next morning. A study of over 400 SIDS victims found that 74 percent died during the early morning hours, and one-third died while an adult was asleep in the same room. None of these infants made an agonized outcry; the death itself went unobserved. SIDS deaths have also occurred in car seats while the infant was sleeping and

---

Crib death is a tragedy arousing deep and troubling emotions.

---

a parent was driving. In some cases, there has been evidence of suffering before death: infants have been found lying in unusual positions in a corner of the crib or grasping blankets.

Incidence

In areas where there are definite seasons, researchers have found, the incidence of crib death is higher in the winter. More SIDS deaths occur among males and low-birth-weight infants than other babies. Infants of mothers who smoke appear to run a greater risk of SIDS. Children of American Indians, Alaskan natives, and economically disadvantaged blacks are twice as likely as white infants to succumb to crib death. There is also evidence that infants of teenage mothers run an increased risk of SIDS. According to one study, the incidence among such babies was about five for every 1,000 live births, compared with two for every 1,000 in the general population. In general, although SIDS strikes families at all socio-economic levels, it is more common among the poor.

Searching for the Cause

The cause of crib death is unknown. Researchers' efforts to explain it have resulted in some 100 different theories. For many years it was thought that breast-feeding provided some protection against these sudden and inexplicable deaths, but a recent study found no connection between bottle feeding and SIDS. Some physicians have voiced concern that the DPT shots—combining vaccines against diphtheria, pertussis (whooping cough), and tetanus—commonly given in infancy may be linked in some way to SIDS deaths; a recent preliminary report from a large study, however, found no convincing evidence of such a relationship.

A major area of research has been the possible role of a virus-caused infection in SIDS. The high frequency of crib deaths in the winter months, along with the fact that about half of SIDS victims show signs of a viral infection of the upper respiratory system, suggests that viruses are somehow involved. Many different viruses have been isolated in these children, however, and no single one has emerged as a likely cause of death.

Another possibility is that SIDS

is an inherited disorder. But here, too, no convincing evidence has been found as of yet.

Crib Death and Apnea

In the last ten years much SIDS research has focused on a possible link with apnea, or temporary interruptions of breathing, during which the baby may turn blue or become limp. Many specialists have thought that episodes of apnea could be considered at least an indication of an increased risk of crib death.

There is now some evidence, however, that if there is a relationship between apnea and SIDS, it is not a direct one. Since the breathing interruptions themselves can be life-threatening, electronic monitors may be attached overnight to infants who suffer from apnea; the monitor will sound an alarm if the baby stops breathing. In areas where apnea monitors have been used extensively, there has been no change in the rate or the number of crib deaths. Although the monitors may help avert death from life-threatening apnea, they clearly do not protect against SIDS.

Parents' grief can be acute; they are often overwhelmed by feelings of guilt and inadequacy.

A study of more than 800 SIDS babies found very little correlation between crib deaths and previous life-threatening apnea episodes: only 5 percent of the babies had at any time before their deaths turned blue or pale, gone limp, or stopped breathing. In addition, studies done with infants who have had such life-threatening episodes indicate that only about 5 percent of them subsequently die during infancy.

Based on these data, it would seem that, at most, about 5 percent of crib deaths may be linked in some way to apnea.

The Impact on Parents

Parents' grief over the loss of a child to SIDS can be acute. Many SIDS parents are young; often this is their first confrontation with death in their immediate family. SIDS parents are usually overwhelmed by feelings of guilt and self-blame and tend to go over and over in their minds the few hours before the death, searching for some way they could have prevented it. Because it is so difficult to accept a death that cannot be attributed to any known cause, the parents' guilt and sense of inadequacy often persist despite assurances from their doctor that they are not at fault. The suddenness of the death, of course, deprives parents of any chance to prepare for the loss as they might in the case of a child suffering from a terminal illness.

People faced with the death of a loved adult often find that reminiscing helps them work through their grief. But an infant's death generally cancels out the short-lived happiness surrounding the child's birth. The parents' anticipation of the birth, their joy at the birth itself, and their hopes and plans for the family's future, now so cruelly negated, are often buried beneath grief and anger and are not discussed. Friends are also typically reluctant to stir up such memories.

Although mothers have traditionally been the primary care givers for infants, researchers are increasingly studying the father-infant relationship as well, and the reactions a father has when his baby suddenly dies. Fathers who have not been as involved as their wives with the daily care of the infant often have less insight into the realities of child rearing and less knowledge of health risks. When confronted with crib death, they may therefore be less prepared to accept the fragility of an infant's life and their own lack of control over their child's destiny. Thus, fathers may experience confusion, helplessness, and anger in a different way from their wives.

Fathers also tend to require

Older children are especially vulnerable in the period following the death of a sibling.

---

different outlets for their grief, presumably because of traditional demands by society that men be more stoic and less emotional than women. A recent study of 28 fathers who had lost children to SIDS found that the men felt a need to keep busy—they worked extra hours, took on additional jobs, and enrolled in more courses than usual. Many of the fathers experienced feelings of diminished self-worth and blamed themselves for not being involved enough in the care of their child.

The Impact on Siblings

The brothers and sisters of a SIDS baby have a difficult time as well. Often they cannot comprehend the concept of death. The mysterious force that has broken into the security of the family and taken away the baby can fill siblings with fear and dread—including the fear of their own death. The role of older brother or sister that in many families has been carefully prepared for is harshly disrupted.

Children feel especially vulnerable during the period following the infant's death. The family unit has changed, along with communication between their father and mother. Usually, the parents' behavior toward the surviving children also shifts, and the children must attempt to adapt. A recent report found that surviving siblings of SIDS victims experienced changes in their relations with their parents, in their social interactions, and in their sleep patterns in the period following the death.

Most often, parents become overprotective of or permissive toward surviving children. Occasionally, however, in an unconscious attempt to avoid the pain of possible further loss, parents withdraw from their attachment to their other children. As in most cases of family trauma, the needs of children are best served when parents can maintain some consistency of attitude and degree of firmness.

It is best if the parents work through their reactions to the baby's death before deciding to have another child.

Having Another Child

The decision to have another child after a SIDS death is a complex and emotion-laden one. Preferably, the parents should overcome their grief and work through their reactions to the death before having another baby; if so, the family environment for the next child will be healthier. Parents are too often advised to have a "replacement" child quickly. But a lost child cannot be replaced. Moreover, parents who try to have another child immediately sometimes find their grief compounded by frustration: the mother may experience difficulty in conceiving or may have a spontaneous abortion. Research suggests that women who

attempt to conceive another child in the first year after losing a baby to SIDS have a higher than usual rate of infertility and spontaneous abortion.

There appears to be a difference in attitude between fathers and mothers of SIDS babies regarding the urgency of a subsequent pregnancy. Fathers seem rather quick to focus on having another child. This may be related to a difficulty in expressing grief outright, or to their feelings of helplessness— they may be seeking renewed evidence of their virility or, more broadly, some sense of power over events.

After another child is born, parents are often frightened of any minor illness the infant may develop. When the baby has a slight cold or when parents face a relatively simple decision, such as

whether to change to a different formula or move to a new house, they often seek medical advice for reassurance. They are likely to check on their infant frequently during the night; they may become anxious if they do not hear the baby moving about. In general, these reactions are entirely natural.

Further information on crib death can be obtained by writing to the National Sudden Infant Death Syndrome Foundation at 2 Metro Plaza, Suite 205, 8240 Professional Place, Landover, Md. 20785, or by calling the foundation at (800) 221-SIDS. A good source of information and help in Canada is the Canadian Foundation for the Study of Infant Deaths; its address is P.O.B. 190, Station R, Toronto, Ontario M4G 3Z9, and its phone number is (416) 488-3260. ☐

New Help for Infertility

Susan Walton

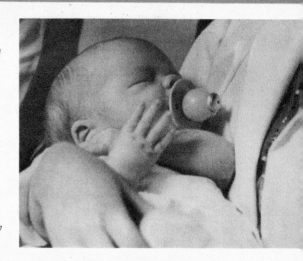

The first embryo-transfer baby born in the United States.

Ten years ago, couples who tried and failed to have children through fertility drugs or corrective surgery had only two choices—remaining childless or adopting. The introduction of a technique called in vitro fertilization—which produced the first "test-tube" baby in 1978—gave new hope to childless couples, especially those whose infertility was caused by damage to the woman's fallopian tubes. Now, a new technique called embryo transfer (or ovum transfer) will offer other infertile couples the opportunity for parenthood.

Embryo transfer involves the removal of an egg or embryo (an already fertilized egg) from one woman, and its implantation in another woman, who carries the fetus to term and delivers it. Genetically, a child born of this procedure has the characteristics of the woman who donated the egg and of the man whose sperm fertilized it—usually the husband of the woman who bears the child.

In early 1984, physicians in Australia and the United States reported the birth of three babies from donated eggs. The two groups used different methods to obtain and fertilize the eggs. Regardless of the method used, embryo transfer will offer a chance of becoming pregnant to women whose ovaries are not functioning. It could also provide couples in which the woman is the carrier of a genetic defect or disease—the gene for hemophilia, for example—with a way to eliminate the threat of inherited disease while still allowing her to bear a child.

The First Success

The birth of the world's first embryo transfer baby was reported in January 1984 by Dr. Carl Wood and colleagues at Monash University and Queen Victoria Medical Centre in Melbourne. The Australian researchers used the same technique that is basic to in vitro fertilization (IVF). In IVF, scientists surgically remove an egg from a woman's ovary and place it in a glass dish with sperm from her husband. Fertilization then occurs. After some 30 hours, the resulting embryo is implanted in the mother's uterus. The embryo transfer procedure used by Dr. Wood's team differed from IVF in one important way: the egg was removed from a donor woman and, after it was fertilized by sperm from a recipient woman's husband, was implanted in the recipient woman.

The woman who donated the egg in this first case was a 29-year-old participant in Monash's IVF program. The researchers removed four eggs from her ovary (a number of eggs are retrieved routinely in IVF) during a surgical procedure called laparoscopy. With her permission, the surgeons removed an additional egg to be donated to a woman whose infertility was even more intractable.

The recipient was a 25-year-old woman who had undergone premature menopause and whose ovaries consequently produced no eggs. She was otherwise healthy, and the researchers viewed her as a good candidate for embryo transfer.

But it was not only the absence of eggs that had to be corrected. Before the transfer could take place, the researchers had to induce artificially in the recipient the other physiological changes that make the body receptive to pregnancy. To effect those changes, the woman took daily doses of two hormones, estrogen and progesterone. The "artificial menstrual cycle," developed by a biochemist on Dr. Wood's research team, in effect mimicked the changes in levels of the hormones that occur in a natural menstrual cycle, until the patient was brought to the point where she could become pregnant. That the patient did become pregnant in the absence of the natural hormones proves, Dr. Wood said, that of the many hormones produced by the body, only estrogen and progesterone are needed to sustain early pregnancy.

When the woman who was to receive the embryo had been hormonally prepared for pregnancy (this had been timed to coincide with removal of eggs from the donor), the researchers took the donated egg and fertilized it in a glass dish with sperm from the recipient's husband. After the embryo was implanted in the recipient's uterus, it developed into a healthy baby boy.

A Different Method

In California, Dr. John Buster and colleagues at the Harbor-UCLA Medical Center in Torrance used a different technique to produce the same result. Again, an egg from one woman was fertilized and then implanted in a second woman, who carried it to term. The fertilization, however, took place not in a glass laboratory dish but in the uterus of the donor.

The first successful pregnancy using this technique was in a woman in her 30's who had spent more than eight years trying unsuccessfully to become pregnant. She was afflicted with endometriosis, a disease in which the endometrium (the lining of the uterus) begins growing outside the uterus. Although it does not always cause infertility, endometriosis is one of the most common obstacles to pregnancy.

The donor was matched with the recipient according to hair and eye color, as well as blood type and Rh factor (a blood component that can cause difficulties if it is present in the fetus and not in the woman carrying it). The donor underwent artificial insemination with sperm from the recipient's husband. Then, five days later, the physicians performed a procedure called uterine lavage, or washing. They flushed out the embryo and implanted it into the uterus of the recipient. Another factor in choosing the donor was

that her hormonal cycle coincided with that of the recipient, who was therefore prepared to begin a pregnancy at the time of the transfer. The woman who received the embryo had a normal pregnancy and delivered a healthy baby boy in January 1984. Two months later, Dr. Bustee's team announced the birth of another child—a girl—to a woman who also had undergone the procedure.

Both the Australia method and the California one have advantages and disadvantages, physicians note. The California researchers list some major medical advantages that their technique has over the other. It is a "simple office procedure," they say, requiring no anesthesia or surgery (laparoscopy to remove the egg from the donor), and it may have a higher success rate than that currently achieved by IVF (about 20 percent at the best clinics). In support of the last statement, Dr. Buster cited experience with embryo transfers

How Embryo Transfer Works
Australian Method

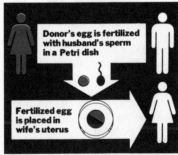

Donor's egg is fertilized with husband's sperm in a Petri dish

Fertilized egg is placed in wife's uterus

California Method

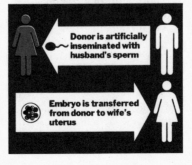

Donor is artificially inseminated with husband's sperm

Embryo is transferred from donor to wife's uterus

in livestock breeding: "Similar techniques have been successful in 14 species of animals with success rates of up to 60 percent per transfer," he said.

The lavage method does have its drawbacks. If the flushing process does not successfully wash the embryo out of the donor's uterus, she will be left with an unwanted pregnancy—possibly a dangerous ectopic pregnancy, in which the fetus grows outside the uterus, often in one of the fallopian tubes. It was this possibility that led the Australian team to stick with the in vitro system for the time being, Dr. Wood said.

The Australian physicians also are trying to make the process easier for donors. Up till now eggs have generally been retrieved by laparoscopy, in which one instrument (called a laparoscope) is used to enable the physician to view the ovaries, while another (a suction tube) is used to remove the egg or eggs. This operation requires two incisions and use of a general anesthetic. The Melbourne team is beginning to use another technique. The new method permits physicians to retrieve eggs with a needle, guided by ultrasonic imaging, in which high-frequency sound waves are sent through the patient's abdomen to create an image of her internal organs. The procedure is more economical and can be done under a local anesthetic.

Several modest changes in procedure have also led to improved fertilization. Dr. Wood's team has simplified the substance on which the embryo is nourished before implantation, decreasing the number of chemicals used from more than 200 to 20. They have also begun culturing the donor egg for several hours before the sperm is added. That practice may, as Dr. Wood puts it, "imitate that last little bit of maturing" that would normally take place in the ovary.

195

Frozen Embryos

The methods used by both the Australian and California doctors could benefit from another achievement announced by the Melbourne team in April 1984—the successful birth of a child from an embryo that had been frozen for several months. The Australians began freezing embryos because of concerns that disposing of unused ones generated by the IVF program might be unethical. (Because of the use of fertility drugs, IVF participants generally produce several eggs at once.) As the technique, known as cryo-preservation, became more advanced, the doctors tried to implant a thawed embryo. After one failed attempt, they were able to implant a thawed embryo (in the woman from whom the egg had come originally) that developed normally.

There are many potential advantages of freezing embryos. First, if eggs are removed surgically from a donor or a woman undergoing IVF of her own eggs, the "extras" may be preserved for use if the first implantation does not result in successful pregnancy. Thus, the need for repeated surgery would be either reduced or eliminated. Second, in embryo transfers, there would be no need to synchronize the hormonal cycles of donor and recipient, since the embryo could be retrieved, frozen, and then thawed and implanted when the recipient was ready. The Australian researchers hope eventually to be able to freeze unfertilized eggs as well as embryos.

The freezing of embryos, Dr. Wood points out, is not without risk. "One of the dangers is that there is just a possibility that we will do it at a point that would disrupt the chromosomes."

Embryo Transfer Programs

In July 1984, the first embryo transfer program in the United States officially opened, at the Infertility Center of New York. The program, which is a for-profit operation, reported a huge initial response from couples wanting to participate. As of early 1985, no embryo transfers had actually been done, but the center hoped to begin performing the transfers in the near future.

In order to qualify for the embryo transfer program, couples must be found suitable medically and psychologically. If the couple is deemed suitable, they work with staff members from the center in choosing a donor. The donors—recruited through

---

> ## Embryo transfer lets some infertile women bear children, even if they cannot produce eggs of their own.

---

advertisements in local newspapers—are matched on the basis of physical type, education, and other factors, and they are screened for medical conditions, past or present, that would rule out the use of their eggs. The donors are also evaluated to determine their emotional stability; one concern is that donor mothers may change their minds at the last minute about surrendering the embryo.

The New York program will use the lavage method, which does not require hospitalization for either donor or recipient. The cost of a complete transfer has not yet been determined, and it is likely that the expense will vary for each couple, depending on the amount of medical attention needed.

A Chicago-based firm called Fertility and Genetics Research Inc., which funded the Harbor-UCLA embryo transfer ex-periments, plans to open two or three embryo transfer clinics in 1985. Fertility and Genetics Research is intended to be a profit-making venture, and officials of the company announced that they would apply for patents on the embryo transfer procedures and equipment that had been developed at Harbor-UCLA.

Ethical Issues

The announcement about patents provoked some criticism from within the medical community, which for several years has been debating the propriety of patenting new developments in medicine. The decision to seek the patents is just one of several ethical and legal issues sur-rounding embryo transfer and related technologies. In Australia, a public controversy erupted in 1984 over two frozen embryos belonging to a wealthy Los Angeles couple who had died in a plane crash a year earlier without leaving any instructions for the embryos' disposition. Questions were raised about whether the embryos had a right to live or to inherit the estate of their "parents."

In the United States, although no such situation has yet arisen, an article in the September 1984 issue of the journal Fertility and Sterility warned physicians that "in perhaps no other area of medicine are there so many separate statutes and regulations that potentially apply." What is more, the applicable statutes were enacted to cover fetal research and abortion, not in vitro fertilization and embryo transfer, which have wholly different aims.

Conflicting laws and ethical dilemmas, however, are not likely to act as a deterrent to the thousands of childless couples who are eager to join embryo-transfer programs. For some, at least, the new technology renews a hope they had abandoned years ago. □

Teenage Suicide WHY?

Richard H. Seiden, Ph.D., M.P.H.

Since 1950 the suicide rate among young people in the United States has tripled, from about four per 100,000 to a current rate of over 12 suicide deaths per 100,000 for those between 15 and 24 years of age. Approximately one out of every nine deaths in this age group is attributed to suicide—a rate that gives youthful suicide the status of an epidemic. Today, there are more than 5,000 officially documented suicides every year among Americans 15-24 years old. This is a minimum figure; there are many more cases that are not reported as suicide because of the stigma associated with suicidal death. In Canada, the statistics are equally grim, with over 700 suicide deaths each

Every suicide threat should be taken seriously.

year in the 15-24 age group, representing a rate of almost 16 per 100,000.

Even if the more than 5,000 officially recorded U.S. suicides were a true reflection of the situation, the figure would not begin to approach the number of attempts at suicide by youths. It is estimated that attempts number close to 250,000 every year in the United States alone.

The high number of attempted suicides, compared with the

number of suicide deaths, reflects the fact that many adolescent suicide attempts are actually cries for help—dramatic efforts made by young people to change their lives, rather than reflections of a straightforward, actual wish to die. Nevertheless, every suicide attempt should be taken seriously, and no such incident should ever be dismissed as a mere gesture or attention-getting device. It is a plea for help in what seems to the adolescent to be a desperate situation.

Whatever the actual numbers may be, we know that suicide among young people is an unnecessary, premature, and stigmatizing death. The burden it leaves on the survivors is terribly profound. Indeed, the entire

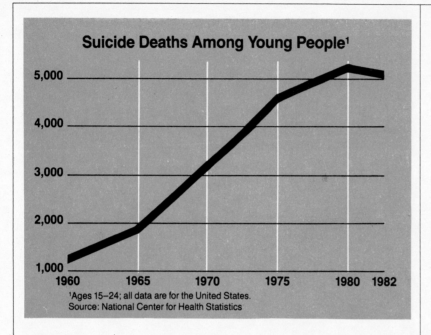

Suicide Deaths Among Young People[1]

[1]Ages 15–24; all data are for the United States.
Source: National Center for Health Statistics

depending on factors such as age, race, sex, socioeconomic status, and geographic location.

Epidemiological studies clearly demonstrate that race and sex are important variables in teenage suicide. The suicide rate among young whites is currently about twice as high as that among nonwhites of the same age group. The sex differential is even more striking, with males committing suicide three times more than females of the same age (although girls make more nonfatal attempts than boys). Socioeconomic status is another key variable. Suicide is more frequent among the well-to-do than among the poor. This analysis indicates that young, affluent white males are at the

---

The suicide rate among young people in the United States has tripled in the last 30 years.

---

greatest risk. Yet from all outward appearances, this group should be among the most favored in the population.

Research does not point to a particular personality type that makes people suicide-prone. Suicide occurs among people with widely varying personalities.

Recognizing Suicidal Behavior

Adolescent suicide fantasies are so widespread that they must be considered normal from a statistical viewpoint. Yet there is a great difference between fleeting daydreams and behavior that acts out such thoughts. What often seems to tip the balance between fantasy and an actual suicide attempt is the type of coping mechanisms and the social support network that a young person has to help him or her through the inevitable

---

community—parents, friends, siblings, neighbors, teachers—may be affected.

Clusters of Suicide

Major outbreaks of suicide among high school students in the United States were widely reported in the press in 1984. In the Dallas suburb of Plano, there were 11 suicide deaths in the 1983–1984 school year. Clear Lake City, Texas, near Houston, experienced a string of six youthful suicides within 2½ months. And three neighboring counties north of New York City were rocked by 11 suicides between February and October.

All these outbreaks were centered in affluent suburbs of major metropolitan areas, so that material need and economic despair can be ruled out as a root cause in these cases. However, it has been suggested that life in such communities can lead to psychological despair in some youths confronted with rootlessness, divorce, the pursuit of material possessions at the cost of family closeness, and a weakening of traditional values. Such despair is often seen as a prelude to suicide attempts.

There is also a strong element of imitation in much adolescent peer group behavior, and in these suicide outbreaks there does seem to be some evidence that later victims knew of and were influenced by the earlier cases.

These recent outbreaks are still under study, and researchers have not yet reached a full consensus on the causes. However, there is complete agreement on one general aspect—in the United States the leading method of teenage suicide has been firearms, especially handguns. Because they so often prove lethal, these weapons have turned impulsive youthful suicide attempts into fatalities. When a gun is used as the means of suicide, there is little chance for intervention and rescue.

Groups at Risk

One means of understanding the youthful suicide epidemic is to study it with the tools used to understand other epidemic conditions—the epidemiological approach. This approach is based on the knowledge that disease does not occur at random. Instead, certain groups are more susceptible than others are,

stresses of growing up. The teenager who has many friends, a full social life, and people in whom to confide is in a much better position to deal successfully with life's problems than one who is socially isolated, friendless, and without a peer support group.

Social isolation is not the only danger signal. A youngster who is experiencing disturbances of appetite, who can't sleep, or who seems excessively moody and despondent may be experiencing psychological depression, a condition frequently arising from a sense of hopelessness and strongly linked to suicide attempts. Many depressed young people try to improve their condition through mood-altering drugs, with alcohol the cheapest and most easily obtained.

Unfortunately, alcohol is itself a depressant; its excessive use tends to compound the problem, leading to an aggravated sense of worthlessness and despair.

"Tunnel Vision"

The depression and despair that personal problems may provoke can be especially dangerous in young people, who may react to them impulsively. Older people with similar problems but greater experience with the ups and downs of life are more likely to believe that the passage of time can heal wounds and bring about changes in undesirable aspects of life. The young, in contrast, are more likely to be afflicted with a sort of tunnel vision, believing that things will never change, that their situation will never improve. To youths who feel this way, suicide, rather than patience and endurance, can seem the "solution" to what is really a temporary problem.

Causes of Depression

There are numerous factors that can contribute to youthful depression; a broken home, excessive drug use, romantic rejection, and underemployment are only a few. One other factor that markedly affects this age group is academic stress. Most Americans between the ages of 15 and 24 are students, and academic expectations and the pressure to get good grades frequently figure in suicidal crises at this stage of life.

The effects of such stress in Japanese society, where strong emphasis is placed on academic achievement, have been well

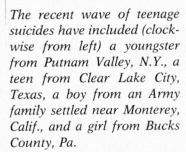

The recent wave of teenage suicides have included (clockwise from left) a youngster from Putnam Valley, N.Y., a teen from Clear Lake City, Texas, a boy from an Army family settled near Monterey, Calif., and a girl from Bucks County, Pa.

199

documented. Japan has the unwanted distinction of being the only country in the world where suicide rates peak in the youthful years (in all other countries they peak in late middle age). In Japan there is tremendous competition for admission into the most prestigious universities. Those who fall by the wayside in this competition can expect to spend their working lives in lower status jobs, since the highly stratified social structure does not allow much opportunity for a second chance. Thus, when the university admission lists are published each year, there is a rash of suicides among those who have not been chosen and who feel they have let down themselves and their families. Japan's example strikingly illustrates the strains that academic expectations—both personal and parental—can place upon an individual and the sense of failure that can lead to suicidal behavior.

Many adolescents attempt suicide not because they wish to die—but because they need help.

Preventive Action

Parents must adjust to the fact that children entering the teenage years are involved in a process of freeing themselves from parental control. They spend more time with their peer group, and their parents exercise relatively less influence in their lives. This is why the greatest emphasis in suicide prevention is now placed on programs based in the school. Such programs seek to educate young people, as well as teachers and parents, to recognize warning signs and respond effectively.

Special help is available from local suicide prevention or crisis centers in many communities.

Every suicide threat should be taken seriously. It is untrue that people who talk about committing suicide aren't serious about it. In fact, most people who take their own lives have given warnings previously that have gone unheeded or been misunderstood. Sometimes it may be a veiled expression, such as "You'd be better off without me," or perhaps an indirect clue, such as suddenly giving away favored possessions. In many cases teenagers who make suicide threats are testing to see if anybody really loves them, whether anybody cares if they live or die. At such a time, a willingness to listen and not criticize can have extremely beneficial results.

Parents, a teacher, or a friend who suspects a youth is contemplating suicide can try to encourage the person to begin talking about the problem with a simple question like "You seem to be a little down in the dumps lately; is something bothering you?" If the answer is yes, a follow-up question might be "Do you feel, at times, that it's just not worth trying anymore?" Further questions can be even more specific: "Some people think about suicide when things seem really bleak; have you been so depressed that that thought has occurred to you?" If this kind of discussion confirms that the youth may be thinking of suicide, professional help should be sought.

Professional Help

In general, psychiatrists, psychologists, and social workers are the people who can provide valuable professional help. However, not all of these practitioners are specifically trained to work with suicidal patients.

Specialized, competent help is available from local suicide prevention or crisis centers in many communities. These centers are staffed by trained volunteers who provide confidential services around the clock and without charge. In addition to emergency telephone counseling to deal with crises, the centers offer information and referral services, maintaining files of local therapists who are trained to work with suicidal patients. The most important consideration is to act promptly: early intervention and treatment afford the best chance of preventing a needless death and dealing with the underlying problem.

U.S. government actions and research on teenage suicide have increased. In 1984 the U.S. Senate's Juvenile Justice Subcommittee conducted hearings on teenage suicide. The U.S. Centers for Disease Control has established a Violence Epidemiology Branch with a focus on youth suicide, and the U.S. National Institute of Mental Health is sponsoring studies of the problem through its suicide research unit. Legislative hearings have been conducted at state and local levels as well, and, most significantly, there has been a mushrooming of school-based suicide prevention programs throughout the nation.

Additional information on the topic of suicide prevention and referrals to local programs are available from the American Association of Suicidology, 2459 South Ash, Denver, Colo. 80222. In Canada, information and referrals are available from the Canadian Mental Health Association's Suicide Education Information Center, Suite 103, 723 14th Street, N.W., Calgary, Alberta T2N 2A4.

FRACTURES & SPRAINS & STRAINS

Steven P. Roy, M.D.

In the last few decades, millions of adults who once were sedentary have taken up exercise, and children's participation in organized sports has reached an all-time high. All of this stepped-up activity, added to ordinary hazards like a slip in the shower or a spill on the ice, accounts for vast numbers of injuries each year to bones, muscles, and joints, causing pain, annoyance, and medical expense. This article will discuss some of the most common injuries that occur and how to treat them.

To begin with, a number of definitions are in order. A fracture is a crack in a bone, whether the bone is completely or only partly broken through. (The term is interchangeable with "broken bone.") Fractures come in different types. They may be described as "open" or "compound" if the skin is torn and as "closed" or "simple" if the skin is intact. Children often suffer what is called a greenstick fracture (so named because of its resemblance to the breaking of a branch on a young tree), where the bone is cracked on one side and bent out of place, but not completely broken through.

A sprain is an injury to the ligaments—the thick, strong fibers that attach one bone to another—while a strain involves a tearing of the muscles themselves or of the tendons, the tissues that join muscles to bones. Sprains and strains are divided into three categories, according to their severity. A first-degree, or minor, sprain or strain involves a slight tearing of some fibers of the ligament, muscle, or tendon that leaves the strength of these tissues unimpaired. In a second-degree (moderate) sprain or strain, the tissues are more seriously torn, and some strength is lost. In a third-degree (severe) sprain or strain, the tissues are completely torn.

Fractures

Some fractures are obvious, while others may be hard to detect. For instance, if the main bone in the lower leg (the tibia) is fractured, the bone will not move in the ordinary way. There will be marked tenderness in the area of the fracture, and swelling may develop soon after the injury. On the other hand, a fracture around the ankle is often difficult to detect, since it is not easily distinguished from a sprain. The only way to be sure is to X-ray the affected joint.

TYPES OF FRACTURES

SIMPLE
Skin over broken bone is not torn

COMPOUND
Broken bone protrudes through skin

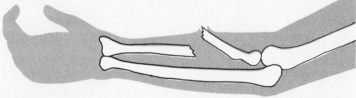

GREENSTICK
Bone is cracked on one side and bent, but not completely broken through

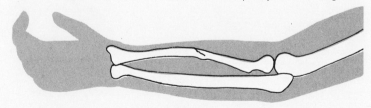

Whenever there is at least a suspicion of a fracture, certain steps should be taken at once. Weight must be kept off the injured joint or limb, and the bones should be splinted using any suitable material that is readily available (such as a piece of wood or an umbrella). Ice may be applied to the area of the injury, although it should never be used on toes or fingers, as circulation may be impaired. The injury should be examined by a doctor and should be X-rayed as soon as possible.

First aid for an open fracture, where a fragment of bone is actually protruding from the skin, includes covering the wound with a clean dressing and applying pressure if there is profuse bleeding. If medical or paramedical help is not available, you should try to splint the limb after the wound has been covered. (If a splint is not available, an uninjured leg can be tied to the injured one above and below the site of the fracture.) The patient should then be taken to an emergency room, where he or she can be examined and treated. Open fractures usually need to be surgically cleaned

because infection through the open skin can lead to major complications.

If X rays confirm the presence of a closed fracture, the fractured bone is usually immobilized in a cast. The traditional plaster-of-paris cast is seldom used these days; its place has been taken by

---

Considerably less force is usually needed to cause a sprain or a strain than to break a bone.

---

a variety of plastic and fiberglass materials that are water-resistant, stronger, and longer-lasting—and also weigh much less.

The length of time a fracture takes to heal varies widely, depending on such factors as the severity and type of the fracture, whether it is open or closed, and the particular bone involved. For example, the long bones in the legs generally take considerable time—often 12 weeks or more—

to heal satisfactorily, while the smaller bones in the forearm may take only four to six weeks. As a rule, fractures in young children heal at a remarkable rate, while those of older children do so less rapidly. Once adulthood is reached, however, age does not seem to have much effect on the rate of healing.

Sprains

In everyday situations, sprains and strains are far more common than fractures, since they can be caused by much less force than is usually needed to break a bone. Rapid swelling of the joint usually indicates a serious sprain; if a pop is heard or felt by the patient, it is a further sign of serious injury.

Ankle sprains are far more common than other types. They usually involve an inward twisting of the foot and ankle (an inversion sprain), which causes injury to the outside, or lateral, ligaments. If you injure your ankle, do not put weight on that leg until you are examined by a doctor. Ice should be applied to the area of greatest tenderness, and the limb should be kept elevated high above the level of

the heart. The ice serves to relieve pain and reduce swelling and internal bleeding from damaged blood vessels; elevation helps in draining away excess fluid. Leave the ice in place for about 20 minutes and then wrap a firm elastic bandage around the injury to help further in reducing swelling. The ice can be reapplied for a 20-minute period each hour.

Further treatment depends partly on how bad the injury is. Severe, or third-degree, ankle sprains may require the use of a cast. In less severe sprains, it is often better to apply a splint, which will allow up and down movement but spare injured ligaments the stress of side-to-side motion. A stretching and strengthening program to rehabilitate the muscles around the ankle is one of the most important aspects of treatment. This therapy should be continued for at least four weeks so that the patient can return to a full range of activity with no discomfort, and with less risk of a repeat sprain.

If you sprain your knee, the leg has to be splinted in order to prevent any further damage to the ligaments. Again, do not put weight on the affected leg until it has been examined by a doctor. In the meantime, ice should be applied, along with an elastic bandage.

In a first-degree or second-degree sprain, the knee often has to be placed in a special brace or cast for one to six weeks, during which time exercises are begun to keep the thigh muscles working well. A full and vigorous rehabilitation program is as important following a knee sprain as after an ankle sprain. At the same time, the patient's activity should be restricted until the injured leg is as strong as the other leg, with the muscles as well developed.

A third-degree sprain of the knee ligaments (in other words, complete tearing of one or more of the ligaments) frequently requires surgery in which the ends of the ligaments are tied together to allow proper healing. The decision to perform surgery depends on the ligament involved, the age and activity level of the patient, and whether there are associated injuries. If cartilage (tough, fibrous connective tissue) is thought to be torn, the doctor may decide on an arthrogram. In this test, dye (and often air) is injected into the knee joint to outline the cartilage, making any tearing visible on an X ray.

Another increasingly common medical procedure is known as arthroscopy. With this technique, the surgeon, using a thin tube with a bright light and with a magnifying eyepiece at one end, can look into the knee joint and assess the damage to ligaments and cartilage. Various surgical procedures, especially one to remove torn cartilage, can also be performed by means of the arthroscope.

The time it takes fractures to heal can vary.

There are times when what seems to be a sprain is not a sprain at all, particularly when the victim is an adolescent or preadolescent. In the case of adults, ligaments are more likely to be injured than bone whenever force is applied to a joint.

However, when the same amount of force is applied to a child's joint, a fracture may occur through the growth line (the area from which long bones grow). These growth lines consist of cartilage and usually remain open until age 14 or 15 in a girl and up to age 18 in a boy. Whether it is a sprain or a fracture through the growth line, the symptoms may be similar, and the immediate treatment should be the same—splinting and applying ice to the affected limb.

Strains

Muscle strains are most common in athletic activities and in other situations that involve sudden or intense exertion. The well-known hamstring "pull," felt as a sudden sharp pain behind the thigh, is a good example. Middle-aged people are subject to sudden tears of the calf and other muscles. Even the Achilles tendon, which joins the muscles of the calf to the heel bone, may suddenly snap. In any of these injuries, you feel a sharp pain deep in the affected muscle—a pain frequently likened to a "shot in the back of the leg." You may well look around in surprise at first, to see what hit you. The affected muscle or tendon quickly makes weight-bearing

difficult and painful. At this point you should refrain from walking without the support of crutches and should apply ice to the area of maximum discomfort for 20 minutes. This should be followed by application of an elastic bandage and elevation of the limb. Again, you should seek medical guidance on physical therapy and on how best to return to full activity. Ice, bandaging, and elevation are also appropriate treatment for an arm strain; a sling will help keep the arm immobilized until medical attention can be sought.

Overuse Injuries

With the increase in athletic activity in recent years, the so-called overuse syndrome has become more common. This term really means that you pushed too far or too fast, that you were trying to do more than your body was capable of handling at a particular time. Frequently, overuse involves the tendons, which become inflamed and swell up, leading to pain and difficulty in moving the joint fully. One of the best examples of this type of injury is rotator cuff tendinitis, which affects the shoulder tendons. This condition frequently affects the professional baseball pitcher, but it is even

more common among "weekend athletes," particularly those who were previously inactive for a long time.

The initial treatment for rotator cuff tendinitis is to apply ice for about 20 minutes three times a day and to avoid painful movements. An arm sling may be useful, and aspirin can help

Casts are now usually made of synthetic materials that are stronger, lighter, and longer-lasting than the traditional plaster of paris.

decrease the inflammation and reduce discomfort. If the symptoms have not subsided after a few days, the patient should be examined by an orthopedist.

Another frequent overuse injury is a stress fracture. This is an actual hairline crack in a bone, which develops from the repeated pull of the muscle on the bone. There is localized pain and tenderness in one particular spot directly on the bone, but an X ray at the time of the injury, will not show evidence of a fracture. (An X ray taken a few weeks later, however, will show that the bone was fractured, since it will reveal the new bone being formed as healing takes place.) A special test called a bone scan will show up a stress fracture and may be done if it is considered essential to make the diagnosis. This test involves injecting a minute amount of radioactive material into the veins. The material is taken up by the bones where a great deal of new bone is being created, such as at the site of a stress fracture; the fracture shows up as a "hot spot" on the scan. □

The Best First Aid: RICE

If you suffer a sprain or strain, you should take the following steps as soon as possible. The acronym RICE will help you remember them.

Rest: Stop using the injured limb or joint immediately.

Ice: Apply ice (for no more than 20 minutes at a time) to reduce pain and swelling.

Compression: To further reduce swelling, wrap an elastic bandage around the injured area.

Elevation: Keep the limb or joint above the level of the heart to help drain excess fluid.

ULCERS
Causes and Cures

M. Michael Eisenberg, M.D.

Ulcers are ubiquitous in Western civilization. Perhaps as many as 20–40 million people in the United States alone suffer from them. Whether or not you develop an ulcer may be affected to some extent by your sex, your personality, the way you react under stress, your diet, and your genes. It isn't surprising that some of us have ulcers. The real surprise is that we all don't.

What Is an Ulcer?

The term "ulcer" can refer to a sore on the surface of any body organ or tissue, but it is most commonly understood to mean a peptic ulcer, that is, an inflammatory sore in the lining of the gastrointestinal tract. The sore penetrates at least through the mucous lining of the tract and into the surrounding muscle tissue. Sometimes the ulcer may even penetrate the wall of the stomach or intestine, causing a complete perforation. Ulcers generally vary in size from one-quarter to three-quarters of an inch in diameter.

Peptic ulcers are usually found in the portions of the gastrointestinal tract that are bathed by acid stomach juices. In order to digest food, the stomach secretes hydrochloric acid and pepsinogen, a substance that hydrochloric acid converts into

Portions of this article are adapted from *Ulcers*, by M. Michael Eisenberg, M.D. Copyright © 1978 by M. Michael Eisenberg, M.D. Used by permission of Random House, Inc.

the enzyme pepsin. Enzymes are substances that act as catalysts to bring about certain chemical changes in other substances, for example, to help decompose food. Under normal circumstances, the tissues lining the gastrointestinal tract are shielded from the corrosive action of stomach acid and pepsin by various defensive mechanisms that keep the stomach from digesting itself. When the defense mechanisms are defective or insufficient, however, the lining of the gastrointestinal tract becomes vulnerable to the very juices that digest food, and an ulcer may develop.

Two Types of Ulcers

The two common locations for ulcers in the gastrointestinal tract are in the duodenum (duodenal ulcer) and in the stomach itself (gastric ulcer). A duodenal ulcer, the most common type of peptic ulcer, is usually found in the first inch or so of the duodenum, the chamber in the digestive tract into which the stomach empties its contents. Although primarily a disorder of adults, it is seen with alarming frequency in children. Most often, it occurs between the ages of 16 and 25. Duodenal ulcers are more common in men than in women, although this appears to be changing. The disorder tends to be lifelong; there may be long periods during which the patient suffers no symptoms, but these respites are

generally temporary. Sooner or later, unless medical treatment is intensive and continuous or unless the overproduction of acid is permanently altered by surgery, the ulcer will probably flare.

The second most common form of peptic ulcer occurs in the stomach itself, usually on the right side of the stomach, known as the lesser curvature. Although a gastric ulcer is caused by the same sort of self-digestion that gives rise to a duodenal ulcer, it has several key features that make it different. Ulcers in the stomach are only about one-fourth as common as those in the duodenum. However, in up to 40 percent of cases, a gastric ulcer occurs in conjunction with a duodenal ulcer. Although it is sometimes seen in children, gastric ulcer is primarily an adult disease, and it tends to develop when people are in their 40's, 50's, 60's, or even older.

Gastric, like duodenal, ulcers tend to predominate in males, but the trend is less pronounced with gastric ulcers. The levels of acid that the stomach secretes tend to be very high in patients with duodenal ulcers but normal or less than normal in those with gastric ulcers. This suggests that in gastric ulcer cases even normal or small amounts of acid overwhelm a defective defense mechanism; with duodenal ulcers, in contrast, high amounts of acid overwhelm normal defense mechanisms.

Are You Ulcer-Prone?

Some elements in a patient's habits or physiological makeup can clearly be defined as causing ulcers. Producing too much stomach acid is one. Taking large amounts of the drug cortisone or any drug that causes stomach irritation, such as aspirin, may be another. A third may be genetic background. Other elements that contribute to being ulcer-prone are less clearly established, such as personality, type of work, and diet. A number of studies name psychological stress as a factor, such as the stress imposed by work or family difficulties. Some individuals' personalities may also make them ulcer-prone, but as with stress most researchers maintain that the connection between personality and ulcers has not been clearly established.

Each of the factors may independently exert only a small influence. In pairs or groups, though, they may represent a more important basis for susceptibility, since the factors tend to reinforce one another.

Common Symptoms

The single most consistent symptom in patients with peptic ulcers is pain. Most often described by patients as a gnawing, burning, or aching sensation, the pain can also feel like soreness or hunger pangs. With duodenal ulcers, the pain usually occurs in the middle of the abdomen, often just below the breastbone. It is intermittent, and it generally comes on between meals or when the stomach is empty during the night. Food often relieves the symptoms of a duodenal ulcer, and people sometimes learn that keeping the stomach full helps prevent the development of pain or relieves it once it occurs. The pain can sometimes be severe and unrelenting, especially in a prolonged attack; even back pain may occur.

The pain from a gastric ulcer is generally more constant. It can begin during or soon after meals. Not only is food less likely to relieve the symptoms, it can sometimes bring them on. The pain is often centered in the middle abdomen and slightly to the left; back pain is very rare. Nausea, bloating, vomiting, and burping tend to be more common with gastric ulcers.

Diagnostic Techniques

The most valuable technique for determining whether an ulcer is present is the barium X-ray study.

The patient swallows a small amount of chalk-like dye, which usually allows the ulcer to be seen on an X ray. The technique is safe and valuable; although less accurate than actual visual examination with a special instrument called an endoscope, it is easier for the patient and more widely available. X-ray pictures are also valuable to the doctor because they allow the physician to evaluate the ulcer from time to time to determine if there are changes in its size or its depth.

The endoscope is an optical instrument approximately the thickness of the human thumb. When local anesthesia is used to numb the membranes in the back of the throat and the pharynx, the instrument can be easily and safely passed into the patient's stomach and duodenum. This makes it possible for the physician to evaluate the condition of the lining and can provide views

WHERE ULCERS OCCUR

Esophagus

Vagus Nerves

Common Site of Gastric Ulcers

Common Site of Duodenal Ulcers

Stomach

Antrum

Duodenum

of the inside of the gastro-intestinal tract that are almost as good as directly seeing it with the naked eye. Also important is the fact that a camera can be connected to the endoscope, making possible a permanent record.

Medications and Diet

A bewildering variety of medications have been advocated over the years for the management of peptic ulcers. Today, however, only a few categories of drugs survive as acceptable treatment. Among them are acid neutralizers (antacids) and acid suppressants. The basic actions of antacids are the neutralization of acid by chemical reaction and the physical absorption of acid. Because the stomach is constantly secreting new acid, as well as emptying itself on a relatively continuous basis, the usual antacid given by prescription or sold over the counter acts for only 20–40 minutes. This does not mean that pain cannot be relieved for longer than that, but only that the acid itself is buffered, or controlled, for that length of time. With nonhospitalized patients, it is impossible to monitor and control stomach acid with antacids 24 hours a day. It is no surprise, therefore, that there is little agreement among physicians as to which antacid is best or even whether antacids have any significant effect at all on the long-term course of the disease.

We know that the less acid the stomach produces, the easier it is to neutralize it. Thus, the most commonly used and most effective medications available for the management of peptic ulcers work by suppressing the production of acid rather than neutralizing the acid after it has been produced. Called H_2 blockers, they act on important cell structures in the lining of the stomach to interrupt the pathways by which acid production is triggered. Cimetidine (sold under the brand name Tagamet) and ranitidine (brand name, Zantac), are the two most commonly prescribed drugs for the suppression of acid production. They are both extremely effective when taken according to a physician's directions, and although these drugs do not cure ulcers, they can very effectively manage an ulcer over long periods of time.

The subject of diet for people with ulcers is complex. For example, there is the question of whether deficiency of certain foods is a factor in the development of ulcers, as well as the more traditional question of which foods can aggravate or cause an ulcer. Although dietary deficiencies may be of some importance in causing ulcers, as yet no firm conclusions can be drawn. Protein deficiency and, in particular, an insufficient intake of vitamins A, B complex, and C are often blamed for ulcers. However, these observations have been based on experiments done with animals, and there are no carefully controlled studies with people that support such findings.

A more controversial topic of ulcer research is whether certain foods may or may not cause or aggravate an ulcer. It has been shown that people have very individualized responses to certain foods, so there is no general agreement as to which foods are capable of aggravating or causing an ulcer. Nevertheless, doctors usually recommend that patients exclude spices, such as black pepper and chili powder, and highly seasoned foods from their diet, at least during the first few days of an ulcer attack. Coffee, tea, cocoa, cola drinks, and alcohol can stimulate secretion of stomach acid; as a result, they may also be restricted.

Despite the small amount of hard information that exists on diet and ulcers and the fact that the rationale for a bland diet is weak and poorly supported by scientific evidence, most physicians have concluded that there is some value in frequent small feedings of bland foods for patients who are suffering an acute ulcer attack.

Surgery for Peptic Ulcers

Medication taken according to a doctor's direction can usually manage a peptic ulcer very well, but there are circumstances in which surgery does become necessary, particularly if certain complications develop. It is estimated that somewhere between 2 and 5 percent of all people suffering from peptic ulcers ultimately require surgery.

Surgery is indicated in the following cases: bleeding from the ulcer that cannot be controlled, blockage of the stomach outlet as a result of severe scarring and distortion by the ulcer, perforation of the stomach or duodenum by an ulcer that has burned its way completely through the lining of the gastrointestinal tract, and "intractability." Intractability means that diet, medication, rest, and avoidance of stress, among other therapies, can no longer control the ulcer and that a more certain and more permanent means of control is required.

Several types of ulcer surgery exist. In one, known as subtotal gastrectomy, the lower part of the stomach (the antrum) is removed, together with a significant number of the acid-secreting cells. Between two-thirds and three-fourths of the stomach may be removed. The operation is used for gastric ulcers under certain specific circumstances but less and less frequently for duodenal ulcers.

Another surgical technique is to cut the nerves that control acid secretion. These nerves, called the vagus nerves, run from the brain to the gastrointestinal tract and are an important link in the pathway that allows the central nervous system to affect your stomach acid secretion. Interruption of these pathways (vagotomy) is now a common operation for peptic ulcers. Complete severing of the vagus nerves may be combined with enlarging of the outlet of the stomach or bypassing of the

Although medications will not cure an ulcer, they can effectively relieve its symptoms.

outlet of the stomach to compensate for some of the muscle flabbiness that occurs after the nerves are cut. The operation (vagotomy and a drainage procedure) is extremely safe and is successful 97 percent of the time.

Severing of the vagus nerves to the stomach is combined with a limited (50 percent or less) removal of the antrum in a procedure known as vagotomy and antrectomy. This is the single most effective way to cure an ulcer. It is not quite as safe an operation as vagotomy and drainage, but it virtually ensures permanent relief. This operation is generally reserved for patients under the age of 60, in relatively good physical condition, who have aggressive ulcers.

Highly selective vagotomy—or as it is sometimes called, parietal cell vagotomy—is a newer operation that removes only the nerve stimulus to the cells that secrete acid. This leaves the nerves to the muscular pump of the stomach and other parts of the stomach intact. Surgeons have considerably less experience with this operation than with those previously described, and opinions of its effectiveness in the management of ulcers vary widely. □

Treating Burn Victims

Roger W. Yurt, M.D.

Whether from hot grease splattering out of a skillet, a backyard barbecue explosion, or a house fire, more than 2 million people in the United States and Canada suffer burn injuries each year. Burns are one of the leading causes of injury in young children, and most burns occur in the home. Burns can be caused by exposure to the sun; by flames, scalding liquids, or direct contact with a hot object; by exposure to chemicals; and by contact with electrical currents. In recent years, dramatic medical advances have been made in the care of burn victims.

Types of Burns

Burns are classified by the depth of the injury (although at times this may be difficult to determine, even by an experienced burn surgeon). First-degree, or superficial, burns—the least severe type—cause the skin to become red and dry. Only the surface of the thin outer layer of the skin—called the epidermis— is affected. Most cases of sunburn, for example, are superficial burns. Partial-thickness, or second-degree, burns often cause blisters. These burns affect deeper portions of the epidermis but spare enough

of it to allow healing without a skin graft, the surgical transfer of a piece of skin from an unburned area of a patient's body to the site of the injury.

The most severe type of burn is a full-thickness, or third-degree, burn. This causes the loss of the epidermis, the dermis (the deep skin layer), hair follicles, and sweat glands; healing cannot occur without a skin graft. Third-degree burns, although extremely serious, are not painful to the touch because the nerve endings in the skin have been destroyed. Skin with third-degree burns may be whitish, blackish, or charred in appearance.

With burns caused by contact with flames, hot liquids, or hot

---

Each year, millions of people suffer burn injuries.

---

objects, the extent of damage is usually visible. Once the victim is no longer in contact with the source of heat or fire and the skin has cooled, no further injury results. Burns from exposure to chemicals may be more de-ceiving. If the chemical is not

completely washed away from the skin, tissues below the top layer of skin may continue to be injured or destroyed. The effect of burns from contact with an electrical source may vary. Some are similar to flame burns while others can cause deep damage to muscles, nerves, bones, or even internal organs like the heart.

The Entire Body Is Affected

The severity of a burn injury also depends on the size of the area that is damaged. The skin is the largest and one of the most important organs in the body. The larger the surface area affected, the greater the risks involved.

Burns that involve 25 percent or more of the adult body surface area (10 percent or more for children) are considered major burns and require immediate medical attention because they can cause shock. Shock is a life-threatening state of collapse in the body, with symptoms that include rapid shallow breathing, a pale face, rapid heartbeat, and cold hands and feet. Shock is associated with, among other things, loss of body fluids—one of the consequences of burns.

Burns damage blood vessels, making them more permeable. This in turn causes plasma (water, salt, and protein components of blood) to leak into surrounding tissues (a condition called edema) and into the burn area. If a large amount of fluid is lost from the bloodstream and is not replaced, then the volume of blood will decrease and shock will follow. Patients with burns over a large area of the body therefore must be given replacement fluids intravenously. The amount of fluid needed depends on the patient's weight and the amount of body surface involved. A burn victim may require a great deal of fluid. For example, in the first 24 hours after the accident, an average-sized adult male with a 50-percent surface-area burn may need almost 4 gallons. It is not unusual for patients with a large burn to gain 15 percent of their body weight in the first 24 hours because of replacement fluids—which would be a 22½-pound weight gain for a 150-pound patient. The requirement for large amounts of fluids persists, though not to as great an extent, until burn wounds are healed or grafted.

Normal skin keeps foreign material out of the body. After a burn injury, the bacteria, viruses, and fungi that are always on the skin can enter the body. The moisture and dead cells at the burn site also provide ideal growing conditions for bacteria. In addition, burns affect the body's defense mechanisms; the white blood cells and other components of the blood that fight infection do not function properly. The combination of greater vulnerability to bacteria and other infection-causing agents and lowered resistance means increased risk of infection for the burn patient.

Damage to the skin from a burn can have consequences for all the organs of the body. By approximately five days after a major burn, the body's metabolic rate (the rate at which the body consumes energy) may have increased as much as twofold. This means that the heart has to pump twice as much blood as usual; other organs are placed under a similar burden. Since nearly twice as much energy is being used by the body, twice as much energy in the form of food must be taken in to supply these needs. This stress on the body continues until the burn wound is healed.

First Aid

The first priority for both major and minor burns is to stop the burning process. If, for example, your clothes are on fire, you should not run, but drop to the ground and roll to smother the flames. Then remove the smoldering clothing. (However, you should not attempt to remove any charred clothing that is stuck to the skin.) In the case of burns from chemicals, the burned area should be washed continuously with clean water until a physician can be consulted. Save the container the chemical came in or a sample of the agent itself so the doctor can determine the substance that caused the burn and prescribe treatment accordingly.

If a burn is the result of an electrical shock, the victim must be removed from the power source. Either turn off the power or remove the person from the source with a nonconducting object such as a plastic rod. Do not directly touch a victim who is still in contact with a live electrical current—or else you might be hurt, too.

Minor burns are treated by running cool water over the burned area. Small blisters (the size of a quarter or smaller) may be left unbroken. Larger blisters, however, may become infected if they are not treated; these blisters are usually removed by a physician, and an antibiotic cream is applied. The wound is then covered with a dry sterile dressing. Household items such as butter, oil, or lard should *not* be applied to burns. Such substances have no beneficial effect on the burn wound and must be removed later—a process that can be difficult and painful—and they may serve as a breeding ground for bacteria on the wound.

Burns resulting from contact with chemicals or electrical currents and any possible third-degree burns of any size should be treated immediately by a physician. Second-degree burns that are more than about 1 inch to 1½ inches in diameter should also be examined by a doctor.

Victims of major burns should be wrapped in a clean sheet or blanket and kept warm to avoid the risk of hypothermia (decreased body temperature), which can develop quickly. For the same reason, water or cool bandages should not be used on burns covering large areas. Hypothermia can lead to several problems, including irregular heartbeat or even cessation of heartbeat and breathing. Burns from electrical sources may also cause the heart to stop working. In these cases, burn victims may require cardiopulmonary resuscitation (CPR), which should be performed only by someone who has been trained in the technique.

Hospital Care

Although advances in medical care have shortened the hospital stays of burn victims, patients with severe burns often must remain in a medical facility for a considerable amount of time. Physicians estimate that one day of hospital recovery time is needed for each 1 percent of surface area burned. During hospitalization, the primary goals of the medical team are to provide the best conditions for healing and to remove deeply burned tissue and replace it with skin grafts.

Optimal burn care depends on a team approach involving several medical specialties. For this reason, special centers for burn care have been set up at hospitals throughout the United States and Canada. These centers are fully equipped to provide both immediate treatment of life-threatening conditions and long-term rehabilitation.

The Burn Center at the New York Hospital–Cornell Medical Center, for example, has four surgeons who specialize in burn care and four surgical residents. At least one nurse is available to each severely injured patient 24 hours a day. Full-time occupational and physical therapists work with patients from the day of admission to the day of discharge, and often for months thereafter, to help them overcome disabilities caused by scarring and regain joint mobility. Specially designed pressure garments may be used to decrease the cosmetic and functional consequences of scarring. When scars become thickened, they do not allow joints to move.

Dietitians, social workers, and psychiatrists are also assigned to the New York Hospital Burn Center. All of these individuals contribute their expertise to the team effort to provide the best possible recovery for the patient.

Two additional roles of the New York Hospital Burn Center, as well as other such centers, are education and research. Educational programs are provided not only to update and train the center's staff but also to teach burn care and prevention in the community. Laboratory and clinical research enables the staff to bring the latest advances to the aid of patients.

Advances in Treatment

Advances in the medical sciences and in burn care specifically have significantly increased burn patients' chances of survival and recovery and have reduced the risks of serious complications. Intravenous replacement of the large volume of fluid lost after

burn injuries has virtually eliminated deaths that prior to the late 1950's were caused by burn-related shock. The development in the late 1960's and early 1970's of improved antibiotics, including creams and ointments that could be applied to the burn wound, was a significant step in decreasing the incidence of infection.

Recent studies have analyzed the tremendous metabolic demands and, hence, nutritional requirements of burn patients. In particular, the pioneering work done during the 1970's at the U.S. Army Institute of Surgical Research in San Antonio has provided the basis for the use of diet and nutrition in treating patients with extensive burns. Bleeding from the stomach after a burn injury, as a result of stomach ulcers, was at one time a major complication for almost all

---

Advances in burn care have greatly increased patients' chances of recovery.

---

victims of major burns. However, it is no longer generally considered a serious risk, thanks to improved nutritional care and recognition of the importance of decreasing acidity in the stomach.

Grafts

Because of improvements in treatment, surgery to remove damaged tissue and replace it with skin grafts can now be performed within a matter of days after the burn occurs. In the past, delays of weeks were common for patients with third-degree burns. Third-degree burn wounds must be covered with skin grafts to replace destroyed skin tissue and to prevent infection and fluid loss. Outer layers of the patient's own skin, called donor skin, are removed

from unburned areas of the body (called donor sites). The healthy skin is then transplanted to the wound area.

Several major burn centers now have skin banks that supply skin from another person (allograft skin), obtained from cadavers. Allograft skin is used only as a temporary cover for the wound, since the body will eventually reject skin tissue that is not its own, but it allows time for the patient's skin to grow at previous donor sites. The patient's skin can be reharvested from these sites approximately once every three weeks. Allograft skin is frequently in short supply, and therefore xenograft skin (skin from a different species—usually pigskin) is often used as a graft instead, again only as a temporary substitute for the patient's own skin. Commercially available synthetic skin has been refined to the extent that it is now useful as a temporary covering for second-degree burns; there has been some success reported in its use on third-degree burns as well.

The primary limitation on grafting with patients' own skin (called autologous grafting) has been that there is sometimes not enough unburned skin area available for use as donor sites. There have been promising reports in the last few years that a kind of artificial skin—made, in part, of collagen (a protein that is a normal skin component) obtained from cowhide—can be applied to burn wounds. This material, fabricated so that its structure resembles that of the normal dermis, can serve as a medium for the growth, at the wound site, of a "neodermis." To protect against infection and fluid loss, the artificial skin is covered with an outer layer of silicone rubber, which is removed after a few weeks. Small pieces of the patient's epidermis are then transplanted to the area, and a new epidermis grows.

Research efforts at the New York Hospital–Cornell Medical

First Aid Tips

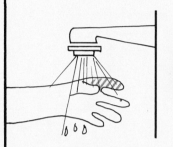

For minor burns, run cool water over burned area.

Do not apply butter, oil, or lard to burns.

Do not remove charred clothing stuck to burned skin.

See a doctor immediately for chemical, electrical, or possible third-degree burns.

Wash chemical burns continuously with clean water until a doctor is contacted.

Keep victims of major burns warm by wrapping them in a clean sheet or blanket.

Do not use water or cool bandages on major burns (except chemical burns).

Center have focused on developing a "universal" skin—a readily available permanent skin replacement. This involves an attempt to cause human skin cells grown in the laboratory to lose their antigenicity—the property that allows the body's immune system to detect the difference between its own cells and those from others. If the technique is successful, such skin could be grown, preserved, and grafted without concern for rejection. The result of preliminary experiments have been encouraging; however, additional study is required.

A potential new treatment for victims of extensive burns using a type of test-tube skin has received wide attention. In August 1984, the results of this approach in two young brothers from Wyoming, who had been severely burned over 95 percent of their bodies, were reported from the Shriners Burn Institute in Boston. Doctors applied sheets of skin grown in the laboratory from tiny patches of the boys' own skin. The sheets were grown from individual cells in test tubes. After several weeks, about one-half of a square foot of the test-tube grown skin was applied to the wounds of each boy, in sheets measuring 2 by 3 inches. Additional test-tube grown skin was grafted onto the boys' bodies in a series of operations.

The new skin, which is thinner than normal skin because it does not have a dermis, covers about half of one boy's body surface and more than half of his brother's; the rest of the boys' injured skin healed naturally or was replaced with grafts from the healed areas. (The boys still face years of additional therapy.) A team of researchers and surgeons decided to use the treatment, still considered highly experimental and never attempted on such a scale before, when it was deemed the only hope for the boys' survival.

The disruption of normal body processes that is associated with severe burns exceeds that of any other injury or disease. Recent advances in grafting techniques, skin synthesis, and care of the burn patient have been dramatic, but clearly the ideal solution is prevention of burn injuries in the first place. □

The Uses of STEROIDS

Thomas H. Maugh II, Ph.D.

In the early days of World War II, U.S. Army Air Force planners were shaken by reports that German pilots were able to fly at higher altitudes than their American counterparts and were less susceptible to the increased gravitational forces generated during sudden dives and strafing runs. The Americans feared that the Germans were achieving this increase in endurance by using a newly discovered substance, then known as Compound E, that is normally produced in minute amounts by the body's adrenal glands. To meet the German challenge, the U.S. National Research Council undertook a crash program to synthesize large quantities of Compound E—now more widely known as cortisone.

The rumors about German pilots later proved false, and the U.S. government abandoned the project. Private research efforts continued, however, and the first laboratory synthesis of cortisone was achieved in 1944. Scientists continued to improve their procedures until they were able to produce enough cortisone to study its effects.

In 1948, a 29-year-old house-wife bedridden by severe rheumatoid arthritis was given a single injection of cortisone. Four days later she climbed out of her hospital bed and went on a shopping spree. Thus began the age of steroid therapy—an age that has all too often been marked by high hopes for effective therapy followed by disappointment because of the severe side effects that resulted.

Steroids in the Body

Cortisone is just one of a family of naturally occurring and synthetic chemicals and hormones that together are known as steroids. They share a complex chemical structure and play a

---

Steroid abuse by athletes is a serious problem.

---

major role in the regulation of bodily functions and in the treatment of disease. Steroid hormones are produced and secreted in the body by the testes, ovaries, placenta, and adrenal glands (located on top of the kidneys).

Among the many different naturally occurring steroids are the sex hormones (such as estrogen, progesterone, and testosterone); various alcohols in the skin that are transformed into vitamin D when exposed to sun-light; fats, such as cholesterol; certain heart-stimulating hor-mones, such as digitoxigenin; and the corticosteroids, which are derived from the cortex (outer part) of the adrenal glands and which include cortisone, hydrocortisone, and aldosterone.

Steroids have many different roles in the body. The sex hormones control the sexual development of embryos after conception and regulate the process of reproduction in adults. The corticosteroids regulate the retention of water and salts by the body and the utilization of carbohydrates—a function that is shared by insulin. They play a major role in triggering the body's reaction to stress, and they influence the electrochemical functioning of brain cells.

Corticosteroids also have a major effect on the functioning of the immune system, par-ticularly on inflammation—a reaction to injury, infection, or irritation that is characterized by redness, pain, heat, and swelling. Elevated concentrations of steroids suppress virtually all actions of the body's immune system. This not only can reduce inflammation, but also can minimize damage caused by malfunctioning of the immune system and increase the body's tolerance of transplanted organs. It can, however, also increase susceptibility to infections.

Treatment With Steroids

Because steroids are present everywhere in the body and affect so many of its systems, it is not surprising that naturally occurring and synthetic steroids are among the most widely used drugs. They are probably best known for their use in oral con-traceptives and for their abuse by weight lifters and other athletes, but they have many other uses. Most are related not to the hormonal aspects of steroids, but rather to their ability to reduce inflammation and undesirable activity of the immune system.

Steroids are used in the treatment of rheumatoid arthritis; cancers of the blood and lymphatic system, such as leukemia and Hodgkin's disease; chronic liver disease and inflammatory bowel diseases, such as colitis; and autoimmune diseases, in which the immune system attacks the body's own cells. Other disorders for which steroids may be prescribed include allergies, certain lung diseases, and neurologic disorders, such as multiple sclerosis. The drugs are also used in combination with other treatments after organ transplants, to prevent the body's immune system from rejecting the new organ.

Side Effects

The steroids would indeed be wonder drugs were it not for one major problem: because they have so many diverse effects in the body, they have a large number of undesirable side effects when used as drugs. For many minor diseases for which steroid therapy might seem a promising treatment, the side effects of the drugs are potentially worse than the disease itself.

Among those side effects are osteoporosis (a weakening of the bones caused by loss of calcium), loss of function by the adrenal and other glands, and increased retention of salts and water, producing swelling. Other side effects include retarded growth in children, undesirable growth of hair, and muscle weakness. There is some evidence also that prolonged use of high levels of certain synthetic steroids may cause cancer. Because of these side effects, steroids now receive only limited use in the treatment of arthritis, and their use in other illnesses is restricted as much as possible.

If steroids must be used, there are two ways to work around the problem of side effects. The most common approach is to gradually reduce the dose the patient is receiving until the minimum effective amount is reached. When possible, that small dose is given every other day, which allows the body's

hypothalamus, pituitary, and adrenal glands a day to recover so that they do not atrophy. Timing is also important. The body's production of hydrocortisone and other steroids varies regularly over a 24-hour period, so that concentrations of steroids in the blood are highest in the morning and lowest at night. When steroids are administered in the morning, during the period of highest normal concentrations, side effects are further minimized.

The second alternative is to use topical preparations—creams, ointments, and drops that come into contact with only the specific areas that need treatment. Because relatively little of the steroid reaches the bloodstream, such preparations cause fewer side effects. Topical preparations are commonly used to treat contact allergies and dermatitis and for inflammations of the eye. Steroid enemas are used for treating intestinal inflammation when the inflammation is near the rectum.

Over-the-counter drugs containing steroids are generally thought to be safe not only because they are topical, but also because they contain very low concentrations of the relatively weak steroid hydrocortisone. However, patients must be

careful with topical drugs that are prescribed by physicians and contain higher concentrations of steroids. If these preparations are applied to the skin for an extended period of time, significant quantities can be absorbed into the body, affecting the adrenal glands and causing thinning of the skin.

Stimulating Production

In acute flare-ups of certain disorders, such as multiple sclerosis, arthritis, and allergies, steroids often do not provide sufficient relief. In such cases, the hormone ACTH (adrenocorticotropic hormone, or corticotropin) is often used. ACTH is a substance normally secreted by the pituitary gland to increase the secretion of steroid hormones by the adrenal glands. When it is given, typically by injection, it stimulates the production of natural steroids and provides relief from flare-ups of these disorders. Its side effects can be even more severe than those of steroids, however, and it is used only for short-term therapy.

Birth Control

The use of steroids in oral contraceptives has revolutionized the practice of birth control. During the 2½ decades since its

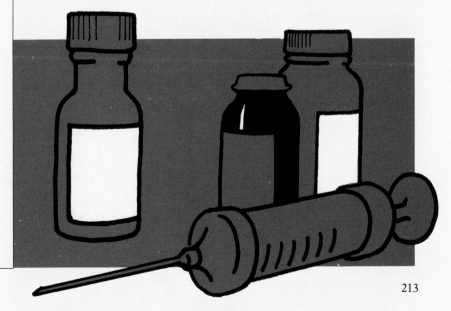

213

introduction, the pill has proved to be highly effective in the prevention of pregnancy—only about four pregnancies will occur among every 1,000 women who use the pill for one year if prescription directions are followed precisely. And despite fears, the pill has also proved to be remarkably free of side effects, partly because estrogen and the other female sex hormones used in oral contraceptives do not produce as many side effects as the corticosteroids and partly because the dose given in oral contraceptives is much smaller.

There has been concern that use of the pill increases susceptibility to breast cancer, but the results of several studies have been inconclusive. For the moment, the worst that can be said is that the use of oral contraceptives containing high levels of progesterone may result in a slightly increased risk of breast cancer. Most such preparations, however, are no longer used.

Use of oral contraceptives slightly increases the risk of blood clots and stroke (the risk is greater in smokers than in non-smokers). Recent studies also suggest that there is a slightly increased risk of cancer of the cervix. In all of these cases, the increased risk is less than the normal risk associated with childbirth.

Oral contraceptives also appear to confer some incidental health advantages. They reduce the risk of pelvic inflammatory disease by 50 percent, and studies have shown that the pill offers some protection against cancer of the endometrium (lining of the uterus) and ovaries.

Other Uses of Estrogen

Estrogen is sometimes prescribed for women over the age of 40 to control severe symptoms of menopause or as hormone replacement therapy after a hysterectomy. It has been found that these women have a significantly reduced rate of heart attacks. (Paradoxically, the incidence of heart attacks in men has been found to be highest among those who have the highest concentrations of naturally occurring estrogen in their blood.)

Women may also be given estrogen to prevent or treat osteoporosis, which is common after menopause or hysterectomy. (Although corticosteroids can cause bone thinning, estrogen protects against it.) Estrogen is often successful in preventing osteoporosis in young women who have had hysterectomies. Results have not been as encouraging when the hormone is given to older women whose bones have already started to become thinner. The possible risks of estrogen must therefore be taken into account before older women are treated.

Steroid Abuse by Athletes

The male sex hormones, such as testosterone and its synthetic derivatives, have relatively limited use in medicine. They are most often prescribed in low doses to correct hormonal imbalances or to prevent muscle atrophy in people recovering from surgery or starvation. They are, however, widely abused by athletes.

Male hormones have two primary effects, masculinization and muscle-building, or anabolic, effects. Many athletes and some scientists believe that the anabolic steroids, when taken over long periods of time, increase strength, endurance, and muscle mass in both men and women. Many studies, however, suggest that these effects are illusory, and there is no firm evidence that the anabolic steroids actually improve athletic performance.

There is little doubt, however, that some effects of anabolic steroids on athletes are disastrous. Among those effects are significant weight gains, osteoporosis, liver disease, heart disease, and either temporary or permanent infertility accompanied, in males, by atrophy of the testes. In adolescents, use of steroids can result in diminished stature because bone growth is halted prematurely. There seems little question that anabolic steroids should never be used by athletes. ☐

Some Common Steroids: ALDOSTERONE CORTISONE ESTROGEN HYDROCORTISONE PROGESTERONE TESTOSTERONE

Facts About MULTIPLE SCLEROSIS

William A. Sibley, M.D.

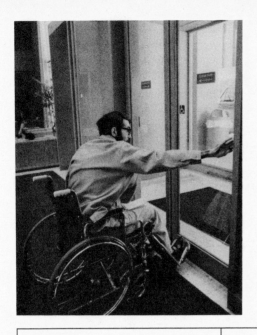

For Ray, life was full of promise. Just 30 years old, he was a successful insurance salesman with a wife and two young children. One morning, however, he awoke and found that both hands were numb and tingling; he shook them, fully expecting the abnormal feeling to disappear quickly, but it persisted. Three days later, his hands and arms still numb, he went to his physician, who examined him and found nothing unusual. In two weeks the numbness began to subside, and in four weeks everything was back to normal. Ray almost forgot the episode.

About two years later, he suddenly noticed while driving his car that everything appeared double: he saw two cars where only one existed. If he covered one eye, the double vision disappeared. His eye doctor ordered some tests, but in one month the double vision disappeared; Ray had been able to work in the meantime with a patch over one eye.

Again he felt perfectly well; he jogged each morning and kept his tennis game in good shape. But one afternoon about six months after the eye problem, he became aware of a numbness in his feet. Within a few hours he had difficulty walking and was admitted to a hospital with paralysis of both legs. A neurologist did a complete examination, including a spinal tap, in which fluid is withdrawn from the spinal canal (with a needle) for analysis. The diagnosis was multiple sclerosis. Ray's legs improved in about eight weeks, but thereafter he needed a cane to walk safely.

Evidence suggests that MS is an autoimmune disease.

The following three years saw two more attacks of leg weakness which were so disabling that he found it necessary to use a wheelchair in order to travel more than a few hundred feet. The mildest exertion left him very fatigued, and he was forced to give up his job. Slowly over the next several years his legs became weaker and stiffer. Ten years after the initial episode of hand numbness Ray was confined to a wheelchair; his arms were strong but awkward, and his speech was slurred.

What Is Multiple Sclerosis?

Ray's disease—multiple sclerosis, or MS—is a disorder of the central nervous system (the brain and spinal cord) that affects primarily young adults. MS symptoms generally arise between the ages of 20 and 40; it is unusual for the disease to begin before 15 or after 55. Some of the more common symptoms are loss of vision in one or both eyes, double vision, vertigo (dizziness), weakness or numbness of the limbs, facial numbness, slurred speech, loss of coordination, and paralysis. Bowel and bladder problems may also be present.

The symptoms of MS result from the progressive destruction of myelin, the fatty insulating material that forms a sheath around many nerve fibers in the brain and spinal cord. The myelin sheath speeds up the passage of nerve impulses along the fiber, and destruction of the sheath interferes with the transmission of nerve messages.

The irregular patches of damage to the myelin in MS are called plaques; the number of plaques increases with the severity of the illness.

An Unpredictable Course

Different MS sufferers may have different symptoms, and a given individual's symptoms may vary over time. It is nearly impossible to predict the disease's course. There are, however, several general statements that can be made. In the early stages of the disease, periods in which new symptoms crop up often alternate with periods of improvement. New plaques tend to form in widely separated clusters, and new symptoms arise rapidly over a period of minutes or hours. The symptoms typically remain unaltered for six to 12 weeks (though sometimes less) and then are likely to fade. The periods of improvement are called remissions, and the attacks of new symptoms are known as exacerbations. The remission of symptoms is possible because the nerve fibers themselves are not usually affected in the early stages of the disease.

Remission is often complete after the first few attacks of new symptoms; occasionally, a remission occurring after initial onset of the illness will last 20 years or more, though this is exceptional. The average patient has about one attack, or exacerbation, every two years during the first ten years or so. Attacks are generally less frequent after that, although this does not necessarily indicate improvement; it may be, instead, that new damage to already affected nerve pathways may not be as dramatically expressed in new symptoms. Thus, in the later years of the illness, distinct exacerbations are seldom seen. Rather, as more and more plaques develop, persistent symptoms without periods of real remission are usual, and the illness in most cases worsens very

slowly. This is known as the slowly progressive phase of the disease.

Multiple sclerosis can in advanced stages lead to severe disability, especially paraplegia, or paralysis of the legs and lower part of the body. MS is the second most common cause of paraplegia in North America and Europe. (Automobile accidents are first.) A person with advanced MS may also develop ataxia of the arms—an inability to control the arm muscles—and speech problems like scanning speech, in which a lack of control over emphasis and inflection gives speech heavily accented patterns similar to those of scanning poetry aloud.

There is no way to predict whether a person who develops MS will become disabled. About a third of all cases involve a form of the disease called benign MS; symptoms are mild, and there is no permanent disability.

Who Gets MS?

MS has occurred in all major racial groups (except the Eskimo and Bantu) but is most common by far in northern Europeans and people of northern European ancestry. It is rare among Orientals and among African blacks, though not among blacks in the United States. The disease is less common in tropical than in temperate climates. In the United States, the number of cases tends to be lower in southern states than in northern ones. MS occurs in nearly twice as many women as men.

It is possible that heredity plays a role in MS, since the majority of individuals with the disease have a certain gene, called DR2, that occurs much less commonly among other people. This gene appears most frequently in northern Europeans, particularly Scandinavians. In the United States about 55 percent of MS patients have the DR2 gene, compared to only 18 percent of the general population. At most,

however, inheritance seems to account for no more than a susceptibility to the disease, since only 0.05 percent of Americans actually get MS.

Many researchers suspect that some unknown environmental factor may trigger MS—not only because the incidence of MS is higher in certain geographical areas, but also because increases in MS rates in relatively limited areas often seem to be linked to the introduction of a new environmental element. On the Faeroe Islands in the North Atlantic, MS was rare prior to World War II, even though the islands' population is of Scandinavian descent; but in the two decades following the British wartime occupation of the islands, more than 40 cases were recorded among island natives. In Key West, Fla., an unusually high rate of MS for a subtropical climate was recently reported; state officials announced a study of the outbreak.

Research Into Causes

Despite intensive research efforts over the past three decades, the precise cause of the disease remains unknown. At present, the preponderance of evidence suggests that MS is an autoimmune disorder, in which the immune system, the body's defense against foreign invaders like viruses, goes awry and attacks the body's own tissues, in this case the myelin sheaths on nerve fibers.

This hypothesis is supported by several pieces of evidence. One intriguing fact is that the DR2 gene is located on the human chromosome that determines immune responsiveness. Another is that MS patients have fewer suppressor T lymphocytes during periods of exacerbation. (Suppressor T lymphocytes are special white blood cells that help regulate the working of the immune system by inhibiting it from reacting excessively.)

If MS is an autoimmune

disease, the immune system's breakdown might possibly be triggered by a viral infection. According to this theory, a virus provokes an immune reaction not only against itself but also against some protein in the myelin of the central nervous system. In a recent eight-year study, it was found that exacerbation rates for multiple sclerosis were two to three times higher in the five weeks following common viral infections like colds and flu than during periods when no viral infection had occurred.

Another piece of evidence that MS may somehow be related to a viral infection is that high levels of immunoglobulin G have been observed in the spinal fluid of almost all patients with advanced cases; immunoglobulin G is a major type of antibody, a substance produced by the body to help ward off foreign invaders. Increased immunoglobulin G in the spinal fluid is associated with various infectious diseases, including those caused by viruses. Also, some studies have found that MS patients have increased levels of certain antibodies against measles virus.

If a virus does play a role in MS, it is more likely an indirect one, involving an autoimmune reaction, than a direct one. Thus far, scientists have not been able to isolate a virus that could directly produce the disease. Efforts to transmit MS to apes have not been successful, and no virus has been detected in the tissue of MS patients. These failures do not entirely rule out direct viral infection, but it is clear that MS is not a contagious disease.

Diagnosing Multiple Sclerosis

The symptoms typical of MS can also be produced by other disorders and so are not in themselves proof positive that multiple sclerosis is present. Before making a diagnosis of MS, the doctor will carry out a neurological examination to look

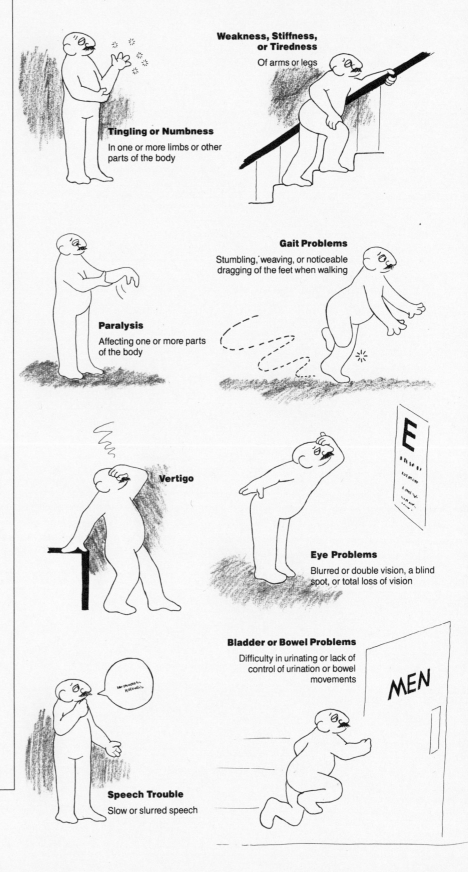

POSSIBLE WARNING SIGNS OF MS

Tingling or Numbness
In one or more limbs or other parts of the body

Weakness, Stiffness, or Tiredness
Of arms or legs

Paralysis
Affecting one or more parts of the body

Gait Problems
Stumbling, weaving, or noticeable dragging of the feet when walking

Vertigo

Eye Problems
Blurred or double vision, a blind spot, or total loss of vision

Bladder or Bowel Problems
Difficulty in urinating or lack of control of urination or bowel movements

Speech Trouble
Slow or slurred speech

for the plaques that are the distinguishing feature of the disease. There is, however, no single test that can clearly establish their presence in all cases. Most often the examination will include a spinal tap. The fluid thereby obtained may reveal an increased quantity of immunoglobulin G, or the immunoglobulin G may exhibit, upon analysis, a distinct banding of proteins called oligoclonal bands; these findings can point to the presence of MS as well as to other diseases, which must then be ruled out.

In more and more cases, plaques can be detected, and a diagnosis of MS confirmed, with the use of computerized tomography (CT, or CAT, scanning) or of the more recently introduced technique of magnetic resonance imaging (MRI), which "sees" more plaques than a CT scan.

In some difficult cases, diagnostic techniques known as evoked reponse testing are used. These tests measure the travel time of nerve impulses in the central nervous system by recording the brain's responses to sensory stimuli. Since destruction of myelin in MS characteristically slows the transmission of nerve. impulses, evoked responses can provide evidence of myelin damage. The most useful diagnostic test of this kind is the visual evoked response, which can reveal damage to the myelin sheath of the optic nerve.

Diagnosis may be especially difficult in the early stages of MS, particularly if the patient's only symptoms are numbness and tingling. In many such cases a neurological examination may reveal no abnormality; with insufficient evidence for a diagnosis of MS, physicians often suspect an emotional cause.

It is very important that a diagnosis of MS be made by a neurologist—a physician familiar with the other diseases of the nervous system that may produce similar symptoms.

The Search for a Cure
Unfortunately, there is as yet no cure for MS. Nor does there exist a treatment capable of preventing exacerbations or progression of the disease, although several forms of therapy, based primarily on viral and autoimmune theories of its origin, are currently being studied. Scores of remedies have been advocated during the past 50 years, usually because a few patients improved after trying them. Most have now been discarded as useless. The natural tendency for MS symptoms to temporarily improve without treatment has made the evaluation of therapies very difficult.

Corticotropin (ACTH), a pituitary gland hormone, has been shown to be capable of shortening the duration of acute attacks. So have cortisone and other corticosteroids, which are hormones (or synthetic drugs resembling them) that are produced by the adrenal glands. But with continued use these substances generally lose their effectiveness, and they also can produce dangerous side effects. In any event, they do not halt progression of the disease.

Powerful immunosuppressive drugs, such as azathioprine (brand name, Imuran) and cyclophosphamide (Cytoxan or Neosar), have been tried and show some promise, but further study is required. Safer immunosuppressants, such as cyclosporine, may prove more effective. A drug called 4-aminopyridine may be able to help improve the transmission of nerve impulses in MS patients and is currently being tested.

Several recent studies found that injections of alpha-interferon, a substance produced naturally by the body to fight certain viruses, reduced the number and intensity of MS attacks in some cases. Such findings are considered preliminary but encouraging.

A technique that is called plasmapheresis, devised as a potential treatment for autoimmune diseases, has been used experimentally in MS patients. In this technique, blood plasma is withdrawn, the antibodies are removed, and the plasma is then returned. The value of plasmapheresis is still unproven.

Helping Victims Cope
Although MS cannot be cured, the psychological and physical burdens it places on its victims can be eased so that they can live as normal a life as possible. Psychotherapy or counseling is available to help MS sufferers adjust to their situation. In general, doctors advise their MS patients to seek prompt treatment for infections and to avoid extreme temperature changes—as well as very high temperatures (including hot baths)—which can make symptoms worse. Various treatments exist for relieving specific problems. As noted above, ACTH and corticosteroids may in some cases be used on a short-term basis to speed recovery from attacks. For weakened muscles and limbs, massage and physical therapy are often recommended, and drugs that relax muscles are sometimes prescribed to combat muscle spasms. In the case of serious urinary problems, a tube, or catheter, may be inserted into the bladder to draw off urine—although permanent use of a catheter is generally not recommended, because of the danger of infection. Those who are severely disabled by the disease require nursing care.

More information about current research and treatment can be obtained from the National Multiple Sclerosis Society, 205 East 42nd Street, New York, N.Y. 10017, and from the Multiple Sclerosis Society of Canada, 7th Floor, 130 Bloor Street West, Toronto, Ontario M5S 1N5. ☐

STUTTERING

M. N. Hegde, Ph.D.

Stuttering is a common disorder of speech, so common that probably everyone has seen a child or an adult struggle while trying to say some very simple words. The disorder, sometimes called stammering, has a long history. Mention of a speech problem that could very well have been stuttering can be found in ancient and classical writings. Some think that Moses was a stutterer, and the disorder was known to the Greek philosopher Aristotle. Sir Isaac Newton, Winston Churchill, and King George VI of England all stuttered, and country singer Mel Tillis is a stutterer. (Surprisingly, people who stutter when they speak can usually sing, or read in unison with another person, without difficulty.)

What Is Stuttering?

Stuttering is a disorder of fluency, the rhythm and flow that characterizes normal speech. Within limits, speech is continuous: fluent speech flows smoothly, with few interruptions, and without much effort. The interruptions that do occur are not very long. Such brief and infrequent interruptions appear natural, and listeners seem to understand them. To some extent, such interruptions are even necessary. Speakers must pause, if only to take a breath, and fluency may be interrupted while they think about what to say or how to say it.

A stutterer's speech, however, is interrupted too often, for too long, and for no apparently good reason. The person knows what to say, and how, but just cannot say it smoothly. In fact, the person might stutter the most when absolutely sure of what to say. For example, giving one's own name and address may turn out to be a traumatic event.

Most interruptions of fluency are called disfluencies, and there are many types of them. Some are repetitions of parts of words ("ta-ta-time"), whole words ("time, time"), or phrases ("I am, I am going"). Prolongation of the first sound of a word ("sssoup") is also a form of disfluency. Even the very common habit of interjecting syllables ("um"), words ("well"), or phrases ("you know") is considered a disfluency. In addition, a stutterer's speech may contain pauses of extended duration. Words may be broken, as in "be (pause) cause." The speaker may leave too many sentences unfinished or keep revising the sentences. These and other disfluencies disrupt the continuity and smoothness of speech.

Practically everyone has some disfluencies, but stutterers have more of them. Some experts think that people who do not stutter have very few part-word repetitions and sound prolongations, while stutterers' speech is more likely to contain these types of disfluencies. A speaker who exhibits excessive disfluencies of any kind runs the risk of being labeled a stutterer.

The disfluencies of stutterers may be accompanied by muscular tension, particularly in the face, neck, and chest, and such reactions as quivering or puckering of the lips, knitting of the eyebrows, and tensed blinking of the eyes. Associated behaviors show a tremendous variety and number. During stuttering, speakers may wring their hands, jerk their heads, or clench their fists. Their faces may be distorted, and body posture may be tensed or awkward. There may also be irregular and labored breathing.

A Common Problem

The prevalance of stuttering varies with age. In children under the age of six or seven, the incidence may be as high as 4 to 5 percent; it is lower in adults. There are more than 15 million stutterers in the world—about 1 million in the United States alone. Stutterers can be found in almost all cultures, nations, and societies.

Stuttering affects four times as many males as females, and it tends to run in families. In terms of developing stuttering, a female stutterer poses a greater risk to her children, especially to her sons. And if one identical twin stutters, the other is also likely to be a stutterer.

How Stuttering Develops

Stuttering typically begins in childhood, sometimes as early as age two but, in a majority of cases, between the ages of four and six. As children grow older, the risk of developing stuttering decreases. Onset of stuttering in adults is rare, and some experts think that the condition may not be the same as that found in children.

Some children who begin to stutter may do so for only six months or less, which indicates that in certain cases stuttering can be outgrown without professional help. Unfortunately, it is hard to predict who will outgrow the problem and who will need treatment.

One of the earliest signs of stuttering is an increased number of disfluencies. Associated behaviors, such as tension and facial grimaces, may not appear until later. At first, parents may ignore or not really notice these disfluencies. Gradually, though, the disfluencies may increase significantly in number and occur in a wider variety of situations. Some of the associated behaviors may show up or become more prominent. By this time, the parents are probably alarmed, and they begin to think of their child as a stutterer. They may offer the child suggestions, such as "think before you speak," "take a deep breath," or "slow down." Soon, the parents realize that they cannot control the stuttering and that their suggestions sometimes actually worsen the symptoms. When it is time to enter the first grade, the child may be a full-fledged stutterer with a number of associated behaviors.

Profound Effects

Stuttering can have profound effects upon the life of the person who stutters. At the very beginning, however, the effects are on the parents, who get emotionally upset and may not know how to handle either their child's stuttering or their own reactions. When some of their attempts to control the youngster's stuttering fail, they feel frustrated.

The child soon becomes aware of the problem and begins to experience some negative effects. The child's self-confidence, schoolwork, and social life may all be affected. When attempts at speaking prove frustrating, the

---

Professional help for stuttering should be obtained early.

---

child may feel inadequate. Any criticism or negative reactions from parents, teachers, and friends further complicate the problem.

The worst effect may be a tendency on the part of the child to avoid social situations; the youngster might shun friends and begin to avoid opportunities to speak. As adults, stutterers might continue to avoid speaking situations. It may become harder for them to succeed in college and find a good job.

What Causes Stuttering?

A wide range of theories has been set forth to explain why people stutter. Some of these theories stress the importance of hereditary factors. Others explain stuttering on the basis of learning and conditioning. Support for this explanation comes from the fact that treatment designed to change stuttering behavior by teaching a new way of speaking is often successful. Neither the hereditary nor the conditioning theory specifies the exact cause of stuttering.

Still other theories point out the importance of brain mechanisms as a cause of stuttering. The brain controls speech, which is a highly complex activity requiring fine coordination of rapid muscular movements. Stuttering may occur when the brain is unable to regulate speech in a smooth and coordinated way.

No single theory is accepted by a majority of experts. In fact, most experts think that stuttering is caused by more than one factor. There may be an inherited tendency to stutter, and some minor brain disorder may be a part of this predisposition. It is equally likely that environmental events are also important. Stuttering generally begins at a time when the child is trying to master the language. Certain environmental pressures and stresses at this critical time may contribute to the development of stuttering.

At the very least, it is known that certain conditions trigger stuttering. For example, such external events as talking to strangers, before an audience, and on the telephone often increase stuttering.

Treatment

Historically, the treatment of stuttering has not been very successful. Such methods as hypnosis, psychotherapy, counseling, and anxiety-reducing drugs have not produced lasting fluency. Equally ineffective is the electronic metronome (in a hearing-aid type of device), which induces rhythmic speech as the wearer speaks in time to its steady beat. Other devices that produce a mechanically generated masking noise to prevent stutterers from hearing their own voice have shown only a temporary effect.

Research in recent years, however, has produced a set of techniques that are known to be effective in reducing or even eliminating stuttering in a majority of cases. Most of these methods teach the stutterer certain skills that are necessary to maintain fluent speech. Professional help should be sought as soon as possible for any stuttering problem; waiting can be detrimental. It is now possible to treat very young children successfully. In addition, recently developed treatment procedures can give significant relief to adults who have stuttered all of their lives and have tried many types of therapy without success.

Since fluent speech consists of a complex series of steps, the treatment of stuttering usually takes several months. The stutterer is taught how to use the breath-stream to maintain a smooth and continuous flow of speech. The sound should be produced by the larynx in a gentle manner to avoid an excessive tightening of the vocal cords. Treatment is given in a carefully planned sequence of steps. Often, the first step is to induce slow, smooth, and easy production of single, simple words. The person then learns longer words, phrases, and sentences. Slow and stutter-free speech is encouraged, and finally, fluency in normal-sounding speech is established. Once the stutterer is able to maintain fluency in the therapist's presence, additional procedures are used so that the fluency can be generalized and maintained in everyday situations.

In very young children, fluency can be systematically encouraged without necessarily teaching specific speech skills. Parents, acting with the guidance of therapists, can help by praising the child whenever the youngster is able to speak without

FAMOUS STUTTERERS

Celebrated stutterers include (from left) British statesman Winston Churchill, physicist Isaac Newton, and popular country singer Mel Tillis.

stuttering. In addition, parents should ignore stuttering when it occurs unless they have received special training in handling it.

In general, to ease the frustrations of someone who stutters, friends and relatives should be patient and should avoid telling the stutterer to "take it easy." They should try to maintain eye contact during conversations and should never fill in a word for the stutterer, which adds to a feeling of time pressure.

How to Get Help

The successful treatment of stuttering depends on a number of factors, such as the severity of the problem, the cooperation of family and friends, the motivation of the patient, and the expertise of the speech and language pathologist treating the stutterer. In many U.S. states, these

pathologists are licensed, and they are certified by the American Speech-Language-Hearing Association.

By law, public schools in the United States must provide speech therapy to stutterers, as well as to those students with other speech problems. Speech therapy is available as well in many hospitals and rehabilitation facilities. Colleges and universities that train speech and language pathologists generally operate clinics for people with speech problems, and private clinics can be found in many locales.

For further information, contact the American Speech-Language-Hearing Association, 10801 Rockville Pike, Rockville, Md. 20852 (301-897-5700) and the National Council of Stutterers, P.O. Box 8171, Grand Rapids, Mich. 49508 (616-241-2372). ☐

What is PREMENSTRUAL SYNDROME?

Judith M. Abplanalp, Ph.D.

Premenstrual syndrome, or PMS—the name given to a large collection of physical and emotional symptoms experienced by some women in the week or two before their menstrual periods—has been widely publicized of late. PMS is not yet well understood by health professionals. However, the mere fact that many professionals now recognize PMS as a legitimate condition has meant much to women whose complaints of physical discomfort and emotional upsets were for years shrugged off by most physicians as part and parcel of woman's lot or as evidence of psychological conflicts.

Despite the large amount of attention it has received recently, premenstrual syndrome means different things to different people—including the women who believe they suffer from it, the researchers who study it, the physicians who treat it, and the counselors who help women cope with it. There is no generally accepted definition of the term, and not all women who believe they are afflicted with PMS experience the same difficulties. The number, type, timing, severity, and course of the symptoms are all matters of lively controversy—as are the treatments, none of which has been scientifically proved to be effective. There are various theories, too, about what actually causes PMS. In addition, there is still some controversy over whether it is a distinct medical disorder at all.

Nevertheless, it appears that about 40 percent of women of childbearing age are beset to some degree with at least some of the symptoms grouped under the PMS banner; a small percentage of these women suffer premenstrual problems severe enough to affect their daily lives significantly. (There is some evidence that the incidence of suicide, accidents, and child abuse among women may increase just before menstruation.) PMS seems to be most prevalent in women in their 30's and 40's, although it has been reported in young girls beginning as early as the first period. It has been noted as a problem even for women who have undergone simple hysterectomies (removal of the uterus, with the ovaries left intact).

A Host of Symptoms

Premenstrual difficulties, which tend to occur a week or two before a woman's period begins, fall into three categories—emotional, physical, and behavioral. The emotional problems include anxiety, irritability, nervousness, depression, tearfulness, anger, and hostility. The physical complaints most frequently reported are bloating or swelling of the breasts, abdomen, and extremities, breast tenderness, headache, fatigue, constipation, and back pain. As for behavior, a woman with PMS may avoid social activities and have a tendency to pick fights, especially with her spouse, lover, or children; there may also be a tendency to violence.

Other common symptoms include both increases and decreases in sexual desire, clumsiness and coordination difficulties, decreased concentration, acne, and food cravings (especially for sweets, salty foods, and junk foods). Up to 150 symptoms have been associated with PMS, making a clear description difficult.

Another factor that makes a precise description of PMS difficult is that the reported symptoms are likely to vary both among different women and within the same woman during different menstrual cycles. It is in fact quite rare to find that, over the course of many consecutive menstrual cycles, a woman experiences absolutely identical symptoms of the same degree of intensity or at the exact same part of the cycle.

Why so much variability? A number of ideas are currently the focus of investigation. Stress may play a significant role. Some women report that their PMS symptoms are noticeably worse when they are experiencing personal difficulties such as job pressures, marital conflicts, or problems with children. The same women report significant easing of PMS symtoms at times when life seems to be less worrisome.

Diagnosis

Given the large number and the variability of possible symtoms, diagnosis of PMS is not a clear-cut matter. No laboratory test is available to detect PMS, and it is difficult to establish a diagnosis on the basis of a regular medical history alone. For many doctors, it is the timing of the symptoms, not the number or type, that is most important in diagnosing PMS. If the symptoms tend to occur shortly before a woman's period begins, and if the onset of menstruation brings significant relief, PMS is frequently suspected.

A doctor will often ask a woman believed to be suffering from PMS to keep a menstrual calendar or diary. Several forms of calendars have been developed. Most include a list of symptoms or changes reported by the majority of those women thought to have PMS. For every day the calendar covers, the patient notes the presence or absence of each item on the list and rates each symptom's severity. It is generally recommended that the patient keep the diary for at least two complete menstrual cycles and that no treatment be undertaken until this basic information has been collected and analyzed.

The doctor's analysis of the calendar information must take into account the symptoms that are most bothersome to the patient. The points in the cycle at which the various symptoms occur must be noted, as well as whether any are present throughout the entire cycle. In addition, the doctor should note whether the pattern is the same or similar for all of the cycles covered and how severe the symptoms are when they are at their worst.

Physicians must, of course, determine that other physiological disorders or serious emotional problems are not primarily responsible for the reported symptoms. Glandular disorders such as hyperthyroidism (overactivity of the thyroid gland), migraines, or conditions like endometriosis—in which the lining of the uterus begins to grow outside that organ—may affect or be affected in some way by a woman's menstrual cycle. Women who are severely depressed, who are chronically anxious, or who suffer from certain other types of mental illness may believe they have PMS because they find that their emotional distress is intensified before their periods. Most investigators, however, believe

Up to 150 symptoms have been linked with PMS.

that the problems faced by these women should not be confused with emotional changes that are experienced *only* premenstrually by women who are symptom-free during the remainder of the menstrual cycle.

On the other hand, it has been suggested that women suffering from severe depression are likely to have or to develop PMS. And some investigators have noted the reverse tendency—that women who become very depressed premenstrually may be more vulnerable than others to full-blown depression that is not limited to one phase of the menstrual cycle. Another theory that has been put forward holds that postpartum depression—after the birth of a baby—may indicate potential subsequent development of PMS.

PMS must also be differentiated from dysmenorrhea, or pain during the menstrual period. Some women who report problems during the premenstrual phase may also experience dysmenorrhea, but the two are not necessarily related.

Possible Causes

The causes of PMS are one of the most controversial areas of study of this puzzling syndrome. Many different viewpoints have been expressed over the past 50 years.

According to some psycho-analytic explanations, PMS is caused by a woman's basic rejection of her femininity or sexuality. The psychoanalyst Karen Horney in the 1930's took distressing preperiod symptoms to indicate a woman's unconscious denial of her desire for children. More recently, others, including many feminists, have seen PMS in a broader social and cultural context. They feel that the syndrome's perplexing symptoms may reflect negative cultural beliefs about menstruation, including the notion that the monthly cycle (once popularly known as the "curse") indicates inferiority. There are also theories that PMS may be related to emotional conflicts arising from passive acceptance of the traditional woman's role.

Various physiological causes have been hypothesized as well. Some researchers believe that PMS occurs in some women as a reaction to ovulation—the release of an egg from an ovary approximately midway through the menstrual cycle and the hormonal and physical changes that accompany it. According to this theory, the symptoms that constitute PMS would not be present if ovulation did not occur. Indeed, some women have found that using birth control pills, which suppress ovulation, has alleviated premenstrual problems. Other drugs that affect the chemical action of the ovaries are currently under study as possible methods of relieving PMS symptoms.

Another theory is that PMS results if there are abnormally low levels of the hormone progesterone just before menstruation. (Production of progesterone rises following ovulation and then falls off if fertilization does not take place.) Fluctuations in other hormones, including estrogen, have also been blamed, as has a possible problem in the ratio of progesterone to estrogen.

Also currently under study are alterations in levels of certain brain chemicals, including endorphins (which block pain) and neurotransmitters (substances that transmit messages from one nerve cell to the next); the relation of these chemicals to hormonal changes is being investigated. Finally, some think that nutritional factors, such as a vitamin B_6 deficiency, may affect a premenstrual woman's mood and physical state.

The attempt to account for all PMS symptoms with one theory has thus far proved unsuccessful and may in fact be too simple an approach. Given the varying patterns of the symptoms, it is quite possible that there is no single cause of the many problems generally accepted as part of PMS and that some combination of the various theoretical causes is responsible.

Relieving PMS

Since there is neither a formally agreed-upon definition nor a generally accepted cause of PMS, it is not surprising that the list of PMS treatments currently in use rivals in length the list of symptoms. There may be no single effective treatment for all PMS cases. In addition, it should

be noted that women who suffer only mild symptoms may not require medical treatment at all.

Hormones are often prescribed to relieve PMS. One of the pioneers of PMS research, British gynecologist Katharina Dalton, advocates large supplements of natural progesterone, given by injection or suppository. Dalton, who has treated thousands of British women, claims a 95 percent cure rate with this treatment. However, as of yet progesterone has not been proved effective in carefully controlled scientific studies, and some researchers are skeptical about it.

Bromocriptine (sold under the brand name Parlodel) also has been used with some frequency. Bromocriptine inhibits the release of the hormone prolactin (an

---

Recognizing that PMS is a valid problem can in itself help relieve symptoms.

---

excess of which can interfere with the menstrual cycle), and treatment often successfully relieves certain PMS symptoms, such as swollen or tender breasts. Drugs that act against body chemicals called prostaglandins, which control the functioning of certain smooth muscles, including the uterus, have been tried as a treatment for PMS. These drugs, such as ibuprofen (sold commonly as Motrin in prescription form and as Advil and Nuprin in nonprescription form), are often prescribed for menstrual cramps but have also been found effective in relieving premenstrual uterine and intestinal cramping, joint pain, and headache, among other symptoms. A product from the health food store, efamol, or oil of evening primrose, has also

become popular in dealing with PMS.

Most nutritional programs to combat food cravings and mood swings call for eating smaller and more frequent meals—six rather than three a day, for example—as well as cutting down on salt, sugar, alcohol, and caffeine. Vitamin B_6 supplements are given to remedy a deficiency that may contribute to both physical and emotional premenstrual problems. Exercise is often recommended along with these dietary changes. In treating specific symptoms, diuretics (for bloating and fluid retention) and antidepressants may be prescribed by physicians.

Psychotherapy has been found to be very useful, as have relaxation training and other stress reduction techniques, even if only to enable women to handle PMS symptoms more easily. Sometimes the realization, achieved through counseling or support groups, that PMS is a valid problem shared by many other women can make a great deal of difference—enough difference, in fact, that in some cases no other treatment may be necessary. In much the same way, a diagnostic menstrual diary can often assure a woman that her symptoms are not made up, vague, or random but real and cyclic; keeping the diary may restore some sense of control and may thus in itself prove therapeutic.

One of the problems in evaluating treatments for PMS is that patients are likely to report an improvement, for a short period of time, in response to any treatment whatsoever—even to placebos like sugar water. Researchers must take this into account in designing their studies. Until the mysteries of PMS are unraveled, however, treatment must be based on what seem to be the most effective tools and must address the individual needs of each patient. □

HELP FOR COCAINE USERS

Thomas H. Maugh II, Ph.D.

T he use of cocaine is often considered an innocuous pastime of the affluent and the famous. Most users believe that cocaine is harmless if they do not smoke or inject it. According to medical research, this is clearly not true. Nevertheless, cocaine use is a massively escalating problem.

One of every ten Americans has tried cocaine at least once, and more than 5 million now use it at least once a month. It has spread into virtually every geographic area and social class. According to Dr. Arnold Washton of New York City's Regent Hospital, cocaine "is now the drug of choice of middle-class America. Cocaine is the drug of the 1980's as marijuana was the drug of the 1960's."

Quitting Cocaine

The number of people who want to stop using cocaine is also growing, judging from calls to the "cocaine hot line," a telephone service that offers help and advice. The hot line (the number is 800-COCAINE) was established in May 1983 by Dr. Mark Gold of Fair Oaks Hospital in Summit, N.J. By early 1985, the service had received more than 775,000 calls, most from users who wanted to quit.

Many casual cocaine users in the United States have been helped to break the habit by self-help groups such as Narcotics Anonymous in the East and Cocaine Anonymous on the West Coast; both of these groups are modeled after the long-established Alcoholics Anonymous. Heavier users, however, require medical assistance. Physicians have slowly reached the conclusion that although cocaine does not produce the same kind of physical dependence as heroin, it is every bit as addictive, if not more so, in a psychological sense. When cocaine addicts quit "cold turkey," they suffer withdrawal symptoms that can include overeating, excessive sleep, depression, and, above all else, an intense craving for more cocaine.

Unfortunately, notes Gold, "there is no consensus about what constitutes appropriate therapy for cocaine abuse." Recently, however, approaches to treating the cocaine abuser have begun to separate into two distinct categories.

One group of doctors argues in favor of chemical intervention; they believe that cocaine use can be controlled if patients take newly recognized drugs that block its effects, much as methadone blocks the effects of heroin. The second group of doctors contends that drugs are of little treatment value; they hold instead that the best results are obtained by using relatively drastic psychotherapeutic techniques to change the patterns of behavior that originally led to the patient's cocaine abuse.

Drugs to Fight Drugs

Drug therapy for cocaine use is based on a still incomplete understanding of cocaine's effects on the brain. The most important of these effects seems to be a disruption of communication between brain cells, which interact by means of chemical messengers called neurotransmitters. When a cell receives a message, it sends the neurotransmitter back so it can be used again.

Most investigators now think that cocaine both stimulates the synthesis of neurotransmitters and blocks their return. The neurotransmitters then accumulate in abnormally high quantities at the receiving cells, flooding and overstimulating them. This flooding is thought to produce the euphoria associated with cocaine use.

Because of the overproduction of neurotransmitters, the brain eventually runs out of the chemicals used to synthesize them, and the person develops a severe depression. "Cocaine users find themselves in a vicious cycle," says Dr. Jeffrey Rosecan of the Columbia-Presbyterian Medical Center in New York City. "To alleviate this depression, they get high again. This depletes the stores of neurotransmitters in their brains even more, making the depression worse the next time they come down."

Rosecan thinks that this process can be short circuited by the use for a number of months of the antidepressant drug imipramine (also sold as Tofranil). He stumbled on this effect while treating patients for cocaine-related depression, when several patients being treated with imipramine reported that they could no longer get high.

Rosecan recently reported what he termed "incredibly dramatic results." Of 14 patients who used 5 grams or more of cocaine each week and who were treated with imipramine, 12 stopped using cocaine entirely or significantly reduced their usage over a ten-week period. The doctor said that the results were "especially impressive because none of the patients were hospitalized: all returned to their communities where they were subject to the temptations that hooked them on cocaine in the first place." Most are still drug free more than a year later.

Since that report, Rosecan has treated several more patients with imipramine for two to three months, with a success rate of more than 80 percent. The antidepressants apparently bind to the brain cell areas otherwise affected by cocaine, thereby blocking cocaine's effects.

Rosecan was not the first to use antidepressants to treat cocaine users. That distinction goes to Dr. Forest Tennant of the UCLA School of Medicine. In 1983, Tennant reported that he had used the antidepressant drug desipramine (sold under the brand names Norpramin or Pertofrane) to treat 14 patients, but only for about a week while they were undergoing the acute phases of withdrawal (detoxification).

Tennant has subsequently begun using the drug as well for maintenance therapy after detoxification, and he has treated some patients for several months. He recently reported that nearly 75 percent of approximately 100 patients—people who had used cocaine between four and 12 times a day—have become cocaine free.

Four Types of Users

Antidepressants have also been used successfully for detoxification by Drs. Herbert Kleber and Frank Gawin of the Yale University School of Medicine. But they use, in addition, either of two other drugs, together with psychotherapy, to keep their patients from returning to cocaine. They divide abusers into four general categories.

One group has what is called a cyclothymic disorder. These patients are similar to manic-depressives, who undergo wide swings in mood, but their swings are less severe. Such individuals typically use cocaine to control and extend their manic periods. Kleber and Gawin have found that lithium, a drug that is also used for manic-depressives, can prevent many of these patients from returning to cocaine use.

Those in the second group

treated by Kleber and Gawin suffer from a type of attention-deficit disorder—impulsiveness and an inability to concentrate, similar to hyperactivity in children. These individuals use cocaine for stimulation and to "mellow out." For them, relapse can often be prevented by the use of methylphenidate (Ritalin), the amphetamine-like drug used to treat hyperactive children. Methylphenidate can have unfortunate side effects, however, and its use is sharply limited.

The final two categories into which the Yale University doctors divide their patients are individuals who are medicating themselves for depression, and everybody else; together, these categories comprise about 60 percent of cocaine users. Kleber and Gawin have treated about 20 such individuals with desipramine; 75 to 80 percent of them became drug free.

Kleber emphasizes, however, that all his patients also receive a special form of psychotherapy that takes into account the social and psychological problems that lead to cocaine abuse. In late 1984, Kleber and Gawin began new, controlled studies to test the effectiveness of lithium and desipramine.

Changing Behavior

All of the work with various medications has drawn some critical fire. Dr. Washton of Regent Hospital objects to the conditions under which studies like Rosecan's were conducted. Rosecan did not monitor patients' urine samples, to check for the presence of cocaine in their bodies. Rather, he relied on their subjective reports. (Tennant and Kleber have monitored urine.)

Investigators also must be careful, Washton says, not to see as successful drug therapy what is really just the "conditioning phenomenon," in which patients who have begun to recognize the negative aspects of cocaine use report reduced euphoria or even negative reactions when they use the drug again. Washton is also concerned about possible over-doses of the antidepressants and about harmful interactions between them and cocaine. Rosecan, Kleber, and Tennant contend that they have observed no harmful side effects.

To help cocaine users break the habit, Washton uses a three-stage program of behavior altera-tion that is more extensive than the psychotherapy programs used by most physicians treating cocaine abuse. The first stage is the signing of a treatment con-tract, in which the patient agrees to attend the program for six months and to refrain from cocaine use. The penalty for a major relapse or for failure to provide urine specimens is hospitalization or release from the program.

The second stage of Washton's program is relapse prevention, in which the patient is educated about how to cope with stress and other factors that might cause a return to drug use. An important component of relapse prevention is recognition of a series of events often seen in withdrawal from cocaine (or from use of other drugs, smoking, or overeating): a one-time relapse will initiate a cascade of reactions that include feelings of failure, guilt, and finally a "what's the difference" attitude that produces a return to addictive behavior. The patient must be educated in advance that such a relapse is likely to occur, says Washton, and convinced that one slip does not make someone a hopeless addict.

After the patient has refrained from cocaine use for six months, the individual undergoes con-ventional psychotherapy to control the underlying problems that led to cocaine use in the first place and that might cause a relapse. With this program, Washton has obtained a success rate of about 85 percent. It should be noted, however, that Washton's patients are typically individuals with high incomes who are referred by spouses or employers and who have much to lose by continuing their cocaine use.

A counselor at 800-COCAINE, a telephone hot line at Fair Oaks Hospital in Summit, N.J., advises people who want to stop a cocaine habit.

Tougher Programs

Some researchers think that a more severe regimen than Washton's may be necessary. According to Dr. Thomas Crowley of the Colorado University Health Sciences Center, many addicts say the cocaine high is the most compelling experience they have ever had. Therefore, Crowley contends, the "immediate positive effect for the user is so strong that any other positive effects which might be used to aid withdrawal," such as a sum of money to be refunded to the patient if treatment succeeds, are not sufficient to overcome it. "It is necessary," he says, "to make the adverse consequences of a relapse so great that the patient has a strong incentive to remain drug free."

Crowley achieves this with a technique known as contingency contracting. In this approach, an addict who is a physician, for instance, might write a letter addressed to the state licensing board stating, "I am a cocaine abuser and I hereby surrender my license." The letter is left with the therapist, and the patient agrees to undergo periodic urine sampling. If the cocaine is found in the urine or if the patient refuses to provide a sample, the letter is mailed. For six months after joining the program, the patient is also given counseling like that provided by Washton.

Crowley recently reported results of a study in which 32 patients submitted to con-tingency contracting and 35 others received conventional therapy. In the first group, 31 patients completely abstained from cocaine use, while none of the 35 people in the second group remained abstinent and in therapy. Some therapists think Crowley's methods are too harsh, but he emphasizes that they have been used primarily for individuals who "are rather desperate, who feel that they have lost control and need some type of external control."

In the past, the main factors preventing cocaine use have been the drug's high price and its relatively low availability. Unfortunately, both of those factors are changing for the worse. At the same time, however, society is beginning to recognize the potentially de-structive effects of cocaine use, meaning that the demand for therapy will probably continue to grow rapidly. □

LEFT-HANDEDNESS

Pat Costello Smith

Individuals as different as Albert Einstein and Marilyn Monroe, Ben Franklin and Babe Ruth, Queen Victoria and Jack the Ripper had one trait in common: all were left-handed.

The majority of human beings use their right hands for most skilled tasks. Yet throughout history a small minority, despite cultural and social opposition, have persistently preferred their left. The left-handed, who make up 5 to 10 percent of the world's population, have long interested scientists searching for clues to the mysterious workings of the human brain. Some investigators now believe that left-handedness may be associated with particular abilities and talents, as well as with certain disabilities and disorders.

A Right-Handed World

Living in a right-handed world, the left-handed must deal with dozens of objects, ranging from watch stems and school desks to can openers and corkscrews, that are designed for the convenience of the other-handed majority. Although few modern parents and teachers try to force children who show a preference for the left hand to switch to the right, the left-handed are still subtly and sometimes not so subtly reminded of their nonconformity. Consider such derogatory phrases in the English language as "left-handed compliment," "two left feet," and "so easy that you can do it with your left hand." Yet various studies have shown that left-handers, far from being "out in left field," are represented at disproportionately high rates in several skilled occupations. Being different does not mean being second best.

Searching for Causes

What causes left-handedness? Some researchers believe it may

> **The left-handed are of major interest to scientists studying the human brain.**

be inherited; others, that it may result from environmental factors before or during birth. And according to yet another theory, the male sex hormone testosterone is associated with left-handedness, as well as with learning disabilities and disorders of the immune system.

The common element in all these theories is that they link left-handedness and right-handedness to differences in the organization of the brain's two sides, or hemispheres. Physicians studying patients who had suffered brain damage found that injuries to one hemisphere of the brain caused paralysis on the opposite side of the body. Thus, it was learned that the left hemisphere receives sensory signals from and directs movement on the right side of the body, and the right hemisphere controls sensation and movement on the left side.

In 1861, Paul Broca, a French physician and anthropologist, observed that most brain-damaged patients who suffered from aphasia, or speech impairment, had sustained injury to the brain's left hemisphere. Broca's examination of the brains of aphasic patients after death corroborated his observations: the damaged area causing speech impairment was always in the left

228

hemisphere. Broca's discovery of a center of speech in the left hemisphere was the first indication of the dominance of one hemisphere over the other in controlling particular functions.

Scientists theorized that in right-handed people language and handedness were controlled by the left, or "dominant," hemisphere of the brain, to which the right hemisphere was subservient. In the left-handed, they assumed, language and handedness were controlled by the right hemisphere.

After World War II, however, scientists studying patients who had sustained head wounds or suffered strokes found to their surprise that aphasic left-handers did not always have right-hemisphere damage. More than 50 percent had left-hemisphere injuries, indicating that many left-handers must control speech from the left rather than the right side of the brain. Investigators noted, too, that left-handers recovered from aphasia better than right-handers, no matter which hemisphere was damaged; this suggested that at least some of the left-handed had speech centers in both hemispheres.

Studies of patients undergoing brain surgery and of split-brain patients—those in whom the corpus callosum, the connection between the two hemispheres, had been severed—confirmed that almost all right-handers and most left-handers have left-hemisphere speech control. The remaining left-handers have speech control either in the right hemisphere or in both. Clearly, left-handers' brains are not simply the reverse of those of right-handers. But the cause of left-handedness remains unclear.

Some investigators believe that left-handedness can result from damage to the left hemisphere before or during birth; the right hemisphere, in this view, then takes over the specialized functions of language and handedness. But this does not account for those left-handers who process speech in the left or in both hemispheres.

It seems unlikely that left-handedness is directly inherited. Most left-handers are born to right-handed parents, and only half of the children of two left-handed parents are left-handed. Also, in 16 percent of identical twins, one twin is right-handed and the other left-handed. However, heredity may be involved in some complex way. An English psychologist, Marian Annett, has suggested that a single gene causes both left-hemisphere speech dominance and right-handedness. In the absence of this gene, speech dominance and handedness could go either way.

Recent studies of brain structures have pointed to

Left-handers must deal with living in a world designed for right-handers.

---

another possible explanation of left-handedness. Such studies have revealed that the hemispheres are not of equal size or shape. The left hemisphere is usually larger (wider toward the back) in both right-handed and left-handed people, but left-handers are more likely to have hemispheres that are more nearly symmetrical or to have somewhat larger right hemispheres. It is probable that these structural differences underlie handedness.

Disabilities and Disorders

Scientists have noted that male left-handers outnumber females (by about two to one), that a disproportionate number of people with learning disabilities are left-handed, and that learning disabilities occur much more frequently in males than in females. Dr. Norman Geschwind, a neurologist at Harvard Medical School and one of the pioneers in the study of brain structure, language, and behavior, hypothesized that left-handedness and developmental learning disabilities, as well as disorders of the immune system, may all be associated with the male sex hormone testosterone.

According to Geschwind's theory, high levels of testosterone in the fetus—more likely in males than in females—delay growth of the left hemisphere, thereby favoring random hemispheric dominance and left-handedness. A marked delay, Geschwind believed, may result in language disorders, such as dyslexia, a condition in which intellectually capable individuals have reading difficulties.

Geschwind also theorized that testosterone may slow down the development of the immune system in the fetus, leading to increased susceptibility to immune disorders. These disorders include allergies, in which the immune system reacts abnormally to environmental substances, and autoimmune diseases, in which the immune system attacks the body's own cells. One of the problems with Geschwind's theory, however, is that autoimmune diseases are more common in young women

---

Research reveals a disproportionate number of left-handers in fields like math, music, and engineering.

---

than in young men. But according to Geschwind, testosterone has a protective influence on the immune system after puberty—by which time handedness and learning disabilities have been well established. Male susceptibility to immune diseases occurs later in life, when testosterone levels decline.

From 1981 to 1983, Geschwind and his colleagues studied individuals who were strongly left-handed and strongly right-handed—that is, people who used only the left hand or only the right hand for all the tasks on a handedness test. Learning disabilities were found to be about ten times more frequent in the left-handers; left-handers also had more autoimmune diseases, especially of the thyroid and bowel, and greater frequencies of allergies and migraine headaches. (According to Geschwind, migraines, at least in some cases, may have an immunological basis.) Finally, the strongly left-handed reported larger numbers of relatives with learning disabilities and immune system disorders.

In some other studies, left-handers have been found to have greater tendencies than right-handers toward alcohol abuse, smoking, schizophrenia, and suicide.

Special Talents

The foregoing research notwithstanding, investigators have taken pains to point out that being left-handed is not a biological disadvantage. Left-handedness has, in fact, been linked with many kinds of giftedness, including mathematical ability and musical talent. Research has revealed a disproportionate number of left-handers in skilled occupations, such as architecture, athletics, engineering, art, and music.

Many scientists think these data reflect the functioning of the brain's right hemisphere, which in many left-handers is dominant over or shares functions with the left side of the brain. The right hemisphere is believed to

specialize in spatial functions— the processing of complex visual patterns and spatial relationships. These are, of course, abilities needed by architects, engineers, and artists. And there is much evidence that musical aptitude is a right-hemisphere function; for example, patients whose left hemispheres are damaged are able to sing even when they are unable to speak.

It has been proposed that motor functions as well as language may be controlled by both hemispheres in some left-

handed people. Such left-handers are believed to have better manual dexterity in both hands, giving them an advantage over right-handers in athletic competition. However, this theory has been countered with the argument that in certain sports—tennis, boxing, and to some extent baseball, for example—the left-handed have a tactical advantage over right-handers that has nothing to do with manual dexterity. In baseball, left-handers have an edge as batters (because they stand closer to first base), pitchers, and first basemen, although in the shortstop, second base, and third base positions, left-handers are at a distinct disadvantage.

Banding Together

Living in a world that turns to the right, left-handers can rely on many special shops and mail-order houses that sell products designed specifically for them. All kinds of left-handed items, including household utensils and tools, are available.

Three U.S. organizations provide information for and about left-handers and seek to promote public awareness of left-handers and their accomplishments. These organizations (listed below) also aid in the development of left-handed products, sponsor or conduct research into the causes and effects of left-handedness, and assist parents and teachers in the education of left-handed students. Each of these organizations has its own newsletter, and one, Lefthanders International, publishes a quarterly magazine. □

Sources of Further Information

League of Lefthanders, P.O. Box 89, New Milford, N.J. 07646.
Lefthanders International, 3601 S.W. 29th Street, Suite 201, Topeka, Kan. 66614.
Southpaw's International, P.O. Box 31170, Birmingham, Ala. 35222.

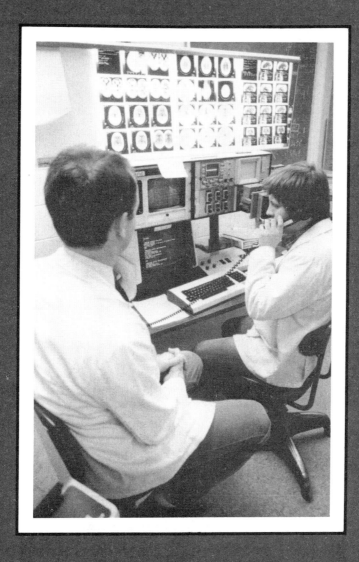

HEALTH AND MEDICAL NEWS

Aging and the Aged

Over the last several years, interest in the study of aging and age-related diseases has grown along with the number of older people in North America. (People over age 65 now number about 11 percent of the population in the United States and 10 percent in Canada, and the proportion is expected to continue to rise.) Under the auspices of the U.S. National Institute on Aging and a number of private foundations, much time and effort have been devoted to research on aging. As a result, there have been many significant contributions to knowledge about aging and how to treat the problems associated with it.

Preventing Disease and Promoting Health

Recent research has shown the value of a variety of preventive health measures for the aged. Vaccines are one such approach. For example, the type of pneumonia caused by pneumococcal bacteria is a significant cause of illness and death among older people, but there is a vaccine that can protect over 70 percent of those inoculated against this disease; it is now recommended for all people over 65 who have not been previously vaccinated. The influenza vaccine is also safe and effective for the aged and should be given to everyone over age 65 each fall, since the types of influenza viruses in circulation tend to vary each year. Finally, the largest number of cases of tetanus in the United States each year occur in people over 65 who have never been inoculated; these people should be immunized with the tetanus vaccine.

Although research has not shown that exercise prolongs life, it may be beneficial to the elderly. In addition to improving their sense of well-being, exercise makes the heart work more efficiently and helps retard the bone loss that occurs with aging. It may also improve the body's use of sugar in the type of diabetes that does not require injections of insulin (called non-insulin-dependent, or adult-onset, diabetes), as well as for normal elderly people.

Proper diet is also important to the elderly, but uncertainty surrounds the issue of what is the ideal body weight for an older person. Research done with rats over several years suggested that rats fed a low-calorie diet with adequate nutrients live longer, resist infection better, and are less subject to tumors and bone loss than rats allowed to eat their fill. Whether this applies to people is uncertain. Before doctors suggest that people go out and starve themselves, it is worth looking at a study done at the National Institute on Aging. Researchers examined life insurance survival tables and found that the greatest longevity for 20-year-olds was in the group who were at or slightly below their ideal body weight. In older people, however, the highest survival rate was among people who were 10 to 15 percent over their ideal body weight, suggesting that a slight increase in fat tissue with age may be beneficial.

Whatever the final answer on weight will be, it is certain that there are a number of dietary supplements that are important for the aged. Although the recommended daily dietary allowance of calcium for older individuals is 800 milligrams per day, absorption of calcium decreases with age. Therefore, the average elderly woman should take over 1,000 milligrams of calcium daily (about the amount contained in a quart of milk) to help prevent osteoporosis, a progressive loss of bone tissue especially common in elderly women. The ability to absorb and produce vitamin D, which helps the body absorb calcium, also decreases with age, and those over 65 should take in 15 milligrams daily. The amount of fiber in the diet should also be adequate, and protein intake should be increased in times of stress or illness, since the aged break down the protein that makes up much of the body more quickly when ill and do not replace it as quickly in times of stress.

Although doctors disagree on the necessity of routine physical exams, the elderly should regularly undergo certain medical tests. A Canadian task force that studied the need for routine medical tests recently updated its recommendations for screening procedures in patients over 65. A yearly blood pressure test, and visual and hearing checks every two or three years, were recommended for everyone; women should also have a breast exam every year and a Pap test every three years, and men should have an annual rectal exam.

Advances in Therapy

A number of therapies for problems common in the aged have been found to be valuable and safe for elderly people. For example, a group of cancer researchers recently found that older people tolerate chemotherapy for a variety of tumors as well as the young, except that their red blood cells are slightly more likely to be harmed. It is likely that doctors will begin to give older patients doses of chemotherapy similar to those given younger cancer victims, instead of the lower doses the elderly now generally receive. Recent studies also suggest that open-heart surgery—coronary artery bypass or heart valve replacement—can be performed safely in the elderly, with 95 percent or more of the patients surviving the operation if surgery is done on a nonemergency basis.

Men with certain types of prostate cancer require radical surgery, which until recently left most of them impotent. Researchers at Johns Hopkins have developed a technique which preserves various nerves that are generally destroyed in prostate surgery; as a result, many men can retain their potency. In addition, in the past, those patients with prostate cancer that had spread beyond the prostate gland itself (metastasized) were treated with estrogens (female sex hormones) or castration. Little else was available if these treatments failed. However, recent work with a synthetic version of the hormone LHRH suggests that this agent may be very useful in the future for prostate cancer that has metastasized.

Dealing With Urinary Incontinence

Recent research has clarified the causes of urinary incontinence (the inability to control urination) in the aged and has suggested several promising treatments. Urinary incontinence is a common—though often unreported—cause of problems in the elderly. Recent surveys suggest that it may occur more than occasionally in 20 percent of older women and 10 to 15 percent of elderly men. It is a problem for about half of all nursing home residents and is responsible for about 5 percent of nursing home costs—a total of $1 billion annually in the United States alone. In addition to the fact that it is aesthetically unpleasant and a cause for withdrawal from social life, incontinence can lead to rashes, bedsores, urinary infections, and other complications.

The most common causes of incontinence include a bladder that contracts before it is full (called detrusor instability) and the loss of urine when there are increases in pressure within the abdomen, which can be caused by coughing, sneezing, or lifting. The latter problem, known as stress incontinence, is usually caused in women by injuries sustained years earlier during childbirth and in men following prostate surgery. Another frequent reason for incontinence is a bladder which does not empty urine properly (a noncontracting bladder). Some patients have a combination of detrusor instability and stress incontinence.

Many patients with detrusor instability can now be treated effectively with drugs that inhibit bladder contraction. These include oxybutynin chloride (brand name, Ditropan), imipramine (Tofranil), and nifedipine (Procardia). In addition, some patients can benefit from the use of electrical nerve stimulation units when they feel the urge to void and wish to inhibit it. Patients use these units to stimulate nerves located on the surface of the skin that affect the sphincter muscle of the bladder.

Over 90 percent of female patients with mild to moderate stress incontinence can be treated with estrogen creams applied to the vagina, together with exercises to strengthen muscles in the pelvic floor. If this fails, incontinence can often be cured with surgery, and artificial sphincters are being investigated as well. Finally, patients with a noncontracting bladder may benefit from drugs that cause contraction of the bladder muscle and relaxation of the bladder outlet. If these medi-

Senior citizens visiting a university planetarium inspect a star projector. They are participants in the Elderhostel movement, which sponsors education programs on college campuses for older people.

cations fail, patients may be taught to use a catheter to empty their own bladders periodically. By all of these means, over 50 percent of patients with incontinence can be cured or have their condition improved. For those who do not respond, a variety of protective garments are now available.

Understanding Alzheimer's Disease

Although the exact cause of Alzheimer's disease remains a mystery, there are new clues as to its origin, and experiments with treatment are going on. The condition—also called senile dementia of the Alzheimer type—is common. In the United States, an estimated 5 percent of people over 65, and 20 percent of those over

80, are afflicted with this slow, progressive deterioration of the brain, which leads to memory loss, confusion, and a general decline in mental powers.

Research into various aspects of the disease continues to progress, resulting in some concrete knowledge. For instance, aluminum poisoning was once thought to be involved in the disease, but it is no longer considered to be a significant cause. It is known that Alzheimer's disease is more common in patients with Down's syndrome, and inheritance appears to play a role as well. Although a viral infection has never been shown to cause Alzheimer's, current research is investigating whether tiny infectious particles called prions may be involved. Recent studies also suggest that in Alzheimer's patients, the immune system, whose normal function is to resist infection, may attack tissues in the brain. Abnormalities have also been demonstrated in the brain's formation of proteins, in the use of sugar by the body, and in the white and red blood cells.

A number of chemical deficiencies in the brain have been found in Alzheimer's patients. For instance, they have a deficiency, in certain parts of the brain, of acetylcholine (ACH), a neurotransmitter, or substance that helps in the transmission of nerve impulses from one cell to another. Other patients, particularly those who develop the disease early, have a deficiency of other neurotransmitters, including those known as norepinephrine, somatostatin, and GABA.

The evidence of such deficiencies has led to experimental therapies. A recent study showed some short-term benefit for certain patients when they were given drugs that prevent ACH breakdown (known as anticholinesterase drugs), in combination with the substance lecithin (which the body uses to produce ACH). In addition, research is going on with certain antidepressant drugs that increase the amounts of the neurotransmitter norepinephrine available to the nerve endings in the brain. Naloxone (Narcan), a drug that blocks the effect of morphine-like substances called endorphins that normally circulate in the body, has also been tried with some success. And compounds called ergoloid mesylates (Hydergine), which are derived from a fungus, appear to stabilize or slightly improve brain function in some patients. Although the benefits of most of these drugs are marginal or inconsistent, they hold hope for better medications in the future.

New Knowledge About Parkinson's Disease

More is being learned about Parkinson's disease, which increases in frequency with age and affects many elderly people. It begins insidiously; the first thing most patients notice is loss of dexterity for skilled movements or a mild tremor. The disease then progresses gradually. When it is fully developed, patients have a "pill-rolling" tremor of the thumb and fingers, excessive muscular stiffness, reduced speed of movement, difficulty with balance, and abnormalities in speech and writing. Parkinson's disease is like Alzheimer's in that it is associated with a neurotransmitter deficiency. In this case, the substance in question is called dopamine, and the deficiency results from degeneration of cells in an area at the base of the brain.

Most cases of Parkinson's are of unknown cause. However, valuable information on this issue was obtained after a Parkinson's-like syndrome was discovered in a number of intravenous drug abusers on the West Coast in 1982. Investigation revealed that the syndrome was caused by an impurity—a substance called MPTP—in the "artificial heroin" they took. This substance produces a condition very similar to Parkinson's disease when it is injected into monkeys, thus providing a way of studying the condition in laboratory animals. These studies suggest that poisons in the environment may be involved in some cases of the illness, opening the way for further investigation into its causes.

Research into means of treating Parkinson's disease also continues. In the past, the main form of treatment for the condition has been an orally taken drug called

Growth of the Older Population

millions of Americans 65 and over and percentage of total population

Year	Millions	Percentage
1900	3	4%
1950	12	8%
1980	26	11%
2000	35	13%
2050	67	22%

levodopa, which is converted to dopamine in the brain. However, the effect of the drug eventually wears off, and some patients experience an "on-off phenomenon," in which the medication is sometimes effective and sometimes ineffective. Recent work has shown that the variable effectiveness of levodopa in some patients may come about because absorption of the drug is affected by certain foods. Some amino acids in the diet, for example, may keep levodopa from crossing from the bloodstream into the brain. Scientists are currently looking at ways to modify the diet and prevent such problems. Doctors have also been investigating the use of continuous intravenous infusions of levodopa, to provide a steady dosage more similar to the brain's natural production of dopamine.

Newer drugs that stimulate dopamine receptors (the areas on nerve cells where dopamine does its work) are also being assessed. One, bromocriptine (Parlodel), is available by prescription. Others, including lisuride and pergolide, are not yet sold in North America. These medications may be useful in patients who become resistant to levodopa.

Animal experiments have been used to test devices that are implanted in the brain, where they deliver dopamine directly to the area where it is needed. Scientists are also exploring the possibility of transplanting dopamine-producing cells into the brain. Finally, substances called gangliosides, which are normally found in the tissues of the central nervous system, have been shown in animals to cause regeneration of the nerve cells that degenerate in Parkinson's. These may be used therapeutically in humans in the near future.

How to Treat Osteoporosis

Osteoporosis continues to be a significant problem for the elderly, particularly women. The progressive loss of bone mass that occurs in this condition results in back pain because of compression fractures of the spine (when one of the vertebrae making up the spine is so weak that it collapses into itself) and also leads to fractures of the wrist and hip. These can all be significant causes of illness and death in the elderly, but better ways to detect the condition and treat it—or even prevent it—are now available.

Bone mass has to decrease 30 to 40 percent before it can be detected on regular X rays, and at this stage the disease is often far advanced and difficult to treat. However, new techniques, such as dual photon absorptiometry, which can measure bone density, and computerized tomographic (CT) scanning of bone, hold promise for earlier detection.

In the spring of 1984, the U.S. National Institutes of Health held a conference on osteoporosis. The panelists attending issued a consensus statement on the best way to deal with the condition, and the conference came out with several recommendations. The first step in preventing fractures is to reduce dangers in the home that can lead to falls, such as loose rugs, poorly lighted stairs, or haphazardly placed furniture. Most elderly women should take extra vitamin D, and if they do not have medical conditions that make it inadvisable (such as kidney disease or a history of kidney stones), they should also take in at least a gram of calcium daily. Regular exercise also appears to be helpful in the prevention of age-related bone loss.

The panelists stated that estrogen therapy is appropriate for any woman with premature menopause (either naturally occurring or resulting from surgery) and also for any woman who understands the possible side effects and need for follow-up. On the other hand, estrogens are not a good idea for people with a history of blood clots in the veins (thrombophlebitis), breast cancer, disease of the gallbladder or bile ducts, or severe heart disease. Most doctors no longer feel that estrogen therapy increases the risk of breast cancer, but there is a slightly higher occurrence of endometrial cancer (cancer of the lining of the uterus). With proper follow-up, however, almost all cases can be caught at an early stage and treated easily by surgery. Such follow-up includes a regular pelvic exam, an annual endometrial biopsy (a simple procedure that can be done in the doctor's office), and prompt reporting of any vaginal bleeding. Recent research suggests that the use of estrogens cyclically in combination with another hormone, progesterone, may lessen or eliminate the risk of endometrial cancer. And the diuretic drug hydrochlorthiazide may also prove valuable in preventing postmenopausal bone loss.

If osteoporosis has become established, treatment revolves around the use of rest, painkillers, estrogen, calcium, and vitamin D. Tests are being conducted to assess the value of fluoride, calcitonin (a hormone normally present in the body), growth hormone, and a variety of other substances, alone or in combination, for treating osteoporosis.

GRAYDON S. MENEILLY, M.D.

Alcoholism

Alcoholism is a major public health problem throughout the world. A recent report issued by the U.S. Alcohol, Drug Abuse, and Mental Health Administration estimated that the cost of alcohol abuse to the U.S. economy in 1980 was $89.5 billion. When this figure was updated for inflation and population growth, it was estimated that alcohol abuse cost the United States $116.7 billion in 1983. According to Canadian government estimates for 1981 (the latest year for which figures are available), excessive alcohol consumption cost that country $6.25 billion (Canadian). These estimates include both the direct costs to society—such as the outlays for alcoholism treatment and those expenses resulting from motor vehicle accidents, crime, and social welfare programs—and the indirect costs—for instance, those resulting from reduced productivity. (Problem drinking reduces productivity by an estimated 21 percent below that of otherwise similar people who do not drink heavily.)

Liver Disease and Alcohol Abuse

The connection between alcohol abuse and the development of liver disease has been known since the 16th century, but the exact cause-and-effect relationship between them remains unclear. A recent study by a team of Danish doctors helps clarify the conditions in which severe liver disease can develop.

Several stages of liver disease can occur in the alcoholic. Fatty liver is one of the earliest; at this stage, the liver cells become swollen with fat, enlarging the entire organ. A more serious stage of liver disease is alcoholic hepatitis, an inflammation of the liver cells. This disease can be diagnosed only by doing a liver biopsy—removing a small piece of tissue and examining the cells

As part of the national effort to reduce the number of deaths from drunk driving, this bartender displays and even wears warning slogans.

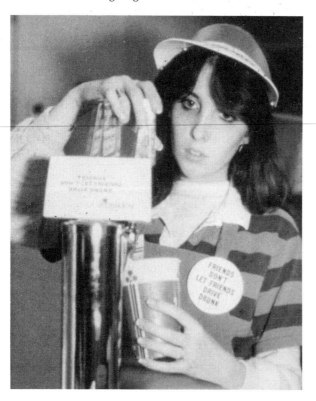

under a microscope. The most severe type of liver damage is cirrhosis of the liver, in which extensive scarring occurs, and the scar tissue replaces the normal liver cells. The liver consequently is unable to fulfill many of its major functions.

It has remained a puzzle why, despite very heavy alcohol intake, only a fraction of alcoholics develop cirrhosis. The Danish study provides evidence that the development of cirrhosis is independent of both the length of time people have abused alcohol and the amount of alcohol they consume (providing that a minimum of 50 grams of alcohol—four or five average drinks—was consumed daily). In the study, a group of alcohol-abusing men was observed over a period of ten to 13 years. About 2 percent of the men developed cirrhosis each year.

Blood tests that were done did not help doctors predict which of the men would develop the disease, but microscopic examination of liver biopsy specimens was useful. If the biopsy showed that the patient had alcoholic hepatitis, his risk of developing cirrhosis was increased nine-fold. And the men with fatty livers also had increased risks of developing cirrhosis. In the past, doctors usually considered this stage of liver disease to be of little consequence and thought that the liver cells would return to normal if the person stopped drinking. There is now a major cause for concern that an enlarged liver may be a more serious medical complication than had been previously believed. It remains to be determined whether—as many doctors suspect—other factors interact with alcohol to increase the risk of developing cirrhosis.

Drinking's Effect on Memory

Drinking alcohol has long been known to affect memory, but researchers and alcoholics alike may have been wrong in their ideas about just how memory is affected. An extreme example of memory impairment associated with drinking is the alcoholic blackout—the complete inability to recall events experienced during intoxication—which may occur in both alcoholics and nonalcoholics. At one time, blackouts were thought to be caused by psychological problems. The drinker supposedly repressed the memory of what happened when drinking because the events were emotionally negative. It has now been shown that this is not the case: alcohol may cause the drinker to forget events with no emotional significance. The extent of the amnesia depends on the person's blood alcohol level, but the amount of alcohol needed to disrupt memory is relatively small. For example, a study using college students as subjects found that a blood alcohol level as low as 0.04 percent disrupts memory function (legal intoxication is usually defined as 0.1 percent).

Experiments have shown that alcohol's primary ef-

Drawings by children of alcoholic parents can reflect the profoundly troubling impact of alcoholism on the whole family.

fects relating to amnesia are on memory formation, so that people have difficulty forming new memories when intoxicated. This differs from traditional beliefs of alcohol's effects on memory. Heavy drinkers tend to believe that drinking makes them forget their problems, but this is not the case.

Depression and Suicide

Several studies have shown that alcoholics who are currently drinking may be prone to depression. Even alcoholics who stop drinking may be affected. This was revealed by a recent study that found a high incidence of depression in alcoholics who had refrained from drinking for at least a year.

Alcoholics may also be prone to suicide. A large study of suicide and alcoholism, conducted by Swedish investigators, pointed out that the frequency of suicide in alcoholics is considerably higher than in the general population. It has been estimated in the United States that up to 30 percent of all deaths among alcoholics are suicides, and an estimated 35 percent of all suicides occur in alcoholics.

In order to better understand the factors that might help to predict whether an alcoholic will commit suicide, the Swedish researchers evaluated more than 1,300 alcoholics admitted for the treatment of alcoholism for the first time. The patients were followed for 30 years, during which time over 500 deaths occurred, of which 88—or 16 percent—were officially registered as

suicides. Characteristics of those who killed themselves included depression, feelings of illness or unhappiness, and an increased frequency of peptic ulcers.

An Increased Risk of Cancer

It is generally believed that alcohol intake increases a person's risk of developing cancer of the mouth, pharynx, larynx, and esophagus. The association between drinking alcohol and getting cancer in other parts of the body, such as the colon, rectum, and lung, has remained more controversial, but there is new evidence that they are linked. Investigators studied more than 8,000 men and discovered an increased occurrence of cancer of the rectum in those consuming more than 15 liters (about 16 quarts) of beer per month. The study also noted an increased incidence of lung cancer among people who consumed large amounts of wine or whiskey, even when age and cigarette smoking were taken into account. The authors caution, however, that there may be other factors, such as diet, in the case of the lung cancer findings.

Early Death From Alcohol

Recent information from the U.S. National Center for Health Statistics indicates that from 1968 through 1978, there were approximately 23,000 deaths attributed to acute alcoholism and more than 3,400 deaths caused by alcohol poisoning. Although these made up only a minuscule percentage of total deaths in the United States,

237

they should have been preventable. During this 11-year period, the proportion of such deaths increased somewhat, especially among males, and it was highest among rural males. The greatest number of such deaths occurred around the Christmas and New Year holidays.

Although the average age at death for acute alcoholism was about 50, nine such deaths occurred among children under the age of ten. The average age at death for alcohol poisoning was also about 50, but 18 deaths occurred in those under the age of ten. Nearly all deaths from acute alcohol poisoning are accidental; many people are unaware that alcohol in excess amounts is poisonous and can be fatal.

A large study reported in 1984 of nearly 8,000 Swedish urban men provided important information on premature death and alcohol. The men were followed for a period of 3½ to eight years. During that time, 218 deaths occurred, of which 55 were alcohol related. The alcoholics died as a result of accidents, suicide, pneumonia, medical complications such as pancreatitis (inflammation of the pancreas) or cirrhosis, and numerous other complications of alcoholism. Blood tests (done when the men entered alcoholism prevention programs) showed that those who died from alcohol-related problems had high blood levels of gamma glutamyl transpeptidase, a liver enzyme that is elevated in heavy drinkers. In contrast, low blood levels of cholesterol and creatinine (a product of the body's use of the amino acid creatine) were associated with alcohol-related death. The authors proposed that these blood tests be used preventively, in a manner similar to blood pressure measurements for patients with hypertension. That is, the tests could be used to discover which alcoholics were at high risk for complications, and the people would then be warned that they had an increased risk of future problems that could lead to early death. The tests could also be used over a long period of time to monitor the progress of patients being treated for alcoholism.

Are There Benefits From Drinking?

Cigarette smokers who do not drink are more than twice as likely to develop a severe degree of emphysema in central portions of the lungs, compared with smokers who regularly consume alcohol. This surprising finding was recently reported by researchers from Duke University who set out to investigate the relationship between smoking and emphysema. The researchers analyzed autopsy results and correlated the signs of emphysema with the subjects' drinking and smoking histories. They found that the heaviest drinkers were the least likely to have suffered from emphysema in the central lobes of the lungs.

The investigators speculated that alcohol may protect patients from developing emphysema by inhibiting the activity of the lungs' inflammatory cells, which release into the lung enzymes that break down proteins. In nonsmokers, the body is able to neutralize the protein-destroying enzymes. Smokers, however, have more inflammatory cells in their lungs; if the enzymes the cells release are not properly neutralized, they can bring about the destructive changes of emphysema. The authors of the study do not recommend regular alcohol consumption for preventing emphysema, because of the many deleterious effects heavy drinking can have on the body. Rather, they think a drug might be developed which inhibits the inflammatory cells as alcohol does, but without the toxic or habit-forming effects of alcohol.

Progress in Understanding Alcoholism

Extensive research has been conducted in the past on alcohol's physical effects on the body, particularly on the liver. More recent research has focused on the effects of alcohol on the brain, especially in people whom earlier studies have shown to be at high risk for becoming alcoholics—that is, the sons of alcoholics. Researchers in both New York and California have been evaluating the brain waves aroused by outside events, in particular a type of brain wave called P3, which appears when people are asked to perform specific tasks. There seems to be a difference in the P3 wave pattern in the sons of alcoholics as compared with boys whose fathers were not alcoholics, both when the sons were given drinks and when they were not. It remains to be seen whether the difference in P3 waves can be used to predict future alcohol abuse. It will probably be several years before this question can be answered.

Meanwhile, psychological studies of the sons of alcoholics continue. No differences have been found so far between sons of alcoholics and sons of nonalcoholics in personality tests or in blood alcohol concentrations after drinking under standard conditions. Researchers do, however, report differences in individuals' subjective responses to drinking. Recently, two groups of college students were evaluated—nonalcoholic sons and brothers of alcoholics, and nonalcoholic students without family histories of alcoholism. After drinking small amounts of alcohol, the two groups did not differ significantly in their blood alcohol levels. But the relatives of alcoholics reported less intense feelings of intoxication after drinking, especially during the two hours after the blood alcohol levels began to drop. The investigators caution that the group studied was small and that the observations should be checked with a larger group of people, including females. Whether such a subjective response to alcohol can be used to identify people at high risk for alcoholism remains to be determined.

T. M. WORNER, M.D.

Arthritis and Rheumatism

Arthritis and rheumatism—general terms for over 100 different conditions that affect the joints—are increasingly being recognized as a leading cause of decreased productivity and lost work days. One out of every seven people in the United States and Canada has sought medical care for these disorders, and each year, Americans spend over $1 billion on ineffective quack cures. Meanwhile, as many as 70 new arthritis drugs slowly advance through the cumbersome U.S. Food and Drug Administration approval process—which can take ten years or more of research for each medication, at an average cost of $70 million per drug. Recently, this situation has led to new efforts to improve the process, so as to reduce the high cost of new drugs and encourage research leading to improved therapy.

Understanding and Treating Rheumatoid Arthritis

Better understanding of the different drugs used to treat rheumatoid arthritis have led to fewer complications for patients. Rheumatoid arthritis is a chronic inflammatory joint disorder of unknown cause that can be severely disabling. It cannot be cured, but with appropriate treatment, many patients are able to carry out the usual activities of daily life. In most mild cases, basic treatment consists of rest, physical therapy, and aspirin or aspirin-like drugs called nonsteroidal anti-inflammatory agents. These alternatives to aspirin can be used for all types of inflammatory arthritis and rheumatism; at high dosages, these drugs can suppress inflammation as well as control pain.

The difficulty with such drugs, as well as with aspirin, is their side effects, notably gastric upset or bleeding at the high dosages required for anti-inflammatory effect. Recent studies with an endoscope—an instrument that allows doctors to look into the stomach—emphasize the high frequency of silent (that is, symptomless) peptic ulcer disease that occurs with long-term use. Newer treatments for these problems include sucralfate (brand name, Carafate), a drug used for peptic ulcers, which can help prevent one of the things that can result from the use of anti-inflammatory medications, the depletion of a substance called prostacyclin. Prostacyclin is necessary to protect the mucous cells that line the stomach from the potentially harmful effects of gastric acid.

In recognition of the potential for gastric upset, newer anti-inflammatory drugs incorporate methods of delivery, such as special coatings, that allow them to bypass the upper gastrointestinal tract and to be absorbed in the lower bowel. Another possibility being investigated are "pro-drugs," substances that would pass through a troubled upper gastrointestinal tract in an inactive chemical form, and then, after absorption, be converted by the liver into an active anti-inflammatory form. Older, nonaspirin salicylates—drugs of the aspirin family, like salicylsalicylic acid (sold as Mono-Gesic and Disalcid)—appear to be the safest of all anti-inflammatory agents, and the least likely to cause gastric problems when taken at anti-inflammatory levels.

The drugs called corticosteroids aroused great enthusiasm as a treatment for arthritis in the late 1940's when the first of them, cortisone, was introduced, but they later fell into disfavor when their serious side effects were noted. They have now come full cycle, and today there is an increased appreciation of low doses of corticosteroids as a treatment for rheumatoid arthritis and other inflammatory joint disorders. For instance, one major rheumatic disorder of the elderly, polymyalgia rheumatica, characterized by pain and stiffness in the muscles, has been shown to respond dramatically to such low-dose therapy. Early use of a combination of calcium, fluoride, and vitamin D provides enhanced protection against and treatment for the loss of bone tissue that is a frequent side effect of corticosteroid therapy in women past menopause.

Not only have scientists gained better understanding of the effects of drugs used in rheumatoid arthritis—they have also gathered some clues regarding the possible cause of the disease. In rheumatoid arthritis, the body's immune system, which normally acts to protect against infection, attacks the lining of the joints. Scientists have suspected that a virus might cause the change in the immune system that leads to rheumatoid arthritis, and in 1984 researchers reported finding a small type of virus called a parvovirus in tissue taken from a rheumatoid arthritis patient. The virus produced a crippling disease when it was injected into baby mice, and tests with cells taken from 14 other rheumatoid arthritis patients suggested that 13 of them had been exposed to the virus. The association of the virus with the disease is still tentative, however.

Treating Degenerative Joint Disease

Osteoarthritis, also known as degenerative joint disease, remains the most common form of arthritis. Although it is often attributed to "wear and tear" on the cartilage that normally cushions the joints—a degeneration that can come with advancing age—osteoarthritis can occur in middle life as well as in later years. It may also occur in a secondary form because of a specific factor, like a strenuous occupation, an injury, or a form of destructive arthritis such as rheumatoid arthritis. Any of these activities or conditions can lead to the deterioration of cartilage that occurs in this disorder.

The sequence of bodily changes in osteoarthritis, in which the cartilage develops tiny cracks or pits and also suffers a loss of its ability to absorb fluid properly, has been well documented. However, as with rheumatoid

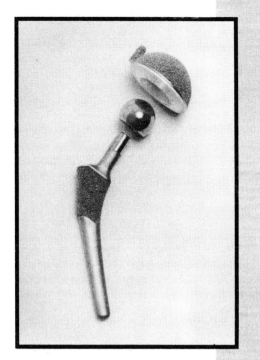

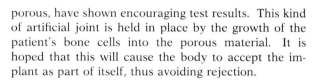

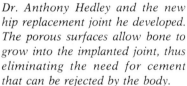

Dr. Anthony Hedley and the new hip replacement joint he developed. The porous surfaces allow bone to grow into the implanted joint, thus eliminating the need for cement that can be rejected by the body.

arthritis, no corrective treatment has yet been developed to treat the disease directly. Instead, anti-inflammatory drugs are used to treat the symptoms. Recent studies suggest, however, that their long-term value is impaired because aspirin and other anti-inflammatory drugs interfere with the body's synthesis of a type of protein called proteoglycan, which serves as a building block of cartilage structure. The possibility that the medication has this effect is a cause of concern since proteoglycan is necessary to healthy joints, which are threatened by the progression of osteoarthritis.

Protecting affected joints, weight control, and keeping the ligaments, muscles, and other tissues surrounding the joints as healthy as possible through physical therapy remain the main factors of a conservative treatment program for degenerative joint disease. In the past, when such approaches proved unsuccessful and the patient suffered discomfort and a loss of function, artificial joints were used. Enthusiasm for the replacement of badly diseased joints by artificial ones (generally made of stainless steel and plastic) has lessened somewhat of late for more active, younger patients because the body tends to reject methyl methacrylate, the "bone glue" used to hold the artificial joint in place. But newer designs, in which the portion of the artificial joint that comes in contact with the patient's bones is

porous, have shown encouraging test results. This kind of artificial joint is held in place by the growth of the patient's bone cells into the porous material. It is hoped that this will cause the body to accept the implant as part of itself, thus avoiding rejection.

Controlling Gout

Gout, or gouty arthritis, is one arthritic disease in which therapy can control the cause as well as the symptoms. The pain of gout—traditionally and most commonly in the big toe, though it can occur in other joints as well—is caused by deposits of uric acid salts in the affected joint. It can be controlled over the long term by lowering the elevated levels of uric acid found in the blood of gouty patients. (Uric acid is a by-product of the body's use of certain essential amino acids; it is removed from the blood by the kidneys and excreted in the urine, but people with gout either produce excess amounts of uric acid or do not dispose of it efficiently.)

A drug called allopurinal (also sold as Lopurin and Zyloprim) can reduce the body's production of uric acid, while other drugs called uricosuric agents—which include probenecid (Benemid) and sulfinpyrazone (Anturane)—can increase its secretion in the urine. Such drugs can be used alone or in combination, depending on specific circumstances, and will prevent the recur-

240

rence or worsening of gout attacks. However, gout cannot be cured: lifelong treatment is required once the disease has appeared.

Gout can be treated successfully, but the treatment provides an example of some of the difficulties posed by medical progress. A wide variety of medical tests have been developed and are now frequently used to screen for various problems; the tests generally include one for uric acid in the blood. If a doctor finds that a patient has a high uric acid level together with joint pain, the diagnosis is very likely to be gout—but this is not necessarily correct. Uric acid levels can vary throughout the day, and some people appear to be able to tolerate continued high levels without ill effects. In such a case, the joint symptoms may have another cause, which would go untreated while the patient was exposed to the possible side effects of the drugs used for treating gout, as well as being marked with the stigma of having a chronic disease.

Lyme Disease

Lyme disease, a type of infectious arthritis caused by a bacterial infection that is transferred to humans by the bite of an infected tick, appears to be on the rise. Health officials in New York State (the disease is particularly common in the Northeast) reported in early 1985 that 434 cases of Lyme disease had been confirmed in the state in 1984, more than double 1983's 168 cases. New Jersey health officials also reported an increasing incidence of the illness.

The first sign of the disease is a skin rash near the site of the tick bite. Flu-like symptoms may follow, and if the infection is not treated, it can have serious effects on the heart, the nervous system, or the joints, where it can lead to recurring arthritis symptoms. About 60 percent of those infected will develop arthritis symptoms anywhere from two weeks to two years after the infection occurs, if treatment is not given. However, treatment with antibiotics—tetracycline or penicillin—usually shortens the duration of the skin rash and prevents the more serious complications. It is important that such treatment begin early; it may not be effective if it is delayed.

Nonprescription Arthritis Drug Approved

The most commonly prescribed arthritis drug, a simple analgesic called ibuprofen, has recently been approved for over-the-counter sale in the United States. It is now available in low dosages under the brand names Nuprin and Advil. (The drug continues to be sold in prescription form, under the brand names Motrin and Rufen.) This approval signifies a new level of concern for the consumer with arthritis and rheumatism.

Unregulated use of the medication could lead to two problems, however. The low dose of the drug recom-

mended on nonprescription packaging will provide relief for the "minor pains of arthritis and rheumatism," but it will not suppress inflammation. Thus, the more serious form of arthritis could remain undertreated, with deterioration of the joints and other problems more likely to occur. On the other hand, going past the suggested over-the-counter doses, to doses even higher than recommended for anti-inflammatory action, could lead to gastrointestinal damage and other dangerous side effects, without the safeguards of medical monitoring and laboratory checks. More recently, kidney failure has been found in certain people taking ibuprofen, raising the risks of such abusive practices. The need for the consumer to be properly informed about arthritis or rheumatism and its management is evident.

SANFORD H. ROTH, M.D.

Bioethics

Bioethics is the study of ethical issues in medicine and the biomedical sciences. In recent years, cases involving children have been prominent in the field. For example, questions have arisen when parents of newborns have chosen to forgo potentially life-saving therapy on religious grounds or because of a belief that their child's life will not be worth living. In the most recent cases involving children, the emphasis has been on having them—the rapidly emerging technologies of human reproduction.

Reproduction and Its Moral Dilemmas

The practice of adoption gave rise to the generally accepted and understood distinction between biological parenthood and social parenthood. Technological developments of the last 20 years—especially since 1978, when the first baby conceived outside a human body was born—have made the traditional social, legal, and ethical notions of parenthood inadequate.

There are now five logically and practically separate aspects of parenthood. The first is the male's genetic contribution—his sperm. Artificial insemination by donor (AID), in which a woman receives the sperm of an often anonymous man, has been available since the 1960's. The second aspect is the female's genetic contribution—the ovum, or egg. Eggs can be taken surgically from a woman's ovary and, after fertilization, used by her or donated to another woman. The site where fertilization takes place is another component of parenthood. No longer is fertilization confined to a woman's fallopian tubes. It can now take place in a glass laboratory dish, as done with in vitro fertilization, the practice that produces so-called test-tube babies.

The fourth aspect is the womb in which the fetus develops. A fertilized egg can be taken from a woman's uterus or a glass dish and placed in another woman's womb. In cases of surrogate motherhood, a woman agrees to be impregnated by the sperm of an unrelated man by AID and to surrender the baby—her own biological child—to the genetic father at birth. The adults who actually rear the child are the last aspect of parenthood. These are the child's "social" parents; they may, but need not have been, involved in any of the other steps.

The practical existence of these different factors—the result of recent advances in reproductive medicine—has raised fundamental ethical and legal questions about the nature of parenthood, the rights and duties of biological and social parents, the rights of offspring, and the moral status of embryos.

"Orphaned" frozen embryos. In 1981, Mario and Elsa Rios, a wealthy Los Angeles couple, went to the Queen Victoria Medical Centre clinic in Melbourne, Australia, to seek the help of fertility specialists there. The doctors removed a number of eggs from Mrs. Rios's ovary (she was given drugs that cause several eggs to ripen simultaneously), and three were fertilized. One embryo was placed in her womb, and the remaining two were frozen in liquid nitrogen for use in a subsequent attempt should the implant fail. It did fail, but before the Rioses informed the clinic what they wanted done with the two frozen embryos, they died in a plane crash in 1983.

Only in 1984 did the clinic learn of the Rioses' fate and ask what to do with the embryos. The situation was further complicated by revelations that the couple—who had not drawn up wills—had left an estate worth perhaps $1 million, and Mario Rios had a son by a previous marriage who claimed the inheritance. The son's attorney further claimed that the sperm used to fertilize the embryos were those of an anonymous donor, and not of Mario Rios.

Many women volunteered to have the fertilized embryos implanted, and the clinic was faced with an unprecedented dilemma: deciding whether frozen embryos of deceased parents have any "right" to be adopted. Would the embryos, if they were eventually born, have any legal claim on the Rios estate? Who "owned" the frozen embryos?

An Australian government commission in September 1984 recommended that the embryos be thawed and disposed of, but some weeks later the state legislature enacted legislation requiring that the embryos be made available for implantation. No steps had been taken by early 1985. Most experts believe that the embryos are not viable, since the freezing techniques in use in 1981 were comparatively primitive. (The first successful birth of a frozen embryo was in March 1984.) Although couples entering the program in Melbourne must now specify what is to be done with any frozen embryos in case of their death or separation, clinics in other parts of the world, including the United States, are beginning to use the freezing process. An ethical and legal consensus must be reached on the issues raised by the Rios case.

Bearing someone else's child. Some men who want to have and raise a biological child do not have a relationship with a woman who is able or willing to be the mother of that child. The man may be married and have a wife who is unable to bear children, or, as in the case of Alexander Malahoff, he may not be married at all. Malahoff made an agreement with Judy Stiver, a married woman, in which she agreed to be artificially inseminated with his sperm, to carry his child, and to surrender the infant to Malahoff at birth. For her services, Mrs. Stiver was to receive $10,000 plus medical expenses.

Ultimately, the child was born with microcephaly—an abnormally small head—and mentally retarded. Malahoff insisted on a blood test to determine paternity, and the results were revealed simultaneously to Malahoff and the Stivers on Phil Donahue's television show. Malahoff, the test showed, was not the father, and it appeared that Mr. Stiver was. The baby is now in the Stivers' custody while the Stivers and Malahoff sue each other.

An estimated 100 to 150 babies have been born under surrogate motherhood agreements in the United States since the practice began in the late 1970's. Few have received the publicity of the Stiver-Malahoff case, but all raise difficult ethical and legal questions. Who has the greater right to a child, the male who contributes his sperm, or the woman who contributes her egg and her womb for nine months? Who is responsible for a child born with a serious illness or birth defect? Even if we permit the practice of voluntary surrogate motherhood, is it ethically acceptable to allow payment for it, or does this turn child-bearing into a commodity? If payment is permitted, should the state be involved in enforcing contracts for child-bearing "services"?

Approximately half of the U.S. states have laws banning payment to a mother who gives up her child for adoption. Although these laws were not intended to cover surrogate motherhood, the courts may decide they apply, as did a Michigan appeals court in 1981. However, a trial court in Kentucky ruled otherwise in 1983, saying that a natural (biological) father could not be said to be "buying" his own child. New legislation would clarify the legal situation, but it would be difficult to pass in light of controversy about the issue; some people believe surrogate motherhood arrangements should be banned entirely, while others feel it should be regulated by the government.

Who owns donated sperm? Artificial insemination by donor has been available since the 1960's, and it has

Surrogate motherhood can involve moral dilemmas, as in the case of Alexander Malahoff (right), who hired Judy Stiver (seated with her husband at left) to be artificially inseminated with his sperm. When the baby was born mentally retarded, Malahoff insisted on a paternity test. The results, revealed on Phil Donahue's television program, showed that the child was not his.

resulted in approximately 250,000 births in the United States alone. Many states have laws governing AID, and the practice seems to have been generally accepted as legitimate, although many issues remain unresolved. A case in Marseille, France, raised legal questions about the practice of AID in 1984.

Corinne Parpalaix's husband died of cancer in 1983, but before he had begun his regimen of cancer therapy, he left a sample of his sperm with a sperm bank in Marseille. Mrs. Parpalaix requested that she be inseminated with her late husband's sperm, but the sperm bank refused, on the grounds that he had left no such instructions. A French court ruled otherwise, saying that this "secretion containing the seeds of life" belonged to Mrs. Parpalaix. There is no guarantee, however, that a court in the United States—or, for that matter, another French court—would decide the next case in a similar fashion.

Baby Fae and the Baboon Heart

On October 26, 1984, Dr. Leonard Bailey, a surgeon at California's Loma Linda University Medical Center, transplanted a baboon's heart into the chest of an infant suffering from hypoplastic left heart syndrome, in which the left side of the heart is drastically underdeveloped. The condition is almost always fatal, and it appeared that without some radical intervention, the child who came to be known as Baby Fae soon would die.

After years of experimenting with transplanting hearts between animal species, Dr. Bailey was convinced that the time was ripe for an attempt on a human infant. A baboon heart was chosen, presumably because baboons were readily available as laboratory animals, even though other primates—especially chimpanzees—are more closely related genetically to humans.

The operation was a technical success, as the baboon heart began to pump blood through the infant's frail body. The next three weeks followed a trajectory from optimism to despair. The struggle to prevent the heart from being rejected, without damaging the child's other organs with high dosages of the drugs needed to suppress her immune system, finally failed, and she died on November 15.

From the first day, the hope engendered by the experiment was tempered by nagging questions about its ethical justification. Three principal questions emerged. The first is whether the scientific groundwork for the experiment had been properly laid. It is an internationally recognized principle that scientists do risky experimental procedures on human beings only after extensive research on animals has answered all the questions that can be answered without using human subjects. Doubts have been raised about whether this was done in the case of Baby Fae, particularly since Dr. Bailey had had little success getting grants for, or

243

publishing papers on, his research on cross-species transplants.

The second question is whether a more promising treatment for Baby Fae's condition was available. One option was a surgical repair procedure, which requires two operations to correct the defect. It remains risky but has shown considerable promise. Another possibility was a human heart transplant; many experts believe that a human heart is more likely to be accepted by a patient's immune system than one from another species. As it happens, another infant heart reportedly was available at that time, although there is not enough information to judge whether it would have been suitable for Baby Fae. The fact remains that the Loma Linda team did not even investigate the possibility.

The third question is whether the fully informed consent of Baby Fae's parents was obtained for the experiment. Without it, the procedure would be unethical and probably illegal. Spokesmen for Loma Linda maintain that the consent was thorough and even was obtained twice to ensure that the parents had had time to mull it over. In March 1985, a U.S. National Institutes of Health report concluded that the parents had been adequately informed but that the doctors had overstated the infant's chance for survival.

The case of Baby Fae is a tragic reminder of the limits of medical technology and of the need for very careful scrutiny of the ethics of research.

THOMAS H. MURRAY, PH.D.

Blood and Lymphatic System

A major advance appears to have been made in the struggle against the devastating illness known as AIDS. Scientists have identified the disorder's probable cause, thereby making possible the development of blood tests for detecting it. Other research news includes encouraging reports on new treatments for a disorder affecting blood platelets, tiny cells in the blood that are responsible for preventing leakage of blood from small vessels and for initiating the formation of blood clots in the body. Advances have also been made in the study of the special proteins in the blood called coagulation factors, which help maintain the delicate balance in the healthy body between the tendency of blood to clot (thereby permitting the repair of damaged blood vessels and preventing life-threatening bleeding from minor injuries, such as cuts) and its tendency to flow freely (thereby dissolving unwanted clots).

AIDS Virus and Blood Tests

In AIDS (short for acquired immune deficiency syndrome) the immune system, the body's defenses against disease, breaks down, resulting in an increased suscep-

tibility to otherwise rare infections, to a malignant skin condition called Kaposi's sarcoma, and to cancer of the lymphatic system. A person with AIDS suffers from an imbalance between certain groups of lymphocytes, the white blood cells responsible for regulating the immune system. Since first attracting the attention of doctors a few years ago, the disorder has spread in epidemic proportions. Many scientists searching for what causes the imbalance in the immune system suspected that a virus might be at fault.

In spring 1984, researchers at the U.S. National Cancer Institute reported the isolation of a likely candidate for such a virus in the blood of patients with AIDS. They named this virus HTLV-III (human T-cell lymphotropic virus type III). Scientists at the Pasteur Institute in France had previously identified a virus suspected of causing AIDS and had dubbed it LAV (lymphadenopathy-associated virus). Most experts believe the two viruses are essentially the same and that this LAV/HTLV-III virus is indeed the primary cause of AIDS. The discovery of the virus had enormous implications for the fight against the disorder. At the very least, it meant that a specific test could probably be developed to identify blood contaminated with the AIDS virus. The isolation of the virus also potentially opened the way to creating a vaccine that could prevent the disease from developing. For such a vaccine to become a reality, however, several more years of research will probably be needed.

In mid-1984, five U.S. drug and biotechnology companies were issued licenses by the federal government for the development of an AIDS test for use by blood banks and research institutions. Donated blood found by such a test to show signs of possible exposure to the AIDS virus could be discarded, thereby virtually eliminating the chance that the virus might be transmitted through blood transfusion.

With the development of a blood test seemingly imminent, the U.S. National Heart, Lung, and Blood Institute began a massive program of collecting blood samples from healthy donors, with the samples being stored for future analysis. With the availability of a suitable test, the samples are to be examined for the presence of signs of the AIDS virus. It is hoped this will help answer crucial questions about how both the virus and AIDS develop over time and are transmitted from one person to another. The program should also make possible long-term follow-up of people who may have been exposed to the virus. In addition, the testing may detect persons who have contracted the virus, but whose immune systems have mounted a successful defense against it.

In early March 1985 the U.S. Food and Drug Administration authorized the marketing of two firms' versions of a test developed for blood banks. A controversy had arisen, however, over exactly how the test should be used, in view of its limitations. The test was designed to detect the presence in blood of antibodies developed by the immune system in response to exposure to the AIDS virus; it did not indicate if the virus itself was present. A positive test result did not necessarily mean that true infection had occurred. Moreover, the test would not catch blood from infected individuals who fail to develop detectable antibodies.

Blood Substitute

In recent years, the search for an artificial replacement for human blood has intensified, and considerable testing has been performed on the most promising candidate yet found, a substance called Fluosol-DA. For transfusions, Fluosol-DA has many potential advantages over blood. It can be stored for long periods of time, carries no risk of disease transmission, and can be used without regard for the patient's blood type.

When Fluosol-DA was introduced, considerable optimism was voiced about its ability to perform many of the functions of human blood. Much of this optimism, however, has not been borne out. Fluosol-DA does not contain such necessary parts of the blood as important proteins and coagulation factors. And researchers have now shown that it cannot carry oxygen as well as blood can. In addition, in 1984 a careful, scientifically well-designed study of the effects of Fluosol-DA in people with severe anemia showed no clear-cut difference between the new substitute and the intravenous solutions normally used. Thus, it seems that Fluosol-DA may at most be useful as a replacement for blood only in certain specific situations.

Blood Platelets

New treatments for platelet disorder. In the platelet disorder known as idiopathic thrombocytopenic purpura or ITP, which occurs mostly in young women, platelets are produced normally but are destroyed by the body's immune system. The resultant lack of platelets can lead to serious bleeding problems. The conventional treatments for ITP—administering so-called glucocorticoid hormones (which belong to the large group of hormones known as corticosteroids) or removing the spleen, the organ in which the platelets are destroyed—have not been entirely satisfactory. Up to one-fourth of all patients with the disorder do not respond to them.

Researchers have, however, reported success with the use of a synthetic male hormone called danazol in some patients who do not respond to conventional therapy. Danazol was found to increase the number of platelets in the blood. The hormone has few side effects; both male and female patients who were studied tolerated it well. Besides its use in ITP patients who fail to respond to conventional therapy, danazol has shown promise as

an effective treatment for people whose immune systems destroy their red blood cells.

When ITP occurs in pregnant women, therapy becomes more difficult. Besides the risk of bleeding it creates for the mother, it temporarily lowers the unborn child's platelet count, so that there is risk of bleeding in the infant during labor and delivery. In addition, many treatment options, including danazol, cannot be used because of their potential for harming the development of the fetus.

Researchers in Japan and France have successfully tried a new approach to this problem. Prior to the time of delivery, they treated a number of pregnant women who had ITP with a combination of high doses of a substance known as immunoglobulin G and glucocorticoid hormones. A short-term rise in the mother's platelet count was produced, permitting the safe delivery of the infant. Immunoglobulin G is a natural substance the body produces to fight infection and the invasion of foreign substances. Although scientists still do not fully understand how it works in cases of ITP, it seems to be an effective, safe treatment for pregnant women with the disorder.

Preventing clot formation. Researchers have found that the ability of platelets to form a clot may be related in some way to the degree that the mineral calcium enters the platelets. People with a blood clot in the leg, for example, have been demonstrated to have more calcium entering their platelets than normal individuals. On the other hand, nifedipine (Procardia), a drug known as a calcium blocker because it blocks the movement of calcium into cells, has been shown to limit the calcium influx into platelets. Use of the drug may decrease the possibility that platelets will contribute to the formation of a blood clot. Although many questions about such an application of calcium blockers remain to be answered, there may be a place for these drugs in the prevention and treatment of clots in blood vessels and of disorders associated with abnormal platelet activity.

Coagulation Factors

Treating hemophilia. A deficiency in coagulation factors can lead to serious bleeding disorders. One of the most common hereditary diseases of this kind is so-called classical hemophilia, or hemophilia A, which is caused by a deficiency of a particular coagulation factor—that known as factor VIII. People with hemophilia have a lifelong tendency to bleed excessively and generally require frequent transfusions of factor VIII concentrate so that their blood will clot more readily. The concentrate is obtained from the blood of thousands of donors, a process that carries the risk of transmitting to the recipient diseases that the donors may be carrying, such as AIDS and the serious liver disorder hepatitis.

To avoid this problem, researchers have for some time sought to produce a safe, effective factor VIII with genetic engineering techniques.

In 1984 two research teams each announced the copying, or cloning, of the entire gene responsible for the production of factor VIII in the body. The cloned gene was inserted into animal cells in a laboratory, and the cells then produced the factor VIII protein. Cloning the factor VIII gene was the most crucial step toward the goal of achieving mass production of factor VIII for use by hemophiliacs. Although production on a commercial scale may still be years away, hope now exists that it will be possible to treat hemophiliacs without the risks of disease transmission.

Testing for liver cancer. Most of the coagulation factors are produced in a normally functioning liver. Researchers recently found that when a cancer originates in the liver, the organ may start to produce an abnormal form of a coagulation factor called prothrombin. This abnormal prothrombin, known as des-gamma-carboxy prothrombin, seems to be present only in individuals with cancer originating in the liver. The researchers concluded that testing for the presence of the abnormal coagulation factor may help doctors distinguish this type of cancer from other conditions that affect the liver, such as hepatitis or cancer that has spread to the liver from other organs. In addition, the abnormal coagulation factor may provide a useful means of following the progress of patients during treatment for liver cancer. WILLIAM L. STERNHEIM, M.D.

Bones, Muscles, and Joints

Like other medical specialties, orthopedic surgery—which is concerned with conditions of the bones and joints as well as with correcting skeletal deformities—has felt the impact of the rapid pace of technological advance. Electronic engineering, for example, has made possible revolutionary imaging methods that enable the physician to see an internal injury with a clarity of detail never before possible. Artificial joints are lasting longer, thanks in part to computer-assisted design improvements and the development of new, more durable materials. Surgical and rehabilitation techniques have benefited as well. The result of all of these advances has been the chance for an improved life for the orthopedic patient.

Helping Victims of Spinal Injury

Victims of injuries to the spine often provide tragic testimony to the toll exacted by certain contemporary activities. Fast driving and increasingly popular recreations such as hang gliding and motorcycle riding contribute to accidents causing these terrible injuries and the paralysis—whether of the legs (paraplegia) or arms and legs (quadriplegia)—that may accompany them. For the patient and family, the effects can be devastating. Society at large pays a price as well, both in the loss of a productive person and in the enormous costs—often lifelong—of caring for these patients.

In the past, because there was so little likelihood that those who suffered spinal injury (or trauma) would recover significant function, treatment was usually rather passive. The patient was generally immobilized in a plaster cast to allow the fracture or dislocation to heal, and care centered on managing the medical and surgical problems that stemmed from the initial injury. As technological innovations have improved the chances that patients will have some recovery of function, however, doctors and researchers have taken a more aggressive approach toward treatment and rehabilitation. As a result, more and more spinal trauma patients are now leading full, productive lives.

Research efforts. Experimental work in this area generally focuses on two approaches. In the first, techniques are being evaluated to promote healing of the spinal cord itself. For instance, some research suggests that cooling the injured spinal cord may promote its ultimate recovery, presumably because the metabolic demands (that is, the chemical needs and activity) of any tissue are higher at normal body temperature than when cooled. Drugs that have this effect are being investigated. This type of work is still in its infancy, however, and results cannot yet be applied to patient care. The second approach, which seeks ways to minimize the effects of the injury to the spinal cord, has already led to practical benefits for the patient. For example, some surgeons now use early surgery to relieve pressure exerted by bone or disk material (the cushion of connective tissue between the vertebrae that make up the spine) on a partially damaged cord. Such pressure, if untreated, could cause progressive loss of nervous system function. The exact conditions under which such early surgery should be performed are currently being studied.

Diagnosis. The enormous progress made in electronics in recent years, particularly with computers, has contributed to greater accuracy and safety in diagnosing spinal cord injuries. Computerized tomography (CT, or CAT, scanning)—a technique that uses computers and X rays beamed at the body from different angles to create cross-sectional images—has already become familiar. Each year, as a result of increasingly rapid computers and better programming, there is an improvement in the quality of the images that CT scanners produce. Thus, the somewhat risky technique of myelography, in which a dye is injected into the spinal canal before an X ray is taken, is now often replaced by

CT scanning to enable the physician to see the nature of the injury.

There is a disadvantage to CT scanning: there is significant X-ray exposure for the patient. A still newer computer-assisted technique called magnetic resonance imaging (MRI) thus holds the promise of even greater safety for patients because X rays are not used. In MRI, the part of the body being studied is exposed to a magnetic field and then to weak radio-frequency energy. The nuclei of the atoms of certain elements that occur in body tissues, like hydrogen and phosphorus, change their alignments in response to these energy fields. In so doing, they give off signals that are "read" by a computer and transformed into an image. MRI shows actual body structure, as CT scans do, but MRI has the additional advantage of giving physiological information as well.

Early MRI scanners for medical use have focused on detecting hydrogen, which is abundant in the body, occurring especially in water, carbohydrates, and fats. Since fats are a common building material for nerves, the nervous system is well visualized by MRI. (Advanced MRI models are expected to have an improved capability to detect other atoms abundant in body tissue, and they thus will provide increasing information about body function.) MRI is potentially useful in diagnosing spinal fractures because nervous tissue is shown well and because the scanner detects disruption of the bone marrow—the soft material filling the bone cavity—when bleeding into the marrow causes a weaker signal to be emitted to the computer. While at present MRI images are often not as clear as CT scans, refinements are being made at an extremely rapid pace, and medical workers anticipate that the technique will further improve their ability to diagnose injuries to the spine as well as other portions of the body.

Surgery and rehabilitation. The most impressive gains in caring for patients with spinal trauma involve surgical management and physical rehabilitation. One such advance is the trend toward using traction and early surgery to relieve pressure on the spinal cord. Another improvement involves so-called halo fixation, in which a metal ring attached to the skull with four screws is held with metal supports to a strong but light vest. This holds the neck and upper chest portion of the spine rigidly immobile while a fracture or surgical repair is allowed to heal.

Surgical techniques for immobilizing the upper chest and lower back portions of the spine have also been improved. Such developments permit the spine to heal with proper alignment, but free the patient of the restrictions of wearing a body cast. Intersegmental wiring is one such technique that markedly improves spinal stability without a body cast. A rigid rod is attached to the spine with wire passed around each spinal seg-

ment. Because there are risks in placing many wires next to the sensitive nerve components, the technique is generally restricted to cases where the spine is unstable. As wider experience with intersegmental wiring leads to improvements in its safety, use of the method may well spread.

Exciting efforts in rehabilitation, an essential part of the care of the patient with a spinal injury, are also under way. For example, researchers using computers to send electrical impulses to paralyzed leg muscles have enabled some paraplegics to walk, even if only for a few moments and with assistance.

However, most of the rehabilitation techniques in use are not new. Although they do reflect recent advances in materials and electronics, they generally are based on older principles, such as having the patient wear braces for support, retraining the person in getting the injured body part moving again, and using devices to assist the patient. New instruments utilizing electronics include voice-controlled devices (for example, a computer that can be instructed by voice to dial a telephone or adjust the angle of a quadriplegic's bed), newly engineered "smart" wheelchairs, and modified motor vehicles. The true "innovation" in all this is simply a change in attitude: there is now an aggressive, concentrated effort on the part of rehabilitation physicians and physical and occupational therapists to teach patients, by all available techniques, the skills they need to take maximum advantage of their remaining functions. With this vigorous approach, even patients with injuries as devastating as a spine fracture can, with motivation, learn to care for themselves, drive a car, and lead productive lives.

Advances in Synthetic Joints

Among the benefits that orthopedic patients are reaping from space-age technology are improvements in design and composition of synthetic joints, leading to longer-lasting joint replacements. Developments with total hip replacement (arthroplasty), first performed in England in the early 1960's by Sir John Charnley, provide a good example.

Charnley's success, after a quarter-century of work on the problem, was based on his understanding of mechanics, his superb intuition, and a little luck in assembling the technology he needed. The synthetic joint he finally developed was made of a plastic, polyethylene, combined with stainless steel and held in place in the body with methyl methacrylate, a substance originally used as a dental cement.

The basic hip replacement procedure developed by Charnley is still in use today, refined rather than radically changed since its introduction. Advanced computers are now being used to help create better-fitting artificial hips and other joints as well. The materials used to make synthetic joints have changed as well, with "super alloys" involving the metal titanium (which is used in spacecraft) and microcrystalline, high-performance chrome-cobalt alloys. Since these materials withstand heavy use longer than conventional materials, their use should mean greater durability for joint components.

Methyl methacrylate, the cement used to hold hip implants (and most major joint implants) in place remains the weak link in the procedure. Because it does not provide a permanent bond, the artificial joint tends to loosen, and further surgery is required. The thrust of recent efforts has been to avoid this problem by designing cementless joints—if bone can be encouraged to bond to the synthetic joint itself, no cement would be needed. Some researchers are coating synthetic joint components with a porous metal mesh or bead lattice, while others are using ceramic coatings; all of these promote the growth of the patient's own bone into the replacement joint. Early trials with such implants are currently going on, and the U.S. Food and Drug Administration recently approved the first type of cementless hip component—made of a chrome-cobalt alloy coated with beads—for general use. Early results with it are excellent.

Keeping Broken Bones Strong

Another area that has benefited from the development of new materials is the healing of fractures. Surgeons sometimes have to attach rigid metal plates to bone fragments to promote the healing of the fractures. This type of fixation may lead to a condition called disuse osteoporosis—calcium loss from the bone protected by the metal plate. This occurs because the plate, not the bone, is receiving the stress (from recovering function) that bone needs if it is to repair itself and remain healthy. In principle, plates made of more flexible materials could minimize the problem. Some researchers are working on such semirigid materials, while others experiment with materials that ultimately would be reabsorbed by the body. This would avoid the problem because the stress would be returned gradually to the healing bone as the plate is weakened and absorbed by the body.

Electricity for Healing Soft Tissues

Although using electricity to heal bone fractures is becoming more and more widespread, its extension to treating injuries in soft tissues—tendons, muscles, and ligaments—is still considered experimental. However, at least one Canadian physician, in Halifax, has treated over 100 patients (usually athletes) by implanting in the injured area a small battery that emits a constant electrical current. The pulse of the battery—which is removed after about six months—apparently promotes

healing and strengthens the muscles and other soft tissues that tend to weaken through disuse in a cast. (Patients do not wear a cast in this method—merely a dressing around the area.) Patients are said to recover quickly from their injuries. Although some patients' bodies reject the implant, for many, the method appears to offer quicker and stronger recovery from some of the injuries affecting an increasingly athletic population.

See also the Spotlight on Health article FRACTURES, SPRAINS, AND STRAINS.   ERIC L. HUME, M.D.

Cancer

The most exciting recent developments in cancer research have been advances made by scientists toward understanding what causes the disease. Since a number of different disorders are grouped together under the name "cancer," the story of how normal cells in the body are transformed into cancer cells is a complicated one. The story involves the cells' genes and the biochemical roles they play. But it now appears that an understanding of the basic processes by which cancer arises and develops is at hand, a prospect that opens new vistas in the areas of diagnosis, treatment, and prevention.

Meanwhile, research has continued in such areas as possible treatment applications of laboratory-produced versions of certain substances naturally produced by the human body's immune system. Further evidence has been found linking the synthetic hormone diethylstilbestrol (DES) with cancer. And some experts have cast doubt on widely reported claims that recent years have seen a marked increase in the percentage of cancer patients being cured.

Unlocking the Causes of Cancer

Cancer and heredity. Understanding the recent explosion in knowledge about how normal cells become cancerous requires first stepping back a few years in time. Scientists had long suspected that alterations in the basic genetic material of the cell, DNA (deoxyribonucleic acid), played an important role in causing malignancy. Cancer seemed to run in families, strongly indicating a hereditary factor. In addition, many things known to give rise to cancer, including certain chemicals (carcinogens) and certain kinds of radiation, had been shown to have direct effects on DNA. Studying the cell's genetic material, however, was a difficult task because of the extraordinary complexity of DNA. It represents a kind of code, whose components are genes. Each gene potentially codes for a single protein important for body function—that is, it provides instructions for making the protein. Genes are located in structures called chromosomes (which occur in duplicate, in pairs). The total number of genes in a complete set of human chromosomes is enormous.

Identifying cancer genes. New experimental approaches devised in the last several years, however, have allowed scientists to identify a series of genes, perhaps no more than 30, that appear to play a direct role in the development of cancer. These genes, called oncogenes ("onco-" means tumor), were suspected to exist after it had been shown that viruses that cause tumors in animals could transform normal cells into malignant ones by controlling the functioning of the cells' genes.

Oncogenes were initially isolated by a method called DNA-mediated gene transfer. In this technique, DNA purified from human cancer cells was inserted into normal mouse cells in a laboratory dish. Some of the mouse cells appeared to become cancerous; when injected into mice, they developed into sarcomas (cancers of connective tissue). In this manner, it was shown that the DNA in human tumor cells carried the ability to transform a normal mouse cell into a malignant cell. Since it is possible to distinguish human from mouse DNA, the transferred human DNA was then isolated and the single gene that was involved in this process was identified.

Using the same approach, transforming activity was found in cancers as diverse as those originating in the lungs, breast, and bladder, as well as in various leukemias, lymphomas (tumors of the lymphatic system), and sarcomas. The next step was to compare these isolated genes with genes from animal viruses that were known to transform normal cells into malignant cells. The first human oncogene that was identified (it was isolated from a bladder cancer) was discovered to be identical to a transforming gene originally found in a rat sarcoma virus. This gene was labeled the H-ras gene.

With the isolation of a group of genes apparently directly involved in causing cancer, researchers then began searching for these genes in normal cells. The original oncogene isolated, the H-ras gene, was found to be present in all normal cells, and located on a particular chromosome. Because the chromosome occurs in duplicate, everyone has two H-ras genes in each cell of the body. Since we all have these genes but do not all develop cancer, there must be some difference between the genes as they appear in the normal cell and the genes as they appear in a malignant cell. Scientists have found some initial answers as to what this crucial difference might be.

Chromosome changes in cancer cells. It was discovered many years ago that the chromosomes of cancer cells have an abnormal appearance. Some of the observed chromosome abnormalities, or changes, occur consistently in particular types of cancer. For example, in most cases of chronic myelogenous leukemia, two

Cancer victims are proving that "disabled doesn't mean unable." Jeff Keith, who lost a leg to bone cancer in 1974 at the age of 12, has played lacrosse for Boston College and finished a coast-to-coast run to raise funds for the American Cancer Society and the National Handicapped Sports and Recreation Association.

chromosomes have exchanged some of their material (this is called reciprocal translocation.) Another example is Burkitt's lymphoma, a cancer affecting children, most commonly in western Africa. All malignant Burkitt cells have such a chromosome defect.

The list of the chromosome defects found in association with individual cancers has grown greatly in the last few years with the introduction of the technique called extended banding for the analysis of human chromosomes. Many scientists now believe that the malignant cells in virtually all cases of acute leukemia have chromosome changes of various kinds.

New techniques have also made it possible to study the chromosomes of other types of cancers. It has been found, for example, that in virtually all cases of so-called small-cell lung carcinoma, cells have suffered a loss, or deletion, of part of a specific chromosome. (This is a type of lung cancer that is strongly associated with cigarette smoking.) The part of the chromosome that is lost is adjacent to one of a number of "fragile" points in the human chromosome. At such points DNA characteristically breaks after exposure to certain carcinogens. The same break that occurs in this type of lung cancer can be observed in cells exposed in the test tube to the carcinogens of cigarette smoke. It was in this manner that a definite link was established between a known environmental carcinogen, a unique chromosome change, and the human cancer most strongly associated with both.

Recent studies have shed much light on possible connections between these chromosome changes in cancer cells and oncogenes. It was discovered, for example, that in certain situations an oncogene is involved directly in a translocation. In the translocation characteristic of Burkitt's lymphoma an oncogene moves from one chromosome to the other. In a Burkitt cell, the protein this oncogene codes for (its protein product) is found at much higher levels than in normal cells.

An example of a different kind of process is provided by cells from neuroblastoma, a nervous system cancer that occurs in children. Here, the oncogene involved appears to be present in many copies, a phenomenon known as gene amplification. And more oncogenes mean more protein product. Thus, while various mechanisms may be involved in chromosome changes, the common result is an altered level, usually an increase, of the protein product of the oncogene.

A different, more subtle kind of genetic change that leads to cancer involves the mutation of a tiny part of a gene's DNA. A single mutation in the DNA can alter the gene's protein product. Although it differs from the normal protein by only a single amino acid (the building blocks of proteins), this mutant protein is capable of transforming a normal cell into a cancer cell.

Cancer and viruses. When researchers found that some human cancers involve oncogenes identical to those in viruses causing cancers in animals, the hunt for

Dr. J. Michael Bishop, a cancer researcher at the University of California at San Francisco, displays a model of a tumor virus; new knowledge about such viruses has led to considerable progress in understanding how they cause disease.

a virus-cancer connection in humans intensified. Much information had already been discovered about how viruses produced cancer in animals. The known animal cancer viruses belonged to a group called retroviruses; the basic genetic material of these viruses is not DNA but a closely related substance called RNA (ribonucleic acid). A retrovirus (which may or may not be carrying an oncogene) that infects a cell may make a DNA copy of its genetic information, which may then be inserted into the DNA of the infected cell, thereby altering it. A problem confronting researchers, however, was that there was no solid proof of a retrovirus causing cancer in humans.

But the situation has changed in the past few years. Retroviruses have now been found that are directly involved in causing certain leukemias and lymphomas. These viruses are called human T-cell lymphotropic viruses (HTLV's) because they affect T lymphocytes, which are a type of white blood cell important in the body's immune system.

The disease found in the United States that has recently been associated with the virus known as HTLV–I is very similar to cancers originally seen in southern Japan and subsequently observed in the Caribbean and in Central and South America. This difficult-to-treat disease—called adult T cell lymphoma/leukemia—most commonly affects young blacks and is characterized by swollen lymph glands, skin rashes, in many cases a high level of calcium in the blood, and a predisposition to infections. A second class of human retrovirus, termed HTLV–III, has been isolated from individuals suffering from the disorder known as AIDS (acquired immune deficiency syndrome), which involves a breakdown of the body's immune system.

Considerable progress has been made recently in understanding why these two similar viruses cause such different diseases—in the first case, the T lymphocytes proliferate (a malignancy of the immune system), and in the second, they are destroyed. Researchers are currently devoting considerable effort to the development of vaccines against both viruses.

Cancer genes and cell growth. Cancer seems fundamentally to be a problem of growth and development. When oncogenes were found in all human DNA, it was strongly suspected that they played a role in the normal growth, development, and specialization of cells.

Strong evidence in support of this view has been obtained recently. First, it has been shown that H-ras genes essentially identical to those found in humans are present in organisms as primitive as yeast. The fact that this genetic material was conserved as the process of evolution unfolded suggests that it is of fundamental biological importance. More directly, scientists discovered that an oncogene originally isolated from a sarcoma occurring in monkeys is also present on a human

chromosome. This gene codes for a protein identical to a growth-stimulating substance called platelet-derived growth factor. More recently, an oncogene that codes for a protein linked with another growth-stimulating substance (epidermal growth factor) has been found.

It is thus now possible to imagine how a malignancy might develop. Some change occurs in the gene that codes for a normal growth factor, such as a mutation or a chromosome translocation, a change in the gene's actual location on the chromosome. In some cases, the change leads to greatly increased production of the gene's protein product. This suggests that either increased amounts of a normal protein product or perhaps an abnormal protein might sometimes be involved in a cell's becoming malignant. Consistent with this hypothesis, it has been shown recently that certain oncogene protein products when injected into normal cells have caused the cells to appear malignant and have increased the cells' growth rate. Thus, according to this theory, a cell, unchecked by its growth-control mechanisms, produces increased amounts of a substance that normally stimulates the cell's growth and reproduction. The consequent abnormal growth pattern results in the accumulation of primitive cells in the condition called cancer.

The importance of this concept of cancer cannot be overestimated, for it has major implications for prevention, diagnosis, and treatment. Treatment approaches such as radiation therapy or drug therapy (chemotherapy) are based on the notion that normal cells and cancer cells are biologically different, and so will be affected by a treatment in different ways. Scientists' newest findings, however, suggest that the differences between malignant and nonmalignant cells may be very subtle indeed. This may in fact account for doctors' lack of success in treating many patients. A more complete understanding of the way in which cancer develops cannot but aid in the development of the safe and successful treatment for which everyone hopes.

New Hopes for Cancer Treatment

Advances in biomedical technology have made available to researchers large quantities of pure biological substances, enabling these substances to be studied for possible use in cancer treatment. These include so-called biologic response modifiers (naturally occurring substances that can enhance or stimulate the working of the body's immune system) and monoclonal antibodies.

Interferon and interleukins. Among the biologic response modifiers being tested regarding their possible ability to enhance the immune system's resistance to cancer are various kinds of interferon (an antiviral protein) and interleukins.

A laboratory-produced form of the interferon called

alpha-interferon, for example, has yielded significant improvements in the condition of patients with cancers of the blood and bone marrow, including multiple myeloma, some lymphomas, and a rare cancer called hairy-cell leukemia. Some patients with other cancers, such as malignant melanoma, have also responded well. Although the initial inflated expectations that had been voiced regarding interferon's ability to combat tumors have not been realized, the substance has proved of some effectiveness and seems likely to be combined in certain future cancer treatments with chemotherapy or with other biologic response modifiers.

A very different kind of substance is interleukin-2, or T-cell growth factor, which is also being tested in patients with cancer (as well as those with AIDS). Interleukin-2 has, in tests with animals, been able to stimulate the immune system to recognize and destroy malignant cells.

Monoclonal antibodies. Cancer researchers have for many decades been searching for a treatment that would be specifically targeted at malignant cells. Such a targeted treatment should not only be more successful but also offer less danger—since normal cells would not be damaged. The development of monoclonal antibodies through genetic engineering techniques was a major step forward toward this goal. The immune system naturally produces a wealth of different antibodies that help it do battle with different foreign substances that invade the body; each antibody has a specific target. With the monoclonal technique, which yields many copies of a hybrid antibody-producing cell derived from an animal, pure antibodies of great specificity can be produced in the laboratory in virtually unlimited amounts. The importance of this advance was recognized in the awarding of the 1984 Nobel Prize in physiology or medicine to three European scientists who were instrumental in bringing it about.

The monoclonal antibodies produced so far have been used not only in research but also to some degree in diagnosing and treating patients with various leukemias and lymphomas and with colon cancer and malignant melanoma.

But since the monoclonal antibodies used to date have been derived from mouse cells, they have produced allergic reactions in some patients. And despite some success in helping cancer patients, improvements due to the antibodies have in general been only partial and short-lived. Most researchers now believe that the future of monoclonal antibodies in cancer therapy lies in using them as a vehicle to carry chemotherapy drugs, poisons (toxins) for killing targeted cells, or radioactive substances that serve as easily detectable "tags" permitting the location of the antibodies in the body to be observed. Much current research, therefore, is directed toward the formulation of such antibody combinations,

as well as toward production of monoclonal antibodies from human cells.

Developments in 1984 included a report on the high sensitivity of the technique called monoclonal antibody imaging: radioactively tagged monoclonal antibodies injected into a patient and traced by an electronic scanner detected microscopic cancer cells that had strayed from a tumor to other parts of the body and had not been found in other diagnostic tests. In addition, two different monoclonal antibodies able to detect a common form of bladder cancer have been developed and are being studied further for their diagnostic value.

Vitamin C Ineffective Against Cancer

In the early 1970's the Nobel Prize–winning chemist Linus Pauling began advocating the use of large doses of vitamin C as a treatment for cancer. The evidence in favor of vitamin C was circumstantial, but the claim that it could be effective drew wide public attention thanks to the authority lent it by Pauling's reputation of solid achievement in several fields of science. (He has also argued that the vitamin can be helpful against colds, influenza, mononucleosis, and heart disease.) A careful 1979 study at the Mayo Clinic in Rochester, Minn., found that vitamin C was not able to ease symptoms or lengthen survival time in advanced cancer, but Pauling stood his ground. To meet certain objections he raised to their study, the Mayo group carried out another. This extremely rigorous study, published in January 1985, showed the vitamin to have no effect against advanced cancer of the large intestine (a particular cancer that Pauling had found to respond well to vitamin C treatment). The case against vitamin C's effectiveness thus seems very strong.

DES Update

A major study reported in late 1984 found yet another possible link between cancer and the drug diethylstilbestrol. A synthetic estrogen, or female sex hormone, DES in the United States was until 1971 prescribed to pregnant women to prevent miscarriages. After a number of cases of cancer of the vagina were reported in daughters of women who had taken the drug, the U.S. Food and Drug Administration in 1971 warned that it should not be prescribed to pregnant women. Researchers subsequently found that daughters born to DES mothers run an increased risk of cancer of both the vagina and the cervix.

The new study showed a late-developing increased risk of breast cancer in the women who took DES while pregnant. They were found to have, beginning about two decades after exposure to the drug, a 40 to 50 percent greater chance of breast cancer than women who did not take the drug. This increase, however, is relatively moderate: the risk for DES mothers is still not as great as that for women who have close relatives with breast cancer. The number of deaths due to breast cancer in DES mothers was not found to be significantly higher than for non-DES mothers; since, however, the cancer risk appears to increase with time, figures for breast cancer deaths associated with DES may climb.

A recently completed seven-year study confirmed that the incidence of cervical and vaginal cancer in women whose mothers took DES and who were thus exposed to the drug in the womb is distinctly greater than for unexposed women—about two to four times as great, in fact. On the other hand, another recent study found no evidence that the sons of DES mothers show more infertility, other reproductive abnormalities, or cancer of the testicles than other men, although this had been suspected at one time.

Are We Winning the War on Cancer?

There is a growing debate over how much progress has actually been made during the last quarter-century or so in treating and curing cancer. Many experts believe the gains have been substantial. Others admit that there have been advances in fighting some types of cancer but claim that the overall picture is not encouraging; figures apparently showing markedly improved survival rates, they say, are misleading and do not reflect reality.

The U.S. National Cancer Institute reported in late 1984 that, overall, cancer survival rates had continued to improve, if somewhat moderately, during the preceding ten years. Of those patients whose cancers were diagnosed between 1976 and 1981, 49 percent were expected to live at least five years from the time of detection. (For most types of cancer, survival for five years after detection is considered to be a rough indication that the cancer may have been cured.) For those diagnosed from 1973 to 1975, the figure was 48 percent. The rate had been 42 percent for 1970 to 1973 and 38 percent for 1960 to 1963.

These statistics might suggest that greater strides were made before the increased funding from the federal government's war on cancer, declared in 1971, could have had any effect. Many factors, however, must be taken into consideration before drawing conclusions. For one thing, figures for the earlier years were based on data collected from a much smaller number of hospitals. That "sample" of hospitals was less comprehensive, and less representative, and so the resulting statistics might be less accurate. Also, the overall survival rate statistics are affected by what types of cancer are most prevalent in a given period. For example, the incidence of lung cancer is now rising; chances of surviving this particular form of cancer are still relatively slim. This in itself may be lowering overall survival rates.

Those experts who regard the survival figures as misleading believe that the apparent gains are largely a consequence of changing definitions of cancer and improving tumor detection methods. They argue, for example, that doctors are increasingly able to detect diseases that look like cancer, and are counted as cancers, but are not deadly. People with these types of diseases would survive at least five years whether they were treated or not. In addition, as one of the analysts has put it, "the survival clock is being started earlier." In other words, more cancers are now detected at earlier stages, generally ensuring at least five-year survival for those with long-acting cancers, such as breast cancer. Finally, some experts claim, nonfatal cases are more likely to be registered today than two or three decades ago, while the accuracy for reporting fatal cases has not markedly changed. This alone would account for some of the improvement in survival rates.

Many doctors contend that although such factors may have affected the statistics, there still has been a genuine overall improvement in survival rates. How the debate is ultimately resolved has implications for policymakers. If, for example, treatment results are indeed found to be showing less improvement than official statistics suggest them to be, some have argued that it might be desirable to devote more resources to alternative approaches to fighting cancer, such as prevention. Many cancer researchers feel that this allocation of resources should not be at the expense of basic scientific research into cancer biology. It is their strong sense that an understanding of the basic biological mechanisms involved in cancer, many of them discussed in this article, is at hand. With this information should come new progress in the diagnosis and treatment—as well as the prevention—of cancer.

DAVID R. PARKINSON, M.D.

Childbirth

See OBSTETRICS AND GYNECOLOGY.

Child Psychology and Development

Advances in child psychology are helping to answer long-standing questions about inborn and learned abilities and the impact the environment has on a child's social, perceptual, and intellectual development. Researchers are discovering that newborn babies have far more abilities than was once believed, and there is enhanced understanding of how an infant's different senses interact to provide the child with a unified per-

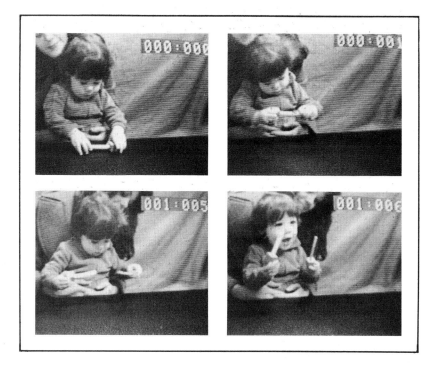

This 14-month-old child is pulling apart a toy in 6 seconds a day after seeing an adult doing the same thing. It has now been demonstrated that children this young can remember and imitate behavior, even after a 24-hour time lapse; it was previously believed that such ability did not appear until 1½ to two years of age.

ception of the external world. Conditions affecting the development of parent-infant attachments and the consequences these bonds have on the child's later social functioning also continue to be investigated.

Interactions of the Senses

In the past 20 years developmental psychologists have vastly increased their understanding of how the individual senses function in infants and young children. Researchers are now turning their attention to the interrelations among the senses. How, they are asking, do infants and young children coordinate information received from the different senses?

Touch and vision. One-month-old infants may be able to relate information picked up by touch and by sight. This was the finding of one recent experiment in which investigators removed the nipples from ordinary pacifiers, replaced them with small rubber spheres or spheres with nubs on them, and gave infants one or the other pacifier to explore in their mouths. After 90 seconds, the pacifiers were carefully removed. Each infant was then shown two shapes, only one of which matched the shape on the pacifier the infant had had in its mouth. The infants looked longer at the shape matching the pacifier they had held in their mouths, suggesting that the infants could recognize by sight the objects they had previously felt. Since the infants in this study were only one month old, the investigators hypothesized that experience may not be necessary for human

beings to coordinate information from two different senses and that there may be an innate ability to code information in a form accessible by two perceptual systems.

Hearing and vision. An infant's perception of adult speech has often been treated as an exclusively auditory phenomenon (that is, connected to hearing). But recent findings suggest that vision may also play a role. A team of investigators at the University of Washington examined a possible connection between hearing and vision by testing whether infants could relate vowel sounds to the lip shapes that cause them. Four-month-old infants were shown a film in which two adult faces appeared side by side. The faces each made a different mouth movement: one, forming the vowel sound "ah," had a wide, open mouth, while the other, forming the vowel sound "ee," had the lips narrowly opened with the corners pulled back. Meanwhile, a loudspeaker placed midway between the two faces played the two vowel sounds. Evidently, very young infants have some primitive lipreading skills: based on the comparative length of time the babies looked at the face making the specific vowel sound they were hearing, most of the infants could relate the sounds to the appropriate mouth shape.

Help for handicapped infants. The fact that information picked up through one sense may complement that received through another—or that one sense may serve as a substitute for another—has various potential practical applications for handicapped babies. For example, it may be possible to help deaf infants through the combined use of lipreading and special vibratory devices that deliver tactile stimulation to the skin. Such techniques of sensory substitution have already proven effective with adults.

Blind infants may also be helped in a way that is being explored by a team of researchers in Scotland. They adapted a device called a sonic guide, which is used by blind adults, for use with young infants. The sonic guide is essentially a sophisticated echolocation device that emits waves of ultrasound signals and converts reflections from nearby objects into audible sounds. The device is arranged such that an object's distance is related to the signal's pitch, and an object's size is related to the signal's loudness. In addition, the nature of the sound gives information about the texture of the object, and the direction of the object is specified by which of the two ears receives the audible signal first.

The remarkable thing discovered by the Scottish researchers was that blind infants, some as young as 16 weeks old, used this device with relative ease to track objects, turning their heads toward the objects. One of the infants even reached out and hit a small object dangling on a wire in front of him. Wearing the sonic guide, the same infant turned back and forth toward his mother, bringing her in and out of his sound field. Smiling, he repeated this behavior several times, giving the researchers and the mother the strong impression that he was playing a kind of auditory peekaboo game.

The Nature and Role of Imitation

The determination of which skills are learned by observation, which are innate, and which develop through other means has always been a central concern of child psychologists. Today, addressing these questions directly through laboratory experiments, they have concluded that imitation plays a powerful role in shaping the actions of babies.

Jean Piaget, one of the fathers of modern child psychology, considered the imitation of facial expressions to be a developmental milestone, occurring shortly before the time of the first birthday. Piaget theorized that imitating a facial expression was a difficult task, requiring considerable learning and experience on the part of the youngster. Because infants cannot directly compare their own actions with those of others, they would need to play interactive games with adults—like touching an adult's face and then their own—before they could learn to relate the expressions they see to their own unseen movements.

But according to new evidence, imitation of facial expressions seems to be one of the starting points of early psychological development, rather than a developmen-

tal goal reached after many months of experience. In the late 1970's, researchers reported experimental evidence showing that infants as young as two to three weeks old could imitate both facial and manual gestures, such as opening their mouths, sticking out their tongues, pursing their lips, and moving their fingers in a specific way. Infants performed these gestures significantly more often after they had seen an adult demonstrate them than they did spontaneously, without seeing the demonstration.

It was possible, of course, that the infants had already learned to imitate certain gestures when they dealt with their parents in their first weeks of life. Another, more recent study therefore was conducted at the University of Washington with 40 newborns, all under 72 hours old; the youngest was only 42 minutes old. Like the older babies in the first experiment, the newborns imitated the adult's facial expressions. The conclusion was that the ability to imitate such gestures is an innate one, which does not require weeks or months of learning and experience.

Imitation would play a very limited role in development if children copied adult behavior only immediately after witnessing it and could not duplicate the behavior at a later time. The ability for delayed, or deferred, imitation has traditionally been assumed to appear at about 1½ to two years of age; younger children have been thought to lack the necessary memory and capacities. However, a new study of 120 children indicates that babies as young as 14 months old may have this ability. One group of children watched an adult pull apart a small toy and put it back together again. A second group of children did not see this. The next day, each child was given one of the toys. The babies who had seen the adults take apart and reassemble the toy were about five times more likely to pull apart the toy—and with impressive speed—than were those who had not witnessed the adults' actions. This illustrates the deep influence that adult models can have on young children. Although these 14-month-old children had not seen the experimenter before and were exposed to only a short demonstration, their behavior was directly influenced by what they saw the adult do, even after a delay of 24 hours.

Attachments: Secure and Insecure

Over the past two decades, the study of parent-infant attachment relationships and their impact on the child's developing personality has greatly expanded. Research in this field has been widely reported in the press largely because of growing concern over such issues as the prevention of child abuse and neglect and the effects of maternal employment and day care on children. Recent research has led to a greater understanding of disturbances in the relationship between parent and infant, the possible connections between such disturbances and the risk of maltreatment, and the effect of the overall relationship on the child's functioning. (Most research has focused on the mother and infant, but this is slowly changing. The impact of fathers is now being studied as well.)

A mother's responsiveness and sensitivity to her baby's needs and signals have generally been thought to be critical factors in the development of their relationship, in the closeness of their bond. Some mothers, however, are less able to respond sensitively to their babies. For example, it has been believed that depressed mothers and their children are more likely to develop insecure or tenuous relationships because of the mothers' periodic emotional withdrawal or unavailability.

This was recently confirmed in a report by researchers at the U.S. National Institute of Mental Health, who found that only about one-quarter of the infants whose mothers were well or had minor depression showed insecure attachments. In contrast, over half of the children whose mothers had major depression, and over three-fourths of those whose mothers suffered from manic-depression, showed insecure attachments. The length of the mother's illness, the severity of her episodes of depression, and whether or not the mother was a single parent all were found to be significant factors in predicting whether the child's attachment to the mother would be secure or not. The research also indicated that the child's early relationships with other people are strongly affected by the emotional stability of the mother.

Studies reported in 1984 by the Harvard University Child Maltreatment Project revealed that approximately 70 percent of children who had been maltreated—either physically abused or severely neglected—had insecure relationships with their mothers. (The disturbances in the mother-child bond were not found to result from economic disadvantage, however.) In addition, whereas by the age of about 19 months most children are able to recognize themselves in a mirror, the maltreated children at this age were not yet able to do so. Psychologists consider this ability to be an indication of a developing sense of oneself as a separate person.

Current research is also focusing on the stability of the parent-child relationship over time—whether or not, for example, the security or insecurity of the relationship fluctuates in response to changes in the home environment or in the parent's actions, and how significant such fluctuations might be. Psychologists are also examining the effects of secure and insecure parent-child relationships on the child's behavior, and they have discovered some continuity between early responses to parents and later social behavior.

Later, in preschool settings, children with secure bonds seem to be more friendly and more able to deal with school activities and with peers; they are judged by teachers and parents to have greater self-control and more resiliency in the face of challenge or frustration. Not surprisingly, children (especially boys) who as infants had insecure relations with their parents, tend, by comparison, to exhibit behavioral problems when they are four to six years old. A strong network of friends can in some cases offset or circumvent such difficulties for the child.

An infant's degree of security does not appear to be solely a trait or an ingrained personality characteristic; it is instead a reflection of the present and past quality of care-giving, and it is clear that parenting is affected by a host of complex, interacting factors. The stability of attachment during infancy and its importance for later personality functioning are strongly affected by outside factors that directly and indirectly influence the child and the family. That family harmony, family and neighborhood support systems, parental employment status and patterns, and parental attitudes toward children affect the central parent-child relationship is clear. The extent of these factors' influence remains to be established. We may then begin to understand more clearly how these early attachments, in turn, influence social and emotional development as the child matures.

ANDREW N. MELTZOFF, PH.D.
and MARK T. GREENBERG, PH.D.

Dentistry

See TEETH AND GUMS.

Diet

See NUTRITION AND DIET.

Digestive System

Researchers have found new evidence that certain sugar substitutes may produce gastrointestinal problems—involving, for example, the stomach or small and large intestines—in some individuals. A recent U.S. government study, however, seemed to quiet doubts about the safety of the artificial sweetener aspartame. Developments of interest to people who have been drinking little or no milk, a richly nutritious food, because of trouble digesting milk sugar include a finding that they may be able to eat yogurt and the new availability of enzyme tablets that may help some digest dairy products. Other research news includes documentation of a relatively high incidence of gastrointestinal problems, including bleeding, in marathon runners.

Sugar Substitutes and Gastrointestinal Disorders

Sorbitol. So-called sugar-free food products have become quite popular because they are lower in calories and are less likely to cause tooth decay than products containing ordinary table sugar. Technically known as sucrose, ordinary sugar is composed of the simple sugars glucose and fructose. One sweetener widely used in "sugar-free" products is sorbitol, a substance derived from glucose.

Sorbitol is poorly absorbed by the small intestine, and doctors have known for some time that consuming it in large enough amounts (20 to 50 grams) may produce an ailment called osmotic diarrhea. (A piece of sugarless gum or mint made with sorbitol contains 1.3 to 2.2 grams of the sweetener; thus, about nine to 15 pieces would contain 20 grams, or about 4 teaspoonfuls, of it.) Moreover, fermentation of sorbitol by bacteria in the large intestine may cause other gastrointestinal symptoms.

A study of seven healthy adults, however, revealed that the ingestion of even smaller quantities of this sweetener may result in gastrointestinal distress. Five of the seven experienced gas and bloating after taking 10 grams of sorbitol in a water solution. Four suffered more severe symptoms (cramps and diarrhea) after taking a solution containing 20 grams. As little as 5 grams of sorbitol in water produced gas and bloating in three of the seven.

Children who eat sugarless foods may be particularly likely to ingest amounts of sorbitol that are large for them; their smaller body weight makes them potentially more sensitive to any adverse effects. An outbreak of diarrhea among children that was linked to dietetic candy containing sorbitol was reported in New Hampshire in 1984. Eight of nine neighborhood playmates, ranging in age from five to 13 years, developed stomach cramps and diarrhea shortly after each child had eaten three to 16 pieces of the candy. Only one of the eight received medical attention; the remaining seven recovered without treatment within two or three hours after the symptoms began. Three other children, who had eaten only one piece of candy, did not become ill, nor did four others who had eaten no candy at all. The amount of sorbitol in each piece of candy was a little over 3 grams.

Thus, people experiencing diarrhea or other symptoms of stomach or intestinal upset should consider their use of food products containing sorbitol. Sorbitol has not been linked with side effects other than diarrhea and gastrointestinal discomfort.

Fructose. Fructose, often used commercially as a sweetener instead of sucrose because of its lower cost,

Aspartame, a new low-calorie sweetener sold under the brand names NutraSweet and Equal, is now widely used, as are other sugar substitutes.

may also cause gastrointestinal symptoms. Fructose is sweeter than sucrose; it is not a low-calorie sweetener. Over a decade ago an inexpensive industrial process was developed for making corn syrup with a high fructose content from corn starch; the process converts glucose into fructose. The availability of this high-fructose corn syrup has resulted in the increasing use of this substance by soft-drink manufacturers. By 1979 high-fructose corn syrup accounted for about 12 percent of the total U.S. sweetener market (not including non-caloric sweeteners); it was estimated by the U.S. Department of Agriculture that for 1984 the figure would be about 29 percent.

In one study of the effects of fructose, five of 16 healthy persons who drank a solution containing 50 grams of the sweetener (about the same as in 18 to 30 ounces of a soft drink) developed abdominal cramps or diarrhea because the fructose was not completely absorbed by the small intestine. In comparison, none of 15 people who took a similar amount of sucrose developed symptoms. The study suggests that fructose, in the quantities found in some soft drinks, may cause gastrointestinal symptoms in people with a limited intestinal capacity to absorb this sugar.

Aspartame. Aspartame, a relative newcomer to the U.S. sweetener market, is made from two of the building blocks of proteins, the naturally occurring amino acids aspartic acid and phenylalanine. Sold under the brand names NutraSweet and Equal, the substance is about 180 to 200 times sweeter than sucrose. Unlike the artificial sweetener saccharin, it has no aftertaste and has not been linked with cancer. Since a very small amount of it is generally enough to produce the desired sweetness, it adds few calories to the diet. At present, the products in which it is most widely used include soft drinks, tabletop sweeteners, and dried beverage mixes.

There have been, however, numerous reports of alleged adverse health effects of aspartame. In an effort to obtain additional data, over 500 complaints received by the U.S. Food and Drug Administration were analyzed by the Centers for Disease Control of the U.S. Public Health Service. Most of the complaints fell into one of the following areas: central nervous system effects (headache or irritability), gastrointestinal effects (nausea or diarrhea), rashes and hives, and menstrual problems. (There were also some reports that aspartame contributes to depression.) The CDC study, released late in 1984, concluded that most of the illnesses were mild, that the symptoms reported were common in the general population, and that there was no evidence for the existence of serious, widespread, or adverse health consequences from the use of aspartame. It was pointed out that although a small segment of the population may be especially sensitive to aspartame, this is not an unusual phenomenon for any substance, and extensive studies would probably be required to determine just which individuals have a high sensitivity. In general, people who think they are allergic to aspartame can easily avoid it, since products containing the substance are clearly labeled.

Options for People Who Can't Digest Milk

Some individuals can't drink milk because they are allergic to milk proteins. But many more have trouble drinking it because they simply do not have enough of the enzyme called lactase that breaks down the main sugar, lactose, found in dairy products. Lactase deficiency does not normally affect young children but is the most common cause of milk intolerance in adolescents and adults. Researchers estimate that approximately 80 percent of the adult population of the world is unable to digest lactose adequately. In the United States, about 20 to 25 percent of adults are thought to be affected.

The nature of milk intolerance. When lactose-intolerant people consume milk, and milk products, in the usual amounts, they tend to develop such symptoms as abdominal cramps, gas, bloating, or diarrhea within 15 minutes to three hours after eating. Some lactase-deficient individuals are sensitive even to very small quantities of dairy products.

Lactase is made by cells that line the surface of the small intestine. A lactose-tolerant individual has enough lactase to break down lactose into the simple sugars glucose and galactose, which can then be absorbed by the digestive system. In people who do not have sufficient lactase in the small intestine, the lactose passes undigested and unabsorbed (along with intestinal fluid) into the large intestine, where it is fermented by bacteria into substances that cause the characteristic symptoms. Exactly which symptoms occur, and how intense they are, depend on the amount of lactose ingested and the degree to which lactase is lacking. But symptoms will definitely develop in those who take in more lactose than they can tolerate.

Most people who are sensitive to lactose can tolerate small amounts of milk—for example, the amount used in coffee—but not large quantities. Generally, one 8-ounce glass of milk, containing about 12 grams of lactose, will produce symptoms in 50 percent of those who are lactase-deficient; 90 percent will have symptoms after drinking 32 ounces of milk.

Avoiding lactose in the diet. A simple way to deal with the problem of lactose intolerance is to avoid foods containing milk sugar. But this means doing without the many nutritional benefits offered by milk. One alternative for people sensitive to lactose is to consume milk and milk products in small amounts that they can tolerate. The level of intolerance can be discovered by trial and error: at first, very small quantities of foods containing lactose are tried, and the amounts are gradually increased until an adverse reaction develops. Some lactase-deficient people are able to consume as much milk (or other dairy products) daily as a normal individual by dividing the total amount into small servings that are eaten throughout the day. Another alternative is to eat more dairy products that are lower in lactose than ordinary milk; examples are hard cheeses (such as cheddar and Swiss), yogurt, sour cream, and buttermilk. Stores in some areas also now offer special lactose-reduced products, including ice cream and cottage cheese.

Those individuals who are so sensitive to milk sugar that they need to follow a lactose-free diet should keep in mind that milk products (and therefore lactose) may be present in a number of nondairy processed foods (for example, muffins and instant potatoes). It is thus a good idea to obtain a lactose-free diet plan from a dietitian or nutritionist.

Yogurt. A recent study suggests that yogurt has a special advantage enabling it to be tolerated by many lactase-deficient people who cannot drink milk without adverse effects. Samples of milk and commercial, unflavored yogurt, containing equal amounts of lactose, were given to ten lactose-intolerant individuals. Tests revealed that the lactose in the yogurt was absorbed better than that in the milk and that less gas and diarrhea were experienced after eating the yogurt than after drinking the milk. Apparently, yogurt contains lactase that comes from the bacteria responsible for the yogurt fermentation process; once the yogurt reaches the small intestine, the lactase is activated in amounts sufficient to digest 50 to 100 percent of the lactose content of the yogurt.

Adding lactase. Another way to deal with lactose intolerance is to drink milk that has been pretreated with lactase. (Such milk has a sweet taste that some people find unpleasant.) Ready-to-drink pretreated milk is now sold in some areas. In addition, milk (and many other dairy products) can be pretreated at home with a lactase product, sold without prescription. Numerous studies have shown that symptoms are significantly reduced in lactose-intolerant persons who drink milk to which a few drops of this liquid lactase are added at home 24 hours beforehand.

Lactase can also be added to milk at mealtimes (although larger quantities are required). The effectiveness of this more convenient approach was confirmed by a combined U.S.-Mexican study published in 1984 which found that adding a lactase product made from yeast (sold as LactAid) to milk five minutes before drinking it reduced or eliminated symptoms in ten of 12 milk-intolerant persons.

A different approach to the problem is to add lactase directly into an individual's system. Just such a product, a tablet form of LactAid, was recently introduced in the United States and Canada. A person takes it just before drinking milk or eating other foods containing lactose. Consumers' experience with the tablets, and further studies by researchers, will determine whether they are as practical and effective an aid for lactose-intolerant people as the manufacturer claims.

See also the feature article MILK: GOOD FOR EVERYONE?

Gastrointestinal Effects of Running

It is estimated that there are over 35 million runners in the United States. There is no question that running is a good way to gain aerobic fitness: it increases the body's capacity to use oxygen during exercise and enhances the overall efficiency of the heart and lungs. It is also effective for burning excess body fat and toning muscles. In some people, however, running may produce gastrointestinal problems.

New documentation of the extent of these problems came in late 1984 with the publication of results of a survey of participants in an Oregon marathon. Out of 1,700 runners who were requested to fill out a questionnaire, over 700 responded. The questionnaire asked about their overall experiences with gastrointestinal symptoms during or immediately after long-distance running. The respondents ran an average of 46 miles a week. More than a third of them said they relatively often felt the urge to have a bowel movement while running or just afterward. Bowel movements after running were relatively common for 35 percent of those surveyed, and diarrhea after running for 19 percent; 18

percent sometimes had to interrupt a hard run for a bowel movement, and 10 percent had to do so for diarrhea. These gastrointestinal "disturbances" were more common in women than in men and in younger than in older runners. Bloody bowel movements associated with running occurred relatively often in about 1 to 2 percent of those surveyed. Among other gastrointestinal symptoms that were noted, heartburn was more common during running than after it; vomiting and nausea occurred more frequently during hard runs and after running than during easy runs.

A British study that was published several months before the Oregon survey indicated that bleeding into the digestive tract may be a relatively common occurrence during long-distance running. Out of some 300 runners in a marathon race who were surveyed, only one had a bloody bowel movement. So-called occult blood (blood present in amounts too small to be visible to the naked eye), however, showed up more often. Stool samples from 39 randomly selected marathon runners, taken both before and after running, were examined for occult blood. Three of the runners (8 percent) were found to have such hidden blood in their stools after the marathon; none of the three had had occult blood in their stools before the race. The exact cause of the bleeding remains to be established.

Further research is needed to confirm these findings on gastrointestinal problems in runners, to explain the cause and significance of the symptoms, and to develop recommendations to prevent their occurrence.

See also the Spotlight on Health article ULCERS: CAUSES AND CURES. DANIEL PELOT, M.D.

Drug Abuse

Although many experts believe that drug abuse in the United States has on the whole leveled off, it remains a serious public health problem, and there is some evidence that its extent has been underestimated. Efforts at prevention are increasingly focusing on reducing the demand for illicit drugs, as well as eliminating the supply. Researchers are paying growing attention to the abuse of such drugs as antianxiety medications and stimulants. A new study suggests that angel dust, whose abuse has reached epidemic proportions in some areas, may be even more dangerous than previously thought. Recent advances in the treatment of drug abuse include the approval by the U.S. government of a new nonaddicting drug, naltrexone, that can be used in many cases of heroin addiction.

The Magnitude of the Problem

A survey of mental disorders in adults that was made public in October 1984 cited drug abuse as the fourth

Clara Hale, at 78, presides over a Harlem home for the youngest heroin addicts of all—those who were exposed to the drug before birth. President Ronald Reagan singled out her work for special praise in his 1985 State of the Union address.

most common psychiatric problem in the United States (after anxiety disorders, mood—or "affective"—disorders, and alcohol abuse). Also indicative of the extent of drug abuse is a recent increase in the number of cocaine users applying for treatment of drug-related problems, as well as a continuing strong demand for treatment of narcotic dependence of all kinds in most large metropolitan areas, especially in the eastern United States. Medical problems from marijuana use occur infrequently, but use has remained high.

An encouraging sign was the latest results (reported in early 1985) from an annual survey of drug use among high school seniors. The survey, sponsored by the U.S. National Institute on Drug Abuse (NIDA), showed a small overall decline in the use of illegal drugs since the previous year, a continuation of a trend that, many experts think, may foreshadow a future period of decreased use and abuse. The trend may be similar in Canada; recent surveys taken among Canadian adolescents suggest a stabilization or even a decline in the use of marijuana and other drugs.

A development in Mexico in November 1984, however, had disturbing implications for the question of the extent of drug abuse. In a series of raids, authorities there seized more than 10,000 tons of marijuana—reportedly the largest recorded drug seizure ever. The amount captured, most of it destined for the U.S. market, was nearly as much as was previously thought to be used in the United States in an entire year. Since the statistical methods used to estimate nationwide marijuana use are the same as those applied to most other illegal drugs, the size of this "catch" forced federal officials to wonder if they had vastly underestimated the use of all illicit drugs in the United States.

Prevention: Restraining Supply and Demand

The Reagan administration has been pursuing a vigorous but uphill campaign to hold back the flood of illegal drugs entering the United States from other countries by exerting political and economic pressure on foreign governments and using military personnel and equipment to stop drug smuggling. In one of the most important heroin cases ever developed by the U.S. government, over 30 alleged members of a heroin ring run by organized crime were arrested in 1984. The ring was said to have brought $650 million worth of heroin (street value) into the United States since 1979. (Since a string of pizza restaurants was used as a cover, the case was dubbed the pizza connection.) Eastern and midwestern cities were reportedly the main markets for the ring.

A major anticrime bill that was passed by Congress and signed by the president in October 1984 established a National Drug Enforcement Policy Board, under the chairmanship of the attorney general, to coordinate the enforcement efforts of federal antidrug agencies. Among other provisions, the bill sharply raised federal penalties for drug violations and increased the government's power to confiscate the property of convicted drug dealers.

A few months earlier, legislation was enacted removing the drug methaqualone from the U.S. retail market. Prior to the enactment of the law, authorities had successfully prosecuted 40 to 60 individuals who were dispensing the drug illegally under the guise of running "stress clinics." Sold under the trade name Quaalude, methaqualone was popular with some drug users because it was thought to produce a dreamlike state and also to enhance sexual relations. Its legitimate use was as a sleeping medication. Methaqualone is still available in Canada, although under more strict regulation than most prescription drugs.

In spite of these gains, drug abuse prevention efforts based on supply reduction alone face serious obstacles. A report on controlling drug use in adolescents that was published in 1984 by the Rand Corporation, a major U.S. consulting firm, concluded that it is nearly impossible to stop the distribution of illegal drugs when demand for them is strong and users are ready to pay high prices. The report emphasized the importance of programs to reduce the willingness of young people to experiment with drugs (although the evaluation of such programs is still in an initial stage) and to improve early treatment of addicts. The authors of the report suggested that a type of antismoking program that has been effective with adolescents—the "social influence model"—might be successfully adapted to anti–drug use programs. In this approach, peer disapproval (that is, disapproving attitudes of other young people toward smoking) and the effects of smoking on appearance and personal hygiene are stressed.

An educational campaign aimed at acquainting preteens with the health hazards of marijuana has been begun by the American Lung Association in conjunction with the American Council for Drug Education. In the program—called Marijuana: A Second Look—children aged nine to 11 (and their parents) are taught how marijuana can damage the lungs and are advised not to let their lungs "go to pot." A wide variety of other prevention programs are under way, started by, for example, parents' and youth groups and religious organizations and sometimes involving public service advertising campaigns. All these efforts attempt to encourage young people to avoid drug use, often by pointing out its hazards while emphasizing the positive aspects of more traditional life-styles.

Research Efforts

Although funds for treating drug abusers have been reduced for some programs, there was a 15 to 17 percent increase in federal funding of drug abuse research in the United States in fiscal year 1984, with a similar increase approved for fiscal year 1985. Research has focused largely on learning more about the underlying biological mechanisms of addiction, studying short-term and long-term drug effects, and developing more effective treatments.

Many scientists in the United States and other countries, for example, have been examining the endorphins. These are substances produced by the body that have morphine-like effects in suppressing pain. It is thought that a better understanding of how they act may lead to more effective treatment for many psychiatric disorders, including drug dependence.

Antianxiety drugs and stimulants. Another active area of research is study of the benzodiazepines, a class of antianxiety drugs that includes such commonly used tranquilizers as diazepam (Valium) and chlordiazepoxide (Librium). Some benzodiazepines have a significant potential for abuse, especially among people who are dependent on other sedatives or on narcotics.

Researchers have discovered that cells in the central nervous system have special "receptors" that combine with drugs like diazepam to initiate a process that reduces anxiety. (A receptor is a cell structure that has an affinity for reacting with a particular substance.) It has also been found that as many as 43 percent of people who take these drugs for an extended period of time (eight months or longer), even when using them in recommended doses, have withdrawal symptoms if the drug is discontinued abruptly. Scientists are seeking to better understand these withdrawal reactions and the way in which the drugs act upon the benzodiazepine receptors. This research could result in improved treatment for anxiety as well as in an increased knowledge of what happens in the body in a variety of psychiatric conditions, including anxiety states and narcotics dependence.

The abuse of over-the-counter stimulant medications such as phenylpropanolamine (PPA) or PPA-caffeine combinations has provoked growing concern, and research on their physiological effects and abuse potential is increasing. These drugs are widely sold in the United States as appetite suppressants (for example, Dexatrim and Codexin) or as mild stimulants. (Appetite suppressants containing PPA have never been allowed on the market in Canada.) Taking advantage of the demand among drug abusers for amphetamines, a group of powerful stimulants, some individuals in the illicit drug trade have manufactured capsules and tablets containing high doses of PPA or PPA-caffeine combinations, which are sold as amphetamine "look-alikes." With over 50 case reports of serious adverse reactions to such look-alikes, there is reason to believe that they should be more stringently controlled.

Marijuana and cocaine. Also receiving more detailed study are the subtle effects of marijuana, such as marijuana "hangover," as well as such possible long-term behavioral effects as the "amotivational syndrome," in which the marijuana user appears to lose all desire to engage in productive activities. It remains to be determined, however, whether this syndrome is caused by marijuana per se or is simply a personality trait shared by people who choose to smoke marijuana regularly. The widespread use of marijuana makes an understanding of such effects extremely important.

Research is proceeding on more effective treatments for cocaine abuse. Some pilot studies have indicated that antidepressant medications such as imipramine (Tofranil) or desipramine (Norpramin, Pertofrane), as well as lithium (often used to treat manic-depressive illness), may reduce the euphoria and other stimulant effects produced by cocaine, and that cocaine abusers treated with these drugs do better than those who receive standard treatments alone.

Angel dust. Many users of angel dust—whose technical name is phencyclidine, or PCP—claim it causes a giddy euphoria, and some speak of feelings of invincibility. A painkiller, PCP is known to have numerous effects on the central nervous system; people using it may experience hallucinations or delusions and may develop a condition resembling schizophrenia. When taken in high enough doses, it can produce coma, convulsions, and even death.

A study published in mid-1984 raised the possibility that PCP may also damage the immune system, the body's defenses against foreign invaders like bacteria and viruses. Under laboratory conditions, several kinds of white blood cells that play key roles in the immune system were exposed to PCP. Among other things, it was found that the drug slowed the production of antibodies by the so-called B cells, and cut in half the production of the important substance interleukin-1 by the cells known as monocytes. Further research is necessary to confirm these findings and, if they hold up, to clarify their implications. It is possible, of course, that PCP in the body may not affect white blood cells in the same way as in the laboratory.

Effectiveness of Treatment

Methadone. Two widely used approaches to treating drug addiction were recently assessed. Participants in a series of meetings sponsored by NIDA evaluated methadone maintenance, the most commonly used treatment for opiate dependence (that is, dependence on a drug derived from opium, such as morphine, heroin, and codeine). This approach seeks to combat addiction to, say, heroin (and its grave social consequences) by supplying addicts with methadone, a long-acting, synthetic narcotic that is taken by mouth rather than by injection. The methadone is administered under controlled conditions in a structured treatment program to help ease the addict's withdrawal from dependence. Methadone maintenance has provoked considerable controversy because it substitutes the legal use of one narcotic (methadone) for the illegal use of another (heroin).

The NIDA review supported earlier findings that methadone maintenance can provide significant benefit to the addict and also highlighted the complexity of social, psychological, legal, and administrative problems involved in methadone treatment programs. It emphasized the need to study the differences in staffing patterns, admission and discharge policies, and disciplinary procedures among these programs and the effect of these differences on success in treating addicts. A study under way at Temple University in Philadelphia to evaluate 12 different methadone programs is addressing some of the issues and findings that resulted from the NIDA meetings.

Therapeutic communities. The second major NIDA review evaluated the effectiveness of treatment in a therapeutic community, where addicts trying to overcome their drug habit live together under supervision, receiving moral support from each other as well as training and counseling to help them redirect their lives. It was found that patients treated in such programs tend to show important gains in controlling their drug use and antisocial behavior, in their employment status, and in their feelings about themselves and others; these gains were maintained over a 12-month, posttreatment follow-up period. In general, persons with more severe psychiatric symptoms did not make as much progress as those who were less psychiatrically impaired, and patients who spent more time in treatment had better results than those remaining for shorter periods. Even patients who left prematurely showed gains, although they were not as substantial as those made by individuals who completed the entire program.

Naltrexone Approved

Naltrexone, a long-acting drug that blocks the effects of heroin (and other opiates) and the addict's craving for it, was approved for marketing in late 1984 by the U.S. Food and Drug Administration. Like methadone, naltrexone (which is sold under the name Trexan) is taken orally; unlike methadone, it is not itself addicting. Naltrexone is administered only after the addict has been "detoxified" and no heroin remains in the body. Since naltrexone has no euphoric effect of its own and keeps the addict from feeling the euphoria produced by heroin, some addicts prefer not to be treated with it. So far, it has been especially useful in treating highly motivated individuals, such as middle-class or upper-class addicts who have a lot to lose if they fail to break their narcotic dependence; naltrexone programs have had less success with so-called street addicts.

Some experts have voiced concern about possible adverse effects of naltrexone on people with liver problems, which many narcotics addicts have. A number of researchers who have worked with the drug, however, say most addicts don't have "active" liver disease. For such opiate addicts, they claim, naltrexone poses no significant risk of liver damage if taken in the recommended dosage.

See also the Spotlight on Health article HELP FOR CO-CAINE USERS.　　　　　GEORGE E. WOODY, M.D.,
A. THOMAS MCLELLAN, PH.D.,
and CHARLES P. O'BRIEN, M.D., PH.D.

Drugs

See MEDICATIONS AND DRUGS; DRUG ABUSE.

Ears, Nose, and Throat

Researchers in otolaryngology—the field dealing with diseases of the ears, nose, and throat and with surgery of the head and neck—have been exploring new treatments to help a damaged larynx, or voice box, function more normally, alleviate facial paralysis, and eliminate or reduce vertigo caused by the disorder known as Ménière's disease. Among other developments, the U.S. government has approved for marketing a device capable of opening up the world of sound to many persons suffering from severe deafness, and a major study has shed new light on how the sense of smell varies with age.

New Help for Larynx Problems

The larynx is a complex organ in the neck that plays a role in both breathing and speech and protects the windpipe (the air passage, or airway, leading to the lungs) by keeping out food and other foreign substances. Within the larynx are the vocal cords. These two folds of tissue have two basic positions: when held together they are capable of producing speech; when held apart, they allow free breathing. Problems that may keep the larynx from functioning normally include inflammation (laryngitis), the development of a tumor, and damage caused by an injury or by surgery to remove a tumor. If the vocal cords are unable to come together completely, the speech produced is weak or

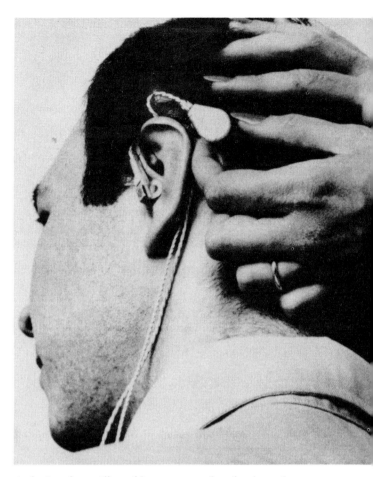

A device that will enable some people who have been totally deaf to hear many sounds—though not clearly enough to understand speech—was approved by the U.S. Food and Drug Administration in November 1984. Called a cochlear implant, it transforms sounds into electrical impulses that are transmitted directly to the nerves of the inner ear.

breathy; in addition, solid food or liquids that are swallowed may accidentally enter the windpipe. Considerable recent research has focused on treatment for this vocal cord problem, with existing techniques being improved and new ones developed.

An approach that has been used for some time is the injection of substances such as Teflon into weakened vocal cords to provide additional bulk and improve speech. One of the newest techniques along these lines employs a gel material similar to that contained in some soft contact lenses. Injections of the material have been tried on patients suffering from shrinking, or wasting, of the vocal cords and paralysis of the muscles that bring the vocal cords together. The use of a microscope ensures precise control of the surgical instruments. The

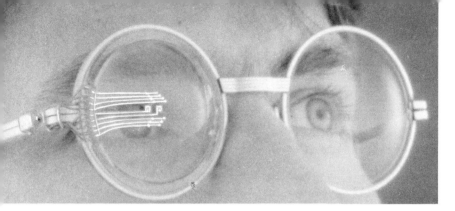

Visible Sound

Still in an experimental stage are computerized eyeglasses that will allow deaf people to "see" speech. The autocuer is designed to help lip readers distinguish between sounds the speaker may pronounce with lips in virtually the same position. A microphone on the glasses transmits signals to a microcomputer worn by the viewer; visual signals are displayed on the glasses (and can be positioned near the speaker's mouth). In the photos shown here, the speaker is saying "he" at left and "ge" as in "get" at right.

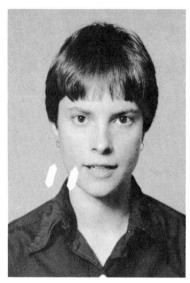

injections have been generally successful, their effectiveness depending on the severity and cause of the patient's original disability. The complications have been minimal. Researchers expect that additional suitable materials will be developed in the future.

Other research has focused on the problem of vocal cords being fixed in a closed position. Individuals with this problem have almost always had to undergo a tracheotomy—an operation in which an incision is made through the skin and into the windpipe (trachea)—so that a tube can be introduced for breathing purposes. During the past 50 years, numerous procedures have been proposed for moving one vocal cord to the side in order to widen the airway in the larynx and make breathing easier. These procedures have generally required extensive surgery. In 1984 researchers reported the development of a simpler technique that uses a carbon dioxide laser and does not require any incision in the neck. The laser is aimed through the mouth into the larynx and, under precise control with the aid of a microscope, removes some tissue from the vocal cord, thereby reducing the cord's bulk. Surgical stitches are then placed in the larynx and pulled sideways to increase the width of the airway. In most cases where the procedure was tried, the patients were able to have their tracheotomy tubes removed and to begin breathing normally within several weeks.

Alleviating Facial Paralysis

Paralysis of one side of the face is a very debilitating problem that can have serious effects on a person's mental health and relations with others. The cause of the paralysis is not always known—for example, in the condition known as Bell's palsy—but some progress is being made with treatment. Researchers have reported new surgical techniques for reanimating the paralyzed face by grafting nerves and muscles from other areas of the body. A nerve graft restores motion to the muscles around the eye, enabling it to open and close. A muscle from the cheek area, together with its nerves, is used to provide support for the muscles around the mouth. These new techniques not only restore motion to the face but also enhance the patient's control of the facial muscles, making it possible to move the upper and lower portions of the face separately. People who undergo this treatment require up to two years of rehabilitation training before the success of the surgery can be completely assessed.

Implants That Bring Sound to the Deaf

One of the most exciting research stories in the treatment of ear, nose, and throat disorders continues to be the rapid development of cochlear implants for the deaf. These are miniaturized electronic devices, whose components include a microphone (to convert sound into electrical energy), a processing unit, and one or more surgically implanted electrodes that provide electrical stimulation to nerve cells in the hearing portions—the cochlea—of the inner ear. People who have received a cochlear implant hear sounds, but not clearly enough to understand speech. They can, however, sense the duration and rhythm of certain intense sounds, as well as variations in volume. If they are trained to read lips, they can understand more of what a speaker says than can a lip-reader who lacks the device. With the implant, for example, they may be able to hear the stress a speaker places on certain words or the difference in intonation between a question and a simple statement.

Various cochlear implants are being tried experimentally. One type, developed by Dr. William House of the House Ear Institute in Los Angeles in conjunction with the 3M Company, was approved for marketing by the U.S. Food and Drug Administration in November 1984; it is designed for totally deaf adults who cannot be helped by a hearing aid. In general, the progress made during the past five years in cochlear implants suggests that they will have an important role in the future rehabilitation of people with severe deafness.

See also the feature article HEARING IMPAIRMENT *and* MEDICAL TECHNOLOGY.

Surgical Treatment of Vertigo

Encouraging results have been achieved with a new surgical treatment of Ménière's disease. One of the most difficult disorders to treat in otolaryngology, Ménière's disease is usually characterized by tinnitus (ringing in the ears), vertigo (a sense of spinning movement of the patient or the environment), and fluctuating hearing loss. These symptoms probably result from a fluid imbalance in the chambers of the inner ear. During the past 50 years, numerous surgical techniques have been tried for reducing or eliminating them. Unfortunately many of the procedures have been only partially successful or have introduced new damage in the process of attempting to alleviate the symptoms.

One recent research effort has involved surgical treatment with a technique called retrolabyrinthine vestibular neurectomy, a procedure by which the surgeon cuts one of the nerves running from the ear to the brain that register balance. This approach attempts to eliminate the perception of vertigo while preserving the patient's hearing. Of 49 patients on whom the procedure was tried, 71 percent had no vertigo after the operation, and 23 percent were much improved.

New Data on the Sense of Smell

Does the sense of smell change with age? There has been no lack of studies on this question, but they have been limited ones, with contradictory results. Recently, however, a major, large-scale study of smell at almost all ages was completed. It showed that the sense of smell is indeed affected by age.

Researchers tested almost 2,000 people between the ages of five and 99 and found that, on the average, the ability to identify odors peaks between the ages of 20 and 50. The ensuing decline in olfactory ability turns into a sharp drop after 70. In the group tested, signs of major impairment of the sense of smell were seen in over half of those between the ages of 65 and 80 and in more than 75 percent of those older than 80. The researchers noted that, given these findings, it is little wonder that many older persons claim that food does not seem to be as flavorful as it used to be. They also commented that the decline in the sense of smell with age could mean that many elderly individuals are less able to detect fires and leaking gas in the home.

Another finding of the study was that at all ages females tended to identify odors better than males. In addition, smokers' sense of smell was less accurate than nonsmokers'.

Removing Tonsils and Adenoids to Ease Breathing

If children's tonsils or adenoids—located at the back of the throat—become swollen (as a result, say, of infection), the airway from the nose through the throat can be obstructed, making breathing difficult. In the past, removing the offending tonsils or adenoids by surgery was a common way of dealing with severe cases of this problem. But these operations have come under increasing scrutiny during the past two decades or so, with many respected physicians questioning whether the results of the procedures are sufficiently beneficial to patients to justify performing them. Evidence has been reported, however, that the operations may indeed benefit some children. And a technique called nocturnal sonography (sleep monitoring) seems to be of use in clarifying the nature of the obstruction problem.

In one form of this technique, each child's breath sounds are recorded for a two-hour period during sleep; a computer analysis of the sounds helps determine the degree of airway obstruction. The technique makes it possible to identify those who require more time to inhale than to exhale, a symptom of increased obstruction. X rays of the neck also assist in assessing the narrowing of the airway caused by swollen tonsils and/or adenoids.

Among a group of children who had had their tonsils and adenoids removed to alleviate airway obstruction of varying degrees, it was noted that 70 percent showed improvement in nighttime breathing patterns. Also, parents reported that the children snored less and had fewer episodes of interrupted breathing during sleep.

FRANK E. LUCENTE, M.D.

Environment and Health

The worst industrial disaster in history, a leak at a pesticide plant in Bhopāl, India, killed thousands of people, injured at least 150,000 more, and caused deep concern about the possible dangers posed by similar factories in the United States and other countries. The best environmental news of 1984 was that tens of thousands of children, who are considered most at risk for problems linked with high blood levels of lead, are likely to enjoy better health over the next few years because of the U.S. government's decision to phase out the use of leaded gasoline. Also of significance was a plan designed by the U.S. Environmental Protection Agency (EPA) to protect the nation's underground supply of drinking water from toxic materials. Health in the United States is also likely to be improved by restrictions on the toxic substance dioxin.

Industrial Chemicals: Hazards and Fears

Tragedy in Bhopāl. In what was described as the worst peacetime industrial disaster in history, on December 3, 1984, a tank at a plant owned by the Union Carbide Corporation in Bhopāl, a city of over 670,000 in central India, leaked toxic fumes. Over 2,000 people were killed and many thousands more injured. Countless numbers of domestic animals were killed or injured as well. The repercussions were felt in the United States and in other countries where similar plants exist.

The Bhopāl plant manufactured a pesticide in the group known as carbamates, developed as a biodegradable substitute for the now banned pesticide DDT. The immediate cause of the deaths and illnesses was methyl isocyanate, a chemical used to make the pesticide. One of the gases associated with methyl isocyanate is phosgene, the poison gas used during World War I. In Bhopāl, the methyl isocyanate was made up ahead of time and stockpiled in underground tanks.

As many as 150,000 to 200,000 people may have required medical care as a result of the gas leak. Victims suffered eye injuries, such as corneal irritation, corneal infection, and temporary blindness, and respiratory distress, such as lung inflammation and swollen larynxes. Long-term illnesses and injuries, such as blindness, mental retardation, and so-called secondary infections, were feared but had not materialized several months after the accident. However, follow-up for a number of years will be needed to fully determine all of the effects of the gas leak.

Methyl isocyanate is produced at other sites around the world, including a Union Carbide plant in Institute, W.Va. The cancer rate in the area around Institute is reportedly 25 percent higher than that of the United States as a whole, and this has been linked by some to the release of about 280 pounds of methyl isocyanate into the air every year. An investigation of leaks of the chemical from the plant is under way.

Lack of data on health risks. Very little is known about methyl isocyanate, but this is not uncommon for various chemicals, despite their widespread use in industry. According to experts at the U.S. National Academy of Sciences, little or nothing is known about the vast majority of chemicals on the market, including the ingredients contained in pesticides like those produced at the Union Carbide plants. Since 1976, the Toxic Substances Control Act has required testing of new chemicals, but the law contains no provisions for the many compounds that predate the law. Most research on chemicals is done by the companies that produce them. (Drugs, cosmetics, and food additives are subjected to even less investigation.)

Reports issued in July 1984 by the General Accounting Office (GAO), an arm of Congress, stated that toxic chemicals were insufficiently monitored by the federal government. Under the Toxic Substances Control Act, the EPA is responsible for assessing and controlling the health risks involved in the manufacture, use, and disposal of chemicals. But according to the GAO, only a small number of the 60,000 chemicals on the market have been controlled for possible risks by the EPA. The GAO also criticized the agency for its tendency to assess new chemicals only on the basis of their proposed uses; the possible effects of any uses other than those that are initially proposed are not taken into account by the EPA.

New Legislation on Toxic Wastes

Given the enormous task of guarding the public and environmental health from the seemingly ever-growing list of toxic materials, one of the more hopeful steps taken in 1984 was the passage by Congress of an amendment to the Resource Conservation and Recovery Act of 1976, one of the primary antipollution laws in the United States. The amendment, the only major environmental legislation enacted in 1984 and the first such legislation in several years, reauthorizes and strengthens the 1976 law. It eliminates loopholes that allowed small businesses to dump hazardous wastes; these small concerns must now come under federal regulation.

The amendment also restricts disposal of toxic materials in landfills, and it forbids the recycling of toxic chemicals in other substances, such as the combining of wastes with home heating oil or the mixing of dangerous substances with waste oil that is used to control dust on roads. It was the spreading of such road oil, in this case containing dioxins, that led to the contamination of the community of Times Beach, Mo., a situation that received widespread attention in late 1982 and 1983.

Protection of Drinking Water

Perhaps the biggest public health threat facing the United States in coming years is the contamination of supplies of drinking water by the seepage in of toxic substances from underground storage tanks, waste dumps, and other sources. A study by the congressional Office of Technology Assessment concluded that perhaps half of the nation's population now relies on water supplies that may become contaminated. According to the study, cancer, liver and kidney damage, and nervous system diseases could result from the contaminated water supplies, in addition to other adverse social, environmental, and economic effects.

In California, for instance, the underground drinking water supply of 500,000 people in the Los Angeles area is expected to be contaminated by a variety of heavy metals, pesticides, and other toxic wastes by 1987; officials say it may now be too late to prevent this from happening. And in Woburn, Mass., a town near Boston, clusters of possibly pollution-associated leukemia cases have occurred near contaminated water supplies.

A program announced in August 1984 by the EPA to safeguard water supplies will rely on a combination of state and federal controls, and the state and federal governments will share the costs equally. No new mandatory standards were imposed; instead, the purpose of the program is to coordinate various water protection efforts and the use of different environmental laws. Under the program, underground water supplies will be divided into three categories, with each category receiving a different level of protection. Supplies that are relied on by large populations for drinking or that support ecological systems very vulnerable to contamination will be given the strongest protection legally possible. The location of hazardous waste disposal sites near these water supplies will be forbidden. The second category includes underground water supplies currently in use; these will continue to be protected according to existing regulations. Highly contaminated or saline supplies form the third category; since they are not likely to be used for public water systems, they will be neither protected nor cleaned up.

Dioxins Restricted as Hazardous

Effective in mid-1985, the EPA is extending its regulatory authority over all types of dioxin—there are actu-

Victims of the disastrous leak of methyl isocyanate gas in Bhopāl, India, are helped away from the area of the Union Carbide plant where the leak occurred. At least 2,000 people were killed and tens of thousands were injured in what was described as the worst peacetime industrial disaster in history.

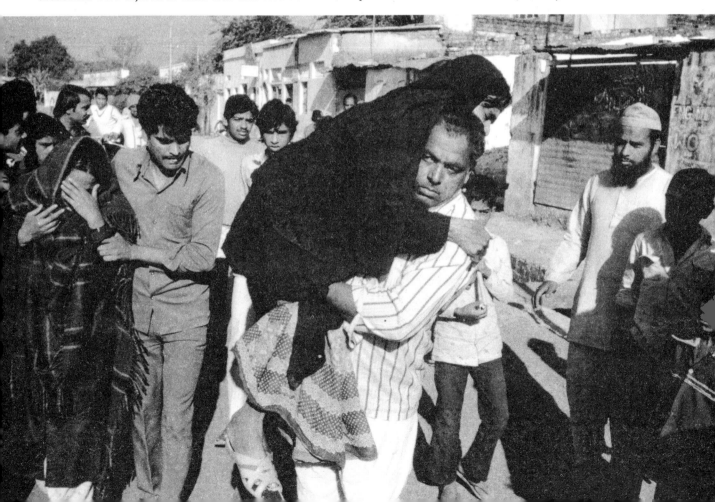

Contamination of well water in New Jersey because of seepage from chemical waste dumps, industrial plants, and underground gasoline tanks has forced thousands of residents to install family water coolers.

ally 75 dioxin compounds, only some of which are dangerous—by designating them as hazardous wastes. These compounds include the type used in the dioxin-contaminated waste oils that several years ago were spread on roads in various communities like Times Beach. The new regulations, first proposed in 1980, also cover related compounds known as furans. Prior to the new rules, only one type of dioxin (called 2,3,7,8-TCDD) was regulated by the EPA.

Dioxin is a component of the herbicide 2,4,5-T and the defoliant known as Agent Orange. The use of these substances in the past and the possible link of such use to disease formed the basis of a number of lawsuits in the United States and Canada in 1984 and 1985. The most visible was a $180 million out-of-court settlement between seven chemical companies that manufactured Agent Orange and thousands of veterans exposed to it during the Vietnam war. The veterans claimed that the herbicide had caused cancers, liver damage, skin and nerve problems, and birth defects. In the settlement, the chemical companies did not admit any direct link between the herbicide and the veterans' health problems; nevertheless, the case and its settlement encouraged other suits. In Canada, for instance, over 100 former employees of the New Brunswick Electric Power Commission, or their survivors, are suing over exposure they had to Agent Orange during the 1950's and 1960's when they were involved in a weed eradication program to clear the way for power lines. The suit claims that the herbicide contributed to the high rate of death seen among the exposed employees and that it has also caused health problems including cancer, heart attacks, and arthritis among many workers who are still living.

Restrictions on Creosote Proposed

In July 1984, the EPA announced that it would permit only trained and certified workers to handle and use three wood preservatives known to cause cancer and birth defects in laboratory animals—creosote, pentachlorophenol, and inorganic arsenic compounds. Although most creosote is used for preserving wood, 14 million pounds a year are used for such purposes as herbicides in gardens, as insecticides, and as fungus inhibitors on rope and canvas. Now the EPA has proposed banning all uses of creosote other than for preserving wood. U.S. consumers and processors have used about 1 billion pounds of the three compounds a year, accounting for 97 percent of all wood preservatives and more than one-third of all pesticides.

Under the proposed restrictions—which were pending early in 1985—sale of most wood products treated with any of the three compounds would still be permitted, but all such materials would have to bear labels stating that fact and giving information on risks and best methods for use. Outdoor furniture, sun decks, and other treated wood products that are likely to come into frequent contact with human skin would have to be sealed with shellac or varnish. Older equipment originally treated with one of the preservatives should present no health hazard, nor will fence posts painted with creosote below the soil line be able to pollute the grounds farther than about one-half inch away, according to health authorities.

The Asbestos Problem

In 1984 the extent of asbestos in private and public buildings, especially schools, became more apparent, and the possible health risks aroused some controversy. Asbestos was once widely used as insulation in walls, ceilings, floor tiles, and heating ducts.

Asbestos has been closely associated with several diseases. One is asbestosis, in which asbestos particles, which are smaller than dust particles, lodge in the lungs, scar them, and prevent them from functioning properly. Another disease is mesothelioma, a rare cancer of the abdominal cavity. Asbestos is also known to cause lung cancer. A 1984 Canadian study—undertaken after the deaths of some 70 former workers at an Ontario plant, where they were engaged in making asbestos-cement pipes—confirmed hazards of asbestos fibers in the workplace. The study recommended a ban on the manufacture of asbestos textiles; the researchers found textile weaving to be the most hazardous process involving asbestos. The study found that although asbestos posed an occupational hazard, the risk of whatever asbestos exists in the average home was no greater than that of smoking half a cigarette a year. This conclusion was disputed for a number of reasons.

In the United States, there is increasing concern over the complex health and economic issues involved in dealing with asbestos. It has been debated, for example, whether or not the federal government should require the removal of asbestos from school walls and ceilings, whether such removal would create a greater hazard than leaving the asbestos in place, and how removals could be carried out with the least possible health risks to workers and to the building's regular occupants. Coping with asbestos in school buildings—where a substantial amount of asbestos is located—presents problems. It has been estimated that perhaps 15 million to 36 million students in the United States are exposed to possibly dangerous levels of asbestos in school buildings. Removal of the asbestos is expensive—it could cost as much as $3 billion to rid all the country's schools of asbestos. And that very removal process may itself pose a significant hazard. In one typical case, the opening of many schools in New Jersey was delayed in the fall of 1984 because a statewide asbestos-removal program had not been completed during the summer recess, and local school boards were unsure if opening the schools was safe.

The federal government has not as yet developed a comprehensive, detailed plan for safe removal of asbestos, nor have most states. However, the EPA is developing guidelines for assessing the hazards of asbestos materials and working out standards for certifying contractors to remove asbestos safely. In the courts, both personal injury cases and class action suits have been filed against various asbestos producers.

Finally, it turns out that family pets are not only fellow sufferers of asbestos hazards but also serve as a kind of an early warning system for their human housemates. According to an epidemiologist at the University of Pennsylvania, since animals develop tumors more rapidly than humans do, asbestos-related cancers in pets may identify owners who will be at high risk in the future—despite any steps they may take. A number of such instances have been documented.

Leaded Gas

Under new rules issued by the EPA in March 1985, the maximum permissible content of lead in gasoline will be reduced to 0.5 grams per gallon by July 1, 1985, and to 0.1 grams per gallon by January 1, 1986. As a result, there will be a 90 percent reduction in the lead content of gasoline by 1986; prior to the issuing of the new regulations, 1.1 grams of lead were allowed per gallon of gas. The EPA also stated that it was considering instituting a complete ban on leaded gas by the year 1988.

When the EPA first proposed the reduction in mid-1984, the agency said the purpose of the new regulations was "to end the use of lead as a gasoline additive to prevent unacceptable health effects and misfueling while protecting engines designed strictly for the use of leaded fuel." Both high and low levels of lead have been associated with health problems, including brain, liver, and kidney damage, especially in young children. In addition, a number of studies have shown that even small amounts of lead can cause a reduction in the IQ (intelligence quotient) of children.

The new regulations were deemed necessary because of the unexpected, continued demand for and use of leaded gasoline. The EPA in 1973 first announced a gradual phaseout of lead in gasoline, to be completed by the early 1990's. When the present limit was instituted as part of that phaseout, in 1982, officials assumed that there would be a total of no more than 21 billion grams of lead released into the air by 1987; new cars would have emission controls and would require unleaded gasoline, and fewer and fewer older cars using leaded gas would be on the road. However, there is illegal use of leaded fuel by about 13 percent of U.S. cars designed to use unleaded gas. This has raised the estimate of lead released to 36 billion grams. Such illegal use also damages emission control devices, causing the newer cars to pollute the air more than those with no emission control systems at all—producing great amounts of hydrocarbons, carbon monoxide, and oxides of nitrogen, the major air pollutants the control devices were designed to check.

Lead was developed as a gasoline additive to boost the octane rating of gas at little additional cost; fuel with increased octane burns more smoothly and provides better ignition, more power, and reduced engine knock. Some 30 million older vehicles still expected to be on the road in 1987 will not be able to run properly without leaded fuel. However, people whose cars can run on unleaded gas have been switching to leaded fuel, not only because of the extra power leaded gas gives to their cars but also because it typically is less expensive to buy than unleaded gas. Experts point out, though, that since lead also fouls spark plugs and other engine parts of the cars designed for using unleaded gasoline, the increased repair costs usually negate the initial savings.

Leaded gasoline has been banned outright by countries of the European Economic Community; phaseout is to be complete by 1986. Also, in 1984 the city council in Chicago voted to prohibit the sale of leaded gasoline in the city, making it the first large municipality in the United States to do so. When the new nationwide reductions go into effect, benefits are expected to include fewer and lower medical bills, and overall costs savings are estimated at $1.8 billion in 1986 alone. At the same time, the lower-leaded gas will help the nation meet clean air standards.

There is increasing evidence of lead's deleterious effects on the body. Researchers in Pittsburgh and Boston found in a study of over 4,300 women giving birth that there was an association between blood lead levels and mild malformations in the infants. Blood samples were taken from the umbilical cords during labor and then analyzed for lead content. These results were correlated with hospital records of the condition of the newborns. The abnormalities found included small skin growths, benign tumors, and undescended testicles. The physicians stated that although no particular malformation was associated with the umbilical cord lead levels and the malformations might not be significant in themselves, the presence of such abnormalities may be a marker for impaired development.

In addition, a smaller amount of lead in the blood than was once believed hazardous may indeed be dangerous. In February 1985, the U.S. Centers for Disease Control (CDC) issued new guidelines lowering the blood levels of lead in children that the agency considers either elevated (and possibly dangerous) or poisonous. The CDC lowered the level it defines as elevated from 30 micrograms of lead per deciliter to 25 micrograms per deciliter. (A microgram is about 35 billionths of an ounce; a deciliter is roughly a fifth of a pint.) The CDC also lowered the blood lead level it defines as poisonous from 50 micrograms per deciliter to 35. The agency recommended that all children be screened for possibly high lead levels.

The Adverse Effects of Stress

Scientists are finding increasing links between people's health and the stresses and hazards of ordinary life. These range from the long-term effects of an economic recession to ailments caused by crowded living conditions. It has long been known that stress has a negative effect on the human body—whether it is "good" stress, like that caused by a marriage or promotion, or "bad" stress, such as that from the loss of a job or a divorce.

A study at the University of Wisconsin has found a chemical change within the body that occurs with stress. The chemical involved is called acetylcholine, and it is classified as a neurotransmitter—a substance that transfers messages from one nerve to another in the brain. Acetylcholine apparently decreases during periods of stress, and this has the same effects on some muscles as the normal decrease of acetylcholine that occurs in aging. (Lowered levels of this chemical also may be implicated in Alzheimer's disease, a condition that involves progressive memory loss among middle-aged and older people.) A deficit of acetylcholine slows reflexes and causes weakness in certain inactive muscles, mainly in the legs and arms. (Muscles that are in constant use, like the diaphragm, are not affected in this way.) The good news for people under stress, who may be at risk of this, is that exercise appears to reverse these negative effects.

Stress also has been linked to increased death rates during the three years following a heart attack. Researchers in New York City interviewed over 2,300 men two to three months after their heart attacks. The investigators found that men who were socially isolated and had high rates of stress in their lives—including enforced retirement, unfulfilling previous work experience, financial difficulty, or a distressing divorce in the family—were four times as likely to die within the three years following the heart attack as men who had strong family, social, and community ties and low levels of stress. The research team also found that social isolation and stress were most marked among the least educated patients studied and lowest among the best educated. Neither depression nor the strongly competitive, aggressive behavior known as Type A, which has been associated with heart disease, appeared to have an effect on the pattern of death in the time period studied. People cannot always control the stress-producing aspects of their lives, but perhaps patients who have suffered heart attacks can be helped to deal better with those aspects and reduce the risks involved.

Crowding. In many urban areas, crowded conditions are common—and are a source of considerable stress. In the past, some have believed that residents of crowded neighborhoods prefer living that way. A recent study of San Francisco's Chinatown provides anecdotal evidence that counters such beliefs. According to the study, Chinatown residents say that crowding makes them ill (comments included "it gives me a headache" and "it causes breathing problems"), forces them to behave in antisocial ways (like yelling at their children and being short-tempered), and causes frustration and depression. Most of those who said they wanted to move away from the neighborhood gave crowding as the reason.

Researchers suggest that both crowded homes and

crowded neighborhoods are stressful, but crowded housing is much more so. Crowded neighborhoods provide some benefits, such as shopping and transportation; however, community interactions are usually short-term and superficial. On the other hand, the resident of a crowded home is continuously subjected to cramped, intimate surroundings; such a living arrangement offers virtually no benefits at all. Also, long exposure to crowding does not appear to make it more tolerable. On the contrary, those Chinatown residents who had been raised in the extremely crowded conditions of Hong Kong hold more negative attitudes toward crowding than other residents.

Poor economic conditions. The health consequences of another source of stress, an economic recession, may not appear for many years, often as many as ten, according to a study done for the congressional Joint Economic Committee by a public health expert at Johns Hopkins University. He reported that recession and unemployment are linked to increased incidence of violence, antisocial behavior, and suicide and a rise in admissions to mental hospitals. Also, during a recession, tension and anxiety are widespread: workers concerned about keeping their jobs or overburdened because of other workers' layoffs tend to experience a level of stress that is nearly equal to that among the unemployed. There are increases in personal habits that have a harmful effect on health, such as drinking alcohol and smoking cigarettes.

The researcher noted that there is a peak in deaths from heart disease three years after a recession and another peak ten years after a recession. Deaths from cirrhosis of the liver also rise. The professor focused on the recession of 1973–1974, but he predicted that the recession of 1981–1982 would have similar effects and expressed the hope that the impact of the state of the economy on health would be taken into account by policy planners.

See also the feature article STRESS IN THE WORKPLACE.

The Effects of Smoking on Nonsmokers

The effects of tobacco smoke on nonsmokers are causing concern among health professionals. A 1984 Japanese report confirmed the extent of the problem, concluding that health hazards are directly proportional to nonsmokers' exposure to cigarette smoke—this is known as passive smoking—both inside and outside the home. Researchers at Kyoto University measured urinary levels of the substance cotinine, which the body makes out of nicotine. Because cotinine is easily identified and is produced only when there is nicotine in the body, the scientists thought that testing for it was the best way to explore the effect of passive smoking on the body. They discovered that the levels of cotinine were high in nonsmokers who lived with or worked with

smokers. The researchers recommended that people refrain from smoking in the presence of children and nonsmokers, both at home and at work, and that smoking in public places be restricted as much as possible. They acknowledged, however, that people would continue to smoke and that ventilation is inadequate in most buildings.

According to an EPA study reported in late 1984, tobacco smoke is the most hazardous cancer-causing air pollutant in the United States. The EPA estimated that anywhere from 500 to 5,000 nonsmokers per year succumb to fatal lung cancers caused by breathing other people's cigarette smoke. The tobacco industry has disputed these findings.

Mining and Lung Cancer

Diseases that have long developmental periods, such as cancer, are often difficult to connect to one occupation or activity. Nevertheless, a number of studies have provided evidence that uranium mining is responsible for a high incidence of lung cancer among miners. Inhalation of radon, a radioactive gas given off by many substances, including uranium-bearing ore, is thought to cause the cancer. However, some have criticized the research done on radon's role because other cancer-causing agents may have been involved. For instance, in the past, many of the miners studied have been smokers.

Two studies published in June 1984, however, have confirmed that radon is carcinogenic by itself, independent of other agents, and have shown that cigarette smoking markedly enhances radon's carcinogenic effects. One study, by a research team at the University of New Mexico and the National Institute for Occupational Safety and Health, has confirmed a very strong link between uranium mining and lung cancer in nonsmoking Navahos. The scientists concluded that since American Indians have lower rates of lung cancer than other segments of the U.S. population, and since the rate of smoking among Navahos is very low, the higher than expected rates of lung cancer they found among nonsmoking Navaho uranium miners must be considered largely occupational in origin. The study also noted that the miners with cancer developed it during a period when permissible levels of radon were higher than they now are; those who began mining since lower levels were instituted are probably somewhat less likely to develop lung cancer.

The second study, of Swedish iron miners, found that the total amount of time the men spent in underground iron mining, and hence the cumulative amount of exposure to radon and its radioactive products, were directly related to the risk of developing lung cancer. The scientists involved in this study warned, in addition, that high levels of radon and its products released by home insulation into indoor air may cause a significant public health problem in terms of increased cases of lung cancer.

See also the Spotlight on Health article ARE VDT'S DANGEROUS? ELLEN THRO

Epidemiology

The dominant story in epidemiology, the medical field dealing with the occurrence and spread of disease in populations, continues to be the devastating disorder known as AIDS (for acquired immune deficiency syndrome). Research efforts have produced considerable new knowledge about the probable cause of the disease, although a cure still seems a distant goal. Other recent developments include advances in scientists' understanding of the liver disease hepatitis, new studies on links between exercise and health, and increasing efforts to deal with day-care centers' potential role in spreading disease.

The AIDS Epidemic

From several points of view, recent developments in research on AIDS have made the disease appear more serious than was formerly evident. Nevertheless, there is some cause for optimism because of rapid strides being made in understanding the nature of the disorder, which involves a breakdown in the immune system— the body's defense against infectious disease.

There is rapidly mounting evidence that a virus dubbed lymphadenopathy-associated virus (LAV) in Europe and human T-cell lymphotropic virus type III (HTLV-III) in the United States is the cause of AIDS. The virus has been found in the affected tissues (lymph nodes) of AIDS patients and has been shown to damage the specific immune system cells affected early in the course of the disease.

As with other infections, people infected with the AIDS virus produce antibodies specific to the virus. These antibodies—substances that fight the invading infectious organism—have become progressively more common in population groups that run a higher than average risk of developing AIDS, such as homosexuals, but not in other groups. For example, antibodies to LAV have increased in prevalence in groups of homosexual men in San Francisco, rising from 1 percent in 1978 to 25 percent in 1980 and 65 percent in 1984. The occurrence of these antibodies in the general popula-

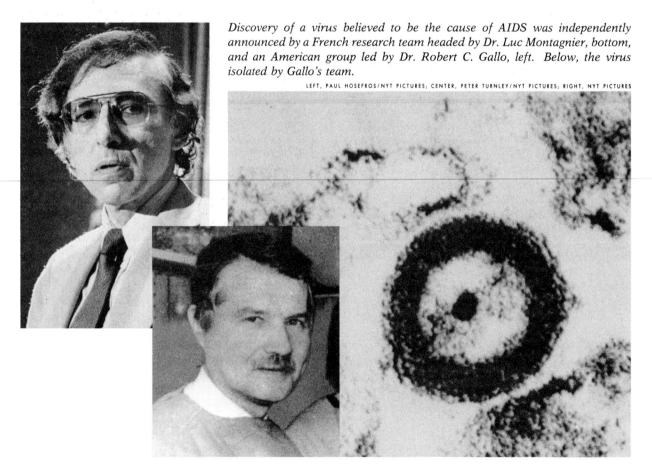

Discovery of a virus believed to be the cause of AIDS was independently announced by a French research team headed by Dr. Luc Montagnier, bottom, and an American group led by Dr. Robert C. Gallo, left. Below, the virus isolated by Gallo's team.

LEFT, PAUL HOSEFROS/NYT PICTURES; CENTER, PETER TURNLEY/NYT PICTURES; RIGHT, NYT PICTURES

tion remains very low. It is not known what percentage, if any, of the persons with antibodies to the AIDS virus will go on to develop clinical AIDS in the future, nor is it known what percentage of them are carriers of the virus and, hence, able to spread it to others.

One recent report described a patient with early symptoms of AIDS infection ("lymphadenopathy syndrome"—involving the lymph nodes) who later recovered: the AIDS symptoms gradually disappeared—and laboratory tests ceased finding signs of the disorder— even though antibodies to the virus remained. How many persons with early AIDS symptoms make such an apparent recovery is not known, but the fact that it can occur is encouraging.

Perhaps the aspect of the AIDS picture most puzzling to epidemiologists is that heterosexual Haitians and Central Africans seem to have a relatively high chance of developing the disorder. One possible explanation for this is that some combination of malnutrition and an overload of antibody-stimulating infections leads to damage to the body's immune system. According to this hypothesis, the overstressed and damaged immune system can no longer resist certain types of infection and cancer, and AIDS symptoms develop as a result.

This explanation is compatible with factors known to apply to other groups at increased risk for AIDS—sexually active male homosexuals, intravenous drug abusers, and patients receiving frequent transfusions of blood or blood products. Persons in all of these groups may be exposed to an unusually large number of infections, such as hepatitis. It would seem that, for AIDS to occur, two circumstances must exist: the virus must have entered the body, and the individual's immune system must be overstressed or damaged. If this explanation is correct, it might mean that the AIDS epidemic is not likely to spread to any great extent beyond the current high-risk groups. The majority of people, after all, do not belong to groups likely to be exposed to the infection and do have healthy immune systems. On the other hand, since the AIDS virus can damage the immune system, and since scientists do not know how likely this is to occur in persons with normal immune systems, health authorities remain worried about the possibility of AIDS spreading to the general heterosexual population.

Recent findings have shown that the suspected AIDS virus can spread from mothers without AIDS symptoms (but with antibodies to—and presumably, therefore, present or past infection with—the AIDS virus) to their infants, who may then develop the disease. Together with other findings this suggests that there is a "carrier" state for the infection—a condition in which a person is apparently well but can still transmit the infection to others. Moreover, this carrier state can exist despite the presence of defensive antibodies in the blood, so that

the task of developing a vaccine against AIDS infection may prove very difficult.

In early March 1985 the U.S. government approved for marketing two versions of a blood test for use by blood banks and other organizations to screen donated blood for the presence of antibodies to the AIDS virus. Although the test had certain limitations, there was hope it might reduce the chances of transmitting the disease through contaminated blood or blood products. By February 1985 over 175 U.S. cases of AIDS had been attributed to such transmission.

Among the AIDS cases diagnosed in the United States before July 1982, more than 76 percent have proved fatal. The total number of AIDS cases in the United States passed 8,500 in February 1985, and the numbers reported per quarter year continued to increase. Over 180 cases had been reported in Canada by February 1985. Growing numbers of AIDS cases have also been registered in Europe, although the incidence rate there is still less than 10 percent of the U.S. rate.

Hepatitis

Delta hepatitis. In late 1983 and 1984 an unusually severe epidemic of the type of hepatitis known as hepatitis B occurred in Worcester, Mass.; about 12 percent of those infected died. The epidemic was considered significant because it was the first one in the United States in which a virus called the delta agent was found definitely to have been responsible for increased severity of the disease. Scientists have established that the delta virus cannot cause disease by itself; it can infect a person only if infection caused by the hepatitis B virus is present. Studies in Europe have shown that the risk of dying from hepatitis B is usually much higher if there is an associated delta hepatitis infection.

Transfusion hepatitis. In 1984, U.S. government researchers claimed to have identified a virus that is the probable cause of most cases of hepatitis acquired through blood transfusions. The form of hepatitis involved—called non-A, non-B—accounts for 90 percent of the transfusion-acquired hepatitis cases, and 40 percent of all hepatitis cases, in the United States. The discovery of the virus raised hopes that scientists could proceed to develop a diagnostic test for blood suspected of contamination with the virus (which would help prevent transmission of the disease to recipients of blood transfusions) and, might eventually be able to produce a vaccine.

Another group of researchers—at the New York Blood Center—also claimed to have identified a virus responsible for non-A, non-B hepatitis. Although it is possible the two viruses discovered are the same, some researchers have theorized that transfusion-related non-A, non-B hepatitis may be caused by more than one agent.

Possible Rise in Rocky Mountain Spotted Fever

Rocky Mountain spotted fever is a serious disorder caused by a microorganism that is transmitted to humans by the bite of certain ticks. The disease is sometimes fatal but can usually be treated effectively with antibiotics if it is diagnosed in time. Despite its name, most of the cases of Rocky Mountain spotted fever have been in the southeastern United States, Oklahoma, and Texas. Up to 1970, the reported annual incidence of the disease in the United States was approximately one case for every 650,000 people. The rate then started growing, finally leveling off around 1978 at about one case reported per year for every 200,000 people. It is possible that this rise was simply a reflection of improved diagnosis and reporting of the disease. If, however, the rise in reported cases represented a true increase in incidence, it might be accounted for, at least in part, by the growing popularity of such activities as camping, hiking, and jogging, which entail increased human contact with areas likely to be infested with ticks.

Success in Preventing Rubella

Rubella, or German measles, is seldom a serious disease for a child or adult who becomes infected with it, but if a pregnant woman contracts it, particularly in the first three months of pregnancy, the dangers to the fetus are many and serious—they include abnormalities of the eyes, heart, and brain. In newborn children these rubella-caused abnormalities are called congenital rubella syndrome (CRS). The rubella immunization program in the United States is aimed primarily at preventing CRS rather than postbirth infection. In the late 1960's, as many as 60 or more cases of CRS were reported annually. Although the numbers were considerably lower throughout much of the 1970's, it was not until 1980 that there was a big drop—to 14 cases. Only two cases, according to preliminary data, were reported for 1984. It is difficult to know, however, what proportion of this decrease is due to immunization and what proportion to abortion of fetuses exposed to rubella.

Measles Upsurge

Despite a nationwide immunization effort and the availability of an effective vaccine, the incidence of measles in the United States rose in 1984. According to preliminary data, 2,239 cases were reported, compared with 1,497 (the lowest figure ever) in 1983—an increase of about 50 percent. The cases reported in 1984 occurred in 26 states.

Public health officials are hopeful, however, that measles will eventually yield to preventive efforts and be eliminated in the United States—a goal originally set for October 1, 1982. The number of cases reported in recent years is far smaller than before the measles vaccine was introduced; between 1950 and 1962, for example, cases averaged over 525,000 reported each year. Experts suggest that special emphasis should be directed toward immunizing such groups as young adults (between 20 and 24 years old) and preschoolers (from 16 months to four years old). According to detailed figures for the first three-quarters of 1984, 75 percent of the measles cases reported in these two age groups were preventable. Recent epidemics of measles on college campuses—for example, at Boston University and at Principia College in Illinois—have caused some institutions to take measures requiring their students to be immunized.

The Role of Exercise in Health

Various recent studies of the effects of exercise, especially jogging, on health have yielded interesting (but not definitive) results. One study, for example, found that even moderate exercise can help middle-aged and older men add years to their expected lifespan. Another study suggested that high blood pressure is less likely to develop in men and women who exercise. Studies of this kind, however, are sometimes open to criticism. One problem is that the individuals surveyed may not be truly representative of all people, thereby skewing the results. If among those studied there seems to be a link between exercise and good health, this could be because the healthy ones might be more likely to take up exercising, while those with heart disease or other disorders, even in an early phase, might be less likely. Thus, it might be that the chances of not developing disease determine the willingness to exercise, rather than the other way around.

Nonetheless, most doctors and other experts do believe that regular, prudent exercise can be of help in lowering death rates. On the other hand, there is little doubt that exercise can also sometimes cause sudden death by heart attack. One recent study, for example, showed that although men who exercise strenuously run a lower overall risk of heart attack, if they do suffer an attack, it is much more likely to occur while they are exercising than at other times.

Recreational and Occupational Health Hazards

Water slides. A relatively new potential health hazard people may encounter at, for example, amusement parks is the water slide. In the state of Washington, surveys showed that one particular slide was the source of an unusual number of severe injuries, including spinal and skull fractures, concussions, sprains, bruises, and cuts. In an attempt to reduce the risk of injury, some curves on the slide were changed, the outlets were rounded, the wearing of helmets was required, and warning signs were posted. The changes appeared to reduce the incidence of injuries, but it is difficult to say how effective they actually were, since the changes coincided with reduced use of the slide as a result of cooler weather and the return of children to school.

Because water slides are a relatively new recreational device, there are as yet no tested, uniform design standards. Thus, it is advisable for people playing on water slides to be in good physical condition and to be careful to use them only as instructed.

Health risks on the job. Each year an estimated 10 million Americans suffer an injury at work, of which about 30 percent are severe and some 10,000 are fatal. Approximately 21,000 workers suffered amputations in 1982, about 93 percent losing fingers and 4 percent hands or toes. Also frequently occurring are fractures, cuts, various injuries from highway motor vehicle accidents, loss of eyes, electrocution, gunshot wounds, and injuries from explosions. Mining and quarrying are the most hazardous major occupations with respect to fatal injuries, closely followed by agriculture and construction.

Risks From Raw Milk

Public health officials continue to be alarmed about the drinking of raw milk. There is a persistent, although unsubstantiated, belief that raw milk has more nutritional benefits than pasteurized milk. In the past, outbreaks of such diseases as typhoid fever, scarlet fever, diphtheria, and tuberculosis were associated with the drinking of raw milk. Fortunately, such outbreaks are now rare.

In 1984, however, infections with the bacteria known as *Salmonella dublin* and *Campylobacter jejuni* were again found to be linked with the drinking of raw milk. An even more disturbing development has been the appearance of a possibly new diarrheal disorder associated with drinking raw milk. More than 100 people in the vicinity of a Minnesota town experienced chronic diarrheal illness that gradually improved but that, in most cases, still had not fully disappeared many months after the onset of the disease. Although the cause of this chronic diarrhea has not been determined, many experts strongly suspect that it was due to drinking raw milk. Thus, even in the 1980's people who drink raw milk run a substantial risk of acquiring an infectious disease—a risk that would be virtually eliminated by using only pasteurized milk.

Infectious Diseases in Day-Care Programs

With more and more American women who have children of preschool age getting jobs, the number of children between the ages of three and five enrolled in day-care programs is expected to reach about 10 million by 1990, up from 5 million in 1974. Such programs can be of benefit to many children—by helping ensure that they are adequately fed and by giving them a chance to develop their social skills and learning abilities. But day-care settings also provide opportunities for the spread of infectious diseases, especially among younger children still in diapers—a situation that has drawn increasing attention from epidemiologists.

Diseases spread by the respiratory route, such as colds or influenza, have long been known to be easily picked up in gatherings of children, including school classes. But recently concern has been aroused particularly by diseases spread by oral contact with fecal contamination—the diarrheal diseases. These include illnesses caused by bacteria, viruses, and parasites. One new problem came to light in 1984 in Seattle. There, public health workers found that an outbreak of diarrhea in a day-care setting that would often be attributed to a viral cause was actually due to a rare subtype of the bacterium *Escherichia coli*. The bacterium was known to be a source of disease in developing countries and, rarely, in nurseries for newborns in the United States, but it had not previously been fully documented as a cause of disease in day-care settings.

Another type of illness that has attracted attention is hepatitis. A recent study in Arizona found that 40 percent of the 1,008 cases of hepatitis A reported during a ten-month period occurred in persons closely associated with day-care settings.

Epidemiologists and day-care administrators in the United States are beginning to work together in order to control the problem presented by infectious diseases. Several state and local health departments are developing disease-control programs for day-care settings.

Herpes in the Classroom

Several U.S. cities have recently been the scene of bitter controversy over the admission to preschools of children said to be suffering from herpes. In three cases that attracted national attention, the child's presence resulted in a boycott of the school by some students and teachers because of fears that the child would be a dangerous source of infection to classmates and teachers.

Such fears reflect widespread misunderstanding of the diseases involved. Two of the three children reportedly had a virus known as herpes simplex. There are actually two principal types of herpes simplex virus, and they can cause sores in different areas of the body. Cold sores in the mouth or on the lips (herpes labialis) are most often due to type 1; the genital lesions known as genital herpes are usually caused by type 2. The third child was said to have a related virus called cytomegalovirus. These viruses are extremely common: there is evidence, for example, that half of U.S. children under the age of five, and perhaps three-quarters of adults, have been exposed to type 1 herpes simplex virus. About half of those exposed never develop any

A three-year-old Maryland victim of herpes, John Bigley, is escorted to an empty classroom by his parents. The other five students in his special education group, as well as the teacher, boycotted the class because of their fears of being infected. Several incidents of this kind have occurred around the United States.

symptoms of disease. The rest experience outbreaks of blisters, which may recur. Ordinarily, infections with herpes simplex virus or cytomegalovirus are hazardous only for newborns, in whom they sometimes lead to mental retardation, blindness, or even death.

Herpes simplex is contagious when the infection is in an active state, generally represented by the presence of sores. But direct contact with the virus is required for the disease to spread. One of the children at the focus of the recent controversy was apparently infected shortly after birth when she was kissed by her mother, who had a cold sore. Since very young children often

like to roughhouse or hug and kiss one another, it may be a good idea to keep such a child home during an active infection. Older children sufficiently responsible not to expose others to secretions from their blisters may generally be allowed to go to school even during flare-ups.

It is useful to keep in mind some simple facts: Infection with herpes simplex type 1 is particularly common and seldom serious. Infection with type 2 is often a venereal disease and can be especially dangerous to newborns. Even type 2, however, is not usually serious in children of school age.

Aspirin Warning for Reye's Syndrome

Reye's syndrome is a rare complication of influenza and chicken pox in children. It is characterized by abnormal behavior and subsequent coma. Death occurs in about one-fourth of all cases. First described in 1963, the disorder has been a medical mystery.

In 1980 there emerged evidence of a possible connection between aspirin and Reye's syndrome. Three separate studies arrived at the same conclusion: children with influenza or chicken pox who took aspirin were more likely to develop the syndrome. The relative risk of getting the disease was estimated to be approximately four times as great for ill children who took aspirin. A pilot study conducted by the U.S. Centers for Disease Control and released in 1984, however, found the difference in risk to be much greater: children with chicken pox or influenza who take aspirin may be 25 times as likely to develop Reye's syndrome.

In January 1985, Margaret Heckler, the head of the U.S. Department of Health and Human Services, asked aspirin manufacturers to put warning labels on packages of aspirin and aspirin products. Manufacturers agreed to alter the wording on product labels and to include an appropriate warning about Reye's syndrome, despite controversy over the proper interpretation of the studies. More research is needed to clarify the relationship between Reye's syndrome and aspirin.

The Battle Against Malaria

In the past few years India, Pakistan, Africa, and Central America have recorded significant increases in the incidence of malaria. Efforts to control the disease have been hampered by two developments: the parasites that cause malaria are becoming increasingly resistant to the principal antimalarial drug, chloroquine, and the mosquitoes that spread the parasites are developing resistance to insecticides.

By learning more about the mosquito's biology researchers hope to develop biological methods of mosquito control. Meanwhile, work is proceeding toward a vaccine against the disease. Genetic engineering techniques were recently used to reproduce a protein capable of stimulating immunity to one of the three forms of the most common malaria parasite—the sporozoite form, which enters the human body through the bite of a mosquito. According to some estimates, this advance could lead to a vaccine's being tested in one to two years, and, if successful, the vaccine could be available for inoculation programs after about five years. Developing an effective vaccine of this kind, however, is a formidable task. Such a vaccine would have only a short time in which to work against the sporozoites (from the time they are injected into the bloodstream by the mosquito until they enter body cells). Furthermore, to prevent malaria, it must not allow even a single sporozoite to survive.

JAMES F. JEKEL, M.D., M.P.H.
and STEVEN D. HELGERSON, M.D., M.P.H.

Eyes

Technical advances in eye surgery as well as lower costs were major reasons for the growing trend toward outpatient surgery for cataract removal. Increasing attention was paid to prevention of the large number of eye injuries caused by racket sports, and a unique airborne eye hospital continued to make important contributions to eye care around the world.

Outpatient Surgery for Cataracts

One of the important developments in current ophthalmic practice is the fast-growing trend toward the performance of eye surgery—in particular, cataract surgery—on an outpatient basis. Cataract surgery is the most common major ophthalmic surgical procedure, and in fact, it is one of the most frequently performed major surgical procedures of any kind in the United States, with an estimated 700,000 operations done each year. Moreover, most patients who undergo cataract surgery are over 60 years old, and since the United States within the next 15 years will add about 7 million people to its aged population, the number of cataract operations is expected to increase steadily.

A cataract is a clouding of the crystalline lens of the eye that reduces vision. In cataract surgery (referred to as cataract extraction), this cloudy lens is removed and usually replaced with a hard plastic lens called an intraocular lens implant—a kind of permanent contact lens. Traditionally, cataract surgery was performed in a hospital, with a one-night stay before the operation and several days of hospitalization after surgery, although the length of hospital stay for cataract operations has steadily declined over the past 20 years. In outpatient cataract surgery, the patient goes to the outpatient facility the day of surgery and is usually sent home several

hours after the operation. Patients are then seen by the surgeon in the doctor's office for the next two or three days to ensure that no complications requiring treatment have developed.

Improved technology. A number of factors have encouraged the trend toward outpatient ophthalmic surgery, probably the most important being the improvement in ophthalmic surgical technology in the past 20 years. For example, the operating microscope is now used on a routine basis; indeed, many parts of the modern cataract operation could not be performed without it. This instrument gives the surgeon much greater control over surgical technique and permits the cataract incision to be sutured (closed with stitches) with the greatest amount of precision. In addition, the development of ophthalmic microsurgery has permitted the use of finer sutures and more delicate instruments, making the cataract operation less traumatic to the eye.

Techniques for removal of the cloudy lens itself have changed radically over the past ten years. A decade ago, most cataracts were removed by a method called intracapsular extraction, a technique in which a cryogenic (freezing) probe was used to remove the lens and the capsule surrounding it (the transparent capsule) from the eye. Although this technique produced excellent results in most cases, it has been largely replaced by another method, extracapsular cataract surgery, in which a suction device is used to remove the cloudy inner contents of the lens, while leaving the back surface of the surrounding capsule in place as a support for the plastic intraocular lens implant. Some of the suction devices also use ultrasound to remove the lens contents.

The development of safe and effective plastic intraocular lens implants to replace the cataract is yet another technological advance. Previously, cataract extraction was followed by the use of thick cataract spectacles to restore the focusing power lost when the lens was removed. However, these did not restore absolutely normal vision. Intraocular lenses have changed this and provide an effective and convenient means of vision correction, so that patients are now requesting surgery to improve their vision at an early stage of cataract development. The lenses themselves have improved steadily since 1975; at present, they are implanted in more than 75 percent of patients undergoing cataract operations in the United States, and their use has both hastened and improved patients' recovery after surgery.

The economic impetus. The second major impetus toward outpatient surgery of all kinds, including cataract surgery, is economic. In general, outpatient surgical procedures are less costly than those associated with inpatient hospitalization. The average cost for an inpatient cataract operation in the United States, for example, is over $3,000, not including the surgeon's fee. When the same procedure is done on an outpatient basis, the average cost per operation is well under $1,000. It is estimated that if all cataract surgery currently performed on an inpatient basis were moved to an outpatient setting, the annual savings in the United States would be over $1 billion. A large percentage of cataract surgery in the United States is sponsored by medicare, and medicare programs in a number of states now mandate that cataract surgery be performed on an outpatient basis, unless the patient's medical condition makes inpatient surgery imperative.

From the patient's point of view, outpatient cataract surgery has a number of advantages. For example, there is less interference with the patient's normal activities, and the fear of hospitalization that some patients experience is eliminated. However, not all patients are satisfactory candidates for outpatient cataract surgery, and those who have serious medical problems requiring careful monitoring, who are frail and may find the increased travel necessitated by outpatient surgery difficult, and who live alone may prefer the inpatient procedure.

It should be noted that outpatient surgery is increasingly favored for a variety of ophthalmic surgical procedures. However, not all operations lend themselves to outpatient surgery. In particular, complicated operations involving retinal detachment or the use of the surgical technique known as vitrectomy will certainly continue to require in-hospital management.

If outpatient surgery is performed, it may be done in a hospital facility or in ambulatory surgical centers physically separate from a hospital and sometimes associated with a clinic or doctor's office. An estimated 200 outpatient ophthalmic surgical units are currently in operation in the United States, and it is anticipated that outpatient ophthalmic surgery will increase rapidly within the next two years.

A Foldable Lens Implant

The U.S. Food and Drug Administration has approved clinical investigation of the safety and effectiveness of intraocular lenses made of silicone. Unlike the rigid plastic intraocular lenses now implanted at the time of cataract surgery, silicone lenses are flexible and can be folded over for insertion; thus, they can be placed in the eye through an incision that is considerably smaller than that required for a conventional intraocular lens implant. In general, a smaller incision means a speedier healing process and quicker restoration of normal vision. The new study should add important information on silicone lenses to the limited experience doctors currently have with patient use.

Lasers Approved for Cataract Surgery

In 1984, neodymium-YAG lasers (which use yttrium, aluminum, and garnet—a synthetic diamond) produced by three manufacturers were approved by the FDA as being safe and effective for posterior capsulotomy, a type of cataract surgery. The YAG laser, which like all lasers produces brief, powerful pulses of light, is the newest type of laser technology to find widespread therapeutic use in ophthalmology.

In contrast to the argon laser, a heating laser used primarily in ophthalmology to destroy abnormal blood vessels in the eye, the YAG laser can be used instead of an instrument to actually cut membranes inside the eye. In extracapsular cataract surgery, the contents of the lens are removed while the lens's transparent capsule is left in place. If this part of the lens capsule left behind becomes cloudy (as it does in up to half of cataract extractions), another operation may be needed to open the capsule; it was for this procedure that use of the YAG laser was approved. The 1984 approvals were for lasers made by Coherent Medical, Coburn Inc., and American Medical Optics Division of American Hospital Supply Corporation.

Surgery with the YAG laser can usually be done on an outpatient basis, without anesthesia and without the risk of infection. Thus, there is considerable interest in other applications—for example, for cutting membranes deeper in the eye or for making openings in the

Racquetball champion Marty Hogan models protective eyeguards that meet new safety standards.

COURTESY OF LEADER SPORT PRODUCTS

iris of the eye (a procedure known as iridotomy)—that are still being studied. YAG lasers are manufactured by more than 20 suppliers in the United States and abroad. Each brand of laser must be separately approved by the FDA.

Standards Set for Protective Eyewear

The National Society to Prevent Blindness estimates that, for participants between the ages of 25 and 64, racket sports account for 29 percent of eye injuries that occur in a selected group of sports that have a high risk of injury to the eye. In recognition of this fact, the Eye Safety Subcommittee of the American Society for Testing and Materials (now officially called the ASTM) has approved performance standards for protective lenses to be used in tennis, squash, and racquetball. The chairman of the subcommittee reported that a wide variety of eye injuries can result from racket sports, including lacerations of the cornea, hemorrhages inside the eye, cataracts, and torn or detached retinas. In some instances, these injuries can lead to temporary loss of vision or even blindness.

Many of the protective lenses currently on the market did not pass laboratory testing during the subcommittee's standards-setting process. For instance, eyeguards with lensless eye openings fared poorly because a ball or racket can still reach the eye. High-speed photography was used to determine the speed of balls and rackets during actual playing conditions. The speed of a badminton shuttlecock in an overhead smash was found to be the highest, 145 miles per hour. The speed of a squash ball was 140 mph, that of a racquetball 125 mph; a tennis ball was 110 mph and a handball, 60 to 70 mph.

The ASTM standard specifies that lenses must withstand 22 foot-pounds of pressure, compared with the industrial safety glasses standard of 0.6 foot-pounds. Polycarbonate was the toughest material tested. The standard also specifies that there must be no fogging or distortion within the lenses, and the central 30 degrees of the field of vision must be unobstructed.

Previously, the Eye Safety Subcommittee was instrumental in creating standards for ski goggles and baseball masks, and it also drafted a safety standard for hockey masks. The use of these face protectors has been credited with eliminating 70,000 eye and face injuries in hockey each year. Protective eyewear should be used by all participants in racket sports.

Project Orbis: Eye Care Around the World

Project Orbis is a flying eye hospital that brings the latest in ophthalmic diagnostic and surgical techniques to nations around the world. Since 1982 the DC–8 winged hospital has visited more than 45 cities in over 35 countries spread over four continents. More than 160 U.S. ophthalmologists, nurses, and technologists have participated in the project, and more than 2,800 treatments, including major surgery and laser procedures, have been provided.

The plane is equipped with the latest in ophthalmic technology; in addition to sophisticated surgical and laser apparatus, the plane has facilities for sterilization and refrigeration, a recovery room, a fully equipped audiovisual and educational center, and a library. Orbis was not designed to treat a large number of patients, however, but rather to impart skills to doctors in the host countries who would, in turn, provide improved care to their local patients. About 2,500 host country physicians have attended seminars and observed modern surgical techniques. As each of these physicians treats new patients over a period of years, the "multiplier effect" of Orbis's work becomes clear. Educational activities are supplemented by the Orbis staff's assessment of local needs when visiting a country, as well as by their visits to local hospitals.

Project Orbis has a number of other goals as well. One is to reduce blindness: it is estimated that two-thirds of the blind people in the world today could be cured with modern ophthalmic surgery. Orbis also seeks to increase public awareness of blindness and its prevention, primarily by means of the publicity associated with an Orbis visit to a community, and to promote international good will.

Supported primarily by private foundations, corporations, and individuals, together with a supplemental grant from the U.S. Agency for International Development, Orbis is headquartered in New York City and has an annual budget of $3.5 million. As the airborne hospital embarked on its 50th mission in the spring of 1985, it continued to generate worldwide interest as one of the most successful private initiatives ever undertaken in the field of international eye care.

See also the Spotlight on Health article CONTACT LENSES. CARMEN A. PULIAFITO, M.D.

Food

See NUTRITION AND DIET.

Genetics and Genetic Engineering

Genetic engineering—the manipulation of DNA (deoxyribonucleic acid), the basic genetic substance of cells—has in just a few years gone from an experimental science to a growth industry. The principal techniques of genetic engineering have become so commonplace that the focus of attention in the field has already switched from basic research to identifying products that can be profitably made.

Signs of the field's rapid development are the number of products already on the market or undergoing testing and scientists' expectations that replacement of defective genes as a treatment for disease will soon be tried in humans. One of the more notable recent research achievements was the successful biosynthesis of a blood-clotting substance needed by hemophiliacs.

Meanwhile, in other areas of heredity research, another shot was fired in the longtime battle over whether a person's intelligence is determined more by heredity or by environment.

Genetic Engineering to the Marketplace

Among the products of genetic engineering already being marketed are a biosynthetic form of human insulin, several animal growth hormones, and two vaccines against diarrhea in animals. A number of potential products are being tested in humans. These include several forms of interferon, a substance produced naturally in body cells that acts against viruses; human growth hormone, for treating individuals whose bodies do not produce enough on their own; interleukin–2, a compound normally produced by white blood cells that may be useful in treating diseases thought to involve a malfunctioning of the body's immune system, such as multiple sclerosis, rheumatoid arthritis, and AIDS (acquired immune deficiency syndrome); and tissue-type plasminogen activator, a substance that helps dissolve heart attack–producing blood clots. Sales of biotechnology-derived health products totaled $35 million in 1983, and it is expected that they will grow to $900 million by 1988.

DNA Probes

A potentially enormous market exists for products used to detect disease and to test, or "assay," for the presence of viruses, proteins, hormones, cells, and other materials. One approach along these lines involves the use of DNA probes. The DNA probe is based on the fact that when two strands of DNA are similar in such a way as to form what is called a complementary pair, they bind together tightly. To perform an assay with a DNA probe, a strand of DNA (the probe) complementary to the DNA of the virus, bacterium, or gene being sought is combined with a sample of blood, urine, or tissue from the individual being tested. If the virus, bacterium, or gene is present, its DNA will combine with the probe to form a pair whose presence can be monitored. This provides a very specific means of determining whether, for example, the individual is carrying a particular disease-causing organism.

DNA probe kits for a number of viruses—including the one that causes the liver disorder known as hepatitis B and the one believed to be responsible for AIDS—are already being sold to research scientists. Also available are probes for specific oncogenes (genes thought to be responsible for the onset of cancer) and for genes associated with such diseases as diabetes, muscular dystrophy, and the hereditary nervous-system disorder known as Huntington's chorea (sometimes called Huntington's disease).

Automated Testing for DNA Defects

An automatic genetic analyzer that can detect defects in an individual's DNA overnight, instead of taking days to weeks as with current manual techniques, has been developed at Georgetown University. The apparatus, which is also more accurate than current methods, is based on DNA probe technology but completely automates the process, using up to nine probes simultaneously.

The machine shows promise of allowing gene identification to be performed in a physician's office rather than at the few specialized university laboratories that now do it. The device might be used, for example, to screen people to determine if a genetic predisposition to a disease makes it inadvisable for them to work in a certain environment, such as in a chemical factory. The analyzer must undergo clinical testing and then be submitted to the U.S. Food and Drug Administration for review of its reliability. Subject to receiving FDA approval, it will be manufactured and marketed by AN-CON Genetics of Melville, N.Y.

Gene Therapy

One of the most exciting, and controversial, prospects offered by the rapid progress of genetic engineering is gene therapy—treatment of an inherited disease by replacing defective genes linked to the disorder with normal genes created in the laboratory. With the possibility of trying gene therapy techniques in humans seeming closer than ever, the U.S. National Institutes of Health in January 1985 published a set of proposed guidelines for such research. A final set was to be issued after a period of public comment on the proposals. The guidelines were in the form of points that researchers would be expected to consider in their applications to NIH for approval and funding of their work (for example, such points as the risks and benefits of the therapy, experimental methods, and animal testing).

The idea of gene therapy has generated considerable debate because of ethical problems it might involve. Fears have been voiced that gene therapy represents a potentially dangerous intrusion by scientists into the natural processes that determine human characteristics. The proposed guidelines, however, applied only to somatic-cell gene therapy—that is, to replacement of genes in body cells of individual patients. Changes in the genes of these cells cannot be passed on to the patient's children. According to a report released in December 1984 by Congress's Office of Technology Assessment, this form of gene therapy is essentially like standard treatments and poses no more ethical problems than they do. "It can be viewed," said the report, "as simply another tool to help individuals overcome an illness." By contrast, changes caused by replacing genes in reproductive cells (eggs or sperm) could be inherited by the next generation, possibly raising serious ethical questions. Such gene therapy, however, is not feasible now. If it should become practical, it would require intense public review.

New Help for Hemophiliacs

People suffering from the hereditary disorder hemophilia are subject to excessive and potentially fatal bleeding from cuts or wounds because their blood does not clot properly. The most common form of the disease is classical hemophilia, or hemophilia A, which afflicts 20 out of every 100,000 males. Individuals with classical hemophilia have a deficiency of the protein called factor VIII, which promotes clotting. The bleeding problem can be controlled with regular injections of the protein. But the factor VIII given to hemophiliacs at present is extracted from donated human blood at great expense and with some risk. The injections may cost $5,000 to $10,000 a year, and since the blood used

comes from a great number of donors, it carries a relatively high risk of being contaminated by viruses such as those thought to cause hepatitis and AIDS.

In 1984, researchers associated with two biotechnology companies reported that they had succeeded in reproducing the entire gene responsible for the production of factor VIII in humans. They were able to incorporate the gene copies into animal cells in the laboratory; the cells responded by producing factor VIII. The achievement is particularly remarkable since the gene is very large and the factor VIII protein is an immense and complex molecule, consisting of more than 2,300 amino acids.

So far, only small amounts of the biosynthetic factor VIII are being produced. Techniques for making large quantities of high purity need to be developed, and the product must be proved to be both safe and effective in actual use. But the possibility now exists that in just a few years an inexpensive and risk-free form of factor VIII will be on the market.

Prenatal Detection of Sexual Ambiguity

Scientists at the Cornell Medical Center in New York City have identified the defective gene responsible for some cases of a hormonal disorder called congenital adrenal hyperplasia (CAH). This disorder is the most common cause of a condition in which newborn baby girls are genetically female and have female internal re-

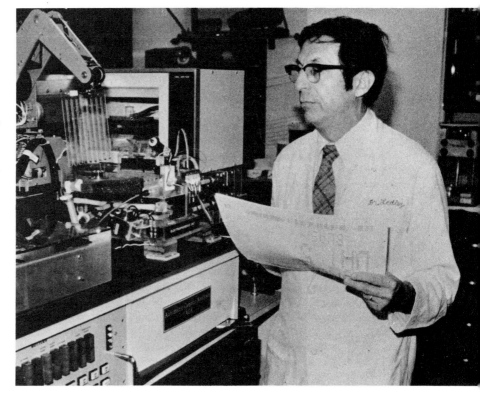

The automatic genetic analyzer with its inventor, Dr. Robert S. Ledley of Georgetown University. The new machine is expected to enable doctors to screen patients in their offices for genetic defects.

productive organs, but possess external genital organs that look like male genitals. The condition is caused by an overproduction of male sex hormones by the adrenal glands during the first 14 weeks of pregnancy. A study conducted in Italy found one case of CAH in every 7,000 people. (CAH causes other medical problems as well, in both males and females.)

At present CAH can be diagnosed in the fetus with the help of amniocentesis, which involves taking a sample of the amniotic fluid surrounding the fetus. But this procedure cannot be done until after the stage of pregnancy during which the abnormal genitals develop. The Cornell researchers feel that, in at least a limited number of cases of CAH, the newly identified gene might eventually be used in conjunction with a recently devised but still experimental method (chorionic villi sampling) that permits analysis of fetal cells as early as the sixth week of pregnancy. If the defect can be detected this early, they hope, it may become possible to prevent the masculinization process from taking place—through, say, hormone treatment in the mother.

Intelligence and Heredity

Is intelligence, as measured by an IQ test, inherited, or is it determined by the environment in which a child is raised? In other words, which is more important—nature or nurture? A new contribution to this old controversy offers evidence, drawn from information collected in Denmark, that supports the view that nature may control intelligence but the environment may have a larger influence on educational achievement.

In what is believed to be the first study of its kind on adults, scientists compared two groups of men. One group consisted of 127 pairs of brothers (or half brothers) who had been raised by different parents because of adoption. The second group comprised 27 pairs of men unrelated by blood; the members of each pair had been adopted and reared together as brothers. It was decided to study Danes because in Denmark siblings separated by adoption could be located through an adoption registry and because information about individuals' IQ and educational achievement could be obtained from mandatory intelligence tests and medical examinations conducted by Danish draft boards when youths are between the ages of 18 and 26. Only males were studied because females are not subject to draft board examination.

The researchers' findings accorded with the theory that genetic factors play a dominant role in intelligence. The IQ's of full siblings (brothers who had both biological parents in common) who had been raised apart showed the same types of relationships as those of full siblings raised together; that is, if one brother had a high IQ, the second was also likely to have a high IQ, and so on. Brothers who shared only a genetic mother

or genetic father showed less correlation, while those who were genetically unrelated but had been reared as brothers showed no correlation. Educational achievement, on the other hand, while showing some relationship to intelligence, was more strongly linked to the social class of the adopting family. The scientists cautioned that their findings should be regarded as tentative since the number of siblings studied was relatively small. THOMAS H. MAUGH II, PH.D.

Glands and Metabolism

Scientists are continuing to identify new examples of the chemical messengers called hormones and to refine their knowledge of old ones. Released into the bloodstream by the organs called endocrine glands, hormones are carried to various body tissues. The messages, or signals, they deliver influence a wide range of processes in the body, including its use of various nutrients and response to disease. It is becoming more and more evident that many body tissues besides the classical endocrine glands—the pituitary, thyroid, parathyroids, islets of Langerhans (in the pancreas), adrenals, and gonads—have an endocrine function. Recently, for example, much attention has focused on a hormone produced by the heart. And new findings have been reported about a hormone that is capable of influencing the body's use of calcium in various tissues and is derived from vitamin D through transformations in the liver and kidneys.

Other recent research has focused on the use of steroids for treatment of illness. Steroids are a group of chemically related substances that include sex hormones and several hormones released by the adrenal glands. Synthetic steroids make up a large class of drugs, widely used for various purposes.

The Heart as a Gland

Based on recent findings, the heart can now be called an endocrine organ. A substance produced in the atria (the heart chambers that receive blood from the veins and pump it into the chambers called ventricles, which in turn pump it into the arteries) causes increased excretion of salt in the urine ("natriuresis"); it also inhibits the adrenal glands' production of aldosterone, a hormone that promotes retention of salt by the body. This "atrial natriuretic factor," also called atriopeptin or auriculin, is released when the atria are stretched because of taking in a large volume of blood. Auriculin tends to reduce the load on the heart by increasing salt and water loss, thus lowering the total volume of circulating blood.

In 1984 auriculin was identified as one of the small proteins known as peptides, its composition was determined, and it was artificially reproduced in the laboratory. A test has been developed that can detect auriculin in normal blood. As a regulatory chemical found in the bloodstream, it can properly be called a hormone. Further study of this hormone may provide insight into diseases where fluid retention is a problem, such as congestive heart failure and cirrhosis of the liver, and may lead to new methods for treating fluid retention and high blood pressure.

A Hormone From Vitamin D

The revolution in scientists' knowledge about vitamin D continues. For some time it has been known that the liver transforms vitamin D into a hormone precursor (a substance that the body uses to manufacture some hormone). This hormone precursor is converted into the hormone calcitriol by, normally, the kidneys. (A synthetic form of calcitriol is marketed under the brand name Rocaltrol.)

Calcitriol, which has an important part to play in regulating the body's use of calcium, is beneficial in treatment of the bone softening (osteopenia) that accompanies kidney failure, when the kidneys become unable to form the hormone. Calcitriol is also useful in treating other types of bone disease. Many doctors are excited by the prospect that it may prove effective in some cases of osteoporosis, the thinning of bones that is common in postmenopausal women and that, since it can result in fractures and destruction of bone, is a major cause of illness and death.

On the other hand, the presence of excessive amounts of calcitriol may cause abnormally high levels of calcium in the blood and urine, which can lead to such problems as kidney stones.

There is now good evidence that the high blood calcium seen in sarcoidosis (a disease of unknown cause characterized by the formation of inflammatory nodules in the lungs or other parts of the body) and in other long-lasting inflammatory diseases is a result of calcitriol production in the diseased tissues. Studies have revealed that calcitriol has an unexpected effect: it inhibits the activity and proliferation of certain inflammatory cells. (These cells, which include several types of white blood cells, are a vital part of the body's defense against infection and its repair of injury; they are also the cause of a number of serious diseases when the inflammatory response, unable to resolve the problem that triggered it, becomes chronic.) Thus, the high calcitriol levels found in cases of sarcoidosis may represent the body's attempt to control the disease.

Treatment With Steroid Drugs

Ever since it was discovered that cortisone, a hormone produced by the adrenal glands, could dramatically suppress the symptoms of rheumatoid arthritis and other inflammatory diseases, cortisone-like products have been employed to treat a host of illnesses in which symptoms are brought about by inflammation. The name "corticosteroids" has been applied to this group of steroid drugs to indicate that they are produced in the cortex, or outer shell, of the adrenal glands. Nowadays, synthetic corticosteroids are preferred to cortisone because they are able to provide a more selective anti-inflammatory action, with fewer side effects. Still, serious side effects do occur, including reduced resistance to infection, osteoporosis, growth retardation in children, and aggravation of diabetes. Such effects become more common during prolonged treatment. When a doctor considers recommending the use of corticosteroids, their benefits are weighed against their adverse effects. New light on these benefits and risks was shed by several studies of corticosteroid treatment reported in 1984.

Easing side effects from cancer therapy. The potent drugs used in drug therapy, or chemotherapy, for cancer frequently cause severe nausea and vomiting, for which the usual antinausea medications are ineffective. Researchers compared the corticosteroid dexamethasone and a conventional antinausea drug called prochlorperazine (both sold under various brand names) to see which was more effective in controlling these chemotherapy side effects. The results seemed conclusive: dexamethasone was better. Of the 42 patients who took part in the study, 25 had no nausea while on dexamethasone, but only 14 were protected by prochlorperazine; a total of 29 did not vomit while on the corticosteroid, but with the conventional drug the figure was only 18. No serious adverse effects were seen with dexamethasone, as is generally the case when steroid treatment is brief.

Toxic shock syndrome. The serious and occasionally fatal illness known as toxic shock syndrome is caused by a localized infection with a strain of bacteria that produces a potent poison, or toxin. A few years ago, the disorder received a great deal of publicity because of its appearance in women who used certain tampons that were conducive to the establishment of the infection in the vagina. When a group of women with toxic shock syndrome who received corticosteroid treatment were compared by researchers with a similar group of women who did not, the duration and severity of illness were significantly less in the corticosteroid-treated group. Again, the period of corticosteroid treatment was brief—usually three to four days—and was associated with no adverse effects.

Septic shock. When a bacteria-caused infection becomes so severe that the infectious bacteria can be found in the bloodstream, a profound state of shock—a life-threatening state of collapse with low blood pressure and poor blood circulation—may result. This infection-related shock is called septic shock. In animal experiments, as well as some studies with humans, corticosteroids have appeared to be effective against septic shock, while other studies with humans have shown no benefit, or even harm.

A rigorous study focusing on this problem was recently conducted, in which people with the symptoms of septic shock were randomly assigned to receive dexamethasone, another potent corticosteroid called methylprednisolone (sold under various names), or no steroid therapy. The long-term outcome was the same for all three treatments, and about three-fourths of the members of each group died. Also, the corticosteroid groups had a higher incidence of new infections by organisms resistant to the drugs used in treatment, more patients with high sugar levels in the blood, and more with digestive tract bleeding. These findings underline the importance of the fact that indiscriminant use of steroids is to be avoided.

Of the patients who recovered, however, those who were treated with corticosteroids recovered more quickly, leaving open the possibility that some patients with septic shock may benefit from such drugs, as did the patients with toxic shock syndrome mentioned above.

Chronic hepatitis. There has been general agreement that corticosteroids are effective in treating some types of chronic hepatitis (inflammation of the liver). In the kind of hepatitis produced by alcoholism (alcoholic hepatitis), however, research results are varied, with the weight of the evidence being against any benefit from steroid treatment. In a recent reexamination of the effectiveness of steroid therapy in alcoholic hepatitis, the corticosteroid methylprednisolone was compared with a placebo (a medically inactive substance) and with oxandrolone (Anavar), a synthetic steroid related to the male sex hormones. The corticosteroid was found to provide no advantage over the placebo. Oxandrolone, though, did improve long-term survival and seemed particularly effective in patients with moderate cases of the disease.

Oxandrolone is one of several so-called anabolic, or tissue-building, steroids, which mimic the effect of the male sex hormone testosterone and stimulate growth of muscle and other tissues but are much less potent than testosterone in causing masculinization (beard growth, baldness, deep voice, and so on). These drugs have gained notoriety recently because of their abuse by some athletes. They may have a role in treatment of some types of wasting diseases, anemia, and osteoporosis. Further research is needed to determine how they may be most appropriately used in the treatment of hepatitis.

See also the Spotlight on Health article THE USES OF STEROIDS. WILLIAM L. GREEN, M.D.

Government Policies and Programs

Efforts to control the soaring cost of health care for both government and individual patients continued to cause controversy in both Canada and the United States. In Canada, legislation designed to preserve universal access to the national health insurance system was enacted over the opposition of most of the provincial governments, which suffered financial penalties for allowing hospitals or doctors to charge higher fees than those specified by Ottawa. In the United States, Congress imposed a 15-month freeze on fees charged by physicians under medicare, the federal program of health insurance for the elderly and disabled; the freeze was challenged in court by the American Medical Association and other groups. Congress also enacted new legislation intended to ensure that medical treatment is not withheld from severely handicapped newborn infants.

United States

"Baby Doe" controversy. The "Baby Doe" issue (so called because the families involved are usually granted anonymity by the courts) continued to produce a legal controversy involving the federal government, doctors and hospitals, "right-to-life" advocates, and the parents of handicapped babies. "Baby Doe" raises the thorny question of whether seriously handicapped newborn infants must always be given life-prolonging treatment. The Reagan administration has asserted the government's right to ensure such treatment, but regulations enacted toward this end have faced difficulties in the courts.

In May 1984, a U.S. district court judge struck down the latest of these regulations, issued by the U.S. Department of Health and Human Services (HHS) in February. The judge ruled that HHS had overstepped its authority by using a 1973 civil rights law (the Rehabilitation Act of 1973) as the basis for its rule. Under the HHS regulation, doctors and nurses in hospitals were required to report suspected cases of neglect in treatment of handicapped infants. The administration appealed the court decision, but the ruling was upheld by an appeals court in December.

In the meantime, the issue was taken up by Congress. A House-Senate conference committee developed compromise "Baby Doe" legislation that became part of a child abuse bill signed into law by President Ronald Reagan in October. The legislation expands the definition of child abuse to include withholding of medical care from a handicapped infant and permits the prosecution of medical personnel involved. It also states that when medical procedures, in the physician's "reasonable medical judgment," would only prolong the infant's dying, the parents and physician may decide the best course of action. The measure gave responsibility for investigating cases of suspected medical neglect to state child protective agencies, and it specified that states receiving federal funds for child abuse prevention and treatment must adopt procedures for handling medical neglect cases. New "Baby Doe" regulations, based on this legislation, and requiring treatment and nutrition of most handicapped newborns, were proposed by HHS in December.

New disability benefit legislation. As a result of a bill passed by Congress in September 1984, the government will now have to prove that an individual's medical condition has improved before it can terminate social security disability benefits. Under the legislation, recipients threatened with loss of benefits will continue to receive payments until all avenues of appeal are exhausted. The legislation also extended a moratorium on review of benefits being paid to mentally impaired people until new eligibility standards can be developed.

The legislation came in response to the Reagan administration's removal of nearly 500,000 people from the disability rolls on the grounds of ineligibility between 1981 and 1984. Court rulings that the removals were unjustified had resulted in restoration of benefits in about half the cases. The new measure is expected to allow review of an additional 100,000 cases where disability benefits had been cut off, although the Reagan administration urged the courts to interpret the law in a manner that would favor benefit curtailment.

In a related development, in December 1984 a federal appeals court overturned a district court ruling that had restored disability benefits to several thousand people.

FDA drug review. A 22-year effort by the FDA to identify prescription drugs that do not perform as claimed was virtually finished during 1984. The review, which cost $40 million, scrutinized more than 3,400 prescription drugs and more than 16,000 therapeutic claims. During the course of the study, nearly 1,100 products were taken off the market because their effectiveness could not be proved.

New drug regulations. Legislation signed by President Reagan in October 1984 will make it easier for manufacturers to gain FDA approval for the sale of generic drugs—usually less expensive, non–brand-name versions of prescription drugs. Generic products often sell for 50 to 80 percent less at retail than comparable brand-name drugs. The same bill provided a benefit to the brand-name drug manufacturers by extending the patent terms for new discoveries.

The Orphan Drug Act, signed into law in 1983, offers such incentives as tax credits to encourage drug companies to develop and market medications to treat rare, or "orphan," diseases. However, full implementation of

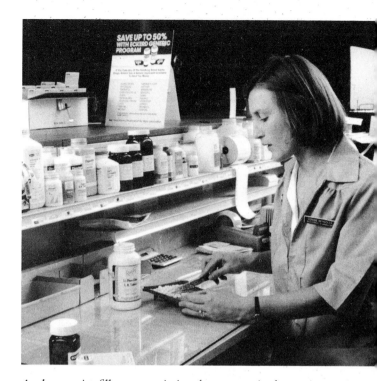

A pharmacist fills a prescription for a generic drug. A new law makes it easier for such drugs to gain the approval of the U.S. Food and Drug Administration. Generic drugs, while essentially identical to their brand-name competitors, are considerably less expensive, as the chart below indicates.

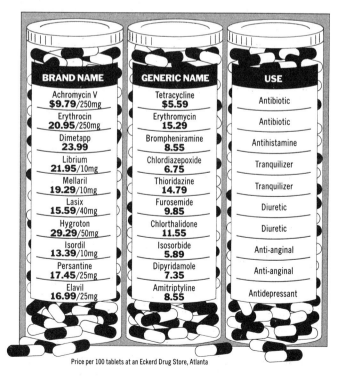

BRAND NAME	GENERIC NAME	USE
Achromycin V **$9.79**/250mg	Tetracycline **5.59**	Antibiotic
Erythrocin **20.95**/250mg	Erythromycin **15.29**	Antibiotic
Dimetapp **23.99**	Brompheniramine **8.55**	Antihistamine
Librium **21.95**/10mg	Chlordiazepoxide **6.75**	Tranquilizer
Mellaril **19.29**/10mg	Thioridazine **14.79**	Tranquilizer
Lasix **15.59**/40mg	Furosemide **9.85**	Diuretic
Hygroton **29.29**/50mg	Chlorthalidone **11.55**	Diuretic
Isordil **13.39**/10mg	Isosorbide **5.89**	Anti-anginal
Persantine **17.45**/25mg	Dipyridamole **7.35**	Anti-anginal
Elavil **16.99**/25mg	Amitriptyline **8.55**	Antidepressant

Price per 100 tablets at an Eckerd Drug Store, Atlanta

the measure was delayed because a clear definition of eligible diseases was lacking. To this end, Congress in 1984 passed legislation that defined orphan diseases as those affecting fewer than 200,000 people. One drug approved under the new legislation was pimozide (Orap), for treatment of Tourette's syndrome. This rare neurological disease causes involuntary muscular movements and vocalization, with a third of its victims involuntarily shouting obscenities. Pimozide may help the 30,000 to 50,000 victims of Tourette's syndrome for whom haloperidol (Haldol), the standard drug treatment, is not effective.

In September 1984, the FDA announced that it was adopting new rules for the marketing of new forms of existing drugs. The action came after the deaths of 38 newborn infants had been linked to the administration of an intravenous vitamin E solution. Under the existing regulations, since the intravenous vitamin E was an altered form of a drug already on the market, it did not require separate FDA approval. Under the revised regulations, new products will no longer be presumed safe because they are related to drugs now on the market. Manufacturers and distributors of all existing marketed prescription drug products are required to report important adverse reaction information about such products to the FDA immediately.

In response to criticism that it was not adequately monitoring problems arising from the use of FDA-approved medical devices, such as cardiac pacemakers and anesthesia equipment, the FDA issued new regulations requiring that manufacturers notify the agency within five days of death or serious injury associated with such products.

Hospital construction. Approval of construction of new hospital and other health care facilities and of major renovation or the addition of major new services at existing facilities is a state government function. In 1983, in order to force hospitals to agree to joint planning and sharing of services and equipment, New York State imposed a freeze on all new hospital construction. In 1984, several large teaching and specialty hospitals in New York City agreed to a number of cost-cutting concessions demanded by the state in return for permission to proceed with their building plans.

The state acted on the advice of the city's federally funded Health Systems Agency (HSA), a private non-profit body that examines building and capital improvement proposals by private and public hospitals. Among the concessions agreed to by the hospitals were the elimination of excess beds, merging of a number of costly services, and scaling down of building plans. However, the state overruled an HSA recommendation that the prestigious Memorial Sloan-Kettering Cancer Center not be allowed to acquire a magnetic resonance imaging machine, a sophisticated and expensive diag-

nostic device. The HSA had recommended denial of the new machine to Sloan-Kettering on the grounds that it would duplicate one recently installed in a nearby hospital.

A new Ohio law gives state officials increased control over health facility construction. The legislation allowed the state to end a six-month moratorium on hospital construction, expanded the definition of covered health care facilities to include freestanding emergency centers, and authorized the state, under certain circumstances, to impose unrelated conditions in return for approval of a proposed hospital construction or expansion project. For example, the state may require that a hospital eliminate some beds in the obstetric department in return for permission to remodel a surgical wing.

Ohio also received HHS approval in August 1984 for reinstatement of Health Systems Agency units in the state. Federal funding of the units was received by February 1985. The request for reinstatement came from Governor Richard F. Celeste, elected in 1982. The state's previous governor, James A. Rhodes, had eliminated the state's ten HSA units in 1981, saying that the state was fully capable of handling its own health facility planning and charging that many HSA recommendations were "arbitrary, capricious, and politically motivated."

In West Virginia, a three-person Health Care Cost Review Authority that serves as the health planning agency for the state became operational on July 1, 1984. Authority members, who are appointed by the governor for six-year terms, have the power to veto virtually all hospital capital expenditures as well as to set hospital rates. The authority was created by a law enacted in 1983.

Medicare. A 15-month freeze, effective July 1, 1984, on fees paid to doctors for care of the elderly and disabled under medicare was imposed by Congress as part of the Deficit Reduction Act of 1984. The legislation established two physician classifications—participating and nonparticipating. Participating physicians must agree to accept a fee schedule established by the government for services to medicare patients. The participating physician will be reimbursed directly by the government for 80 percent of the set fee; the patient will pay the remaining 20 percent. A nonparticipating physician can charge rates that are higher than those set by medicare, provided they are not higher than the rates previously charged by that physician. In either case, physicians may not raise rates for medicare patients through September 1985. Penalties of up to $2,000 can be levied for each violation.

To encourage physician participation, the measure called for publication of directories of participating physicians and establishment of toll-free telephone lines to provide names of participants. Participating physicians would be able to use direct phone lines for electronic filing of claims and would be allowed an increase in their medicare-reimbursable fees after the freeze expires in 1985.

The constitutionality of the freeze is being challenged in court by the American Medical Association and several other medical groups; the American Association of Retired Persons is encouraging physicians to accept the frozen fees. Physicians who oppose the measure claim that it rewards those who had already been charging higher fees and punishes those who had kept their fees low.

October 1, 1984, marked a full year since establishment of medicare's new prospective payment system (PPS), which reimburses hospitals a flat fee for each admission of a medicare-covered patient. The size of the fee is based on so-called diagnosis-related groups—468 categories of medical conditions for which uniform payment schedules have been set. This contrasts with the traditional method of billing, in which fees are based on length of hospital stay and services received while hospitalized. PPS was intended to cut down on medicare hospitalization costs by reducing unnecessary services and unnecessarily long hospital stays. Hospitals were phased into participation in the program throughout the year, with the last group joining in July. Hospitals in Maryland, Massachusetts, New Jersey, and New York were exempted from the program because of previously implemented state cost-control measures.

The Health Care Financing Administration (HCFA) reports that PPS has been successful in shortening the average hospital stay for medicare patients in participating hospitals from 9.5 days to 7.5 days; HCFA also reported virtually no change in the number of hospital admissions of medicare patients in participating hospitals. HHS Secretary Margaret Heckler credited PPS with helping to slow the annual average rate of health care inflation; the rate dropped from 6.4 percent in 1983 to 6.1 percent in 1984. PPS and other changes in medicare financing are expected to keep the federal government's hospital insurance trust fund from going bankrupt before 1995, but serious financial problems are still projected for the late 1990's.

New federal regulations that took effect February 1, 1985, were expected to bring at least 200,000 medicare recipients into health maintenance organizations, or HMO's, during the year. These groups offer comprehensive medical care for a fixed, prepaid fee. The new rules allow medicare to pay in advance for care provided by HMO's, at a rate equal to 95 percent of the average annual medicare cost per patient in the HMO's service area.

Child Health Assurance Program (CHAP). Coverage for children and pregnant women by the state-administered medicaid program was mandated by Congress in 1984 as part of a $435 million increase in the program's funding over three years. This expansion of medical care benefits for the poor was included in the Deficit Reduction Act of 1984.

Under the expanded program, states must now provide coverage to first-time pregnant women, to pregnant women in two-parent families where the principal wage earner is unemployed, and to children under age five in two-parent families where the family income is below a state's poverty line. Some states had previously denied benefits to some or all individuals in these categories.

The bill also increased federal reimbursement to the states under medicaid, by allowing a 1981 reduction in matching funds to expire.

HHS funding. Just days before adjourning in October 1984, Congress approved a $78.4 billion appropriation for programs within the Department of Health and Human Services for fiscal 1985. This figure represented an increase of $4.3 billion over fiscal 1984 and was $2.8 billion more than President Reagan had proposed. The legislation continues to bar medicaid funding for abortions, except when the life of the mother is endangered.

Also approved by Congress was a $1.6 billion three-year block grant for state-run alcohol, drug abuse, and mental health programs. The legislation stipulates that there be a new emphasis on treatment of substance abuse by women and on mental health services for severely disturbed children and adolescents.

Brain death. New York became the 38th state to recognize through either legislation or court decision that a person whose brain has ceased to function may be declared legally dead even if breathing and heartbeat are being maintained artificially. The ruling came in a decision by the state's highest court, which upheld manslaughter convictions in two shotgun deaths; the defendants had claimed the victims had died not of bullet wounds but because doctors, determining the wounded individuals were "brain dead," had disconnected them from respirators and removed various organs for transplants.

Acceptance of brain death has been encouraged by the American Medical Association, the American Bar Association, and the President's Commission for the Study of Ethical Problems in Medicine and Biomedical and Behavioral Research. Without such a definition of death, physicians are in a legally ambiguous position when they turn off respirators and other devices of patients who exhibit no brain waves.

National Organ Transplant Act. Under the National Organ Transplant Act, signed into law in October 1984, Congress authorized the spending of $31 million to help patients in need of organ transplant surgery. The legis-

287

New Cigarette Warnings

SURGEON GENERAL'S WARNING: Smoking Causes Lung Cancer, Heart Disease, Emphysema, And May Complicate Pregnancy.

SURGEON GENERAL'S WARNING: Quitting Smoking Now Greatly Reduces Serious Risks to Your Health.

SURGEON GENERAL'S WARNING: Smoking By Pregnant Women May Result in Fetal Injury, Premature Birth, And Low Birth Weight.

SURGEON GENERAL'S WARNING: Cigarette Smoke Contains Carbon Monoxide.

lation requires HHS to establish a national computerized registry for matching available organs with potential recipients. Money was allocated to establish and expand local and regional organ procurement organizations, and HHS was instructed to create a task force to report to Congress during 1985 on various issues raised by the expense of lifesaving transplant surgery. The legislation also makes the sale or purchase of human organs a federal crime.

Cigarette labeling. Cigarette manufacturers must now provide stronger warnings about the health risks of using their products. Under legislation passed by Congress in 1984, the previously mandated general warning on cigarette packages, "The Surgeon General Has Determined That Smoking Is Dangerous to Your Health," will be replaced during 1985 by four more specific labels that will be rotated every three months (see above).

BARBARA SCHERR TRENK

Canada

Canada Health Act. After a long conflict between the federal and provincial governments over Canada's health insurance system, the Canada Health Act was passed into law by Parliament in April 1984. However, controversy over the act did not end with its enactment, as a number of provinces refused to go along with its provisions.

Prior to its December 1983 introduction in Parliament by the then ruling Liberal Party, the Canada Health Act had been several years in the making and was the highlight of former Health Minister Monique Bégin's political career. The act's main purpose is to discourage so-called extra-billing and hospital user fees, practices whereby doctors or hospitals charge additional fees directly to the patient above those reimbursed by medi-

care, Canada's publicly funded health insurance system. The act tightens Ottawa's hold on medicare and allows for financial penalties to be assessed on provinces that continue to permit extra fees for medical care. The most controversial part of the act allows Ottawa to deduct $1 in the medicare grant to a province for every $1 collected in the province through user fees or extra-billing.

The penalties went into effect July 1, 1984, and as of early 1985, only Newfoundland and Labrador, Prince Edward Island, Nova Scotia, the Northwest Territories, and the Yukon Territory had received full medicare grants. The other seven provinces were losing a total of Can$9.5 million per month from their federal medicare grants, because they continue to allow doctors to extra-bill their patients, hospitals to charge user fees, or both.

The provinces have responded in various ways to the loss of medicare funds. Manitoba considered legislation to ban extra medical charges, and Ontario studied ways to modify its policy of permitting the province's doctors to extra-bill. Saskatchewan began talks with its provincial medical association. In addition, Alberta, which was losing more than Can$1 million per month in federal grants, continued a campaign to discourage its doctors from extra-billing. New Brunswick argued with the federal health department that user fees are not primarily intended to raise money but to encourage people to visit their family doctors rather than hospital outpatient facilities. British Columbia, one of the two provinces that forbids extra-billing (Quebec is the other), still allows hospital user fees. The province, however, has introduced a temporary 8 percent personal income tax increase, called the Health Care Maintenance Tax, that will make up for medicare funds lost as a penalty for user fees.

Meanwhile, Health Minister Bégin—who viewed the Canada Health Act as "a move to head off the eventual collapse" of the medicare system—resigned her post in July 1984, believing her job to be complete. This occurred during the federal election campaign, which eventually saw the Liberals lose as the Progressive Conservative Party scored a stunning victory. The provincial health ministers, who had been opposed to the Canada Health Act, were confident that their relations with Ottawa would improve under Conservative Prime Minister Brian Mulroney, and they welcomed the incoming government. These ministers told Ottawa not to forget that Canada owes its outstanding health care system to the provinces. (Health care in Canada has been a provincial matter since the country was formed in 1867). They asked the new Conservative federal health minister, Jake Epp, to reflect on what they consider to be the damage the Canada Health Act has done to the health care system in the country. Epp responded by telling the provincial health ministers he hoped they would decide to get rid of extra medical charges, but he reassured them that he would not interfere with their jurisdictions or tell them how to run their medicare plans.

Generic drugs. The long-running battle in Canada between manufacturers of brand-name drugs and manufacturers of generic drugs reached a new peak as a federal inquiry examining the nation's pharmaceutical industry came to a close in November 1984. However, by early 1985, the commission had yet to sift through the more than two weeks of presentations and evidence and publish its conclusions.

At issue is the dispute over whether the government should continue a 15-year practice of allowing companies operating in Canada to sell low-priced generic copies of brand-name drugs patented by multinational firms. This compulsory licensing, as it has become known, allows Canadian drug firms to copy a brand-name drug, providing that the generic manufacturer offers sufficient evidence that the generic will be equivalent to the original and pays the patent holder or inventing company a 4 percent royalty.

The influx of generic drugs since compulsory licensing became law in 1969 brought prices for pharmaceuticals down drastically. Supporters of compulsory licensing claim that repeal of the act would cost consumers, who have grown accustomed to having pharmacists automatically sell them the lower-priced generic versions of prescribed drugs. Opponents of compulsory licensing, particularly the Pharmaceutical Manufacturers Association of Canada, say that such a low royalty fee undermines patent protection and forces the companies that develop the drugs to introduce them at relatively high prices so research-and-development costs can be recovered over a reasonably short time.

In making its recommendations, the commission investigating the issue must decide how much money generic drugs have saved consumers and the extent to which multinational pharmaceutical companies have lost money because of the generic competition.

Abortion. Dr. Henry Morgentaler, the Quebec physician often credited with keeping the abortion issue alive in Canada, suffered both a victory and a defeat in 1984. In November, Morgentaler and two colleagues were cleared by an Ontario Supreme Court jury of charges of conspiring to procure a miscarriage, the term used in the Canadian Criminal Code to describe an abortion. Morgentaler's attorney had admitted that the doctor had broken the law but said he did so because of "necessity." However, a month later, the Ontario government announced that it would appeal the acquittal because, Ontario Attorney General Roy McMurtry said, "to leave the verdict unchallenged would indicate the law was wrong."

Morgentaler had been charged in Ontario following a July 1983 raid on his Toronto abortion clinic. Under a 1969 law, abortions in Canada are permitted only in hospitals where a therapeutic abortion committee (TAC) reviews each case and determines that the woman's life or mental or physical health is threatened. Morgentaler's clinic is not an accredited hospital and does not have a TAC. In the 1970's, Morgentaler was acquitted on abortion charges three times in Quebec. In 1985, he faced abortion-related charges pending against him in Manitoba as well as the Ontario government's appeal of the late 1984 case.

Heroin. The use of heroin as a painkiller will most likely be legal again in Canada some time in 1985. In December 1984 Health Minister Epp said that a proposal to lift the ban against the medical use of heroin would be submitted to Parliament early in 1985; Epp said that he expected it to win swift approval. The announcement was welcomed by the Canadian Medical Association (CMA), which had recommended the immediate approval of heroin for medical uses at a meeting in August 1984.

The use of heroin to ease pain in terminally ill patients has been under dispute since the 1950's. Canada, cooperating with the U.S. government's crackdown on the black market for drugs, banned heroin in 1954. However, heroin supporters claim that, though highly addictive, the drug is the most potent agent against pain and induces a euphoria that relieves the depression that often afflicts terminally ill patients. Dr. William Ghent

Abortion rights crusader Dr. Henry Morgentaler, flanked by supporters, heads for a Toronto police station in December 1984 to surrender on charges that he had conspired to perform abortions. He had won acquittal on a similar charge a few weeks before, after losing a constitutional challenge to Canada's antiabortion laws earlier in the year.

of Kingston, Ontario, who chaired the CMA's Council on Health Care when the CMA recommended licensing the medical use of heroin, maintained that the Canadian government's ban on heroin was based on a mistaken belief that such a ban would reduce illicit use of the drug. RHONDA BIRENBAUM

Gynecology

See OBSTETRICS AND GYNECOLOGY.

Heart and Circulatory System

Recent research dealing with heart disease, the main cause of death in the United States, has been marked less by innovation in treatment and prevention than by refinements and improved understanding of existing therapies. New findings have been forthcoming on the effectiveness of, and best techniques for, coronary bypass surgery. Also, further evidence has been obtained for the effectiveness of balloon angioplasty, a procedure for clearing a clogged artery by inflating a tiny balloon in it. Some researchers have been exploring the complicated relationship between vigorous exercise and sudden death from heart disease. Meanwhile, events in late 1984 and early 1985 sparked new public interest in techniques for replacing a diseased heart: these events included the second and third implantations of a permanent artificial heart and the transplanting of a baboon heart into a baby girl.

Coronary Bypass Surgery

Results have become available from several large studies conducted during the past ten years that bear on various questions associated with coronary bypass surgery, particularly regarding how long the operation remains effective, and how this may vary depending on surgical technique. Coronary bypass surgery is used to treat some patients in whom the blood vessels supplying the heart have become narrowed, largely by fatty deposits. The surgeon literally bypasses the blockage by sewing, or grafting, a blood vessel from elsewhere in the body (often a leg vein) between the unobstructed portions of the coronary vessels, thus creating a new path by which blood can flow to the heart.

Coronary bypass for persons with angina. It is now well established that the coronary bypass operation is an effective method for relieving the symptoms of angina pectoris—that is, chest discomfort or pain due to insufficient blood supply to the heart muscle—and for restoring a more active life-style to individuals disabled by these symptoms. Researchers have also shown that it prolongs life in certain groups of angina patients:

those who have severe coronary vessel narrowings in strategic locations that threaten large amounts of healthy heart muscle with damage and those who have sustained significant prior heart damage. Since most of the studies on which these findings are based have followed the patients for five to seven years, their conclusions are valid only for that span of time.

Clogging of the bypass. The hardening and clogging of the arteries leading to the heart—a condition known as coronary atherosclerosis—proceed slowly but often surely. The underlying problem is not necessarily altered by creating bypass grafts, which merely act as alternative "plumbing" for carrying blood to the heart muscle. These grafts are subject to the same accumulation of atherosclerotic material that led to the original blockages in the patient's coronary arteries, and so the grafts may themselves become significantly narrowed over time. Several researchers have addressed this problem in reporting on ten to 15 years of follow-up data from patients who underwent bypass surgery shortly after the operation's introduction in the late 1960's. Their findings have important practical implications that should help to improve the long-term outlook for persons undergoing this type of surgery.

Cardiologists from the Montreal Heart Institute, for example, performed X-ray studies of coronary vessels and bypass grafts in a number of patients who had undergone coronary bypass surgery ten years earlier and whose bypass grafts were known to be functioning well one year after surgery. Ten years after surgery, somewhat fewer than one-third of the grafts had closed completely, and another one-third were narrowed by material that appeared to be the type that causes atherosclerosis. Only 50 (38 percent) of the 132 bypass grafts studied were unaffected by the atherosclerotic process. Significant additional narrowing due to the continuing atherosclerotic process was also seen in almost 50 percent of the coronary arteries that had not been bypassed originally because they were normal or only minimally narrowed at the time. Disease progression in both the bypass grafts and the coronary arteries was most common in those patients who had the highest levels of cholesterol in their blood.

The Montreal researchers suggested that the way to prevent or slow the clogging of the coronary arteries and bypass grafts may be to reduce excess cholesterol in the blood by changing the patient's diet, administering cholesterol-lowering medications, or both. The fact that so many of the bypass grafts had narrowed or closed ten years after surgery suggests that patients' long-term health after bypass surgery depends to a great extent on controlling the same factors that contributed to the need for surgery in the first place.

The best vessel for the graft. Since the early days of bypass surgery, surgeons have debated over what vessels would make the best grafts. Most settled on using the patient's saphenous veins, located near the surface of the legs, while others favored the two internal mammary arteries, which begin, one on each side of the chest, from a branch of the aorta (the major artery leading from the heart) and pass down the sides of the breastbone, supplying blood to the inner surface of the chest wall. The internal mammary artery has certain theoretical advantages—for example, since it is an artery (rather than a vein), it may be better suited structurally than the saphenous vein to withstand the high pressures involved in blood flow through the coronary arteries. In addition, its use does not require the surgeon to make an incision in the leg; it is accessible from the same incision made to perform the bypass operation. The internal mammary artery, however, does have disadvantages: it can generally be grafted to only one of the three major coronary arteries, and removing it from the chest wall is a tedious procedure that takes more time than using the leg veins.

Now, however, an overriding advantage of using the internal mammary graft over the vein graft—its longevity—has been revealed in long-term follow-up studies of bypass surgery conducted in Montreal, Cleveland, and Portland (Ore.). Ten years after surgery, between 70 and 90 percent of the internal mammary grafts were still open and functioning, compared with only 45 to 50 percent of saphenous vein grafts. Furthermore, in contrast to saphenous vein grafts, the internal mammary artery rarely develops significant narrowing due to atherosclerosis, even ten years after surgery. The internal mammary artery is most frequently grafted to that one of the three major coronary arteries that supplies blood to the greatest quantity of heart muscle. Thus, since the internal mammary artery remains unobstructed over a relatively long period, using this artery should help to lower the frequency of the large and often fatal heart attacks that may occur when blood flow to this region of the heart is shut off. If use of the internal mammary graft becomes routine, the long-term results of coronary bypass surgery should improve.

Effectiveness of Balloon Angioplasty

Recent refinements in another method of improving blood flow to the heart, and encouraging reports on follow-up of patients who have undergone the procedure, appear to signal a broader role for the technique, thus offering physicians a wider choice of treatment strategies. In this method—balloon angioplasty (also called percutaneous transluminal coronary angioplasty)—a thin tube, or catheter, is passed through an artery in the leg into an obstructed coronary artery. A small, deflated balloon at the tip of the catheter is positioned at the point within the artery where the narrowing has occurred and is then inflated and deflated several times to compress the fatty material causing the blockage, thus reducing the obstruction and improving the flow of blood to the heart muscle. A great advantage of this technique is that while the coronary bypass operation is major surgery, balloon angioplasty requires neither general anesthesia nor a major incision. If it is successful, the patient may leave the hospital in two to three days and resume full activity immediately.

First performed in 1977 by Dr. Andreas R. Grüntzig in Switzerland, balloon angioplasty could originally be used in only about 5 to 10 percent of all patients who required bypass surgery, and was successful in only 60 to 70 percent of the cases in which it was employed. This picture has now changed dramatically. Advances in catheter design and balloon material, along with the experience gained by surgeons over the past several years in performing the technique, have greatly increased the number of cases in which it can be used and have improved its overall success rate.

In many medical centers up to 40 percent of all patients who before the introduction of angioplasty would have had coronary bypass surgery are now undergoing the balloon procedure instead. In addition, in patients having the type of coronary artery disease that is most likely to benefit from balloon angioplasty, success rates now approach 90 percent in many medical centers. Within two to six months after the procedure up to a third of patients may develop the same symptoms they originally experienced, because the dilated (widened) artery renarrows. But over 90 percent of these arteries can be redilated; the success rate for these repeat procedures is about 60 to 70 percent. A follow-up report on Dr. Grüntzig's original group of angioplasty patients that was published in 1984 found that if the dilated site in the artery had not renarrowed six months after the procedure was performed, then there was less than a 10 percent likelihood of a subsequent recurrence in the next five to seven years.

Such favorable follow-up results bode well for the future of balloon angioplasty as a supplement or replacement for bypass surgery. As has been noted, many bypass grafts have only a limited life span because they gradually become clogged through atherosclerosis. While second and even third bypass operations can be and frequently are performed, repeat operations are usually more difficult and more risky than the first bypass procedure. This is because scarring may have occurred in the chest cavity from the previous operation and because additional segments of leg veins may be unavailable for use as bypass grafts. Therefore, the longer the first bypass operation can be safely postponed—for example, by buying time with a less radical procedure like balloon angioplasty—the better the long-term outlook (ten to 20 years) for the patient may be. This is particularly true for younger patients.

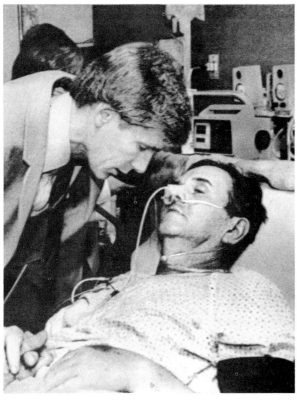

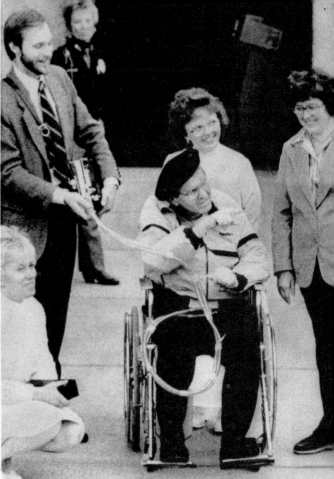

In patients with disabling angina, the physician can often identify one or two severe narrowings, within one or two major coronary arteries, that are responsible for an inadequate supply of blood to the heart muscle and, consequently, for the symptoms the patient is experiencing. Although the patient may have other, less severe coronary narrowings, widening these most critical ones by balloon angioplasty may relieve the symptoms and postpone the need for a bypass operation. Since repeated angioplasties involve less risk and discomfort (and are less expensive) than repeated bypass operations, it should be possible to perform several angioplasty procedures over the years, as the need arises, although the effectiveness of this strategy remains to be proved.

Exercise and Heart Disease

The role of vigorous physical exercise in both preventing and precipitating (triggering) sudden death from cardiac, or heart-related, causes has long been a subject of great controversy. The debate took on a new intensity in 1984 when the 52-year-old author and jogging enthusiast Jim Fixx whose *Complete Book of Running* (1977) had helped start a national exercise trend, suddenly and unexpectedly died while running.

Jim Fixx personified the controversy. As a young man he had been overweight and had smoked heavily.

Moreover, he had a family history of early cardiac death—his father had died at 43 of a heart attack—and thus was in a high-risk group for an early heart attack himself. Autopsy findings showed advanced atherosclerosis. The unanswered question was whether his years of vigorous running prolonged his life or hastened his death.

Today's widespread enthusiasm for regular, vigorous physical exercise has its roots in several scientific findings. In general, regular exercise promotes weight loss, improves the condition of the heart and blood vessels, and—as a result of these two effects—may help to lower blood pressure. Several studies have suggested that regular physical exercise can raise the level of the so-called "good" cholesterol (high-density lipoprotein cholesterol, a kind of cholesterol different from the type implicated in the development of a atherosclerosis) in the blood and thereby help to lower the risk of coronary heart disease. Finally, several large-scale studies have suggested that habitual vigorous exercise is associated with a lowered risk of sudden cardiac death.

Nevertheless, the sudden death of apparently healthy individuals during vigorous exercise is not uncommon. Furthermore, the effects of vigorous exercise in persons who have been diagnosed as having coronary heart disease remains unclear, because no study has yet shown that vigorous exercise by cardiac patients either lowers

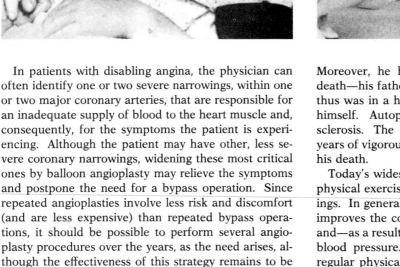

Artificial Hearts

At Humana Hospital Audubon, Louisville, Dr. William C. De-Vries briefs artificial heart recipient William J. Schroeder on his condition (far left); Schroeder suffered a stroke after a few weeks of high-spirited recovery. Left, Schroeder takes a brief ride around the hospital grounds with the aid of a portable power system for his heart. At right, Murray P. Haydon, who received a similar artificial heart on February 17, 1985, admires a picture of his new-born grandson the day after surgery.

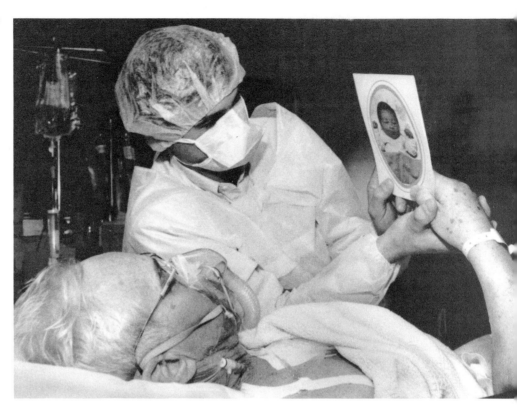

the risk of future heart attacks or promotes longevity. In fact, vigorous exercise by people with impaired blood flow to the heart muscle or previous heart damage can cause a serious shortage of blood flowing to the heart muscle, critical irregularities of the heart beat, or even sudden death.

In one recent study, researchers examined 133 cases of out-of-hospital cardiac arrest among married men for a 14-month period in an attempt to determine what role various levels of habitual physical exercise play in precipitating or preventing sudden cardiac death in men without a known history of heart disease or other serious health problems. They found that the risk of sudden cardiac death during intense physical activity was higher than the risk during lower levels of physical activity. While this was true no matter what the individual's level of habitual physical activity, the risk of sudden death during vigorous activity was ten times higher for those with a low level of habitual physical activity than in those men at the highest level of habitual activity. In the latter group, the slight, temporary, increased risk of sudden death during acute vigorous activity was outweighed by a reduced risk of sudden cardiac death when the men were not exercising.

These findings suggest some precautions for reducing the chances of sudden death during vigorous physical exercise. The greatest risk of such death appears to oc-

cur in those who do not exercise regularly. In practical terms, it is clear that an inactive person older than 25 or 30 who is contemplating beginning an exercise program should consult his or her physician first. Persons who are at risk for premature coronary artery disease—those who smoke cigarettes or have high blood pressure, diabetes, high levels of blood cholesterol, or a family history of premature coronary heart disease or sudden death—should be examined by a physician carefully (and should perhaps take a stress test) before embarking on an exercise program.

A detailed physical examination is also a must for anyone experiencing symptoms that suggest the presence of coronary heart disease or other forms of heart disease. Such an individual should probably, at least in the beginning, exercise only under the supervision of trained medical or paramedical personnel, in a setting where emergency resuscitation equipment is readily available.

Most important, physical activity should start at a very low level and be built up very slowly. By gradually attaining a higher level of conditioning a person may lower the risks involved in sudden vigorous activity. Finally, a detailed medical evaluation will probably be able to identify those individuals for whom the risks of vigorous physical activity even in a supervised setting outweigh its potential benefits.

Replacing the Diseased Heart

The most dramatic recent developments in cardiovascular medicine involved the most radical approach to treating persons with incurable, far-advanced disease of the heart muscle: replacing the failing heart.

Transplanting human hearts. Heart transplants, performed at barely a handful of medical centers until the last several years, are now carried out in many large metropolitan medical centers. Improvements in transplant procedures, along with the introduction of new drugs (especially cyclosporine) for combating the body's efforts to reject the new heart, have raised the chances of survival, while more sophisticated means of obtaining and distributing donor hearts (for example, by coordination through a network of computerized clearinghouses for information on organ availability) have helped widen patient access to heart transplants. Patients who receive properly matched human heart transplants and who are otherwise healthy now have as much as an 80 percent chance of being alive one year after the transplant is performed, and almost half of them are alive and gainfully employed five years after.

Artificial hearts. Despite this encouraging progress, tens of thousands of people in the United States die yearly from irreversible heart muscle disease who were unable to benefit from a heart transplant because of the shortage of suitable donor hearts or the high cost of the procedure. This fact has stimulated an intensive search for a practical artificial device that could perform the heart's pumping function without damaging other organ systems and thereby offer the patient a chance for an extended and more comfortable life.

The quest culminated in December 1982 in the first permanent implantation of a totally artificial heart in a human by a surgical team, headed by Dr. William C. DeVries, at the University of Utah Medical Center. Dr. Barney Clark, a 61-year-old retired dentist dying of cardiomyopathy (weakness of the heart muscle), lived 112 days after implantation of a plastic-and-aluminum "Jarvik-7" artificial heart, eventually succumbing to complications arising from severe, preexisting lung and kidney disease, not to failure of the artificial heart.

The second such device (again a Jarvik-7) was implanted in retired government worker William J. Schroeder, 52, of Jasper, Ind., on November 25, 1984, by the same physicians, this time at the Humana Heart Institute (located within the Humana Hospital Audubon) in Louisville, Ky. Like Barney Clark, Schroeder suffered from far-advanced cardiomyopathy (as well as diabetes), and was expected to live only a matter of days without the heart implant. His progress after surgery was at first remarkably rapid—within two days he was breathing on his own and asking for a beer, and he was soon walking, with assistance. But on December 13 he suffered a serious stroke, possibly as a result of a blood clot that formed within the artificial heart. With some speech and memory loss persisting from the stroke, together with a noticeable change in mood from his former ebullience, the future course of Schroeder's recovery was uncertain. In any event, for as long as he would live he would need to remain attached by two hoses to the 323-pound system powering his new heart, except for brief periods of relative freedom allowed by a small, portable power system that represented the major difference between Schroeder's implant and that used in Barney Clark. On March 17, 1985, Schroeder marked his 113th day with the implant, surpassing Clark's period of survival.

The third artificial heart implantation took place on February 17, 1985, at Humana. The recipient of the device, again a Jarvik-7, was Murray P. Haydon, a 58-year-old retired factory worker from Louisville who was suffering from terminal cardiomyopathy. The operation took only 3½ hours, half the time required for Schroeder's surgery and four hours less than Clark's. In late February, after a monitoring tube was removed from Haydon's chest, the tiny hole that then remained in the remnant of his natural heart (left in place as an anchor for the Jarvik-7) failed to close as expected; bleeding into the chest resulted, and Haydon on March 2 underwent surgery to shut the hole. Clark and Schroeder had also suffered bleeding complications—in each case of a different nature.

Controversy erupted in early March 1985 when a different artificial heart was implanted in a dying man at the University of Arizona Medical Center in Tucson. Neither the device nor the doctor who performed the operation had received the necessary approval from the U.S. Food and Drug Administration. The FDA sent a letter of "mild rebuke" to the university medical center and began an investigation to determine if further action was called for.

The patient, Thomas Creighton, a 33-year-old automobile mechanic, had received a human heart transplant on March 5. His body rejected the transplant, and the surgical team, hoping to buy enough time to obtain another human heart, made an emergency implant of the unapproved artificial heart. This device, developed by Dr. Kevin Cheng, a Phoenix dentist, had previously been tried only in calves, for 12 hours at the longest. After about 11 hours with the device, Creighton received a new transplant. He died on March 8, reportedly of complications (accumulation of fluid in the lungs and subsequent heart failure) stemming from his being on a heart-lung machine for over ten hours before receiving the Phoenix heart.

A few days after Creighton's death, Dr. William S. Pierce of Pennsylvania State University's Hershey Medical Center received FDA approval for experimental use of an artificial heart developed by him and his associates. This "Penn State heart" is intended as a temporary device, to keep patients alive until a transplant can be performed.

The role that the Jarvik and other types of artificial heart devices will eventually play in treating heart disease will depend on the results of long-term follow-up on how the devices perform in a substantial number of patients, as well as on further technological developments and on how and whether society decides to provide the immense financial resources needed to make these devices widely available.

Animal-to-human transplant. A different approach to the replacement of a failing heart was taken by doctors at Loma Linda University Medical Center in California. In October 1984 they transplanted the heart of a young female baboon into a baby identified only as Baby Fae, who had been born with a usually fatal congenital heart abnormality known as hypoplastic left heart syndrome. This transplant was widely greeted with shock among both the public at large and the medical community, the latter because of the scarcity of published experimental data suggesting that using an animal heart would be an effective procedure. The baby lived for 20 days after the surgery, eventually succumbing both to her body's rejection of the transplanted heart and to complications from the drugs given in an attempt to prevent the rejection process.

Final judgment regarding the appropriateness of this method of organ replacement for various forms of heart disease, as well as regarding whether further attempts in humans are justified, must await both publication of additional scientific data and public consideration of the ethical issues raised.

See also the feature article NEW SUCCESSES IN TRANSPLANTS. JOHN F. SCHNEIDER, M.D.

Kidneys and Urinary System

Progress in recognizing, treating, and—ultimately—preventing diseases of the kidneys and urinary system often depends on how skillfully the knowledge gained from laboratory work is applied to patient care. Examples include recent findings concerning the actions of bacteria as applied to urinary tract infections, and research in physiology as applied to problems of the body's salt and water balance and to progressive chronic kidney disease.

Bacteria and Recurrent Urinary Tract Infections

An important advance has been made in understanding why some people suffer more severe or more frequent urinary tract infections than do other persons. Urinary tract infections occur when disease-causing bacteria multiply in the kidney, ureter and urethra (the tubes

carrying urine into and then out of the bladder), bladder, or male prostate gland. They are probably the second most common type of infection (after respiratory tract infections), occurring in both men and women but more commonly in women.

A recent series of studies focused on the ability of bacteria to adhere (stick or bind) to cell surfaces in the urinary tract as well as in other body systems. It was found in both adults and children that the bacteria associated with urinary tract infections are more likely to adhere tightly to urinary tract cells from patients with recurrent infections than from individuals without a history of such infections. This adherence occurs through hairlike projections from the bacteria called pili or fimbriae. Further studies have shown that the pili of certain disease-causing bacteria "recognize" sites on human cell walls that act as specific attachment receptors for the bacteria. Moreover, a study of patients with apparent kidney infections showed that over 90 percent of the bacteria responsible for the infections were able to recognize one particular receptor (called the P-antigen receptor). In contrast, only 7 percent of similar bacteria cultured at random from stool specimens of healthy individuals had this potential for adhering to the cells. Since organisms that cause urinary tract infections usually arise in the stool, this finding indicates the importance of the pili for the P-antigen in the bacteria's ability to make its way to the kidney to establish an infection there. Studies applying these findings to patient care are under way to determine if it is possible to block these attachment sites in patients who suffer recurrent infections, possibly by immunizing individuals with substances derived from the bacterial pili.

ANF: New Treatment for Kidney Disease?

ANF—a recently discovered substance that appears to play an important role in regulating the body's content of salt and water—someday may be useful in treating a number of medical conditions, including high blood pressure and disorders related to impaired blood flow in the kidney.

One of the kidney's major functions is maintaining a delicate balance of sodium (an element that is a major component of table salt) and water in the space surrounding cells. This is accomplished both by conservation, when dietary intake of sodium and water falls, and by increased excretion, when intake increases. Preservation of this balance is regulated in part by two hormones that function through their action on the kidney: antidiuretic hormone from the hypothalamic region of the brain, which causes water to be retained, and aldosterone from the adrenal glands, which promotes salt retention. There is evidence that ANF—which stands for atrial natriuretic factor and which was first de-

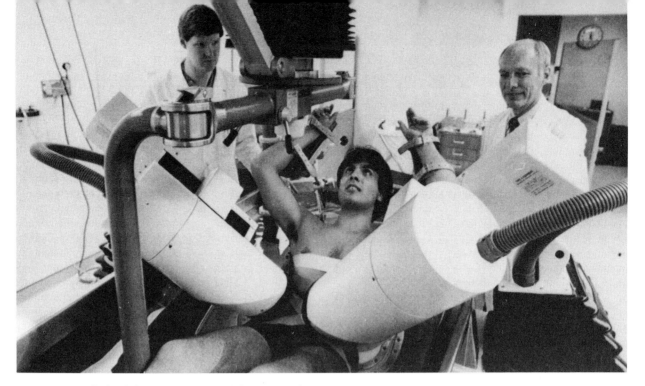

A machine called a lithotripter, approved for use in the United States in late 1984, smashes kidney stones with shock waves, making surgery unnecessary. The device is expected to save millions of dollars in health care costs every year.

scribed in 1981—may be a third hormone in this system.

Early experiments with rats demonstrated that the injection of crude extracts of tissue from the atrial (entrance) chambers of the heart led to a rapid, temporary increase in the excretion of sodium, potassium, and water from the kidney; extracts of tissue from the heart's pumping chambers, the ventricles, did not have the same effect. The increase in sodium excretion caused by ANF was 30–40 times greater than that which occurred with other salt-excreting substances produced by the body. More recently, ANF has been isolated from the atria of human hearts, showing that it exists in people as well as in rats.

The principal activity of ANF appears to be two-fold: it causes a striking increase in the flow of plasma across the tiny filtering units (glomeruli) of the kidneys, resulting in increased water and salt excretion, and it relaxes the blood vessels, particularly those subject to narrowing in response to certain stimuli. Extensive efforts are now under way to study the characteristics of ANF. Exploration of its possible uses in treating a wide variety of disorders of blood pressure control and kidney function will certainly follow.

Protein in Chronic Progressive Kidney Failure

Most patients with chronic kidney failure (that is, patients with irreversible and usually progressive loss of kidney function) appear to lose their remaining kidney function at a rate that is relatively constant in any one person, regardless of the nature of their underlying dis-

ease. While this rate varies widely among patients, it can be calculated for an individual patient from the results of a simple blood test for a substance called creatinine. The cause of this seemingly orderly, progressive kidney deterioration has puzzled scientists for some time. It now appears that restricting protein (and possibly phosphate) in the diet of such patients may slow this steady loss of kidney function, and a theory has been offered that may explain why.

The theory, which has important implications for the treatment of chronic kidney disease, was proposed by researchers at Harvard Medical School and involves the approximately 1 million tiny units called nephrons that perform the filtering and excretion work of each kidney. When the initial stage of kidney failure causes the loss of some nephrons, their work load is taken up by the remaining healthy nephrons, a "shift" accomplished by means of increased blood flow through the remaining nephrons. A sequence of events then occurs, according to this hypothesis, in which the increased flow of proteins across the glomerular capillary walls stimulates new material to form around the cells; this material clogs and causes the loss of more nephrons, starting the cycle over again. A similar mechanism may cause the decline in kidney function that occurs with age, in diabetes, and in other diseases leading to a chronic wasting of the kidneys.

Thus, it appears that protein may play an important role in this still-theoretical process, and restricting the amount of protein in the diet has in fact been found to slow kidney deterioration related to both age and disease in laboratory experiments with animals. (Restricting phosphate in the diet may also be beneficial, although the reasons are not yet understood.) Protein restriction used to be widely used to control symptoms of the severe toxic condition called uremia in patients with advanced kidney disease, before the availability of dialysis and kidney transplants. Studies are now under way in patients with early chronic progressive kidney disease to determine if restricting the protein and phosphate in their diets can prevent or minimize progressive kidney deterioration. Preliminary reports indicate some success with such diets in postponing the need to begin dialysis or to undergo a transplant.

Aluminum-Related Disease in Dialysis Patients

Aluminum has been of relatively little interest to medical scientists through the years. The metal is not dangerous to healthy individuals, since it is poorly absorbed from the gastrointestinal tract and promptly excreted by the kidneys. However, it now appears that aluminum causes a devastating disorder in patients receiving long-term dialysis treatment for far advanced kidney disease. (In dialysis, the patient's blood is passed through a filtering system that removes waste products from it.)

The central nervous system syndrome known as dialysis dementia or dialysis encephalopathy was first seen about ten years ago, usually in patients who had been on dialysis for at least two to four years. The patients first developed slurred speech or stuttering and impaired memory; these symptoms soon progressed to include periodic muscle spasms, hallucinations, psychosis, severe seizures, and deteriorating mental function, ending in the total loss of mental powers and death. The fact that this syndrome occurred in patients at a limited number of dialysis centers suggested that some element of the physical environment of these centers was the cause. Investigation eventually revealed that the tap water used to prepare the dialysis solution at centers where the syndrome was observed was contaminated by aluminum; it entered the patients' bloodstreams during dialysis, and their damaged kidneys could not excrete it. Autopsies confirmed that the gray matter (a type of brain tissue) of patients who died from dialysis dementia had significantly higher concentrations of aluminum than did the gray matter of dialysis patients who died from other causes.

Often accompanying the dementia syndrome was a form of progressive bone softening (called osteomalacia) that caused worsening bone pain, muscle weakness, and a susceptibility to multiple fractures that was resistant to treatment with vitamin D. Aluminum exposure also appeared to be involved in this condition.

Aluminum may occur naturally in tap water or it may be added to clarify the local water supply as part of a city's routine water treatment procedure. Now that its tragic effects in hemodialysis are known, processes called deionization and reverse osmosis are being used to remove nearly all the aluminum from the tap water of dialysis centers affected by the problem. If the aluminum-related syndrome stops occurring, as it appears it has, then at least this medical aspect of the dialysis patient's life should become a little less precarious than it has been.

Kidney Stone Crumbler Approved

The lithotripter (literally, stone crusher), a device developed in West Germany that uses shock waves of sound energy to crumble kidney stones, was approved in December 1984 by the U.S. Food and Drug Administration. Once the stones have been disintegrated they can be passed from the body, thus providing almost immediate relief without the risks and discomfort of surgery. Although the lithotripter (which weighs four tons) costs close to $2 million, the savings in surgical costs alone for this common and painful condition are expected to provide rapid payback of the initial outlay.

See also the feature article New Successes in Transplants. Marvin Forland, M.D.

Liver

The liver, the body's largest internal organ, plays a variety of essential roles. It stores and filters the blood, produces bile for the digestion of fats, converts sugar to a different form for storage and eventual release to meet the body's energy needs, and produces proteins for blood clotting. Diseases of the liver constitute a public health problem of global scale. Researchers continued efforts to find effective treatment for the many serious complications of cirrhosis, to understand the causes of hepatitis, and to refine vaccines against hepatitis B, its most widespread form.

Treating Bleeding from Cirrhosis

Cirrhosis of the liver is a condition characterized by the excessive formation of fibrous tissue, followed by hardening and contraction of the organ. A frequent, serious, and often fatal complication of cirrhosis is esophageal varices—that is, internal bleeding from swollen blood vessels (varices) lining the esophagus (food pipe). This recurrent bleeding is the result of high blood pressure that occurs in the portal vein when the scarred condition of the liver prevents blood from the intestines from passing through the vein; the blood is then forced into other paths of flow. Drugs called beta blockers, commonly used to treat high blood pressure and heart disease, are being tested for their effects in lowering blood pressure in the portal vein.

Several studies by a French team have found that the oral administration of one such drug, propranolol (brand name, Inderal), reduces the risk of recurrent bleeding in patients with cirrhosis. However, a more recent study, conducted in Britain with patients having cirrhosis from a variety of causes (many of them more severely affected than the patients studied by the French researchers), did not find any significant reduction in the frequency of bleeding, although the patients did have a drop in blood pressure. Clearly, additional work is needed to confirm that propranolol is effective, and under what specific conditions. Other drug therapies for esophageal bleeding, including the hormone somatostatin, are also being investigated as alternatives to surgical treatment.

Encouraging results in treating esophageal bleeding continue to be reported for the technique of sclerotherapy. In this procedure, a flexible fiberoptic tube called an endoscope is passed through the mouth into the esophagus, enabling the physician to see the enlarged veins. Then, using a long, flexible needle, the doctor injects the veins with a solution that causes blood clots to form, thus preventing or stopping further bleeding. Specialists using this technique report considerable success in stopping bleeding from esophageal varices and in reducing complications from the procedure. Sclerotherapy appears to reduce death from bleeding in some studies, although not the overall death rate from liver failure.

Patients with cirrhosis are also at increased risk of dying from pneumococcal pneumonia (a form of pneumonia caused by the pneumococcus bacterium). A 1984 study, however, demonstrated that persons with alcoholic cirrhosis (the majority of cirrhosis patients) can develop immunity to the bacterium if they receive the pneumococcal vaccine. Therefore, it may soon be recommended that patients with cirrhosis receive this vaccination to protect them from yet another of the disease's complications.

Progress Toward Preventing Hepatitis

Hopes were raised in 1984 that scientists using the techniques of genetic engineering will produce a cheap, safe, and effective vaccine against hepatitis B (serum hepatitis) in the not too distant future. Work also proceeded toward increased understanding of the other forms of hepatitis.

Hepatitis B vaccines. Hepatitis is, literally, an inflammation of the liver. In its hepatitis B form it is a global problem; besides the primary disease the hepatitis B virus can cause chronic liver disease, cirrhosis, and liver cancer. The estimated 200 million people who carry the virus that causes hepatitis B but who may or may not show symptoms of it vastly complicate the public health problem. There is no known treatment for the infection, leaving prevention as the only practical control strategy.

Although a vaccine (called Heptavax-B) against hepatitis B has been on the market for the past few years, developments in 1984 cast doubt that it was the hoped-for breakthrough in preventing the disease. The series of three injections is expensive, costing about $100. Furthermore, because it is made from donated human blood, there is an unfounded but nevertheless widespread fear that vaccination could bring exposure to organisms that cause other diseases, such as AIDS (acquired immune deficiency syndrome). Thus, some people have been reluctant to receive the vaccine. In addition, reports from two hepatitis vaccination programs raised questions about the vaccine's effectiveness. Researchers in Boston reported that 4 percent of vaccinated health care workers failed to produce antibodies (substances that fight diseases) against the hepatitis B virus after they were vaccinated and therefore had to be revaccinated. Results of a study of vaccinated kidney dialysis patients (another high-risk group) were also disappointing.

Thus, the report in mid-1984 by a team of workers from the Merck Institute for Therapeutic Research that an experimental synthetic vaccine against hepatitis B had been developed and was being tested in humans (healthy adults at low risk for contracting the disease) was especially welcome. The scientists had used gene-splicing techniques to modify the genetic makeup of a strain of yeast, creating yeast that produced a substance that caused people to produce antibodies against the hepatitis B virus. If the yeast-derived vaccine proves effective, it is likely that it can be produced inexpensively and without risk of contamination. Other research teams are following different approaches to creating a synthetic vaccine, so it seems only a matter of time until a practical means of preventing hepatitis B and its devastating complications is at hand.

Understanding other forms of hepatitis. Hepatitis occurs in other forms as well, including hepatitis A (infectious hepatitis), characterized by a very low mortality rate, complete recovery, and lifelong immunity to further infection; non-A, non-B hepatitis, the form thought to be involved in most cases of hepatitis from blood transfusions; and delta hepatitis, apparently responsible for flare-ups of hepatitis B in carriers of the hepatitis B virus who previously appeared to be healthy. It is now known that the delta virus, discovered in 1977, cannot act alone; rather, it requires the "helper" effect of the hepatitis B virus to cause infection. It has also recently been shown that infection with the delta virus can make cases of hepatitis B more severe. The first U.S. outbreak of severe hepatitis B in which the delta agent was clearly shown to have contributed to the severity of the disease began in Worcester, Mass., in 1983 and continued into 1984; some deaths were reported. Little is known about how delta hepatitis spreads or what its long-term effects are.

There was some progress toward understanding the non-A, non-B form of hepatitis when two separate groups of researchers claimed in 1984 to have discovered a non-A, non-B virus. It was not yet known whether the two teams had found the same virus or two different ones.

Shortages and Cost in Liver Transplants

Thanks to a difficult but well-established surgical technique and increasing experience in using drugs to prevent the body from rejecting a transplanted organ, patients receiving liver transplants (usually for terminal liver disease) have a steadily improving outlook for recovery. Two major problems remain. First, there is a severe shortage of donor livers, partly as a result of hard-to-meet requirements: a liver suitable for transplant must come from a healthy donor and must be implanted only hours after the donor's death. At present, public education programs, such as the Liver Donor Awareness Campaign sponsored by the American Liver Foundation, are the focus of efforts to increase the supply of donor livers. The second problem encompasses issues of cost and selection of patients. These may be even more difficult to resolve than the shortage of livers when a transplant that can cost over $200,000 is viewed in a setting of finite health care resources.

See also the feature article NEW SUCCESSES IN TRANSPLANTS.   DAVID B. FALKENSTEIN, M.D.

Lungs

See RESPIRATORY SYSTEM.

Medical Technology

Doctors and engineers working together have produced the first artificial inner ear to win U.S. government approval for marketing and provided the second and third recipients of a permanent artificial heart with a power unit more mobile than their predecessor's. While a team of doctors reported treating two burn victims with large amounts of laboratory-grown skin, other researchers explored ways of using beams of charged atoms, space satellite imaging techniques, and audible sound in medical diagnosis or treatment.

Artificial Inner Ear Brings Sound to the Deaf

Piercing the barrier of silence that separates the deaf from the world of sounds has proved a formidable task, but several teams of scientists report that they are making progress. A notable step forward came in November 1984 when the U.S. Food and Drug Administration approved for marketing an "electronic inner ear" for adults. More sophisticated models are already being tested in patients. The devices, named cochlear implants for the snail-shaped organ (the cochlea) of the inner ear where they do their work, are designed for those whose deafness is caused by damage to, or a lack of, the tiny hair cells within the cochlea. (As many as 200,000 Americans may suffer from severe deafness of this kind.) These cells convert sound waves to electrical impulses, which are then sent to the brain.

Although the implants are still a long way from enabling deaf people to understand individual spoken words, they can convey changes in inflection, rhythm, and volume, thereby significantly enhancing the understanding achieved through lipreading. And they make audible such sounds as car horns and sirens—safety factors that a hearing person takes for granted.

Instead of amplifying sound and delivering it to the outer ear as a traditional hearing aid does, the new devices mimic the action of the hair cells by picking up sound from a small microphone worn on clothing or eyeglasses, processing the resulting signal through a battery-powered device that may be carried in a pocket or on a belt, and then transmitting it from a coil behind the ear to a miniature receiver implanted under the skin. The transmitted signal is then converted to electrical impulses, which are conveyed by a short wire, or electrode, to the cochlea, where they stimulate the endings of the auditory nerve. From there, the impulses move to the brain, where they are perceived as sound.

The model now available commercially, developed by the House Ear Institute in Los Angeles and the 3M Company of St. Paul, Minn., uses a single electrode inserted just a few millimeters into the inner ear to stimulate the nerve, while other models being developed employ several electrodes, which tend to be longer. Some researchers feel that the increased number of electrodes, as well as improvements in processing the signal, should eventually enable the device to receive and transmit natural sound with greater clarity, thus improving the ability of a person with an implant to discriminate between words. But the effectiveness and long-term safety of the more sophisticated devices are still being explored.

New Artificial Heart Recipients

In November 1984 a mechanical heart slightly larger than a natural heart and weighing three-quarters of a pound was implanted in the chest of William J. Schroeder, a 52-year-old retired federal government worker from Jasper, Ind. It was the second time a permanent artificial heart has been placed in a human patient. Dr. William C. DeVries, the surgeon who had implanted the first device in 1982 in Dr. Barney Clark (who survived for almost four months), headed the team that replaced Schroeder's diseased heart.

DeVries carried out a third implant in February 1985. This time the recipient was Murray P. Haydon, a 58-year-old Louisville, Ky., resident and retired factory worker. Haydon's operation was considerably briefer than Clark's and Schroeder's.

Like Clark, Schroeder and Haydon received a "Jarvik-7" air-driven plastic and aluminum pump, connected by hoses, via two incisions in the abdomen, to a power unit. A major advantage in their case was the availability of a new 12-pound portable battery-powered air compressor unit, allowing, for limited periods, relative freedom of movement. The size of a camera bag, it can be worn over the shoulder and used for up to three hours to keep the mechanical heart functioning. When not using the power pack, the artificial heart recipient has to be tethered to a cumbersome 323-pound refrigerator-sized air compressor, sharply limiting mobility. Several groups of researchers are working to develop an artificial heart featuring a miniaturized drive system installed permanently inside the chest that would be linked to a portable battery pack worn around the waist. But such a model is probably still years away from being tried in humans.

The Jarvik-7 mechanical heart consists of two hollow chambers, each with a flexible diaphragm. As air is received from the external power unit, the diaphragms alternately swell and collapse, thus pumping blood through the body's circulatory system. Clark's artificial heart had two-piece valves, which proved faulty. The later devices had stronger, one-piece valves made of titanium. The next model, the Jarvik-8, is expected to be available in more than one size, including a version for persons with small body frames.

DeVries performed his pioneering first implant at the University of Utah Medical Center in Salt Lake City. But in the summer of 1984 he moved his program to the Humana Heart Institute (located within the Humana Hospital Audubon) in Louisville, after the corporation backing the private, for-profit institution pledged to underwrite 100 of the implant procedures, which may cost from $100,000 to $250,000 apiece.

See also HEART AND CIRCULATORY SYSTEM.

Massive Burns Healed With "Test Tube" Skin

An estimated 15,000 persons in the United States are severely burned each year. A chief goal in the treatment of such burns is to get the wound closed fast—before infection sets in and vital body fluids are lost. Cadaver skin, pigskin, and "artificial skin" made of collagen (a fibrous protein found in natural skin) and a carbohydrate substance have been used as temporary coverings, but for long-lasting closure, the best sealant

is a strip of the patient's own skin, taken from an unscathed area of the body. When massive burns leave healthy skin in short supply, surgeons may be forced to harvest strips over and over again from the same spots on the body, waiting each time for the few weeks it takes to regrow new cells. Sometimes there simply is not enough healthy skin to go around.

A group of Boston doctors reported in August 1984 that an experimental technique involving growing small patches of the burn victim's skin into larger sheets in the laboratory had successfully met a tough real-world challenge. For each of two young brothers (one five years old, the other six) who had been badly burned over 95 percent of their bodies, enough grafts of this laboratory-grown skin tissue were provided to cover about half of the burned area. (Other sections healed naturally or received grafts from already healed areas.) The laboratory-grown skin generally "took" well. "The smooth supple skin generated on the face and hands," said the doctors, "was particularly impressive." The technique had been previously used on some patients with much smaller burns.

The laboratory-grown skin grafts are made primarily of epithelial cells, the chief components in the top layer of normal skin. To produce the new covering, a piece of the patient's top skin layer the size of a postage stamp is minced and chemically treated to break it up into individual cells, which are mixed with enzymes, nutrients, and fibroblasts, cells from the deeper layer of skin that seem to provide important growth factors for the epithelial cells. The separated cells are then allowed to multiply and grow into continuous sheets in laboratory dishes. Within several weeks, enough of the material can be grown to cover a child's entire body. Because the grafts are derived from the patient's own cells, the risk that the body will reject them as foreign tissue is eliminated.

It is too soon to tell how effective the laboratory-grown skin will be in the long run. The fact that it consists of only the outer layer of skin, for example, may in time pose a problem. The inner layer (which may possibly, however, eventually develop beneath the new covering) is thought to be important in lending durability and elasticity to healthy, normal skin.

See also the Spotlight on Health article TREATING BURN VICTIMS.

Brain Surgery With Ion Beams

Beams of high-speed ions (electrically charged atoms) that penetrate the brain without destroying healthy tissue are being studied as a possible supplement to surgery in treating fragile, tangled blood vessels that can cause paralysis, coma, and even death if they burst. The technique, now being tested at several centers in the United States and Europe, is still experimental, but

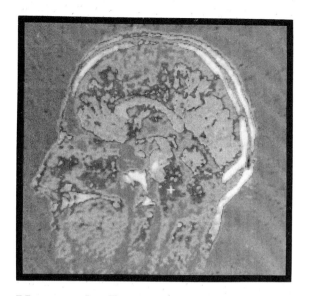

Magnetic Resonance Imaging Sharpens Its Focus

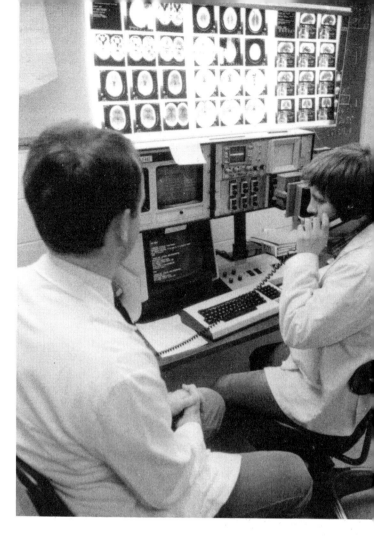

Above, the human head as seen by the scanning technique called MRI. Doctors at right review a series of such scans, which can help diagnose a tumor by revealing its difference from normal tissues. Computer programs originally developed for enhancing information sent back from space by satellites are being adapted to make MRI pictures clearer; the improvement may make it possible to distinguish between benign and malignant tumors without a surgical biopsy.

seems promising as a way of preventing bouts of bleeding in patients in whom these tangled clusters of dilated blood vessels, called arteriovenous malformations (AVM's), are too deep within vital portions of the brain to be removed safely by surgery.

Scientists at the Lawrence Berkeley Laboratory in California who have been working with the technique have been using helium ions. The ions are pushed to a high speed by the laboratory's synchrocyclotron particle accelerator, and the resulting beams are focused on a tiny area in the patient's head. While X rays lose energy as they pass through tissue to reach a target in the body, the ion beams deposit nearly all of their power at the target AVM, whose precise site has been pinpointed by computer-aided imaging. Researchers at Massachusetts General Hospital in Boston have been using high-speed protons in a similar manner. (The protons are positively charged ions of ordinary hydrogen.) In both versions of the procedure, the beams are thought to slightly damage cells lining the abnormal vessels—just enough to trigger a scarring that thickens the vessel walls over a matter of months, rendering them more resistant to rupture.

Such ion beams have also been used in recent years to destroy tumors buried within the pituitary gland, pancreas, esophagus, eyes, spinal cord, and kidneys and to relieve severe pain from cancer by destroying parts of brain cells involved in pain sensation.

Satellite Imaging Improves Body Mapping

The same computer technology that helps a satellite to "see" the difference between the contours of a timber stand and a rich deposit of minerals, and then relay the message in the form of a clear and colorful image, may be used to improve the pictures of the human body constructed through the technique of magnetic resonance imaging, or MRI (also known as nuclear magnetic resonance scanning).

In the last several years MRI has undergone remarkably rapid refinement as a diagnostic tool that complements—and may, in certain diseases, eventually supplant—such well-established methods of seeing "into" the body as traditional X-ray studies and CT (computerized tomography) scanning. MRI tends to be better than X rays at visualizing soft tissues, as well as organs concealed by bones.

The effectiveness of MRI arises from the fact that the water content—and hence the hydrogen content, since hydrogen is a major component of water—of each type of tissue differs. In MRI the patient being scanned is

301

placed within the cylindrical opening of the MRI scanner and exposed to a high-power magnet. All the nuclei of the hydrogen atoms within the portion of the body being scanned align themselves with the magnetic field, much as iron filings line up on a sheet of paper held over a dime store magnet. Low-energy radio waves are then applied. These are absorbed by the hydrogen nuclei, which are thereby knocked out of alignment. When the radio waves are turned off, the nuclei "relax," releasing tiny amounts of energy that are converted by computer into an image based on the intensity of the signal produced by each type of tissue. For example, fat emits a stronger signal and appears somewhat brighter than muscle, and much brighter than bone. The time used by each nucleus to realign itself also shapes the signal. (Some researchers are also constructing magnetic resonance images from signals emitted by elements other than hydrogen in body tissues— phosphorus and sodium, for example. Such scans are expected to add significantly to MRI's usefulness in studying the functioning of the body.)

But, while this new technology provides a wealth of information about the structure and chemistry of body tissues without exposing the patient to the potentially hazardous radiation of X rays, at its present state of development the resulting images can be somewhat fuzzy or difficult to interpret.

Enter the computers from the U.S. National Aeronautics and Space Administration's Landsat program (run since mid-1984 by the National Oceanic and Atmospheric Administration), whose satellites have circled the globe since the 1970's, sending back information about the earth's surface. The same computers that highlight the contrasts between water and soil can also pick up the distinct biochemical "signature" of a tumor that is different from the surrounding tissue. By assigning a different color to each signature, the computer can produce images that look almost like freshly cut slices of the human body.

Dr. Michael Vannier, a radiologist at Washington University in St. Louis and a former NASA engineer, collaborated with the space agency in one of the projects that is bringing space technology to medicine. The most obvious use for the color-coded tissue maps, Vannier says, is in helping radiologists see the precise outline of a particular organ or collection of tissues and in facilitating earlier diagnosis of disease than is now possible. For example, if the computer can search a brain scan for blood's signature, it can rapidly show the exact limits of a blood clot, information not accurately available from an MRI scan not enhanced by signature coding. Vannier believes the technique will eventually permit the physician to determine whether or not a tumor is malignant without having to perform a surgical biopsy.

Vannier has worked with NASA to adapt the Landsat color-coding computer program to the computer used in commercial MRI systems that are appearing in increasing numbers in hospitals and radiology clinics throughout the United States. (Although such systems have been used on an experimental basis for several years, not until relatively recently has the Food and Drug Administration authorized their marketing for general clinical use; two manufacturers' scanners were approved in March 1984, and by early 1985 the number of approvals had reached five.) Only when this adaptation is accomplished, he says, will it be possible to fully explore the practical value of the marriage between MRI and satellite imaging.

"Sounding" Joints for Healthy Function

With the help of an experimental device called an acoustic arthromodulograph, researchers at the University of Minnesota are using audible sound waves beamed along bones to check for malfunctions in joints. Their first tests of the device in humans were with patients suffering from pain in the hinge of the jaw (the temporomandibular joint), which is involved in many dental problems.

To check this joint, the operator places a buzzer over the cheekbone and turns on the sound, producing a clear tone. Since the sound is audible, its frequency is much lower than that used in ultrasound scans. Most of the sound waves cross the joint to the jawbone, where they are picked up through the skin with a receiving microphone. The sound received as the jaw opens and closes has the same frequency as the original sound. The bone and tissues through which the sound-wave signal passes, however, cause variations in its shape and other characteristics, providing an "acoustic profile." The receiver converts this modulated sound-wave signal to electrical impulses that can be used to graph the pattern of the joint's functioning as a series of peaks and valleys.

Side effects are considered unlikely. People who listen to a radio through earphones or attend a symphony or rock concert administer much more sound to their bones than the acoustic arthromodulograph transmits.

Potential uses of the device include diagnosing hip problems in the elderly, monitoring the fit of artificial hip joints, and checking for arthritic deposits in various joints throughout the body. The sound waves may also help scientists improve their knowledge of how healthy joints withstand the stress of everyday wear and tear. If early successes achieved in animal and human tests are a sign of things to come, the acoustic arthromodulograph could prove to be an inexpensive and useful alternative to the X-ray studies, CT scans, fiberoptic instruments, and exploratory surgery currently used to detect and evaluate joint defects.

DEBORAH FRANKLIN

Medications and Drugs

Several recently introduced drugs, the first of their kind to become available, offer new ways to manage heart failure and circulatory problems. Among other new products recently approved for use by the U.S. Food and Drug Administration (FDA), the Health Protection Branch of Health and Welfare Canada, or both, are drugs for treating diabetes and infections, as well as a new type of birth control pill.

Drugs for Cardiovascular Problems

Intermittent claudication is a condition in which people suffer severe leg pain while walking. This occurs when a person's arterial capillaries—among the circulatory system's tiniest vessels—cannot deliver enough oxygenated blood to meet the needs of the exercising muscles. A drug is now widely available to treat this problem. The medication, pentoxifylline, is the first of a new class of drugs that improve the blood's ability to flow through the capillaries. It went on the market in the United States (under the brand name Trental) a year after it became available in Canada and several years after its introduction in Europe.

Pentoxifylline makes the blood less sticky and helps to soften the red blood cell membranes. This makes it easier for the more flexible red cells to bend, twist, and squeeze their way through the narrow arterial capillaries that carry oxygen and nutrients to muscle cells. Larger amounts of oxygen reach the muscles, relieving muscle aches, cramps, and fatigue and enabling individuals with intermittent claudication to walk longer distances without discomfort. People treated with pentoxifylline have suffered few side effects. Digestive discomfort, the most common complaint, can be minimized by taking the medication with meals. Although this is a relatively safe drug, it is chemically related to caffeine and similar stimulants, and there have been occasional cases of angina, low blood pressure, and heart rhythm irregularities when claudication patients who also had diseased heart and brain blood vessels were given pentoxifylline.

Amrinone (brand name, Inocor), the first of a new class of drugs for treating congestive heart failure, was introduced in both the United States and Canada. When injected intravenously, the drug increases the strength with which the disease-weakened heart muscle contracts. In patients who had failed to improve when treated with standard heart stimulants like digoxin, amrinone has increased the amount of blood being supplied to body tissues.

Injections of amrinone act promptly to relieve shortness of breath caused by the buildup of fluid in the lungs—a common complication in heart failure patients. The drug does this by acting upon both the heart and the blood vessels. It reduces congestion in the veins of the lungs by helping the heart to pump more blood, and it dilates (widens) blood vessels, making it easier for the heart to pump the blood.

One of the adverse effects of injected amrinone is a reduction in the number of circulating blood platelets (small blood particles that play an essential role in blood clotting), which can lead to episodes of bleeding. However, laboratory tests can readily detect any drop in platelets before the number falls far enough for a hemorrhage to occur. If blood tests do show a decrease in the number of platelets, doctors can reduce the patient's dosage of amrinone or stop treatment. The patient's heart rate, heart rhythm, and blood pressure should be checked frequently for abnormalities that may require the discontinuation of treatment.

Labetalol, a drug for treating high blood pressure, became available in 1984 in the United States (as Normodyne and Trandate), a year after its introduction in Canada. The drug has a currently unique dual action. It functions as a so-called beta blocker in that it blocks nerve impulses that stimulate the heart, and it also acts as an alpha blocker, blocking nerve impulses that narrow the blood vessels. The combined actions of the drug result in a rapid drop in blood pressure. When injected intravenously during an emergency situation, the drug begins to reduce dangerously high pressure levels within minutes. Taken orally, it lowers pressure in an hour or two, much more rapidly than beta blockers can.

Like pure beta blockers such as propranolol (Inderal), labetalol must be used with caution, if at all, by patients with bronchial asthma, chronic bronchitis, and emphysema because it may set off bronchial spasm. However, the drug is less likely to cause excessive slowing of the heartbeat and reduction in the pumping power of the heart than are ordinary beta blockers. Some people have been forced to discontinue labetalol therapy because of side effects that include dizziness and weakness when patients stand up as well as male sexual dysfunction.

Tocainide (Tonocard) is chemically similar to lidocaine, the drug most commonly used to control heart rhythm irregularities in hospitalized heart attack patients under intensive care. Unlike lidocaine, which must be injected, tocainide can be taken orally. Thus, it was recently approved for long-term use by patients with persistent heart rhythm irregularities arising in the heart's ventricles, or main pumping chambers. Most patients tolerate tocainide quite well once its dosage has been individually adjusted. However, adverse effects develop in about one out of every five patients and can be severe enough to require discontinuing treatment. The most common side effects are lightheadedness, dizziness, tremors, and nausea.

A rare but more serious adverse effect of tocainide is a decrease in the number of infection-fighting white blood cells. If blood tests taken during the first weeks of therapy reveal a significant drop in white cells, the drug may have to be discontinued. Patients are told to watch for signs of infection such as sore throat, chills, and fever. They should promptly report these to their doctor, as well as any persistent cough, wheezing, and shortness of breath, which could be signs of lung damage occasionally caused by tocainide. The drug must be discontinued if chest X rays show lung changes.

The drug clonidine, which reduces high blood pressure, is now available in a new form—a patch that is applied to the skin. Each clonidine-containing patch of this so-called transdermal therapeutic system, called Catapres-TTS, delivers enough of the drug to keep a patient's blood pressure under continuous control for seven days. Patients who use the patches have had few side effects. Itching and skin redness do sometimes occur at the site of application; if discomfort persists and blisters develop, the patch may have to be removed. If this proves necessary, the patient should be switched to the standard oral form of clonidine since discontinuing clonidine therapy abruptly can lead to a rebound rise in blood pressure.

Cholestyramine (Questran), an agent that lowers blood cholesterol, was used in a ten-year study of cholesterol and the risks of developing coronary heart disease sponsored by the U.S. National Heart, Lung, and Blood Institute. Results of the study, reported in 1984, showed that a group of men who took the drug daily, in addition to eating a low-cholesterol diet, had a greater decrease in blood cholesterol levels than a similar group that followed the diet but did not take the drug. Those using cholestyramine regularly also suffered fewer heart attacks, and their death rate from coronary artery disease was lower than that of the men who only followed the low-fat diet.

Tools To Fight Infections

A new antibacterial combination containing the antibiotic amoxicillin and the compound potassium clavulanate, a drug that keeps the antibiotic from being inactivated by bacterial enzymes, is now marketed as Augmentin in the United States and as Clavulin in Canada. The manufacturer claims that the product is able to eliminate more strains of resistant bacteria than other oral drugs of the beta-lactam class of antibiotics (drugs of the penicillin and cephalosporin families). By inhibiting the so-called beta-lactamase enzymes of the amoxicillin-resistant bacteria, the clavulanate component protects the antibiotic from being broken down. The bacteria then become susceptible to the antibacterial action of amoxicillin.

The new combination is effective for treating upper and lower respiratory infections, including sinusitis caused by strains of bacteria resistant to amoxicillin alone, such as strains of *Hemophilus influenzae*, as well as acute bronchitis and bronchopneumonia caused by more common organisms. Skin infections caused by many resistant strains of the bacterium *Staphylococcus aureus* have also been cured by this mixture of amoxicillin and clavulanate, as have amoxicillin-resistant strains of *Escherichia coli*, the cause of many urinary tract infections.

Two other new antibiotics resistant to beta-lactamase enzymes, cefonicid sodium (Monocid) and ceforanide (Precef), became available for injection in serious infections. Both are second-generation cephalosporins—members of a subclass with higher antibacterial action than the first generation drugs of this family against such bacteria as *Hemophilus influenzae* and *Escherichia coli*. Neither of these new cephalosporins is quite as active as the first-generation group against bacteria such as *Staphylococcus aureus*. Nor do they strike down as many strains of bacteria as do drugs of the third generation of cephalosporins now available. Still, cefonicid sodium and ceforanide are adequately effective for treating a wide variety of bacterial infections, and they have certain special properties that make them the preferred medicines for treating some types of infections. For instance, they rapidly reach their peak levels in the blood and in the fluids bathing infected tissues, and they also stay at effective antibacterial levels for long periods of time. In fact, cefonicid has the longest-lasting action of all cephalosporins, and it is the first drug of this family to require only one daily dose. Ceforanide need be injected only once every 12 hours—less often than other previously available second-generation cephalosporins.

Because of their long-lasting action, both of these drugs are considered especially effective for preventing infections following surgery. The drugs are injected about an hour before the operation to provide effective antibacterial activity during and after procedures in which bacterial contamination commonly occurs—bowel surgery, for instance. In some situations in which infections could be especially serious—like open-heart surgery or procedures for replacing a knee or hip—these cephalosporins are administered as a preventive measure both before and after the operation is performed.

A drug to treat a serious lung disease that is often fatal to people with AIDS (acquired immune deficiency syndrome) was recently approved for use in the United States. The drug—pentamidine isethionate (Pentam 300)—was previously used abroad for treating certain tropical infections. In the United States, it will be given to treat lung infections caused by the parasite *Pneumocystis carinii*, which rarely causes pneumonia in the general population but commonly causes fatal infections in people with impaired immune defenses. In addition to AIDS patients, this includes people with leukemia or Hodgkin's disease and patients being given prolonged treatment with corticosteroids, anticancer agents, or other drugs that suppress the immune system.

Pentamidine has reportedly helped save the lives of a high proportion of patients lacking immune defenses who are suffering from pneumocystic lung infections. However, the drug causes adverse reactions in half of those who receive it, and some of the reactions, such as a sudden drop in blood pressure, can be life-threatening. Patients getting an intravenous infusion of pentamidine therefore must have their pressure monitored while the drug is being dripped slowly into a vein. Kidney and liver damage and a decrease in the number of blood platelets have also resulted.

In January 1985, the first oral drug for the treatment of genital herpes was approved by the FDA. The drug, acyclovir (brand name, Zovirax), had previously been available as an intravenous solution and as an ointment for the treatment of initial herpes infections. The new capsule form is intended for treating the initial infection and also for recurrent infections. Although acyclovir is not a cure for herpes, it does relieve herpes symptoms (such as blister-like sores, pain, and itching) and significantly reduces virus shedding, or the release of the virus by cells, which means that the period in which the infection is contagious is shorter.

New Diabetes Drugs

The FDA recently approved two oral drugs for lowering blood sugar in Type II diabetes (the type that generally does not require insulin). One of the drugs, glyburide, which has been available in Canada as Euglucon, is now marketed in the United States as DiaBeta and as Micronase. The other medication is glipizide (Glucotrol), currently not available in Canada. Both of these drugs, which have been widely used abroad for many years, are said to offer some advantages over the four first-generation drugs of this class. Glyburide and glipizide are much more potent than the earlier drugs and are effective when taken in much smaller doses. They lower the glucose (sugar) level quite rapidly and produce longer-lasting control of blood sugar levels. Glipizide is taken half an hour before breakfast; it is quickly and completely absorbed and reaches peak levels in one to three hours. Glyburide, which is taken with the day's first meal, begins to act somewhat more slowly. Since the effects of both drugs last about 24 hours, they need be taken only once a day.

Both of these new second-generation drugs are said to be safer than other drugs of this class for diabetes patients with poor kidney function. However, caution is still required in patients with impaired liver or kidney function, since these conditions can cause drugs to accumulate in the body and may cause hypoglycemia (low blood sugar).

These second-generation drugs are also claimed to have advantages over the widely used older diabetes drug chlorpropamide (Diabinese). Unlike chlorpropamide, neither glyburide nor glipizide causes water retention. Both tend instead to produce a mild diuretic, or fluid-eliminating, effect. In addition, people taking the newer drugs do not suffer adverse effects such as flushing when drinking alcoholic beverages.

New Oral Contraceptives

A new type of birth control pill, the triphasic oral contraceptive, made its first appearance in products called Ortho-Novum 7/7/7, Tri-Norinyl, and Triphasil. Like

A worker inspects tablets of glyburide (brand names, DiaBeta and Micronase), a recently approved medication for diabetes that is more potent than earlier drugs of its class and also causes fewer side effects.

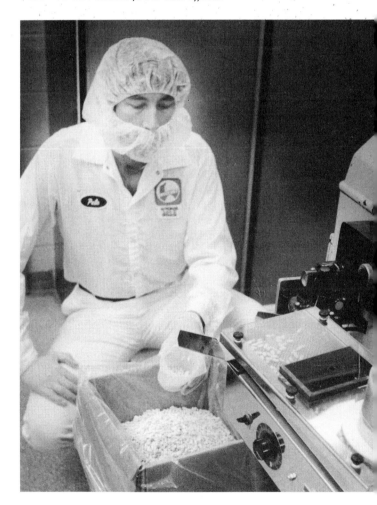

earlier forms of the pill, these oral contraceptives contain two types of synthetic sex hormones, estrogens and progestins. However, they differ from previous formulas by containing three different dose levels of progestins in the 21 tablets scheduled to be taken each month. The progestin content of the tablets varies in accordance with the times during the 21-day dosage cycle when women are directed to take them.

The purpose of the three adjustments in progestin dosage is to mimic the changing blood levels of the natural hormone progesterone that occur in the course of a normal menstrual cycle. This, in turn, helps to prevent bleeding between menstrual periods. Women have often discontinued use of previously introduced birth control pills—the constant dose (uniphasic) or the biphasic oral contraceptives—because of such bleeding.

The three currently available triphasic birth control pills are highly effective in preventing pregnancy. It is hoped that their very low total content of estrogens and progestins will also help to reduce the risk of serious side effects that sometimes occur with higher dose pills. However, such an increase in safety has not yet been proven.

Drugs Used in Anesthesiology

A number of drugs were recently introduced for use in surgery and anesthesia. One, sufentanil (Sufenta), is a powerful new opium-like pain reliever, hundreds of times more potent than morphine and most other narcotic painkillers. The drug is not used routinely for relief of pain in medical situations but was approved for use in anesthesiology in two major ways. First, small doses may be injected into a vein and supplemented by other drugs to produce balanced anesthesia (anesthesia that uses a combination of drugs), a procedure that prepares patients for abdominal, gynecologic, or orthopedic surgery. And high doses of the drug can be given alone to produce deep, prolonged, general anesthesia during open-heart surgery and other types of cardiovascular operations, as well as in certain neurosurgical procedures. ·

An advantage claimed for sufentanil is that patients' blood pressure and heart rates do not rise but tend to stay stable. Respiration is deeply depressed, but patients can be kept fully supplied with oxygen by a respirator. At the end of long operations performed under sufentanil anesthesia, any continued respiratory depression can be counteracted by repeated injections of the drug naloxone (Narcan), without interfering with sufentanil's prolonged postoperative painkilling effects. Like the less potent related painkiller fentanyl, sufentanil tends to make chest wall muscles rigid. However, this can be counteracted by giving the patient a skeletal muscle relaxant.

Atracurium (Tracrium) and vercuronium (Norcuron),

two new skeletal muscle relaxants, were recently introduced for use during anesthesia and surgery. They are said to be suitable for use with all kinds of anesthetics and in most surgical procedures that require a good deal of muscular relaxation. They are also often used when the anesthesiologist wants to relax the patient's jaw muscles in order to insert a breathing tube into the trachea (windpipe). Both of these new drugs are said to have various advantages over standard drugs used to block transmission of nerve impulses to skeletal muscles. When injected into a vein, they do not cause the patient's blood pressure to drop, as sometimes occurs with the standard muscle-paralyzing drug tubocurarine. Nor do the new drugs cause the patient's heart rate to race, as do such other muscle relaxants as pancuronium and gallamine.

In addition, unlike all other relaxant drugs of their type, the new agents do not rely on the kidneys for their elimination from the body. Thus, these drugs are safer for patients suffering from kidney failure, as the drugs do not accumulate in the body and delay the patient's recovery from muscle paralysis. In fact, patients receiving these drugs ordinarily recover muscle function in about one-third the time required with most other relaxants. However, neither of the new medications has as short an action as the older drug succinylcholine, which is still the preferred relaxant for short procedures that require only brief periods of muscle relaxation.

Drugs for Rare Disorders

Pimozide (Orap), a drug previously available in Canada, has been approved for U.S. use in treating those over 12 years of age who have Tourette's syndrome, a rare neurologic disorder marked by involuntary muscular contractions and, sometimes, disruptive behavior. The drug is to be used only in the minority of patients who have first failed to respond to haloperidol (Haldol), the standard drug for this condition. Pimozide is a so-called orphan drug, one which the FDA puts on a "fast track" approval procedure under terms of the 1983 Orphan Drug Act; the measure permits hastened testing, among other incentives, to encourage pharmaceutical companies to develop drugs useful only to small numbers of patients.

Pimozide suppresses both motor and vocal symptoms of Tourette's syndrome, including the involuntary shouting of obscenities that often makes it difficult for victims to function in a normal social environment. Although the drug does not cure the underlying neurochemical defect that causes the condition, it relieves the symptoms and helps patients take part in the normal activities of daily life.

Patients and their families should be informed about the potentially serious side effects of pimozide. These include symptoms similar to those of Parkinson's disease (stiffness, tremors, and difficulty in movement), which can be controlled with medication or by reducing the drug's dosage. A more serious drug reaction is tardive dyskinesia, a condition marked by irreversible, bizarre, involuntary movements.

Desmopressin, a drug previously available in nasal inhalant form for treating diabetes insipidus (a disease in which the body loses large amounts of water because of a hormone deficiency), became available as a sterile solution for intravenous infusion. Now marketed as Stimate, this drug, when injected, stimulates the body to produce certain blood clotting factors and can help control bleeding episodes in patients with certain types of hemophilia. The advantage for these patients is that they are not exposed to the risk of hepatitis, which can occur when they receive substances to aid blood clotting that are prepared from donated blood.

When infused intravenously, desmopressin stimulates a rise in the clotting factors to peak levels in 15 to 30 minutes. This helps to stop bleeding promptly during and after minor surgical procedures, and it controls hemorrhages that occur spontaneously or as a result of injuries. There are occasionally temporary side effects such as facial flushing and headaches. However, since desmopressin can cause water retention and raise blood pressure, caution is required when dealing with infants, the elderly, and patients with hypertension or coronary artery disease.

Over-the-Counter Painkiller

Ibuprofen, an anti-inflammatory painkiller that has been available only in prescription form for ten years (under the brand names Motrin and Rufen), is now sold in lower dosages in the United States in nonprescription form. It is the first over-the-counter painkiller introduced in the United States in 30 years. (As of early 1985, ibuprofen was still sold only as a prescription drug in Canada.) Like aspirin, ibuprofen—available over-the-counter as Advil and Nuprin—effectively relieves pain and reduces inflammation. However, there are possible side effects, and some criticism was voiced over the fact that the warning label does not list all of them. For example, ibuprofen can aggravate high blood pressure and may cause kidney problems in susceptible people, such as the elderly, people with diabetes, and those taking diuretics. In addition, people who are unable to take aspirin should not take ibuprofen. Ibuprofen has had an excellent track record as a prescription drug, but as with any drug, consumers should exercise caution when using it.

Morning Sickness Drug Cleared

In March 1985, a federal court jury held that the drug Bendectin—once widely used to treat morning sickness—did not cause birth defects in children whose mothers took the drug. The trial consolidated some 1,000 suits brought against the drug's manufacturer by parents of children born with defects. The manufacturer had discontinued production of Bendectin in 1983, although it contended that no solid evidence linked the drug with birth defects.

MORTON J. RODMAN, PH.D.

Mental Health

Research on the chemistry and anatomy of the brain is providing psychiatrists with new insights into biological abnormalities associated with mental disorders, as well as a better understanding of the drugs used to treat these illnesses. At the same time, research into the prevalence of mental illness in society and the value of social support for psychiatric patients, and into the effects of disasters on the mental health of those who live through them, is helping to clarify the relation between society and the mental health of the individual.

How Prevalent Is Mental Illness?

During 1984, the first results were published from a study, supported by the U.S. National Institute of Mental Health, to determine how frequently psychiatric disorders occur in the general population. These results, based on surveys in New Haven, Conn., Baltimore, and St. Louis, indicated that perhaps a third of all Americans suffer from a psychiatric illness at some point in their life.

The study, which will involve some 17,000 people, was undertaken as a basis for psychiatric research and policy-making, and also because of wide disagreement among earlier studies. These had yielded estimates of the proportion of the population with a psychiatric disorder ranging from 10 percent to more than 80 percent. Thus, there was a need for a careful determination of the number of people who have specific psychiatric disorders. Information was gathered in household interviews, and diagnoses were determined according to the current edition of the American Psychiatric Association's *Diagnostic and Statistical Manual of Mental Disorders.*

The proportion of people interviewed who reported that they had had a psychiatric illness at some time in their life was found to range, in the three cities, from 29 to 38 percent. The most common disorders were alcohol abuse or dependence (11 to 16 percent), phobias (8 to 23 percent), and depression (6 to 10 percent). From 1 to 2 percent of those interviewed were found to have suffered from schizophrenia at some time in their life. By a margin of approximately five to one, men were more likely than women to exhibit chronic antisocial behavior or alcohol-related problems. On the other hand, women were twice as likely as men to suffer from depression or phobias.

The study also examined the proportion of people who had had a psychiatric disturbance within the preceding six months. These numbers were naturally lower than those for the incidence of mental disorders over a lifetime, but they nevertheless ranged from 15 to 23 percent, with the most common diagnoses being phobias, alcohol abuse or dependence, and depression. Furthermore, the majority of those with a recent disorder had not sought to be treated for it during the six-month period studied. Even among people with severe conditions, such as schizophrenia, only half had received any treatment. In the six months, just 6 to 7 percent of all adults studied had visited a general medical doctor or a mental health specialist because of a mental health problem.

Social Support for Psychiatric Patients

There has been growing recognition that while antipsychotic medications are remarkably effective in controlling some of the disruptions in thinking and perception that characterize schizophrenia, such as delusions and hallucinations, they are less effective for treating what are called negative symptoms, which include difficulty in making decisions and in carrying on the functions of everyday life. Many mental health professionals now believe that such factors as the quality of family support and the patient's own strategy for dealing with symptoms may affect the patient's ability to adjust to the illness. In particular, patients who are able to sit back and observe their own condition, to evaluate how they are doing, and to develop strategies for avoiding a worsening of symptoms seem to handle their illness better. Simple strategies such as avoiding stressful situations or recognizing that the illness is getting worse and seeking support or more medication can sometimes be quite effective. Some patients with schizophrenia do better than others; close to half of them may show significant periods of improvement, during which they function quite well.

A number of approaches have been developed to help the families of patients with chronic mental illness understand the patient's problems better and assist the patient in coping with them. These approaches include teaching the family about the illness, the importance of medication, and the warning signs of a worsening of the condition. Other approaches emphasize ways in which the family can have a positive influence on the patient's behavior. Family members are urged to provide consistent encouragement for improvements in behavior, and to avoid giving way to demoralizing outbursts of anger at the patient's failures. In still other approaches, the stress is on problem-solving and communication

skills—that is, helping the patient and family members learn how to express themselves and listen to each other in ways that improve communication, rather than make them defensive and angry. Although they are not viewed as cures for the illness, such approaches can be helpful in decreasing the need for a patient's return to inpatient hospital care.

In recent years the number of organizations, or networks, composed of families who have members with chronic mental illness has grown. Such groups provide information about services available to the mentally ill, hold meetings for mutual support, produce educational materials, and lobby with local, state, and federal governments. The groups have formed a national organization called the National Alliance for the Mentally Ill, with headquarters at 1200 15th Street, N.W., Suite 400, Washington, D.C. 20005.

Exercise and Mental Illness

There has been growing interest in both normal and pathological uses of regular exercise, such as running, in relation to psychiatric problems. A number of psychiatrists have noted that regular exercise seems to help individuals suffering from milder forms of anxiety and depression, which seem to be made worse by stress. The body's reaction to stress includes physiological changes—such as elevation of the heart rate and blood pressure—to prepare one for physical activity. But the stressful situations routinely encountered in the modern world are more likely to require intellectual activity and dealings with other people than physical action. Regular exercise seems to help discharge the accumulation of physical excitability brought on by stress.

A few people, on the other hand, exercise in a way that worsens their problems. Some patients with anorexia nervosa combine running with their pathological refusal to eat; the exercise accelerates their dangerous weight loss. Individuals suffering from anorexia nervosa, most often young women, usually have a severely distorted view of their own body, seeing themselves as obese even when emaciated. When they become extremely underweight, they are vulnerable to sudden death because of, among other things, infections and imbalances in chemicals in the blood. Therapy for anorexia may include inpatient care and careful monitoring of behavior and encouragement of proper nutrition both in and outside the hospital. Family therapy is often used to try to get at the roots of the problem.

Controlling the Urge to Smoke

Psychological methods such as training in self-hypnosis have been used for some time to help people stop smoking. There has been increasing interest in the use, along with such methods, of chewing gum containing nicotine since the product won approval from the U.S. Food and

Drug Administration in January 1984 (it has been available in Canada for several years). The gum can help people make a gradual reduction in their nicotine intake while they are taught to manage stress and control the urge to smoke. Preliminary evidence indicates that a combination of nicotine chewing gum with psychological techniques may be more effective for helping people stop smoking than psychological techniques alone, although the latter are often sufficient. The nicotine-gum approach is especially helpful for those who experience symptoms such as irritability and an intense craving when they stop smoking.

Psychological Help for Cancer Patients

A number of studies have demonstrated the effectiveness of psychological methods for helping patients cope with cancer and its associated problems. Several studies have demonstrated that group support for cancer patients can be very valuable, helping them to share (and thereby perhaps reduce) fears about the illness, solve problems of communications with doctors and family members, reconstruct social networks (which are often damaged by a serious illness like cancer), and plan the best use of their time while undergoing treatment. Techniques such as self-hypnosis can be effective in reducing pain, as well as the nausea and vomiting that often accompany chemotherapy.

Biology and Psychiatry

Psychiatric researchers continue to explore the association between biochemical abnormalities and mood disturbances such as depression and manic-depressive illness (in which periods of depression alternate with periods of overexcitement). Several of the neurotransmitters—the chemicals that communicate nerve impulses from one nerve cell to the next—have been implicated in these illnesses. For example, a deficiency of the neurotransmitter norepinephrine, which is similar to the stimulant amphetamine, has been associated with depression. Antidepressant drugs appear to increase the availability of norepinephrine by preventing its chemical breakdown or keeping it longer in the synapses (the minuscule gaps between nerve cells across which the neurotransmitters travel, thereby allowing one nerve cell to stimulate another). However, this picture has been complicated by the discovery that drugs that affect the brain's use of other neurotransmitters, such as serotonin, also alleviate depression. Recent studies have suggested that mood is affected not simply by the amount of these chemicals, but rather by the dynamic balance among the different neurotransmitters and the nerve cells which use them to communicate (each nerve cell generally responds to one particular neurotransmitter, and nerve cells responding to a particular transmitter seem to form networks, or "sys-

tems"). Thus, the total rate of production and degradation of a whole series of neurotransmitters may be involved in mood disorders. Changes in one neurotransmitter system produce alterations in others, which may try to compensate for differences brought about either by illness or its treatment. While great strides are being made in understanding the biochemical bases of some mood disorders, the picture is growing increasingly complex as more is learned.

An important study published in 1984 provided preliminary evidence of an inherited biological abnormality in patients with manic-depressive illness. Skin cells taken from such patients were found to have an increased number of receptors (portions of the cell membrane that respond to a particular substance) for a neurotransmitter called acetylcholine, as compared to normal relatives. This study suggests that there may be similar differences on the surfaces of nerve cells in the brains of these patients and thus that this chemical may be involved in their mood swings. The study is important not only because it suggests that there may be an identifiable biological difference in patients with disorders of mood but also because it suggests modification in the biochemical theory of disorders of mood. Previously, the neurotransmitters norepinephrine and serotonin had been the primary ones implicated in depression. It now appears that acetylcholine—found commonly throughout the body, as well as in the brain—also plays a role in regulating emotion. The dry mouth and blurred vision often experienced by patients on antidepressant drugs are the effects of blocking the function of acetylcholine; the blocking action may also be helping to relieve depression.

This study adds to the growing evidence that abnormalities in the ways nerve cells communicate are related to the major mental illnesses. Similarly, abnormalities in the sensitivity of receptors to the brain chemical called dopamine have been implicated in schizophrenia.

A new study using the method called positron emission tomography (PET scanning), which allows assessment of the brain's metabolic activity, confirmed earlier findings that people with schizophrenia show relatively greater activity in the back of the brain than in the front. (An increase in activity in the back of the brain, rather than a decrease in the front, accounted for most of the difference.) Patients with manic-depressive illness showed similar results, and both groups were different from normal people used for comparison. Thus, several techniques are showing some consistent abnormalities among patients with severe psychiatric illness.

New Studies on Alcoholism

Recent research on alcoholism indicates that recovery of mental functions when an alcoholic becomes abstinent can be a slow process, taking years. Such findings may give hope to former alcoholics that even though recovery is slow, improvement may continue. There is also evidence, however, that some difficulties with memory may persist indefinitely.

Other research has indicated that relatives of alcoholics show some differences in brain functioning from relatives of nonalcoholics. Among other differences, the relatives of alcoholics are less likely to show impairment of mental functions than other people when given something to drink. The research suggests that there are genetic differences between the groups, and possibly a genetic vulnerability to alcoholism among the family members of alcoholics, who are known to be at increased risk for alcoholism.

Computers and Psychiatry

There has been a dramatic increase in the use of computers in psychiatric care and research. The recent emphasis has been on developing computer systems for making clinical data more accessible throughout treatment, and, increasingly, psychiatric-interview and psychological-test programs have been developed; patients sit at a computer terminal and use the keyboard to answer questions shown on the screen. The test and interview programs are not meant as substitutes for a person-to-person interview with a trained clinician, but they do provide standardized information that can be used as background by the clinician and in research.

The Effects of Trauma

There is expanding interest in the effects on mental health of traumatic experiences, such as accidents or natural disasters, rape or other physical assaults, combat experience, and physical abuse in childhood. Mental health professionals now recognize a condition known as post-traumatic stress disorder, which includes a preoccupation with the traumatic experience to the extent that it interferes with normal activities, a numbing of responsiveness to or a lack of interest in daily life, a loss of the ability to feel pleasure, avoidance of situations reminiscent of the traumatic event, and the widely publicized "flashback reaction," or a temporary belief that one is reliving the distressing event. Some scientists believe a biological mechanism may account for many of the symptoms of post-traumatic stress disorder. They point to analogies between the helplessness learned by animals that have been subjected to repeated electric shock with no chance of escape and the psychic numbing in survivors of overwhelming trauma. They postulate that chemicals similar to morphine may be secreted in the brain and alter traumatized people's sensitivity to stimuli, making them less receptive to normal stimuli because they have been forced to react to extraordinary ones.

The psychological effects of major catastrophic events have recently been studied systematically—events such as the 1979 Three Mile Island nuclear accident and the atrocities committed in Cambodia in the late 1970's by the Pol Pot regime. Studies have shown that although everyone involved is affected by such events, not every survivor develops a post-traumatic stress disorder. Factors that seem to make some people more vulnerable than others include lack of social support (family and friends), lower educational and income levels, being unemployed, being the mother of preschool or school-age children, and having a previous history of physical or psychiatric illness. In other words, those whose normal lives are relatively unburdened tend to cope better with the sudden effects of a disaster. Only a small minority of victims become psychiatrically disabled as a result of the disaster; most go through only a brief period of anxiety and depression, which is a normal response to the trauma.

There has also been renewed interest in the extent and psychological effects of another type of trauma—the sexual abuse of children. Recent studies in the United States and Canada have indicated that such abuse is unfortunately not uncommon and that up to a third of all girls have had some experience of sexual abuse. Further, studies show that children tend to blame themselves rather than their parents for the abuse. Thus, they suffer especially from parental hostility and blame, even from the nonabusing parent, who not infrequently has some awareness that abuse is occurring.

Other traumatic events in childhood may also have lasting effects. Recently reported studies of the children kidnapped in a school bus in Chowchilla, Calif., in 1976 and buried in a truck underground for several days reveal lasting effects on the victims five years later. The children had persistent nightmares and apparently permanent alterations in the ways they relate to other children. Although repeated trauma is clearly worse than a single incident, either can have lasting and serious effects.

Freud and Child Abuse

Substantial and not always sympathetic interest in Sigmund Freud and the origins of psychoanalysis was revived by several books and magazine articles. They charged that Freud had abandoned his initial belief that neurosis was the result of childhood sexual trauma because of his mishandling of an early patient. Freud used hypnosis in his early work to help patients relive experiences which had been repressed from consciousness but which seemed symbolically connected to their symptoms. Often when such patients relived a traumatic earlier event, such as a sexual assault by a parent or caretaker, allowing themselves to experience the

A family hurriedly leaves home after warnings about the release of radiation from the Three Mile Island nuclear plant. The majority of people undergoing traumatic experiences of this kind go through at least a brief period of anxiety and depression; a small percentage suffer serious psychiatric problems.

painful feelings associated with the event but long repressed, their symptoms, such as periods of amnesia or physical weakness, improved. Freud initially thought that a sexual trauma was always responsible for these neurotic symptoms, but after ten years of espousing this unpopular theory, he retracted it. He came to believe that his use of hypnosis and psychoanalysis had elicited a combination of real and unreal memories from his patients. At times they had reported fears and fantasies as facts.

Freud's recent detractors accused him of changing his point of view to avoid confronting his own responsibility for obtaining an unnecessary surgical procedure for a patient. The operation was mishandled by a trusted mentor of Freud, Wilhelm Fliess, and the patient was disfigured and nearly bled to death. Freud thereupon allegedly changed his theories so that he could account for the patient's bleeding as a result of her own "hysteria." However, Freud maintained close contact with the patient for many years, and indeed referred patients to her when she became a psychoanalyst herself. He did not revise his theory until eight years after her operation.

Legal Issues

Appeals courts in a number of states have limited the admissibility of evidence obtained through the use of hypnosis. This technique has been used increasingly by mental health professionals and the police to enchance the memory of witnesses and victims of crime. The classic use of hypnosis in such cases involves helping a traumatized victim who has repressed memories of the event to relive or review it, while controlling the accompanying feelings of fear, pain, and helplessness. For example, hypnosis was used to help the bus driver who was kidnapped along with the schoolchildren in Chowchilla, Calif., recall a license plate. Unfortunately, a number of instances of abuse of hypnosis have occurred, in which the technique was used to alter a witness's apparently accurate recollection of an event rather than to enhance the person's recall.

Deliberate misuse of the technique aside, there is substantial debate about the reliability of any testimony obtained with the aid of hypnosis. One study found that while hypnosis did produce an increase in correct memories, it also produced a greater increase in incorrect memories. People capable of being hypnotized may be vulnerable to pressure to provide new information and may respond with a mixture of accurate and inaccurate recall. Accuracy, of course, is a problem with any kind of eyewitness testimony.

The use of hypnosis in criminal cases certainly involves risks—of contaminating real memories with "pseudomemories" or of allowing the witness to report uncertain memories as real. At the same time, there are circumstances, especially when severe emotional trauma occurs, when useful additional information may be obtained.

Controlling the Costs of Care

The impact of the diagnosis-related groups (DRG's) being introduced as a basis for reimbursement in U.S. government–funded health care programs such as medicare has begun to be examined. Under this system, hospitals receive a preset payment based on the patient's diagnosis rather than payment for the amount of treatment actually provided. The preset payments are determined largely by estimates of how much treatment is necessary for given diagnoses.

The DRG system, however, presents problems, particularly for psychiatric facilities. Psychiatric patients with the same diagnosis may require widely differing amounts of treatment, depending on such factors as family and other social support, socioeconomic status, prior psychiatric and medical history, and age. Furthermore, while an effort by the hospital to include diagnoses for other conditions which occur at the same time can increase reimbursement, the DRG system is still likely to penalize hospitals that provide more comprehensive care or make care available to more difficult patients. Certain patients with very complex or difficult problems could conceivably find it difficult to obtain care under such a system.

Psychiatric illness, in particular, often affects a patient's cooperation with treatment, which in turn may affect the patient's recovery. Moreover, a series of recent court decisions have upheld the right of psychiatric patients to refuse medication (except in emergencies), although drug treatment may be the most efficient way to manage the particular illness. For all of these reasons, there is concern among mental health professionals about the effects of the DRG system on the quality and availability of psychiatric care.

See also the feature article IDENTIFYING MENTAL PROBLEMS. DAVID SPIEGEL, M.D.

Nutrition and Diet

Two important recent health news stories concerned nutrition—the conclusive evidence that lowering the level of the fatty substance cholesterol in the blood will reduce the incidence of coronary heart disease, and the tragic famine in Africa. Both developments called for large-scale public action: many experts believe that heart disease can be reduced significantly if people learn to control their cholesterol levels, and massive efforts are needed in Africa not only to prevent the deaths of thousands more people from starvation, but also to ensure that those who survive will not be handicapped for the rest of their lives.

Cutting Down on Cholesterol

In early 1984, the results of a landmark study sponsored by the National Heart, Lung, and Blood Institute were published, offering the first conclusive evidence that lowering the level of cholesterol in the blood would reduce a person's chances of developing coronary heart disease—one of the leading causes of death in the Western world. Although it was previously known that coronary heart disease was directly related to the level of cholesterol in the blood—called serum cholesterol—what was missing was hard scientific evidence on how the risk would be affected if a group of people lowered their blood cholesterol level.

In the study, some 3,800 men with high serum cholesterol were followed carefully for seven to ten years. All were placed on a standard low-fat, low-cholesterol diet; in addition, half received a cholesterol-lowering drug. The results were dramatic: there was a significant drop in coronary heart disease, including heart attacks and angina, in the group that received the drug.

Cholesterol deposits are mainly responsible for atherosclerosis, or hardening and blockage of the arteries; if a coronary artery becomes completely blocked, the blood supply is cut off, leading to a heart attack. Many public health officials have advocated a change in the American diet in an effort to reduce the risk of atherosclerosis and heart attacks.

In December 1984, the National Heart, Lung, and Blood Institute convened a panel of experts in various health fields, which reviewed information on cholesterol and drew up recommendations for the general population. The panel, noting that it had been shown "beyond a reasonable doubt" that lowering blood cholesterol levels would reduce the high rate of heart disease in the United States, recommended that Americans adopt diets with a much smaller amount of fat. The panel set target levels for serum cholesterol that are significantly lower than both the levels many doctors have considered acceptable and the level that is average for middle-aged Americans. For instance, the panel recommended a cholesterol level of 180 milligrams per deciliter of blood for people under the age of 30 and a level of less than 200 milligrams per deciliter for those age 30 and over; the current average U.S. level is 220–230 milligrams for middle-aged adults. A number of steps were recommended to help people reach these goals, with more aggressive actions advised for those with very high cholesterol levels, including cholesterol-lowering drugs if diet and exercise were not effective in these individuals.

Dietary changes were recommended for everyone. All people over the age of two were told to reduce their intake of dietary fat from the current average of 40 percent of total calories to 30 percent of total calories. Less than 10 percent of the fat in the daily diet should be in the form of saturated fat (the type found, for example, in meat and dairy products), and the amount of cholesterol eaten each day should be no more than 250–300 milligrams.

For all this to be accomplished, the panelists said, "the eating habits of the entire family must be changed." For example, people should drink low-fat or skim milk, eat less red meat and more fish and poultry (with the skin removed), and limit their consumption of butter and oil, egg yolks, and fatty sauces and salad dressings.

The panel also suggested wide-ranging public health measures to help implement their recommendations. These include national programs to educate physicians, other health professionals, and the public about the significance of lowering cholesterol and the ways to go about it. Blood cholesterol testing should be standardized, once various screening methods have been assessed, and routine cholesterol measurement considered. In addition, government food programs, the food industry, and restaurants (including fast-food restaurants) should provide more appetizing low-fat and low-cholesterol choices, and food labels should list the fat and cholesterol content of the products.

The panel report has its critics; some experts believe that there are insufficient data to recommend a diet and life-style change for everyone and imply that everyone will benefit from such a change. There are many risk factors for heart disease, including cigarette smoking, high blood pressure, and physical inactivity. Cholesterol may be only another factor to consider in any individual case.

The Benefits of Fish Oils

Recently, important evidence has been accumulating linking a reduced incidence of heart attacks to eating relatively large amounts of marine oils. These oils, derived mainly from fish, are polyunsaturated like most vegetable oils but at the same time are rich in one particular fatty acid, called eicosapentaenoic acid (EPA).

Studies have shown that Greenland Eskimos have a low incidence of coronary heart disease even though their diet is quite high in fat. When these Eskimos move to Denmark and spend several years eating the typical Danish diet, which is also high in fat, their incidence of heart disease reaches the higher level of native Danes. This change appears to be caused by the type of fat consumed. In Denmark the typical Western diet prevails—high in saturated fat from meat and dairy products. But in Greenland, the diet is much richer in marine oils from fish. Eating this high marine oil diet significantly lowers the serum cholesterol level of the Eskimos below that of people living in Denmark.

Further studies have been conducted during the past few years with animals and with human volunteers. These investigations have shown that EPA not only lowers serum cholesterol but also inhibits the aggregation, or clumping, of platelets, small particles in the blood that play an essential role in the clotting process. This slows down the formation of clots that block arteries and may lead to heart attacks. The actual means by which EPA works is still not clear. Some evidence suggests that this fatty acid (and perhaps others in marine oils) stimulates the platelets to make substances that inhibit them from clumping together at the site of fatty buildup in arteries narrowed by atherosclerosis. When platelets fail to aggregate, clots will not develop in these areas as easily.

There is currently not enough evidence to recommend the routine use of EPA. Certain theoretical disadvantages to its use exist. For instance, since EPA inhibits blood clotting, bleeding time will increase. Although this may be beneficial to people who are at risk for atherosclerosis, it may be detrimental to anyone who has a tendency to bleed, who is in an accident, or who requires surgery. More research into this possible bleeding problem is needed. However, from what is already known, marine oils may play an important role in the future in the treatment and perhaps even the prevention of atherosclerosis.

Warning on Obesity

It is not news that obesity can be a killing disease. Many people, however, do not take seriously enough the hazards of being overweight. A useful reminder that these hazards are very real came in February 1985 from a panel of experts convened by the U.S. National Institutes of Health to review the available data.

The panel said that even small amounts of extra weight may cause problems for some people. Otherwise healthy adults who exceed the desirable weight for their sex, height, and body frame by at least 20 percent are candidates for treatment by their doctors. Severely obese individuals—those who are 40 percent or more overweight—run a particularly high risk of developing obesity-related disorders. Health problems made more likely to occur by obesity include high blood pressure, some kinds of cancer, gall bladder disease, arthritis, respiratory and menstrual abnormalities, and Type II diabetes (the form of diabetes in which the body cannot make effective use of the insulin it produces). The panel also noted that obesity can be a heavy psychological burden, constituting for many a social and emotional handicap.

Using Radiation to Preserve Foods

When the use of the cancer-causing pesticide EDB (ethylene dibromide) was banned recently in the United States and Canada, the possibility of broadening the approved uses of radiation as a food preservative and insecticide gained impetus. In February 1984, the U.S. Food and Drug Administration (FDA) submitted a proposal to allow food suppliers to use up to 100,000 rads of radiation to kill insects in fruits and vegetables and prevent the spoiling of food. (A rad is a unit of energy absorbed from radiation.) A final decision on the proposal is expected in 1985.

The FDA already allows limited use of food radiation. Small amounts were approved in the 1960's to kill insects in wheat and flour and to prevent sprouts on potatoes, but the process was not used commercially. And in 1983, the irradiation of some spices at up to 1 million rads was approved to control bacteria and kill insects. The new proposal, in addition to allowing higher radiation doses for other foods, would increase the permitted radiation of spices to 3 million rads. In announcing the new proposal, federal officials noted that 30 years of research into the irradiation of foods had shown that the process leaves no radioactive residue on foods and does not lessen their nutritional value.

In the irradiation process, fruits and vegetables are placed on a conveyor belt and carried past sources of radiation—gamma rays emitted by the radioactive substances cobalt-60 or cesium-137 or electron beams generated by an accelerator. The radiation levels are high enough to either kill or reduce the rate of growth of bacteria, mold, and insect larvae but are much too low to make the food radioactive.

Proponents of food irradiation say that it could save at least a quarter of the world's food supply that is lost each year to insects and spoilage. In the future, they say, it might eliminate the need for some dangerous chemical additives, such as nitrites in bacon and other cured meats. Irradiated food is now available in over 20 countries, has been deemed safe by such groups as the World Health Organization and the Food and Agriculture Organization of the United Nations, and has been extensively tested and used to prepare food for U.S. astronauts.

However, some challenge the safety of food irradiation. Critics believe, for instance, that too little is known about the chemical changes that radiation causes in foods. The process may create chemical compounds called unique radiolytic products, which, according to some scientists, require further testing for possible dangerous or cancer-causing effects. In response to this, the FDA cites scientific literature on the safety of irradiation and says that the changes it causes in foods are of no more consequence than those that occur in storage or canning. Another concern lies in whether food that has been treated with radiation will be labeled as such or not.

Protein Diet Warning

In April 1984, the FDA issued requirements that all very-low-calorie protein diet products (those which supply fewer than 400 calories a day) carry prominent warnings that using the product as a total diet without medical supervision "may cause serious illness or death." Low-calorie products intended to supplement other foods must bear warnings that they be used only as directed and not as the sole basis of a daily diet. The FDA took action after reports of illnesses and deaths linked to the diet products.

The FDA ruling primarily involves protein powder diets, which are mixed with water and which supply from 300 to 500 calories a day. These powdered diet foods—one of the best known is the Cambridge Diet—contain protein, carbohydrates, vitamins, and minerals, but the small number of calories can cause conditions similar to those of semistarvation: heart rhythm irregularities, liver abnormalities, anxiety, and even death.

The liquid protein diets popular in the late 1970's, which also were very low in calories and which caused some 60 deaths, are no longer sold. However, the FDA regulation will apply to them as well if they are revived.

Diseases From Selenium Deficiency

An important story with enormous public health significance reached its culmination in 1984. Few have learned about this nutritional discovery because it has had very little mention outside the scientific literature, and even there it has received little attention because most of the reports have been published in journals from the People's Republic of China. The discovery involves two diseases, Keshan disease and Kaschin-Beck disease, which have been known for many years in China.

Keshan disease, named for the town in which it was discovered, primarily affects the heart, causing a degeneration of the heart muscle and its replacement by fibrous connective tissue. It affects mostly young women and children. Kaschin-Beck disease—described in ancient Chinese medical reports from at least 2,000 years ago—results in a severe chronic and very debilitating form of arthritis. (The condition is called "big joint disease" in the areas of China where it occurs.) Kaschin-Beck disease affects young children, causing severe deformities and permanent disability.

About ten years ago, a team of Chinese scientists began to study Keshan disease. They noted that the disease was confined to one large belt of territory extending from northeast to southwest China. They also realized that within this geographic area, many of the cattle had been dying of a muscle disease similar to a disorder that affected cattle in the United States and was reported to be caused by a deficiency of the mineral selenium. The scientists determined that the entire population (several hundred million people) living within this belt were selenium-deficient as a result of a virtual absence of selenium in the soil and hence, in the food supply. Selenium dietary supplements were given to several thousand people, and Keshan disease virtually disappeared from them. A large-scale-supplementation program is currently under way in China in an attempt to eradicate the disease. Based on further research into the causes of Keshan disease, scientists believe that it occurs when one or more viruses that are not usually harmful are able to infect the heart of a selenium-deficient person.

Recently a team of Chinese scientists has turned its attention to the crippling effects of Kaschin-Beck disease, which is prevalent not only in the same regions as Keshan disease but also in the Soviet Union near the Chinese border. In fact, the disease is named after the two 19th-century Russian physicians who first described it. Again, it has been determined that the disease affects only people who are selenium-deficient, and a large-scale selenium supplementation program is being planned for the areas that are not included in the Keshan disease program. Whether an agent such as a virus is involved in this disease is not yet known.

Famine in Africa

For the last few years, mass starvation involving millions of people has been occurring in a vast area of northern Africa. The nations of the world have been trying to mobilize and coordinate a massive relief effort, but it is clear that the conditions that have led to this famine still exist and that a long-term plan designed to prevent a similar recurrence is urgently needed. Hundreds of thousands of people have already died, the mortality rates being highest among the very old and

Ethiopian famine victims search for bits of edible plants in the near-barren soil; millions of African children are at risk of permanent effects from severe malnutrition, including stunted growth and brain damage.

depletion of muscle mass. The second type is called kwashiorkor (a name coined in Africa to describe the loss of hair pigment that is a common sign of this form of malnutrition). Children suffering from kwashiorkor retain water and their bodies swell (a condition called edema). They fail to grow and often develop severe skin rashes and brittle hair that has lost its color. Finally, the liver may accumulate fat, leading to severe, often fatal, liver disease. Both infantile marasmus and kwashiorkor are usually accompanied by severe diarrhea, which depletes the body of water and of certain minerals. If the diarrhea is not controlled, death can occur rapidly. In addition, either form of malnutrition increases a child's susceptibility to infection and decreases his or her resistance once infection strikes. Relatively innocuous childhood diseases, such as measles and chicken pox, are major killers when they strike a population of severely malnourished children.

Even if children survive a bout of marasmus or kwashiorkor, the disease may have inflicted permanent damage on their brains and other organs during a critical period in their development. Severe early malnutrition will harm brain cells and inhibit the secretion of certain important brain hormones. The result is a brain that has not developed properly, and the damage is irreversible. We can therefore expect that a grim legacy of the present famine will be a generation of children who will be stunted in their growth, will have permanent brain damage, and will exhibit functional handicaps for the rest of their lives.

A famine of this proportion also will markedly lower the birth rate. In many ways this is fortunate, since compelling evidence from various studies suggests that the fetus is particularly vulnerable to the effects of severe maternal malnutrition. Much of this information is based on knowledge about a severe famine that occurred in 1944 and 1945 in the Netherlands. Germany imposed a food blockade on a number of Dutch cities such as Rotterdam in retaliation for a general strike by transport workers. The ensuing famine lasted nine months until the Netherlands was liberated. The Dutch maintained excellent hospital records during this period, and these records have recently been examined. Several important observations on the effects of maternal malnutrition on the growth and subsequent development of the fetus have been made.

First, it is clear that the famine resulted in a significant drop in birth weight. The fetus is generally considered to be most vulnerable to the effects of maternal malnutrition during the last trimester (three months) of pregnancy, but even fetuses who were exposed to the famine during the first or second trimester were smaller at birth than infants who were born either before or after the famine. It is also clear from research done during the past few years that the fetus is more vulner-

the very young. In addition, millions of infants and young children are suffering the effects of severe malnutrition. Most of these infants will survive. Thus, it is important to focus not only on the present acute crisis but on the long-term problems that will confront the survivors. Fortunately, a great deal is known about the problem of severe protein-calorie malnutrition in infants and children. Unfortunately, it takes a tragedy of the magnitude of the African famine to galvanize action based on this knowledge.

There are two distinct forms of severe protein-calorie malnutrition in infants and children, both of which are occurring during the present emergency. The first, called infantile marasmus, is characterized by failure to grow, severe emaciation with loss of all body fat, and

able to maternal malnutrition than the mother. Data from the Dutch famine, as well as from animal experiments, show that the mother's body protects her own body stores at the expense of fetal growth. An explanation for this apparent paradox can be found in the fact that pregnancy has two major functions: first, to provide an environment for the developing fetus, and second, to deposit energy stores in the mother in the form of fat, which ensures that she will be able to produce and maintain an adequate milk supply during lactation. When food is scarce, priorities must be decided. Unless adequate lactation stores are available, the newborn infant will probably die, and thus, creating these stores is the highest priority even if it means some curtailment of fetal growth.

Studies during the last few years have made clear the mechanism by which fetal growth is slowed as a consequence of maternal malnutrition. During pregnancy the mother's body adapts, particularly her circulatory system. The volume of blood circulating through the mother's body increases by about 20 percent to accommodate the demands of the growing uterus and its contents, the expanding breasts, and the other tissues of reproduction. This places an extra demand on the heart, which responds by pumping blood more efficiently. At the same time this extra blood is redirected so that the blood flow to the uterus and the placenta, the organ that joins the fetus to the uterus, is markedly increased. Thus, the mother's body is adapting in order to establish an adequate blood supply to the fetus. During periods of food restriction, such as the famine occurring in Africa today, adequate adaptation does not take place. The blood supply is reduced, and hence, nutrients are delivered to the fetus poorly. It is not a question of too little food being available, because the mother's body contains ample reserves. It is a question of inability to deliver the food efficiently to the fetus.

Fetal growth retardation resulting in low birth weight always increases infant mortality. This was found in the Dutch famine and is the major cause of the high infant death rate seen among poorer segments of the Western population today. Even if the famine in Africa were to cease today, those infants who were currently developing in the uterus would have a higher death rate.

One important finding to come out of the studies of the Dutch famine leaves a faint ray of hope in an otherwise bleak situation. Those children who were developing in the uterus during the Dutch famine were examined 20 years later and found to have normal IQ scores. This is in stark contrast to the results in certain countries of the Third World, where low IQ's and poor school performance have been reported in children who were born to mothers suffering from malnutrition. The reason for the successful outcome in the case of the Dutch children is that the famine was an acute situation immediately followed by recovery and a return to the relatively stimulating environment provided to all children in the Netherlands. Unfortunately, the famine in Africa is the final catastrophe in a long history of deprivation and poverty. The results of all of the studies conducted during the past two decades show that unless fundamental changes occur in the economic and social conditions which led to the famine, millions of children are destined to grow up physically and mentally handicapped.

See also the feature articles MILK: GOOD FOR EVERYONE? *and* VEGETARIANISM *and the Spotlight on Health articles* THE IMPORTANCE OF FIBER *and* HOW TO PRESERVE NUTRIENTS IN FOOD.

MYRON WINICK, M.D.

Obstetrics and Gynecology

There has been increasing concern in the last few years that the cessation of menstruation that often accompanies strenuous athletic training by women may have ill effects on their health, and researchers have indeed found signs of osteoporosis—a progressive thinning of bone tissue—in nonmenstruating female athletes. Another area of great concern is an increasingly common infection of the fallopian tubes, which appears to be the cause of the rising rate of ectopic pregnancy—a dangerous condition in which a fertilized egg becomes implanted outside the uterus.

Exercise and Menstruation

There has been considerable interest recently in the potential hazards, both short-term and long-term, of women engaging in intensive athletic exercise and conditioning that results in a reduction or cessation of menstruation. Approximately a third of female long-distance runners, swimmers, gymnasts, and ballet dancers stop menstruating during intensive training periods. One researcher reported that fully 69 percent of female athletes participating in the 1980 Summer Olympics had menstrual abnormalities during training and competition. According to various other studies, 25 to 40 percent of highly trained endurance athletes menstruate fewer than three times a year. Although many female athletes believe this to be advantageous to their performance, concern remains that the disturbances and changes that occur in the hormonal cycles affecting menstruation may have ill effects on the women's future fertility. There is also concern that the hormonal disturbances could cause loss of bone tissue.

Low estrogen levels. There is a wide consensus that the common denominator in the loss of menstrual periods (technically called amenorrhea) is a reduction in the body's production of the female hormone estrogen, as well as a disturbance in the rhythmic nature of the production, which normally correlates with the phases of the menstrual cycle. The actual cause of the low estrogen levels found in exercise-related amenorrhea is uncertain, but experts have tended to focus attention on either of two possibilities. The first is a reduction in the synthesis and release, by the pituitary gland, of the hormones called gonadotropins that regulate estrogen production. It is also possible that strenuous exercise disturbs the process by which certain substances are converted into biologically active estrogen by fat tissue.

Exercise may well affect different hormones in the body, including some of those involved in the menstrual cycle. Recent evidence suggests that exercise causes the pituitary gland to increase its production of the opium-like "natural painkillers" called beta endorphins and the hormones ACTH, which helps regulate the body's reaction to stress. Scientists aren't sure why there is an increase in beta endorphins, but the rise is considered to be stress-related. (There is a possible relationship between an increased number of beta endorphins and the well-known "runner's high," the sense of euphoria and well-being experienced by many runners.) Exercise also appears to raise levels of the hormone prolactin, which is important in milk production and in regulating levels of another hormone, progesterone. The gonadotropins known as FSH and LH, on the other hand, appear to be reduced in the bloodstream as a result of exercise. This suggests that the disruption in their regulatory role is responsible for the low estrogen levels and the cessation of menstruation.

Another possible reason that has been widely discussed to explain why estrogen levels are so low during intensive exercise is a decrease in body fat. Approximately one-third of the estrogen circulating in a woman's body is normally produced in fat tissue. When there is a decrease in such body fat, the tissue appears to continue to produce estrogen. But it seems to shift its production from that of the biologically most active type of estrogen, called estradiol, to a much less active form. This apparently affects the intricate hormonal arrangements that bring about and regulate the menstrual cycle. The less active estrogen does "signal" the pituitary gland that estrogen is being produced, and the pituitary indeed responds as it should by decreasing its secretion of the gonadotropins that stimulate estrogen production. This feedback mechanism is a normal part of the menstrual cycle. But the less active estrogen fails to bring about the cyclic changes in reproductive organs that normally occur in menstruation. For instance, estrogen normally makes the lining of the uterus (the endometrium) build up and thicken, helping to ready it for the implantation of a fertilized egg if conception has occurred; if there has been no conception,

Female athletes who train intensively may stop menstruating for varying lengths of time; doctors are studying whether this condition might affect bone tissue.

the lining is shed during menstruation. But the less active estrogen fails to make the uterine lining grow—and without a thickened uterine lining, there can be no menstruation. This hypothesis to account for exercise-induced amenorrhea remains controversial, and the most recent studies have failed to show any consistent correlation between amenorrhea and the ratio of fat to lean body mass.

Whatever the exact causes of the low estrogen levels, they have important medical implications. It is probable that an athlete's first menstrual period is significantly delayed by intensive exercise training that begins before puberty. This delay has been calculated at 0.4 months for each year of the girl's age during premenstrual training. In addition, the young athlete tends to have a longer time between menstrual periods once they do begin. However, after nonmenstruating athletes stop participating in a strenuous training program, there does not appear to be an unduly long delay in the resumption of their periods. And a recent study found no correlation between the length of time the athlete had no periods and the length of time required for menstruation to begin again. As for fertility, a ten-year follow-up study of formerly amenorrheic female athletes suggests that their fertility is comparable to that of the general population.

Possible bone loss. While exercise-related amenorrhea thus appears to have little if any effect on fertility once menstruation resumes, it does appear to be associated with loss of bone density, or osteoporosis. Over time, this could lead to an increased risk of fractures or to compression of the weakened vertebrae, which causes shortened stature and the "dowager's hump" seen in women with severe osteoporosis. It has been well established that estrogen protects against osteoporosis; the condition is most common in women who no longer produce the hormone, that is, those who have passed menopause or had a hysterectomy. However, athletes with low estrogen levels may not be doomed to weak bones. It has been suggested that although their estrogen levels are reduced, their bone mineral content might be protected by the known effects of physical activity, which helps to build up bone mass, or at least to prevent its loss. This suggestion is reinforced by evidence that physical activity can help inhibit and even apparently reverse early osteoporosis in postmenopausal women.

One study of 14 nonmenstruating athletes in their 20's demonstrated that their bone mass, as measured by the density of the vertebrae of the lower back, was significantly reduced compared to that of 14 athletes whose menstrual cycles were normal. The mass of the radius bone of the forearm did not appear to be affected, but the loss of vertebral bone mass was significant. In fact, the average mineral density of the nonmenstruating athletes' vertebrae was comparable to what might be expected of 51-year-old women. And two of the 14 nonmenstruating athletes demonstrated a vertebral bone density so low that they were considered to be at risk for fractures. The percentage of body weight made up of fat tissue was not significantly different in the two groups, the women had all had their first periods at about the same age, and their physical characteristics, such as height and weight, were comparable. It is of interest, however, that the nonmenstruating athletes on average ran almost twice as far each week as did the others (41.8 miles, compared with 24.9 miles).

The estrogen estradiol and the hormones progesterone and prolactin were on the average significantly lower in the nonmenstruating group. Those with the lowest estradiol concentrations, however, did not necessarily have the greatest loss of vertebral bone tissue. This reflects the fact that there is considerable individual variation in the effects of estrogen on bone mass.

More research is needed, and concern remains about the potential for osteoporosis in those athletes who develop amenorrhea during their training programs.

PID and Ectopic Pregnancy

Acute pelvic inflammatory disease (PID) and its effects have become a major scourge of young women. This infection of the fallopian tubes (it may also involve the cervix, uterus, or ovaries) is often caused by the bacteria that causes gonorrhea, but other infectious organisms—usually more than one type in any given case—can also be responsible. During the past decade there has been an increase in the prevalence of PID, as well as in the prevalence of an important after-effect of the disease—ectopic pregnancy, or implantation of a fertilized egg outside the uterus, usually in a fallopian tube. Damage to the fallopian tubes by PID leaves women much more vulnerable to ectopic pregnancy. There are a number of reasons why PID is so much more common today. They include greater freedom of sexual behavior and a decline in the use of so-called barrier methods of contraception—such as the condom or diaphragm—that tend to protect against the transmission of the infecting organisms.

A 1984 study of PID analyzed information from a general hospital discharge survey conducted by the U.S. National Center for Health Statistics. The researchers collected data on those women who had been discharged from the hospital with a diagnosis of PID during the years 1975 through 1981. By studying hospital records, the researchers determined that the rate of hospitalization for PID rose gradually during this seven-year span and averaged 5.3 hospitalizations per 1,000 women aged 15 to 44 years. Women aged 25 to 34 consistently had the highest rate, but their rate declined slightly over the seven years; meanwhile, the incidence of PID in women between the ages of 15 and 24 distinctly rose. By five-year age groups, the 20-to-24-year-olds had the highest average rate, at seven hospitalizations per 1,000 women.

The impression of the study group was that a change in the type of infectious organisms causing the disease may be one reason for the rising number of hospital admissions for PID. Gonorrheal bacteria appear to bring about fewer cases of PID today than in the past, while another kind of sexually transmitted bacteria called chlamydia accounts for a greater proportion of cases. Chlamydia infections are generally milder than those caused by the bacteria of gonorrhea, so the early phase of PID may go unnoticed. Undetected and untreated initially, the pelvic infection may then have more serious consequences, such as pelvic abscesses, that require hospital admission and often surgery. An additional reason for the increase in PID cases found by the survey may be a new attitude on the part of some doctors. Physicians who have come to realize the serious long-term implications of PID are more likely to treat it aggressively, using intravenous antibiotics that require short-term hospital admission, when this diagnosis is suspected.

Perhaps the most troubling aspect of the greater number of PID cases has been a corresponding increase in the occurrence of ectopic pregnancies, which according to recent data more than doubled in the United States during the 1970's, from 4.5 per 1,000 reported pregnancies in 1970 to 10.5 in 1980. This has tragic implications: ectopic pregnancy is now the leading cause of maternal death during the first three months of pregnancy. Both PID and ectopic pregnancy also tend to threaten a woman's future fertility. Although the dramatic success of in vitro (or "test-tube") fertilization programs offers new hope for many women whose fallopian tubes have been damaged by PID or ectopic pregnancy, the prevention of pelvic infection through a reduction in sexually transmitted diseases remains a major health objective.

See also the Spotlight on Health articles NEW HELP FOR INFERTILITY *and* WHAT IS PREMENSTRUAL SYNDROME?
P. HARDING, M.D.

Pediatrics

Awareness is increasing that many steps can be taken to avoid accidental injury or death in children. Studies were completed on the prevalence and benefits of breast-feeding and on the value of a new program to help children with asthma take a more active role in controlling their illness. A dramatic animal-to-baby heart transplant was performed.

Infant Feeding and Infant Health

A task force of physicians and other specialists appointed by the U.S. Department of Health and Human Services to review the scientific evidence on the relationship between infant feeding practices and infant health reported its findings in 1984. Focusing both on the United States and on developing countries, the task force found breast-feeding on the increase in the former but declining in popularity in the Third World. It confirmed the ability of breast milk to provide the infant some protection against certain infections, and it identified topics on which further research is needed.

Popularity of breast-feeding. The task force reported that in the 1940's, breast-feeding was a commonly practiced form of infant feeding in the United States, especially among disadvantaged women. A decline in breast-feeding occurred over the next 30 years, as infant formulas became widely popular. This decline was most rapid among the disadvantaged, and the current

resurgence of breast-feeding is lowest among them. In the developing nations, the current decline in breast-feeding is most pronounced among urban women.

A number of factors—some obvious and some subtle—may influence a woman's decision to breast-feed or bottle-feed her baby: attitudes toward breast exposure in public, her husband's influence, friends' attitudes and advice, the need to work outside the home, and the state of the mother's health. Although it has been suggested that advertising for commercial formulas and the marketing practices of the manufacturers of these formulas have a negative influence on the decision to breast-feed, the task force found little or no hard evidence that these factors have any significant impact.

Influence of feeding method on health. There is no question that breast milk is the best milk for babies. It is nutritionally balanced, easy for the infant to digest, and sanitary. It also contains antibodies that protect the baby from some infections. However, although there is some positive association between breast-feeding and the health of infants born in the United States in the past ten years, the task force noted that in a population with good sanitation, good nutrition, and access to medical care, the additional benefit from breast-feeding is modest. Breast-feeding has been shown to protect infants from gastroenteritis (inflammation of the lining of the stomach and intestines) and appears to provide some protection against middle ear infections, but evidence that it protects infants against other infections or against allergies is less clear.

Some problems may also be associated with breast milk. Infants who are fed exclusively on breast milk do require supplemental food after four to six months to maintain normal growth; those who have breast milk but no other food for nine to 12 months may experience a slowing of growth or may grow erratically. Since breast milk is deficient in vitamins D and K and in iron, some infants may develop vitamin or iron deficiencies if fed exclusively on breast milk, without supplements. In the distant past, when few humans lived in areas of the world with winter climates, a baby's need for vitamin D might have been supplied by sunshine, but many of today's babies, because of climate, urbanization, or convention, do not receive much exposure to the sun. In recognition of these deficiencies, pediatricians generally add vitamin D and iron supplements to a breast-fed infant's diet.

Another area of concern about breast milk has to do with the presence of chemicals in the mother's body. For example, mothers taking medication may pass the drug to their infant, although in diluted strength and usually in small amounts. Pediatricians and obstetricians are aware of this hazard and often can adjust a mother's medication schedule to allow her to continue breast-feeding.

Commercial formulas are not without problems. In the past some formulas were found to be deficient in certain nutrients, but manufacturers have corrected these deficiencies, and their products are considered safe and nutritious. Nevertheless, all formulas are made from either cow's milk or soy products and therefore may be difficult for some infants to digest. Powdered formula mixed with unclean water can be a health threat (a problem more common in the Third World than in the United States). And no formula can provide the infant with infection-fighting antibodies.

Future research. The task force suggested a number of areas in which further research is needed. For example, since babies born to disadvantaged U.S. families have higher rates of illness and death than infants in the rest of the U.S. population and might therefore be expected to benefit most from the positive health effects of breast-feeding, it would be important to have more detailed knowledge of the infant feeding practices of this segment of the population. More information is also needed about normal growth in breast-fed infants, since current U.S. growth standards were developed in the 1950's and 1960's, when almost all babies were bottle-fed. In order to encourage more mothers to breast-feed their babies, it is important to learn how to alter negative influences on this choice; therefore, further research was recommended on the factors that contribute to a woman's decision to breast-feed or bottle-feed.

Teaching Children to Live With Asthma

Among diseases affecting children, asthma is one of the leading causes of school absences, emergency room visits, and hospitalizations. However, a new program that teaches children with asthma how to take more responsibility for managing the disease may be able to help these children both reduce the severity of asthmatic attacks and increase their self-esteem.

The asthmatic episodes that disrupt some children's lives can be triggered by any one of a number of stimuli: an allergic reaction, exercise, air pollutants, an infection, or even emotional stress. In such an episode, the air passages of the lungs (bronchi and bronchioles) become narrowed because the surrounding muscle layer contracts and the lining of the passages swells from increased production of a thick, sticky mucus. The child can breathe air into the lungs but has trouble getting it out through the narrowed air passages; the sound of the child's breathing as the air forces its way through is the wheezing people commonly associate with asthmatic attacks. These episodes occur rather suddenly and, if not relieved promptly, can continue for several days and require hospitalization. Difficulty in breathing is a frightening experience, and treatment is protracted and expensive.

In the past several years, it has become standard medical practice to attempt to prevent sudden asthmatic attacks by having the child take medication on a regular basis, whether the child is wheezing or not. This approach, called maintenance therapy, has been effective for many children, enabling them to remain free of attacks for very long periods (ranging from weeks to months). Children who take medicine all the time, however, tend to perceive themselves as sickly or weak and "different" from others. Most allow their parents to be responsible for managing their illness and thus remain more dependent than other children of the same age. Parents of children with asthma also feel "different" because of an ever-present fear of an imminent crisis. They see the child as vulnerable and sickly, and feel powerless to help.

Since the late 1970's there has been an increasing effort to address these problems through educational programs. In 1981 and again in 1983, the U.S. National Institutes of Health held a conference to review the variety of self-management programs for children with asthma that began to be developed. Although all these programs were thought to be beneficial, there was no formal evaluation of how well they worked. In 1984, however, researchers at the University of California at Los Angeles did perform a careful evaluation of a program they had developed called ACT, for Asthma Care Training. ACT, now an educational and support program of the Asthma and Allergy Foundation of America, was found to be highly beneficial.

The UCLA researchers worked with two groups of children with asthma (all elementary-school age) who required medication at least one week out of every month. One of the groups, with their parents, attended three asthma education sessions, each session lasting 1½ hours. The children and their parents were interviewed prior to the classes to determine how much they understood about asthma, what they thought about their health in general, what they did when an asthma attack occurred, and who gave out and kept track of the medication. The second group was asked the same questions but was given a different educational program—the ACT program. Consisting of five one-hour sessions, attended at weekly intervals, it emphasized teaching the children how to "take charge" of their disease, rather than feeling helpless.

In the ACT sessions, asthma control was compared to driving a car, with the colors of traffic lights used to simplify the training. The children were first taught to code their symptoms green, yellow, or red, according to severity. Then, each measure that might be used in asthma management—medication, relaxation techniques, breathing exercises, control of environmental factors, calling the doctor—was assigned a color: red, yellow, or green. The items in the green category were those with which the children should be able to "keep going" on their own (for example, maintenance medications). The yellow-coded items, standing for "caution, slow down," were those to be used to treat mild symptoms (such as practicing breathing-control exercises or moving out of the room to change the environmental factors). The red, or "stop," items were those needed to treat a major asthmatic attack (such as using more potent medications or calling the doctor). The children were taught to use the green-coded items independently and to consult with their parents when symptoms worsened, possibly requiring measures in the yellow category to be begun. Thus, the children and their parents were taught to share the decision-making responsibility, so that both gained confidence in their ability to manage the disease.

The UCLA researchers found that children and parents who took both types of training sessions benefited—gaining a better understanding of asthma and coming to realize that the children were not as ill as had been believed. However, the group that learned the ACT color-coding approach to asthma management showed additional benefits. The children in this group became less dependent on their parents for care, needed fewer visits to hospital emergency rooms, and spent fewer days in the hospital than before receiving ACT training, gains that also made for more peace of mind and considerably less expense for the families.

Organ Transplants

Organ transplants in young children remained in the news. The fact that a kidney transplant has become a standard procedure, and that the number of hospitals performing pediatric liver transplants has continued to grow, has in one sense provided access to these operations for more children with serious or terminal organ disease. At the same time, it has intensified the already severe shortage of donor organs. As with adult organ transplants, requirements for matching tissue types between donor and recipient—and for care, speed, and complicated logistics in getting the donor organ to the patient—are stringent. In addition, in pediatric transplants the donor organ must be small enough to fit the recipient's body. Since mortality rates for children in the developed countries are low, the pool of donor organs for children is even smaller than for adults.

One theoretically possible way to ease the shortage of donor organs is to use organs from animals as well as humans. In October 1984, Dr. Leonard L. Bailey of the Loma Linda (Calif.) University Medical Center surprised the medical community—and the general public—by transplanting the heart of a baboon into an infant, identified only as Baby Fae. She had been born with a fatal heart defect called hypoplastic left heart syndrome, in which the left ventricle of the heart, the main pumping chamber supplying blood to the body, fails to develop.

Hypoplastic left heart syndrome currently accounts for 25 percent of deaths from heart disease in the first month of life.

Dr. Bailey, one of many pediatric cardiologists and cardiac surgeons to have wrestled over the years with the problem of how to treat the syndrome, became convinced that the solution was a heart transplant. He believed, however, that the likelihood of finding matching donor hearts from similar-sized human infants was practically nil, and after substantial animal experimentation, he felt that an animal-to-human implant was a viable alternative.

Another type of treatment was possible for Baby Fae: a two-stage surgical procedure developed by Dr. William I. Norwood, a pediatric surgeon at the Children's Hospital of Philadelphia. In this procedure, the surgeon reroutes the blood coming from the heart in order to use the well-developed vessels and pumping chamber on the right side (which are normally used to send blood to the lungs) to do all the pumping to both the lungs and the rest of the body. The first operation is performed shortly after birth and the second after the baby has grown sufficiently to tolerate further corrective surgery. The procedure is complex and its success very uncertain, although it is regarded as promising.

Despite the use of drugs to combat rejection of the transplanted organ, Baby Fae died 20 days after the baboon heart implant. Dr. Bailey's efforts raised a number of difficult medical and ethical questions. Among these questions was whether enough animal experiments had been performed to justify trying an implant in a human baby, whether a search should have been made for a human donor heart for Baby Fae, and whether her parents were fully informed of their options before agreeing to the implant. A U.S. government report issued in March 1985 found shortcomings in the hospital's consent form signed by Baby Fae's parents but concluded that the parents had "understood the alternatives available as well as the risks."

See also the feature article NEW SUCCESSES IN TRANSPLANTS.

Preventing Injuries and Accidents

Since accidents account for nearly half of all deaths in children between the ages of one and 14 in the United States, accident prevention should be at the forefront of society's efforts to improve child health and welfare. For a long time, it was thought that because accidents are, by definition, unpredictable, preventive efforts would be largely futile. Today, there is abundant evidence that they can make a difference.

A good example is provided by the hundreds of poison control centers in the United States and Canada, whose work has been credited with achieving a dramatic reduction in childhood deaths from poisoning.

Alive After Drowning

When four-year-old Jimmy Tontlewicz was rescued after 20 minutes beneath the ice of Lake Michigan, doctors induced a coma to prevent the brain swelling that can follow near-drowning and raised the boy's temperature gradually from the 85 degrees to which it had fallen. The low temperature helped make his survival possible by reducing his brain's need for oxygen. At left, Jimmy as he appeared several months later when he was undergoing speech, physical, and psychological therapy.

In addition to providing 24-hour first-aid advice by telephone and referring children to appropriate emergency treatment facilities, the centers carry on extensive educational campaigns. In part as a result of their efforts, there is now general awareness of the importance of storing cleaning supplies, medications, and other dangerous substances out of children's reach, and laws requiring childproof containers for medications have become common.

Attention has also focused recently on the accident potential of many common items of baby furniture and equipment, including cribs, carriages and strollers, and baby walkers. Another such item is the accordion-style baby gate, used to block off staircases or doorways. These collapsible gates, with fairly large diamond-shaped openings, have been responsible for the death by strangulation since 1975 of at least eight U.S. chil-dren who had caught their heads in the openings. Production of these gates was halted, effective February 1985, by an agreement between manufacturers and the U.S. Consumer Product Safety Commission; safer gates, with openings far too small for a baby's head to get caught in, were already on the market.

Mattel Inc., a major toy manufacturer, introduced a process that renders the small loose parts of its toys easily visible on X-ray films. Thus, a physician treating a child who has swallowed the toy part can quickly find the object without having to resort to more drastic measures, including exploratory surgery. Mattel developed the process in cooperation with the Committee on Accident and Poison Prevention of the American Academy of Pediatrics.

In the United States, the automobile is the major cause of accidental deaths in children. Whether as passengers or pedestrians, infants and children are more vulnerable than any other segment of the population to injury by or in a car. To address this problem, the American Academy of Pediatrics began a vigorous educational and legislative program in 1980, now called "Make Every Ride a Safe Ride." Its aims are to ensure that newborns leave the hospital in approved infant safety seats, to increase the use of safety seats for children aged one to four, to reduce teenage auto injuries and deaths, and to support mandatory seat belt legislation. By the beginning of 1985, all U.S. states except Wyoming required that young children, usually up to the age of four, be restrained, while a passenger in any car, in a car seat or seat belt that meets federal standards. Media campaigns promoting automobile safety for infants and children were encouraging compliance with these requirements. Despite these efforts, compliance remained low; an official of the National Transportation Safety Board estimated that under 40 percent of people in the United States used safety belts for their children and that 70 percent of those using protective seats were using them incorrectly.

Improvements in Treating Injuries

Pediatricians and pediatric surgeons are devoting increasing attention to an area largely neglected until now, the care of children with major injuries. Its importance was underlined by the surprising results of a four-year study of 34 young patients at the John Hopkins Pediatric Intensive Care Unit in Baltimore, Md.—all of whom survived major head injuries and comas

averaging 15 days in length. Despite conventional medical thinking that children who are comatose for longer than 24 hours cannot recover without serious physical or mental impairment, it appears from this study that if patients are taken quickly to a specialized trauma center, treated aggressively while in a coma, and given long-term follow-up care, many can experience a healthy recovery. Most of the 34 patients in the Johns Hopkins study were eventually able to return to school and resume normal lives.

Although the Johns Hopkins unit that helped the comatose patients was geared especially to treating children, in general, as the emergency care system has evolved in the United States, trauma centers have been established that in most cases were designed specifically to treat multiple injuries in adults. Surgeons, nurses, and paramedics are trained in routine procedures that apply to adults, and a scoring system is in use that permits rescue workers in the field to classify patients quickly according to the nature of their injury and know exactly when and where to move them for specialized care. Such is not the case for infants and children. When paramedics and rescue teams arrive at the scene of an accident in which a child has been injured, they have few guidelines to follow for the care of the youngster. Should the child be given intravenous fluids and interim care at the scene, or be moved immediately to a hospital? And to which hospital? When children are brought to a general hospital, still more questions arise: Should the child receive emergency care and then be moved again to a pediatric facility for

Safe Rides for Children

The use of properly installed auto safety seats for all child passengers could prevent hundreds of deaths and thousands of injuries each year.

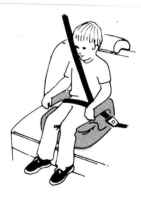

An infant seat should face the rear, preferably in the back seat, and can be used until a child weighs about 20 pounds.

A toddler seat, for children up to about age four, has lap and shoulder belts; a five-point harness is shown here.

A booster seat allows older children to use a regular lap and shoulder belt and still see out the window.

longer-term treatment? Should a scaled-down version of the same procedures used for adults be used to treat the child, or are different, more appropriate techniques available? At present, there are few answers to these questions.

Injuries at different stages of development, from fetus to teenager, require differing medical responses, and the rules for adults do not always apply to children. For example, because an infant's skull is expandable, a severe blow to the head may cause sufficient bleeding in the skull cavity to produce shock. For adults, the usual guideline states that if a patient is in shock and has a head injury, then one should search for blood loss elsewhere in the body. The same arm or leg injury that may be minor in a 20-year-old could result in a deformed limb or later growth problems for a two-year-old, because of the rapid growth of young children's bones. Injury to the abdomen in a child often results in tearing of the liver or spleen because these organs are less well protected than in adults. Thus, careful examination and observation are required to detect potentially serious, even life-threatening injuries that may not at first be obvious.

For all these reasons and others, the pediatric profession is focusing on meeting specific needs in improving the care of injured children. These needs include collection of detailed data on when, where, how, and why children are injured; an evaluation of the outcome of treatment at a pediatric trauma center versus that at a general trauma center; development of a scoring system applicable to children that field paramedics and ambulance personnel can use to decide quickly how urgent a child's injuries are; and a method by which to evaluate the likely effect of an injury on a child's physical and psychological health and development.

Vitamin E Solution Recall

An injectable form of vitamin E for use in premature infants was recalled from the market by its distributor in 1984 after being implicated in the deaths of infants in over 30 U.S. hospitals. There was no definite proof that the product, E-Ferol, caused the deaths. However, the association between administration of E-Ferol and development of unusual symptoms (including fluid accumulation in the abdominal cavity and an enlarged liver and spleen) and subsequent death was sufficiently strong to prompt the drug's withdrawal.

Vitamin E is considered to be of benefit in lessening vision and breathing problems in premature infants, but until the introduction of E-Ferol, could be given only by mouth—a difficult task in babies sometimes weighing as little as one pound. E-Ferol was introduced by its manufacturer in 1983, without U.S. Food and Drug Administration approval, as a variation on an existing product (oral vitamin E supplements).

Infant Heart Drug Approved

An intravenous form of indomethacin, a drug used for years to treat arthritis, is now available to help deal with a life-threatening heart defect in infants. The new form, sold as Indocin IV, was approved for use in the United States by the FDA in February 1985; it has been available as Indocid PDA in Canada since 1984. The drug is expected to help thousands of infants who would otherwise require emergency surgery for the defect. Called patent ductus arteriosus, the defect occurs when a blood vessel in the heart (the ductus arteriosus) that normally closes up at birth fails to close—a condition found mostly in premature infants. Indomethacin has in many cases proved effective in closing the blood vessel.

See also the Spotlight on Health articles CONQUERING CHILDHOOD DISEASES *and* CRIB DEATH.

LOIS A. POUNDS, M.D.

Psychiatry and Psychology

See MENTAL HEALTH; CHILD PSYCHOLOGY AND DEVELOPMENT.

Respiratory System

Home care for those who need the help of a mechanical ventilator to breathe is increasingly becoming a realistic alternative to long-term institutionalization. The importance of the diaphragm and its role in disorders of the respiratory system have attracted new attention, and new research implicates alcohol, even in relatively moderate amounts, in breathing problems during sleep. Lung cancer deaths continue to mount, but first reports were published in 1984 on an effort to detect lung cancer early and, it is hoped, thereby increase the survival rate of those who develop the disease.

Home Care for Lung Disease

Marked technological improvements in the care of patients with lung disease have resulted in the survival of people who formerly would have succumbed, usually while in the hospital. This has occurred, for example, with patients suffering from obstructive lung diseases (those which obstruct the patient's airflow during exhalation, such as emphysema or bronchitis). These patients may have episodes of breathing difficulties so severe that they have to be hospitalized and use a mechanical ventilator—that is, a respirator or breathing machine—to help them breathe. As expertise in intensive-care medicine has grown, episodes of acute respiratory failure requiring mechanical ventilator support are often successfully treated, in that patients who once died now survive the crisis of being unable to breathe without mechanical support. However, after treatment, a small fraction of patients are unable to breathe on their own without the mechanical ventilator; these patients are called ventilator dependent.

It is not only patients with lung disease as such who can become dependent on a ventilator. Patients whose nerves or muscles have been damaged by disease or injury may also have severe breathing problems. In these instances, the lung may be normal, but the "spark plug" or the "bellows" (that is, the nerves or the muscles, respectively) may be so impaired that they cannot support spontaneous breathing. Examples of conditions that can leave patients unable to breath on their own include polio and spinal cord paralysis (usually because of injury).

Cases of ventilator dependence result in an extremely difficult professional, moral, social, and economic situation. Until the past few years, patients unable to breathe on their own had to stay in a hospital or, less frequently, a long-term chronic care facility (a nursing home), where they had constant access to the mechanical support systems they needed. Their lives by necessity were confined to their hospital or nursing-home rooms, with absolute dependence on the medical staff for their care, and with no opportunity for normal social and recreational activities.

For all of these reasons, home care for the ventilator patient is now being considered as a possible option. Recent reports, one of them from Britain, describe the type of activities and organization necessary to rehabilitate some ventilator patients, beginning in the institution and continuing at home. A highly complex unit of services, including medical, rehabilitative, and training care, is required in the hospital, in addition to home support by skilled medical personnel and family members who have been trained to take responsibility for some of the patient's needs. Programs to this end are being set up in selected medical centers in the United States. Reports have indicated that many patients can be rehabilitated to some extent, and some can return home to care for themselves in a limited way. The cost of such services is high, but it is probably much less than any type of long-term institutional care. Not all ventilator-dependent patients are candidates for home care, however. Some patients are unable to care for themselves for physical or emotional reasons. The author of one report suggests that men are less successful than women in accepting ventilator dependence and the loss of their social role as provider for the family.

The Diaphragm: Disease and Damage

In 1984, several articles were published on the diaphragm—the single most important muscle for breathing—and its role in lung disease. Chronic obstructive lung diseases such as emphysema tend to have harmful effects on the function of the diaphragm, which is the large, dome-shaped muscle that separates the thoracic cavity where the lungs are from the abdominal cavity. Emphysema causes enlargement of the lungs' microscopic air sacs and damaging changes in the sac walls; the lungs of people with emphysema may be up to twice the normal lung size. These enlarged lungs push the diaphragm down into a position where it does not operate efficiently. (The diaphragm, like any other muscle, must have the appropriate length and shape for maximum efficiency.)

Recent studies have evaluated the effects of drugs called bronchodilators, which are used in the treatment of emphysema and bronchitis. Both of these conditions cause destructive changes in the airways within the lungs, called bronchi; the bronchodilators act to relax the muscles of the bronchi and improve airflow. Theophylline compounds are a class of bronchodilators of which aminophylline is one type. These compounds are a mainstay in the treatment of the bronchial narrowing found in obstructive lung disease—but they may have another important benefit as well. Recent studies with both people and animals have shown that theophylline compounds improve the strength of the diaphragm and decrease the muscle fatigue found in certain lung diseases. Aminophylline was effective in patients with chronic obstructive lung disease as well as in tests designed to simulate respiratory failure in animals. While these findings will not revolutionize the care of patients with obstructive lung disease, they are significant, as they reemphasize the diaphragm's importance in breathing and the usefulness of drugs that improve diaphragm function.

It is expected that the effect of other drugs on the diaphragm will be assessed in the future. Interestingly, one study that has been done evaluated the effect on diaphragm function of a chemical first cousin of theophylline—caffeine—which was found to have some effect in improving diaphragm function. What effect daily coffee drinking might have on lung function, on the other hand, has yet to be evaluated.

After surgery a number of pulmonary complications can occur, especially in patients who had lung disease before surgery. These complications can include lung collapse and pneumonia; both can lengthen the patient's hospital stay and even increase the risk of death. The diaphragm plays a pivotal role in the development of these complications. It is already recognized that patients breathe more shallowly after surgery because of pain, and continuous shallow breathing without occasional deep breaths can lead to lung collapse or pneumonia. A Canadian study has shown that the diaphragm does not function normally after surgery, and this may be part of the reason for shallow breathing. It is not yet known why the diaphragm does not function properly, but it appears that function improves within 24 to 48 hours in some patients.

Treatment for postoperative problems can include measures to increase the depth of breathing. In a recent Boston study, patients were helped to take deep breaths by regular, supervised deep-breathing exercises, through the use of a measurement device that allowed them to check on how successfully they were breathing deeply, or by intermittent application of air pressure by mechanical means. The study found that vigorous postoperative therapy offers significant improvement in the pulmonary complications that patients suffer. It is thought that diaphragm function may be improved by these maneuvers.

Paralysis of the diaphragm often occurs after spinal cord injuries, usually in patients with a broken neck that results in total paralysis. Such paralysis can also result from direct injury to the nerve controlling the diaphragm, a nerve that runs from the spinal cord through the chest to the diaphragm. Recently, an unusual cause of diaphragm paralysis was reported as a result of open-heart surgery; the nerve to the diaphragm was thought to have been inadvertently injured during the operation. This very uncommon complication resulted in severe shortness of breath, and one patient needed the support of a mechanical ventilator. Fortunately, most of the patients reported on recovered from this type of diaphragm paralysis after a period of weeks or months.

Is there any treatment for other types of diaphragm paralysis? Unfortunately, most diaphragm problems that follow severe spinal cord injury are not reversible, and patients often become ventilator dependent. Since it is the nerves themselves that cease functioning after such an injury, the diaphragm muscle is often still normal. Some doctors have attempted to artificially stimulate the diaphragm in such cases. In one totally paralyzed quadriplegic patient, an electrical nerve stimulator was implanted and the diaphragm stimulated electrically, producing an improvement in breathing. Further study is required, however, before this type of treatment can be widely used.

Sleep and Breathing Problems

Problems with breathing during sleep have gained widespread attention in the last few years. In 1984, new information was reported: alcohol, even in moderate amounts, can cause such breathing irregularities.

Breathing can become irregular or can even stop during sleep, for as long as 60 seconds; if breathing does stop, blood oxygen levels drop, and this can impair the function of the brain, heart, and lungs. A common type of disordered breathing during sleep is the sleep apnea syndrome. Generally, patients are middle-aged men, at times overweight, who have incredibly large numbers of apneas (periods when breathing ceases) at night. Breathing is interrupted because the upper airway is blocked by abnormal relaxation of muscles there. The airway becomes narrowed, and when it becomes totally obstructed, the patient's breathing ceases. The patient then wakes up and begins breathing again. (This is called obstructive apnea; in a less common condition called central apnea, breathing stops because of an interruption in nerve signals to the breathing muscles.) It is not known at this time why some people develop obstructive sleep apnea.

In 1984, a new risk factor—alcohol—was described for the development of sleep apnea. Sleep researchers in Florida reported that the ingestion of alcohol equivalent to a "couple of drinks" causes apnea to occur in men not known to have the syndrome. In patients who do have the syndrome, alcohol, particularly in excessive amounts, may cause a marked worsening of their condition. Some hangover symptoms may also be related to disturbed breathing during sleep.

It appears the alcohol may increase apnea in a number of ways. One study that examined normal people found that under the influence of alcohol, the tongue muscles worked less effectively to keep the airway open during breathing, leading to an increase in apneas. It also appears that alcohol can depress the brain's activity level, interfering with the nervous sytem's messages to all of the muscles used in breathing. Patients with sleep apnea syndrome should be aware of the effect alcohol has on breathing.

Lung Cancer

The number of people dying from lung cancer continues to increase. According to the American Lung Association, almost 140,000 new cases were expected in the United States in 1984, as were more than 120,000 deaths from the disease. The association also reports that lung cancer has now surpassed breast cancer as the cancer causing the most deaths among women in the United States. Cigarette smoking is believed to be the major cause of lung cancer, and prevention of most lung cancer is thought to be possible if people stopped smoking. Unfortunately, programs that help people quit smoking have met with limited success.

The prognosis for survival after lung cancer is diagnosed is grim. Currently less than 10 percent of all patients with lung cancer survive for five years or more. Because people continue to smoke cigarettes and lung cancer survival is so limited, attention has been directed to early detection of lung cancer, usually in people who do not as yet show any symptoms of the disease. It is hoped that catching and treating the disease early will result in saving more lives.

Preliminary reports of a cooperative study by the National Cancer Institute were published in 1984. Three major American hospitals participated in the study, which involved over 30,000 cigarette-smoking men who were at high risk for developing lung cancer. They were screened regularly for five years and followed for five years more. The purpose of the study was to determine whether deaths from lung cancer can be reduced by certain screening procedures.

In the screening procedures that were used in the study, people were evaluated regularly for lung cancer because they were at risk for cigarette smoking, rather than because they showed symptoms. The screening procedures included a regular chest X ray and examination of sputum for tumor cells (a procedure not unlike a Pap test for cervical cancer, except that it is done on a sample of sputum).

The published reports on the cooperative study are still preliminary; it is too early to know what the conclusive results will be. The preliminary data do indicate a greater prevalence of abnormal X ray and sputum examination results in smoking men, and they also indicate that in some patients who developed lung cancer, survival was increased. Whether this was the result of early detection of the cancer is still unknown. Valuable information is expected from these studies.

SUSAN K. PINGLETON, M.D.

Skin

The recognition that people with a certain type of mole run a high risk of developing malignant melanoma promises to reduce the number of deaths from this form of skin cancer. The increasing use of Mohs' surgery, a precise surgical technique for the treatment of skin cancer, is greatly reducing the risk of recurrence and complications from several common forms of cancer. Vitamin A–derived drugs that have proven highly effective in treating many skin diseases may eventually benefit cancer patients as well; however, concern about their safety continues.

Warning Sign of Malignant Melanoma

The incidence of malignant melanoma, a potentially fatal cancer of the pigment-forming cells of the skin, continues to rise at a disturbing rate in the United States. In fact, both the incidence and the mortality rate of this type of skin cancer are rising more rapidly than for any other form of cancer except lung cancer. Although the overall survival rate for malignant melanoma is only about 80 percent, early diagnosis usually makes a cure possible by simple surgical removal of the malignancy. The recent identification of a type of mole, known as a dysplastic nevus, that seems to act as an early warning sign that a person is at risk of developing melanoma promises to facilitate early diagnosis. Thus, for the first time there is hope that the mortality rate for this most pernicious form of skin cancer can be significantly reduced.

The dysplastic nevus was first discovered to be a warning sign in certain families (few in number) who have a dramatically high incidence of malignant melanoma. The members of these families who develop melanoma frequently have this distinctive type of mole, while family members without these moles generally remain melanoma-free. Although most dysplastic nevi remain benign throughout a person's life, they nevertheless become malignant more often than do ordinary moles.

Typical dysplastic nevi are between one-fifth and one-half inch in diameter, slightly larger than ordinary moles. Most are flat, and their borders are often irregular and poorly defined. Their color may be brown, tan, black, or pink, they can occur anywhere on the body, but not uncommonly are found on covered areas, such as the breasts or buttocks. A physician's visual diagnosis of dysplastic nevi can always be confirmed by a biopsy, because the moles have a distinctive appearance under the microscope. Although they begin to appear in adolescence, new ones may continue to appear during adulthood.

The risk of developing melanoma for a member of a melanoma-prone family who has dysplastic nevi has been estimated to approach 100 percent. Fortunately, such families are rare. If they can be identified, and if the members who have these unusual moles are regularly seen by a physician who watches for any change in the moles that might signal approaching malignancy, then it can be expected that the risk of death from melanoma in this group of individuals should virtually be eliminated.

Dysplastic moles also occur in about 2 to 8 percent of the general population. While the chance that a healthy white person in the United States will develop melanoma is estimated at 1 in 150 (the incidence is much lower among blacks), the risk for such an individual with dysplastic nevi has been estimated at 1 in 10. Thus, physicians are now able to identify two groups who have an increased risk for melanoma: a small, high-risk group of persons who have dysplastic moles as well as a family history of melanoma, and a very large, moderate-risk group having dysplastic nevi but no personal or family history of the disease. (Melanoma may also occur in persons having no dysplastic nevi.) In the latter group as in the former, the death rate from melanoma can be reduced if the melanoma-prone individuals can be identified, their moles evaluated regularly by a doctor, and any suspicious or changing pigmented moles removed surgically.

Precise Surgical Technique for Skin Cancer

The surgeon treating skin cancer has a number of traditional approaches to choose from, depending on such considerations as the type and location of the tumor, the age of the patient, and whether or not there has been earlier treatment. These traditional approaches include excision (cutting out the malignancy), curettage and desiccation (scraping and burning), cryosurgery (freezing), and radiation therapy. However, surgeons are now more often choosing yet another technique, called Mohs' surgery (or microscopically controlled surgery). They find that it frequently has significant advantages over the standard methods.

Mohs' surgery is actually not new, having been developed by Dr. Frederick E. Mohs, a Wisconsin surgeon, over 40 years ago. It combines excision of the tumor by removal of successive layers of tissue with the immediate examination of each layer of removed tissue under the microscope. The microscopic examination replaces visual inspection as the way of determining the extent of the cancer. The technique allows the surgeon to, on the one hand, be sure that only diseased tissue is removed and, at the same time, ensure that no cancerous tissue has been left at the edges of the excision. Mohs' surgery has the highest cure rate of all the available treatment techniques, while requiring the smallest possible loss of tissue.

Because this technique is more time-consuming and expensive than others, it is still not employed as the first treatment for most routine cancers. Nor is it frequently used to treat malignant melanoma; because of the high risk that this type of tumor will spread, wide margins of healthy tissue surrounding the tumor are usually removed, and therefore little attempt is made to preserve the maximum amount of uninvolved tissue. However, Mohs' surgery is generally recognized as the treatment of choice for skin cancers that recur after other means of therapy have failed, for tumors that abut a healthy organ that can possibly be saved, or when the border or depth of a tumor is difficult to determine. The proper use of Mohs' surgery promises to reduce serious complications from basal cell and squamous cell carcinomas, the two most common forms of skin cancer.

Update on the Retinoids

Since its approval by the U.S. Food and Drug Administration in 1982, the drug isotretinoin (also known as 13-cis-retinoic acid and sold as Accutane) has revolutionized the treatment of severe cystic acne. This drug is one of a group of compounds, known as the retinoids, that are derived from vitamin A. Isotretinoin, which is available by prescription in Canada as well as the United States, not only clears up severe acne eruptions, but in most cases also produces a prolonged disease-free period after the patient has stopped taking it.

In addition, there is now evidence that the retinoids may be useful in treating many other skin diseases. Already, they are being employed in treating inflammatory diseases of the skin (such as psoriasis and rosacea), as well as diseases that involve faulty production of the outermost, horny layer of the skin (like ichthyosis and Darier's disease). And evidence is increasing that the retinoids may have some potential benefit in the prevention and treatment of skin cancer. These vitamin A derivatives have been demonstrated to affect cell duplication and cell differentiation (the process by which cells develop individual characteristics and functions). In some animal studies, the retinoids have displayed the ability to reverse early cancerous changes in cells. Patients who have the hereditary basal cell nevus syndrome, which puts them at high risk for skin cancer, should prove to be important subjects in whom the anticancer effects of these drugs can be tested. Still newer derivatives of vitamin A are now being produced and studied, holding out the promise of important advances in treating many internal, nondermatologic diseases (such as leukemia), as well as ailments affecting the skin.

Unfortunately, together with these exciting prospects comes continuing concern about the serious side effects of the retinoids. For example, levels of uric acid (a body waste product) and fats in the blood may be raised; elevated uric acid levels can potentially trigger attacks of gout, and elevated fat levels can potentially precipitate attacks of pancreatitis or accelerate the development of atherosclerosis. Other side effects of the retinoids include dry skin, vision problems, and pseudotumor cerebri (a condition that produces the symptoms of a brain tumor), as well as a possible association with inflammation of the large intestine. However, the major focus of concern regarding adverse effects of the retinoids is their role in causing birth defects.

It has long been known that isotretinoin has this effect in animals. Since the drug's approval by the FDA for use in treating acne, a disease that frequently affects women of childbearing age, it has become clear that it causes birth defects and miscarriages in humans as well. By mid-1984, 17 cases of birth defects (including malformations of the brain, ears, and heart) and 20 miscarriages had been attributed to the drug. As a cautionary measure, the FDA advised blood banks not to accept blood donations from persons taking isotretinoin until they had been off the drug for a month (to avoid potential risk to pregnant women who might receive the blood). The manufacturer, Hoffmann–La Roche, strengthened warnings to physicians and patients about the side effects of the drug. Physicians have been urged to reserve use of the drug for severe cases of acne that do not respond to antibiotics or other conventional treatment.

The birth defect–causing effect of isotretinoin does not appear to be prolonged, and conception one month after the drug has been discontinued is considered safe. However, its use by women of childbearing age is to be avoided unless there is no possibility that the patient is pregnant and she is using an effective form of contraception.   EDWARD E. BONDI, M.D.

Smoking

See RESPIRATORY SYSTEM; ENVIRONMENT AND HEALTH.

Teeth and Gums

Strategies to help people overcome their fear of dental examination and treatment received growing attention, as dental phobia clinics were established around the United States. Research on periodontal disease indicated a new way that the tetracyclines, a group of antibiotics, were effective in treating advanced cases. There was increasing concern that the growing use of "smokeless tobacco" would produce an increase in the incidence of oral cancer. Researchers reported progress in developing a new technique for diagnosing disorders of the joints controlling lower jaw movement, and a new ceramic material has been developed to replace gold in "capped" teeth.

Fear of the Dentist

An estimated 5 to 10 percent of Americans have so strong a fear of dental treatment that they never go to a dentist; anxiety and fear keep a much larger number from seeking dental treatment as often as they should.

At the University of Göteborg in Sweden, a team of researchers that included a psychologist as well as a dentist studied 160 dental patients, predominantly women between the ages of 20 and 40, who had avoided all dental care, except in some emergency cases, for an average of 16 years. They found that for 85 percent of the patients the major cause was a traumatic dental experience in childhood, usually involving insensitive professional behavior by the dentist. The remaining patients had acquired their fear as adults, usually because of suffering undue pain from drilling (for example, when teeth were drilled without anesthesia or when the dentist continued to drill a tooth even if the anesthetic was not working), having an injection of an anesthetic, or having a tooth pulled. The patients most admired dentists who were understanding of patients' concerns and who tried to avoid inflicting pain.

Another group of people who avoid dental treatment are those troubled by an exaggerated gagging response when dental instruments are placed in their mouths. In a study conducted at Florida State University in Tallahassee, a group of volunteers who had not gone to a dentist for up to seven years because of their gagging response were helped by behavioral therapy. They received instruction in relaxation procedures and practiced controlled breathing and distraction techniques. After an average of eight 30-minute training sessions, the volunteers were able to tolerate dental instruments without undue gagging, and they resumed regular dental care.

In an effort to make treatment of dental phobias available to the general public, a number of medical centers and dental schools have opened dental phobia clinics. One of these is at Mount Sinai Medical Center in New York City. Treatment begins with relaxation training in the setting of a dentist's examining room. Then a dentist very gradually introduces dental instruments (and eventually the drill) to the scene, while ensuring that the patients employ relaxation techniques to counter their anxiety reactions. The fear response slowly diminishes, until normal dental treatment can take place.

New Role for Antibiotics in Periodontal Disease

In severe forms of rapidly progressing periodontal disease (deterioration of the gum tissue and bony structure that support the teeth), the tetracylines, a family of antibiotics, are often used to supplement office and self-care procedures because of the drugs' effectiveness against particular bacteria associated with this disease. In a series of studies, researchers at the State University of New York at Stony Brook have now demonstrated that tetracycline and minocycline (a member of the same family of drugs) play a second role: they inhibit the activity of the enzyme collagenase, which is produced in the gum area as part of the inflammation that occurs in periodontal disease and which destroys the collagen fibers that make up much of the tissue supporting the teeth in their sockets. Collagenase molecules include ions of calcium and zinc, which are essential for the enzyme's activity. The tetracyclines can bind, or react with, these metals very effectively, resulting in a loss of over 60 percent of enzymatic activity. The Stony Brook investigators have shown that use of the tetracyclines in patients with advanced gum disease results in a much lower level of collagenase activity in the pockets that form around the teeth.

In a related series of experiments with animals, the same researchers demonstrated that the tetracyclines markedly inhibited the production of collagenase in the gum tissue of rats with diabetes. Diabetes has been associated with an abnormally high rate of breakdown of the tissues that support the teeth. The tetracyclines dramatically reduced this breakdown in the laboratory

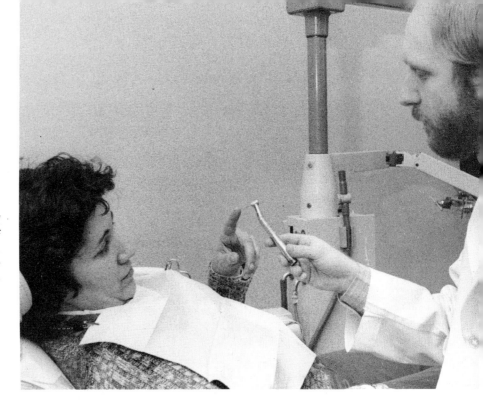

A dentist shows a patient with dental phobia a disconnected drill, as part of a program to help people like her, some of whom have stayed away from the dentist for years, to overcome their fears.

rats, showing a profound effect on gum collagenase both in diabetic rats infected with the bacteria that cause periodontal disease and in those without any bacteria. This new role for the tetracyclines in inhibiting collagenase activity was also demonstrated in a series of laboratory experiments involving collagenase in skin, cartilage, and bone and in preliminary evidence that the antibiotics can help in treating uninfected corneal ulcerations (sores of the cornea) in humans, a disease that is believed to involve collagenase produced on the surface of the eye.

Oral Cancer and Smokeless Tobacco

According to the U.S. Centers for Disease Control in Atlanta, more and more Americans are using chewing tobacco or snuff (pulverized tobacco that may be chewed or placed next to the gum). The use of "smokeless tobacco" has grown at an annual rate of about 11 percent since 1974. It has been estimated that there are 22 million users in the United States, most of them between the ages of 18 and 30. The CDC has warned that smokeless tobacco has been linked to oral cancer (cancers of the lip, tongue, mouth, and pharynx), as well as to tooth loss and gum disease. Users are four times more likely to develop oral cancer than are nonusers, and if finely ground tobacco is placed between the cheek and gum, then users are 50 times more likely to develop cancers in this area than are nonusers.

Although there is still no certainty about which component of the tobacco is responsible for the cancer-causing effect, the most likely possibility is nitrosonornicotine (NNN), which is known to cause tumors in animals. NNN is present in higher concentrations in snuff and chewing tobacco than in cigarette smoke, and the concentration increases when smokeless tobacco mixes with saliva. Over time, NNN may produce changes in the normal cells of the mouth, first causing leukoplakia, a condition in which white patches appear in the mouth, and then a type of cancer called squamous cell carcinoma.

Oral cancers cause about 9,000 deaths a year in the United States, and there is increasing public pressure on the U.S. Food and Drug Administration to compel manufacturers to put warning labels on their smokeless tobacco products. Somewhat less than half of all U.S. patients with mouth cancer are alive five years after treatment is started.

Research at the School of Dentistry of the University of California at San Francisco has shown that patients with squamous cell carcinoma of the mouth have higher levels in their blood than do healthy persons of antibodies to the herpes simplex type 1 virus (the virus that causes cold sores). It was also shown recently that among patients with this form of cancer, the quantity of herpes simplex antibodies at the start of treatment may serve as a predictor of how long they will live after beginning treatment. Patients with pretreatment antibody levels higher than the median (middle) value for those studied had a five-year survival rate of 76 percent. The rate was 44 percent for those below the median.

Diagnosing Jaw Problems

It's not only breakfast cereals that snap, crackle, and pop, according to dental scientists at the University of Connecticut at Storrs and Massachusetts General Hospital in Boston. They found that different disorders of the temporomandibular joints (the hinges of the lower jaw) produce characteristic sounds as the jaw moves.

331

These disorders affect large numbers of people, causing pain and limiting jaw movement.

The three most common problems arise from displaced disk-like structures (menisci) within the joint, arthritis of the joint, and spasm of the muscles that control jaw movement (also called myofascial pain disorder). In the new procedure, named arthrophonometry (literally, measuring the sound of the joint), the investigators placed a special, highly sensitive microphone over the temporomandibular joints and recorded joint sounds during opening, closing, and side-to-side movements. Comparing healthy volunteers with patients suffering from one of the three common types of disorders, the researchers found dramatic differences in the patterns of sound arising from each of the three. These patterns were sufficiently distinct from one another to serve as diagnostic guides.

Arthrophonometry appears to offer many advantages over existing procedures (usually involving X rays, sometimes with a dye being injected into the joint). It is painless, noninvasive (no instruments or substances enter the body), cannot produce any allergic reaction, and does not require exposure to X rays. Also, it can be used to assess the effect of treatment, as well as for initial diagnosis.

Improvements in Dental Materials

Porcelain crowns are frequently used to "cap" broken or badly decayed teeth, since the color of the porcelain matches that of the surrounding teeth. To increase the strength of these crowns, the porcelain is often fused to an underlying gold core. The use of gold adds considerably to the cost of the tooth restoration, however. A specialist in dental materials at the University of Michigan has now found that a newly developed glass-ceramic material has the desired strength to serve as the core of a crown, plus the physical properties to enable it to bond successfully to the outer porcelain layer. The ceramic core has the added advantage of allowing X rays to pass through it, facilitating checkups on the health of the capped teeth (gold cores block X rays).

A group of materials called composite resins are widely used to fill cavities in front teeth because their color blends well with that of natural enamel. Their use in back teeth has been limited, however, because the demands of chewing tend to cause them to wear down rapidly. Attempts have been made to improve the durability of the composites—for example, by adding strontium—but the results of the few long-term (lasting several years) studies on the strengthened composites to date have not been encouraging. The problem of excessive wear was not solved, and discoloration and recurrent decay were found next to the filling.

As efforts to develop better composites for back teeth continue, some specialists are conducting their studies on primary, or baby, teeth. Using baby teeth offers research advantages. First, the composites need to serve as a filling material for only a relatively few years. Second, when the filled baby teeth fall out naturally, the wear on the filling materials can be studied in detail. A recent two-year study of fillings in primary teeth compared strontium-filled composite resins with traditional fillings of amalgam (an alloy of mercury and other metals). Results indicated that the composite resins could be used to fill primary molars for at least two years. During this time span, they withstood wear as well as amalgams, although for just how much longer the composites would be wear-resistant remains to be established. The researchers cautioned that inserting the composites correctly demands exacting techniques (for example, the mouth has to be kept dry, and materials have to be mixed carefully according to manufacturers' directions), but they anticipated that with greater knowledge of proper application, and with improvements in the composites themselves, the usefulness of composite resins could be extended considerably.

Dental Effects of Bulimia

Although many of the harmful effects of bulimia, the "binge-and-purge" eating disorder, are becoming increasingly well known, the profound effect it can have on the teeth has received less attention. This dental effect, however, may lead to earlier diagnosis and treatment of the disorder.

Sufferers from bulimia characteristically indulge in binges of gross overeating, then purge themselves of the food, usually by forcing themselves to vomit. Consequences can include damage to the esophagus, dehydration, and perhaps even life-threatening loss of essential minerals. The ailment is most common among college-age women, with estimates of the proportion affected ranging from 5 to 15 percent. A recent study indicated that an increasing number of people ages 13 to 18 are also bulimic; the prevalence in this group was estimated at 8 percent.

The dental effect of bulimia stems from the fact that the frequent self-induced vomiting characteristic of the disease repeatedly propels gastric juices from the stomach, which contain hydrochloric acid, into the mouth. The acid may then dissolve or erode the enamel on the surfaces of the teeth near the tongue and palate. With this loss of enamel and exposure of the underlying dentin (the inner material making up the mass of the tooth), the teeth become sensitive to cold and sweets, leading bulimics to seek dental help. Thus, the dentist is often in a unique position to identify victims of the disorder at an early stage and to refer the patient promptly for specialized treatment.

See also the Spotlight on Health article STRAIGHTENING TEETH. IRWIN D. MANDEL, D.D.S.

GLOSSARY
CONTRIBUTORS
INDEX

Glossary

Clear, concise definitions of common medical terms that appear in the book.

Acquired immune deficiency syndrome, *see* AIDS.

Acute, relatively severe and lasting for a short time; said of a disease or condition.

Addiction, strong psychological and, usually, physical dependence on a substance such as a drug or alcohol.

Adrenaline, *see* Epinephrine.

AIDS, or acquired immune deficiency syndrome, a disorder of the immune system leading to serious and often fatal complications, including uncontrollable infections and the malignant skin disease Kaposi's sarcoma.

Allergen, a substance that can trigger distressful physical symptoms in people abnormally sensitive (allergic) to it.

Allergy, abnormal sensitivity to certain substances or conditions in the environment.

Amino acid, the chemical unit that is the building block of proteins in plants and animals.

Amniocentesis, a test in which a sample of the amniotic fluid surrounding the fetus is drawn off with a needle and then examined to provide information about the fetus.

Analgesic, a substance that relieves pain without causing loss of sensation or consciousness.

Anemia, a deficiency in the number of red blood cells, which impairs the ability of the blood to carry oxygen throughout the body.

Aneurysm, an enlarged section of a blood vessel, which can cause pain and which can rupture and cause dangerous internal bleeding.

Angina pectoris, or angina, intermittent chest pain, pressure, or constriction that results from insufficient blood and oxygen supply to the heart.

Angiography, a series of X rays made to demonstrate the flow of dye through blood vessels to pinpoint areas where irregularities of the vessels or of the flow through the vessels exist.

Anorexia, lack or loss of appetite. In the emotional disorder called anorexia nervosa, patients, commonly young women, choose to eat little or no food for long periods.

Antibiotic, a type of drug that can destroy or hinder the growth of disease-causing organisms, such as bacteria, yeasts, or certain viruses.

Antibody, a kind of substance, produced by the body's immune system, that fights foreign substances entering the body, such as disease-causing organisms.

Anticoagulant, a substance that inhibits blood clotting.

Antidepressant, a drug administered to prevent or relieve depression.

Antigen, a substance in the body (typically, a foreign substance such as a disease-causing virus) that triggers a reaction by the immune system.

Antihistamine, a type of drug used to relieve allergic and nonallergic reactions caused when certain body cells release a substance called histamine.

Apnea, a temporary cessation of breathing, often occurring involuntarily during sleep.

Arteriosclerosis, or "hardening of the arteries," a condition characterized by localized thickening and loss of elasticity in artery walls, often leading to a decrease or even a complete stopping of blood flow.

Arthroscopy, examination of the interior of a joint with a slender viewing instrument called an arthroscope.

Atherosclerosis, a type of arteriosclerosis in which deposits of fatty materials, such as cholesterol, build up along artery walls, narrowing the passageway through which blood flows.

Autoimmune disease, a disorder in which the body's immune system, which normally defends against foreign substances, attacks the body's own cells, causing serious damage.

Bacteria, tiny organisms which may live in soil, water, organic matter, or living things; some bacteria capable of living in humans are responsible for various diseases.

Benign, favorable for recovery, not life-threatening; often used to describe a noncancerous tumor or growth.

Beta blocker, a drug used to block the effects of nerve impulses or of certain substances, such as adrenaline, circulating in the blood.

Biopsy, the removal and microscopic examination of living tissue for the purpose of diagnosis.

Bipolar disorder, or manic-depressive illness, a psychosis that involves alternating periods of overexcitement and depression.

Blood pressure, the force the blood exerts on the walls of the heart and vessels. Systolic pressure (the higher number in a blood pressure reading) is exerted when the heart contracts, diastolic pressure when the heart is at rest.

Brain death, irreversible cessation of brain functions; now often accepted as a definition of death.

Bronchodilator, a drug that helps to open up air passages in the lungs when they become constricted as a result of a respiratory disease.

Calcium blocker, or calcium antagonist, a drug that blocks the movement of calcium into cells; calcium blockers may be used to steady or slow down heart action or dilate blood vessels by inhibiting calcium uptake by heart muscle tissue or vessel walls.

Calorie, in nutrition, a unit for measuring the energy content of foods; 1 calorie is equivalent to the amount of heat needed to raise the temperature of 1 kilogram of water 1 degree Celsius.

Carbohydrates, certain chemically related substances that are found in many foods; they include cellulose (which acts as roughage in the digestive system) and sugars and starches, which are major sources of energy.

Carcinogen, a substance that causes cancer.

Cardiac arrest, a sudden stopping of effective heart action, most often brought on by an irregular or uncoordinated beating of the heart.

Cardiopulmonary resuscitation, *see* CPR.

Cardiovascular, relating to the system made up of the heart and the blood vessels.

Catheter, a flexible tube that is inserted into a body cavity, passageway, or blood vessel, usually to draw off fluid (such as urine), to introduce a fluid into the body, or to measure blood pressure.

CAT scanning, *see* CT scanning.

Cauterization, the use of an electric current or other agent to seal bleeding vessels or destroy tissue.

Chemotherapy, the treatment of disease with chemicals; usually refers to the use of drugs in battling cancer.

Cholesterol, a substance produced in the body, and also consumed in meat and dairy products, that is an essential component of fat; it has important uses in the body but can contribute to heart disease and strokes when it builds up, in deposits called plaques, in blood vessels.

Chromosome, a threadlike collection of molecules inside body cells, containing DNA, which determines hereditary characteristics.

Chronic, lasting over a long period of time; said of diseases or conditions.

Chronic obstructive lung disease, or COLD, a kind of chronic respiratory disease in which the flow of air to and from the lungs is obstructed.

Coma, a state of unconsciousness so deep the patient cannot be aroused.

Computerized tomography, *see* CT scanning.

Congenital, existing from, and usually before, birth.

Control group, in an experiment, a group of subjects having characteristics generally identical to those of the experimental group, who are not treated with the procedure or substance being tested and whose responses are compared to those of the experimental group.

Coronary, relating to the vessels that carry blood to or from the heart or, more generally, relating to the heart itself.

Corticosteroids, hormones produced by the cortex (outer part) of the adrenal glands or synthetic drugs resembling these hormones. They are part of the general group of substances called steroids. Corticosteroids help regulate the body's use of sugar, fats, and proteins.

CPR, or cardiopulmonary resuscitation, a first aid technique for maintaining air flow into the lungs and circulation of blood and for restarting a patient's breathing and/or heartbeat.

Crib death, *see* Sudden infant death syndrome.

CT scanning, or computerized tomography, a diagnostic technique in which X rays take many pictures of a body structure at different angles, and a computer reconstructs the pictures into a composite cross-sectional image. Also called CAT scanning, for computerized axial tomography.

Cyst, an abnormal sac or pouch in the body, usually filled with liquid or solid material.

Depression, an emotional disorder of varying severity, marked by such symptoms as sadness and dejection, loss of interest in the outside world, difficulty in thinking and concentrating, loss of energy, poor appetite, sleep problems, and recurrent thoughts of death or suicide.

Dialysis, a technique for removing waste products and excess fluid volume from the blood of patients with kidney failure, by connecting the patient to a special machine that acts like a kidney.

Diuretic, a drug that removes excess water from the body by increasing output of urine.

DNA, or deoxyribonucleic acid, a complex, chainlike molecule found in living cells that is the substance of genes; the sequence of chemicals in the DNA molecule determines the characteristics of the individual.

Drug addiction, *see* Addiction.

Electrocardiogram (ECG or EKG), a representation, on paper or on a screen, of the electrical impulses emitted by the heart muscle, used to detect malfunctioning in different parts of the heart; it is made with a machine called an electrocardiograph.

Electroencephalogram, or EEG, a representation, on paper or on a screen, of electrical impulses in the brain, to reveal abnormalities; it is made with a device called an electroencephalograph.

Embolism, blockage of a blood vessel by a blood clot, air bubble, or abnormal particle that has been carried by the bloodstream to the affected area.

Endocrine system, various glands and other organs whose secretions, called hormones, are released into the bloodstream and regulate different body functions.

Endorphins, substances in the brain that act to block pain, apparently by obstructing the transmission of impulses from nerve cell to nerve cell.

Endoscopy, visual examination of a body cavity using a long, slender, lighted instrument called an endoscope.

Enzyme, a substance made by body cells that stimulates specific chemical reactions in the body.

Epinephrine, or adrenaline, a hormone secreted by the adrenal glands that stimulates the heart and blood vessels to increase heart rate and, frequently, blood pressure; it excites the central nervous system and promotes the release of sugar into the blood from the liver to provide energy.

Estrogen, any of various female sex hormones. Estrogen stimulates development of female sex characteristics and acts during the menstrual cycle to provide a suitable environment for possible development of an embryo. It is used in oral contraceptives and for various other purposes.

Fat, soft whitish or yellowish tissue in the body that serves to store energy; also, a constituent of many foods.

Fiber optics, the transmission of light and images along flexible, intertwined glass or plastic fibers. Doctors use fiber-optic instruments to see internal body parts.

Gene, a segment of the DNA molecule that calls for the production of a specific protein, which in turn determines or helps determine a characteristic of the individual.

Gene splicing, or recombinant DNA technology, transfer of genes from one cell or organism to another to change the genetic makeup and, in some cases, induce large numbers of cells to produce a certain substance.

Gland, an organ or group of cells that secretes a useful substance. The secretions of many glands, such as those in the endocrine system, are used elsewhere in the body; in other cases, such as the sweat glands, the substance secreted is eliminated from the body.

Glucose, the chief form of sugar found in the human body and a principal source of the body's energy.

Hardening of the arteries, *see* Arteriosclerosis.

HDL, or high-density lipoprotein, a kind of protein molecule that carries cholesterol in the bloodstream. A high proportion of HDL's in the blood apparently reduces the risk of atherosclerosis. *See also* LDL.

Health maintenance organization, *see* HMO.

Heart attack, or myocardial infarction, destruction of part of the muscle tissue that drives the heart, apparently caused most often by blockage of arteries that supply blood to the heart muscle.

Hemoglobin, an iron-containing molecule, found in red blood cells, that carries oxygen to fuel body cells and carries away the waste product carbon dioxide to be exhaled by the lungs.

High blood pressure, *see* Hypertension.

High-density lipoprotein, *see* HDL.

HMO, or health maintenance organization, a health care service providing comprehensive medical treatment and preventive health care to enrolled members, in return for a fixed, prepaid fee.

Hormone, a chemical substance produced in one part of the body and carried in the bloodstream to a distant organ or tissue, whose activity it influences.

Hypertension, or persistent high blood pressure, a condition in which the blood presses too forcefully against artery walls, because of constricted blood vessels or excessive pumping of blood by the heart.

Immune system, the body system that seeks to destroy foreign invaders (for example, viruses or bacteria); in rare cases, it may attack the body's own cells. It consists of white blood cells, lymph nodes, the spleen, and substances called antibodies produced by white blood cells.

Immunity, resistance or nonsusceptibility to disease.

Infection, invasion of the body by disease-causing, multiplying microorganisms, such as bacteria or viruses.

Inflammation, a response of body tissues to injury or infection, designed to localize and stop the damage and commonly producing pain, redness, and swelling.

Interferon, a class of substances produced in the body that play a role in inhibiting certain viruses from multiplying rapidly.

Invasive, said of diagnostic and treatment techniques that involve making an incision in the skin or inserting some instrument or foreign substance into the body.

In vitro fertilization, or "test-tube" pregnancy, a procedure in which a ripe egg is removed from the woman's ovary, placed in a special culture medium to be fertilized by sperm, and reinserted in the uterus, where it can then develop normally.

Laparoscopy, visual examination of the abdomen with a long, slender, lighted instrument called a laparoscope.

LDL, or low-density lipoprotein, a kind of protein molecule that carries cholesterol in the bloodstream. A high level of LDL's in the blood is associated with increased risk of atherosclerosis. *See also* HDL.

Lesion, damage or abnormal change, caused by injury or disease, in a body tissue or function.

Leukotrienes, naturally occurring chemicals in the body that can help cause inflammation and play a role in allergic reactions.

Low-density lipoprotein, *see* LDL.

Lymphatic system, a body system whose network of vessels carries lymph (excess fluid and particles picked up from body tissue and not reabsorbed into capillaries), filtering it through lymph nodes at various locations and returning it to the bloodstream. Lymph vessels also carry lymphocytes to the bloodstream.

Lymphocyte, a type of white blood cell, usually formed in the tissues of the lymphatic system, that plays a key role in the action of the immune system.

Magnetic resonance imaging, *see* MRI.

Malignant, tending to become progressively worse, life-threatening; commonly applied to cancerous tumors.

Mammography, the use of X rays to detect possible cancer in the breast.

Manic-depressive illness, *see* Bipolar disorder.

Metabolism, sum of physical and chemical processes by which the body consumes energy in the form of nutrients with or without oxygen, to build new tissues and repair worn ones, obtain more energy, and eliminate wastes.

Metastasis, the spread of disease (often cancer) from one part of the body to another.

Microsurgery, surgery carried out with the aid of microscopes and miniaturized instruments.

MRI, or magnetic resonance imaging, a diagnostic technique in which signals are picked up from atoms in the body exposed to a magnetic field and are organized by computer into composite cross-sectional images. Also called NMR (for nuclear magnetic resonance) scanning.

Myocardial infarction, *see* Heart attack.

Narcotic, a drug, such as opium, that depresses central nervous system functioning, thereby dulling pain, inducing sleep, and sometimes producing a euphoric effect.

Neurosis, a class of anxiety-related psychological disorders with symptoms that are distressing but not grossly abnormal.

Neurotransmitter, any of various chemical substances in the nervous system that help in the transmission of nerve impulses from one cell to another.

NMR scanning, *see* MRI.

Noninvasive, said of diagnostic and treatment techniques that do not involve an incision or the insertion of an instrument or foreign substance into the body.

Nuclear medicine, a branch of medicine in which substances "tagged" with small amounts of radioactive elements are inhaled or injected into the body to give information about body functions, diagnose disorders, or inhibit or destroy certain cells.

Nurse practitioner, or NP, a registered nurse who provides nursing care and also qualifies, through additional training, to provide primary medical care under the general supervision of a physician.

Opiate, any narcotic derived from opium, such as morphine, heroin, or codeine; the word is sometimes used for any addictive drug that relieves pain and dulls the senses.

Orthodontics, the branch of dentistry concerned with the prevention and correction of abnormally positioned teeth.

Osteoporosis, a condition in which bones become thin, brittle, and easily broken.

Pap test (Papanicolaou test), a test, especially for diagnosis of cancer of the cervix or uterus, in which cells obtained from the genital tract are examined under a microscope for signs of abnormality.

Pelvic inflammatory disease, *see* PID.

Perinatal, relating to the last several weeks of pregnancy and the first few weeks after birth.

Periodontics, the branch of dentistry concerned with the gums and other tissues that surround and support the teeth.

PET scanning, or positron emission tomography, a diagnostic technique using computerized images to trace the path of compounds inhaled or injected into the body that are tagged with minute amounts of radioactive substances that give off particles called positrons.

Physician's assistant, or PA, a trained health professional who provides primary medical care under the general supervision of a physician.

PID, or pelvic inflammatory disease, an infection of the fallopian tubes, most often transmitted sexually. Infections of the cervix, uterus, and ovaries are also sometimes referred to as PID.

Placebo, an inactive substance, generally one that appears to be medicine and is given to a person in its place.

Plaque, a patch or area that differs from surrounding tissue. Plaque may be a layer of material that builds up on a body surface, such as the teeth or the inside walls of blood vessels. The nonfunctioning tissue that forms around nerve cells in certain nervous system diseases is also called plaque.

Polyunsaturated fat, a fat (such as certain vegetable oils) the molecules of which can take on additional hydrogen atoms; such fats have been linked with reduced levels of cholesterol in the blood.

Positron emission tomography, *see* PET scanning.

Prostaglandins, chemicals produced in most parts of the body that have wide-ranging effects; individual prostaglandins can, among other things, make muscles contract, cause blood vessels to widen or narrow, inhibit or promote blood clotting, and stimulate sensory nerves.

Proteins, chemical compounds, made up of long chains of amino acids, that are essential components of body cells and important to the functioning of the body.

Psychosis, a class of severe mental illnesses characterized by disordered thought processes and loss of contact with reality.

Receptor, a structure on a cell wall or within a cell that can bind with certain substances produced in the body, such as hormones, or with certain drugs, leading to some action, such as a change in the function of the cell.

Recombinant DNA, DNA that has been reconstructed in the laboratory by breaking up and splicing DNA from more than one organism.

RNA, or ribonucleic acid, a chainlike molecule in living cells that helps carry out instructions received from DNA molecules to form new proteins.

Saturated fat, a type of fat—found, for example, in meat and dairy products—whose molecules cannot take on additional hydrogen atoms; saturated fats have been linked with high levels of cholesterol in the blood.

Schizophrenia, a type of severe mental illness involving such symptoms as delusions (especially of persecution), disordered thought, hallucinations, inappropriate emotions, and withdrawal from reality.

Shock, a state of collapse and progressive circulatory failure marked by such symptoms as feeble breathing, pallor, and rapid heartbeat; it is caused by inadequate blood supply or low blood pressure, generally resulting from severe injuries, hemorrhage, or burns.

Sleep apnea, *see* Apnea.

Steroids, a group of natural hormones or drugs resembling them. Different steroids may be used for a variety of purposes—for example, in birth control pills or as drugs to relieve arthritis symptoms.

Stroke, or cerebrovascular accident, a disorder caused by disruption of blood supply to part of the brain, usually because of a blood clot or hemorrhage.

Sudden infant death syndrome, or "crib death," the sudden death of an apparently healthy infant during sleep.

"Test-tube" pregnancy, *see* In vitro fertilization.

Toxic shock syndrome, or TSS, an infectious disease found mainly, though not exclusively, in menstruating women who use tampons.

Tranquilizer, any of a wide variety of drugs that exercise a calming effect but do not ordinarily dull consciousness or induce sleep.

Trauma, injury to the body, caused by an accident or any outside force; also, emotional shock produced by some event.

Tumor, a tissue growth in which cells multiply at a rapid rate; may be either malignant or benign.

Ulcer, a break in the surface of the skin or of a mucous membrane, exposing the tissue underneath and leaving an open sore.

Ultrasound, the use of inaudible, high-frequency sound waves for mapping (or creating a "picture" of) internal organs and structures or for medical treatment.

Vaccine, a preparation containing killed or weakened disease-causing organisms, given to individuals so that they will produce protective antibodies against the disease, and thus be immune to it, over a long period of time.

Vasectomy, a technique for male sterilization in which the duct that carries sperm from each testicle is severed and the ends closed off.

Vasodilator, a drug that relaxes the walls of the blood vessels, allowing blood to flow more easily and thus reducing blood pressure.

Virus, a minute disease-causing organism that can reproduce only when it enters a living host.

Vitamin, one of a number of organic (carbon-containing) substances needed in small amounts to enable the body to perform certain essential functions.

Contributors

Abplanalp, Judith M., Ph.D. Associate Professor, Department of Psychiatry and Behavioral Sciences, University of Texas Medical Branch at Galveston. WHAT IS PREMENSTRUAL SYNDROME?

Allen, Richard E. Writer and editor. CHECKUPS: WHAT TO EXPECT.

Birenbaum, Rhonda. Writer specializing in medicine and science; Contributing Editor, *Medical World News;* Regional Correspondent, *The Medical Post.* GOVERNMENT POLICIES AND PROGRAMS (CANADA).

Bondi, Edward E., M.D. Associate Professor, Department of Dermatology, University of Pennsylvania, Philadelphia. SKIN.

Calladine, Carole E., M.S.S.A. Writer and family counselor. HAVING A SECOND CHILD.

Douglas, Joel P., D.M.D. Assistant Clinical Professor of Orthodontics, Harvard School of Dental Medicine; Staff Associate, Forsyth Dental Center, Boston. STRAIGHTENING TEETH.

Eisenberg, M. Michael, M.D. Director, Department of Surgery, Long Island College Hospital; Professor and Vice-Chairman, Department of Surgery, State University of New York, Downstate Medical Center, Brooklyn, N.Y. ULCERS: CAUSES AND CURES.

Falkenstein, David B., M.D. Staff Physician, Gastroenterology Section, Veterans Administration Medical Center, New York City. LIVER.

Forland, Marvin, M.D. Professor and Deputy Chairman for Clinical Activities, Associate Dean for Clinical Affairs, Department of Medicine, University of Texas Health Science Center at San Antonio. KIDNEYS AND URINARY SYSTEM.

Franklin, Deborah. Science writer and editor. MEDICAL TECHNOLOGY.

Green, William L., M.D. Associate Chief of Staff for Research and Development, Veterans Administration Medical Center; Professor of Medicine, State University of New York, Downstate Medical Center, Brooklyn, N.Y. GLANDS AND METABOLISM.

Greenberg, Mark T., Ph.D. Associate Professor of Psychology, University of Washington, Seattle. CHILD PSYCHOLOGY AND DEVELOPMENT (coauthor).

Harding, P., M.D. Professor and Chairman, Department of Obstetrics and Gynecology, University of Western Ontario. OBSTETRICS AND GYNECOLOGY.

Hegde, M. N., Ph.D. Professor of Communicative Disorders, California State University at Fresno. STUTTERING.

Helgerson, Steven D., M.D., M.P.H. Assistant Clinical Professor of Epidemiology and Public Health, Yale University School of Medicine. EPIDEMIOLOGY (coauthor).

Hume, Eric L., M.D. Assistant Professor of Orthopaedic Surgery, Jefferson Medical College of Thomas Jefferson University, Philadelphia. BONES, MUSCLES, AND JOINTS.

Jekel, James F., M.D., M.P.H. Professor of Epidemiology and Public Health, Yale University School of Medicine. EPIDEMIOLOGY (coauthor).

Lucente, Frank E., M.D. Professor and Chairman, Department of Oto-laryngology, New York Eye and Ear Infirmary, New York Medical College, New York City. EARS, NOSE, AND THROAT.

Mandel, Irwin D., D.D.S. Professor of Dentistry, Director, Center for Clinical Research in Dentistry, School of Dental and Oral Surgery, Columbia University. TEETH AND GUMS.

Mandell, Frederick, M.D. Assistant Clinical Professor in Pediatrics, Harvard Medical School; Senior Associate in Medicine, Children's Hospital, Boston; Vice-President, National Sudden Infant Death Syndrome Foundation. CRIB DEATH.

Maugh, Thomas H., II, Ph.D. Senior Science Writer, *Science* magazine; coauthor, *Seeds of Destruction: The Science Report on Cancer Research.* GENETICS AND GENETIC ENGINEERING; HELP FOR COCAINE USERS; THE USES OF STEROIDS.

McLellan, A. Thomas, Ph.D. Director of Clinical Research, Psychiatric Service, Philadelphia Veterans Administration Medical Center; Associate Professor, Department of Psychiatry, University of Pennsylvania. DRUG ABUSE (coauthor).

Meltzoff, Andrew N., Ph.D. Associate Professor, Department of Psychology, Chairman, Psychology and Psychiatry Research Program, Child Development and Mental Retardation Center, University of Washington, Seattle. CHILD PSYCHOLOGY AND DEVELOPMENT (coauthor).

Meneilly, Graydon S., M.D. Fellow in Gerontology, Division on Aging, Harvard Medical School. AGING AND THE AGED.

Murray, Thomas H., Ph.D. Associate Professor of Ethics and Public Policy, Institute for the Medical Humanities, University of Texas Medical Branch at Galveston. BIOETHICS.

O'Brien, Charles P., M.D., Ph.D. Chief, Psychiatric Service, Philadelphia Veterans Administration Medical Center; Professor, Department of Psychiatry, University of Pennsylvania. DRUG ABUSE (coauthor).

Parkinson, David R., M.D. Physician, Division of Hematology-Oncology, New England Medical Center; Staff Scientist, Cancer Research Center; Assistant Professor of Medicine, Tufts University School of Medicine, Boston. CANCER.

Pelot, Daniel, M.D. Associate Clinical Professor, Division of Gastroenterology, Department of Medicine, University of California at Irvine. DIGESTIVE SYSTEM.

Pingleton, Susan K., M.D. Associate Professor of Medicine, Director, Clinical Investigations, Pulmonary Division, University of Kansas Medical Center, Kansas City. RESPIRATORY SYSTEM.

Pounds, Lois A., M.D. Associate Professor of Pediatrics, University of Pittsburgh School of Medicine. CONQUERING CHILDHOOD DISEASES; PEDIATRICS.

Puliafito, Carmen Anthony, M.D. Instructor in Ophthalmology, Harvard Medical School. CONTACT LENSES; EYES.

Rodman, Morton J., Ph.D. Professor of Pharmacology, Rutgers University, New Brunswick, N.J. MEDICATIONS AND DRUGS.

Roth, Sanford H., M.D. Medical Director, Arthritis Center, Ltd.; Professor and Director, Aging and Arthritis Program, Arizona State University, Tempe. ARTHRITIS AND RHEUMATISM.

Roy, Steven P., M.D. Director, Sports Injuries and Running Clinic of Eugene (Ore.). FRACTURES, SPRAINS, AND STRAINS.

Schneider, John F., M.D. Assistant Professor of Medicine, University of Cincinnati Medical Center; Director, Cardiac Catheterization Laboratory, University Hospital. HEART AND CIRCULATORY SYSTEM.

Seiden, Richard H., Ph.D., M.P.H. Director of Research Programs, Suicide Prevention and Crisis Intervention Service of Alameda County, Berkeley, Calif. TEENAGE SUICIDE: WHY?

Sibley, William A., M.D. Professor of Neurology, University of Arizona College of Medicine, Tucson. FACTS ABOUT MULTIPLE SCLEROSIS.

Smith, Pat Costello. Medical and science writer. LEFT-HANDEDNESS.

Spiegel, David, M.D. Associate Professor of Psychiatry and Behavioral Sciences (Clinical), Director, Adult Psychiatric Outpatient Clinic, Stanford University School of Medicine. MENTAL HEALTH.

Sternheim, William L., M.D. Assistant Professor of Medicine, Division of Hematology, University of Miami School of Medicine. BLOOD AND LYMPHATIC SYSTEM.

Thro, Ellen. Science writer; member, National Association of Science Writers and American Medical Writers Association. ENVIRONMENT AND HEALTH.

Trenk, Barbara Scherr. Writer specializing in health issues. GOVERNMENT POLICIES AND PROGRAMS (UNITED STATES).

Walton, Susan. Science and education writer. NEW HELP FOR INFERTILITY.

Williams, Eleanor R., Ph.D. Associate Professor, Department of Food, Nutrition and Institution Administration, University of Maryland, College Park. HOW TO PRESERVE NUTRIENTS IN FOOD.

Winick, Myron, M.D. R. R. Williams Professor of Nutrition, Professor of Pediatrics, Director, Institute of Human Nutrition, Director, Center for Nutrition, Genetics and Human Development, College of Physicians and Surgeons, Columbia University. NUTRITION AND DIET.

Woody, George E., M.D. Chief, Substance Abuse Treatment Unit, Philadelphia Veterans Administration Medical Center; Clinical Associate Professor, Department of Psychiatry, University of Pennsylvania. DRUG ABUSE (coauthor).

Worner, T. M., M.D. Chief, Medical Section, Alcohol Dependency Treatment Program, Veterans Administration Medical Center, Bronx, N.Y.; Assistant Professor of Medicine, Mount Sinai School of Medicine, City University of New York. ALCOHOLISM.

Yurt, Roger W., M.D. Associate Professor of Surgery, Director, Trauma Center, New York Hospital-Cornell Medical Center, New York City. TREATING BURN VICTIMS.

Index

Page number in *italics* indicates the reference is to an illustration.

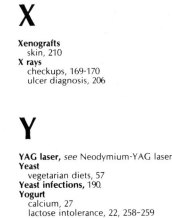

Photo/Art Credits